RELIGION
&
REASON

AN ANTHOLOGY

RELIGION & REASON

AN ANTHOLOGY

BURTON F. PORTER

WESTERN NEW ENGLAND COLLEGE

ST. MARTIN'S PRESS/NEW YORK

Senior editor: Don Reisman
Managing editor: Patricia Mansfield-Phelan
Project editor: Suzanne Holt
Production supervisor: Katherine Battiste
Text & cover design: Sheree L. Goodman

For information, write:
St. Martin's Press, Inc.
175 Fifth Avenue
New York, NY 10010

ISBN: 0-312-04885-8

ACKNOWLEDGMENTS

Acknowledgments and copyrights are listed, by selection number, at the back of the book on pages 526–528, which constitute an extension of the copyright page.

To Barbara
who loves the light

ACKNOWLEDGMENT

I wish to express my gratitude to my wife, whose good sense, warmth, and strength sustained me during the worst period of my life. She is the most real person I know and deserves much more than she has ever received.

Contents

Strong Son of God, immortal Love,
    Whom we, that have not seen thy face,
    By faith, and faith alone, embrace,
Believing where we cannot prove.

—Alfred, Lord Tennyson, *In Memoriam A.H.H.*

Sure he that made us with such large
    discourse,
Looking before and after, gave us not
That capability and godlike reason
to fust in us unused.

—William Shakespeare, *Hamlet,*
Act IV, scene iv, 36–39

RELIGION

&

REASON

AN
ANTHOLOGY

Introduction

The philosophy of religion is philosophic thinking about religion. It attempts to probe the underlying assumptions of personal faith and organized religion to determine whether good reasons exist for belief in a supernatural realm. It examines the nature of that realm, the character of the God who is supreme within it, and the relation of that God to the world—most particularly, to human life. It asks why a loving and almighty God would allow human beings, including innocent children, to suffer; whether prayer makes a difference and how one can tell; what life after death might mean, the survival of the soul after the disintegration of the body; and what role reason plays in judging matters of faith, what Athens has to do with Jerusalem.

Philosophers who explore such questions are sympathetic to the spirit of religion and the remarkably rich traditions, institutions, and forms of worship that have persisted from the beginning of civilization itself. They are also moved by the human yearning for order and purpose in the world, the need for things to make sense in terms of a divine being who controls and orders all events to some meaningful end. At the same time, they are as critical of spiritual claims as any other claims, demanding evidence and reasoned argument to prove that religious statements are true and not just emotionally comforting. They recognize that the desire to believe in a divine being is very great and could induce people to accept ideas they would otherwise dismiss as farfetched, and that religious convictions are often acquired during childhood and, for that reason, assimilated without question.

The task in philosophic thinking about religion, then, is to be receptive to religious belief in light of the significant role it has played in human history and in the human heart, while at the same time maintaining a certain critical awareness in evaluating religious assertions. We must not, of course, be so alert to the possibility of error that we fail to recognize the truth when we come across it. Rather, we should bring a sympathetic intelligence to bear on the phenomenon of religion.

Philosophers, unlike theologians, are not necessarily believers, and, qua philosophers, they strive to operate with minimum assumptions and maximum objectivity, attempting to determine whether the system of beliefs does, in fact, diagram reality. The philosopher begins with questions rather than certainty, wondering above all whether *God* is the name of an actual being or simply an imaginative construct that personifies our hunger for direction, compassion, and immortality. Theologians, on the other hand, are already committed to the worship of God and look for the structure of support that lies within; they seek to comprehend, interpret, elaborate, and refine that religious system. The difference, in short, is that the theologian cries, "Dear God in heaven," while the philosopher says, "Dear God, if there be a God, in heaven, if there be a heaven." Both look for the justifying structure, but only one assumes that it is there.

In poring over this book many readers will be seeking answers to these questions in the writings of outstanding figures in the philosophy of religion, and some will find what they are looking for in a selection that speaks to them directly, an analysis that strikes home. But the chief value of the book lies in the range and depth of possibilities presented for consideration and in the exposure to different ways of thinking, not just the familiar path but the novel option. The writings included constitute a varied array of positions, developed and expressed by outstanding minds, and the critical interplay among those positions should induce reflection in the honest seeker.

The reader, therefore, can hope to gain a deeper understanding of what religious belief entails, what choices exist, and what kinds of logical considerations apply in reaching an intelligent decision.

PART I

The Phenomenon
of Religion

CHAPTER *1*

Early Beliefs

*I*f we want to know when writing began or when the post and lintel architectural style was first used, we can consult various sources. The physical evidence is available to archaeologists, and they have compiled factual records to answer such questions. However, if we want to know when the religious sense first emerged in human consciousness and culture, the problem is much more difficult. The date or even the period of its origin is extremely elusive because the religious sense is an intangible phenomenon.

One approach is to refer to the oldest available indirect evidence, such as funeral and cult objects, temple carvings, sculptures in sanctuaries, and various paintings and engravings dealing with subjects that seem to be religious in nature. For more recent information we can also examine sacred texts and holy writings that reveal the formal beliefs of a people.

However, this method relies on inferences from extant objects to inner spiritual states, which is rather like judging the religious feelings of Catholics by examining censers and priests' vestments. Furthermore, an officially sanctioned bas-relief or written record may not tell us what the people themselves thought or felt, and it is the generally emerging sense of religion that we want to understand.

Another approach is to study contemporary peoples who are in a primitive stage of development and, by analogy, to assume that their state of mind must resemble that of early human beings. The Maori in New Zealand have been studied for this purpose, as have the Tassaday in South America and various tribes in Africa, Indonesia, and the Pacific Islands. However, when we use such a method, we never know whether the parallels are apt. In other words, we can never be sure that these people are primitive in the same way. Furthermore, we have difficulty in deciding which peoples to identify as primitive. The standard of being technologically backward may not do if the society is otherwise well ordered, harmonious, and ideally suited to its environment.

Consequently, we can only speculate with varying degrees of accuracy on the religious forms and feelings of early human beings. This has meant that anthropologists sometimes offer very different interpretations of early religion, leaving the layperson quite confused. Despite the uncertainties, however, some areas of agreement have emerged. Anthropologists generally concur on the main types of religious (and nonreligious) states that characterize the earliest human societies.

One pervasive belief was in *mana,* meaning a supernatural power residing within an object or person that makes it excellent in its particular functioning. For example, a knife with mana will cut extremely well and not break where ordinary knives would; furthermore, the user will have uncanny skill when using such a knife to make kills in the hunt and, when under attack, will find it a fierce weapon. An animal skin with mana will be unusually warm to wear, a hook with mana will catch more fish, and a house with mana will withstand a storm that destroys all other houses. Mana makes things or people uniquely gifted by imbuing them with a strange force. Unlike the secular notion of "luck," the concept of mana entails a feeling of awe and mystery. Good fortune just happens to the lucky person, but individuals empowered with mana have an extraordinary excellence that radiates from their person.

Sometimes related to mana is the idea of *taboo,* which is a prohibition against saying or doing something because of the immediate harm from preternatural powers that would follow. It can be connected to mana in that a high mana object would have properties that are dangerous to the wrong person. In Melanesia and Polynesia, for example, the chief was taboo to the commoners, who would die instantly if they had contact with that much mana. But taboo can also stand for a ban because of supernatural forces that must be respected, and here the connection with mana is less clear. Questions of morality, social customs, or taste might be involved, based on a religious sense of the sacred and profane.

Another religious state or feeling is *animism,* which means a general belief in spiritual beings. The person who accepts animism feels that all objects in the natural world possess consciousness. The rivers, winds, clouds, and mountains, the sun, the moon, and the stars are all filled with souls or spirits that animate their actions. Their movements therefore resemble those of people or animals and can be ascribed to the same motivating force. As the cultural anthropologist James Frazer put it in *The Worship of Nature,* "Every nook and hill, every tree and flower, every brook and river, every breeze that blew and every cloud that flecked with silvery white the blue expanse of heaven" had a spirit within it.

Frazer further believed that the concept of gods was a natural outgrowth of the notion of spirits, so that from animism came polytheism, the belief in multiple gods. This concept in turn was simplified and unified to form the contemporary theory of monotheism. The anthropologist E. B. Tylor also regarded animism as the foundation of religion, and, in *Primitive Cultures,* he was probably the first to speak of it as "the minimum definition of religion."

Be that as it may, animism appears to have been at least as common in early beliefs as mana and taboo, and it persists to this day. We know it in literature as "the pathetic fallacy," whereby poets refer to the gentle stream, the cruel sea, or the maternal earth.

Another early notion was *magic,* which refers to ritualistic techniques of a supernatural kind for controlling events in the natural world. An array of spells, rites, incantations, chants, charms, and special materials are used to affect objects or the behavior of animals or people.

For example, the earliest paintings ever discovered are magical in nature and appear on the walls of caverns in sites such as Altamira in Spain and Font-de-Gaume, Niaux, and Lascaux in France. Many of the paintings in these subterranean galleries show bison, horses, reindeer, and woolly rhinoceroses with spears or arrows in their sides. Such depictions are interpreted as a magical attempt to gain power over the animals in the hunt by casting a spell on them. In the primitive mind, the picture was thought to be the same as the animal, so whatever was done to the one happened to the other. Because the food supply was obviously of paramount importance, rituals must also have been performed over these paintings to further control the hunt through magic.

The propagation of animals or human beings was quite naturally another major concern of early humankind, so magical efforts were employed here also to make the herds multiply and to increase fertility in women. The Paleolithic statuette called the *Willendorf of Venus* falls into this category, for it presents a female figure with large hips and breasts obviously signifying fecundity. And at a site close to St. Girons in the Pyrenees, interlacing heel marks have been found that are taken as evidence of ritualistic dancing, probably to make the various animal species increase. Fertility magic was later used to ensure good crops and to increase the supply of wild fruits and berries.

In interpersonal magic, a distinction is sometimes made between black and white magic, black being used for evil purposes and white for good. If one person tries to harm another, perhaps by putting pins in an effigy of that person, that is clearly black magic. However, if a love potion is used, or a cure is attempted through charms and incantations, then white magic is being practiced.

Another distinction sometimes made is between magic, religion, and science. Following the classification in *The Golden Bough* by James Frazer, magic is like religion and unlike science in that supernatural forces are at work. However, it is also like science and unlike religion because a mechanical system of cause and effect is assumed. One does not persuade a god through prayer and supplication but instead compels the supernatural forces by pulling the right wires. Magicians believe that if they use the proper spells and the proper materials, then the desired effect must occur. If it does not, they conclude that the spell or the materials were wrong, not that magic does not work. Scientists maintain the same type of assumption: if an experiment does not turn out as it should, they conclude that it was not performed properly, not that the scientific method should be questioned. (Frazer sees magic as "false science.")

Still another religious phenomenon that is very widespread, ranging from North America and South America to Africa and Australia, is *totemism*, meaning belief in a kinship or mystical relationship between an individual or clan and some plant or animal. For example, a clan may feel that they have literally or figuratively descended from bears and, consequently, may refrain from eating bear meat or do so only after they have asked forgiveness of the bear spirit, their ancestor. They may dress in bearskin during dances or ceremonies and act out the mating, foraging, or combat of bears.

Among totemic groups marriage is usually exogamous, that is, allowed only outside the totem "kin," so that the lines of descent from various plants or animals become crossed and complex. In the Pacific Northwest the people of each Indian village erect a "totem pole" showing the totemic symbols of each separate clan and the lineage of the entire group.

We see the survival of primitive totemism in heraldic shields and family crests that feature falcons, horses, lions, and so forth, and are halved and quartered to show the family genealogy. Even modern nations often have animal symbols, as do athletic teams, Boy Scout troops, various models of cars, and so on. In each case, the group members (or owners) identify so strongly with the qualities of the symbolic animal that they see themselves as embodiments of that creature, with its daring, speed, dexterity, or strength.

Early religion contains other "prescientific" phenomena, including witchcraft, ancestor worship, and mythological stories, to explain the arrangement or creation of the world. Like mana, taboo, animism, magic, and totemism, they provide a sense of power over happenings in the world that otherwise would seem beyond human control. They also offer an understanding of why things happen as they do, so the world does not appear haphazard and unjust. People feel more secure in believing that an order exists, and that they have a necessary place in the scheme of things. If there are no real accidents, then human life is less vulnerable to disaster; and if everything happens for a reason, then the supernatural and the natural are joined in a satisfying union.

As the philosopher Bertrand Russell observed, human beings fear what nature can do to them, what they can do to one another, and what they can do to themselves through their violent passions. Beliefs, especially of an elemental kind, help people feel less afraid by offering them comprehension and power over the events that affect their lives.

In the selections that follow, William Howells introduces the ideas of mana and taboo, which he regards as the best examples of how "a basic religious feeling . . . takes form as a religious belief." Then E. E. Evans-Pritchard discusses the role of witchcraft in explaining unfortunate events, using as his prime illustration the Azande in northeast Africa.

Following this, Bronislaw Malinowski explores belief in magic, finding it "whenever man comes to an unbridgeable chasm, a hiatus in his knowledge or in his powers of practical control." Clifford Geertz then describes the general role of religion within culture, offering a definition of religion and an empirical account of its functioning.

In the last section, the concepts of myth and mythology are discussed by Ninian Smart and Rudolph Bultmann, which brings our general study of early beliefs up to the biblical period and beyond.

Mana, Taboo, and Witchcraft

1. Mana and Tabu: A Force and a Danger

WILLIAM HOWELLS

There is probably no better example of how a basic religious feeling—a sense of the special, the supernatural—takes form as a religious belief than in the idea of mana. The word itself is from the Pacific, being common to many of the languages of Melanesia and Polynesia, but it has other names in other places. Mana means a kind of force or power which can be in anything, and which makes that thing better in its own special qualities, such as they are, perhaps to the point of being marvelous.

A man who has mana is stronger, or smarter, or more graceful, though mana is not strength or brains or agility. That man's spear or, if he has been civilized, his tennis racket, has mana if it does what is expected of it with particular sureness; but mana is something different from the niceness of balance or the workmanship which has gone into it. At the same time, if the pro who made the spear or the racket consistently turns out first-class spears and rackets, then he obviously has mana of his own, or else he has ways of inducing mana into whatever (spears or rackets) he makes. And there is no difference in the mana which is in the tool, or its owner, or its maker; it simply causes each one to excel in his special way.

Mana, therefore, is an explanation for whatever is powerful, or excellent, or just right. Cole Porter's "You're the Top" reels off a list of things which, if you think of it that way, have mana (Mahatma Gandhi, Napoleon brandy, and cellophane). I need hardly say that if you ever took pains to use a special pen or pencil whenever you wrote a college examination you were thinking along the same lines.

Typically, mana is a sort of essence of nature; it is not a spirit, and it has no will or purpose of its own. It can very well be compared with electricity, which is impersonal but powerful, and which flows from one thing to another, and can be made to do a variety of things, although in itself it remains the same flowing force. In the beliefs of different cults, mana may be supplied by various sources: it may come from gods or spirits, or it may be instilled by the correct ritual, or it may simply exist naturally where it is. But this is only a question of making it conform to other ideas of a cult, and is of no special significance. The one important matter is whether it works. For example, a Melanesian may find a stone; it may have a strange shape, or obtrude itself on his notice in a peculiar way, and he will decide that possibly it has mana. He will take it home and bury it in his garden, and if he gets a particularly fine vegetable crop he will know that he was right, because the stone has transmitted mana (which is far better than fertilizer) to the plot.

In spite of such uses, mana would hardly deserve to be called more than a superstitious explanation of luck, or of other people's successes, if it did not in some cases engender a strongly respectful attitude—if it did not give rise to what can be called a religious sensation and belief, because, though unseen, it influences man to regulate his behavior by it. Among certain tribes, that is what it does.

The Iroquois Indians conceived of a potency, inherent in all kinds of natural objects, called orenda, which word they also used to signify "extraordinary," "wonderful," "ancient," and so on. The manitou of the Algonquins was a good deal the same, and did not mean a personified spirit so much as something in nature which caused a sense of wonder or a momentary thrill. Among the Sioux, wakan or wakonda stood for a better-defined idea, quite like mana as I have described it, although wakan also meant spirits. An Oglala said that wakan meant many things, and would have to be understood from the things that are considered wakan. "When a priest uses any object in performing a ceremony that object becomes endowed with a spirit, not exactly a spirit, but something like one, the priests call it tonwan or ton. Now anything that thus acquires ton is wakan, because it is the power of the spirit or quality that has been put into it. . . . The roots of certain plants are wakan because they are poisonous. . . . Again, some birds are wakan because they do very strange things. . . . In other words, anything may be wakan if a wakan spirit goes into it. . . . Again, if a person does something that cannot be understood, that is also wakan. Drinks that make one drunk are wakan because they make one crazy. . . . Wakan comes from the wakan beings. These beings are greater than mankind in the same way that mankind is greater than animals." Thus wakan, though it is impersonal, can be a power for evil, as well as good.

How the idea of wakan fits into the religious life of the people has been studied in another tribe, the Crows. Typical Indians of the Plains, the Crows lived a nomadic life, normally in small bands, hunting the buffalo; and those actually hunting or fighting did so in even smaller groups. The social structure was loose and informal, and life for each man was intensely personal, with a certain loneliness in it. He had little feeling of acting with a group, and all his rewards and satisfactions were for what he accomplished strictly as an individual. There was in fact only one kind of glory: prestige from his personal feats as a warrior. War was not of our brand, but was composed of chance skirmishes and deliberate raids against traditional enemies, ostensibly to get horses but actually simply to expose oneself to danger, for the greatest achievement was the most foolhardy one. To ride into an enemy camp and cut out and drive off some of its horses was splendid;

to do it alone was more splendid; and to do it alone on foot was most splendid. Many of the Plains tribes had an established scale of bravado (the system of "counting coup"), in which each stunt increased the informal "rank" of a warrior by a given degree and was signalized by an eagle feather cut or painted in a distinguishing way, to be worn on his head. A man with many horses and a history of hairbreadth adventures was a contented and respected personage, and his opposite smarted under public pity, not to say ridicule; the Crows would concede to the latter, however, that it was not his fault, and was due to the fact that he had not been favored with visions.

For visions were the key to all success, and were what every Crow longed for, and thought constantly of, because they brought power. This the Crows called maxpe, which was their word for wakan, and their idea of mana. It was certainly vague and indefinite. Maxpe was given by supernatural beings, who appeared in a vision and awarded it; when a man had it, he was fortunate and powerful thereafter. The spirits might tell him to sing a certain song which they taught him, or to wear something special on his head, when he went out, and if this were so, the power might become associated with that object. But this was not necessary; the power was simply there, at his disposal, because of the vision. . . .

Moslems, particularly North Africans, believe in a power of the same kind, called baraka (holiness). It is a power for many kinds of good, and is quite general: mountains have it, the sea has it; it lives in the sun, moon, and stars, in animals—especially horses—plants, and magic squares. It tends, however, to be personal, associated with such as brides and bridegrooms, the new mothers of twins and triplets, and children generally. And it is sensitive to pollution and destruction by uncleanness of various kinds, or by unrighteousness; and, generally speaking, women and Christians are bad for it, as is fighting or breaking religious laws. The welfare of a country depends on the baraka of the sultan, who may lose it, perhaps to people who kiss his hand.

The Pacific Ocean, as I have said, is the real home of mana. Mana was first brought to the attention of anthropologists by the distinguished missionary-ethnologist Codrington, who studied and described it in Melanesia (New Guinea to the Fiji Islands). The Melanesians see mana in its most general form: a force, as Codrington says, "which acts in all ways for good and evil; and which it is of the greatest importance to possess or control." Much of Melanesia is ghost-ridden; everywhere, in the woods, the streams, the beaches, live the ghosts of the dead, and spirits of a slightly higher order, who are never remote and always near at hand. All of them are full of mana, and act as reservoirs of mana, and act through it. Therefore, if ghosts and spirits can be propitiated, their mana can be controlled. Better yet, however, is mana which has come to reside in a man or an object; the Melanesians are much interested in its tangible aspects because it can be handled directly. If mana exists in a stone or a bone, good; it can be put in the garden or laid on a new canoe; for mana can be conveyed from one object to another, just by keeping them together. The lively interest in ghosts and spirits has an ulterior aim; Codrington justly says that the basis of Melanesian religion is the pursuit of mana.

It was, however, in Polynesia (the islands from New Zealand to Hawaii) that the idea of mana reached its most refined state, even though it did not overshadow other aspects of religion, as it did in Melanesia or among the Crows. The Polynesians, beyond any other people who lacked writing, through the philosophical efforts of their priestly caste made a fully ordered system out of their religious cosmos, so that their theology was comparable to that of the Greeks or the Hindus. A hierarchy ran from the creator of the universe down through later gods to the living chiefs and on to the commoners, and all through this skein was distributed mana, with the greatest amount at the top. It was the basic force of nature through which everything was done, for the gods made weather and the chiefs provided for their people through its preservation and exercise.

The comparison of mana with electricity, or physical energy, is here inescapable. The Polynesian conception of it was not scientific, of course, but it was otherwise completely logical. Mana was believed to be indestructible, although it might be dissipated by improper practices. It came originally from the gods; nevertheless it was not possessed by them any more than by any other being or substance, but was independent of them all. It flowed continually from one thing to another and, since the cosmos was built on a dualistic idea, it flowed from heavenly things to earthbound things, just as though from a positive to a negative pole. It came to the people through the chiefs, who were the direct descendants of the gods, and the chiefs kept it and conducted it to whatever function needed it: ceremony, war, or agriculture. It was not a privilege of the chief that he had so much mana. It was, rather, his function in the scheme of things to serve as reservoir and transmitter of it.

Mana could be contained in any person or thing; however, a man's potential capacity depended on his position in the whole hierarchy. Chiefs were the main vessels, acting as contact between god and man. Priests, or people of high birth, stood next in relative capacity, with commoners low in the scale, and women, who were of the dark, or earthly, half of nature, lowest of all. And, since mana flowed from high to low, an unguarded contact between a chief and a commoner was therefore an evil thing; the chief suffered a loss of mana, which he should preserve for the good of the people, and the commoner, with his limited capacity for mana, might be blown out like a fuse. So contact was avoided, not through any fear of disrespect, but in the public interest, so that the mana of the chief, the tribe's vessel, should not be lowered.

A man's capacity for mana could be increased, however, by study or the acquisition of skill. If he became a master, a tuhuna, in any field, such as canoe building, house building, or knowledge of sacred lore, he acquired mana which helped him in his profession and which did not come via the chief. Mana could also be generated ritually, and so ceremony could increase the mana of a canoe, or of a tuhuna, or of a chief himself, and such ceremonies were important. Handy believes, in fact, that ritual performed for the gods was basically for the purpose of regenerating or increasing the mana of the gods themselves, so that, while they depended on the gods, the people were also able to strengthen the gods by their own exertions.

Tabu [taboo] is another idea which, like mana, the Polynesians thought out carefully, and from which they have given us the word (properly tapu) for our own use. We have taken it to mean something forbidden not by statute but by convention. Obviously there is nothing religious about such an incidental interpretation as this. Among primitive peoples where it has any importance, however, tabu stands for the threat of a powerful evil influence. "Thou shalt do no murder" is both civil and moral law, but is not a tabu in the best sense. "Don't eat mashed potatoes with your fingers" might be our kind of tabu. But "Keep away from the third rail," to someone who lacks a scientific idea of electricity, is a tabu of the original kind.

Tabu was, in Polynesian philosophy, an upset, or anything that caused an upset, in the proper balance of mana, which of course resided in everyone. As Handy says: "Any disturbance of this equilibrium in an individual, either by a surcharge of mana or by a loss of his natural endowment of mana, affected him disastrously." So a commoner was tabu to a chief and a chief was tabu to a commoner, since contact between them would drain off mana from the chief and overload the other. Everyday living for ordinary people was therefore hedged by tabu on either side: above by chiefs and those of royal blood, and below by women or worse—i.e., such things as the evil spirits who were responsible for sickness and death, and who hovered ever ready to take advantage of someone in a delicate or dangerous situation, like a woman in childbirth. To quote Handy again, "What is spoken of as the 'common' needing protection from both divine and corrupt represents the middle ground between the superior and inferior aspects of nature, the common ground of human beings and natural objects, where superior and inferior united in a balanced equilibrium." The effect of tabu on general behavior was very noticeable, especially in the etiquette surrounding a chief.

Everyone had mana in one degree or another; it was located especially in the head, the hair, and the spine. Chiefs, having a tremendous amount by virtue of their close kinship with the gods, constituted an involuntary menace to others, who had to follow strict rules in order not to get an accidental overdose. His barbers necessarily touched the chief's hair, whereat their hands became extremely tabu, to the extent that they could not touch their own heads, or feed themselves, or carry out ordinary actions, until they had been purified and relieved of the tabu by the right ritual. In the same way, a chief's mana ran into everything he used, so that all this became dangerous too. Nobody else could use his furniture, sit in his place, or sleep on his mat; and it was deadly to use his fire to cook with, or even to step over it, or to eat any of his leftover food, or drink out of a castaway cup, no matter how unwittingly any of these things might have been done. This is not theoretical, for there are cases on record from recent times in which a Polynesian had died of dread, and of no other visible cause, simply on discovering that he had inadvertently done one of these things.

In some places the chief was even carried about on a litter, because if he trod a path with his own feet, that path became forever dangerous to commoners. It is clear that without this precaution a chief might make an island of moderate size practically unusable in a short time, so that his only choice was to forgo exercise and keep his feet up. Wherever the tabu idea reached such extremes as this the chief, in spite of his necessary presence as the scion of the gods, must have been an appalling nuisance to everybody, including himself. In fact, in the early nineteenth century, life in Hawaii became so nearly not worth living that Kamehameha II and his people bravely decided to put everything at stake, and all sat down together at one meal, transgressing every tabu. They survived, amid general rejoicing. This seems fatuous enough to us, but to them it was rather like testing an atom bomb in the back yard, in hopes it was a dud. . . .

This same general idea was familiar to the ancients. The Hebrews had it. They had not worked it out upon an expressed belief in mana, which in their case would be merged with the power of Jehovah itself (although the Old Testament suggests such a notion time and again, and a Polynesian would not hesitate to say that Moses was a great tuhuna, palpably suffused with mana). The Hebrews, however, did think and speak of things which were unclean and things which were holy in the same way, as being sacred and untouchable. "Sacred," to us, signifies only the things which are raised up and perfect, the things of heaven, but it first meant those things which are not for human beings to touch. The Hebrews were warned not to go too close when a heathen rite was being held, because they themselves might be "sanctified," i.e., made tabu. Other Hebrew ideas of tabu objects ran close to the Polynesian: dead bodies, mothers after childbirth, most manifestations of sex, warriors, and of course things connected with Jehovah. Any tabu-breaking made the sinner unclean until he could be purified, and tabu objects like new mothers or warriors also called for purification.

Leviticus and Deuteronomy of course teem with tabus, and there can be nobody who has not realized that many of them have no reason, for existence, in morals or ethics, as we understand them. That is an essential feature of a tabu; it is not, as I said, a matter of moral law at all, although naturally the two can mingle. To the Hebrews, the pig was an unclean animal, and they could not eat it. What was the sense of this? In constructing Solomon's temple, they could use no tools of iron. What was the sense of that? There probably are reasons, but not moral ones. The Hebrews, in their tribal origins, were not swineherds, and so perhaps the pig was enemy food, and not for them. And iron may have been prohibited for religious purposes among them, as among some other peoples, because iron was something newfangled; when custom had become fixed they were using bronze or stone tools, and that was the way it should be. Such things gradually became a code of religious laws with the force of tabu.

The classic example of tabu in the Old Testament is the case of the unfortunate Uzzah, the son of Abinadab. Jehovah had ordained that, after it was consecrated, only Aaron and his sons might touch the Ark of the Covenant or the things associated with it. But once, as the Ark was being moved, it was shaken by the oxen and Uzzah put out his hand to steady it, and that was the end of him. Now, except that Jehovah had indicated that the Ark was sacred, and therefore dangerous, there was nothing that we can find wrong in what Uzzah did; by every ethical or moral standard in our own philosophy or that of any other people, Uzzah was doing the right thing; he was trying to keep the Ark from harm. Yet he had forgotten the tabu. He touched the tabued object and got the full voltage. It sounds, altogether, as though Jehovah were issuing not a command, but rather a warning, not to touch the Ark. (The idea of its being charged with something like mana is very clear in the Bible.) It is a question whether, in the original viewpoint which this story represents, Jehovah could have helped this anyway; whether He could have saved Uzzah after the Ark had been sanctified (although, as it actually reads, "the anger of the Lord was kindled against Uzzah"). This was not the only time somebody suffered through inability to handle the holiness of the Ark; the Philistines once got hold of it, in one of their innumerable military entanglements with the Israelites, and it caused them an epidemic of the most unpleasant kind. They were then only too glad to return it to the people who had a ritual to cope with it.

Tabu, as an idea, is widespread, though few cultures have rendered it into so well formed a doctrine as that of the Hebrews and the Polynesians. It attaches, in one tribe or another, to all sorts of things. At crises of life people are surrounded by an aura: at birth, adolescence, often at marriage, and of course at death. Varying reasons may be supplied; usually they are occasions when spirits are likely to take an interest in human affairs, an intrusion which is always unwelcome. But the basic feeling is probably simpler. It is a feeling of apprehension at a change, a feeling that the time is out of joint, that the course of everyday life has been deflected and that the situation is delicate and everyone should be careful. Consider birth. Women are forever having babies, but the fact remains that it is a rather extraordinary thing for them to do, and it leaves everyone excited, nervous, and disturbed. If civilized folk continue to go all atwitter over it, it is easy to see why it makes the uncivilized tread warily. Marriage is similar; bride and groom are entering into a highly intimate relationship in which they can exchange all sorts of tabu influences—primitive people will agree with you that there are few things more mysterious or interesting than sex—and it is therefore natural to proceed with the proper ritual caution in joining them.

Here and there, many different kinds of things create this feeling of tabu. Categories of people do so: women, with their strange physiology; warriors, from their connection with blood and death; and strangers, who come in trailing unfamiliar influences after them, upsetting the local balance of such things. Chiefs or kings; blood; special times, places, or things—examples of tabus on these are endless. Tabu foods are a common idea, and the Hebrew type of prohibitions on certain meats, or certain ways of preparing them (not seething the kid in his mother's milk), are widely found in East Africa.

Finally, of course, various actions may be tabu, and it is here that many obvious moral laws come under tabu's cloak. I said before that the two are not necessarily connected, and cited the laws of Moses as containing many cases of tabu without morals. Naturally, however, there is no reason why they should be separate, and every reason why they should tend to coincide. Grossly faulty ethical behavior always revolts human beings, and of course makes them feel that it also revolts the natural order of things which tabu guards, and therefore such acts as killing and incest have become tabu almost everywhere that the conception of tabu has developed. Thus it is that the majority of the laws of Moses are indeed moral laws and show tabu and morals pulling side by side. I refrained from making this point before, in order to emphasize the essential nature of tabu by itself, but it is important and obvious that tabu should always tend to align itself with the social good. . . .

Tabu makes our first argument on behalf of primitive religion; the first chance to answer the question of why anyone should be devoted to such a baseless belief and what earthly good could come of it. A minor reason is the personal one; it is the reassurance which individual people can draw from an explanation which seems sound and is accepted by everyone else. It is a wonderful thing in this life to know what to do and what not to do; especially the latter, because it is less demanding to avoid doing something than to accomplish something. Tabu shows everyone the correct path to walk, and by marking out the pitfalls gives a sense of safety. Not eating the flesh of the marmot, let us say, and accepting a few limitations in dress or behavior, is a small price to pay for the ability to look forward with confidence, knowing that one is in tune with the universe and that one's ills are not likely to be serious.

Furthermore, when misfortune does arrive, tabu will give its believers the explanation for it and the sense of relief that comes from at least knowing the source of trouble. Nobody likes to have teeth pulled, but if a long siege of aches and pains is finally traced to a bad tooth, the sufferer will rush almost joyfully to the nearest painless dentist, glad to have his general ill-health reduced to a particular single cause. This is parallel with the idea of tabu, and tabu will often work in the same way, by the power of suggestion. Of course it may lead to an occasional catastrophe, as when a Hawaiian gave himself over hopelessly to death because he had made a fearful misstep, but even these cases acted to replenish the faith of others in the system's efficacy.

Far greater is the social usefulness of tabu. Whether it is forming a part of Eskimo religion, which is as informal as a broken umbrella, or of the polished sphere of Polynesian philosophy, it is doing yeomen service for the community by constituting an ever-present prop to morale and by supporting the existing structure and knitting it always more firmly together. It does this primarily by setting up a code of behavior the reasons for which are not only accepted by all but profoundly believed in. It is the effects of this in turn that bolster the body politic. For the actual behavior tabu dictates is not the essential thing; at bottom, it simply creates a sense of carefulness and discipline.

Radcliffe-Brown suggests that tabus are an unconscious way of emphasizing certain important values, which are by themselves too intangible to make their importance duly and constantly felt. In order to exist, a society needs the good will and submissiveness of its members, and in a roundabout way tabu gives them the opportunity to feel that and to express it. For example, to a small tribe the birth of a new member, or the death of an older one, is a matter of importance. And birth and death tabus, which are temporary unusual behavior, make each person connected with the event feel its importance and realize that others are also impressed with it. So tabus act as a ritual confirmation of a tribe's community strength.

I should say that it is probably more general than this, and that tabu serves, where it is recognized, to give a common direction to a society and its ideas of conduct, along with a feeling of common responsibility among its members. It enables such a society gradually to mold a system of morals, lending to the latter the force of religious emotion. But over and above this there are tabus without moral need, and these act simply to ensure that everybody is socially in step and in sympathy, without the need of civil enforcement, like law. And they do act this way. It is obvious, of course, that in some cases Polynesian chiefs, being men of intelligence, used the system of tabu to strengthen their prerogatives, but apart from this they were as deeply in the web as everyone else, and they understood that, no matter how burdensome it was personally, they simply had the greatest share in the common responsibility.

We may not be too pleased at the spectacle of a society goose-stepping to a set of tabus. But it may be accepted that they are better than a vacuum. Values of some sort are necessary; we ourselves need our faith in our own law, our type of government, and our institutions in general; these things support us more than we know. Tabus are a potent agent for a society's control of itself, and it would probably not be possible to organize a community of the complexity of, say, the Polynesians, without the aid of tabu or an equally powerful religious substitute. This is the sort of thing that shows religion to be a necessary social invention.

2. Witchcraft Explains Unfortunate Events

E. E. EVANS-PRITCHARD

It is an inevitable conclusion from Zande descriptions of witchcraft that it is not an objective reality. The physiological condition which is said to be the seat of witchcraft, and which I believe to be nothing more than food passing through the small intestine, is an objective condition, but the qualities they attribute to it and the rest of their beliefs about it are mystical. Witches, as Azande conceive them, cannot exist.

The concept of witchcraft nevertheless provides them with a natural philosophy by which the relations between men and unfortunate events are explained and with a ready and stereotyped means of reacting to such events. Witchcraft beliefs also embrace a system of values which regulate human conduct.

Witchcraft is ubiquitous. It plays its part in every activity of Zande life; in agricultural, fishing, and hunting pursuits; in domestic life of homesteads as well as in communal life of district and court; it is an important theme of mental life in which it forms the background of a vast panorama of oracles and magic; its influence is plainly stamped on law and morals, etiquette and religion; it is prominent in technology and language; there is no niche or corner of Zande culture into which it does not twist itself. If blight seizes the groundnut crop it is witchcraft; if the bush is vainly scoured for game it is witchcraft; if women laboriously bail water out of a pool and are rewarded by but a few small fish it is witchcraft; if termites do not rise when their swarming is due and a cold useless night is spent in waiting for their flight it is witchcraft; if a wife is sulky and unresponsive to her husband it is witchcraft; if a prince is cold and distant with his subject it is witchcraft; if a magical rite fails to achieve its purpose it is witchcraft; if, in fact, any failure or misfortune falls upon any one at any time and in relation to any of the manifold activities of his life it may be due to witchcraft. Those acquainted either at firsthand or through reading with the life of an African people will realize that there is no end to possible misfortunes, in routine tasks and leisure hours alike, arising not only from miscalculation, incompetence, and laziness, but also from causes over which the African, with his meager scientific knowledge, has no control. The Zande attributes all these misfortunes to witchcraft unless there is strong evidence, and subsequent oracular confirmation, that sorcery or one of those evil agents which I mentioned in the preceding section has been at work, or unless they are clearly to be attributed to incompetence, breach of a taboo, or failure to observe a moral rule.

When a Zande speaks of witchcraft he does not speak of it as we speak of the weird witchcraft of our own history. Witchcraft is to him a commonplace happening and he seldom passes a day without mentioning it. Where we talk about the crops, hunting, and our neighbors' ailments the Zande introduces into these topics of conversation the subject of witchcraft. To say that witchcraft has blighted the groundnut crop, that witchcraft has scared away game, and that witchcraft has made so-and-so ill is equivalent to saying in terms of our own culture that the groundnut crop has failed owing to blight, that game is scarce this season, and that so-and-so has caught influenza. Witchcraft participates in all misfortunes and is the idiom in which Azande speak about them and in which they explain them. Witchcraft is a classification of misfortunes which while differing from each other in other respects have this single common character, their harmfulness to man.

Unless the reader appreciates that witchcraft is quite a normal factor in the life of Azande, one to which almost any and every happening may be referred, he will entirely misunderstand their behavior towards it. To us witchcraft is something which haunted and disgusted our credulous forefathers. But the Zande expects to come across witchcraft at any time of the day or night. He would be just as surprised if he were not brought into daily contact with it as we would be if confronted by its appearance. To him there is nothing miraculous about it. It is expected that a man's hunting will be injured by witches, and he has at his disposal means of dealing with them. When misfortunes occur he does not become awestruck at the play of supernatural forces. He is not terrified at the presence of an occult enemy. He is, on the other hand, extremely annoyed. Some one, out of spite, has ruined his groundnuts or spoiled his hunting or given his wife a chill, and surely this is cause for anger! He has done no one harm, so what right has anyone to interfere in his affairs? It is an impertinence, an insult, a dirty, offensive trick! It is the aggressiveness and not the eeriness of these actions which Azande emphasize when speaking of them, and it is anger and not awe which we observe in their response to them.

Witchcraft is not less anticipated than adultery. It is so intertwined with everyday happenings that it is part of a Zande's ordinary world. There is nothing remarkable about a witch—you may be one yourself, and certainly many of your closest neighbors are witches. Nor is there anything awe-inspiring about witchcraft. We do not become psychologically transformed when we hear that someone is ill—we expect people to be ill—and it is the same with Azande. They expect people to be ill, i.e., to be bewitched, and it is not a matter for surprise or wonderment.

But is not Zande belief in witchcraft a belief in mystical causation of phenomena and events to the complete exclusion of all natural causes? The relations of mystical to common-sense thought are very complicated. . . . Here I wish to state the problem in a preliminary manner and in terms of actual situations.

I found it strange at first to live among Azande and listen to naïve explanations of misfortunes which, to our minds, have apparent causes, but after a while I learned the idiom of their thought and applied notions of witchcraft as spontaneously as themselves in situations where the concept was relevant. A boy knocked his foot against a small stump of wood in the center of a bush path, a frequent happening in Africa, and suffered pain and inconvenience in consequence. Owing to its position on his toe it was impossible to keep the cut free from dirt and it began to fester. He declared that witchcraft had made him knock his foot against the stump. I always argued with Azande and criticized their statements, and I did so on this occasion. I told the boy that he had knocked his foot against the stump of wood because he had been careless, and that witchcraft had not placed it in the path, for it had grown there naturally. He agreed that witchcraft had nothing to do with the stump of wood being in his path but added that he had kept his eyes open for stumps, as indeed every Zande does most carefully, and that if he had not been bewitched he would have seen the stump. As a conclusive argument for his view he remarked that all cuts do not take days to heal but, on the contrary, close quickly, for that is the nature of cuts. Why, then, had his sore festered and remained open if there were no witchcraft behind it? This, as I discovered before long, was to be regarded as the Zande explanation of sickness. Thus, to give a further example, I had been feeling unfit for several days, and I consulted Zande friends whether my consumption of bananas could have had anything to do with my indisposition and I was at once informed that bananas do not cause sickness, however many are eaten, unless one is bewitched. . . . I shall record here a few examples of witchcraft being offered as an explanation for happenings other than illness.

Shortly after my arrival in Zandeland we were passing through a government settlement and noticed that a hut had been burnt to the ground on the previous night. Its owner was overcome with grief as it had contained the beer he was preparing for a mortuary feast. He told us that he had gone the previous night to examine his beer. He had lit a handful of straw and raised it above his head so that light would be cast on the pots, and in so doing he had ignited the thatch. He, and my companions also, were convinced that the disaster was caused by witchcraft.

One of my chief informants, Kisanga, was a skilled wood carver, one of the finest carvers in the whole kingdom of Gbudwe. Occasionally the bowls and stools which he carved split during the work, as one may well imagine in such a climate. Though the hardest woods be selected they sometimes split in process of carving or on completion of the utensil even if the craftsman is careful and well acquainted with the technical rules of his craft. When this happened to the bowls and stools of this particular craftsman he attributed the misfortune to witchcraft and used to harangue me about the spite and jealousy of his neighbors. When I used to reply that I thought he was mistaken and that people were well disposed towards him he used to hold the split bowl or stool towards me as concrete evidence of his assertions. If people were not bewitching his work, how would I account for that? Likewise a potter will attribute the cracking of his pots during firing to witchcraft. An experienced potter need have no fear that his pots will crack as a result of error. He selects the proper clay, kneads it thoroughly till he has extracted all grit and pebbles, and builds it up slowly and carefully. On the night before digging out his clay he abstains from sexual intercourse. So he should have nothing to fear. Yet pots sometimes break, even when they are the handiwork of expert potters, and this can only be accounted for by witchcraft. "It is broken— there is witchcraft" says the potter simply. . . .

In speaking to Azande about witchcraft and in observing their reactions to situations of misfortune it was obvious that they did not attempt to account for the existence of phenomena, or even the action of phenomena, by mystical causation alone. What they explained by witchcraft were the particular conditions in a chain of causation which related an individual to natural happenings in such a way that he sustained injury. The boy who knocked his foot against a stump of wood did not account for the stump by reference to witchcraft, nor did he suggest that whenever anybody knocks his foot against a stump it is necessarily due to witch-craft, nor yet again did he account for the cut by saying that it was caused by witchcraft, for he knew quite well that it was caused by the stump of wood. What he attributed to witchcraft was that on this particular occasion, when exercising his usual care, he struck his foot against a stump of wood, whereas on a hundred other occasions he did not do so, and that on this particular occasion the cut, which he expected to result from the knock, festered whereas he had had dozens of cuts which had not festered. Surely these peculiar conditions demand an explana-tion. Again, if one eats a number of bananas this does not in itself cause sickness. Why should it do so? Plenty of people eat bananas but are not sick in consequence, and I myself had often done so in the past. Therefore my indisposition could not possibly be attributed to bananas alone. If bananas alone had caused my sickness, then it was necessary to account for the fact that they had caused me sickness on this single occasion and not on dozens of previous occasions, and that they had made only me ill and not other people who were eating them. Again, every year hundreds of Azande go and inspect their beer by night and they always take with them a handful of straw in order to illuminate the hut in which it is fermenting. Why then should this particular man on this single occasion have ignited the thatch of his hut? I present the Zande's explicit line of reasoning—not my own. Again, my friend the wood carver had made scores of bowls and stools without mishap and he knew all there was to know about the selection of wood, use of tools, and conditions of carving. His bowls and stools did not split like the products of craftsmen who were unskilled in their work, so why on rare occasions should his bowls and stools split when they did not split usually and when he had exercised all his usual knowledge and care? He knew the answer well enough and so, in his opinion, did his envious, backbiting neighbors. In the same way, a potter wants to know why his pots should break on an occasion when he uses the same material and technique as on other occasions; or rather he already knows, for the reason is known in advance, as it were. If the pots break it is due to witchcraft.

We must understand, therefore, that we shall give a false account of Zande philosophy if we say that they believe witchcraft to be the sole cause of phenomena. This proposition is not contained in Zande patterns of thought, which only assert that witchcraft brings a man into relation with events in such a way that he sustains injury.

My old friend Ongosi was many years ago injured by an elephant while out hunting, and his prince, Basongoda, consulted the oracles to discover who had bewitched him. We must distinguish here between the elephant and its prowess, on the one hand, and the fact that a particular elephant injured a particular man, on the other hand. The Supreme Being, not witchcraft, created elephants and gave them tusks and a trunk and huge legs so that they are able to pierce men and fling them sky high and reduce them to pulp by kneeling on them. But whenever men and elephants come across one another in the bush these dreadful things do not happen. They are rare events. Why, then, should this particular man on this one occasion in a life crowded with similar situations in which he and his friends emerged scatheless have been gored by this particular beast? Why he and not someone else? Why on this occasion and not on other occasions? Why by this elephant and not by other elephants? It is the particular and variable conditions of an event and not the general and universal conditions that witchcraft explains. Fire is hot, but it is not hot owing to witchcraft, for that is its nature. It is a universal quality of fire to burn, but it is not a universal quality of fire to burn *you*. This may never happen; or once in a lifetime, and then only if you have been bewitched.

In Zandeland sometimes an old granary collapses. There is nothing remarkable in this. Every Zande knows that termites eat the supports in course of time and that even the hardest woods decay after years of service. Now a granary is the summerhouse of a Zande homestead and people sit beneath it in the heat of the day and chat or play the African hole game or work at some craft. Consequently it may happen that there are people sitting beneath the granary when it collapses and they are injured, for it is a heavy structure made of beams and clay and may be stored with eleusine as well. Now why should these particular people have been sitting under this particular granary at the particular moment when it collapsed? That it should collapse is easily intelligible, but why should it have collapsed at the particular moment when these particular people were sitting beneath it? Through years it might have collapsed, so why should it fall just when certain people sought its kindly shelter? We say that the granary collapsed because its supports were eaten away by termites. That is the cause that explains the collapse of the granary. We also say that people were sitting under it at the time because it was in the heat of the day and they thought that it would be a comfortable place to talk and work. This is the cause of people being under the granary at the time it collapsed. To our minds the only relationship between these two independently caused facts is their coincidence in time and space. We have no explanation of why the two chains of causation intersected at a certain time and in a certain place, for there is no interdependence between them.

Zande philosophy can supply the missing link. The Zande knows that the supports were undermined by termites and that people were sitting beneath the granary in order to escape the heat and glare of the sun. But he knows besides why these two events occurred at a precisely similar moment in time and space. It was due to the action of witchcraft. If there had been no witchcraft people would have been sitting under the granary and it would not have fallen on them, or it would have collapsed but the people would not have been sheltering under it at the time. Witchcraft explains the coincidence of these two happenings.

Magic, Ritual, and Symbolism

3. Magic

BRONISLAW MALINOWSKI

In spite of the various theories about a specific non-empirical and prelogical character of primitive mentality there can be no doubt that as soon as man developed the mastery of environment by the use of implements, and as soon as language came into being, there must also have existed primitive knowledge of an essentially scientific character. No culture could survive if its arts and crafts, its weapons and economic pursuits were based on mystical, non-empirical conceptions and doctrines. When human culture is approached from the pragmatic, technological side, it is found that primitive man is capable of exact observation, of sound generalizations and of logical reasoning in all those matters which affect his normal activities and are at the basis of his production. Knowledge is then an absolute derived necessity of culture. It is more, however, than a means to an end, and it was not classed therefore with the instrumental imperatives. Its place in culture, its function, is slightly different from that of production, of law, or of education. Systems of knowledge serve to connect various types of behavior; they carry over the results of past experiences into future enterprise and they bring together elements of human experience and allow man to co-ordinate and integrate his activities. Knowledge is a mental attitude, a diathesis of the nervous system, which allows man to carry on the work which culture makes him do. Its function is to organize and integrate the indispensable activities of culture.

The material embodiment of knowledge consists in the body of arts and crafts, of technical processes and rules of craftsmanship. More specifically, in most primitive cultures and certainly in higher ones there are special implements of knowledge—diagrams, topographical models, measures, aids to orientation or to counting.

The connection between native thought and language opens important problems of function. Linguistic abstraction, categories of space, time and relationship, and logical means of expressing the concatenation of ideas are extremely important matters, and the study of how thought works through language in any culture is still a virgin field of cultural linguistics. How primitive language works, where it is embodied, how it is related to social organization, to primitive religion and magic, are important problems of functional anthropology.

By the very forethought and foresight which it gives, the integrative function of knowledge creates new needs, that is, imposes new imperatives. Knowledge gives man the possibility of planning ahead, of embracing vast spaces of time and distance; it allows a wide range to his hopes and desires. But however much knowledge and science help man in allowing him to obtain what he wants, they are unable completely to control chance, to eliminate accidents, to foresee the unexpected turn of natural events, or to make human handiwork reliable and adequate to all practical requirements. In this field, much more practical, definite, and circumscribed than that of religion, there develops a special type of ritual activities which anthropology labels collectively as magic.

The most hazardous of all human enterprises known to primitive man is sailing. In the preparation of his sailing craft and the laying out of his plans the savage turns to his science. The painstaking work as well as the intelligently organized labor in construction and in navigation bears witness to the savage's trust in science and submission to it. But adverse wind or no wind at all, rough weather, currents and reefs are always liable to upset his best plans and most careful preparations. He must admit that neither his knowledge nor his most painstaking efforts are a guaranty of success. Something unaccountable usually enters and baffles his anticipations. But although unaccountable it yet appears to have a deep meaning, to act or behave with a purpose. The sequence, the significant concatenation of events, seems to contain some inner logical consistency. Man feels that he can do something to wrestle with that mysterious element or force, to help and abet his luck. There are therefore always systems of superstition, of more or less developed ritual, associated with sailing, and in primitive communities the magic of sailing craft is highly developed. Those who are well acquainted with some good magic have, in virtue of that, courage and confidence. When the canoes are used for fishing, the accidents and the good or bad luck may refer not only to transport but also to the appearance of fish and to the conditions under which they are caught. In trading, whether overseas or with near neighbors, chance may favor or thwart the ends and desires of man. As a result both fishing and trading magic are very well developed.

Likewise in war, man, however primitive, knows that well-made weapons of attack and defense, strategy, the force of numbers, and the strength of the individuals ensure victory. Yet with all this the unforeseen and accidental help even the weaker to victory when the fray happens under the cover of night, when ambushes are possible, when the conditions of the encounter obviously favor one side at the expense of the other. Magic is used as something which over and above man's equipment and his force helps him to master accident and to ensnare luck. In love also a mysterious, unaccountable quality of success or else a predestination to failure seems to be accompanied by some force independent of ostensible attraction and of the best laid plans and arrangements. Magic enters to insure something which counts over and above the visible and accountable qualifications.

Primitive man depends on his economic pursuits for his welfare in a manner which makes him realize bad luck very painfully and directly. Among people who rely on their fields or gardens what might be called agricultural knowledge is invariably well developed. The natives know the properties of the soil, the need of a thorough clearing from bush and weed, fertilizing with ashes and appropriate planting. But however well chosen the site and well worked the gardens, mishaps occur. Drought or deluge coming at most inappropriate seasons destroys the crops altogether, or some blights, insects, or wild animals diminish them. Or some other year, when man is conscious that he deserves but a poor crop, everything runs so smoothly and prosperously that an unexpectedly good return rewards the undeserving gardener. The dreaded elements of rain and sunshine, pests and fertility seem to be controlled by a force which is beyond ordinary human experience and knowledge, and man repairs once more to magic.

In all these examples the same factors are involved. Experience and logic teach man that within definite limits knowledge is supreme; but beyond them nothing can be done by rationally founded practical exertions. Yet he rebels against inaction because although he realizes his impotence he is yet driven to action by intense desire and strong emotions. Nor is inaction at all possible. Once he has embarked on a distant voyage or finds himself in the middle of a fray or halfway through the cycle of garden growing, the native tries to make his frail canoe more seaworthy by charms or to drive away locusts and wild animals by ritual or to vanquish his enemies by dancing.

Magic changes its forms; it shifts its ground; but it exists everywhere. In modern societies magic is associated with the third cigarette lit by the same match, with spilled salt and the need of throwing it over the left shoulder, with broken mirrors, with passing under a ladder, with the new moon seen through glass or on the left hand, with the number thirteen or with Friday. These are minor superstitions which seem merely to vegetate among the intelligentsia of the western world. But these superstitions and much more developed systems also persist tenaciously and are given serious consideration among modern urban populations. Black magic is practiced in the slums of London by the classical method of destroying the picture of the enemy. At marriage ceremonies good luck for the married couple is obtained by the strictest observance of several magical methods such as the throwing of the slipper and the spilling of rice. Among the peasants of central and eastern Europe elaborate magic still flourishes and children are treated by witches and warlocks. People are thought to have the power to prevent cows from giving milk, to induce cattle to multiply unduly, to produce rain and sunshine and to make people love or hate each other. The saints of the Roman Catholic Church become in popular practice passive accomplices of magic. They are beaten, cajoled and carried about. They can give rain by being placed in the field, stop flows of lava by confronting them and stop the progress of a disease, of a blight or of a plague of insects. The crude practical use made of certain religious rituals or objects makes their function magical. For magic is distinguished from religion in that the latter creates values and attains ends directly, whereas magic consists of acts which have a practical utilitarian value and are effective only as a means to an end. Thus a strictly utilitarian subject matter or issue of an act and its direct, instrumental function make it magic, and most modern established religions harbor within their ritual and even their ethics a good deal which really belongs to magic. But modern magic survives not only in the forms of minor superstitions or within the body of religious systems. Wherever there is danger, uncertainty, great incidence of chance and accident, even in entirely modern forms of enterprise, magic crops up. The gambler at Monte Carlo, on the turf, or in a continental state lottery develops systems. Motoring and modern sailing demand mascots and develop superstitions. Around every sensational sea tragedy there has formed a myth showing some mysterious magical indications or giving magical reasons for the catastrophe. Aviation is developing its superstitions and magic. Many pilots refuse to take up a passenger who is wearing anything green, to start a journey on a Friday, or to light three cigarettes with a match when in the air, and their sensitiveness to superstition seems to increase with altitude. In all large cities of Europe and America magic can be purchased from palmists, clairvoyants, and other soothsayers who forecast the future, give practical advice as to lucky conduct, and retail ritual apparatus such as amulets, mascots, and talismans. The richest domain of magic, however, is, in civilization as in savagery, that of health. Here again the old venerable religions lend themselves readily to magic. Roman Catholicism opens its sacred shrines and places of worship to the ailing pilgrim, and faith healing flourishes also in other churches. The main function of Christian Science is the thinking away of illness and decay; its metaphysics are very strongly pragmatic and utilitarian and its ritual is essentially a means to the end of health and happiness. The unlimited range of universal remedies and blessings, osteopathy and chiropractic, dietetics and curing by sun, cold water, grape or lemon juice, raw food, starvation, alcohol or its prohibition—one and all shade invariably into magic. Intellectuals still submit to Coué and Freud, to Jaeger and Kneipp, to sun worship, either direct or through the mercury-vapor lamp—not to mention the bedside manner of the highly paid specialist. It is very difficult to discover where common sense ends and where magic begins.

The savage is not more rational than modern man nor is he more superstitious. He is more limited, less liable to free imaginings and to the confidence trick of new inventions. His magic is traditional and he has his stronghold of knowledge, his empirical and rational tradition of science. Since the superstitious or prelogical character of primitive man has been so much emphasized, it is necessary to draw clearly the dividing line between primitive science and magic. There are domains on which magic never encroaches. The making of fire, basketry, the actual production of stone implements, the making of strings or mats, cooking and all minor domestic activities, although extremely important, are never associated with magic. Some of them become the center of religious practices and of mythology, as, for example, fire or cooking or stone implements; but magic is never connected with their production. The reason is that ordinary skill guided by sound knowledge is sufficient to set man on the right path and to give him certainty of correct and complete control of these activities.

In some pursuits magic is used under certain conditions and is absent under others. In a maritime community depending on the products of the sea there is never magic connected with the collecting of shellfish or with fishing by poison, weirs, and fish traps, so long as these are completely reliable. On the other hand, any dangerous, hazardous, and uncertain type of fishing is surrounded by ritual. In hunting, the simple and reliable ways of trapping or killing are controlled by knowledge and skill alone; but let there be any danger or any uncertainty connected with an important supply of game and magic immediately appears. Coastal sailing as long as it is perfectly safe and easy commands no magic. Overseas expeditions are invariably bound up with ceremonies and ritual. Man resorts to magic only where chance and circumstances are not fully controlled by knowledge.

This is best seen in what might be called systems of magic. Magic may be but loosely and capriciously connected with its practical setting. One hunter may use certain formulae and rites, and another ignore them; or the same man may apply his conjurings on one occasion and not on another. But there are forms of enterprise in which magic must be used. In a big tribal adventure, such as war, or a hazardous sailing expedition or seasonal travel or an undertaking such as a big hunt or a perilous fishing expedition or the normal round of gardening, which as a rule is vital to the whole community, magic is often obligatory. It runs in a fixed sequence concatenated with the practical events, and the two orders, magical and practical, depend on one another and form a system. Such systems of magic appear at first sight an inextricable mixture of efficient work and superstitious practices and so seem to provide an unanswerable argument in favor of the theories that magic and science are under primitive conditions so fused as not to be separable. Fuller analysis, however, shows that magic and practical work are entirely independent and never fuse.

But magic is never used to replace work. In gardening the digging or the clearing of the ground or the strength of the fences or quality of the supports is never scamped because stronger magic has been used over them. The native knows well that mechanical construction must be produced by human labor according to strict rules of craft. He knows that all the processes which have been in the soil can be controlled by human effort to a certain extent but not beyond, and it is only this beyond which he tries to influence by magic. For his experience and his reason tell him that in certain matters his efforts and his intelligence are of no avail whatever. On the other hand, magic has been known to help; so at least his tradition tells him.

In the magic of war and of love, of trading expeditions and of fishing, of sailing and of canoe making, the rules of experience and logic are likewise strictly adhered to as regards technique, and knowledge and technique receive due credit in all the good results which can be attributed to them. It is only the unaccountable results, which an outside observer would attribute to luck, to the knack of doing things successfully, to chance or to fortune, that the savage attempts to control by magic.

Magic therefore, far from being primitive science, is the outgrowth of clear recognition that science has its limits and that a human mind and human skill are at times impotent. For all its appearances of megalomania, for all that it seems to be the declaration of the "omnipotence of thought," as it has recently been defined by Freud, magic has greater affinity with an emotional outburst, with daydreaming, with strong, unrealizable desire.

To affirm with Frazer that magic is a pseudo-science would be to recognize that magic is not really primitive science. It would imply that magic has an affinity with science or at least that it is the raw material out of which science develops— implications which are untenable. The ritual of magic shows certain striking characteristics which have made it quite plausible for most writers from Grimm and Tylor to Freud and Lévy-Bruhl to affirm that magic takes the place of primitive science.

Magic unquestionably is dominated by the sympathetic principle: like produces like; the whole is affected if the sorcerer acts on a part of it; occult influences can be imparted by contagion. If one concentrates on the form of the ritual only, he can legitimately conclude with Frazer that the analogy between the magical and the scientific conceptions of the world is close and that the various cases of sympathetic magic are mistaken applications of one or the other of two great fundamental laws of thought, namely, the association of ideas by similarity and the association of ideas by contiguity in space or time.

But a study of the function of science and the function of magic casts a doubt on the sufficiency of these conclusions. Sympathy is not the basis of prag-matic science, even under the most primitive conditions. The savage knows scientifically that a small pointed stick of hard wood rubbed or drilled against a piece of soft, brittle wood, provided they are both dry, gives fire. He also knows that strong, energetic, increasingly swift motion has to be employed, that tinder must be produced in the action, the wind kept off, and the spark fanned immedi-ately into a glow and this into a flame. There is no sympathy, no similarity, no taking the part instead of the legitimate whole, no contagion. The only associa-tion or connection is the empirical, correctly observed and correctly framed con-catenation of natural events. The savage knows that a strong bow well handled releases a swift arrow, that a broad beam makes for stability and a light, well-shaped hull for swiftness in his canoe. There is here no association of ideas by similarity or contagion or *pars pro toto*. The native puts a yam or a banana sprout into an appropriate piece of ground. He waters or irrigates it unless it be well drenched by rain. He weeds the ground round it, and he knows quite well that barring unexpected calamities the plant will grow. Again there is no principle akin to that of sympathy contained in this activity. He creates conditions which are perfectly scientific and rational and lets nature do its work. Therefore in so far as magic consists in the enactment of sympathy, in so far as it is governed by an association of ideas, it radically differs from science; and on analysis the similarity of form between magic and science is revealed as merely apparent, not real.

The sympathetic rite although a very prominent element in magic func-tions always in the context of other elements. Its main purpose always consists in the generation and transference of magical force and accordingly it is performed in the atmosphere of the supernatural. As Hubert and Mauss have shown, acts of magic are always set apart, regarded as different, conceived and carried out under distinct conditions. The time when magic is performed is often determined by tradition rather than by the sympathetic principle, and the place where it is performed is only partly determined by sympathy or contagion and more by super-natural and mythological associations. Many of the substances used in magic are largely sympathetic but they are often used primarily for the physiological and emotional reaction which they elicit in man. The dramatic emotional elements in ritual enactment incorporate, in magic, factors which go far beyond sympathy or any scientific or pseudo-scientific principle. Mythology and tradition are everywhere embedded, especially in the performance of the magical spell, which must be repeated with absolute faithfulness to the traditional original and during which mythological events are recounted in which the power of the prototype is invoked. The supernatural character of magic is also expressed in the abnormal character of the magician and by the temporary taboos which surround its execution.

In brief, there exists a sympathetic principle: the ritual of magic contains usually some reference to the results to be achieved; it foreshadows them, anticipates the desired events. The magician is haunted by imagery, by symbolism, by associations of the result to follow. But he is quite as definitely haunted by the emotional obsession of the situation which has forced him to resort to magic. These facts do not fit into the simple scheme of sympathy conceived as misapplication of crude observations and half-logical deductions. The various apparently disjointed elements of magical ritual—the dramatic features, the emotional side, the mythological allusions, and the anticipation of the end—make it impossible to consider magic a sober scientific practice based on an empirical theory. Nor can magic be guided by experience and at the same time be constantly harking back to myth.

The fixed time, the determined spot, the preliminary isolating conditions of magic, the taboos to be observed by the performer, as well as his physiological and sociological nature, place the magical act in an atmosphere of the supernatural. Within this context of the supernatural the rite consists, functionally speaking, in the production of a specific virtue or force and of the launching, directing, or impelling of this force to the desired object. The production of magical force takes place by spell, manual and bodily gesticulation, and the proper condition of the officiating magician. All these elements exhibit a tendency to a formal assimilation toward the desired end or toward the ordinary means of producing this end. This formal resemblance is probably best defined in the statement that the whole ritual is dominated by the emotions of hate, fear, anger, or erotic passion, or by the desire to obtain a definite practical end.

The magical force or virtue is not conceived as a natural force. Hence the theories propounded by Preuss, Marett, and Hubert and Mauss, which would make the Melanesian mana or the similar North American concepts the clue to the understanding of all magic, are not satisfactory. The mana concept embraces personal power, natural force, excellence and efficiency alongside the specific virtue of magic. It is a force regarded as absolutely *sui generis,* different either from natural forces or from the normal faculties of man.

The force of magic can be produced only and exclusively within traditionally prescribed rites. It can be received and learned only by due initiation into the craft and by the taking over of the rigidly defined system of conditions, acts, and observances. Even when magic is discovered or invented it is invariably conceived as true revelation from the supernatural. Magic is an intrinsic, specific quality of a situation and of an object or phenomenon within the situation, consisting in the object being amenable to human control by means which are specifically and uniquely connected with the object and which can be handled only by appropriate people. Magic therefore is always conceived as something which does not reside in nature, that is, outside man, but in the relation between man and nature. Only those objects and forces in nature which are very important to man, on which he depends and which he cannot yet normally control elicit magic.

A functional explanation of magic may be stated in terms of individual psychology and of the cultural and social value of magic. Magic is to be expected and generally to be found whenever man comes to an unbridgeable gap, a hiatus in his knowledge or in his powers of practical control, and yet has to continue in his pursuit. Forsaken by his knowledge, baffled by the results of his experience, unable to apply any effective technical skill, he realizes his impotence. Yet his desire grips him only the more strongly. His fears and hopes, his general anxiety, produce a state of unstable equilibrium in his organism, by which he is driven to some sort of vicarious activity. In the natural human reaction to frustrated hate and impotent anger is found the *materia prima* of black magic. Unrequited love provokes spontaneous acts of prototype magic. Fear moves every human being to aimless but compulsory acts; in the presence of an ordeal one always has recourse to obsessive daydreaming.

The natural flow of ideas under the influence of emotions and desires thwarted in their full practical satisfaction leads one inevitably to the anticipation of the positive results. But the experience upon which this anticipatory or sympathetic attitude rests is not the ordinary experience of science. It is much more akin to daydreaming, to what the psychoanalysts call wish fulfillment. When the emotional state reaches the breaking point at which man loses control over himself, the words which he utters, the gestures to which he gives way, and the physiological process within his organism which accompany all this allow the pent-up tension to flow over. Over all such outbursts of emotion, over such acts of prototype magic, there presides the obsessive image of the desired end. The substitute action in which the physiological crisis finds its expression has a subjective value: the desired end seems nearer satisfaction. . . .

4. Religion as a Cultural System

CLIFFORD GEERTZ

> *Any attempt to speak without speaking any particular language is not more hopeless than the attempt to have a religion that shall be no religion in particular. . . . Thus every living and healthy religion has a marked idiosyncrasy. Its power consists in its special and surprising message and in the bias which that revelation gives to life. The vistas it opens and the mysteries it propounds are another world to live in; and another world to live in—whether we expect ever to pass wholly over into it or no—is what we mean by having a religion.*
>
> —Santayana, Reason in Religion (1906)

As we are to deal with meaning, let us begin with a paradigm: *viz.*, that sacred symbols function to synthesize a people's ethos—the tone, character and quality of their life, its moral and aesthetic style and mood—and their world-view—the picture they have of the way things in sheer actuality are, their most comprehensive ideas of order. In religious belief and practice a group's ethos is rendered intellectually reasonable by being shown to represent a way of life ideally adapted to the actual state of affairs the world-view describes, while the world-view is rendered emotionally convincing by being presented as an image of an actual state of affairs peculiarly well-arranged to accommodate such a way of life. This confrontation and mutual confirmation has two fundamental effects. On the one hand, it objectifies moral and aesthetic preferences by depicting them as the imposed conditions of life implicit in a world with a particular structure, as mere common sense given the unalterable shape of reality. On the other, it supports these received beliefs about the world's body by invoking deeply felt moral and aesthetic sentiments as experiential evidence for their truth. Religious symbols formulate a basic congruence between a particular style of life and a specific (if, most often, implicit) metaphysic, and in so doing sustain each with the borrowed authority of the other.

Phrasing aside, this much may perhaps be granted. The notion that religion tunes human actions to an envisaged cosmic order and projects images of cosmic order onto the plane of human experience is hardly novel. But it is hardly investigated either, so that we have very little idea of how, in empirical terms, this particular miracle is accomplished. We just know that it is done, annually, weekly, daily, for some people almost hourly; and we have an enormous ethnographic literature to demonstrate it. But the theoretical framework which would enable us to provide an analytic account of it, an account of the sort we can provide for lineage segmentation, political succession, labor exchange or the socialization of the child, does not exist.

Let us, therefore, reduce our paradigm to a definition, for although it is notorious that definitions establish nothing in themselves they do, if they are carefully enough constructed, provide a useful orientation, or reorientation, of thought, such that an extended unpacking of them can be an effective way of developing and controlling a novel line of inquiry. They have the useful virtue of explicitness: they commit themselves in a way discursive prose, which, in this field [anthropology] especially, is always liable to substitute rhetoric for argument, does not. Without ado, then, a *religion* is:

(1) a system of symbols which acts to (2) establish powerful, pervasive and long-lasting moods and motivations in men by (3) formulating conceptions of a general order of existence and (4) clothing these conceptions with such an aura of factuality that (5) the moods and motivations seem uniquely realistic.

1. . . . A SYSTEM OF SYMBOLS WHICH ACTS TO . . .

Such a tremendous weight is being put on the term "symbol" here that our first move must be to decide with some precision what we are going to mean by it. This is no easy task, for, rather like "culture," "symbol" has been used to refer to a great variety of things, often a number of them at the same time. . . .

So far as culture patterns, i.e., systems or complexes of symbols, are concerned, the genetic trait which is of first importance for us here is that they are extrinsic sources of information. By "extrinsic," I mean only that—unlike genes, for example—they lie outside the boundaries of the individual organism as such in that intersubjective world of common understandings into which all human individuals are born, pursue their separate careers, and leave persisting behind them after they die. By "sources of information," I mean only that—like genes—they provide a blueprint or template in terms of which processes external to themselves can be given a definite form. As the order of bases in a strand of DNA forms a coded program, a set of instructions or a recipe, for the synthesization of the structurally complex proteins which shape organic functioning, so culture patterns provide such programs for the institution of the social and psychological processes which shape public behavior. Though the sort of information and the mode of its transmission are vastly different in the two cases, this comparison of gene and symbol is more than a strained analogy of the familiar "social heredity" sort. It is actually a substantial relationship, for it is precisely the fact that genetically programmed processes are so highly generalized in men, as compared with lower animals, that culturally programmed ones are so important, only because human behavior is so loosely determined by intrinsic sources of information that extrinsic sources are so vital. To build a dam a beaver needs only an appropriate site and the proper materials—his mode of procedure is shaped by his physiology. But man, whose genes are silent on the building trades, needs also a conception of what it is to build a dam, a conception he can get only from some symbolic source—a blueprint, a textbook or a string of speech by someone who already knows how dams are built, or, of course, from manipulating graphic or linguistic elements in such a way as to attain for himself a conception of what dams are and how they are built.

This point is sometimes put in the form of an argument that cultural patterns are "models," that they are sets of symbols whose relations to one another "model" relations among entities, processes or what-have-you in physical, organic, social or psychological systems by "paralleling," "imitating" or "simulating" · them. . . .

2. . . . TO ESTABLISH POWERFUL, PERVASIVE AND LONG-LASTING MOODS AND MOTIVATIONS IN MEN BY . . .

So far as religious activities are concerned . . . two somewhat different sorts of dispositions are induced by them: moods and motivations.

The major difference between moods and motivations is that where the latter are, so to speak, vectorial qualities, the former are merely scalar. Motives have a directional cast, they describe a certain overall course, gravitate toward certain, usually temporary, consummations. But moods vary only as to intensity: they go nowhere. They spring from certain circumstances but they are responsive to no ends. Like fogs, they just settle and lift; like scents, suffuse and evaporate. When present they are totalistic: if one is sad everything and everybody seems dreary; if one is gay, everything and everybody seems splendid. Thus, though a man can be vain, brave, willful and independent at the same time, he can't very well be playful and listless, or exultant and melancholy at the same time. Further, where motives persist for more or less extended periods of time, moods merely recur with greater or lesser frequency, coming and going for what are often quite unfathomable reasons. But perhaps the most important difference, so far as we are concerned, between moods and motivations is that motivations are "made meaningful" with reference to the ends toward which they are conceived to conduce, while moods are "made meaningful" with reference to the conditions from which they are conceived to spring. We interpret motives in terms of their consummations, but we interpret moods in terms of their sources. We say that a person is industrious because he wishes to succeed, we say that a person is worried because he is conscious of the hanging threat of nuclear holocaust. And this is no less the case when the interpretations invoked are ultimate. Charity becomes Christian charity when it is enclosed in a conception of God's purposes; optimism is Christian optimism when it is grounded in a particular conception of God's nature. The assiduity of the Navaho finds its rationale in a belief that, as "reality" operates mechanically, it is coercible; their chronic fearfulness finds its rationale in a conviction that, however "reality" operates, it is both enormously powerful and terribly dangerous.

3. . . . BY FORMULATING CONCEPTIONS OF A GENERAL ORDER OF EXISTENCE AND . . .

That the symbols or symbol systems which induce and define dispositions we set off as religious and those which place those dispositions in a cosmic framework are the same symbols ought to occasion no surprise. For what else do we mean by saying that a particular mood of awe is religious and not secular except that it springs from entertaining a conception of all-pervading vitality like mana and not from a visit to the Grand Canyon? Or that a particular case of asceticism is an example of a religious motivation except that it is directed toward the achievement of an unconditioned end like nirvana and not a conditioned one like weight-reduction? If sacred symbols did not at one and the same time, induce dispositions in human beings and formulate, however obliquely, inarticulately or unsystematically, general ideas of order, then the empirical differentia of religious activity or religious experience would not exist. A man can indeed be said to be "religious" about golf, but not merely if he pursues it with passion and plays it on Sundays: he must also see it as symbolic of some transcendent truths. And the pubescent boy gazing soulfully into the eyes of the pubescent girl in a William Steig cartoon and murmuring, "There is something about you, Ethel, which gives me a sort of religious feeling," is, like most adolescents, confused. What any particular religion affirms about the fundamental nature of reality may be obscure, shallow or, all too often, perverse, but it must, if it is not to consist of the mere collection of received practices and conventional sentiments we usually refer to as moralism, affirm something. If one were to essay a minimal definition of religion today it would perhaps not be Tylor's famous "belief in spiritual beings," to which Goody, wearied of theoretical subtleties, has lately urged us to return, but rather what Salvador de Madariaga has called "the relatively modest dogma that God is not mad."

Usually, of course, religions affirm very much more than this: we believe, as James remarked, all that we can and would believe everything if we only could. The thing we seem least able to tolerate is a threat to our powers of conception, a suggestion that our ability to create, grasp and use symbols may fail us, for were this to happen we would be more helpless, as I have already pointed out, than the beavers. The extreme generality, diffuseness and variability of man's innate (i.e., genetically programmed) response capacities means that without the assistance of cultural patterns he would be functionally incomplete, not merely a talented ape who had, like some under-privileged child, unfortunately been prevented from realizing his full potentialities, but a kind of formless monster with neither sense of direction nor power of self-control, a chaos of spasmodic impulses and vague emotions. Man depends upon symbols and symbol systems with a dependence so great as to be decisive for his creatural viability and, as a result, his sensitivity to even the remotest indication that they may prove unable to cope with one or another aspect of experience raises within him the gravest sort of anxiety.

There are at least three points where chaos—a tumult of events which lack not just interpretations but *interpretability*—threatens to break in upon man: at the limits of his analytic capacities, at the limits of his powers of endurance, and at the limits of his moral insight. Bafflement, suffering and a sense of intractable ethical paradox are all, if they become intense enough or are sustained long enough, radical challenges to the proposition that life is comprehensible and that we can, by taking thought, orient ourselves effectively within it—challenges with which any religion, however "primitive," which hopes to persist must attempt somehow to cope.

Of the three issues, it is the first which has been least investigated by modern social anthropologists (though Evans-Pritchard's classic discussion of why granaries fall on some Azande and not on others, is a notable exception). Even to consider people's religious beliefs as attempts to bring anomalous events or experiences—death, dreams, mental fugues, volcanic eruptions or marital infidelity—within the circle of the at least potentially inexplicable seems to smack of Tyloreanism or worse. But it does appear to be a fact that at least some men— in all probability, most men—are unable to leave unclarified problems of analysis merely unclarified, just to look at the stranger features of the world's landscape in dumb astonishment or bland apathy without trying to develop, however fantastic, inconsistent or simpleminded, some notions as to how such features might be reconciled with the more ordinary deliverances of experience. Any chronic failure of one's explanatory apparatus, the complex of received culture patterns (common sense, science, philosophical speculation, myth) one has for mapping the empirical world, to explain things which cry out for explanation, tends to lead to a deep disquiet—a tendency rather more widespread and a disquiet rather deeper than we have sometimes supposed since the pseudo-science view of religious belief was, quite rightfully, deposed. After all, even that high priest of heroic atheism, Lord Russell, once remarked that although the problem of the existence of God had never bothered him, the ambiguity of certain mathematical axioms had threatened to unhinge his mind. And Einstein's profound dissatisfaction with quantum mechanics was based on a—surely religious—inability to believe that, as he put it, God plays dice with the universe.

But this quest for lucidity and the rush of metaphysical anxiety that occurs when empirical phenomena threaten to remain intransigently opaque is found on much humbler intellectual levels. Certainly, I was struck in my own work, much more than I had at all expected to be by the degree to which my more animistically inclined informants behaved like true Tyloreans. They seemed to be constantly using their beliefs to "explain" phenomena: or, more accurately, to convince themselves that the phenomena were explainable within the accepted scheme of things, for they commonly had only a minimal attachment to the particular soul possession, emotional disequilibrium, taboo infringement or bewitchment hypothesis they advanced and were all too ready to abandon it for some other, in the same genre, which struck them as more plausible given the facts of the case. What they were *not* ready to do was abandon it for no other hypothesis at all; to leave events to themselves.

The second experiential challenge in whose face the meaningfulness of a particular pattern of life threatens to dissolve into a chaos of thingless names and nameless things—the problem of suffering—has been rather more investigated, or at least described, mainly because of the great amount of attention given in works on tribal religion to what are perhaps its two main loci: illness and mourning. Yet for all the fascinated interest in the emotional aura which surrounds these extreme situations, there has been, with a few exceptions such as Lienhardt's recent discussion of Dinka divining, little conceptual advance over the sort of crude confidence type theory set forth by Malinowski: *viz.*, that religion helps one to endure "situations of emotional stress" by "open[ing] up escapes from such situations and such impasses as offer no empirical way out except by ritual and belief into the domain of the supernatural." The inadequacy of this "theology of optimism," as Nadel rather drily called it, is, of course, radical. Over its career religion has probably disturbed men as much as it has cheered them; forced them into a head-on, unblinking confrontation of the fact that they are born to trouble as often as it has enabled them to avoid such a confrontation by projecting them into a sort of infantile fairy-tale world where—Malinowski again—"hope cannot fail nor desire deceive." With the possible exception of Christian Science, there are few if any religious traditions, "great" or "little," in which the proposition that life hurts is not strenuously affirmed and in some it is virtually glorified.

As a religious problem, the problem of suffering is, paradoxically, not how to avoid suffering but how to suffer, how to make of physical pain, personal loss, worldly defeat or the helpless contemplation of others' agony something bearable, supportable—something, as we say, sufferable.

The problem of suffering passes easily into the problem of evil, for if suffering is severe enough it usually, though not always, seems morally undeserved as well, at least to the sufferer. But they are not, however, exactly the same thing—a fact I think Weber, too influenced by the biases of a monotheistic tradition in which, as the various aspects of human experience must be conceived to proceed from a single, voluntaristic source, man's pain reflects directly on God's goodness, did not fully recognize in his generalization of the dilemmas of Christian theodicy Eastward. For where the problem of suffering is concerned with threats to our ability to put our "undisciplined squads of emotion" into some sort of soldierly order, the problem of evil is concerned with threats to our ability to make sound moral judgments. What is involved in the problem of evil is not the adequacy of our symbolic resources to govern our affective life, but the adequacy of those resources to provide a workable set of ethical criteria, normative guides to govern our action. The vexation here is the gap between things as they are and as they ought to be if our conceptions of right and wrong make sense, the gap between what we deem various individuals deserve and what we see that they get—a phenomenon summed up in that profound quatrain:

> The rain falls on the just
> And on the unjust fella;
> But mainly upon the just,
> Because the unjust has the just's umbrella.

Or if this seems too flippant an expression of an issue that, in somewhat different form, animates the Book of Job and the Baghavad Gita, the following classical Javanese poem, known, sung, and repeatedly quoted in Java by virtually everyone over the age of six, puts the point—the discrepancy between moral prescriptions and material rewards, the seeming inconsistency of "is" and "ought"— rather more elegantly:

> We have lived to see a time without order
> In which everyone is confused in his mind.
> One cannot bear to join in the madness,
> But if he does not do so
> He will not share in the spoils,
> And will starve as a result.
> Yes, God; wrong is wrong:
> Happy are those who forget,
> Happier yet those who remember and have deep insight.

The problem of evil, or perhaps one should say the problem *about* evil, is in essence the same sort of problem of or about bafflement and the problem of or about suffering. The strange opacity of certain empirical events, the dumb sense-lessness of intense or inexorable pain, and the enigmatic unaccountability of gross iniquity all raise the uncomfortable suspicion that perhaps the world, and hence man's life in the world, has no genuine order at all—no empirical regularity, no emotional form, no moral coherence. And the religious response to this suspicion is in each case the same: the formulation, by means of symbols, of an image of such a genuine order of the world which will account for, and even celebrate, the perceived ambiguities, puzzles and paradoxes in human experience. The effort is not to deny the undeniable—that there are unexplained events, that life hurts or that rain falls upon the just—but to deny that there are inexplicable events, that life is unendurable and that justice is a mirage. The principles which constitute the moral order may indeed often elude men in the same way as fully satisfactory explanations of anomalous events or effective forms for the expression of feeling often elude them. What is important, to a religious man at least, is that this elusiveness be accounted for, that it be not the result of the fact that there are no such principles, explanations or forms, that life is absurd and the attempt to make moral, intellectual or emotional sense out of experience is bootless.

The Problem of Meaning in each of its intergrading aspects (how these aspects in fact intergrade in each particular case, what sort of interplay there is between the sense of analytic, emotional and moral impotence, seems to me one of the outstanding, and except for Weber untouched, problems for comparative research in this whole field) is a matter of affirming, or at least recognizing, the inescapability of ignorance, pain and injustice on the human plane while simultaneously denying that these irrationalities are characteristic of the world as a whole. And it is in terms of religious symbolism, a symbolism relating man's sphere of existence to a wider sphere within which it is conceived to rest, that both the affirmation and the denial are made.

4. . . . AND CLOTHING THESE CONCEPTIONS WITH SUCH AN AURA OF FACTUALITY THAT . . .

There arises here, however, a profounder question: how is it that this denial comes to be believed? how is it that the religious man moves from a troubled perception of experienced disorder to a more or less settled conviction of fundamental order? just what does "belief" mean in a religious context? Of all the problems surrounding attempts to conduct anthropological analysis of religion this is the one that has perhaps been most troublesome and therefore the most often avoided, usually by relegating it to psychology, that raffish outcast discipline to which social anthropologists are forever consigning phenomena they are unable to deal with within the framework of a denatured Durkheimianism. But the problem will not go away, it is not "merely" psychological (nothing social is), and no anthropological theory of religion which fails to attack it is worthy of the name. We have been trying to stage Hamlet without the Prince quite long enough.

It seems to me that it is best to begin any approach to this issue with frank recognition that religious belief involves not a Baconian induction from everyday experience—for then we should all be agnostics—but rather a prior acceptance of authority which transforms that experience. The existence of bafflement, pain and moral paradox—of The Problem of Meaning—is one of the things that drive men toward belief in gods, devils, spirits, totemic principles or the spiritual efficacy of cannibalism (an enfolding sense of beauty or a dazzling perception of power are others), but it is not the basis upon which those beliefs rest, but rather their most important field of application.

In tribal religions authority lies in the persuasive power of traditional imagery; in mystical ones in the apodictic force of super-sensible experience; in charismatic ones in the hypnotic attraction of an extraordinary personality. But the priority of the acceptance of an authoritative criterion in religious matters over the revelation which is conceived to flow from that acceptance is not less complete than in scriptural or hieratic ones. The basic axiom underlying what we may perhaps call "the religious perspective" is everywhere the same: he who would know must first believe.

But to speak of "the religious perspective" is, by implication, to speak of one perspective among others. A perspective is a mode of seeing, in that extended sense of "see" in which it means "discern," "apprehend," "understand" or "grasp." It is a particular way of looking at life, a particular manner of construing the world, as when we speak of an historical perspective, a scientific perspective, an aesthetic perspective, a common-sense perspective, or even the bizarre perspective embodied in dreams and in hallucinations. The question then comes down to, first, what is "the religious perspective" generically considered, as differentiated from other perspectives; and second, how do men come to adopt it.

If we place the religious perspective against the background of three of the other major perspectives in terms of which men construe the world—the common-sensical, the scientific and the aesthetic—its special character emerges more sharply. What distinguishes common-sense as a mode of "seeing" is . . . a simple acceptance of the world, its objects and its processes as being just what they seem to be—what is sometimes called naive realism—and the pragmatic motive, the wish to act upon that world so as to bend it to one's practical purposes, to master it, or so far as that proves impossible, to adjust to it. The world of everyday life, itself, of course, a cultural product, for it is framed in terms of the symbolic conceptions of "stubborn fact" handed down from generation to generation, is the established scene and given object of our actions. Like Mt. Everest it is just there and the thing to do with it, if one feels the need to do anything with it at all, is to climb it. In the scientific perspective it is precisely this givenness which disappears . . . Deliberate doubt and systematic inquiry, the suspension of the pragmatic motive in favor of disinterested observation, the attempt to analyze the world in terms of formal concepts whose relationship to the informal conceptions of common-sense become increasingly problematic—there are the hallmarks of the attempt to grasp the world scientifically. And as for the aesthetic perspective, which under the rubric of "the aesthetic attitude" has been perhaps most exquisitely examined, it involves a different sort of suspension of naive realism and practical interest, in that instead of questioning the credentials of everyday experience that experience is merely ignored in favor of an eager dwelling upon appearances, an engrossment in surfaces, an absorption in things, as we say, "in themselves": "The function of artistic illusion is not 'make-believe' . . . but the very opposite, disengagement from belief—the contemplation of sensory qualities without their usual meanings of 'here's that chair,' 'That's my telephone' . . . etc. The knowledge that what is before us has no practical significance in the world is what enables us to give attention to its appearance as such . . ." And like the common-sensical and the scientific (or the historical, the philosophical and the autistic), this perspective, this "way of seeing" is not the product of some mysterious Cartesian chemistry, but is induced, mediated, and in fact created by means of symbols. It is the artist's skill which can produce those curious quasi-objects—poems, dramas, sculptures, symphonies—which, dissociating themselves from the solid world of common-sense, take on the special sort of eloquence only sheer appearances can achieve.

The religious perspective differs from the common-sensical in that, as already pointed out, it moves beyond the realities of everyday life to wider ones which correct and complete them, and its defining concern is not action upon those wider realities but acceptance of them, faith in them. It differs from the scientific perspective in that it questions the realities of everyday life not out of an institutionalized scepticism which dissolves the world's givenness into a swirl of probabilistic hypotheses, but in terms of what it takes to be wider, non-hypothetical truths. Rather than detachment, its watchword is commitment; rather than analysis, encounter. And it differs from art in that instead of effecting a disengagement from the whole question of factuality, deliberately manufacturing an air of semblance and illusion, it deepens the concern with fact and seeks to create an aura of utter actuality. It is this sense of the "really real" upon which the religious perspective rests and which the symbolic activities of religion as a cultural system are devoted to producing, intensifying, and, so far as possible, rendering inviolable by the discordant revelations of secular experience. It is, again, the imbuing of a certain specific complex of symbols—of the metaphysic they formulate and the style of life they recommend—with a persuasive authority which, from an analytic point of view, is the essence of religious action. . . .

5. . . . THAT THE MOODS AND MOTIVATIONS SEEM UNIQUELY REALISTIC

But no one, not even a saint, lives in the world religious symbols formulate all of the time, and the majority of men live in it only at moments. The everyday world of common-sense objects and practical acts is, as Schutz says, the paramount reality in human experience—paramount in the sense that it is the world in which we are most solidly rooted, whose inherent actuality we can hardly question (however much we may question certain portions of it), and from whose pressures and requirements we can least escape. A man, even large groups of men, may be aesthetically insensitive, religiously unconcerned and unequipped to pursue formal scientific analysis, but he cannot be completely lacking in common-sense and survive. The dispositions which religious rituals induce thus have their most important impact—from a human point of view—outside the boundaries of the ritual itself as they reflect back to color the individual's conception of the established world of bare fact. The peculiar tone that marks the Plains vision quest, the Manus confession or the Javanese mystical exercise pervades areas of the life of these peoples far beyond the immediately religious, impressing upon them a distinctive style in the sense both of a dominant mood and a characteristic movement. Religion is sociologically interesting not because, as vulgar positivism would have it, it describes the social order (which, insofar as it does, it does not only very obliquely but very incompletely), but because, like environment, political power, wealth, jural obligation, personal affection, and a sense of beauty, it shapes it.

The movement back and forth between the religious perspective and the

common-sense perspective is actually one of the more obvious empirical occurrences on the social scene, though, again, one of the most neglected by social
anthropologists, virtually all of whom have seen it happen countless times. Religious belief has usually been presented as an homogeneous characteristic of an
individual, like his place of residence, his occupational role, his kinship position,
and so on. But religious belief in the midst of ritual, where it engulfs the total
person, transporting him, so far as he is concerned, into another mode of existence, and religious belief as the pale, remembered reflection of that experience in
the midst of everyday life are not precisely the same thing, and the failure to realize
this has led to some confusion, most especially in connection with the so-called
"primitive mentality" problem. Much of the difficulty between Lévy-Bruhl and
Malinowski on the nature of "native thought," for example, arises from a lack of
full recognition of this distinction; for where the French philosopher was concerned with the view of reality savages adopted when taking a specifically religious
perspective, the Polish-English ethnographer was concerned with that which they
adopted when taking a strictly common-sense one. Both perhaps vaguely sensed
that they were not talking about exactly the same thing, but where they went
astray was in failing to give a specific accounting of the way in which these two
forms of "thought"—or as I would rather say, these two modes of symbolic
formulation—interacted, so that where Lévy-Bruhl's savages tended to live, despite his postludial disclaimers, in a world composed entirely of mystical encounters, Malinowski's tended to live, despite his stress on the functional importance of
religion, in a world composed entirely of practical actions. They became reduc-
tionists (an idealist is as much of a reductionist as a materialist) in spite of
themselves because they failed to see man as moving more or less easily, and very
frequently, between radically contrasting ways of looking at the world, ways which
are not continuous with one another but separated by cultural gaps across which
Kierkegaardian leaps must be made in both directions.

For an anthropologist, the importance of religion lies in its capacity to
serve, for an individual or for a group, as a source of general, yet distinctive conceptions of the world, the self and the relations between them on the one hand—its
model *of* aspect—and of rooted, no less distinctive "mental" dispositions—its
model *for* aspect—on the other. From these cultural functions flow, in turn, its
social and psychological ones.

Religious concepts spread beyond their specifically metaphysical contexts
to provide a framework of general ideas in terms of which a wide range of
experience—intellectual, emotional, moral—can be given meaningful form. The
Christian sees the Nazi movement against the background of The Fall which,
though it does not, in a casual sense, explain it, places it in a moral, a cognitive,
even an affective sense. A Zande sees the collapse of a granary upon a friend or
relative against the background of a concrete and rather special notion of witchcraft and thus avoids the philosophical dilemmas as well as the psychological stress
of indeterminism. A Javanese finds in the borrowed and reworked concept of *rasa*
("sense-taste-feeling-meaning") a means by which to "see" choreographic, gusta-
tory, emotional and political phenomena in a new light. A synopsis of cosmic

order, a set of religious beliefs is also a gloss upon the mundane world of social relationships and psychological events. It renders them graspable.

But more than gloss, such beliefs are also a template. They do not merely interpret social and psychological processes in cosmic terms—in which case they would be philosophical, not religious—but they shape them. In the doctrine of original sin is embedded also a recommended attitude toward life, a recurring mood and a persisting set of motivations. The Zande learns from witchcraft conceptions not just to understand apparent "accidents" as not accidents at all, but to react to these spurious accidents with hatred for the agent who caused them and to proceed against him with appropriate resolution. Rasa, in addition to being a concept of truth, beauty and goodness, is also a preferred mode of experiencing, a kind of affectless detachment, a variety of bland aloofness, an unshakeable calm. The moods and motivations a religious orientation produces cast a derivative, lunar light over the solid features of a peoples' secular life.

The tracing of the social and psychological role of religion is thus not so much a matter of finding correlations between specific ritual acts and specific secular social ties—though these correlations do, of course, exist and are very worth continued investigation, especially if we can contrive something novel to say about them. More, it is a matter of understanding how it is that men's notions, however implicit, of the "really real" and the dispositions these notions induce in them, color their sense of the reasonable, the practical, the humane and the moral.

Mythology and the Mythical

5. The Mythic Dimension

NINIAN SMART

When the Christian Church was making its way in the Roman Empire it had to struggle against the Greek, Roman, and other religions, all of which had complicated stories of the gods. The Christians often spoke of these stories rather disparagingly, because they were not based (said they) upon fact, as were the stories contained in the Bible—particularly the story of Christ and his resurrection. The Greek word for stories was *mythoi* from which we get "myths." As a result of this Christian campaign against myth we still tend to think of myths as "false stories." It is odd, incidentally, how even the word "stories" sometimes gets this sense, as when we say of someone that "she is only telling stories." But as we have seen, modern students of religion commonly use the word "myth" in a neutral sense to mean a story of divine or sacred significance, without implying that it is false or true.

For the fact is that the stories of the Bible, which are in many cases historically based, fulfill a function similar to some of the stories about the gods of Greece and Rome and elsewhere. The term "myth" is used to highlight this likeness of function among stories in different religions or cultures. Thus an Indian text says *Iti devā akurvata ity u vau manusyāh:* "Thus did the gods do, and thus too human beings do." This briefly conveys the thought that the myth of divine action presents an example of how humans should act. The gods are thus seen as paradigms. Likewise, in the Christian tradition the stories of Christ and of some of the heroes of the Old Testament become patterns for the faithful to follow. Other religions have a story of how death came into the world, and we are reminded in this of the events in the Garden of Eden. So in this and other ways it is artificial to separate supposed false myths about the divine from "true" stories as found in the Bible or elsewhere. There are important questions to be asked about truth, but these come later.

But we are, of course, looking at these matters from the perspective of the second half of the twentieth century. We have our own way of looking at stories, and we should see what this is before we consider the nature of traditional myths.

As we shall see, stories remain crucial to our world, though they now have evolved into different kinds and styles from those older myths. . . .

THE POWER OF MYTH

The myth is something which is told or enacted through a ritual like a kind of drama, and which exists in an unquestioned atmosphere. It is uttered with the implicit idea "This is how things are and this is how things have been." Unlike history, although not unlike some theories of history, myth can tell about the future—what the end of the world will be like, for instance. Very often the story of the human race and of the cosmos is depicted as framed by "first things"—the creation of the world, the making of the first humans, and so on—and by the "last things" at the end. Thus the Christian Bible begins with Creation and ends in Revelation, with the final summing up of things and the judgment by Christ.

Not only are myths "given," that is, they are told with authority—a breathless air of unquestionable truth—but they also often play strange tricks with things and people. In the Garden of Eden there are a mysterious tree and a speaking serpent, for instance. Myths often contain a set of symbols, that is to say beings and actions which have a meaning beyond themselves. So it is that Adam is not just a man, but stands for all men and women, and the action of eating the fruit has some half-known deep meaning which implies that by this act Adam and Eve are liable to experience death. Nothing here is quite what it seems to be: to decipher its meaning we need to look to what may be called "symbolic depth." In order to understand the mythic dimension we have to know something of the language of symbols in religion and human life. The work of Jung is fertile in this area, for he tries to give psychological insight into the kinds of symbols which he found to exist crossculturally, both in the East and the West.

Because symbols are important in traditional religion, as well as in literature, where they find a new life, it is not surprising that religious art, poetry, and music often convey aspects of the meaning of life. Thus, a branch of inquiry in the field of religion is "iconography," the study of the visual symbols of faith. And secular worldviews which most resemble traditional religions also express themselves through art, music, and poetry. Thus Marxism produces socialist realism, a particularly heroic style of art which invests matter with a kind of shining light and in fact brings out the symbolic importance of production, revolutionary war, and so forth in the furthering of socialism and the consummation of human history.

I have spoken so far mainly about the "telling" of myths. But often myths are not just told in a verbal transaction: they are acted out in ritual. Thus, in the Christian tradition the events of the Last Supper are acted out in the Mass (the Eucharist or Lord's Supper). The story is conveyed in action. The myth is the script for a sacred drama. Many ancient myths are scripts in this sense, and it is no coincidence that Greek drama emerged out of the sacred enactment of myths. The old stories were given a freer and more secular form in the tragedies of Aeschylus and his successors. Some scholars earlier in this century belonged to what was called the "myth and ritual school"; they argued that myth is always to be seen in a ritual context. Although this point of view is too sweeping, it has been illuminating to see how creation myths in the ancient Near East (for instance in Babylon), were reenacted annually at the great spring festivals (for the spring, too, is a miracle of re-creation). . . .

It is perhaps wise to pause here to look at some of the most important kinds of traditional myths.

Some explain the origin of the cosmos as a creation, usually by the thought or the word of a divine Being. Some tell of the emergence of the cosmos out of some preexisting chaos or undifferentiated matter. For instance, in some ancient Indian myths the world is conceived of as an egg: the splitting apart of the egg gives rise to the cosmos. Others see the cosmic order as a result of the dismemberment of a primeval human being, or a sea monster (like Tiamat in ancient Near Eastern myth). Water often plays a vital part because, as many studies have shown and as we have seen, water in numerous cultures is the symbol of chaos. Out of chaos comes order, the cosmos itself. Although the Genesis story, which is woven together out of various myths, has been put together in order to show in the most striking possible way the creation of the world out of nothing, and by the sovereign decision of God, here too we have reference to an earlier "something"—the waters over which the spirit of God brooded, and which symbolize a primeval chaos.

The stories of the beginning or emergence of the cosmos are one variety of a major and vital category of myths, namely those that tell about origins—for instance, how an institution (like keeping the Sabbath) arose, or how a particular kind of plant or animal came into being. Important in particular are those stories dealing with the origin of death. Here is a fine example of this type, which Mircea Eliade quotes in *From Primitives to Zen*, from Sulawesi in Indonesia: In the beginning the sky was close to the earth. One day the creator God let down a stone on the end of a rope, but the first man and woman refused it and wanted something else. So he let down a banana, which they eagerly accepted. Then God told them that because they had refused the stone and taken the banana they would be like the latter. Whereas the stone does not change, a banana plant dies while its offspring continue. This then is how death came into the world.

There are a large number of symbolic themes here. The idea that the sky, the divine home, is close to the earth, the human race's home, suggests that there is not, in the beginning, an alienation between humans and God, but they exist in a much closer relationship. The notion that the first man and woman's action affects the rest of their race ties in with a common theme that the symbolic first being not only represents, but somehow sums up in his or her own person the rest of the race. The fact that the first humans did not know what they were doing in choosing the attractive and edible banana suggests that God tricked them: this is in line with the belief that immortality is a divine thing and not for human beings to aspire to. The idea that what they choose is what they come to resemble (especially since in eating the banana they would somehow assimilate its essence) is a common one in mythic and symbolic thinking: like affects like.

The idea that the sky and earth were once close is linked to a common theme in which the High God withdraws upward, perhaps as a result of some stupidity or offense on the part of the first humans. After that the High God leaves the real work of shaping and guiding the affairs of the cosmos to lesser gods.

Themes of destruction are also important and thus in some worldviews there are periodic creations and destructions of the world (this is most developed in the Indian tradition). Among cataclysms are great floods which are spoken of in a variety of cultures. Sometimes the theme of disaster ties in with the forecast of a period of peace and bliss to follow—hopes which, in a number of religions, have helped to inspire revival movements and sometimes rebellion.

There are all kinds of myths which tell of the exploits of the gods, heroes, and other supernatural beings who control and infest the cosmos and surround human life: these are often the material for great epics, as in the Indian and Greek traditions.

Although it is true that stories about origins are important in the field of myth, they are not the only type. In this respect Eliade exaggerates, and he also perhaps makes too much of the theme of "in that time." Not all myths stress that there is something timeless out of which time-bound things came.

Still, Eliade and Jung attempt to show how the world of archaic myth remains relevant to us today—that the symbolic themes which appear in myths are rooted deep in the human psyche and perception of the world. A major way in which Eliade has helped to illuminate myth is by making us take seriously the manner in which time and space symbolize so much in our world. Thus the whole pattern of our thought about height and depth, center and periphery, shows something of our almost instinctive orientation to the world. And it is no coincidence to find so many myths which portray a mountain, with the upper reaches the abode of the gods or God, as at the center of the world—Mount Olympus in ancient Greece, Mount Zion in Israel, Mount Meru in the Indian tradition.

But although we can recognize how myths have traditionally played a vital part in fashioning a worldview (in fact the worldviews of many small-scale societies are expressed predominantly through myths), there are now limits on their credibility. They no longer seem to speak with that breathless air of authority, and once they lose this they cease to be living myths and become curiosities, tales, plots for dramas and movies, perhaps, the raw material for speculation about human symbol-systems. Is it not the case that secular stories, such as the theories of history which we alluded to earlier, replace the traditional myths? And do not fiction and drama now offer an alternative to the older myth-telling?

Still, there is a place where the traditional mythic forms live on in a vigorous way: in the scriptures of the great living religions. Once myths are taken out of the lips and hands of the storyteller and organized into scriptures, they have a new and different life. Thus, the Bible for the Jew or the Christian, the Koran for the Muslim, the Lotus Sutra for many Mahayanists, the Vedas and Gita for Hindus, the Book of Mormon for the Mormons—these and other sacred and revealed writings have a life of their own in inspiring those faithful who look to them for guidance. They are stories which are given the stamp of authority by God or the Buddha or another High God, and they are preserved in a form which invites interpretation and commentary. In fact, it is often through the commentaries that these works become significant to us. For one thing, commentaries often enable us to understand the doctrinal underpinnings of myth. Thus, if we look at a myth of creation by itself it may seem rather simple-minded: if God made the world, we ask, what out of? But doctrine helps to give sense to the idea that the world developed out of the divine Being himself, or that it was created out of nothing, since the divine Being experiences no limitations but can do anything. In effect what happens in the major religions is that the myth comes to exist alongside of and in interaction with the more abstract ideas of the doctrinal dimension.

For the most part, then, the dominant traditional myths now find their authority and their location in sacred books. New religious movements of the modern period accordingly create their own scriptures—such as the Book of Mormon, the Unification Church's Divine Principle, and so on. And it is precisely because these myths have been so recorded and preserved that they are open to the scrutiny of modern historical scholarship. When the myths themselves take the form of historical narratives, whether about Moses, Jesus, Muhammad, or other great founding figures, then the same tension which we spoke about earlier in relation to national histories should arise even more acutely here. Will modern history puncture some of our cherished beliefs? Once the critical historian looks on scriptures as mere documents, will their authority not come into question?

THE INTERPRETATION OF MYTH

There has come about, in the last hundred and fifty years or so, the modern study of the New Testament, where the problems of history and myth are most acute. The main documents of the early Church, and in particular the Gospels, were selected from a wide and growing range of writings which tried to interpret the life and message of Jesus. But they were selected not primarily as biographies or pieces of historical writing. The Gospels were meant to present the authentic Jesus of Christian experience, and were to be used in the course of worship, as they still are. Also, they were clothed in the language of the day (the Hellenistic Greek understood in much of the eastern part of the Roman Empire—maybe Jesus understood it, in addition to his native Aramaic) and in the metaphors of the age. Those who wish to stay loyal to the tradition may want to restate the message of the Gospel in different language for today.

Take two examples. When the New Testament says that Jesus ascended into heaven, do we think of him as literally going upward? Thanks to science and technology, we now have an idea about what "up there" is like which was not available to the original writers and hearers of the Scriptures. They thought of a three-decker universe—heaven above, the earth here, and the underworld below. Did Jesus go up like a modern rocket? Where is heaven—after you have gone up twenty or a hundred or a thousand or a million miles? In the older mythic sense, it was easy to think of the sky as being where God lives. Even if we think of heaven in terms of its being "the place where God is," our view of the cosmos, our cosmology, has altered. So how do we express what those writers and hearers were trying to say and think? Do we want to say that God exists, as it were, in a fourth or fifth dimension, outside space and time, yet always near us?

Let us consider another example. The Bible says that God is king, or like a king. The imagery of the kingdom of God is very strong. In those days kings had real power, but they do not today. At best they are constitutional monarchs, like the Queen of England—rich, full of prestige, a vibrant symbol, but without any genuine political power. The nearer equivalent to the old kingship is the U.S. Presidency. So do we now say: "God is our President"? If we simply use the actual language of the past, then, since meanings and circumstances have changed, the language now has a different force. So if you stick to the literal letter of the Bible you may be changing the meaning of what it was saying, is saying.

These problems of translating in order to reveal and express the original meaning are referred to as the study of *hermeneutics*. This derives from a Greek word for interpretation, and ultimately from the name *Hermes*, Greek god of messages. Hermeneutics is the theory of interpretation.

The modern probing of the New Testament as history has caused some arguments. Some feel that this secular approach to the text damages the authority of the Bible; they wish to reaffirm the unerring character of the text because it is inspired by God. Others feel that in order to be at home in the modern world we must arrive at a new understanding of the Bible which takes modern scholarship into account. The former are rather loosely called "fundamentalists"; the latter are often called "liberals." The fundamentalists too, of course, have a hermeneutical problem, for when they take the Bible at face value, aren't they reading the text with the eyes of twentieth-century people? And in doing so aren't they reading a lot of today's attitudes into the Bible?

Perhaps the most influential attempt to come to terms with the challenge of modern probings is that of Rudolf Bultmann (1884–1976). He introduced a program of what he called "demythologization." This means trying to see what the mythic and symbolic language of the Bible conveys, and then restating it without the mythological clothing of the original text. Thus, as we have noted, the Bible treats the universe as having three levels—heaven above, earth, and hell below. This picture is now at best just a metaphor, for how can we literally go "down" to hell? For Bultmann this three-decker universe no longer fits modern feeling or thought: we now see ourselves differently, on a blue- and white-clad sphere, the beautiful planet Earth, swimming in space around a star near the periphery of a galaxy in a huge and expanding cosmos which teems with galaxies. This picture is beyond anything the Jews of Jesus's day imagined. But it does not mean that we have to abandon the idea that Jesus brought something extraordinary into the world, and that he is the central figure in God's unfolding revelation of himself to human beings. These are the Christian claims. Here we must remember that Bultmann is not writing as a historian of religion, but more as a Christian theologian, that is, one who is trying to express and clarify in intellectual terms the Christian faith. But he has important things to say which are of great interest to the worldview analyst and student of religions.

Bultmann had to face the question of how we are to state the Christian faith once we have gotten rid of those mythic elements he thought modern folk could not accept—miracles like turning water into wine, walking on the water, casting out devils, ascending into heaven, being born of a virgin through a miraculous conception, and so forth. In order to explain the true and inner meaning of these mythic representations of the truth about Jesus, he went to modern philosophy. Bultmann saw Christ's resurrection as enabling the Christian to participate in a new and authentic way of life. This new freedom cuts through the false values which stem from treating persons as objects and ourselves as members of the crowd. Although science can deal with the world of things and so can be objective, the personal dimension of existence has a different nature. When I truly talk to *you*, you are no longer a thing or a type, but a person who responds. Thus, too, with the human being's relationship to God: it is a relationship of love, and what the Jewish thinker Martin Buber (1878–1965) called the I-Thou encounter. Myths in part reveal the personal nature of God, for they deal with the material world as shot through with spiritual and miraculous powers; but they also can be taken "objectively," as though they are just about objects and events, and not about what they are pointing to. Faith is personal and is a relationship to a Person. It does not arise from belief in mere outer events, however objectively wonderful.

Whether it is possible to accept Bultmann's rather sharp differentiation between the objective and the subjective, and between science and faith, is open to debate. There is also some question as to whether his modern talk of living authentically really gets to the heart of what the Gospel writers meant. But his project of restating the Christian faith is interesting, for it poses questions of deep importance for us if we want to estimate correctly the power and future of traditional religious worldviews.

First, the rise of modern scientific and technical thought means that most of those who accept traditional myth are compelled, in one way or another, to make a distinction between the language of faith and that of science—between differing spheres of human experience and understanding. Bultmann does this in terms of the spheres of persons and of things. The Bible, in the last resort, is about persons and about God, the supreme Person: it is not a textbook of biology or of physics. So the myth of creation is about our relationship to God as our Father; it is not meant to be a material account of how the cosmos evolved.

But if we begin to make a sharp divide between myth and science, we already have a different frame of mind from that of the original myth-makers. The myths now have a new context, and so a new meaning. Our world has already been split up into differing compartments, and it needs some kind of theory to put the compartments together. In earlier days Christianity had a similar problem in the face of Greek philosophy. For Bultmann the theory is supplied by modern philosophy. So Christian faith has to be given a rather abstract framework, and explained through such terms as "authentic" and "personal existence."

Which brings us to a second thought about myth. If we are to follow Eliade and Jung, the ultimate meaning of myths has to do with deep impulses in our psyches. They have to do with how we can come to terms with our feelings, and how we can achieve personal integration and wholeness. For Bultmann, too, faith is a very personal and individual affair. But traditionally myth has a much more communal meaning. A myth is not just about me: it is about us. Thus in the Bible we have the story of how the children of Israel came to be and how they entered into a special relationship to God. Tribal myths deal not just with the creation of the cosmos, but with the creation or emergence of the tribe. This is where national histories resemble traditional myths. We should not, of course, underestimate the importance of the personal and individual side of religion. It is very relevant to the modern world. But it is also good to recognize that religion needs to make sense of the history of the human race: it needs to give an account of where we are and where we are going. The attraction of Marxism is that it provides such an account. For the most part, Christianity and other religions have tended not to interpret the times, and so have not seen the meaning of the human race's transition to modernity and the emergence of the global city. There are exceptions, however. The French Jesuit Teilhard de Chardin (1889–1955) created a picture of the evolutionary process leading up to the human race as we now know it, and beyond to a new and higher unity of the planet bound together by perfect love, which he saw in Christian terms as the coming of Christ. His vision was an attractive one to many traditional Christians because it brought science and faith together in a new way. Evolution was God's mechanism for spiritual progress. But the vision was also regarded as going beyond orthodox Catholic teaching, and his writings were for that reason condemned by the Church. He raised an important question, however: What accounts of the past and future are capable of gripping us in this modern and more skeptical period? What myths have that air of authority, that "reality" which makes us believe them, and not just treat them as interesting and perhaps insightful ways of conveying meanings in a poetic way?

For the fact is that human beings have the impulse to find out who they are by telling a story about how they came to be. Myth thus is the food which feeds our sense of identity. And when we see our identity and our destiny in relation to the unseen world—God or the dharma or the Tao or nirvana—then myth is given an added impulse, for we imagine the invisible through the visible and give life to our faith through symbols. They are thrown up at the point where our feelings and the cosmos intersect, just as myths which give us a past and a future arise at the point where I intersect with my fellow human beings.

6. The Task of Demythologizing the New Testament Proclamation

RUDOLPH BULTMANN

A. THE PROBLEM

1. *The Mythical View of the World and the Mythical Event of Redemption*

The cosmology of the New Testament is essentially mythical in character. The world is viewed as a three-storied structure, with the earth in the centre, the heaven above, and the underworld beneath. Heaven is the abode of God and of celestial beings—the angels. The underworld is hell, the place of torment. Even the earth is more than the scene of natural, everyday events, of the trivial round and common task. It is the scene of the supernatural activity of God and his angels on the one hand, and of Satan and his daemons on the other. These supernatural forces intervene in the course of nature and in all that men think and will and do. Miracles are by no means rare. Man is not in control of his own life. Evil spirits may take possession of him. Satan may inspire him with evil thoughts. Alternatively, God may inspire his thought and guide his purposes. He may grant him heavenly visions. He may allow him to hear his word of succour or demand. He may give him the supernatural power of his Spirit. History does not follow a smooth unbroken course; it is set in motion and controlled by these supernatural powers. This aeon is held in bondage by Satan, sin, and death (for "powers" is precisely what they are), and hastens towards its end. That end will come very soon, and will take the form of a cosmic catastrophe. It will be inaugurated by the "woes" of the last time. Then the Judge will come from heaven, the dead will rise, the last judgement will take place, and men will enter into eternal salvation or damnation.

This then is the mythical view of the world which the New Testament presupposes when it presents the event of redemption which is the subject of its preaching. It proclaims in the language of mythology that the last time has now come. "In the fulness of time" God sent forth his Son, a pre-existent divine Being, who appears on earth as a man.[1] He dies the death of a sinner[2] on the cross and makes atonement for the sins of men.[3] His resurrection marks the beginning of the cosmic catastrophe. Death, the consequence of Adam's sin, is abolished,[4] and the daemonic forces are deprived of their power.[5] The risen Christ is exalted to the right hand of God in heaven[6] and made "Lord" and "King".[7] He will come again on the clouds of heaven to complete the work of redemption, and the resurrection and judgement of men will follow.[8] Sin, suffering and death will then be finally abolished.[9] All this is to happen very soon; indeed, St Paul thinks that he himself will live to see it.[10]

All who belong to Christ's Church and are joined to the Lord by Baptism and the Eucharist are certain of resurrection to salvation,[11] unless they forfeit it by unworthy behaviour. Christian believers already enjoy the first instalment of salvation, for the Spirit[12] is at work within them, bearing witness to their adoption as sons of God,[13] and guaranteeing their final resurrection.[14]

[1] Gal. 4. 4; Phil. 2. 6ff.; 2 Cor. 8. 9; John 1. 14, etc.
[2] 2 Cor. 5. 21; Rom. 8. 3.
[3] Rom. 3. 23–26; 4. 25; 8. 3; 2 Cor. 5. 14, 19; John 1. 29; 1 John 2. 2, etc.
[4] 1 Cor. 15. 21f.; Rom. 5. 12ff.
[5] 1 Cor. 2. 6; Col. 2. 15; Rev. 12. 7ff., etc.
[6] Acts 1. 6f.; 2. 33; Rom. 8. 34, etc.
[7] Phil. 2. 9–11; 1 Cor. 15. 25.
[8] 1 Cor. 15. 23f., 50ff., etc.
[9] Rev. 21. 4, etc.
[10] 1 Thess. 4. 15ff.; 1 Cor. 15. 51f.; cf. Mark 9. 1.
[11] Rom. 5. 12ff.; 1 Cor. 15. 21ff., 44b, ff.
[12] Ἀπαρχή: Rom. 8. 23, ἀρραβών: 2 Cor. 1. 22; 5. 5.
[13] Rom. 8. 15; Gal. 4. 6.
[14] Rom. 8. 11.

2. The Mythological View of the World Obsolete

All this is the language of mythology, and the origin of the various themes can be easily traced in the contemporary mythology of Jewish Apocalyptic and in the redemption myths of Gnosticism. To this extent *the kerygma is incredible to modern man, for he is convinced that the mythical view of the world is obsolete.* We are therefore bound to ask whether, when we preach the Gospel to-day, we expect our converts to accept not only the Gospel message, but also the mythical view of the world in which it is set. If not, does the New Testament embody a truth which is quite independent of its mythical setting? If it does, theology must undertake the task of stripping the Kerygma from its mythical framework, of "demythologizing" it.

Can Christian preaching expect modern man *to accept the mythical view of the world as true?* To do so would be both senseless and impossible. It would be senseless, because there is nothing specifically Christian in the mythical view of the world as such. It is simply the cosmology of a pre-scientific age. Again, it would be impossible, because no man can adopt a view of the world by his own volition—it is already determined for him by his place in history. Of course such a view is not absolutely unalterable, and the individual may even contribute to its change. But he can do so only when he is faced by a new set of facts so compelling as to make his previous view of the world untenable. He has then no alternative but to modify his view of the world or produce a new one. The discoveries of Copernicus and the atomic theory are instances of this, and so was romanticism, with its discovery that the human subject is richer and more complex than enlightenment or idealism had allowed, and nationalism, with its new realization of the importance of history and the tradition of peoples.

It may equally well happen that truths which a shallow enlightenment had failed to perceive are later rediscovered in ancient myths. Theologians are perfectly justified in asking whether this is not exactly what has happened with the New Testament. At the same time it is impossible to revive an obsolete view of the world by a mere fiat, and certainly not a mythical view. For all our thinking to-day is shaped irrevocably by modern science. A blind acceptance of the New Testament mythology would be arbitrary, and to press for its acceptance as an article of faith would be to reduce faith to works. Wilhelm Herrmann pointed this out, and one would have thought that his demonstration was conclusive. It would involve a sacrifice of the intellect which could have only one result—a curious form of schizophrenia and insincerity. It would mean accepting a view of the world in our faith and religion which we should deny in our everyday life. Modern thought as we have inherited it brings with it criticism of *the New Testament view of the world.*

Man's knowledge and mastery of the world have advanced to such an extent through science and technology that it is no longer possible for anyone seriously to hold the New Testament view of the world—in fact, there is no one who does. What meaning, for instance, can we attach to such phrases in the creed as "descended into hell" or "ascended into heaven"? We no longer believe in the three-storied universe which the creeds take for granted. The only honest way of reciting the creeds is to strip the mythological framework from the truth they enshrine—that is, assuming that they contain any truth at all, which is just the question that theology has to ask. No one who is old enough to think for himself supposes that God lives in a local heaven. There is no longer any heaven in the traditional sense of the word. The same applies to hell in the sense of a mythical underworld beneath our feet. And if this is so, the story of Christ's descent into hell and of his Ascension into heaven is done with. We can no longer look for the return of the Son of Man on the clouds of heaven or hope that the faithful will meet him in the air (1 Thess. 4. 15ff.).

Now that the forces and the laws of nature have been discovered, we can no longer believe in *spirits, whether good or evil.* We know that the stars are physical bodies whose motions are controlled by the laws of the universe, and not daemonic beings which enslave mankind to their service. Any influence they may have over human life must be explicable in terms of the ordinary laws of nature; it cannot in any way be attributed to their malevolence. Sickness and the cure of disease are likewise attributable to natural causation; they are not the result of daemonic activity or of evil spells.[15] The *miracles of the New Testament* have ceased to be miraculous, and to defend their historicity by recourse to nervous disorders or hypnotic effects only serves to underline the fact. And if we are still left with certain physiological and psychological phenomena which we can only assign to mysterious and enigmatic causes, we are still assigning them to causes, and thus far are trying to make them scientifically intelligible. Even occultism pretends to be a science.

It is impossible to use electric light and the wireless and to avail ourselves of modern medical and surgical discoveries, and at the same time to believe in the New Testament world of spirits and miracles.[16] We may think we can manage it in our own lives, but to expect others to do so is to make the Christian faith unintelligible and unacceptable to the modern world.

The mythical eschatology is untenable for the simple reason that the parousia of Christ never took place as the New Testament expected. History did not come to an end, and, as every schoolboy knows, it will continue to run its course. Even if we believe that the world as we know it will come to an end in time, we expect the end to take the form of a natural catastrophe, not of a mythical event such as the New Testament expects. And if we explain the parousia in terms of modern scientific theory, we are applying criticism to the New Testament, albeit unconsciously.

But natural science is not the only challenge which the mythology of the New Testament has to face. There is the still more serious challenge presented by *modern man's understanding of himself.*

Modern man is confronted by a curious dilemma. He may regard himself

---

[15] It may of course be argued that there are people alive to-day whose confidence in the traditional scientific view of the world has been shaken, and others who are primitive enough to qualify for an age of mythical thought. And there are also many varieties of superstition. But when belief in spirits and miracles has degenerated into superstition, it has become something entirely different from what it was when it was genuine faith. The various impressions and speculations which influence credulous people here and there are of little importance, nor does it matter to what extent cheap slogans have spread an atmosphere inimical to science. What matters is the world view which men imbibe from their environment, and it is science which determines that view of the world through the school, the press, the wireless, the cinema, and all the other fruits of technical progress.

[16] Cp. the observations of Paul Schütz on the decay of mythical religion in the East through the introduction of modern hygiene and medicine.

as pure nature, or as pure spirit. In the latter case he distinguishes the essential part of his being from nature. In either case, however, *man is essentially a unity.* He bears the sole responsibility for his own feeling, thinking, and willing.[17] He is not, as the New Testament regards him, the victim of a strange dichotomy which exposes him to the interference of powers outside himself. If his exterior behaviour and his interior condition are in perfect harmony, it is something he has achieved himself, and if other people think their interior unity is torn asunder by daemonic or divine interference, he calls it schizophrenia.

Although biology and psychology recognize that man is a highly depen- dent being, that does not mean that he has been handed over to powers outside of and distinct from himself. This dependence is inseparable from human nature, and he needs only to understand it in order to recover his self-mastery and organize his life on a rational basis. If he regards himself as a spirit, he knows that he is permanently conditioned by the physical, bodily part of his being, but he distin- guishes his true self from it, and knows that he is independent and responsible for his mastery over nature.

In either case he finds *what the New Testament has to say about the "Spirit"* (πνεῦμα) *and the sacraments utterly strange and incomprehensible.* Biological man cannot see how a supernatural entity like the πνεῦμα can penetrate within the close texture of his natural powers and set to work within him. Nor can the idealist understand how a πνεῦμα working like a natural power can touch and influence his mind and spirit. Conscious as he is of his own moral responsibility, he cannot conceive how baptism in water can convey a mysterious something which is henceforth the agent of all his decisions and actions. He cannot see how physical food can convey spiritual strength, and how the unworthy receiving of the Eucha- rist can result in physical sickness and death (1 Cor. 11. 30). The only possible explanation is that it is due to suggestion. He cannot understand how anyone can be baptized for the dead (1 Cor. 15. 29).

We need not examine in detail the various forms of modern *Weltan- schauung,* whether idealist or naturalist. For the only criticism of the New Testa- ment which is theologically relevant is that which arises *necessarily* out of the situation of modern man. The biological *Weltanschauung* does not, for instance, arise necessarily out of the contemporay situation. We are still free to adopt it or not as we choose. The only relevant question for the theologian is the basic assumption on which the adoption of a biological as of every other *Weltanschauung* rests, and that assumption is the view of the world which has been moulded by modern science and the modern conception of human nature as a self-subsistent unity immune from the interference of supernatural powers.

Again, the biblical doctrine that *death is the punishment of sin* is equally abhorrent to naturalism and idealism, since they both regard death as a simple and necessary process of nature. To the naturalist death is no problem at all, and to the idealist it is a problem for that very reason, for so far from arising out of man's essential spiritual being it actually destroys it. The idealist is faced with a paradox.

---

[17] Cp. Gerhardt Krüger, *Einsicht und Leidenschaft, Das Wesen des platonischen Denkens* Frankfort 1939, p. 11f.

On the one hand man is a spiritual being, and therefore essentially different from plants and animals, and on the other hand he is the prisoner of nature, whose birth, life, and death are just the same as those of the animals. Death may present him with a problem, but he cannot see how it can be a punishment for sin. Human beings are subject to death even before they have committed any sin. And to attribute human mortality to the fall of Adam is sheer nonsense, for guilt implies personal responsibility, and the idea of original sin as an inherited infection is sub-ethical, irrational, and absurd.

The same objections apply to *the doctrine of the atonement.* How can the guilt of one man be expiated by the death of another who is sinless—if indeed one may speak of a sinless man at all? What primitive notions of guilt and righteousness does this imply? And what primitive idea of God? The rationale of sacrifice in general may of course throw some light on the theory of the atonement, but even so, what a primitive mythology it is, that a divine Being should become incarnate, and atone for the sins of men through his own blood! Or again, one might adopt an analogy from the law courts, and explain the death of Christ as a transaction between God and man through which God's claims on man were satisfied. But that would make sin a juridical matter; it would be no more than an external transgression of a commandment, and it would make nonsense of all our ethical standards. Moreover, if the Christ who died such a death was the pre-existent Son of God, what could death mean for him? Obviously very little, if he knew that he would rise again in three days!

The *resurrection of Jesus* is just as difficult for modern man, if it means an event whereby a living supernatural power is released which can henceforth be appropriated through the sacraments. To the biologist such language is meaningless, for he does not regard death as a problem at all. The idealist would not object to the idea of a life immune from death, but he could not believe that such a life is made available by the resuscitation of a dead person. If that is the way God makes life available for man, his action is inextricably involved in a natural miracle. Such a notion he finds incomprehensible, for he can see God at work only in the reality of his personal life and in his transformation. But, quite apart from the incredibility of such a miracle, he cannot see how an event like this could be the act of God, or how it could affect his own life.

Gnostic influence suggests that this Christ, who died and rose again, was not a mere human being but a God-man. His death and resurrection were not isolated facts which concerned him alone, but a cosmic event in which we are all involved.[18] It is only with effort that modern man can think himself back into such an intellectual atmosphere, and even then he could never accept it himself, because it regards man's essential being as nature and redemption as a process of nature. And as for the pre-existence of Christ, with its corollary of man's translation into a celestial realm of light, and the clothing of the human personality in heavenly robes and a spiritual body—all this is not only irrational but utterly meaningless. Why should salvation take this particular form? Why should this be the fulfilment of human life and the realization of man's true being?

---

[18] Rom. 5. 12ff.; 1 Cor. 15. 21ff., 44b.

B. THE TASK BEFORE US

1. *Not Selection or Subtraction*

Does this drastic criticism of the New Testament mythology mean the complete elimination of the kerygma?

Whatever else may be true, we cannot save the kerygma by selecting some of its features and subtracting others, and thus reduce the amount of mythology in it. For instance, it is impossible to dismiss St Paul's teaching about the unworthy reception of Holy Communion or about baptism for the dead, and yet cling to the belief that physical eating and drinking can have a spiritual effect. If we accept *one* idea, we must accept everything which the New Testament has to say about Baptism and Holy Communion, and it is just this one idea which we cannot accept.

It may of course be argued that some features of the New Testament mythology are given greater prominence than others: not all of them appear with the same regularity in the various books. There is for example only one occurrence of the legends of the Virgin birth and the Ascension; St Paul and St John appear to be totally unaware of them. But, even if we take them to be later accretions, it does not affect the mythical character of the event of redemption as a whole. And if we once start subtracting from the kerygma, where are we to draw the line? The mythical view of the world must be accepted or rejected in its entirety.

At this point absolute clarity and ruthless honesty are essential both for the academic theologian and for the parish priest. It is a duty they owe to themselves, to the Church they serve, and to those whom they seek to win for the Church. They must make it quite clear what their hearers are expected to accept and what they are not. At all costs the preacher must not leave his people in the dark about what he secretly eliminates, nor must he be in the dark about it himself. In Karl Barth's book *The Resurrection of the Dead* the cosmic eschatology in the sense of "chronologically final history" is eliminated in favour of what he intends to be a non-mythological "ultimate history." He is able to delude himself into thinking that this is exegesis of St Paul and of the New Testament generally only because he gets rid of everything mythological in 1 Corinthians by subjecting it to an interpretation which does violence to its meaning. But that is an impossible procedure.

If the truth of the New Testament proclamation is to be preserved, the only way is to demythologize it. But our motive in so doing must not be to make the New Testament relevant to the modern world at all costs. The question is simply whether the New Testament consists exclusively of mythology, or whether it actually demands the elimination of myth if it is to be understood as it is meant to be. This question is forced upon us from two sides. First there is the nature of myth in general, and then there is the New Testament itself.

2. *The Nature of Myth*

The real purpose of myth is not to present an objective picture of the world as it is, but to express man's understanding of himself in the world in which he lives. Myth should be interpreted not cosmologically, but anthropologically, or better still, existentially.[19] Myth speaks of the power or the powers which man supposes he experiences as the ground and limit of his world and of his own activity and suffering. He describes these powers in terms derived from the visible world, with its tangible objects and forces, and from human life, with its feelings, motives, and potentialities. He may, for instance, explain the origin of the world by speaking of a world egg or a world tree. Similarly he may account for the present state and order of the world by speaking of a primeval war between the gods. He speaks of the other world in terms of this world, and of the gods in terms derived from human life.[20]

Myth is an expression of man's own conviction that the origin and purpose of the world in which he lives are to be sought not within it but beyond it—that is, beyond the realm of known and tangible reality—and that this realm is perpetually dominated and menaced by those mysterious powers which are its source and limit. Myth is also an expression of man's awareness that he is not lord of his own being. It expresses his sense of dependence not only within the visible world, but more especially on those forces which hold sway beyond the confines of the known. Finally, myth expresses man's belief that in this state of dependence he can be delivered from the forces within the visible world.

Thus myth contains elements which demand its own criticism—namely, its imagery with its apparent claim to objective validity. The real purpose of myth is to speak of a transcendent power which controls the world and man, but that purpose is impeded and obscured by the terms in which it is expressed.

Hence the importance of the New Testament mythology lies not in its imagery but in the understanding of existence which it enshrines. The real question is whether this understanding of existence is true. Faith claims that it is, and faith ought not to be tied down to the imagery of New Testament mythology.

Bibliography

Ackerknecht, Erwin H. "Problems of Primitive Medicine." *Bulletin of the History of Medicine* 11 (1942): 503–21.

Bartsch, H. W., ed. *Kerygma and Myth*. London: S.P.C.K., 1957.

Boardman, John. *The Oxford History of the Classical World*. Oxford: Oxford University Press, 1986.

Boas, Franz. "The Origin of Totemism." *Journal of American Folklore* 23 (1910): 392–93.

Bronowski, Jacob. *Magic, Science, and Civilization*. New York: Columbia University Press, 1978.

Bultmann, Rudolf. *Jesus Christ and Mythology*. New York: Scribner's, 1958.

---

[19] Cp. Gerhardt Krüger, *Einsicht und Leidenschaft*, esp. p. 17f., 56f.

[20] Myth is here used in the sense popularized by the 'History of Religions' school. Mythology is the use of imagery to express the other worldly in terms of this world and the divine in terms of human life, the other side in terms of this side. For instance, divine transcendence is expressed as spatial distance. It is a mode of expression which makes it easy to understand the cultus as an action in which material means are used to convey immaterial power. Myth is not used in that modern sense, according to which it is practically equivalent to ideology.

Campbell, Joseph, ed. *Myths, Dreams and Religion.* New York: Dutton, 1970.

Cannon, Walter B. "Voodoo Death." *American Anthropologist* 44 (1942): 169–81.

Codrington, Robert H. *The Melanesians: Studies in Their Anthropology and Folklore.* Oxford: Clarendon Press, 1891.

Cook, John W. "Magic, Witchcraft and Science." *Philosophical Investigations* 6 (1983): 37–52.

DeGeorge, Richard T. "Myth and Reason." In *Myth and Philosophy,* edited by George McLean, 28–39. Washington, D.C.: American Catholic Philosophical Association, 1971.

Durkheim, Emile. *The Elementary Forms of Religious Life.* London: Allen and Unwin, 1915.

Eliade, Mircea. *The Sacred and the Profane. The Nature of Religion.* New York: Harcourt, Brace and World, 1959.

———. *Patterns in Comparative Religion.* Translated by Rosemary Sheed. New York: World, 1963.

———. *From Primitives to Zen: A Thematic Sourcebook of the History of Religion.* New York: Harper and Row, 1967.

Elkin, A. P. *The Australian Aborigines: How to Understand Them.* 3d ed. Sydney: Angus and Robertson, 1954.

Evans-Pritchard, E. E. "Religion." In *The Institutions of Primitive Society,* edited by E. E. Evans-Pritchard et al., 37–56. Oxford: Basil Blackwell, 1956.

———. *Theories of Primitive Religion.* Oxford: Oxford University Press, 1965.

Farella, John R. *The Main Stalk: A Synthesis of Navajo Philosophy.* Tucson, Ariz.: University of Arizona Press, 1984.

Firth, Raymond. "Offering and Sacrifice: Problems of Organization." *Journal of the Royal Anthropological Institute* 93 (1963): 12–24.

Frazer, James G. *The Golden Bough: A Study in Magic and Religion.* 3d ed. 12 vols. London: Macmillan, 1911–15.

———. *The Fear of the Dead in Primitive Religion.* 3 vols. London: Macmillan, 1933–36.

———. *The Golden Bough.* 3d ed. New York: St. Martin's Press, 1966.

Freud, Sigmund. *Totem and Taboo: Resemblances between the Psychic Life of Savages and Neurotics.* Translated, with introduction, by A. A. Brill. New York: Moffat Yard, 1918.

———. *The Future of an Illusion.* London: Macmillan, 1920–23.

Geertz, Clifford. *The Religion of Java.* Glencoe, Ill.: Free Press, 1960.

Goldenweiser, Alexander A. "Totemism: An Analytical Study." *Journal of American Folklore* 23 (1910): 179–293.

Hallen, B. *Knowledge, Belief and Witchcraft: Analytic Experiments in African Philosophy.* London: Ethnographica, 1986.

Hallowell, A. Irving. *Culture and Experience.* Philadelphia: University of Pennsylvania Press, 1955.

Hepburn, Ronald W. "Demythologizing and the Problem of Validity." In *New Essays in Philosophical Theology,* edited by Anthony Flew and Alasdair MacIntyre, 227–42. New York: Macmillan, 1955.

Herskovits, Melville J. "African Gods and Catholic Saints in New World Religious Belief." *American Anthropologist* 39 (1937): 635–43.

Howells, W. W. *The Heathens: Primitive Man and His Religions.* Garden City, N.Y.: Doubleday, 1948.

Huxley, Aldous. *Doors to Perception*. New York: Harper, 1954.

Inbody, Tyron. "Myth in Contemporary Theology: The Irreconcilable Issue." *Anglican Theology Review* (April 1976): 139–57.

James, E. O. *Comparative Religion: An Introductory and Historical Society*. London: Methuen, 1938.

Karp, Ivan, and Charles S. Bird, eds. *Explorations in African Systems of Thought*. Bloomington, Ind.: Indiana University Press, 1980.

Keesing, Roger M. "Rethinking Mana." *Journal of Anthropological Research* 40 (Spring 1984): 137–56.

Kitteredge, George Lyman. *Witchcraft in Old and New England*. Cambridge, Mass.: Harvard University Press, 1929.

Kluckhorn, Clyde. "Myths and Rituals: A General Theory." *Harvard Theological Review* 35 (January 1942): 45–79.

———. "Navaho Witchcraft." Peabody Museum Papers, no. 22. Cambridge, Mass.: 1944.

Knox, John. *Myth and Truth*. Charlottesville, Va.: University Press of Virginia, 1964.

Kors, Alan C. *Witchcraft in Europe, 1100–1700*. Philadelphia: University of Pennsylvania Press, 1972.

Kroeber, Alfred L. "Totem and Taboo: An Ethnologic Psychoanalysis." *American Anthropologist* 22 (1920): 48–55.

Lang, Andrew. *The Making of Religion*. London: Longmans, Green, 1898.

Leach, E. R. "Genesis as Myth." *Discovery* 23 (1962): 30–35.

Lethbridge, Thomas Charles. *Witches: Investigating an Ancient Religion*. London: Routledge and Kegan Paul, 1962.

Lévi-Strauss, Claude. "The Structural Study of Myth." *Structural Anthropology*. New York: Basic Books, 1963.

———. *Totemism*. Boston: Beacon Press, 1963.

Lowie, Robert H. *Primitive Religion*. New York: Boni Liveright, 1924.

MacQuarrie, John. *God-Talk*. New York: Harper and Row, 1967.

———. *The Scope of Demythologizing*. New York: Harper and Row, 1968.

Malinowski, Bronislaw. *Myth in Primitive Psychology*. New York: Norton, 1926.

———. *Magic, Science, and Religion*. Boston: Beacon Press, 1948.

McLean, George F., ed. *Myth and Philosophy*. Washington, D.C.: American Catholic Philosophical Association, 1971.

Morgan, William. "Navaho Dreams." *American Anthropologist* 34 (1932): 390–405.

Morley, Sylvanus G. *The Ancient Maya*. 3d ed. Revised by George W. Brainerd. Stanford, Calif.: Stanford University Press, 1956.

Murray, Margaret Alice. *The Witch Cult in Western Europe*. Oxford: Clarendon Press, 1962.

Nadel, S. F. "A Study of Shamanism in the Nuba Mountains." *Journal of the Royal Anthropological Institute* 76 (1946): 25–37.

Nettesheim-Heinrich, Agrippa von. *The Philosophy of Natural Magic*. Secaucus, N.J.: University Books, 1974.

Noss, John B. *Man's Religions*. New York: Macmillan, 1949.

Okafor, Stephen O. "Bantu Philosophy: Placide Tempels Revisited." *Journal of Religion in Africa* 13 (1982): 83–100.

Opler, Morris E. *An Apache Life-Way*. Chicago: University of Chicago Press, 1941.

Parsons, Elsie Clews. *Pueblo Indian Religion.* 2 vols. Chicago: University of Chicago Press, 1939.

Pitois, Christian. *The History and Practice of Magic.* New York: Citadel Press, 1963.

Radcliffe-Brown, A. R. "The Sociological Theory of Totemism." In *Proceedings of the Fourth Pacific Science Congress.* Java, 1929; Batavia, 1930.

Radin, Paul. *Primitive Religion: Its Nature and Origin.* New York: Viking Press, 1937.

Reina, Ruben E. *Shadows, A Mayan Way of Knowing.* New York: New Horizon Press, 1984.

Reinach, Salomon. *Orpheus: A History of Religions.* New York: Liveright, 1930.

Schleiter, Frederick. *Religion and Culture: A Critical Survey of Methods of Approach to Religious Phenomena.* New York: Columbia University Press, 1919.

Schmidt, Wilhelm. *The Origin and Growth of Religion: Facts and Theories.* New York: Lincoln MacVeagh, 1931.

Seabrook, William Buehler. *The Magic Island.* New York: Harcourt, Brace, 1929.

Slotkin, J. S. "Peyotism, 1521–1891." *American Anthropologist* 57 (1955): 202–30.

Swanson, Guy E. *The Birth of the Gods: The Origin of Primitive Beliefs.* Ann Arbor: University of Michigan Press, 1960.

Tambiah, Stanley Jeyaraja. *Magic, Science, Religion, and the Scope of Rationality.* Cambridge: Cambridge University Press, 1990.

Tedlock, Dennis, and Barbara Tedlock, eds. *Teachings from the American Earth: Indian Religion and Philosophy.* New York: Liveright, 1975.

Thorndike, Lynn. *The Place of Magic in the Intellectual History of Europe.* New York: Columbia University Press, 1905.

Tylor, Edward B. *Primitive Culture: Researches into the Development of Mythology, Philosophy, Religion, Language, Art, and Custom.* 2d ed. 2 vols. London: John Murray, 1873; New York: Gordon Press, 1974.

Underhill, Ruth. *Papago Indian Religion.* New York: Columbia University Press, 1946.

Vaillant, George C. *Aztecs of Mexico.* Garden City, N.Y.: Doubleday, Doran, 1941.

Warner, W. Lloyd. *The Family of God.* New Haven, Conn.: Yale University Press, 1961.

Wax, Rosalie, and Murray Wax. "The Magical World View." *Journal for the Scientific Study of Religion* 1 (1962): 179–88.

Webster, Hutton. *Taboo: A Sociological Study.* Stanford, Calif.: Stanford University Press, 1942.

———. *Magic: A Sociological Study.* Stanford, Calif.: Stanford University Press, 1948.

Weisman, Richard. *Witchcraft, Magic, and Religion in Seventeenth-Century Massachusetts.* Amherst: University of Massachusetts Press, 1984.

Winch, Peter. "Understanding Primitive Society." *Ethics and Action.* London: Routledge and Kegan Paul, 1972.

CHAPTER *2*

Religious Systems

As religion developed, it moved from belief in magic, animism, mana, taboo, and so forth into systems of theology in which sacred writings became codified as doctrine. It then became an institutional matter to safeguard the tenets and the ritual. Ideas were accepted as revealed truth concerning the nature of the spiritual realm, especially the character of God (or the gods) and the deity's relationship with human beings and the physical world.

Although considerable controversy exists over exactly how religion evolved, nature worship in its various forms was probably succeeded by polytheism, the belief in multiple gods resembling human beings. It seems an easy transition from the worship of nature in its multiple manifestations to belief in deities who personified natural phenomena. Thus, there was a period in which societies believed in a sun god, as well as a god of harvest, of the hearth, of the sea, of the hunt, of beauty, of swiftness, and so forth. This was especially true of the national religions of ancient Egypt, Greece, and Rome.

Monotheism, the belief in one god, probably originated in Egypt during the reign of Ikhnaton (c. 1372–54 B.C.), although the concept was short-lived. It seems a natural development, in turn, from polytheistic worship. Instead of having a number of gods responsible for various functions or various regions, believers thought a single god combined within himself all attributes and powers.

Thus the important Judeo-Christian tradition of monotheism came into existence, and God was conceived to be a humanlike (anthropomorphic) being of infinite power, wisdom, and love, the creator and sustainer of heaven and earth. The single deity was thought to be eternal, present everywhere and always, transcending all humanity yet immanent within each human soul, sacred and holy, self-existent, and containing all perfections.

This movement toward unity certainly produced a more sophisticated conception of God, but it did present certain problems as well. For example, evil could no longer be attributed to one god and good to another; the same being was responsible for both, and this required considerable explanation. In fact, many seemingly contradictory qualities had to be ascribed to the same deity because, as positive attributes, they should all be possessed by the one supreme being.

60

For example, if God is considered omnipotent (almighty), then we might ask whether that being could choose to behave in a malicious, rather than a loving, way. According to the divine nature, God certainly would not want to, but the question is whether God can act badly or even want to act badly. Does God have the freedom to change the divine nature? Similarly, can God invert moral principles and make loving one's neighbor wrong and hating one's neighbor right—make the good bad and the bad good?

Can God choose to suspend the laws of logic or mathematics—for example, to divide twelve by four and get seven, or to create the world and not create the world at the same time? (The old philosophic chestnut is, "If God is omnipotent, can he create a rock so large that he cannot lift it?" Since this is self-contradictory, the question becomes, Can God do that which is logically impossible?) If we say that God cannot do any of these things, then what becomes of the assertion that the supreme being is all-powerful?

In the same way, if God is omniscient (all-knowing), then God is aware of everything, including the future of the divine will and the decisions every human being will make. But if the future is foreseen, then it must already be fixed and unalterable (how else could it be known?). God's mind therefore cannot change at some later point (in response to prayer, for example), and God cannot do anything other than what is foreseen for the future. And human beings have only the illusion of free will in their lives; in reality, they cannot do other than what is foreseen.

This implies further that God is limited, and that people are not responsible for their actions. They are behaving according to a script or book that God has seen (and perhaps authored), and their choices cannot be different from what they are. They should not, therefore, be rewarded with heaven or punished in hell. (Some theologians have even argued that if human actions are predetermined, then God is responsible for man's sin.) Obviously, these implications of God's omniscience are inconsistent not only with the unlimited power and goodness attributed to God but also with the free will and moral responsibility ascribed to human beings.

In future chapters we consider the problems inherent in conceiving of God as omnipotent, omniscient, and wholly loving, when the creatures in the world that God created are constantly suffering. But this short treatment shows some of the difficulties involved in presenting a consistent account of the nature of God in a monotheistic system.

Some theologians have responded by claiming that the attributes of God are unknowable; others, that God's attributes cannot be literally expressed or communicated—they should be understood symbolically, figuratively, or metaphorically. But to the majority of religious thinkers, some literal meaning exists, and the problem remains of reconciling the disparate parts of God's being.

In dealing with the Judeo-Christian concept of God we must not forget that other religious systems have appeared in the world, attracting milllions of adherents. Hinduism, Buddhism, Islam, Confucianism, Shintoism, Taoism, and other major faiths have thrived for hundreds or thousands of years, most of them predating the Hebrew and Christian religions. Although we will be dealing principally with Western religion, exclusive of Islam, we should not become so Eurocentric that we exclude from our consciousness the other great faiths of the world.

Hinduism, for instance, offers a rival theological system to that of Western religions, and in many ways illustrates the history of belief. It incorporates a number of earlier religious notions of separate gods as described in scriptures called the Vedas—gods such as Varuna, the god of the firmament; Indra, the god of warriors; and Surya, the god of the sun. Some of the gods are wind spirits, some are divinities of light, some control luck, some heaven and hell, some are good (deva) and others extremely bad (sura).

At a later point (between 1000 and 500 B.C.), a sophisticated philosophic system emerged, largely through the sacred writings of the Brahmanas and the Upanishads. In those scriptures a supreme being or soul is identified that is related to the human soul; the goal in living is to reunite the two so that the individual becomes one with the universal spirit. The way to accomplish this ideal union occupies the major part of Hindu philosophy.

For a brief time, largely in response to a challenge from Buddhism, the idea of a number of gods reappeared: Brahma, the creative power; Vishnu, the preserver; and Shiva (with his wife Kali), the destroyer. However, this triad of gods gradually faded in theological importance and became largely symbolic, although they remained a vital part of popular religion. Brahma then became interpreted as an abstract and spiritual force, the world soul described in the Upanishads.

To achieve union with Brahma, believers may take various paths: the Way of Works, the Way of Knowledge, and the Way of Devotion, all of which are thoroughly elaborated. Above all, it is knowledge that matters—specifically, the realization that the self and the universe are one, and that the physical world, including the body, is an illusion that must be renounced. Once one is released from attachment to one's individual person and the world, then enlightenment can occur.

An important dimension of the Hindu system is belief in reincarnation, a series of rebirths in which the soul of a dying person enters the body of a newborn baby. The soul leads a multitude of lives, and the social level of each life depends on the worth, or karma, of the previous existence. That is, the soul of someone who has led a spiritually poor existence previously and has amassed negative karma will be reborn into a low caste; a soul that has lived a very pure life will automatically inhabit a high caste.

Once the highest level is reached, that of priest, the soul is in a position to free itself from the round of rebirths and return to its source in the soul of the universe. It is only at the pinnacle of the hierarchy, the priest stage, that enlightenment is possible, leading to salvation. And salvation is envisioned not as continued existence but as a merging with the All. The spark joins the universal fire; the drop becomes one with the ocean of being.

This philosophic system not only reminds us of the existence of major non-Western religions but also should induce a certain humility about trusting our familiar Western beliefs. In claiming that the religion or denomination we believe in is true, we need to consider other alternatives that seem equally convincing to those raised differently. We need to ask ourselves why we believe as we do and whether our faith is justifiable, and which form of religion contains the "real" truth.

Perhaps more importantly, we should question whether one true religion exists, or whether we live in a pluralistic world in which various religions embody portions of the truth. This would be the approach of openness and tolerance, in which other beliefs are honestly considered and become genuine options for us.

In the following selections, H. J. McCloskey discusses the characteristics of the Judaic-Christian God, including reference to the apparent contradictions that exist between various perfections. Charles Hartshorne's contribution is in terms of "process theology," which conceives of the universe as a continuously changing creation. He views the attributes of God, especially omnipotence, from this organic and evolutionary perspective. Mordecai Kaplan then outlines the modern conception of God, which, to his mind, does not mean a supernatural being but "whatever enhances human life." He says we must discover the "god-hood manifested in our personal and social experience."

T. M. P. Mahadevan offers an outline of Hinduism and Mircea Eliade explains the fundamental ideas behind Buddhism, which should be understood against the backdrop of Hinduism previously described. And Huston Smith discusses Islam, a world religion that has assumed greater prominence in recent years with the resurgence of Shiite fundamentalism and with the increased political role played by the Arab countries.

In the final section, Paul Tillich describes the relationship of Christianity to other religions as marked by "inclusivism" and a "dialectic" rather than by dogmatic exclusivism. John Hick then argues for salvation outside the church and sees a golden thread or common identity running through all religions. He believes that in the future, as ecumenicism increases, different traditions will "no longer see themselves and each other as rival ideological communities."

Judeo-Christian Theism

7. The Nature and Attributes of God

H. J. McCLOSKEY

GOD'S ATTRIBUTES AS LITERALLY ASCRIBED

A great variety of attributes are ascribed to God. Some are purely negative for example, the attributes of being intangible, invisible, and the like. Others are the so-called pure perfections, life, power, intelligence, wisdom, goodness. Others again are of a kind which, if literally interpreted, would involve limitations, for example, being a person, a father, one who loves his creations, and the like. My contention here is that for the problem of evil to arise in its traditional form for the theist, the attributes of power, wisdom and knowledge, as well as goodness must hold of God in a literal sense. Since apologists who accept the problem as a real one often seek to advance solutions by reference to other alleged attributes of God, attributes such as that he is a personal God who loves mankind, and who is capable of personal relationships with his creations, it will be useful here to consider these attributes, and how and in what sense God could be understood to possess them, as well as the more primary attributes of omnipotence, omniscience, and goodness.

Omnipotence

On the face of it the literal ascription of unlimited power to God presents few difficulties. We understand by power the ability to sustain or to bring about a change, an existence, or the destruction of a thing or a state of affairs; a being has power in that it has the ability to do or to refrain from doing something; we have power in so far as we have the ability to do or refrain from doing various things. Omnipotence is often explained as the power to do anything and everything that is possible. As G. H. Joyce notes:

"Even those who affirm the absolute infinity of God's power, admit that there are things which He cannot do: e.g. that He cannot bring it about that two plus two make five, or that the past should not have happened."

And:

"Infinite power can realize all things. The objects excluded from omnipotence are so because they are not things at all, but non-things, and hence incapable of realization by reason of their nonentity, not by reason of lack of power in God. It may be well to illustrate each of these two sources of impossibility. Notions which contain contradictory elements are not being. . . . Again, it is no diminution of omnipotence that God cannot do those things which are inconsistent with infinite perfection, and only possible to a finite agent."

As these statements bring out, in ascribing power—unlimited power or omnipotence to God—the theist is not involved in understanding "power" in some sense other than that in which we speak of the power a man possesses. Omnipotence, or all-power, is power greater than all other beings possess and such as not to be limited in any way by the power of lesser beings whose power is dependent on that of the omnipotent being. An omnipotent being can do anything that is possible. It cannot do what is logically impossible for the logically impossible is not something—as Joyce brings out, the logically impossible is a non-thing. An omnipotent being is often spoken of as an infinitely powerful being. This, I suggest, is to introduce a needlessly obscure notion, that of infinitely, into the account. It is presumably a way of saying that there are an infinite number of possible things that may be done, infinite possibilities for the exercise of power, and that an all-powerful being can do all that is possible. This, I suggest, is unhelpful, as the notion of possibility here is logically subordinate to the notion of unlimited power; the possibilities are all those things an all-powerful being can do. In the light of these considerations, it is surprising that any theist should wish to ascribe power, all-power or omnipotence, to God in any but a literal sense. The sense in which God has power, is that in which we are ascribed power. God's power is simply greater and such as to make our power not simply subordinate to but dependent on his power.

It is possibly because of the paradoxes that arise in respect of God's omnipotence that some theists have sought to explain omnipotence in a non-literal way. Most of the paradoxes turn on a confusion between what an all-powerful being may do and must do, or on incompatibilities between omnipotence and other divine perfections. Thus it is suggested that there is a paradox springing from whether the omnipotent being can destroy itself, or whether it can make something indestructible or immovable—instantaneously or over a period of time—or the like. I suggest that these are not real paradoxes, that either a logical impossibility is being indicated (e.g. with instantaneous self-destruction, creation of an indestructible body), or that God can do what is described, but if he did he would become a being which was no longer omnipotent.

The paradoxes arising from God's omnipotence and his other perfections are most serious. Joyce here observes:

"Yet God's inability to do evil places no restriction on Him or His omnipotence."

I suggest that Joyce is mistaken in respect of omnipotence here. Clearly, an omnipotent being must be able to do what is evil unless by the nature of the case it is logically impossible for it to do so. The question of the possibility of an omnipotent being, being able to change moral and value standards is more puzzling. Many would wish to argue that to do so is logically impossible. My own view is that a synthetic *a priori* impossibility is involved, and hence that it is impossible for a being to be omnipotent in the sense indicated above. Whether the impossibility is a synthetic *a priori* one or not raises many issues that cannot be pursued here. The important issue is that if there are impossibilities of this kind they involve limitations other than those due to logical impossibilities on God. One must either reject God's omnipotence or the fact of synthetic necessary connexions and impossibilities. Many theists are committed to the fact of the latter, whilst seeking to insist on God's omnipotence, in their proofs of the existence of an all-perfect, omnipotent God.

It has also been argued that it is mistaken to argue that God can, by virtue of his omnipotence, do anything at all, for example, something silly. Could an all-powerful being cause a sign to appear in the sky saying "Fortitude beer is best" simply as a result of a whim? I suggest it must be able to do so. That we do not think that God would do so is because we attribute to him other perfections besides omnipotence. This relates to a more general issue which will be discussed later in this Chapter concerning whether the various perfections attributed to God are logically compatible with one another.

Omniscience

The concept of omniscience is also one which presents no difficulty in respect of its literal interpretation, but again, it is one which leads to apparent or actual paradoxes. To be all-knowing means exactly that, namely to know all that has been, all that is, and all that will be, all that can be. Omniscience is implied in omnipotence, for a being which lacked knowledge would lack the power to achieve what it wished to achieve.

The paradoxes which arise from omniscience chiefly relate to the conjunction of omniscience and other perfections of God, most notably, omnipotence and goodness, and to alleged perfections in man, for example, freedom of the will.

Goodness

Another attribute of God is goodness. God is said to be wholly good in the sense of being wholly morally perfect, willing always what is good, as well as being perfect in all other respects. I suggest that there is not difficulty in understanding the notion of perfect goodness, and that there is no need, nor indeed possibility of understanding this goodness in a sense other than that which applies to human beings. God is wholly good in the sense in which moral agents in general, according to their natures and contexts and powers, strive to be good.

The paradox which arises in respect of God's goodness relates to the question as to whether God is contingently or necessarily good. A being who is contingently good but who may conceivably be evil, may be wholly good in one sense, but lack perfection in another. A being who could not be evil, who is not contingently good but such that we can be certain it will always be good, would appear to be superior in goodness. This is how orthodox Christians see the goodness of God. For them, God cannot commit evil. They explain this in terms of there being no possible motives or reasons for evil for God. The problem or paradox that arises here relates to whether God is thereby necessitated to good, and if so, whether the necessitation to goodness is real goodness. A human person necessitated to act virtuously would typically not be deemed to be virtuous (unless one accepts the compatibility thesis, that free will and determinism are not incompatible, a thesis which is commonly founded on the much questioned paradigm case argument, and which I should wish to reject for this and for independent reasons which cannot be gone into here); yet an omnipotent being who *might* be evil, indeed who could be evil, seems less than perfectly good.

The Compatibility of the Perfections of God

This issue, as it arises in this context, is that of the compatibility of complete power, knowledge, wisdom and goodness. Omnipotence involves the power to do anything that is logically possible; perfect goodness involves the impossibility in some sense of doing what is evil. If moral principles are synthetic necessary truths, they impose a limitation on the power of all beings which is a limitation other than that due to logical impossibility. Wisdom imposes a limitation in that a perfect being *cannot do* silly things, by virtue of his perfection, wisdom. Omniscience involves further difficulties in respect of omnipotence and goodness. A being cannot be omnipotent in the sense of achieving what it seeks to achieve without wisdom and knowledge. Yet if the omnipotent being is necessarily omniscient the problem arises as to how an omnipotent being can be wholly good and yet create, with foreknowledge and without pre-determination, beings who will be morally evil.

8. Omnipotence and Other Theological Mistakes

CHARLES HARTSHORNE

FIRST MISTAKE: GOD IS ABSOLUTELY PERFECT AND THEREFORE UNCHANGEABLE

In Plato's *Republic* one finds the proposition: God, being perfect, cannot change (not for the better, since "perfect" means that there can be no better; not for the worse, since ability to change for the worse, to decay, degenerate, or become corrupt, is a weakness, an imperfection). The argument may seem cogent, but it is so only if two assumptions are valid: that it is possible to conceive of a meaning for "perfect" that excludes change in any and every respect and that we must conceive God as perfect in just *this* sense. Obviously the ordinary meanings of perfect do not entirely exclude change. Thus Wordsworth wrote of his wife that she was a "perfect woman," but he certainly did not mean that she was totally unchangeable. In many places in the Bible human beings are spoken of as perfect; again the entire exclusion of change cannot have been intended. Where in the Bible God is spoken of as perfect, the indications are that even here the exclusion of change in any and every respect was not implied. And where God is directly spoken of as strictly unchanging ("without shadow of turning"), there is still a possibility of ambiguity. God might be absolutely unchangeable in righteousness (which is what the context indicates is the intended meaning), but changeable in ways compatible with, neutral to, *or even required by,* this unswerving constancy in righteousness. Thus, God would be in no degree, however slight, alterable in the respect in question (the divine steadfastness in good will) and yet alterable, not necessarily in spite of, but even because of, this steadfastness. If the creatures behave according to God's will, God will appreciate this behavior; if not, God will have a different response, equally appropriate and expressive of the divine goodness.

The Biblical writers were not discussing Greek philosophical issues, and it is at our own peril that we interpret them as if they were discussing these, just as it is at our peril if we take them to be discussing various modern issues that had not arisen in ancient Palestine. It may even turn out on inquiry that perfection, if taken to imply an absolute maximum of value *in every conceivable respect,* does not make sense or is contradictory. In that case the argument of the *Republic* is an argument from an absurdity and proves nothing. Logicians have found that abstract definitions may seem harmless and yet be contradictory when their meanings are spelled out. Example, "the class of all classes." Similarly, "actuality of all possible values," to which no addition is possible, may have contradictory implications. If perfection cannot consistently mean this value maximum, then the Platonic argument is unsound. Nor was it necessarily Plato's last word on the subject.

SECOND MISTAKE: OMNIPOTENCE

God, being defined as perfect in all respects must, it seems, be perfect in power; therefore, whatever happens is divinely made to happen. If I die of cancer this misfortune is God's doing. The question then becomes, "Why has God done this to me?" Here everything depends on "perfect in power" or "omnipotent." And here, too, there are possible ambiguities, as we shall see.

THIRD MISTAKE: OMNISCIENCE

Since God is unchangeably perfect, whatever happens must be eternally known to God. Our tomorrow's deeds, not yet decided upon by us, are yet always or eternally present to God, for whom there is no open future. Otherwise (the argument goes), God would be "ignorant," imperfect in knowledge, waiting to observe what we may do. Hence, whatever freedom of decision we may have must be somehow reconciled with the alleged truth that our decisions bring about no additions to the divine life. Here perfect and unchanging knowledge, free from ignorance or increase, are the key terms. It can be shown that they are all seriously lacking in clarity, and that the theoretical tradition resolved the ambiguities in a question-begging way.

It is interesting that the idea of an unchangeable omniscience covering every detail of the world's history is not to be found definitely stated in ancient Greek philosophy (unless in Stoicism, which denied human freedom) and is rejected by Aristotle. It is not clearly affirmed in the Bible. It is inconspicuous in the philosophies of India, China, and Japan. Like the idea of omnipotence, it is largely an invention of Western thought of the Dark or Middle Ages. It still goes unchallenged in much current religious thought. . . .

TWO MEANINGS OF "GOD IS PERFECT AND UNCHANGING"

The word "perfect" literally means "completely made" or "finished." But God is conceived as the maker or creator of all; so what could have made God (whether or not the making was properly completed)? "Perfect" seems a poor word to describe the divine reality.

To describe something as "not perfect" seems a criticism, it implies fault finding; worship excludes criticism and fault finding. God is to be "loved with all one's mind, heart, and soul." Such love seems to rule out the possibility of criticism. Suppose we accept this. Do we then have to admit that God cannot change? Clearly yes, insofar as change is for the worse and capacity for it objectionable, a *fault* or *weakness*. God then cannot change for the worse. The view I wish to defend admits this. But does every conceivable kind of change show a fault or weakness? Is there not change for the better? We praise people when they change in this fashion. All healthy growth is such change. We are delighted in growth in infants and children. Is there nothing to learn from this about how to conceive God?

It is easy to reply that, whereas the human offspring starts as a mere fertilized single cell and before that as an unfertilized one, God is surely not to be so conceived. However, no analogy between something human and the worshipful God is to be taken in simple-minded literalness. There still may be an analogy between growth as a wholly good form of change and the divine life. For it is arguable that even an infinite richness may be open to increase. The great logician Bertrand Russell expressed this opinion to me, although Russell was an atheist and had no interest in supporting my, or any, theology.

The traditional objection, already mentioned, to divine change was that if a being were already perfect, meaning that nothing better was possible, then change for the better must be impossible for the being. The unnoticed assumption here has been (for two thousand and more years) that it makes sense to think of a value so great or marvelous that it could in no sense whatever be excelled or surpassed. How do we know that this even makes sense? In my view it does not and is either a contradiction or mere nonsense.

Bishop Anselm [of Canterbury] sought to define God's perfection as "that than which nothing greater (or better) can be conceived." In other words, the divine worth is *in all respects* strictly unsurpassable, incapable of growth as well as of rivalry by another. The words are smoothly uttered; but do they convey a clear and consistent idea? Consider the phrase "greatest possible number." It, too, can be smoothly uttered, but does it say anything? It might be used to define infinity; but I am not aware of any mathematician who has thought this a good definition. There are in standard mathematics many infinities unequal to one another, but no highest infinity. "Infinite" was a favorite word among classical theists; but they cannot be said to have explored with due care its possible meanings. In any case "not infinite" is a negation, and the significance of the negative depends on that of the positive which is negated. If being finite is in every sense a defect, something objectionable, then did not God in creating a world of finite things act objectionably? This seems to me to follow.

Do or do not finite things contribute something to the greatness of God? If so, then each such contribution is itself finite. Does this not mean that somehow finitude has a valid application to the divine life? Consider that, according to the tradition, God could have refrained from creating our world. Then whatever, if anything, this world contributes to the divine life would have been lacking. Moreover, if God could have created some other world instead of this one, God must·actually lack what the other world would have contributed. If you reply that the world contributes nothing to the greatness of God, then I ask, What are we all doing, and why talk about "serving God," who, you say, gains nothing whatever from our existence?

The simple conclusion from the foregoing, and still other lines of reasoning, is that the traditional idea of divine perfection or infinity is hopelessly unclear or ambiguous and that persisting in that tradition is bound to cause increasing skepticism, confusion, and human suffering. It has long bred, and must evermore breed, atheism as a natural reaction.

It is only fair to the founders of our religious tradition to remember that their Greek philosophical teachers who inclined to think of deity as wholly unchanging also greatly exaggerated the lack of novelty in many nondivine things. The heavenly bodies were unborn and undying, and changed only by moving in circles; species were fixed forever; the Greek atomists or materialists thought that atoms changed only by altering their positions. Heraclitus, it is true, hinted at a far more basic role for change, and Plato partly followed him. Plato's World Soul, best interpreted as an aspect of God, was not purely eternal, but in its temporal dimension "a moving image of eternity." However, Aristotle, in his view of divinity at least, was more of an eternalist even than Plato, and medieval thought was influenced by Aristotle, also by Philo Judaeus and Plotinus, who likewise stressed the eternalistic side of Plato. Today science and philosophy recognize none of the absolute worldly fixities the Greeks assumed—not the stars, not the species, not the atoms. It more and more appears that creative becoming is no secondary, deficient form of reality compared to being, but is, as Bergson says, "reality itself." Mere being is only an abstraction. Then is there no permanence, does "everything change"? On the contrary, . . . past actualities are permanent. My childhood experiences will be changelessly there in reality, just as they occurred. Change is not finally analyzed as destruction, but only as creation of novelty. The old endures, the new is added.

There are two senses in which freedom from faults, defects, or objectional features, and perfection in *that* sense, may be applied theologically. The divine, to be worthy of worship, must excel any conceivable being other than itself; it must be unsurpassable *by another*, exalted beyond all possible rivals. Hence all may worship God as in principle forever superior to any other being. This exaltation beyond possible rivals applies to both of the two senses of perfection that I have in mind. There are two kinds (or norms) of excellence, which differ as follows. With one kind it makes sense to talk of an absolute excellence, unsurpassable not only by another being but also by the being itself. This is what the tradition had in mind; and there was in it an important half truth. The neglected other truth, however, is that an absolute best, unsurpassable not only by others but by the being itself, is conceivable only in certain *abstract* aspects of value or greatness, not in fully concrete value or greatness. And God, I hold, is no mere abstraction.

The abstract aspects of value capable of an absolute maximum are goodness and wisdom, or what ought to be meant by the infallibility, righteousness, or holiness of God (one attribute variously expressed). We should conceive the divine knowledge of the world and divine decision-making about it as forever incapable of rivalry and in its infallible rightness incapable of growth. God is not first more or less wicked or foolish (or, like the lower animals, amoral, unaware of ethical principles) and then righteous and wise, but is always beyond criticism in these abstract respects, always wholly wise and good in relating to the world. It is not in such attributes that God can grow. This is because goodness and rightness are abstract, in a sense in which some values are not.

Put a man in prison. He is not thereby necessarily forced to entertain wrong beliefs, lose virtue, or make wrong decisions. What he is forced to lose is the aesthetic richness and variety of his impressions. He cannot in the same degree continue to enjoy the beauty of the world. Similarly, a person suffering as Job did is not a happy person, but is not necessarily less virtuous than before. We can go further; ethical goodness and infallibility in knowledge have an upper or absolute limit. Whatever the world may be, God can know without error or ignorance what that world is and can respond to it, taking fully into account the actual and potential values which it involves, and thus be wholly righteous. But if the world first lacks and then acquires new harmonies, new forms of aesthetic richness, then the beauty of the world as divinely known increases. God would be defective in aesthetic capacity were the divine enjoyment not to increase in such a case. Aesthetic value is the most concrete form of value. Everything can contribute to and increase it. *An absolute maximum of beauty is a meaningless idea.* Leibniz tried to define it. Who dares to say that he succeeded? Beauty is unity in variety of experiences. Absolute unity in absolute variety has no clear meaning. Either God lacks any aesthetic sense and then we surpass God in that respect, or there is no upper limit to the divine enjoyment of the beauty of the world.

Plato viewed God as the divine artist, Charles Peirce and A. N. Whitehead termed God the poet of the world. Is the artist not to enjoy the divine work of art, the poet not to enjoy the divine poem? The Hindus attributed bliss to the supreme reality, and many Western theologians have spoken of the divine happiness, but a careful inquiry into the possibility of an absolute upper limit of happiness has not commonly been undertaken. Plato did write about "absolute beauty" but failed to give even a slightly convincing reason for thinking that the phrase has a coherent meaning.

It is not a defect of a Mozart symphony that it lacks the precise form of beauty which a Bach composition has. Aesthetic limitations are not mere defects. The most concrete form of value has no upper limit; there can always be additional values. God can enjoy all the beauty of the actual world and its predecessors, but creativity is inexhaustible and no actual creation can render further creation superfluous. Absolute beauty is a will-o'-the-wisp, the search for which has misled multitudes. This is the very rationale of becoming, the reason why mere static being is not enough. Any actual being is less than there could be. There could be more, let there be more. To suppose that this has no application to God is to throw away such clues to value as we have, turn out the light, and use mere words to try to illuminate the darkness that is left.

TWO MEANINGS OF "ALL-POWERFUL"

The idea of omnipotence in the sense to be criticized came about as follows: to be God, that is, worthy of worship, God must in power excel all others (and be open to criticism by none). The highest conceivable form of power must be the divine power. So far so good. Next question: what is the highest conceivable form of power? This question was scarcely put seriously at all, the answer was felt to be so obvious: it must be the power to determine every detail of what happens in the world. Not, notice, to significantly influence the happenings; no, rather to strictly determine, decide, their every detail. Hence it is that people still today ask, when catastrophe strikes, Why did God do this to me? What mysterious divine reason could there be? Why me? I charge theologians with responsibility for this improper and really absurd question.

Without telling themselves so, the founders of the theological tradition were accepting and applying to deity the *tyrant* ideal of power. "I decide and determine everything, you (and your friends and enemies) merely do what I determine you (and them) to do. Your decision is simply mine for you. You only think you decide: in reality the decision is mine."

Since the theologians were bright people we must not oversimplify. They half-realized they were in trouble. Like many a politician, they indulged in double-talk to hide their mistake even from themselves. They knew they had to define sin as freely deciding to do evil or the lesser good, and as disobeying the will of God. How could one disobey an omnipotent will? There were two devices. One was to say that God does not decide to bring about a sinful act; rather, God decides not to prevent it. God "permits" sin to take place. Taking advantage of this decision, the sinner does his deed. Yet stop! Remember that God is supposed to decide *exactly* what happens in the world. If someone murders me, God has decided there shall be precisely that murderous action. So it turns out that "permits" has here a meaning it ordinarily does not have. Ordinarily, when X gives Y permission to do such and such, there are at least details in the actual doing that are not specified by X (and could not be specified, since human language can give only outlines, not full details, of concrete occurrences). But omnipotence is defined as power to absolutely determine what happens. I have Thomas Aquinas especially in mind here. God gives a creature permission to perform act A, where A is no mere outline but is the act itself in its full concreteness. So nothing at all is left for the creature to decide? What then is left of creaturely freedom?

The most famous of all the scholastics finds the answer, and this is the second of the two devices referred to above. God decides that the creature shall perform act A, but the divine decision is that nevertheless the act shall be performed "freely." Don't laugh, the saintly theologian is serious. Serious, but engaging in double-talk. It is determined exactly what the creature will do, but determined that he or she will do it freely. As the gangsters sometimes say, after specifying what is to be done, "You are going to like it"—in other words, to do it with a will. If this is not the despot's ideal of power, what is?

What, let us ask again, is the highest conceivable form of power? Is it the despot's, magnified to infinity, and by hook or crook somehow reconciled with "benevolence," also magnified to infinity? This seems to have been the (partly unconscious) decision of theologians. Is there no better way? Of course there is.

After all, the New Testament analogy—found also in Greek religions—for deity is the parental role, except that in those days of unchallenged male chauvinism it had to be the father role. What is the ideal parental role? Is it that every detail is to be decided by the parent? The question answers itself. The ideal is that the child shall more and more decide its own behavior as its intelligence grows. Wise parents do not try to determine everything, even for the infant, much less for the half-matured or fully matured offspring. Those who do not understand this, and their victims, are among the ones who write agonized letters to Ann Landers. In trying to conceive God, are we to forget everything we know about values? To read some philosophers or theologians it almost seems so.

If the parent does not decide everything, there will be some risk of conflict and frustration in the result. The children are not infallibly wise and good. And indeed, as we shall argue later, even divine wisdom cannot completely foresee (or timelessly know) what others will decide. Life simply is a process of decision making, which means that risk is inherent in life itself. Not even God could make it otherwise. *A world without risks is not conceivable.* At best it would be a totally dead world, with neither good nor evil. . . .

TWO MEANINGS OF "ALL-KNOWING"

The word "omniscient" seems somewhat less badly tarnished by its historical usage than "omnipotent." Whereas having all power (of decision making) would be a monopoly, implying that the creatures had no such power, having all knowledge has no monopolistic implications. Only one agent can genuinely make a certain concrete decision; in contrast, many agents can know one and the same truth, e.g., that two and three is five, or that Julius Caesar was assassinated by Brutus. Hence that God knows all truth is quite compatible with you or your brother knowing many truths.

With omniscience there is one difficulty: either knowing about the future differs essentially from knowing about the past, and hence even God knows our past decisions in one way and knows about the future of our decision making in another way, or else it is merely our human weakness that for us the future is partly indefinite, a matter of what may or may not be, whereas God, exalted altogether beyond such a "limitation," sees the future as completely definite. If God is to be thought in every respect immutable it is this second option that must be taken; but have we any other reason for rejecting the old Socinian proposition that even the highest conceivable form of knowledge is of the past-and-definite *as* past-and-definite and of the future and partly indefinite *as* future and partly indefinite? Otherwise would not God be "knowing" the future as what it is not, that is, knowing falsely? As we have seen, the arguments for the complete unchangeability of God are fallacious; hence, the arguments for growth in God's knowledge, as the creative process produces new realities to know, are sound. Thus as Fechner, Berdyaev, Tillich, and, probably independently, Whitehead held (and Berdyaev most neatly formulated), our existence from moment to moment "enriches the divine life." And this is the ultimate meaning of our existence.

Is God all-knowing? Yes, in the Socinian sense. Never has a great intellectual discovery passed with less notice by the world than the Socinian discovery of the proper meaning of omniscience. To this day works of reference fail to tell us about this.

9. The Changing Conception of God

MORDECAI KAPLAN

WHAT BELIEF IN GOD MEANS, FROM THE MODERN POINT OF VIEW

To the modern man, religion can no longer be a matter of entering into relationship with the supernatural. The only kind of religion that can help him live and get the most out of life will be the one which will teach him to identify as divine or holy whatever in human nature or in the world about him enhances human life. Men must no longer look upon God as a reservoir of magic power to be tapped whenever they are aware of their physical limitations. It was natural for primitive man to do so. He sought contact with his god or gods primarily because he felt the need of supplementing his own limited powers with the external forces which he believed were controlled by the gods. He sought their aid for the fertility of his fields, the increase of his cattle, and the conquest of his foes. In time, however— and in the case of the Jewish people early in their history—men began to seek communion with God not so much as the source of power but rather as the source of goodness, and to invoke His aid to acquire control not over the external forces but over those of human nature in the individual and in the mass. With the development of scientific techniques for the utilization of natural forces, and with the revision of our world-outlook in a way that invalidates the distinction between natural and supernatural, it is only as the sum of everything in the world that renders life significant and worthwhile—or holy—that God can be worshiped by man. Godhood can have no meaning for us apart from human ideals of truth, goodness, and beauty, interwoven in a pattern of holiness.

To believe in God is to reckon with life's creative forces, tendencies and potentialities as forming an organic unity, and as giving meaning to life by virtue of that unity. Life has meaning for us when it elicits from us the best of which we are capable, and fortifies us against the worst that may befall us. Such meaning reveals itself in our experiences of unity, of creativity, and of worth. In the experience of that unity which enables us to perceive the interaction and interdependence of all phases and elements of being, it is mainly our cognitive powers that come into play; in the experience of creativity which we sense at first hand, whenever we make the slightest contribution to the sum of those forces that give meaning to life, our conative powers come to the fore; and in the experience of worth, in the realization of meaning, in contrast to chaos and meaninglessness, our emotional powers find expression. Thus in the very process of human self-fulfillment, in the very striving after the achievement of salvation, we identify ourselves with God, and God functions in us. This fact should lead to the conclusion that when we believe in God, we believe that reality—the world of inner and outer being, the world of society and of nature—is so constituted as to enable man to achieve salvation. If human beings are frustrated, it is not because there is no God, but because they do not deal with reality as it is actually and potentially constituted.

Our intuition of God is the absolute negation and antithesis of all evaluations of human life which assume that consciousness is a disease, civilization a transient sickness, and all our efforts to lift ourselves above the brute only a vain pretense. It is the triumphant exorcism of Bertrand Russell's dismal credo: "Brief and powerless is man's life. On him and all his race the slow sure doom falls pitiless and dark." It is the affirmation that human life is supremely worthwhile and significant, and deserves our giving to it the best that is in us, despite, or perhaps because of, the very evil that mars it. This intuition is not merely an intellectual assent. It is the "yea" of our entire personality. "That life is worth living is the most necessary of assumptions," says Santayana, "and were it not assumed, the most impossible of conclusions." The existence of evil, far from silencing that "yea," is the very occasion for articulating it. "The highest type of man," said Felix Adler, "is the one who *in articulo mortis* can bless the universe."

The human mind cannot rest until it finds order in the universe. It is this form-giving trait that is responsible for modern scientific theory. That same need is also operative in formulating a view of the cosmos, which will support the spiritual yearnings of the group and make their faith in the goals and objectives of their group life consistent with the totality of their experience as human beings. Out of this process of thought there arise traditional beliefs as to the origin of the world, man's place in it, his ultimate destiny, the role of one's own particular civilization in the scheme of human history, and all those comprehensive systems of belief that try to bring human experience into a consistent pattern.

But there is one underlying assumption in all these efforts at giving a consistent meaning to life, whether they are expressed in the naïve cosmologies of primitive peoples or in the most sophisticated metaphysical systems of contemporary philosophers, and that is the assumption that life is meaningful. Without faith that the world of nature is a cosmos and not a chaos, that it has intelligible laws which can be unravelled, and that the human reason offers us an instrument capable of unravelling them, no scientific theorizing would be possible. This is another way of saying that science cannot dispense with what Einstein has appropriately named "cosmic religion," the faith that nature is meaningful and hence divine. And just as our inquiry into natural law demands the validation of cosmic religion, so also does our inquiry into moral law and the best way for men to live. It implies the intuition that life inherently yields ethical and spiritual values, that it is holy. The God idea thus expresses itself pragmatically in those fundamental beliefs by which a people tries to work out its life in a consistent pattern and rid itself of those frustrations which result from the distracting confusion of ideals and aims, in a word, beliefs by which it orients itself and the individuals that constitute it to life as a whole.

The purpose of all education and culture is to socialize the individual, to sensitize him to the ills as well as to the goods of life. Yet the more successful we are in accomplishing this purpose, the more unhappiness we lay up for those we educate. "As soon as high consciousness is reached," says A. N. Whitehead, "the enjoyment of existence is entwined with pain, frustration, loss, tragedy." Likewise, the more eager we are to shape human life in accordance with some ideal pattern of justice and cooperation, the more reasons we discover for being dissatisfied with ourselves, with our limitations, and with our environment. If, therefore, culture and social sympathy are not to break our hearts, but to help us retain that sureness of the life-feeling which is our native privilege, they must make room for religious faith which is needed as a tonic to quicken the pulse of our personal existence.

Faith in life's inherent worthwhileness and sanctity is needed to counteract the cynicism that sneers at life and mocks at the very notion of holiness. Against such a cheapening of life's values no social idealism that does not reckon with the cosmos as divine is an adequate remedy. How can a social idealist ask men to deny themselves immediate satisfactions for the sake of future good that they may never see in their lifetime, when he leaves them without any definite conviction that the universe will fulfill the hopes that have inspired their sacrifice, or is even able to fulfill them? If human life does not yield some cosmic meaning, is it not the course of wisdom to pursue a policy of "Eat, drink and make merry, for tomorrow we die"?

Belief in God as here conceived can function in our day exactly as the belief in God has always functioned; it can function as an affirmation that life has value. It implies, as the God idea has always implied, a certain assumption with regard to the nature of reality, the assumption that reality is so constituted as to endorse and guarantee the realization in man of that which is of greatest value to him. If we believe that assumption to be true, for, as has been said, it is an assumption that is not susceptible of proof, we have faith in God. No metaphysical speculation beyond this fundamental assumption that reality assures both the emergence and the realization of human ideals is necessary for the religious life.

GOD IS NOT KNOWN UNLESS SOUGHT AFTER

Once this idea is clear in our minds, the next step is to identify those elements in the life about us, in our social heritage and in ourselves, that possess the quality of Godhood. The purpose in setting forth in concrete ethical and rational terms the meaning of God should be twofold: first, to forestall the denial of the divine aspect of reality, and secondly, to counteract the tendency to exaggerate the significance of God-awareness as such, regardless of the irrationality or the immorality of the conduct which accompanies that awareness. *While the immediacy and the dynamic of God-awareness are, no doubt, indispensable to the vital religion, their value is danger- ously overstressed by those of a romantic or mystic turn of mind.*

Nothing less than the deliberate refusal to be satisfied with the negation of life's inherent worth is likely to keep our minds in a receptive mood for the belief in God. But being in a receptive mood is not enough. We shall not come to experience the reality of God unless we go in search of Him. To be seekers of God, we have to depend more upon our own thinking and less upon tradition. Instead of acquiescing passively in the traditional belief that there is a God, and then deducing from that belief conclusions which are to be applied to human experience and conduct, we must accustom ourselves to find God in the complexities of our experience and behavior. "Seek ye me and live."[1] To seek God, to inquire after Him, to try to discern His reality is religion in action. *The ardent and strenuous search for God in all that we know and feel and do is the true equivalent of the behest, "Thou shalt love the Lord thy God with all thy heart, with all thy soul and with all thy might."*[2] Only by way of participation in human affairs and strivings are we to seek God.

We seek God, whenever we explore truth, goodness and beauty to their uttermost reaches. We must take care, however, not to treat these objects of our striving as independent of one another, for then we are likely to pursue some partial truth, some mistaken goodness, or some illusory beauty. The pursuit of truth, unwedded to an appreciation of goodness and beauty, is likely to issue in the sort of personality that can be absorbed in the scientific investigation of the explosive properties of certain chemicals, wholly indifferent as to whether one's conclusions be made to further war or peace, construction or destruction. The well-meaning fanatics of virtue, who inspired the title of one of Bertrand Russell's essays, "The Evil Good Men Do," are typical of the results of seeking goodness while underestimating its relationship to truth and beauty. Their intentions are good, but their behavior reminds us that "the road to hell is paved with good intentions." The exclusive pursuit of beauty results in the type of decadent es-

---

[1] Amos 5:4.
[2] Deut. 6:5.

theticism that fiddles while Rome burns. It issues in an art that is for art's sake rather than for life's sake, and that reaches a *reductio ad absurdum* in forms of artistic expression which communicate no meaning to any except the few artists who happen to subscribe to the same set of artistic dogmas, and to be interested in experimenting with the same techniques.

The penalty for the failure to deal with truth, goodness and beauty as organically related to one another is the failure to reach the conviction of life's true worth. The attainment of that conviction is vouchsafed only to those to whom truth, goodness and beauty are but partial phases of life's meaning. Religion has the one word which seeks to express that meaning in all its depth and mystery. That word is "holiness." It is folly to try to eliminate the concept of holiness from our vocabulary. It is the only accurate term for our deepest and most treasured experiences. The moment any situation evokes from us the awareness that we have to do with something to which no other term than "sacred" is adequate, we are on the point of discovering God. In fact, we already sense His reality.

The part to be played by our religious tradition is to bring to our attention the *sancta* through which the God-awareness has been actualized. But we must take care not to adopt the attitude of the philistine who departmentalizes life into the secular and the holy, and who thereby misses the main significance of holiness, which is compatible only with the wholeness of life. The philistinism which associates sanctity only with certain places and occasions and regards all others as secular is, in effect, a reversion to the primitive magical conception of holiness. Certain sites that, for one reason or another, impressed themselves particularly on the imagination of primitive peoples seemed the special haunts of deity; certain times seemed particularly propitious, others unpropitious for approaching Him. Those were then pronounced holy. In our logical thinking we reject such notions as superstition, having been taught by our Prophets to associate the holiness of God with the thought that "the whole earth is filled with His glory." But our emotional reactions often revert to the attitude of primitive religion, and we then associate holiness only with persons, places and events which have been sanctified by traditional rituals. If, however, we relate the ideal of holiness to the worthwhileness and sanctity of life as implicit in the God idea, we invest places, persons and events with sacredness only as they contribute to our awareness of the sanctity of life as a whole, only as they symbolize the holiness that is in all things.

Every effort to articulate our sense of life's worthwhileness in ritual and prayer is a means of realizing the Godhood manifested in our personal and social experience. The same appreciation of whatever contributes to our joy in living which is voiced in the traditional prayers of praise and thanksgiving still calls for expression. The same hopeful yearning for unrealized good that is voiced in the traditional prayers of petition needs to be articulated, as one of the means toward its ultimate realization. We may have to revise our liturgy to express with greater truth what we sincerely think and feel when we have God in mind, but we cannot dispense with worship. The departure from the traditional idea of God as a self-existent entity necessarily changes the function of prayer, but by no means destroys it. The institution of worship and the resort to prayer did not have to wait for our day to suffer change in their meaning and functioning. From the time that the conception of God as a kind of magnified human being in form or feeling was banned, prayer could not possibly mean what it did in the earlier periods of Jewish religion, when men naïvely believed that God acted directly in answer to any petition that was addressed to Him. Ever since philosophy invaded the field of Jewish religion, it became difficult to pray in the spirit of those who had never been troubled by philosophic scruples. It is unfortunate that medieval Jewish theologians who took such pains to deprecate the naïve idea of God failed to indicate that prayer must undergo changes in form and meaning to correspond with the more philosophical conception of God that they were urging. But their omission does not alter the fact, first, that any affirmative conception of God must necessarily find expression in prayer, and secondly, that the content of the prayer must correspond with the particular conception of God to which we can whole-heartedly ascribe. . . .

Other Major Religions

10. The Message of the Buddha: From the Terror of the Eternal Return to the Bliss of the Inexpressible

MIRCEA ELIADE

THE MAN STRUCK BY A POISONED ARROW . . .

The Buddha never consented to give his teaching the structure of a system. Not only did he refuse to discuss philosophical problems, he did not even issue pronouncements on several essential points of his doctrine—for example, on the state of the holy man in *nirvāṇa*. This silence early made possible differing opinions and finally gave rise to various schools and sects. The oral transmission of the Buddha's teaching and the composition of the canon raise numerous problems, and it would be useless to suppose that they will one day be satisfactorily solved. But if it seems impossible wholly to reconstruct the Buddha's "authentic message," it would be excessive to suppose that the earliest documents already present a radically modified version of his doctrine of salvation.

From the beginning, the Buddhist community (*saṃgha*) was organized by monastic rules (*vinaya*) that assured its unity. As for doctrine, the monks shared certain fundamental ideas concerning transmigration and the retribution for actions, the techniques of meditation that would lead to *nirvāṇa*, and the "condition of the Buddha" (what is called Buddhology). In addition to the community, there existed, even in the Blessed One's time, a mass of sympathizing laymen who, though accepting the teaching, did not renounce the world. By their faith in the Buddha, by their generosity to the community, the laymen gained "merits" that insured them a postexistence in one of the various "paradises," followed by a better reincarnation. This type of devotion is characteristic of "popular Buddhism," and it has great importance in the religious history of Asia because of the mythologies, rituals, and literary and artistic works to which it has given rise.

Essentially it may be said that the Buddha opposed both the cosmological and philosophical speculations of the Brahmans and the *śramaṇas* (magicians) and the different methods and techniques of a preclassic Sāṃkhya and Yoga. As for cosmology and anthropogony, which he refused to discuss, it is obvious that, for the Buddha, the world was created by neither a god nor a demiurge nor an evil spirit (as the Gnostics and Manicheans think; see §§229 ff.), but that it continues to exist, that is, it is continually created by the acts, good or evil, of men. Indeed, when ignorance and sin increase, not only is human life shortened but the universe itself wastes away. (This idea is pan-Indian, but it derives from archaic conceptions of the progressive decadence of the world, which necessitates its periodical renewal.)

As for Sāṃkhya and Yoga, the Buddha borrows and develops the analysis of the Sāṃkhya masters and the contemplative techniques of the yogins while rejecting their theoretical presuppositions, first of all the idea of the Self (*puruṣa*). His refusal to let himself be drawn into speculations of any kind is categorical. It is admirably illustrated in the famous dialogue with Mālunkyaputta. This monk complained that the Blessed One gave no answers to such questions as: Is the universe eternal or noneternal? Finite or infinite? Is the soul the same thing as the body, or is it different? Does the Tathāgata exist after death, or does he not exist after death? And so forth. Mālunkyaputta asks the Master to state his thoughts clearly and, if necessary, to admit that he does not know the answer. The Buddha then tells him the story of the man struck by a poisoned arrow. His friends and relatives fetch a surgeon, but the man exclaims: "I will not let this arrow be drawn out until I know who struck me; also, whether he is a *kṣatriya* or a Brahman . . . , to what family he belongs; whether he is tall, short, or of medium height; from what village or city he comes. I will not let this arrow be drawn out before I know what kind of bow was drawn against me, . . . what string was used on the bow, . . . what feather was used on the arrow . . . , how the point of the arrow was made." The man died without knowing these things, the Blessed One continued, just like one who would refuse to follow the way of holiness before solving one or another philosophical problem. Why did the Buddha refuse to discuss these things? "Because it is not useful, because it is not connected with the holy and spiritual life and does not contribute to disgust with the world, to detachment, to cessation of desire, to tranquility, to profound penetration, to illumination, to Nirvāṇa!" And the Buddha reminded Mālunkyaputta that he had taught only one thing, namely: the four Noble Truths (*Majjhima Nikāya* 1.426).

THE FOUR NOBLE TRUTHS AND THE MIDDLE PATH. WHY?

These four Noble Truths contain the heart of his teaching. He preached them in his first sermon at Benares, soon after the Awakening, to his five former companions (§149). The first Noble Truth concerns suffering or pain (Pali: *dukkha*). For the Buddha, as for the majority of Indian thinkers and holy men after the period of the Upanishads, all is suffering. Indeed, "Birth is suffering, decline is suffering, sickness is suffering, death is suffering. To be joined with what one does not love means to suffer. To be separated from what one loves . . . , not to have what one desires, means to suffer. In short, any contact with [one of the] five *skandhas* implies suffering" (*Majjhima Nikāya* 1. 141). We would point out that the term *dukkha*, usually translated by "pain" or "suffering," has a much broader meaning. Various forms of happiness, even certain spiritual states obtained by meditation, are described as being *dukkha*. After praising the spiritual bliss of such yogic states, the Buddha adds that they are "impermanent, *dukkha*, and subject to change" (*Majjhima Nikāya* 1. 90). They are *dukkha* precisely because they are impermanent.[1] As we shall see, the Buddha reduces the "self" to a combination of five aggregates (*skandhas*) of the physical and psychic forces. And he states that *dukkha* is, in the last analysis, the five aggregates.

The second Noble Truth identifies the origin of suffering (*dukkha*) in desire, appetite, or the "thirst" (*taṇhā*) that determines reincarnations. This "thirst" continually searches for new enjoyments, of which there are three distinct kinds: desire for sensual pleasures, desire to perpetuate oneself, and desire for extinction (or self-annihilation). It is noteworthy that the desire for self-annihilation is condemned along with the other manifestations of "thirst." Being itself an "appetite," the desire for extinction, which can lead to suicide, does not constitute a solution, for it does not halt the eternal circuit of transmigrations.

The third Noble Truth proclaims that deliverance from pain (*dukkha*) consists of abolishing the appetites (*taṇhā*). It is equivalent to *nirvāṇa*. Indeed, one of the names of *nirvāṇa* is "Extinction of Thirst" (*taṇhākkaya*). Finally, the fourth Noble Truth reveals the ways that lead to the cessation of suffering.

In formulating the four Truths, the Buddha applies a method of Indian medicine that first defines a disease, then discovers its cause, and finally presents the methods able to end it. The therapy elaborated by the Buddha constitutes, in fact, the fourth Truth, for it prescribes the means for curing the evils of existence. This method is known by the name of the "Middle Way." And in fact it avoids the two extremes: the pursuit of happiness by the pleasures of the senses, and the opposite way, the search for spiritual bliss by excessive asceticism. The Middle Way is also called the Eightfold Path, because it consists in: (1) right (or just) opinion, (2) right thought, (3) right speech, (4) right activity, (5) right means of existence, (6) right effort, (7) right attention, (8) right concentration.

The Buddha returns tirelessly to the eight rules of the Way, explaining them in different manners, for he addressed different audiences. These eight rules were sometimes classified according to their purposes. Thus, for example, one text of the *Majjhima Nikāya* (1.301) defines the Buddhist teaching as: (1) ethical conduct (*śīla*), (2) mental discipline (*samādhi*), (3) wisdom (*panna*; Skr. (*prajñā*)). Ethical behavior, based on universal love and compassion for all beings, consists, in fact, of the practice of the three rules (nos. 2–4) of the Eightfold Path, namely, just or right speech and thought and right activity. Numerous texts explain what is meant by these formulas. Mental discipline consists of the practice of the last three rules of the Eightfold Path (nos. 6–8): right effort, attention, and concentration. These consist of ascetic exercises of the Yoga type, on which we shall dwell later,

---

[1] Buddhist scholasticism distinguished *dukkha* as ordinary suffering, as suffering caused by change, and as a conditioned state (*Visuddhimagga*, p. 499; cf. Rahula, *L'Enseignement du Bouddha*, p. 40). But, since everything is "conditioned," everything is suffering.

for they are the essence of the Buddhist message. As for wisdom (*prajñā*), it is the result of the first two rules: right view or opinion, right thought.

THE IMPERMANENCE OF THINGS AND THE DOCTRINE OF *ANATTĀ*

By meditating on the first two Noble Truths—on pain and the origin of pain—the monk discovers the impermanence, hence the nonsubstantiality, of his own being. He finds that he is not astray among things (as is, for example, the Vedāntin, the Orphic, and the Gnostic) but shares their modalities of existence; for the cosmic totality and psychomental activity constitute one and the same universe. By employing a pitiless analysis, the Buddha showed that *all* that exists in the world can be classed in five categories—"assemblages" or "aggregates" (*skandhas*); these are (1) the sum total of "appearances," of the sensible (which includes the totality of material things, the sense organs, and their objects); (2) the sensations (provoked by contact with the five sense organs); (3) the perceptions and the notions that result from them (that is to say, cognitive phenomena); (4) psychic constructions, including both conscious and unconscious psychic activity; (5) thoughts (*vijñānas*), that is, the various kinds of knowledge produced by the sensory faculties and especially by the spirit (*manas*) that has its seat in the heart and organizes the sensory experiences. Only *nirvāṇa* is not conditioned, not "constructed," and, consequently, cannot be classed among the aggregates.

These aggregates or assemblages summarily describe the world of things and the human condition. Another celebrated formula even more dynamically recapitulates and illustrates the concatenation of causes and effects that govern the cycle of lives and rebirths. This formula, known as "conditioned coproduction" (*pratītya-samutpāda*; Pali, *paṭicca-samuppāda*), comprises twelve factors ("members"), the first of which is ignorance. It is ignorance that produces the volitions; these, in their turn, produce the "psychic constructions" (*saṃskāras*), which condition the psychic and mental phenomena, and so on and on—up to desire, more especially sexual desire, which engenders a new existence and finally ends in old age and death. Essentially, ignorance, desire, and existence are interdependent, and together they suffice to explain the unbroken chain of births, deaths, and transmigrations.

This method of analysis and classification was not discovered by the Buddha. The analyses of preclassic Yoga and Sāṃkhya, like the earlier speculations of the Brāhmaṇas and the Upanishads, had already dissociated and classified the cosmic totality and psychomental activity into a certain number of elements or categories. Moreover, from the post-Vedic period on, desire and ignorance were denounced as the first causes of suffering and transmigration. But the Upanishads, like Sāṃkhya and Yoga, also recognize the existence of an autonomous spiritual principle, the *ātman* or the *puruṣa*. Now the Buddha appears to have denied, or at least refrained from discussing, the existence of such a principle.

Indeed, a number of texts regarded as reflecting the Master's original teaching deny the reality of the human person (*pudgala*), of the vital principle (*jīva*), and of the *ātman*. In one of his discourses the Master brands as "completely senseless" the doctrine that affirms: "This universe is this *ātman*; after death, I shall be that, which is permanent, which remains, which endures, which does not change, and I shall exist as such for all eternity." The ascetic intent and function of this negation of his are comprehensible: by meditating on the unreality of the person, one destroys ignorance in its very roots.

On the other hand, the negation of a Self, subject to transmigrations but able to free itself and attain *nirvāṇa*, raised problems. This is why the Buddha on several occasions refused to answer questions concerning the existence or the nonexistence of the *ātman*. Thus he remained silent when a wandering monk, Vacchagotta, questioned him concerning these problems. But he later explained to Ānanda the meaning of his silence: if he had answered that a Self exists, he would have lied; moreover, Vacchagotta would have put the Blessed One among the adherents of the "eternalist theory" (that is, he would have made him a "philosopher" like any number of others). If he had answered that there is no Self, Vacchagotta would have taken him to be a partisan of the "annihilistic theory," and, even more important, the Buddha would only have increased his confusion; "for he would have thought: formerly I did have an *ātman*, but now I no longer have one" (*Saṃyutta Nikāya* 4.400). Commenting on this famous episode, Vasubandhu (fifth century A.D.) concluded: "To believe in the existence of the 'Self' is to fall into the heresy of permanence; to deny the 'Self' is to fall into the heresy of annihilation at death."

By denying the reality of the Self (*nairātmya*), one arrives at this paradox: a doctrine that exalts the importance of the act and of its "fruit," the retribution for the act, denies the agent, the "eater of the fruit." In other words, as a late authority, Buddhaghoṣa, put it: "Only suffering exists, but no sufferer is to be found. Acts are, but there is no actor." However, certain texts are less categorical: "He who eats the fruit of the act in a certain existence is not he who performed the act in an earlier existence; but he is not another."

Such hesitations and ambiguities reflect the embarrassment occasioned by the Buddha's refusal to settle certain much-debated questions. If the Master denied the existence of an irreducible and indestructible Self, it was because he knew that the belief in *ātman* leads to interminable metaphysical controversies and encourages intellectual pride; in the last analysis, it prevents obtaining Enlightenment. As he never ceased to repeat, he preached the cessation of suffering and the means of accomplishing it. The countless controversies concerning the Self and the nature of *nirvāṇa* found their solutions in the experience of Enlightenment: they were insoluble by thought or on the plane of verbalization.

However, the Buddha seems to have accepted a certain unity and continuity of the "person" (*pudgala*). In a sermon on the burden and the burden-bearer, he states: "The burden is the five *skandhas*: matter, sensations, ideas, volitions, knowledge; the burden-bearer is the *pudgala*, for example that venerable monk, of such and such a family, such and such name, etc." (*Saṃyutta* 3.22). But he refused to take sides in the controversy between the "partisans of the person" (*pudgalavādin*) and the "partisans of the aggregates" (*skandhavādin*); he maintained a "middle" position. However, belief in the continuity of the person continues, and not only in popular circles. The Jātakas narrate the Buddha's former existences and those of his family and his companions, and the identity of their personalities is always recognized. And how are we to understand the words uttered by Siddhārtha at the very moment he was born—"This is my last birth" (§147)—if we deny the continuity of the "true person" (even if we hesitate to call it the Self or *pudgala*)?

THE WAY THAT LEADS TO NIRVĀṆA

The last two Truths are to be meditated on together. First, one affirms that the halting of pain is obtained by total cessation of thirst (*taṇhā*), that is, "the act of turning away from it (from this thirst), renouncing it, rejecting it, freeing oneself from it, not attaching oneself to it" (*Majjhima N.* 1. 141). One then affirms that the ways that lead to the stopping of pain are those set forth in the Eightfold Path. The last two Truths explicitly state: (1) that *nirvāṇa* exists but (2) that it can be obtained only by special techniques of concentration and meditation. By implication, this also means that all discussion concerning the nature of *nirvāṇa* and the existential modality of the one who has achieved it has no meaning for him who has not reached even the threshold of that inexpressible state.

The Buddha does not put forth a definition of *nirvāṇa*, but he constantly returns to some of its attributes. He affirms that the *arhats* (the delivered saints) "have attained unshakable happiness" (*Udāna* 8. 10); that *nirvāṇa* "is bliss" (*Aṅguttara* 4. 414); that he, the Blessed One, has "attained the Immortal" and that the monks can attain it too: "You will make yourselves present even in this life; you will live possessing this Immortal" (*Majjhima N.* 1. 172). The *arhat*, "even in this life, cut off, nirvanaized (*nibbuta*), feeling happiness in himself, spends his time with Brahman."

So the Buddha teaches that *nirvāṇa* is "visible here below," "manifest," "actual," or "of this world." But he emphasizes the fact that only he among the yogins "sees" and possesses *nirvāṇa* (by this we must understand that he means both himself and those who follow his path, his method). "Vision," called in the canon "the eye of the saints" (*ariya cakkhu*), allows "contact" with the unconditioned, the "nonconstructed"—with *nirvāṇa*. Now this transcendental "vision" is obtained by certain contemplative techniques that were practiced even from Vedic times and parallels to which are found in ancient Iran.

In short, whatever the "nature" of *nirvāṇa* may be, it is certain that no one can approach it except by following the method taught by the Buddha. The yogic structure of this method is obvious, for it comprises a series of meditations and concentrations known for many centuries. But it is a Yoga developed and reinterpreted by the religious genius of the Blessed One. The monk first practices continuous reflection on his physiological life in order to become conscious of all the acts that, until then, he has performed automatically and unconsciously. For example, "inhaling slowly, he thoroughly understands this slow inhalation; exhaling quickly, he understands, etc. And he practices being conscious of all his

exhalations . . . , of all his inhalations; and he practices slowing down his exhalations . . . and his inhalations" (*Dīgha* 2. 291 ff.). Similarly, the monk seeks to
"understand perfectly" what he does when he walks, raises his arm, eats, speaks,
or is silent. This uninterrupted lucidity confirms to him the friability of the
phenomenal world and the unreality of the "soul." Above all, it contributes to
"transmuting" profane experience.

The monk can now attempt with a certain confidence the techniques
properly speaking. The Buddhist tradition classifies them in three categories: the
"meditations" (*jhānas;* Skr. *dhyānas*), the "attainments" (*samāpattis*), and the concentrations (*samādhis*). We shall first describe them briefly and then try to interpret their results. In the first meditation (*jhāna*), the monk, detaching himself
from desire, experiences "joy and felicity," accompanied by an intellectual activity
(reasoning and reflection). In the second *jhāna,* he obtains the calming of this
intellectual activity; in consequence, he experiences inner serenity, unification of
thought, and the "joy and felicity" arising from this concentration. At the third
jhāna, he detaches himself from joy and remains indifferent but fully conscious,
and he experiences bliss in his body. Finally, on entering the fourth stage, and
renouncing both joy and pain, he obtains a state of absolute purity and indifference and awakened thought.

The four *samāpattis* ("attainments" or "contemplations") pursue the process of "purifying" thought. Emptied of its various contents, the thought is concentrated successively on the infinity of space, on the infinity of consciousness, on
"nothingness," and, at the fourth *samāpatti,* it attains a state that "is neither
consciousness nor unconsciousness." But the *bhikkhu* must go even further in this
labor of spiritual purgation by realizing the halting of all perception and of every
idea (*nirodhasamāpatti*). Physiologically, the monk appears to be in a cataleptic
state, and he is said "to touch *nirvāṇa* with his body." Indeed a late author declares
that "the *bhikkhu* who has acquired it has nothing more to do." As for the "concentrations" (*samādhis*), they are yogic exercises of lesser duration than the *jhānas* and
the *samāpattis,* and they serve especially as psychomental training. The thought is
fixed on certain objects or notions in order to obtain unification of consciousness
and suppression of the rational activities. There are various kinds of *samādhi,* each
directed toward a particular goal.

By practicing and mastering these yogic exercises, together with still
others, which we cannot pause to describe, the *bhikkhu* advances on the "path of
deliverance." Four stages are distinguished: (1) "Having Entered the Current" is
the stage attained by the monk who, freed from his errors and doubts, will be
reborn on earth only seven more times; (2) the "Single Return" is the stage of him
who, having reduced passion, hate, and stupidity, will have only one more rebirth;
(3) the stage "Without Return" is when the monk, having definitely and completely freed himself from errors, doubts and desires, will be reborn in a divine
body and will then obtain deliverance; and (4) the final stage is that of the
"Deserving One" (*arhat*), who, purged of all impurities and passions, endowed
with supernatural knowledge and miraculous powers (*siddhis*), will attain *nirvāṇa* at
the end of his life.

TECHNIQUES OF MEDITATION AND THEIR
ILLUMINATION BY "WISDOM"

It would be credulous to think that one could "understand" these yogic exercises, even by multiplying quotations from the original texts and commenting on them at length. Only practice, under the direction of a master, can reveal their structure and their function. This was true in the period of the Upanishads, and it is still true in our day.

However, we will mention some essential points. First of all, these yogic exercises are guided by "wisdom" (*prajñā*), i.e., by a perfect comprehension of the psychic and parapsychic states experienced by the *bhikkhu*. The effort to "attain consciousness" of the most familiar physiological activities (breathing, walking, moving the arms, etc.) is continued in exercises that reveal to the yogin "states" inaccessible to a profane consciousness.

Second, rendered "intelligible," the yogic experiences end by transmuting normal consciousness. On the one hand, the monk is delivered from the errors that are bound up with the very structure of an unilluminated consciousness (for example, believing in the reality of the "person" or in the unity of matter, etc.); on the other hand, by virtue of his supranormal experiences, he attains a plane of comprehension beyond any notional system, and such a comprehension cannot be verbalized.

Third, by progressing in his practice, the monk finds new confirmations of the doctrine, especially the evidence for an "Absolute," a "nonconstructed," that transcends all the modalities accessible to an unilluminated consciousness, the evident reality of an "Immortal" (or "*nirvāṇa*"), of which nothing can be said except that it exists. A late authority very aptly summarizes the experimental (i.e., yogic) origin of belief in the reality of *nirvāṇa*:

> It is vain to maintain that *nirvāṇa* does not exist for the reason that it is not an object of knowledge. Obviously, *nirvāṇa* is not known directly, in the way color, sensation, etc., are known; and it is not known indirectly by its activity, in the way the sense organs are known. Yet its nature and its activity . . . are the object of knowledge. . . . The yogin, entered into contemplation, becomes conscious of *nirvāṇa*, of its nature, of its activity. When he comes out of contemplation, he exclaims: "Oh *nirvāṇa*, destruction, calm, excellent, escape!" The blind, because they do not see blue and yellow, have no right to say that the seeing do not see colors and that colors do not exist.

Probably the Buddha's most inspired contribution was the articulation of a method of meditation in which he succeeded in integrating ascetic practices and yogic techniques with specific procedures for understanding. This is also confirmed by the fact that the Buddha accorded equal value to asceticism-meditation of the Yoga type and to understanding of the doctrine. But, as was to be expected, the two ways—which, furthermore, correspond to two different tendencies of mind—have only seldom been mastered by one and the same person. The canonical texts very early attempted to reconcile them. "The monks who devote themselves to yogic meditations (the *jains*) blame the monks who cling to the doctrine (the *dhammayogas*), and vice versa. On the contrary, they ought to think well of each other. Few indeed are they who spend their time touching with their bodies (that is, 'realizing, experiencing') the immortal element (that is, *nirvāṇa*). Few too are those who see the profound reality by penetrating it by *prajñā* (by intelligence)."

All truths revealed by the Buddha were to be "realized" in the yogic way, that is, to be meditated on and "experienced." This is why Ānanda, the Master's favorite disciple, though unequaled in knowledge of the doctrine, was excluded from the council (§185): for he was not an *arhat*, this is, had not had a perfect "yogic experience." A famous text of the *Saṃyutta* (2. 115) sets Musīla and Nārada, each of them representing a certain degree of Buddhist perfection, face to face. Each had the same knowledge, but Nārada did not consider himself an *arhat*, since he had not experientially realized "contact with *nirvāṇa.*" This dichotomy continued, only becoming more pronounced, through the whole history of Buddhism. Some authorities even affirmed that "wisdom" (*prajñā*) is able by itself to insure the acquisition of *nirvāṇa*, without any need to cultivate yogic experiences. There is perceptible in this apology for the "dry saint"—for the adept delivered by *prajñā* alone—an antimystical tendency, that is, a resistance, on the part of the "metaphysicians," to yogic excess.

We add that the road to *nirvāṇa*—just like the road to *samādhi* in classic Yoga—leads to possession of "miraculous powers" (*siddhis;* Pali, *iddhi*). This confronted the Buddha (as it later did Patañjali) with a new problem. For, on the one hand, the "powers" are inevitably acquired in the course of practice and, for that very reason, constitute precise indications of the monk's spiritual progress: they are a proof that he is in the process of "deconditioning" himself, that he has suspended the laws of nature in whose pitiless mechanism he was being crushed. But, on the other hand, the "powers" are doubly dangerous, because they tempt the *bhikkhu* with a vain "magic mystery over the world" and, in addition, they may cause dangerous confusion among the uninitiated.

The "miraculous powers" form part of the five classes of "Super Knowledges" (*abhijñās*), namely: (1) *siddhi*, (2) the divine eye, (3) divine hearing, (4) knowledge of another's thought, and (5) recollection of previous existences. None of these five *abhijñās* differs from the "powers" that can be obtained by non-Buddhist yogins. In the *Dīgha Nikāya* (1. 78 ff.) the Buddha states that the *bhikkhu* in meditation can multiply himself, become invisible, pass through solid ground, walk on water, fly through the air, or hear celestial sounds, know the thoughts of others, and remember his former lives. But he does not forget to add that possession of these powers bring with it the danger that they will deflect the monk from his true goal, which is *nirvāṇa*. In addition, the display of such powers in no way advanced the propagation of salvation; other yogins and ecstatics could perform the same miracles; even worse, the uninitiated might think that no more than magic was involved. This is why the Buddha strictly forbade displaying the "miraculous powers" before lay people.

THE PARADOX OF THE UNCONDITIONED

If we bear in mind the transmutation of profane consciousness obtained by the *bhikkhu* and the extravagant yogic and parapsychological experiments that he performs, we understand the perplexity, the hesitations, and even the contradictions of the canonical texts in the matter of the "nature" of *nirvāṇa* and the "situation" of one who has been delivered. There has been any amount of discussion to determine whether the mode of being of the "nirvāṇaized one" is equivalent to total extinction or to an inexpressible and blissful postexistence. The Buddha compared obtaining *nirvāṇa* with the extinction of a flame. But it has been observed that, for Indian thought, the extinction of fire does not mean its annihilation but merely its regression to the mode of potentiality. On the other hand, if *nirvāṇa* is supremely unconditioned, if it is the Absolute, it transcends not only the cosmic structures but also the categories of knowledge. In this case, it can be affirmed that the "nirvāṇaized" adept no longer exists (if existence is understood as being a mode of being in the world); but it can also be affirmed that he "exists" in *nirvāṇa*, in the unconditioned, hence in a mode of being that it is impossible to imagine.

The Buddha was right in leaving this problem open. For only those who have entered on the Path and have realized at least certain yogic experiences and have suitably illuminated them with *prajñā* realize that, with the transmutation of consciousness, verbal constructions and the structures of thought are abolished. One then comes out upon a paradoxical and seemingly contradictory plane on which being coincides with nonbeing; consequently, one can affirm, at one and the same time, that the "Self" exists and that it does not exist; that deliverance is extinction and is at the same time bliss. In a certain sense, and despite the differences between Sāṃkhya-Yoga and Buddhism, one can compare the "nirvāṇaized" adept to the *jīvan-mukta*, the "one delivered in life" (§146).

It is important to emphasize, however, that the equivalence between *nirvāṇa* and absolute transcendence of the cosmos, that is, its annihilation, is also illustrated by numerous images and symbols. We have already referred to the cosmological and temporal symbolism of the "Buddha's Seven Steps" (§147). The parable of the "broken egg," used by the Buddha to proclaim that he had broken the wheel of existence (*saṃsāra*)—in other words, that he had transcended both the cosmos and cyclical time—must be added. No less spectacular are the images of the "destruction of the house" by the Buddha and of the "broken roof" by the *arhats*, images that express the annihilation of any conditioned world. When we remember the importance of the homology "cosmos–house–human body" for Indian thought (and, in general, for traditional, archaic thought), we can estimate the revolutionary novelty of the objective proposed by the Buddha. To the archaic ideal of "fixing one's abode in a stable dwelling place" (that is, assuming a certain existential situation in a perfect cosmos), the Buddha opposes the ideal of the spiritual elite with which he was contemporary: annihilation of the world and transcendence of every "conditioned" situation.

However, the Buddha did not claim that he preached an original doctrine. He repeated on many occasions that he was following "the ancient way," the timeless (*akālika*) doctrine shared by the "saints" and the "perfectly awakened" ones of past times. It was another way of emphasizing the "eternal" truth and the universality of his message.

11. Outlines of Hinduism

T. M. P. MAHADEVAN

WHAT IS HINDUISM?

1 A Faith that Enquires

Hinduism, which is the oldest of the world-religions, had its origin in India, and is still professed by the majority of its people. The name had originally a geographical significance. The Persians who invaded India through the northwestern passes of the Himālayas gave the name Sindhu to the region watered by the river Indus, and the word "Hindu" is only a corrupt form of "Sindhu."[1] Hinduism meant the faith of the people of the Indus-land. This significance was lost even in the distant past. Not only did Hinduism become the religion of the whole of India, but it spread far and wide and became the faith of the colonies of Greater India, like Java, Malaya, and Borneo. The indigenous names by which Hinduism is known are *sanātana-dharma* and *vaidika-dharma*. *Sanātana-dharma* means eternal religion and is expressive of the truth that religion as such knows no age. It is coeval with life. It is the food of the spirit in man. The other name, *vaidika-dharma*, means the religion of the Vedas. The Vedas are the foundational Scriptures of the Hindus; and, as we shall learn in the next chapter, they imply not merely the four Vedas, *Ṛg, Yajus, Sāma,* and *Atharva*, but all words that speak of God. "Veda" is a significant name, meaning God-knowledge or God-science. Hinduism regards as its authority the religious experience of the ancient sages of India. It does not owe its origin to any historical personage or prophet. Buddhism, Christianity, and Islam are founded religions. Their dates are definite, since their authors are known. No such date or founder can be cited as marking the beginning of Hinduism. Hence it is called *sanātana* and *vaidika*, ancient and revealed.

Though Hinduism accepts the authority of the Veda, it is not a dogmatic or "authoritarian" religion. "In India religion is hardly a dogma," says Mr. Havell, "but a working hypothesis of human conduct adapted to different stages of spiritual development and different conditions of life." The allegiance to the Veda does not mean the slavery of reason. There is a popular saying to the effect that not even a thousand scriptural texts will be capable of converting a pot into a piece of cloth. A great philosopher by the name of Vācaspati claims authority not for all Scriptures as such but only for purportful Scripture. And for determining the purport one has to use one's intelligence. *Upapatti* or intelligibility in the light of reasoning

---

[1] The word "India," too is derived from "Sindhu" and means the land of the Indus.

is one of the canons of scriptural interpretation recognized by orthodox Hinduism. The variety of views that we find in Hinduism are all due to the freedom of scope that is given for intellectual inquiry. Even from the earliest times rational reflection was allowed to serve as a corrective to religious belief.

The alliance of reason and revelation is responsible for the kinship of religion and philosophy in India. Philosophy, as understood in the West, arises out of intellectual curiosity, a sense of wonder, as they call it. It is a world-view (*Weltanschauung*), a theory of reality. In the East, however, philosophy has always been regarded as a way of life, an avenue to spiritual realization. *Tattva-vicāra* or inquiry into truth is a means to *mokṣa* or spiritual freedom. It is the realization of the fact of moral and physical evil that makes man reflect and ponder over the mystery and meaning of life. Philosophy, like religion, is an answer to practical need. The avoidance of misery and the acquisition of *śānti* (peace) is the supreme human end. Man engages himself in several pursuits for this purpose. He runs after wealth and outer pleasures in the hope that they will give satisfaction. But he soon finds that undisturbed peace is not gained through such methods. He turns inward (*āvṛtta-cakṣuh*) and beholds within himself the resplendent spirit of God who is the seat of supreme felicity and bliss. Thus philosophy in India is the pathway to religion. And by this happy coordination the Hindu thinkers succeeded in preventing philosophy from becoming barren, and religion from becoming blind. It is interesting to note, in this connection, that philosophy is called *darśana* which means "intuition," and religion, *mata* which means "what has been reflected upon."

2 Life-Religion

The charge of pessimism is often leveled against Hinduism. It is said that the Hindu mind takes too grave a view of life and its problems. Life is regarded as fundamentally evil and escape therefrom as the final good. Hinduism does take account of the misery and suffering of the world. It is these in fact that provoke the problems of philosophy and religion. If optimism means an "unjustifiable acquiescence in evil," it is not worth having. The grim side of existence cannot be ignored. It was the perception of woe and evil that led the Buddha to found a religion of hope. *Saṃsāra* (transmigration) is a vicious circle. Even the choicest goods therein have a core of evil. But evil is not the essence of reality. Hinduism admits that there is a soul of goodness in things evil. Transcendence of evil is the end; and it is possible to achieve it even here in this life. It is a peculiar trait of Hinduism that it regards *mokṣa* not as a hypothetical state to be attained after death in some far-off region but as realizable in this life. The Upaniṣad says: "When all the desires that the heart harbours are gone, man becomes immortal and reaches Brahman *here.*"

All the sects of Hinduism, whatever be their creed and dogma, emphasize the need for ethical life as an indispensable condition of spiritual realization. He whose life is disorderly and who maintains no right relations with his fellow-men will not be able to have the vision of God. It will be easier for the camel to pass through the eye of a needle than for the unrighteous man to enter the kingdom of God. Right speech, right thought, and right action are insisted upon by every school of Hindu thought. Conduct counts more than creed. If a person takes care of his morals, right belief will follow. Hinduism, both a philosophy and religion, is not so much a way of thought as a way of life.

3 Universality

The greatest feature of Hinduism, which is at once unique and lofty, is its catholicity. Dictatorship in religion is as much to be detested as other forms of totalitarian ideology. Provincialism of spirit has been the source of bigotry and bloodshed. They are the worshippers of the false God who take the sword in the name of religion. Hinduism realizes this truth and allows the widest freedom in matters of faith and worship. The foreigner is amazed at the almost unending variations in creed that are found in Hinduism. But these variations are an ornament (*bhūṣaṇa*) to the faith and do not import into it any defect (*dūṣaṇa*). The fundamental tenet of Hinduism is: as many minds, so many faiths. The celebrated text of the *Ṛg-veda* that proclaims the One Truth, which is called variously by the sages, we have already quoted. The Upaniṣhads declare that just as cows that are of varied hues yield the same white milk, all the different paths lead to the same goal. "Howsoever men approach me, even so do I accept them; for, on all sides, whatever path they may choose is mine," says the Lord in the *Gītā*. There is a *Smṛti* text that declares, "Some speak of it as Agni, some as Manu, Prajāpati, some as Indra, others as Prāṇa, yet others as the eternal Brahman." Aśoka had this inscribed on his rock pillars: "The king, beloved of the Gods, honours every form of religious faith, but considers no gift or honour so much as the increase of the substance of religion, whereof this is the root, to reverence one's own faith and never to revile that of others. Whoever acts differently injures his own religion while he wrongs another's." Śrī Rāmakrishna made a series of successful experiments with God, realized him in several ways, and taught as the essence of his experience that the different faiths were like the *ghats* that lead to the same Ganges. Mahātmā Gāndhi observed while consecrating a temple in New Delhi: "It must be the daily prayer of every adherent of the Hindu faith that every known religion of the world should grow from day to day and should serve the whole of humanity." This is the tradition of Hinduism—reviling no religion and honouring truth, wherever it may come from and whatever vesture it may wear.

Buddha, the Blessed One, gives the parable of the blind men and the elephant to illustrate that partial knowledge always breeds bigotry and fanaticism. Once a group of disciples entered the city of Śrāvasti to beg alms. They found there a number of sectarians holding disputations with one another and maintaining "This is the truth, that is not the truth. That is not the truth, this is the truth." After listening to these conflicting views, the brethren came back to the Exalted One and described to him what they had seen and heard at Śrāvasti.

Then said the Exalted One:

"These sectarians, brethren, are blind and unseeing. They know not the real, they know not the unreal; they know not the truth, they know not the untruth. In such a site of ignorance do they dispute and quarrel as ye describe. Now in former times, brethren, there was a Rājā (king) in this same Śrāvasti.

Then, brethren, the Rājā called to a certain man, saying: 'Come thou, good fellow! Go, gather together all the blind men that are in Śrāvasti!'

" 'Very good, Your Majesty,' replied that man, and in obedience to the Rājā, gathered together all the blind men, took them with him to the Rājā, and said: 'Your Majesty, all the blind men of Śrāvasti are now assembled.'

" 'Then, my good man, show the blind men an elephant.'

" 'Very good, Your Majesty,' said the man and did as he was told, saying: 'O ye blind men, such as this is an elephant.'

"And to one he presented the head of the elephant, to another, the ear, to another a tusk, the trunk, the foot, back, tail and tuft of the tail, saying to each one that that was the elephant.

"Now, brethren, that man, having presented the elephant to the blind men, came to the Rājā and said: 'Your majesty, the elephant has been presented to the blind men. Do what is your will.'

"Thereupon, brethren, the Rājā went up to the blind men and said to each: 'Have you studied the elephant?'

" 'Yes, Your Majesty.'

" 'Then tell me your conclusions about him.'

"Thereupon those who had been presented with the head answered, 'Your Majesty, an elephant is just like a pot.' And those who had only observed the ear replied, 'An elephant is just like a winnowing basket.' Those who had been presented with the tusk said it was a ploughshare. Those who knew only the trunk said it was a plough. 'The body,' said they, 'is a granary; the foot, a pillar; the back, a mortar; the tail, a pestle; the tuft of the tail, just a besom.'

"Then they began to quarrel, shouting, 'Yes, it is!' 'No, it isn't!' 'An elephant is not that!' 'Yes it is like that!' and so on, till they came to fisticuffs about the matter.

"Then, brethren, that Rājā was delighted with the scene."

Just so are these sectarians who are wanderers, blind, unseeing, knowing not the truth, but each maintaining it is thus and thus.

Those who think that truth is in their exclusive keeping and that their religion is the only approach to God, "see only one side of a thing" like the blind men in the parable. Hinduism does not commit this mistake. It believes in the sanctity and efficacy of all religions.

At the same time the universalism that is envisaged in Hinduism is not an amalgam of all that is good in every religion. A universal religion put together in that way would be a bouquet, exquisite no doubt, but lifeless. Hinduism recognizes different levels of religious experience and arranges them in their order of excellence. Real conversion is vertical—*i.e.*, from the lower to the higher conception of God, and not horizontal—*i.e.*, from one formal faith to another. The spiritual growth is from the crude forms of worship to the highest contemplation of God. Dr. S. Radhakrishnan explains the Hindu attitude by comparing the religions to colleges. "As students are proud of their colleges," he says, "so are groups of their gods. We need not move students from one college to another, but should do our best to raise the tone of the college, improve its standards and refine its ideals, with the result that each college enables us to attain the same goal. It is a matter of indifference what college we are in, so long as all of them are steeped in the same atmosphere and train us to reach the same ideal."

There are various cults in Hinduism and a variety of creeds. But conflict among them is avoided by the twin doctrines of *adhikāra* and *iṣṭa*. *Adhikāra* means eligibility. A person's faith is determined by the kind of man he is. There is no use, for instance, in putting a boy in the Honours Class, if he is fit only for the Pass Course. What is meat for one may be poison for another. A man's creed depends upon his *adhikāra*. And it is his eligibility that determines his *iṣṭa* or ideal. Hinduism prescribes to each according to his needs. Hence it is not to be considered as a single creed or cult, but as a league of religions, a fellowship of faiths.

4 The Spirit of Hinduism

The richness, beauty and greatness of Hinduism lie, no doubt, in its spirit of accommodation. But that does not mean that Hinduism is a medley of ill-assorted creeds, with no cohesion, no common purpose, and no unified understanding. The very fact that it has survived to this day in spite of the vicissitudes of history, and does not show any great sign of decay, proves that there is a soul to it which holds together its different limbs in an indissoluble unity. It is true that Hinduism gathered round it, with the march of time, certain encumbrances and unessentials, as was the case with every other religion. But a unique feature of India's religious history has been the appearance of great reformers—seers of the truth—from time to time, whose especial mission it was to reorganize the people's faith, and infuse in them a sense of unity and purpose. Nowhere else in the world has there been such a galaxy of spiritual leaders who, after having realized the supreme truth, came down to the level of the masses and conveyed to them intimations of the high dignity and glory of their faith.

Is it possible to give a definition of Hinduism, which all its adherents would approve of? What is the greatest common measure of agreement among the Hindu cults? Though it is difficult to express adequately in words the spirit of Hinduism, it is not impossible to indicate its nature. At the outset it should be noted that all Hindus are agreed in their allegiance to the Vedas. Even the Tāntric cults recognize the authority of the Vedas. Many of the latter-day rituals and practices are based on the teachings of the Tāntras, and cannot be traced to the Vedas. Yet the common belief is that the Tantras derived their teachings from certain texts of the Vedas, now lost to us. Whether there were such texts or not, it is clear that, in the view of the Hindus, the Vedas constitute the primary source of Hinduism. The Hindu beliefs and practices, philosophies and faiths are, thus, held to have the sanction of the Vedas behind them.

One of the fundamental beliefs of Hinduism is that there is one all-pervading and all-transcending Spirit which is the basic reality—the source and ground of all beings. This is usually referred to as God (*Iśvara*); but the wise realize it as the impersonal Absolute (*Brahman*). The reality conceived of as God is the cause of the universe—its sole and whole cause. The universe rises from, remains in, and returns to God. There is no other creator alongside of or opposed to God. God does not create the world out of nothing, nor out of any stuff external to him.

It is only a convention that refers to God in the masculine gender. If it is legitimate to address God as Father, it is equally legitimate to address that reality as Mother. In an exquisite passage the *Śvetāśvatara Upaniṣhad* addresses God thus: "Thou art woman; thou art man; thou art the youth and also the maiden; thou as an old man totterest with a stick; being born thou standest facing all directions."

It is God that has taken, as it were, all the forms that we see. This is explained in one of the Upanishads on the analogy of Fire and Wind. Just as the one Fire or the one Wind enters the world and assumes various shapes and configurations, even so the inner Self of all beings takes on the several forms and yet is not exhausted by them. It is, of course, difficult to see God in everything. In fact, to realize the Self in and as all is the highest of spiritual experience. So, as a discipline that will eventually lead to the goal, one is asked to see the face of God in whichever thing that has prowess, splendour and rectitude. Illustrating this truth in the tenth chapter of the *Bhagavad-gītā*, Śrī Kṛṣṇa identifies himself with the best of every kind, *e.g.*, the Himālaya among the mountains, the Gaṅgā among the rivers, Vāsudeva among the Vṛṣṇis, and Arjuna among the Pāṇḍavas. The great mountains and the big rivers, majestic trees and fine animals, heroic men and women—in fact, all things that have excellence, thus, become objects of veneration. When the Hindu worships these or the idols in the shrines, he is aware that it is to God that he really offers his worship. It is wrong, therefore, to characterize Hinduism as an idolatrous religion. The idols are symbols of the invisible Spirit. It is after the devotee has invoked the presence of God therein that they become sacred objects of worship. The Hindu, it is true, bows his head before many a form of the Deity. On that account, however, he is not to be dubbed a polytheist. What the Hindu adores is the One God in the many gods. Even as early as the *Ṛg-veda* we have a philosophical monotheism culminating in monism and non-dualism. What Max Müller characterizes as the henotheism of the Vedas—*viz.*, the worshipping of each divinity in turn, as the occasion demands— is really a tendency toward a philosophical monotheism. The Hindu mind is averse to assigning an unalterable or rigidly fixed form or name to the Deity. Hence it is that in Hinduism we have innumerable god-forms and countless divine names. And, it is a truth that is recognized by all Hindus that obeisance offered to any of these forms and names reaches the one supreme God.

It is the unique conception of the Godhead that we have in Hinduism that led to the formulation of the doctrine of incarnation (*avatāra*). God is not a detached spectator of the world-process. He guides it and actively participates in it, though he is not defiled by it. Whenever there is the need, he incarnates himself, *i.e.* appears in a tangible living form, so that the world may be saved and helped to move higher in its spiritual evolution. Śrī Kṛṣṇa says in the *Gītā*: "Whenever there is a decline of righteousness and a rise of unrighteousness, I incarnate myself. For the protection of the pious, for the destruction of those given to wicked ways, and for establishing righteousness firmly, I am born from age to age." In certain schools of Hinduism such as Śaivism, the doctrine that God is born of parents like mortals is not accepted. But even then it is admitted that God appears in a body when he wants to save a devotee through that way. The spiritual preceptor (*guru*), it is believed, is God in human form. The Hindus hold the teacher in the highest esteem. Whatever honour is shown to God is shown to him also.

Of all the religions of the world it is well-known that Hinduism—with the two other faiths, Jainism and Buddhism, which have stemmed from it—lays the greatest stress on non-violence (*ahimsā*). This is as it should be. If God is all, then all must be sacred, and no injury should be caused to any living being. The highest virtue is non-violence. The implication of this negative term is this: If in order to do some good to a person you have to injure another, then your duty is not to do that good. Saving a being from pain is more of a duty than causing pleasure. Total non-violence is, of course, an ideal. But it is the constant endeavour of the Hindu to approximate to it. If God is Truth (*satya*), non-violence (*ahimsā*) is the way to realize him. "If I were asked to define the Hindu creed," wrote Mahātmā Gāndhi, "I should simply say, search after Truth through non-violent means."

12. Islam

HUSTON SMITH

BASIC THEOLOGICAL CONCEPTS

The basic theological concepts of Islam as outlined in the sweeping strokes of the Koran are at most points identical with those of Judaism and Christianity, its neighbors. We shall confine our attention in this section to the most important four: Allah, Creation, Man, and the Day of Judgment.

As in other high religions, everything in Islam centers in the primal fact of God or Allah. To begin with, Allah is immaterial and hence invisible. For the Arabs this cast no doubt on his reality for they had never learned the art of ignoring everything but what could be seen. As desert dwellers, the notion of invisible hands that drove the blasts that swept the desert and formed the deceptive mirages that lured the traveler to his destruction was always with them.

The Koran did not introduce the Arab to the unseen world of the spirit. What it did by way of innovation was to focus the divine in a single God, a unified Personal Will who overshadows the entire universe with his power and grace. The indelible contribution of Islam to Arabic religion was monotheism.

To the Muslim, we must add, monotheism is Islam's contribution not simply to Arabic religion but to the religion of man in its entirety. Hinduism's prolific images he takes as obvious proof that this religion has never really approached the worship of one God only. Judaism, standing in the tradition the Koran culminates, was correctly instructed in its great *Shema*: "Hear O Israel, the Lord our God, the Lord is One." Alas, from the Muslim perspective the Jews prior to Muhammed's reminder departed tragically from this truth. They reverted to the worship of household gods and golden calves, episodes that figure far more frequently in the Koran than in the Old Testament; in the persons of the Scribes and Pharisees they approached idolatry in their worship of the Law. Christians, for their part, have in Islam's eyes compromised their monotheism by deifying Christ. Islam honors Jesus as a true prophet of God. It even accepts the Christian doctrine of his virgin birth. But at the doctrine of the Incarnation and Trinity it draws the line, seeing these as concessions to man's inclination to seek a compromise between the human and the divine. In the words of the Koran: "They say the God of mercy hath gotten to himself a son. Now have ye uttered a grievous thing. . . . It is not meet for God to have children" (iii: 78, xix: 93). When Jesus claimed to be the Son of God, He was thinking of God's Fatherhood as embracing all mankind. Every human being was to him a child of God. The accretions of councils and theologies have carried Christian doctrine a long way from the simple purity of the Nazarene.

Against all these apostasies the Muslim sees the Koran taking its stand as the grand advocate of God's unity. The strength of the Arab's arms was to wax and wane but again and again the Prophet's vision of a single God triumphed over peoples like the Mongols and the Turks who would subdue his followers in physical combat. Almost every page of the Koran cries out with burning fervor: "Your God is one God. . . . There is no God but He—the Living, the Eternal" (ii: 158, 255).

Islam is so well known for its recognition of the majesty and might of its one God that this point needs little documentation. Allah is almighty, omnipotent, Lord of the worlds, the Author of heaven and earth, the Creator of life and death in whose hand is dominion and irresistible power. Where the outsider has often misjudged Allah is in picturing him as domineering and ruthless; "a pitiless tyrant, who plays with humanity as on a chess-board, and works out His game without regard to the sacrifice of the pieces" is one not atypical Western characterization. Muslims see him otherwise. He who is Lord of the worlds is also

> the Holy, the Peaceful, the Faithful, the Guardian over His servants, the Shelterer of the orphan, the Guide of the erring, the Deliverer from every affliction, the Friend of the bereaved, the Consoler of the afflicted; in His hand is good, and He is the generous Lord, the Gracious, the Hearer, the Near-at-Hand, the Compassionate, the Merciful, the Very-forgiving, whose love for man is more tender than that of the mother-bird for her young.[1]

Because of Allah's grace the world of the Koran, despite its heavy warnings to the unrighteous, is a world of joy. There is air and sun and a confidence not only in ultimate justice but also in help along the way and pardon for the contrite.

> By the noonday brightness, and by the night when it darkeneth, thy Lord hath not forsaken thee, neither hath He been displeased. Surely the future shall be better for thee than the past; and in the end He shall be bounteous to thee, and thou shalt be satisfied. Did He not find thee an orphan, and give thee a home; erring, and guided thee; needy, and enriched thee? (xciii).

Standing beneath God's gracious skies, the Muslim can at any moment lift his heart directly into the divine presence, there to receive both strength and guidance for the living of his days. He has such ready access to the divine because between man and Allah stands nothing.

---

[1] Huston Smith, *The Religions of Man* (New York: Harper, 1958).

Is He not closer than the vein of thy neck? Thou needest not raise thy voice, for He knoweth the secret whisper, and what is yet more hidden. . . . He knows what is in the land and in the sea; no leaf falleth but He knoweth it; nor is there a grain in the darkness under the earth, nor a thing, green or sere, but it is recorded (vi: 12, 59).

Allah, then, is one, immaterial, all-powerful, all-pervading, and benevolent. He is also creator, which brings us to the second basic concept in Islam. In the Islamic conception the world did not emerge, as the Hindus would have it, by some process of unconscious emanation from the divine. It was created by a deliberate act of God's will: "He hath created the heavens and the earth" (xvi: 3). This fact carries two important consequences. First, the world of matter is completely real. It is dependent to be sure on God as its creator, but once originated it is as real as anything there is. Herein lies the basis of Muslim science which during Europe's Dark Age flourished in the Near East as nowhere else. Second, being the handiwork of a God who is both great and good, the world of matter must likewise be basically good. "No defect canst thou see in the creation of the God of mercy; repeat the gaze, seest thou a single flaw" (lxvii: 4). Here we meet a confidence in the material aspects of life and existence which we shall find pervading the other two semitically originated religions, Judaism and Christianity, as well.

Wonderful as is Allah's material creation—and the Koran abounds in lyric descriptions of the majesties of heaven and earth—God's supreme accomplishment lies in the fact that "He hath created man" (xvi: 3). Coming to Islam as we do after surveying Indic and Far Eastern religions, the most important thing to note about the Muslim view of man is its appreciation of both the ultimacy and value of individuality. In the religions of the Far East, the indivisible, all-encompassing cosmic spirit is the primary fact and the fleeting expressions of individuality have no permanence or value. But for Islam individuality is not only fully real but also good in principle. As expressed in the human soul it is also eternal, for once created the soul lives forever. Value, virtue, goodness, and spiritual fulfillment come by expressing one's unique self by virtue of which one is different from anyone or anything else. As a great Muslim philosopher has written, "This inexplicable finite centre of experience is the fundamental fact of the universe. All life is individual; there is no such thing as universal life. God Himself is an individual: He is the most unique individual."

So intense and vivid is the Koran's feel for Allah's power and sovereign will that some interpreters have concluded that it eclipses man's freedom. That there is in Islam a problem of reconciling man's free will with God's omnipotence no Muslim will deny. What he does deny is, first, that the problem is more acute in Islam than in any other developed theology, and second, that it lands the Muslim in fatalism. In the final analysis man is master of his conduct and completely responsible for the decisions he makes. "Whoever gets to himself a sin, gets it solely on his own responsibility" (iv: 111). "Whoever goes astray, he himself bears the whole responsibility of wandering" (x: 103).

This belief in man's freedom and responsibility leads directly to Islam's doctrine of the afterlife. For the Muslim life on earth is the seedbed of an eternal future. It will be followed by a day of reckoning which is foreshadowed in the most awesome terms. "When the sun shall be folded up, and the stars shall fall, and when the mountains shall be set in motion . . . and the seas shall boil . . . then shall every soul know what it hath done" (lxxxi). On that day of judgment each individual will be accountable for the way he has lived. "Every man's actions have we hung round his neck, and on the last day shall be laid before him a wide-open Book" (xvii: 13).

Depending on how it fares in this accounting the soul will then repair either to Heaven or Hell. In the Koran these conditions are described with all the vividness of Eastern imagery. Heaven abounds in deep rivers of cool, crystal water, lush fruit and vegetation, boundless fertility, and beautiful mansions with gracious attendants. Hell's portrayal is at times equally graphic with its account of molten metal, boiling liquids, and the fire that splits everything to pieces. Conservative Muslims take these descriptions literally; others as symbolically as modernist Christians read New Testament passages about pearly gates and streets of gold. In defense of their allegorical interpretation, these liberal Muslims quote the Koran itself: "Some of the signs are firm—these are the basis of the book—and others are figurative" (iii: 5). Also supporting the non-materialistic interpretation of paradise is Muhammed's statement that for the favored of God, to "see his Lord's face night and morning [is] a felicity which will surpass all the pleasures of the body, as the ocean surpasses a drop of sweat." From this view, the joy of joys consists in the beatific vision in which the veil which divides man from Allah will be rent forever and his heavenly glory disclosed to the soul untrammeled by its earthly raiments. In the midst of these subtleties of interpretation, the belief that unites all Muslims concerning the afterlife is that each soul will be held accountable for his actions on earth with his happiness or misery thereafter dependent upon how well he has observed God's laws.

God, Creation, Man, and the Day of Judgment—these are the chief theological pegs on which all the Koran's teachings are hung. In spite of their crucial importance, however, the Koran, as Muhammad Iqbal tells us, is "a book which emphasizes deed rather than idea." It is to these deeds that we turn. . . .

THE FIVE PILLARS OF ISLAM

If a Muslim were asked to summarize the way his religion counsels man to live, he might answer: Islam teaches man to walk in the straight path. The phrase comes from the opening surah of the Koran itself which is recited by every Muslim five times each day:

> *Praise belongs to God, Lord of the Worlds,*
> *The Compassionate, the Merciful.*
> *King of the day of Judgment.*
> *'Tis Thee we worship and Thee we ask for help.*
> *Guide us in the straight path,*
> *The path of those whom Thou hast favored,*
> *Not the path of those who incur Thine anger nor of those who go astray.*

Why the straight path? One meaning is obvious; a straight path is undevious, neither crooked nor corrupt. The phrase contains another meaning, however, which speaks to something distinctive in Islam. The straight path is one that is straightforward, direct and explicit. Compared with other religions, Islam spells out the way of life it proposes; it pinpoints it, nailing it down through explicit injuctions. The consequence is a definiteness about this religion that gives it a flavor all its own. A Muslim knows where he stands. He knows who he is and who God is. He knows what his obligations are and if he transgresses these he knows what to do about it. The world of Islam is the exact opposite of a Kafkaesque world in which man is separated from his destination; he can't get through, the lines are jammed, he doesn't know who he's talking to or who's inside the castle; he knows only that he has done something terrible though he can't find out what it is. Islam has a clarity, an order, a precision which is in sharp contrast to the shifting, relative, uncertain, at-sea quality of much of modern life. Muslims explicity claim this is one of Islam's strengths. God's revelation to man, they say, has proceeded through four great stages. First, through Abraham God revealed the truth of monotheism, God's oneness. Second, through Moses he revealed the Ten Commandments. Third, through Jesus he revealed the Golden Rule, that we are to love our neighbors as ourselves. All these men were authentic prophets; each nailed down indispensable planks in the platform of the God-directed life. One question only remained unanswered. How should we love our neighbor? What does the love of neighbor require in this complicated world in which human interests can cross and tangle like pressure hoses on the loose? A final prophet was needed to answer that question and he was Muhammed. Because God answered this final question through him he deserves the title, the Seal of the Prophets. "The glory of Islam consists in having embodied the beautiful sentiment of Jesus into definite laws."

What, then, is the content of this straight path that spells out the duties of man? We shall divide our presentation into two parts. In this section we shall consider the Five Pillars of Islam, the principles that regulate on the whole the private life of Muslims in their direct relationships with God. In the next section we shall consider the Koran's social teachings.

The first pillar is Islam's creed. Every religion contains convictions that orient its adherents' lives in some way. In some religions these premises are simply assumed; in most religions they are condensed and articulated in some sort of creed. The creed of Islam wastes no words. Brief, simple, explicit, it consists of a single sentence: "There is no God but Allah, and Muhammed is His Prophet." At least once during his lifetime a Muslim must say this creed correctly, slowly, thoughtfully, aloud, with full understanding, and with heartfelt conviction in its truth. In actuality, practicing Muslims repeat it many times each day, but at least once during one's lifetime is mandatory.

The creed contains only two phrases. The first announces the cardinal principle of monotheism. Islam entered the world as a desert religion—stretches of sand as far as the eye could reach, and above, only the blazing sun. This makes a difference. The austerity of the setting as well as its purity carries over into theology. "There is no God but Allah." There is no God but *The* God. More directly still, there is no God but *God*—for the word is not a common noun embracing a class of objects; it is a proper name designating a unique being, a single individual and Him only. In a single stroke, this affirmation demolishes forever God's rivals for man's loyalty. Once for all, it toppled the innumerable idols the Bedouin had worshipped since the dawn of history, and in the Muslim's view sounded toward Judaism and Christianity as well a recall from their near-idolatry of the Torah and Christ.

The second affirmation in Islam's creed—that "Muhammed is [God's] prophet"—speaks at once to the Muslim's faith in the authenticity of Muhammed and in the validity of the book he transmitted. So highly has the Prophet been regarded that his status has at times come near to threatening the monotheism he preached. Come near but not more than that. When Muhammed died there were some who attempted to deify him, but his appointed successor killed the thought with one of the most famous speeches in religious history. "If there are any among you who worshipped Muhammed, he is dead. But if it is God you worship, He lives forever."

The second pillar of Islam is prayer in which the Koran adjures the faithful to "be constant" (xxix: 45).

If we ask why the Muslim is admonished to "be constant" in prayer, the basic reason implied by all the Koran's direct statements is to keep man's life in perspective. The most important and difficult lesson man must learn and continually relearn, the Koran assumes, is that he is not God. Creature rather than creator, man has nevertheless an inveterate tendency to place himself at the center of his universe and live as a law to himself. When he does so, however, when he tries to play God, everything goes wrong. Man is a creature; his life slips into place and stays in proper perspective only when he recognizes this fact. When one asks, therefore, why the Muslim prays, a partial answer is doubtless: in response to the natural yearning of the human heart to pour forth its love and gratitude toward its Creator. But accompanying this desire is a need to keep his life in its proper perspective; to see it in its objective setting; to acknowledge his creatureliness before his creator, and to submit himself to the will of God as rightfully sovereign over his life.

When should a Muslim pray? Five times daily—upon rising, at noon, in mid-afternoon, after sunset, and before retiring. The schedule is not absolutely binding. The Koran says explicitly, for example, that "When ye journey about the earth it is no crime to you that ye come short in prayer if ye fear that those that disbelieve will set upon you." Under normal conditions, however, the five-fold pattern should be maintained. While in Islam no day of the week is as sharply set apart from others as is the Sabbath for the Jews or Sunday for the Christians, Friday most nearly approximates a holy day. Formality is not a pronounced feature in Islam but the closest that Muslims come to a formal service of worship is when they gather on Fridays for noon prayers and collective recital of the Koran. These gatherings are usually in mosques, and visitors to Muslim lands testify that one of the most impressive sights in the religions of man occurs when, in a dimly lighted mosque, hundreds of men stand shoulder to shoulder, then kneel and prostrate themselves toward Mecca. The exact answer to *where* the Muslim should pray, however, is anywhere. "It is one of the glories of Islam," writes an Englishman, "that its temples are not made with hands, and that its ceremonies can be performed anywhere upon God's earth or under His Heaven." Every corner of Allah's universe being equally pure, the faithful are encouraged to spread their prayer rug wherever they find themselves at the appointed hour.

As to *how* the Muslim is to pray, the Koran mentions almost nothing in the way of specifics. Muhammed's personal teachings and practices, however, have crystallized into traditions that, in keeping with Islam's explicitness on almost every point, move in to structure the void. To keep alive the memory of the glorious center where Islam first entered the world in its fullness, Muhammed directed that Muslims should pray facing Mecca. The realization that his brothers are doing likewise creates a sense of participating in a world-wide fellowship even when the Muslim is physically isolated. Paralleling the Christian's purifying rite of Baptism, the Muslim washes himself and spreads his prayer rug before him. Standing erect with hands open on either side of his face and his thumbs touching the lobes of his ears, he recites, "*Allahu akbar*" (God is most great). Still standing he recites the opening *surah* of the Koran (quoted above) followed by other optional selections. Bowing from his hips and placing his hands on his knees, he says, "I extol the perfection of my Lord the Great." He returns to upright position, again repeating, "*Allahu akbar.*" Gliding gently to his knees, he places his hands and his face to the ground. He rises to his knees, sits on his heels, and again returns his hands and his face to the ground. The entire process is repeated several times, with the Muslim creed and optional prayers interpolated between each pair of prostrations. The entire routine is designed to give form to the prayer while allowing ample scope for the most heartful outpouring of devotion before the Almighty Presence.

This brings us to the content of Muslim prayer. Its two great themes are the expression of praise and gratitude on the one hand, and supplication on the other. There is a Muslim saying that every time a bird drinks a drop of water it lifts its eyes in gratitude toward heaven. "All who are in the heavens and the earth celebrate His praises, and the birds, too, spreading out their wings; each one knows its prayer and its praise." Ideally every micro-second of man's life should also be lifted to God in gratitude. In point of fact we repeatedly fall away from this grateful attitude. Five times a day, however, we should bring ourselves back to it. Here is a typical prayer through which the Muslim attempts to do so:

> Thanks be to my Lord; He the Adorable, and only to be adored. My Lord, the Eternal, the Ever-existing, the Cherisher, the True Sovereign whose mercy and might overshadow the universe; the Regulator of the world, and Light of the creation. His is our worship; to Him belongs all worship; He existed before all things, and will exist after all that is living has ceased. Thou art the adored, my Lord; Thou art the Master, the Loving and Forgiving. . . . O my Lord, Thou art the Helper of the afflicted, the Reliever of all distress, the Consoler of the broken-hearted; Thou art present everywhere to help Thy servants. . . . O my Lord, Thou art the Creator, I am only created; Thou art my Sovereign, I am only Thy servant; Thou art the Helper, I am the beseecher; Thou art the Forgiver, I am the sinner; Thou, my Lord, art the Merciful, All-knowing, All-loving.

Turning then to supplication, the devout might combine two traditional prayers as follows:

> O Lord, grant to me the love of Thee. Grant that I may love those that love Thee. Grant that I may do the deeds that win Thy love. Make Thy love to be dearer to me than self, family or than wealth.
>
> O Lord! Grant me firmness in faith and direction. Assist me in being grateful to Thee and in adoring Thee in every good way. I ask Thee for an innocent heart, which shall not incline to wickedness. I ask Thee for a true tongue. I pray Thee to defend me from that vice which Thou knowest, and for forgiveness of those faults which Thou knowest. O my Defender! assist me in remembering Thee and being grateful to Thee, and in worshipping Thee with the excess of my strength. Forgive me out of Thy loving kindness, and have mercy on me; for verily Thou art the forgiver of offences and the bestower of blessings on Thy servants.

The third pillar of Islam is charity. Material things are important in life, but some people have more than others. Why? Islam is not concerned with this theoretical problem. Instead, it turns to the practical question of what should be done about the situation. Its answer is simple. Those who have much should help lift the burden of those who are less fortunate. It is a principle twentieth-century democracy has reached in its concept of the welfare state. Muhammed instituted it in the seventh by prescribing a graduated tax on the haves to relieve the circumstance of the have-nots.

The figure he set was two and one-half per cent. Compared with the tithe of Judaism and Christianity (which being directed more to the maintenance of religious institutions than to the direct relief of human need is not strictly comparable), this looks modest until we discover that it refers not just to income but to holdings. Poorer people owe nothing, but those in the middle and upper-income brackets must annually distribute among the poor one-fortieth of the value of all they possess.

And to whom among the poor should this money be given? This too, characteristically, is prescribed: to those in direst need; to slaves in the process of buying their freedom; to debtors unable to meet their obligations; to strangers and wayfarers; and to those who collect and distribute the alms.

The fourth pillar of Islam is the observance of *Ramadan*. *Ramadan* is a month in the Arabian calendar, Islam's holy month because during it Muhammed received his initial commission as a prophet and ten years later made his historic *Hijrah* from Mecca to Medina. To commemorate these two great occasions, able-bodied Muslims not involved in crises like war or unavoidable journey fast during *Ramadan*. From daybreak to the setting of the sun neither food nor drink passes their lips; after sundown they may partake in moderation. Being a month in a lunar calendar, *Ramadan* rotates around the year. When it falls in the winter its demands are not excessive. When, on the other hand, it falls during the scorching summers, to remain active during the long days without so much as a drop of water is an ordeal.

Why, then, does the Koran require it? For one thing, fasting makes one think, as every Jew who has watched through the long fasts of Yom Kippur will testify. For another thing, fasting teaches self-discipline; he who can endure its demands will have less difficulty controlling his appetites at other times. Fasting underscores man's dependence upon God. Man, says the Koran, is as frail as the rose petal; nevertheless he assumes airs and pretensions. Fasting reminds him vividly of his essential frailty and dependence. Finally, fasting sensitizes compassion. Only those who have been hungry can know what hunger means. If a man has himself fasted for thirty days within the year he will be apt to listen more carefully the next time he is approached by someone in need.

Islam's fifth pillar is pilgrimage. Once during his lifetime every Muslim who is physically and economically in a position to do so is expected to journey to Mecca where God's climactic revelation was first disclosed. The basic purpose of the pilgrimage is to heighten the pilgrim's devotion to God and to his revealed will, but the practice has some beneficial ancillary effects as well. It is, for example, a reminder of the equality between man and man. Upon reaching Mecca pilgrims remove their usual clothes, which tend to carry clear indications of their social status, and don two single sheet-like garments. Everyone as he nears Islam's earthly focus wears the same thing. All distinctions of rank and hierarchy are removed; prince and pauper stand before God in their undivided humanity. Pilgrimage also provides a useful service in international relations. It brings together people from various countries demonstrating that they have in common a loyalty that transcends the loyalties of the warring kingdoms of man. Pilgrims pick up information about their brothers in other lands and return to their own with better understanding of one another.

Such are the five basic supports of the Muslim's faith.

Religious Pluralism

13. Christianity and the Encounter of the World Religions

PAUL TILLICH

The encounter of Christianity with other religions, as well as with quasi-religions, implies the rejection of their claims insofar as they contradict the Christian principle, implicitly or explicitly. But the problem is not the right of rejecting that which rejects us; rather it is the nature of this rejection. It can be the rejection of everything for which the opposite group stands; it can be a partial rejection together with a partial acceptance of assertions of the opposite group; or it can be a dialectical union of rejection and acceptance in the relation of the two groups. In the first case the rejected religion is considered false, so that no communication between the two contradictory positions is possible. The negation is complete and under certain circumstances deadly for the one or the other side. In the second case some assertions and actions of the one or the other side are considered false, others true. This is more tolerant than the attitude of total negation, and it is certainly an adequate response to a statement of facts or ideas some of which may be true, some false, but it is not possible to judge works of art or philosophy or the complex reality of religions in this way. The third way of rejecting other religions is a dialectical union of acceptance and rejection, with all the tensions, uncertainties, and changes which such dialectics implies. If we look at the history of Christianity as a whole, we can point to a decisive predominance of this latter response in the attitude of Christian thinking and acting towards the non-Christian religions. But it is almost impossible to discover a consistent line of thought about this problem. And even less consistent is the attitude of Christianity to the contemporary quasi-religions.* This observation contradicts the popular assumption that Christianity had an exclusively negative attitude toward other faiths. Indeed, nothing is farther from the truth. In this assumption a confusion frequently takes place between the attitude of the Christian churches toward Christian heretics, especially in the late Middle Ages, and their attitude toward

---

*Tillich has in mind especially the movements of fascism and communism.

members of other religions. The demonic cruelty of the former is in contrast with the comparative mildness of the latter. . . .

Jesus' words are the basic confirmation of this principle. In the grand scene of the ultimate judgment (Matt. 25; 31ff.), the Christ puts on his right the people from all nations who have acted with righteousness and with that agape— love which is the substance of every moral law. Elsewhere Jesus illustrates this principle by the story of the Good Samaritan, the representative of a rejected religion who practices love, while the representatives of the accepted religion pass by. And when the disciples complain about people who perform works similar to theirs, but outside their circle, he defends them against the disciples. Although the Fourth Gospel speaks more clearly than the others of the uniqueness of the Christ, it interprets him at the same time in the light of the most universal of all concepts used in this period, the concept of the Logos, the universal principle of the divine self-manifestation, thus freeing the interpretation of Jesus from a particu- larism through which he would become the property of a particular religious group. Further, in the talk with the Samaritan woman, Jesus denies the significance of any particular place of adoration and demands an adoration "in Spirit and in Truth." . . .

In early Christianity the judgment of other religions was determined by the idea of the Logos. The Church Fathers emphasized the universal presence of the Logos, the Word, the principle of divine self-manifestation, in all religions and cultures. The Logos is present everywhere like the seed on the land, and this presence is a preparation for the central appearance of the Logos in a historical person, the Christ. In the light of these ideas Augustine could say that the true religion had existed always and was called Christian only after the appearance of Christ. Accordingly, his dealing with other religions was dialectical, as was that of his predecessors. They did not reject them unambiguously and, of course, they did not accept them unambiguously. But in their apologetic writings they acknowl- edged the preparatory character of these religions and tried to show how their inner dynamics drives them toward questions whose answer is given in the central event on which Christianity is based. They tried to show the convergent lines between the Christian message and the intrinsic quests of the pagan religions. In doing so they used not only the large body of literature in which the pagans had criticized their own religions (for example, the Greek philosophers), but also made free use of the positive creations from the soil of the pagan religions. On the level of theological thought they took into Christianity some of the highest conceptual- izations of the Hellenistic and, more indirectly, of the classical Greek feeling toward life—terms like physis (natura), hypostasis (substance), ousia (power of being), prosopon (persona, not person in our sense), and above all logos (word and rational structure in the later Stoic sense). They were not afraid to call the God to whom they prayed as the Father of Jesus, the Christ, the unchangeable One.

All these are well-known facts, but it is important to see them in the new light of the present encounter of the world religions, for then they show that early Christianity did not consider itself as a radical-exclusive, but as the all-inclusive religion in the sense of the saying: "All that is true anywhere in the world belongs to us, the Christians." And it is significant that the famous words of Jesus, "You, therefore, must be perfect, as your heavenly Father is perfect," (which was always an exegetic riddle) would, according to recent research, be better translated, "You must be all-inclusive as your heavenly Father is all-inclusive." . . .

But in the seventh century something happened which slowly changed the whole situation. The first outside encounter took place with the rise of Islam, a new and passionate faith, fanatically carried over the known world, invading, subjecting, and reducing Eastern Christianity and threatening all Christendom. Based on the Old Testament, pagan, and Christian sources, and created by a prophetic personality, it was not only adapted to the needs of primitive tribes, but also capable of absorbing large elements of the ancient culture, and soon surpassed Western Christianity in culture and civilization. The shock produced by these events can be compared only with the shock produced by the establishment of the Communist quasi-religion in Eastern Europe, Russia, and China, threatening Western Christianity and its liberal-humanist quasi-religious transformation.

The victorious wars of the Islamic tribes and nations forced Christianity to become aware of itself as one religion confronted with another against which it had to defend itself. According to the law that defense narrows down the defender, Christianity became at this point radically exclusive. The Crusades were the expression of this new self-consciousness. . . .

But the encounter of Christianity with a new . . . world religion in the period of the Crusades worked not only for a fanatical exclusiveness; it also worked slowly in the direction of a tolerant relativism. In the same early thirteenth century in which Pope Innocent III gave the model for Hitler's Nürnberg laws against the Jews, there was created by Christian, Islamic, and Jewish forces the near-miracle of a tolerant humanism on the basis of current traditions at the court of Emperor Frederick II in Sicily. It took one to two centuries for similar ideas to come again to the surface, changing the Christian judgment of non-Christian religions in a radical way. . . .

There was, however, always a majority of theologians and church people who interpreted Christianity in a particularistic and absolutistic way. They emphasized the exclusiveness of the salvation through Christ, following the main line of the theology of the Reformers, their orthodox systematizers and their pietistic transformers. In several waves the anti-universalist movements attacked the universalist trends which had become powerful in the last centuries. Every relativistic attitude towards the world religions was denounced as a negation of the absolute truth of Christianity. Out of this tradition (which is not necessarily fundamentalist in the ordinary sense) a strong particularistic turn of theology has grown. It was called in Europe crisis-theology; in America it is being called neo-orthodoxy. Its founder and outstanding representative is Karl Barth. This theology can be summed up from the point of view of our problem as the rejection of the concept of religion if applied to Christianity. According to him, the Christian Church, the embodiment of Christianity, is based on the only revelation that has ever occurred, namely, that in Jesus Christ. All human religions are fascinating, but futile attempts of man to reach God, and the relation to them, therefore, is no problem; the Christian judgment of them is unambiguous rejection of their claim to be based on revelation. Consequently, the problem which is the subject of this book—the encounter of Christianity with the world religions—may be an interesting historical problem, but is not a theological one. Yet history itself forced the problem of Barth, not through an encounter with a non-Christian religion in the proper sense, but through a highly dramatic encounter with one of the radicalized and demoniacal quasi-religions—Nazism. Under Barth's leadership the European Christian churches were able to resist its onslaught; the radical self-affirmation of Christianity in his theology made any compromise with Nazism impossible. But, according to the law mentioned above, the price paid for this successful defense was a theological and ecclesiastical narrowness which blinded the majority of Protestant leaders in Europe to the new situation arising out of the encounters of religions and quasi-religions all over the world. The missionary question was treated in a way which contradicted not only Troeltsch's idea of a cross-fertilization of the high religions, but also early Christian universalism, and it deserves mention that Barth and his whole school gave up the classical doctrine of the Logos in which this universalism was most clearly expressed.

The present attitude of Christianity to the world religions is as indefinite as that in most of its history. The extreme contrast between men like Barth and the theologian of missions, Kraemer, on the one side, and Troeltsch and the philosophical historian, Toynbee, with his program of a synthesis of the world religions, on the other, is symbolic for the intrinsic dialectics of the relation of Christianity to the religions proper. . . .

One thing should have become clear through the preceding descriptions and analyses: that Christianity is not based on a simple negation of the religions or quasi-religions it encounters. The relation is profoundly dialectical, and that is not a weakness, but the greatness of Christianity, especially in its self-critical, Protestant form.

14. God Has Many Names

JOHN HICK

"WHATEVER PATH MEN CHOOSE IS MINE"

I

When you visit the various non-Christian places of worship in one of our big cities you discover—possibly with a shock of surprise—that phenomenologically (or in other words, to human observation) the same kind of thing is taking place in them as in a Christian church. That is to say, human beings are coming together to open their minds to a higher reality, which is thought of as the personal creator and Lord of the universe, and as making vital moral demands upon the lives of men and women. Of course the trappings are very different—in a church men wear shoes and no hat; in mosque, gurdwara and temple, a hat and no shoes; in a synagogue both. In some you sit on a pew, in others on the floor. In some there is singing, in others there is not. Different musical instruments or none are used. More importantly, the supreme being is referred to as God in a Christian church, as Adonai in a Jewish synagogue, as Allah in a Muslim mosque, as Ekoamkar in a Sikh gurdwara, as Rama or as Krishna in a Hindu temple. And yet there is an important sense in which what is being done in the several forms of worship is essentially the same.

In the Jewish synagogue God is worshipped as maker of heaven and earth, and as the God of Abraham and Isaac and Jacob, who led the children of Israel out of Egypt into the promised land and who has called them to live as a light to lighten the world. Worship is very close in form and ethos to Christian worship in the Protestant traditions. Here is a passage of typical Jewish prayer: "With a great love have You loved us, O Lord our God, and with exceeding compassion have You pitied us. Our Father and King, our fathers trusted in You, and You taught them the laws of life: be gracious also to us, and teach us. Have compassion upon us, our Merciful Father, that we may grasp and understand, learn and teach, observe and uphold with love all the words of Your law" (from the Weekday Morning Service in *Service of the Heart: Weekday Sabbath and Festival Services and Prayers for Home and Synagogue*, London: Union of Liberal and Progressive Synagogues, 1967, pp. 40–1).

In Muslim mosques God is worshipped as the maker of heaven and earth, and as the sovereign Lord of the Universe, omnipotent, holy and merciful, before whom men bow in absolute submission. Here is a typical passage of Muslim prayer: "Praise be to God, Lord of creation, Source of all livelihood, who orders the morning, Lord of majesty and honour, of grace and beneficence. He who is so far that he may not be seen and so near that he witnesses the secret things. Blessed be He and for ever exalted" (*Alive to God: Muslim and Christian Prayer*, edited by Kenneth Cragg, London: Oxford University Press, 1970, p. 65). Or again, "To God belongs the praise, Lord of the heavens and Lord of the earth, the Lord of all being. His is the dominion in the heavens and in the earth: he is the Almighty, the All-wise" (*Alive to God*, p. 61).

In Sikh gurdwaras God is worshipped as the maker of heaven and earth, the gracious lord of time and of eternity, who demands righteousness and seeks peace and goodwill between men. Here is part of the Sikh morning prayer:

> God is the Master, God is truth,
> His name spelleth love divine,
> His creatures ever cry: "O give, O give."
> He the bounteous doth never decline.
> What then in offering shall we bring
> That we may see his court above?
> What then shall we say in speech
> That hearing may evoke His love?
> In the ambrosial hours of fragrant dawn
> On truth and greatness ponder in meditation,
> Though action determine how thou be born,

Through grace alone comes salvation.
O Nanak, this need we know alone,
That God and Truth are two in one.   (*Fapji,* 4).

The Hindu temples which have been established in Britain represent the *bhakti* or theistic-devotional form of Hinduism. In them God is worshipped as the ultimate Lord of all, the infinite divine Life known under many aspects and names. Against the background of throbbing music the name of God is chanted again and again by ecstatic worshippers. The language of *bhakti* devotion is emotional and personal. Here is a typical hymn:

O save me, save me, Mightiest,
    Save me and set me free.
O let the love that fills my breast
    Cling to thee lovingly.

Grant me to taste how sweet thou art;
    Grant me but this, I pray,
And never shall my love depart
    Or turn from thee away.

Then I thy name shall magnify
    And tell thy praise abroad,
For very love and gladness I
    Shall dance before my God.

(A. C. Bouquet, ed., Sacred Books of the World,
Pelican Books, 1954, p. 246)

And here is another *bhakti* devotional hymn:

Now all my days with joy I'll fill, full to the brim
With all my heart to Vitthal cling, and only Him.

He will sweep utterly away all dole and care;
And all in sunder shall I rend illusion's snare.

O altogether dear is He, and He alone,
For all my burden He will take to be His own.

Lo, all the sorrow of the world will straightway cease,
And all unending now shall be the reign of peace.

(*Sacred Books of the World,* p. 245)

II

In the light of the phenomenological similarity of worship in these different traditions we have to ask whether people in church, synagogue, mosque, gurdwara and temple are worshipping different Gods or are worshipping the same God? Are Adonai and God, Allah and Ekoamkar, Rama and Krishna different Gods, or are these different names for the same ultimate Being? There would seem to be three possibilities. One is that there exist, ontologically, many gods. But this conflicts with the belief concerning each that he is the creator or the source of the world. A second possibility is that one faith-community, let us say our own, worships God whilst the others vainly worship images which exist only in their imaginations. But even within Christianity itself, is there not a variety of overlapping mental images of God—for example, as stern judge and predestinating power, and as gracious and loving heavenly Father—so that different Christian groups, and even different Christian individuals, are worshipping the divine Being through their different images of him? And do not the glimpses which I have just offered of worship within the various religious traditions suggest that our Christian images overlap with many non-Christian images of God? If so, a third possibility must seem the most probable, namely that there is but one God, who is maker and lord of all; that in his infinite fullness and richness of being he exceeds all our human attempts to grasp him in thought; and that the devout in the various great world religions are in fact worshipping that one God, but through different, overlapping concepts or mental icons of him.

If this is so, the older Christian view of other faiths as areas of spiritual darkness within which there is no salvation, no knowledge of God, and no acceptable worship must be mistaken. This older view, which few still entertain in practice today, was enshrined in the traditional Roman Catholic dogma, *extra ecclesiam nulla salus* (outside the Church no salvation). To quote a classic utterance from this point of view, the Council of Florence in 1438–45 declared that "no one remaining outside the Catholic Church, not just pagans, but also Jews or heretics or schismatics, can become partakers of eternal life; but they will go to the everlasting fire which was prepared for the devil and his angels, unless before the end of life they are joined to the church" (Denzinger, *Enchiridion Symbolorum Definitionum et Declarationum de Rebus Fidei et Morum*, 29th ed., Freiburg, 1952, no. 714). The Protestant missionary equivalent, which likewise is entertained by few today, is the doctrine that outside Christianity there is no salvation. As a fairly recent expression of this, the Congress on World Mission at Chicago in 1960 declared: "In the years since the war, more than one billion souls have passed into eternity and more than half of these went to the torment of hell fire without even hearing of Jesus Christ, who He was, or why He died on the cross of Calvary" (*Facing the Unfinished Task*, ed. J. O. Percy, Grand Rapids, Michigan: Eerdman, 1961, p. 9).

This older view has come to seem increasingly implausible and unrealistic in the light of growing knowledge of other faiths and as a result of better contacts with their adherents. Consequently Christian theologians, perhaps most notably within the Roman communion, have been making strenuous efforts to escape from the unacceptable implications of the older view, though usually without feeling entitled explicitly to renounce it. This is, of course, in accordance with the established ecclesiastical method of developing and changing doctrine. One cannot say that a formerly proclaimed dogma was wrong, but one can reinterpret it to mean something very different from what it was originally understood to mean. Such exercises often display a high level of ingenuity, though no amount of intellectual sophistication can save them from seeming slightly ridiculous or slightly dishonest to the outsider. At any rate, in the attempt to retain the dogma of no salvation outside the Church, or outside Christianity, we have the ideas of implicit, as distinguished from explicit, faith; of baptism by desire, as distinguished from literal baptism; and, as a Protestant equivalent, the idea of the latent Church as distinguished from the manifest Church; and, again, the suggestion that men can only come to God through Jesus Christ but that those who have not encountered him in this life will encounter him in the life to come. Or again there is Karl Rahner's notion of the anonymous Christian (*Theological Investigations*, vol. 5, Darton, Longman & Todd, 1966, ch. 6. Rahner's most recent discussion, reaffirming the notion, occurs in *Theological Investigations*, vol. 14, 1976, ch. 17; see also vol. 16, 1979, ch. 13). The devout Muslim, or Hindu, or Sikh, or Jew can be regarded as an anonymous Christian, this being an honorary status granted unilaterally to people who have not expressed any desire for it. Or again there is the claim that Christianity, properly understood, is not a religion but is a revelation which judges and supersedes all religions. Or finally there is Hans Küng's distinction between the ordinary way of salvation in the world religions and the extraordinary way in the Church. Küng says, "A man is to be saved within the religion that is made available to him in his historical situation. Hence it is his right and his duty to seek God within that religion in which the hidden God has already found him." Thus the world religions are, he says, "the way of salvation in universal salvation history; the general way of salvation, we can even say, for the people of the world religions: the more common, the 'ordinary' way of salvation, as against which the way of salvation in the Church appears as something very special and extraordinary" (*Christian Revelation and World Religions*, ed. Joseph Neuner, Burns & Oates, 1967, pp. 52 and 53). This sounds at first extremely promising. However Küng goes on to take away with one hand what he has given with the other. The ordinary way of salvation for the majority of mankind in the world religions turns out to be only an interim way until, sooner or later, they come to an explicit Christian faith. The people of the world religions are, he says, "pre-Christian, directed toward Christ. . . . The men of the world religions are not professing Christians but, by the grace of God, they are called and marked out to be Christians" (Neuner, pp. 55–6). (For Küng's more recent views, see his *On Being a Christian*, A III.) One is reminded of the British amnesty for illegal immigrants. Although they are unauthorised entrants into the Kingdom of Heaven, the Indian and Pakistani and other foreign worshippers of God will be accepted if sooner or later they come forward to be legally registered by Christian baptism!

III

Thus all of these thinkers, who are trying so hard to find room for their non-Christian brethren in the sphere of salvation, are still working within the presuppositions of the old dogma. Only Christians can be saved; so we have to say that devout and godly non-Christians are really, in some metaphysical sense, Christians or Christians-to-be without knowing it. Although to the ordinary non-ecclesiastical mind this borders upon double-talk, in intention it is a charitable extension of the sphere of grace to people who had formerly been regarded as beyond the pale. As such it can function as a psychological bridge between the no longer acceptable older view and the new view which is emerging. But sooner or later we have to get off the bridge on to the other side. We have to make what might be called a copernican revolution in our theology of religions. You will remember that the old ptolemaic astronomy held that the earth is the centre of the solar system and that all the other heavenly bodies revolve around it. And when it was realised that this theory did not fit the observed facts, particularly the wandering movements of the planets, epicycles were added, circles revolving on circles to complicate the theory and bring it nearer to the facts. By analogy the "no salvation outside Christianity" doctrine is theologically ptolemaic. Christianity is seen as the centre of the universe of faiths, and all the other religions are regarded as revolving round it and as being graded in value according to their distance from it. And the theories of implicit faith, baptism by desire, anonymous Christianity, the latent Church, the "ordinary" and "extraordinary" ways of salvation, and the claim that the Christian religion is not a religion whereas all the others are, are so many epicycles added to this ptolemaic theology to try to accommodate our growing knowledge of other faiths and our awareness of the true piety and devotion which they sustain.

It is worth noting that just as a ptolemaic astronomy could be developed, not only from the standpoint of this earth, but from any of the other planets, so also a ptolemaic theology can be developed not only from a Christian standpoint but equally from the standpoint of any other faith. From, let us say, a Hindu centre one could say that devout Christians are implicit Hindus in virtue of their sincere desire for the truth even though they do not yet know what the truth is; that other faiths provide the "ordinary way" of salvation whilst Hinduism is the "extraordinary" way, in which the truth is manifest which in the others is latent; that Hinduism is not a religion but the eternal truth judging and superseding all religions. The ptolemaic stance can be taken by anyone. But it can only serve as an interim position whilst we prepare our minds for a copernican revolution. Copernicus realised that it is the sun, and not the earth, that is at the centre, and that all the heavenly bodies, including our own earth, revolve around it. And we have to realise that the universe of faiths centres upon God, and not upon Christianity or upon any other religion. He is the sun, the originative source of light and life, whom all the religions reflect in their own different ways.

This must mean that the different world religions have each served as God's means of revelation to and point of contact with a different stream of human life. Such a conclusion makes sense of the history of religions. The first period was one in which the innate religiousness of the human mind expressed itself in the different forms of what we can call natural religion—the worship of spirits, ancestors, nature gods, and often blood-thirsty national deities. But about 800 B.C. there began what Karl Jaspers (*The Origin and Goal of History*, London: Routledge & Kegan Paul, 1953) has called the axial period in which seminal moments of religious experience occurred in each of the four principal centres of civilisation—Greece, the Near East, India, and China—out of which the higher religions have come. In this immensely rich and important band of time the great Hebrew prophets lived; in Persia, Zoroaster; in China, Confucius and the author (or authors) of the Taoist scriptures; in India, the Buddha, and Mahavira, and the writers of the *Upanishads* and later of the *Bhagavad Gita;* in Greece, Pythagoras, Socrates and Plato. And then later, out of the stream of prophetic religion established by the Hebrew prophets there came Jesus and the rise of Christianity, and Muhammed and the rise of Islam.

Now in this axial period, some two-and-a-half thousand years ago, communication between the continents and civilisations of the earth was so slow that for all practical purposes men lived in different cultural worlds. There could not be a divine revelation, through any human means, to mankind as a whole, but only separate revelations within the different streams of human history. And so it is a natural and indeed an inevitable hypothesis that God, the ultimate divine reality, was in this axial period becoming known to mankind through a number of specially sensitive and responsive spirits. In each case the revelatory experiences, and the religious traditions to which they gave rise, were conditioned by the history, culture, language, climate, and indeed all the concrete circumstances of human life at that particular time and place. Thus the cultural and philosophical form of the revelation of the divine is characteristically different in each case, although we may believe that everywhere the one Spirit has been at work, pressing in upon the human spirit.

IV

I shall return presently to this historical view of the different religious traditions to ask what difference it makes that the world has now become a communicational unity. But let me first ask the question that is so important to us as Christians, namely, what does all this imply concerning the person of our Lord? What about the uniqueness of Christ, the belief that Jesus was God incarnate, the second Person of the Holy Trinity become man, the eternal Logos made flesh? Did he not say, "I and the Father are one," and "No one comes to the Father, but by me"? Here, unfortunately, we have to enter the realm of New Testament criticism: and I say "unfortunately" because of the notorious uncertainties of this realm. There are powerful schools of thought, following fashions which tend to change from generation to generation, but no consensus either across the years or across the schools. But this at least can be said: that whereas until some three or four generations ago it was generally accepted among biblical scholars that Jesus claimed to be God the Son, with a unique consciousness of divinity, so that the doctrine of the Incarnation was believed to be firmly based in the consciousness and teaching of Jesus himself, today this is no longer generally held and is indeed very widely thought not to be the case. I am not going to enter into a detailed discussion of the New Testament evidence: I am neither competent to do this, nor is there space. I will only quote some summarising words of Wolfhart Pannenberg in his massive work, *Jesus: God and Man* (London: SCM Press, 1968) where he says that "After D. F. Strauss and F. C. Bauer, John's Gospel could no longer be claimed uncritically as a historical source of authentic words of Jesus. Consequently, other concepts and titles that were more indirectly connected with Jesus' relation to God came into the foreground of the question of Jesus' 'Messianic self-consciousness.' However, the transfer of these titles to Jesus . . . has been demonstrated with growing

certainty by critical study of the Gospels to be the work of the post-Easter community. Today it must be taken as all but certain that the pre-Easter Jesus neither
designated himself as Messiah (or Son of God) nor accepted such a confession to
him from others" (p. 237). Not all New Testament scholars would endorse
Pannenberg's words. But certainly one can no longer regard it as a fact proved out
of the New Testament that Jesus thought of himself as God incarnate. On the
contrary, this now seems to be very unlikely. And certainly we cannot rest anything on the assumption that the great christological sayings of the Fourth Gospel
(such as "I and my Father are one") were ever spoken, in sober historical fact, by
the Jesus who walked the hills and villages of Galilee. It seems altogether more
probable that they reflect the developing theology of the Church towards the end
of the first century.

Now if Jesus himself did not think of himself as God incarnate, one might
well ask whether his disciples ought to do so. But instead of pursuing that question
directly, it seems more profitable to accept that the Son-of-God and God-
Incarnate language has become deeply entrenched in the discourse of Christian
thought and piety, and to ask what *kind* of language it is. Is the statement that Jesus
was God incarnate, or the Son of God, or God the Son, a statement of literal fact;
and if so, what precisely is the fact? Or is it a poetic, or symbolic, or mythological
statment? It can, I think, only be the latter. It can hardly be a literal factual
statement, since after nearly 2,000 years of Christian reflection no factual content
has been discerned in it. Unless, that is, we give it factual content in terms of the
idea of Jesus' Virgin Birth. We could then say that his being the Son of God means
that the Holy Spirit fulfilled the role of the male parent in his conception. But he
would then be a divine-human figure such as is familiar from Greek mythology; for
example, Hercules, whose father was the god Jupiter and whose mother was a
human woman. However, this has never seriously been regarded as the real meaning of the doctrine of the Incarnation. What then is its real meaning? Whenever
in the history of Christian thought theologians have tried to spell out its meaning
in literal, factual terms the result has been heretical. A classic example would be
Appolinaris' theory that Jesus' body and soul were human but that his spirit was
the eternal divine Logos. This was rejected as heresy because it implied that Jesus
was not genuinely human. And all attempts to treat the Incarnation as a factual
hypothesis have likewise been rejected by the Church because they have failed to
do justice either to Jesus' full humanity or to his full deity. Indeed one may say that
the fundamental heresy is precisely to treat the Incarnation as a factual hypothesis!
For the reason why it has never been possible to state a literal meaning for the idea
of Incarnation is simply that it has no literal meaning. It is a mythological idea, a
figure of speech, a piece of poetic imagery. It is a way of saying that Jesus is our
living contact with the transcendent God. In his presence we find that we are
brought into the presence of God. We believe that he is so truly God's servant that
in living as his disciples we are living according to the divine purpose. And as our
sufficient and saving point of contact with God there is for us something absolute
about him which justifies the absolute language which Christianity has developed.
Thus reality is being expressed mythologically when we say that Jesus is the Son of
God, God Incarnate, the Logos made flesh.

When we see the Incarnation as a mythological idea applied to Jesus to express the experienced fact that he is our sufficient, effective and saving point of contact with God, we no longer have to draw the negative conclusion that he is man's one and only effective point of contact with God. We can revere Christ as the one through whom we have found salvation, without having to deny other points of reported saving contact between God and man. We can commend the way of Christian faith without having to discommend other ways of faith. We can say that there is salvation in Christ without having to say that there is no salvation other than in Christ.

V

Let us return, finally, to the historical situation. We have seen that the great world religions arose within different streams of human life and have in the past flowed down the centuries within different cultural channels. They have until recently interacted with one another only spasmodically, and nearly always in hostile clashes rather than in mutual dialogue and friendly interpenetration. But lately this situation has been changing radically. Since the late nineteenth century there has been a positive influence of Christianity upon Hinduism, bearing fruit in a new social concern in India; and an influence of both Hinduism and Buddhism upon Christianity, bearing fruit in our new western appreciation of meditation and the arts of spiritual self-development. And today the world religions are increasingly in contact with one another in conscious dialogue and in deliberate attempts to learn about and to learn from one another. These mutual influences can only increase in the future. It is, I think, very important to notice that each of the world religions is in practice an on-going history of change. Each likes to think of itself as immutable, the same yesterday, today and for ever. But the historian can see that this is not so. Each of the major world faiths has gone through immense historical developments, revolutions and transformations. Each has experienced both times of rapid change, in sudden expansions, schisms, reformations and renaissances, and also periods of relative stability. Islam has perhaps changed less than the others; but even within Islam there have been immense evolutionary developments and also the growth of important divisions. Hinduism has always been able to change, and to absorb new influences into its own life. Christianity and Buddhism have both developed through the centuries almost out of recognition. And in each case there is in principle no limit to the further developments that may take place in the future. In the next period these will occur in a context of interaction. The future of Christianity will be formed partly by influences stemming from Hinduism, Buddhism and Islam; and so also, in a mutually interactive system, with the other world faiths. And all partly also by influences stemming from the secular civilisation within which they will all exist.

Can we peer into the future and anticipate the pattern of development? Obviously, in trying to do so we are guessing. However, such guessing is today dignified by the name of Futurology and large books are written about the state of the planet in, say, the year 2000. These speculations are not random guesses, but are based on the projection of present trends, together with foreseeable emergence of new trends. If secular seers can speculate in these ways about the future of man, why should we not try to consider the forms which the religious life of mankind will take in, say, a hundred years time if the present basic trends continue? I am making the very major assumption, which there is no space to defend here, that man's religiousness is innate and that religion will continue in some form so long as human nature remains essentially the same. But what forms will it take? The broad trend of the present century is ecumenical. Old divisions are being transcended. The deeper essentials in which people agree are tending to seem more important than the matters on which they differ. Projecting this trend into the future we may suppose that the ecumenical spirit which has already so largely transformed Christianity will increasingly affect the relations between the world faiths. There may well be a growing world ecumenism, in which the common commitment of faith in a higher spiritual reality which demands brotherhood on earth will seem more and more significant, whilst the differences between the religious traditions will seem proportionately less significant. The relation between them may thus become somewhat like that between the Christian denominations in this country—that is to say, they are on increasingly friendly terms; they freely visit one another's worship and are beginning to be able to share places of worship; they co-operate in all sorts of service to the community; their clergy are accustomed to meet together for discussion, and there is even a degree of interchange of ministries; and so on.

What are we picturing here as a future possibility is not a single world religion, but a situation in which the different traditions no longer see themselves and each other as rival ideological communities. A single world religion is, I would think, never likely, and not a consummation to be desired. For so long as there is a variety of human types there will be a variety of kinds of worship and a variety of theological emphases and approaches. There will always be the more mystical and the more prophetic types of faith, with their corresponding awareness of the ultimate Reality as non-personal and as personal. There will always be the more spontaneous, warm and Spirit-filled forms of devotion, and the more liturgical, orderly and rationally controlled forms. There will always be the more vivid consciousness of the divine as gracious love or as infinite demand and judgment. And so on. But it is not necessary, and it may in a more ecumenical age not be felt to be necessary, to assume that if God is being truly worshipped by Christians he cannot also be being truly worshipped by Jews and Muslims and Sikhs and by theistic Hindus and Amida Buddhists; or even that if the Ultimate Divine Reality is being validly experienced within the theistic streams of religious life as a personal presence, that Reality may not also be validly experienced within other streams of religious life as the infinite Being-Consciousness-Bliss (*Satchitananda*) of some forms of Hinduism, or as the ineffable cosmic Buddha-nature (the *Dharma-kaya*) of some forms of Buddhism. Let me then end with a quotation from one of the great revelatory scriptures of the world: 'Howsoever men may approach me, even so do I accept them; for, on all sides, whatever path they may choose is mine' (*Bhagavad Gita*, IV, 11). . . .

Bibliography

Adler, Mortimer, J. *Truth in Religion: The Plurality of Religions and the Unity of Truth.* London: Collier Macmillan, 1990.

Anderson, Sir James Norman Dalrymple. *Christianity and World Religions: The Challenge of Pluralism.* Downers Grove, Illinois; Inter-Varsity Press, 1984.

Arberry, A. J. *Revelation and Reason in Islam.* London: Allen and Unwin, 1957.

Babbitt, I. *The Dhammapade.* University Oxford Press, 1936.

Beal, J. *Life of Hiuen-Tsang by Hwui.* London: n.d.

————. *Buddhist Records of the Western World.* London: n.d.

Bennett, W. *Religion and Free Will.* Oxford: Clarendon Press, 1913.

Ben-Yosef, I. A. " 'The East' in the Thought of Martin Buber." *Religions in South Africa* 6 (January 1985): 47–58.

Berdayev, N. *Freedom and the Spirit of Man.* New York: Scribners, 1935.

Bergson, Henri. *Time and Free Will.* New York: Macmillan, 1921.

Brown, Delwin, Ralph E. James, Jr., and Gene Reeves. *Process Philosophy and Christian Thought.* Indianapolis, Ind: Bobbs-Merrill, 1971.

Cahn, Steven M. *Fate, Logic, and Time.* New Haven, Conn.: Yale University Press, 1967.

————. "The Irrelevance to Religion of Philosophic Proofs for the Existence of God." *American Philosophical Quarterly* 6 (1969): 170–72.

Capra, Fritjof. *The Tao of Physics: An Exploration of the Parallels between Modern Physics and Eastern Mysticism.* Berkeley, Calif.: Shambhala, 1975.

Carlyon, Richard. *A Guide to the Gods.* New York: Morrow, 1982.

Ching, Julia. *Confucianism and Christianity: A Comparative Study.* Tokyo: Kodansha International, 1977.

Christian, William. *Oppositions of Religious Doctrines.* New York: Herder and Herder, 1972.

Cobb, John. *Beyond Dialogue.* Philadelphia: Fortress Press, 1982.

Connolly, William E. *The Bias of Pluralism.* New York: Atherton Press, 1969.

Conze, Edward. *Buddhism: Its Essence and Development.* New York: Harper, 1959.

————. *Buddhist Thought in India.* Ann Arbor: University of Michigan Press, 1967.

————. *The Living Thoughts of Gotama, the Buddha.* London: Cassell, 1948.

Coward, Harold G. *Religious Pluralism and the World Religions.* Madras: Radhakrishnan Institute, University of Madras, 1983.

———— ed. *Modern Indian Responses to Religious Pluralism.* Albany: State University of New York Press, 1987.

Copleston, Frederick Charles. *Religion and the One: Philosophies East and West.* New York: Crossroad, 1982.

Cragg, Kenneth. *The House of Islam.* Belmont, Calif.: Wadsworth, 1988.

Creel, Harrlee Glesser. *Confucius, the Man and the Myth.* Westport, Conn.: Greenwood Press, 1972.

d'Arcy, C. F. *God and Freedom in Human Experience.* London: Edward Arnold, 1915.

Davidson, Herbert A. *Proofs for Eternity, Creation, and the Existence of God in Medieval, Islamic, and Jewish Philosophy.* New York: Oxford University Press, 1987.

Davis, Stephen T. *Logic and the Nature of God.* Grand Rapids, Mich.: Eerdman, 1983.

————. "Divine Omniscience and Human Freedom." *Religious Studies* 15 (1979): 303–16.

Dumoulin, Heinrich. *Buddhism in the Modern World.* New York: Macmillan, 1976.

Ehrlich, Stanislaw, and Graham Wootton, eds. *Three Faces of Pluralism: Political, Ethnic and Religious.* Westmead, Farnborough, England: Gower, 1980.

Endress, Gerhard. *An Introduction to Islam.* Edinburgh: Edinburgh University Press, 1988.

Feigl, Herbert and Wilfred Sellars. *Readings in Philosophical Analysis: "The Freedom of the Will."* New York: Appleton, Century, Crofts, 1951.

Ford, Lewis S. "The Infinite God of Process Theism." *Proceedings of the Catholic Philosophic Association* 55 (1981): 84–90.

Geach, Peter T. *Providence and Evil.* Cambridge: Cambridge University Press, 1977.

———. "Omniscience and the Future." Chap. 3 in *Providence and Evil.* Cambridge: Cambridge University Press, 1977.

Gyekye, Kwame. "Al-Farabi on the Logic of the Arguments of the Muslim Philosophical Theologians." *Journal of the History of Philosophy* 27 (January 1989): 135–43.

Hackett, Stuart C. *Oriental Philosophy: A Westerner's Guide to Eastern Thought.* Madison: University of Wisconsin, 1979.

Hartshorne, Charles. *The Divine Relativity.* New Haven, Conn.: Yale University Press, 1948.

———. *Man's Vision of God.* Hamden, Conn.: Archon Books, 1964.

———. *A Natural Theology of Our Time.* La Salle, Ill.: Open Court, 1967.

———. *Creative Synthesis and Philosophic Method.* La Salle, Ill.: Open Court, 1970.

Haydon, Albert E. *Biography of the Gods.* New York: Macmillan, 1941.

Helm, Paul. "Foreknowledge and Possibility." *Canadian Journal of Philosophy* 6 (1976): 731–34.

Hick, John. *God and the Universe of Faiths.* London: Macmillan, 1973.

———. *God Has Many Names.* Philadelphia: Westminster Press, 1980.

———. ed. *Truth and Dialogue in World Religions.* Philadelphia: Westminster Press, 1974.

Hildebrand, D. von. *Christian Ethics.* New York: David McKay, 1953.

Hiriyana, M. *Outlines of Indian Philosophy.* London: Allen and Unwin, 1932.

Hocking, William Ernest. *Living Religions and a World Faith.* New York: Macmillan, 1940.

Holck, Frederick H., ed. *Death and Eastern Thought: Understanding Death in Eastern Religions and Philosophies.* Nashville, Tenn.: Abingdon Press, 1974.

Horner, I. B. *The Early Buddhist Theory of Man Perfected.* London: 1936.

Jacobson, Nolan Pliny. *Understanding Buddhism.* Carbondale: Southern Illinois University Press, 1986.

James, William. "Pluralism and Religion." *Hibbert Journal* 50 (   ): 324–28.

Joseph, Howard, Jack N. Lightstone, Michael D. Oppenheim, eds. *Truth and Compassion: Essays on Judaism and Religion in Memory of Rabbi Dr. Solomon Frank.* Waterloo, Canada: Wilfrid Laurier University Press, 1983.

Joyce, George H. *Principles of Natural Theology.* New York: AMS Press, 1972.

Kane, R. H. "Divine Foreknowledge and Causal Determinism." *Southwestern Journal of Philosophy* 9 (1978): 69–76.

Keith, A. B. *Buddhist Philosophy.* University Press: Oxford: 1923.

Kenny, Anthony. *Will, Freedom and Power.* Oxford: Clarendon Press, 1976.

———. *The God of the Philosophers.* Oxford: Clarendon Press, 1979.

———. "Divine Foreknowledge and Human Freedom." In *Aquinas: A Collection of Critical Essays,* edited by Anthony Kenny, 255–70. Notre Dame, Ind.: University of Notre Dame Press, 1976.

Khamara, Edward J. "In Defence of Omnipotence." *Philosophical Quarterly* 28 (1978): 215–28.

Kitagawa, Joseph, ed. *Modern Trends in World Religions*. La Salle, Ill.: Open Court, 1959.

Knitter, Paul F. *No Other Name?: A Critical Survey of Christian Attitudes toward the World Religions*. Maryknoll, N.Y.: Orbis Books, 1985.

Legge, J. *A Record of Buddhistic Kingdoms*. Oxford: 1886.

Leibniz, G. W. "Theodicy." *Selected Writings in Philosophy*. New York: Appleton-Century, 1939.

Lipner, Julius. "Truth-Claims and Inter-religious Dialogue." *Religious Studies* 12 (1976): 217–30.

Lucas, J. *The Freedom of the Will*. Oxford: Oxford University Press, 1970.

Mahadev, A. *Invitation to Indian Philosophy*. Atlantic Highlands, N.J.: Humanities Press, 1975.

Mavrodes, George I. "Defining Omnipotence." *Philosophical Studies* 32 (1977): 191–202.

McGovern, E. H. *A Manual of Buddhist Philosophy*. vol. 1, *Cosmology*. N.Y.: Clarendon Press, 1923.

McNaughton, William. *The Confucian Vision*. Ann Arbor: University of Michigan Press, 1974.

Morgan, Kenneth W., ed. *The Path of the Buddha: Buddhism Interpreted by Buddhists*. New York: Ronald Press, 1956.

Naravane, Vishwanath Shridhar. *Indian Thought: A Philosophical Survey*. London: Asia Press, 1964.

Netton, Ian Richard. *Allah Transcendent*. New York: Routledge, 1989.

Newman, Jay. *Foundations of Religious Tolerance*. Toronto: University of Toronto Press, 1982.

Orlebeke, C., and L. Smedes, eds. *In God and the Good*. Grand Rapids, Mich.: Eerdmans, 1975.

Palmer, George Herbert. *The Problem of Freedom*. New York: Houghton-Mifflin, 1911.

Pike, Nelson. "Omnipotence and God's Ability to Sin." *American Philosophical Quarterly* 6 (1969): 208–16.

———. *God and Timelessness*. New York: Schocken Books, 1970.

Plantinga, Alvin. *God, Freedom and Evil*. New York: Harper and Row, 1974.

———. *Does God Have a Nature?* Milwaukee: University of Wisconsin Press, 1980.

Ross, James Ross. *Philosophical Theology*. Indianapolis, Ind.: Bobbs-Merrill, 1969.

Ross, Steven L. "Another Look at God and Morality." *Ethics* 94 (October 1983): 87–98.

Rouner, Leroy S., ed. *Religious Pluralism*. Notre Dame, Ind.: University of Notre Dame Press, 1984.

Smart, Ninian. *Doctrine and Argument in Indian Philosophy*. London: Allen and Unwin, 1964.

———. *The Religious Experience of Mankind*. New York: Scribner's, 1969.

———. "The Epistemology of Pluralism: The Basis of Liberal Philosophy." *Philosophical Society Activities* 16 (April/June 1990): 5–14.

Smith, William Cantwell. *Religious Diversity*. Edited by Willard G. Oxtoby. New York: Harper and Row, 1976.

———. *Towards a World Theology*. Philadelphia: Westminister Press, 1981.

Stcherbatsky, T. *Buddhist Logic*. Leningrad: 1932.

Suzuki, D. T. *Outlines of Mahayana Buddhism.* London: 1907.

——. *Studies in the Lankavatara Sutra.* London: 1930.

——. *Mysticism: Christian and Buddhist.* New York: Harper, 1957.

Swinburne, Richard. *The Coherence of Theism.* Oxford: Clarendon Press, 1977.

Tharamangalam, Joseph. "Religious Pluralism and the Theory and Practice of Secularism: Reflections on the Indian Experience." *Journal of Asian and African Studies* 24 (July/October 1989): 199–212.

Tillich, Paul. *Biblical Religion and the Search for Ultimate Reality.* Chicago: University of Chicago Press, 1955.

——. *Dynamics of Faith.* New York: Harper and Row, 1957.

——. *Christianity and the Encounter of the World Religions.* New York: Columbia University Press, 1963.

Tucci, G. *Indo-Tibetica.* Rome: 1932–41.

Vallée Poussin, L. de la. *The Way to Nirvana.* Cambridge, England: 1917.

Voll, John O. *Islam, Continuity and Change in the Modern World.* Boulder, Colo.: Westview Press, 1982; Essex, England: Longman, 1982.

Ward, Keith. "Truth and the Diversity of Religions." *Religious Studies* 26 (March 1990): 1–18.

Watson, Walter. *The Architectonics of Meaning: Foundations of the New Pluralism.* Albany: State University of New York Press, 1985.

Watts, Alan Wilson. *The Spirit of Zen: A Way of Life, Work, and Art in the Far East.* New York: Grove Press, 1958.

Weber, Max. *The Religion of China: Confucianism and Taoism.* Glencoe, Ill.: Free Press, 1951.

Wentz, W. Y. Evans. *Tibetan Yoga and Secret Doctrines.* Oxford University Press, 1935.

Whaling, Frank, ed. *The World's Religious Traditions: Current Perspectives in Religious Studies: Essays in Honor of Wilfred Cantwell Smith.* Edinburgh: T. and T. Clark, 1984.

Whitehead, Alfred North. *Religion in the Making.* New York: Macmillan, 1926.

Wieman, Henry Nelson. *Man's Ultimate Commitment.* Carbondale, Ill.: Southern Illinois University Press, 1958.

Young, Robert. *Freedom, Responsibility and God.* New York: Harper and Row, 1975.

Zimmer, Heinrich Robert. *Philosophies of India.* New York: Pantheon, 1951.

Religious Claims and Criticisms

CHAPTER 3

Classical Proofs for God's Existence

*T*he central question in the philosophy of religion is the existence of God, and in Judeo-Christian thought this means the personal being, omnipotent, omniscient, and omni-good, holy, eternal, and infinite, the creator of all life. Is such a being real or only an imaginative construct, arising from human needs and fears? Voltaire once wrote: "If there were no God, it would be necessary to invent him." Are there good reasons for believing that God is an existent being and not a human invention?

Some believers refuse to address the question, claiming that faith, not reason, brings us to the truth. But not only is this a rational argument against the use of reason (and therefore self-contradictory) but it offers no protection against mistakes. If we argued this way, we would have no reliable method of separating one person's true beliefs from another person's false ones; each individual could claim that his or her views are based on faith and are beyond all reasoning. Furthermore, we would have a welter of different beliefs, many inconsistent with one another, with each claiming to be the final truth. Each would be immune from rational examination, yet they could not all be true. Clearly, this would be an impossible situation.

Although the relation between faith and reason is very complex, many theologians and philosophers have maintained that reason has a legitimate role in religion. They have offered rational arguments as proofs for the religious reality, and although they may not have been willing to abandon their faith when their arguments were criticized as untenable, they did attempt a logical justification for believing in God's existence.

The medieval theologian Saint Anselm presented one of these justifications, called the *ontological argument.* He reasoned that if he had the idea of a being "than which none greater can be conceived," then that being had to exist. He means by such a being God, of course, and so he is claiming that God necessarily exists.

Saint Anselm argues specifically that if he has the idea of a being than which none greater can be conceived, this being must possess all positive attributes. Such a being must be almighty, perfectly wise, wholly loving, and so forth, otherwise Anselm could conceive of a greater entity, one that includes the attributes that are lacking. In addition, if this is truly a being than which none greater can be conceived, Anselm argues, he would have to possess the essential element of existence or, otherwise, not be the being described. The conclusion, then, is that the being Anselm is considering must possess existence, in other words, that God must be acknowledged to exist.

At first reading, Anselm's argument seems bewildering, and he appears to be saying that whatever he thinks of must exist. This was the criticism of a medieval monk named Gaunilon who argued that his ability to imagine a unicorn did not mean there are real unicorns.

However, Anselm's point is more subtle than that. He is not claiming that everything we reflect upon, including centaurs, gremlins, and Santa Claus, must be real, but that in this one unique case existence must be present. For we are thinking of a being than which none greater can be conceived, and here existence is a necessary part of such a being. In more modern terms, if we reflect on what a perfect God would be, we would have to include existence. We may not know everything that perfection entails, but we do know that existence is a necessary part, and that a being without existence could not be called perfect. This means that God, the perfect being, must exist.

If we still feel that something is wrong, that we cannot prove the existence of God just from the thought of God, perhaps our reaction is correct. In fact, those philosophers who criticize Anselm's argument identify this shift as the basic flaw.

Anselm's mistake seems to be that he confuses an idea with the reality the idea refers to. Although the idea of a perfect God must include existence as part of the idea, that does not prove there is an actually existent God behind the idea. Or differently put, the idea of a being than which none greater can be conceived must contain the notion of existence, but that does not imply that an actual being exists as represented by the idea.

More technically put, existence is not an attribute to be added to others in describing a perfect being. It is the positing of a being with its various attributes. As the philosopher Immanuel Kant said, you cannot add to the value of a hundred imaginary dollars by taking a real one out of your pocket.

Because of some of these problems, another version of the ontological argument was proposed by the seventeenth-century French philosopher René Descartes. Sometimes this "Cartesian" argument is classified as causal, but since it does attempt to prove that God exists from the very thought of such a being, it seems basically ontological in character.

Descartes begins his argument with the principle that the greater can produce the lesser, but the lesser cannot produce the greater; that is, you can get less from more, but not more from less. This being so, if we have an idea that is greater than ourselves, then we could not have produced it. God is such an idea, for we as finite beings could not have conceived of the infinite; imperfect man could never have thought of the idea of a perfect God.

Descartes goes on to argue that the only being capable of producing the idea of God in our minds is God. He concludes therefore that God must exist. From the fact that we know of God, yet could not have conceived of that being by ourselves, we must admit the existence of a God who implanted the idea of "himself within us."

Unfortunately, this argument has serious flaws as well. Perhaps the lesser can produce the greater, as in an avalanche caused by a snowball, an acorn that produces an oak tree, or a nuclear explosion that results from a split atom. But whether or not less can produce more in the physical realm, human beings seem able to conceive of things far greater than themselves. Through the power of our imagination we can envision creatures with much greater strength, intelligence, or perception than our own, yet these creatures do not necessarily exist. Using Descartes's argument, we could even "prove" the existence of demons, devils, and Satan.

A second classic argument, which is generally attributed to Saint Thomas Aquinas, concerns the idea of cause and effect, and in its more sophisticated versions, change and unchangingness, and contingency and necessity. The *cosmological argument* proceeds as follows:

The world is arranged in a network of cause-and-effect relations such that every event has a cause which is itself the effect of a prior cause. Whatever occurs, we can legitimately ask what caused it. The tree crashed against the house because it was blown down by the wind; the old man died because his heart failed; the glass shattered because it fell on the stone floor. We can even trace a series of causes and effects backwards in time to see the causal factors that precipitated earlier and still earlier events. The flower grew because of the rich soil, but the soil was deposited by the weathering of rock, and the rock weathered because of the action of wind, water, and ice, which was caused by a changing climate, which in turn was due to . . . and so on.

However, the proponents of the cosmological argument say, this process of finding more and more ultimate causes cannot go on indefinitely; we cannot have an "infinite regress." Something must be shown to be the first cause, responsible for all succeeding links in the chain. There must be a beginning to the series, a *primum mobile* behind everything that occurs, and this first cause can only be God.

This argument seems natural and plausible, and it occurs even to children wondering where things first came from. However, it has been criticized on various grounds by numerous thinkers. First, no logical reason exists for claiming that an infinite regress is impossible. Just as there may not be a last effect (or a last number), there may not be a first cause; in a circular system, for example, the final event becomes the initial one (which is why the ring is a symbol of eternity).

Second, even if a first cause is necessary, that cause may not be God. A natural, rather than a supernatural, force may be responsible. For instance, the creation of the universe may be due to the explosion of the primal atom, something that astronomers refer to as the "big bang" theory. The background noise of that explosion has, in fact, been detected, as well as an unevenness in the radiation which would have allowed energy to form into clusters of stars and planets.

Third, if the argument takes as its premise that everything has a cause, then presumably God has a cause as well and cannot be regarded as an uncaused cause. If, on the other hand, God is an exception to the rule, then there might well be other exceptions. The universe itself might be uncaused, in which case there would be no necessity for postulating a God who caused it.

Many times the advocates of the cosmological argument find themselves arguing in a circle. They claim that everything must have a beginning and that God is that beginning; but when asked how God began, they assert that God did not begin at all, but has always been. When the logical point is made that perhaps the universe also has always been, they object that everything must have a beginning.

The more sophisticated versions, also presented by Saint Thomas, state that the fact of change in the world implies the existence of that which is unchanging, and that the contingency of all things implies that something must exist necessarily. By *contingent* is meant "dependent upon something else for its existence," as distinct from that which is self-existent, or carrying the reason for its existence within itself. These iterations, however, suffer from the same problems as the simple version in terms of cause and effect.

The *teleological argument* is a third traditional justification that has been offered for belief in God; and, like the cosmological argument, it is part of Saint Thomas's Five Ways. This argument turns on the fact of order and harmony in nature, and it claims that if the world shows evidence of design, there must be a cosmic designer. The argument runs that when one examines the natural world, the regularity, balance, and arrangement of objects and events are immediately apparent. Instead of encountering randomness, we see orderliness everywhere.

The temperature and chemical composition of the earth's atmosphere is ideal for maintaining life; if the chemical mixture changed, or the earth were closer or farther away from the sun, life would be impossible. In addition, there is a perfect symbiotic relationship between insects, plants, and animals, so that the organisms within the biosphere are mutually supportive.

Furthermore, each species has exactly what it requires in order to survive: the porcupine has been equipped with quills, the bird with wings, the tiger with sharp teeth and claws, the turtle with an armored shell, the zebra with camouflage, the snake with venom, and so forth. Every class of creature, in fact, has been given the perfect characteristics to meet the needs of the environment. At the anatomical and physiological level, animals have exactly the muscles, organs, and skeletal structure and the circulatory, digestive, reproductive, nervous, and respiratory systems that they require. Even the eye and the heart are marvelous mechanisms, perfectly suited to their functions, as are the fin, the paw, and the hand.

In short, nature provides ample evidence of rational organization in all of its manifestations, which means a cosmic intelligence must exist. For there to be order, there must be an orderer—a plan requires a planner—and if an overall design is apparent, then a divine designer is responsible. God therefore exists as the only being capable of designing this intelligible world.

The teleological argument is extremely persuasive also, and even when philosophers criticize it, they respect its power and commonsense appeal. However, it does have serious weaknesses that make it problematic as a proof of God's existence.

For one thing, the design of the world is far from perfect and the imperfections that abound raise questions about the goodness of a God who created such a system. Not only is there chaos as well as order, but parts of the design involve pain and suffering for the creatures on earth, including human beings. Natural catastrophes (e.g., floods, earthquakes), genetic defects (e.g., blindness, Tay-Sachs disease), illnesses and disabilities (e.g., leukemia, cerebral palsy), savage animals (e.g., tigers, crocodiles), inhospitable environments (e.g., jungles, deserts), and the overwhelming fact of death, leave us in a state of doubt as to the beneficence of the plan. We wonder why a benevolent, almighty God would adopt a design of this kind, or whether the world might simply be the result of natural forces and not designed at all.

This leads to a second criticism, namely, that the order that exists could have come about naturally, not supernaturally. That is, another explanation for the regularity and orderliness in nature, besides that of an intelligent designer, is the scientific one offered by Darwin. According to the theory of evolution, those creatures that had the characteristics called for by the environment managed to survive; they then produced offspring with those same characteristics. Those that did not have the requisite skills, features, or capabilities perished in the struggle for survival, and their genetic line died out. Through this process of natural selection, only the fittest species survived, so it is not at all surprising that the species that exist on earth are fit for survival; if they weren't, they would not exist.

To be surprised that animals are well adapted to their environment would be like finding it uncanny that all Olympic winners are good athletes; obviously, if they weren't good athletes, they would not have won the Olympics. Or to use another parallel, one should not be amazed that so many major cities have navigable rivers; if the rivers had not been navigable, these cities would never have become major ones.

A third criticism that has been offered is that even if the teleological argument were valid, it would not prove a *creator* of the universe but only a cosmic architect who arranged the materials. Both the cosmological and the teleological arguments would have to be sound in order to establish a God who both created and organized the world. What's more, by analogy with human constructions, a number of designers would have been involved in the project. Polytheism, then, might be established, but not monotheism.

After confronting these three classic arguments, the result is rather disappointing. Not all philosophers accept the criticisms, of course, and some champion one or another of the arguments today, but most find them logically flawed for the reasons given.

Now if the ontological, cosmological, and teleological arguments are invalid, does that prove that God does not exist? Clearly not. To disprove an argument for the existence of God is not to disprove God's existence. Rather, we are left with an open question and must seek further for our answer.

In the selections that follow, the ontological argument is presented by

Saint Anselm and Descartes, and a definitive criticism, is leveled by Immanuel Kant. Then the cosmological argument is offered by Saint Thomas Aquinas, with a modern reformulation by Richard Taylor.

Finally, William Paley presents the teleological argument in its most famous form: that if we found a watch on a deserted island, we would assume there had to be a watchmaker; and when we encounter the world, operating in its orderly way, we ought to assume the existence of an earthmaker. David Hume then challenges this view, and Richard Swinburne offers a more reflective, contemporary analysis.

Perfection: The Ontological Argument

15. Proslogion

SAINT ANSELM

PREFACE

Some time ago, at the urgent request of some of my brethren, I published a brief work, as an example of meditation on the grounds of faith. I wrote it in the role of one who seeks, by silent reasoning with himself, to learn what he does not know. But when I reflected on this little book, and saw that it was put together as a long chain of arguments, I began to ask myself whether *one* argument might possibly be found, resting on no other argument for its proof, but sufficient in itself to prove that God truly exists, and that he is the supreme good, needing nothing outside himself, but needful for the being and well-being of all things. I often turned my earnest attention to this problem, and at times I believed that I could put my finger on what I was looking for, but at other times it completely escaped my mind's eye, until finally, in despair, I decided to give up searching for something that seemed impossible to find. But when I tried to put the whole question out of my mind, so as to avoid crowding out other matters, with which I might make some progress, by this useless preoccupation, then, despite my unwillingness and resistance, it began to force itself on me more persistently than ever. Then, one day, when I was worn out by my vigorous resistance to the obsession, the solution I had ceased to hope for presented itself to me, in the very turmoil of my thoughts, so that I enthusiastically embraced the idea which, in my disquiet, I had spurned.

I thought that the proof I was so glad to find would please some readers if it were written down. Consequently, I have written the little work that follows, dealing with this and one or two other matters, in the role of one who strives to raise his mind to the contemplation of God and seeks to understand what he believes. Neither this essay nor the other one I have already mentioned really seemed to me to deserve to be called a book or to bear an author's name; at the same time, I felt that they could not be published without some title that might encourage anyone into whose hands they fell to read them, and so I gave each of them a title. The first I called *An Example of Meditation on the Grounds of Faith,* and the second *Faith Seeking Understanding.*

But when both of them had been copied under these titles by a number of people, I was urged by many people—and especially by Hugh, the reverend archbishop of Lyons, apostolic legate in Gaul, who ordered this with apostolic authority—to attach my name to them. In order to do this more fittingly, I have named the first *Monologion* (or *Soliloquy*), and the second *Proslogion* (or *Address*).

GOD TRULY IS

And so, O Lord, since thou givest understanding to faith, give me to understand—as far as thou knowest it to be good for me—that thou dost exist, as we believe, and that thou art what we believe thee to be. Now we believe that thou art a being than which none greater can be thought. Or can it be that there is no such being, since "the fool hath said in his heart, 'There is no God' "? But when this same fool hears what I am saying—"A being than which none greater can be thought"—he understands what he hears, and what he understands is in his understanding, even if he does not understand that it exists. For it is one thing for an object to be in the understanding, and another thing to understand that it exists. When a painter considers beforehand what he is going to paint, he has it in his understanding, but he does not suppose that what he has not yet painted already exists. But when he has painted it, he both has it in his understanding and understands that what he has now produced exists. Even the fool, then, must be convinced that a being than which none greater can be thought exists at least in his understanding, since when he hears this he understands it, and whatever is understood is in the understanding. But clearly that than which a greater cannot be thought cannot exist in the understanding alone. For if it is actually in the understanding alone, it can be thought of as existing also in reality, and this is greater. Therefore, if that than which a greater cannot be thought is in the understanding alone, this same thing than which a greater cannot be thought is that than which a greater can be thought. But obviously this is impossible. Without doubt, therefore, there exists, both in the understanding and in reality, something than which a greater cannot be thought.

GOD CANNOT BE THOUGHT OF AS NONEXISTENT

And certainly it exists so truly that it cannot be thought of as nonexistent. For something can be thought of as existing, which cannot be thought of as not existing, and this is greater than that which *can* be thought of as not existing. Thus, if that than which a greater cannot be thought can be thought of as not existing, this very thing than which a greater cannot be thought is *not* that than which a greater cannot be thought. But this is contradictory. So, then, there truly is a being than which a greater cannot be thought—so truly that it cannot even be thought of as not existing.

And *thou* art this being, O Lord our God. Thou so truly art, then, O Lord my God, that thou canst not even be thought of as not existing. And this is right.

For if some mind could think of something better than thou, the creature would rise above the Creator and judge its Creator; but this is altogether absurd. And indeed, whatever is, except thyself alone, can be thought of as not existing. Thou alone, therefore, of all beings, hast being in the truest and highest sense, since no other being so truly exists, and thus every other being has less being. Why, then, has "the fool said in his heart, 'There is no God,' " when it is so obvious to the rational mind that, of all beings, thou dost exist supremely? Why indeed, unless it is that he is a stupid fool?

HOW THE FOOL HAS SAID IN HIS HEART WHAT CANNOT BE THOUGHT

But how did he manage to say in his heart what he could not think? Or how is it that he was unable to think what he said in his heart? After all, to say in one's heart and to think are the same thing. Now if it is true—or, rather, since it is true—that he thought it, because he said it in his heart, but did not say it in his heart, since he could not think it, it is clear that something can be said in one's heart or thought in more than one way. For we think of a thing, in one sense, when we think of the word that signifies it, and in another sense, when we understand the very thing itself. Thus, in the first sense God can be thought of as nonexistent, but in the second sense this is quite impossible. For no one who understands what God is can think that God does not exist, even though he says these words in his heart—perhaps without any meaning, perhaps with some quite extraneous meaning. For God is that than which a greater cannot be thought, and whoever understands this rightly must understand that he exists in such a way that he cannot be nonexistent even in thought. He, therefore, who understands that God thus exists cannot think of him as nonexistent.

Thanks be to thee, good Lord, thanks be to thee, because I now understand by thy light what I formerly believed by thy gift, so that even if I were to refuse to believe in thy existence, I could not fail to understand its truth.

A REPLY ON BEHALF OF THE FOOL
by Gaunilo

For example: it is said that somewhere in the ocean is an island, which, because of the difficulty, or rather the impossibility, of discovering what does not exist, is called the lost island. And they say that this island has an inestimable wealth of all manner of riches and delicacies in greater abundance than is told of the Islands of the Blest; and that having no owner or inhabitant, it is more excellent than all other countries, which are inhabited by mankind, in the abundance with which it is stored.

Now if some one should tell me that there is such an island, I should easily understand his words, in which there is no difficulty. But suppose that he went on to say, as if by a logical inference: "You can no longer doubt that this island which is more excellent than all lands exists somewhere, since you have no doubt that it is in your understanding. And since it is more excellent not to be in the understanding alone, but to exist both in the understanding and in reality, for this reason it must exist. For if it does not exist, any land which really exists will be more excellent than it; and so the island already understood by you to be more excellent will not be more excellent."

If a man should try to prove to me by such reasoning that this island truly exists, and that its existence should no longer be doubted, either I should believe that he was jesting, or I know not which I ought to regard as the greater fool: myself, supposing that I should allow this proof; or him, if he should suppose that he had established with any certainty the existence of this island. For he ought to show first that the hypothetical excellence of this island exists as a real and indubitable fact, and in no way as any unreal object, or one whose existence is uncertain, to my understanding.

This, in the mean time, is the answer the fool could make to the arguments urged against him. When he is assured in the first place that this being is so great that its nonexistence is not even conceivable, and that this in turn is proved on no other ground than the fact that otherwise it will not be greater than all things, the fool may make the same answer, and say:

When did I say that any such being exists in reality, that is, a being greater than all others?—that on this ground it should be proved to me that it also exists in reality to such a degree that it cannot even be conceived not to exist? Whereas in the first place it should be in some way proved that a nature which is higher, that is, greater and better, than all other natures, exists; in order that from this we may then be able to prove all attributes which necessarily the being that is greater and better than all possesses.

REPLY TO THE CRITICISMS OF GAUNILO
by Saint Anselm

. . . But, you say, suppose that someone imagined an island in the ocean, surpassing all lands in its fertility. Because of the difficulty, or rather the impossibility, of finding something that does not exist, it might well be called "Lost Island." By reasoning like yours, he might then say that we cannot doubt that it truly exists in reality, because anyone can easily conceive it from a verbal description. I state confidently that if anyone discovers something for me, other than that "than which a greater cannot be thought," existing either in reality or in thought alone, to which the logic of my argument can be applied, I shall find his lost island and give it to him, never to be lost again. But it now seems obvious that this being than which a greater cannot be thought cannot be thought of as nonexistent, because it exists by such a sure reason of truth. For otherwise it would not exist at all. In short, if anyone says that he thinks it does not exist, I say that when he thinks this, he either thinks of something than which a greater cannot be thought or he does not think. If he does not think, he does not think of what he is not thinking of as nonexistent. But if he does think, then he thinks of something which cannot be thought of as nonexistent. For if it could be thought of as nonexistent, it could be thought of as having a beginning and an end. But this is impossible. Therefore, if anyone thinks of it, he thinks of something that cannot even be thought of as nonexistent. But he who thinks of this does not think that it does not exist; if he did, he would think what cannot be thought. Therefore, that than which a greater cannot be thought cannot be thought of as nonexistent.

You say, moreover, that when it is said that the highest reality cannot be *thought of* as nonexistent, it would perhaps be better to say that it cannot be *understood* as nonexistent, or even as possibly nonexistent. But it is more correct to say, as I said, that it cannot be thought. For if I had said that the reality itself cannot be understood not to exist, perhaps you yourself, who say that according to the very definition of the term what is false cannot be understood, would object that nothing that is can be understood as nonexistent. For it is false to say that what exists does not exist. Therefore it would not be peculiar to God to be unable to be understood as nonexistent. But if some one of the things that most certainly are can be understood as nonexistent, other certain things can similarly be understood as nonexistent. But this objection cannot be applied to "thinking," if it is rightly considered. For although none of the things that exist can be understood not to exist, still they can all be thought of as nonexistent, except that which most fully is. For all those things—and only those—which have a beginning or end or are composed of parts can be thought of as nonexistent, along with anything that does not exist as a whole anywhere or at any time (as I have already said). But the only being that cannot be thought of as nonexistent is that in which no thought finds a beginning or end or composition of parts, but which any thought finds as a whole, always and everywhere.

You must realize, then, that you can think of yourself as nonexistent, even while you know most certainly that you exist. I am surprised that you said you did not know this. For we think of many things as nonexistent when we know that they exist, and of many things as existent when we know that they do not exist— all this not by a real judgment, but by imagining that what we think is so. And indeed, we can think of something as nonexistent, even while we know that it exists, because we are able at the same time to think the one and know the other. And yet we cannot think of it as nonexistent, while we know that it exists, because we cannot think of something as at once existent and nonexistent. Therefore, if anyone distinguishes these two senses of the statement in this way, he will understand that nothing, as long as it is known to exist, can be thought of as nonexistent, and that whatever exists, except that than which a greater cannot be thought, can be thought of as nonexistent, even when it is known to exist. So, then, it is peculiar to God to be unable to be thought of as nonexistent. . . .

16. Meditations on First Philosophy
RENÉ DESCARTES

MEDITATION III

If just because I can draw the idea of something from my thought, it follows that all which I know clearly and distinctly as pertaining to this object does really belong to it, may I not derive from this an argument demonstrating the existence of God? It is certain that I no less find the idea of God, that is to say, the idea of a supremely perfect Being, in me, than that of any figure or number whatever it is; and I do not know any less clearly and distinctly that an actual and eternal existence pertains to this nature than I know that all that which I am able to demonstrate of some figure or number truly pertains to the nature of this figure or number, and therefore, although all that I concluded in the preceding Meditations were found to be false, the existence of God would pass with me as at least as certain as I have ever held the truths of mathematics to be.

This indeed is not at first manifest, since it would seem to present some appearance of being a sophism. For being accustomed in all other things to make a distinction between existence and essence, I easily persuade myself that the existence can be separated from the essence of God, and that we can thus conceive God as not actually existing. But, nevertheless, when I think of it with more attention, I clearly see that existence can no more be separated from the essence of God than can its having its three angles equal to two right angles be separated from the essence of a rectilinear triangle, or the idea of a mountain from the idea of a valley; and so there is not any less repugnance to our conceiving a God (that is, a Being supremely perfect) to whom existence is lacking (that is to say, to whom a certain perfection is lacking), than to conceive of a mountain which has no valley.

But although I cannot really conceive of a God without existence any more than a mountain without a valley, still from the fact that I conceive of a mountain with a valley, it does not follow that there is such a mountain in the world; similarly although I conceive of God as possessing existence, it would seem that it does not follow that there is a God which exists; for my thought does not impose any necessity upon things, and just as I may imagine a winged horse, although no horse with wings exists, so I could perhaps attribute existence to God, although no God existed.

But a sophism is concealed in this objection; for from the fact that I cannot conceive a mountain without a valley, it does not follow that there is any mountain or any valley in existence, but only that the mountain and the valley, whether they exist or do not exist, cannot in any way be separated one from the other. While from the fact that I cannot conceive God without existence, it follows that existence is inseparable from Him, and hence that He really exists; not that my thought can bring this to pass, or impose any necessity on things, but, on the contrary, because the necessity which lies in the thing itself, i.e. the necessity of the existence of God determines me to think in this way. For it is not within my power to think of God without existence (that is of a supremely perfect Being devoid of a supreme perfection) though it is in my power to imagine a horse either with wings or without wings.

And we must not here object that it is in truth necessary for me to assert that God exists after having presupposed that He possesses every sort of perfection, since existence is one of these, but that as a matter of fact my original supposition was not necessary, just as it is not necessary to consider that all quadrilateral figures can be inscribed in the circle; for supposing I thought this, I should be constrained to admit that the rhombus might be inscribed in the circle since it is a quadrilateral figure, which, however, is manifestly false. We must not, I say, make any such allegations because although it is not necessary that I should at any time entertain the notion of God, nevertheless whenever it happens that I think of a first and a sovereign Being, and, so to speak, derive the idea of Him from the storehouse of my mind, it is necessary that I should attribute to Him every sort of perfection, although I do not get so far as to enumerate them all, or to apply my mind to each one in particular. And this necessity suffices to make me conclude (after having recognised that existence is a perfection) that this first and sovereign Being really exists; just as though it is not necessary for me ever to imagine any triangle, yet, whenever I wish to consider a rectilinear figure composed only of three angles, it is absolutely essential that I should attribute to it all those properties which serve to bring about the conclusion that its three angles are not greater than two right angles, even although I may not then be considering this point in particular. But when I consider which figures are capable of being inscribed in the circle, it is no way necessary that I should think that all quadrilateral figures are of this number; on the contrary, I cannot even pretend that this is the case, so long as I do not desire to accept anything which I cannot conceive clearly and distinctly. And in consequence there is a great difference between the false suppositions such as this, and the true ideas born within me, the first and principal of which is that of God. For really I discern in many ways that this idea is not something factitious, and depending solely on my thought, but that it is the image of a true and immutable nature; first of all, because I cannot conceive anything but God himself to whose essence existence necessarily pertains; in the second place because it is not possible for me to conceive two or more Gods in this same position; and, granted that there is one such God who now exists, I see clearly that it is necessary that He should have existed from all eternity, and that He must exist eternally; and finally, because I know an infinitude of other properties in God, none of which I can either diminish or change.

For the rest, whatever proof or argument I avail myself of, we must always return to the point that it is only those things which we conceive clearly and distinctly that have the power of persuading me entirely. And although amongst the matters which I conceive of in this way, some indeed are manifestly obvious to all, while others only manifest themselves to those who consider them closely and examine them attentively; still, after they have once been discovered, the latter are not esteemed as any less certain than the former. For example, in the case of every right-angled triangle, although it does not so manifestly appear that the square of the base is equal to the squares of the two other sides as that this base is opposite to the greatest angle; still, when this has once been apprehended, we are just as certain of its truth as of the truth of the other. And as regards God, if my mind were not preoccupied with prejudices, and if my thought did not find itself on all hands diverted by the continual pressure of sensible things, there would be nothing which I could know more immediately and more easily than Him. For is there anything more manifest than that there is a God, that is to say, a Supreme Being, to whose essence alone existence pertains?

17. The Impossibility of an Ontological Proof

IMMANUEL KANT

It is evident from what has been said, that the conception of an absolutely necessary being is a mere idea, the objective reality of which is far from being established by the mere fact that it is a need of reason. On the contrary, this idea serves merely to indicate a certain unattainable perfection, and rather limits the operations than, by the presentation of new objects, extends the sphere of the understanding. But a strange anomaly meets us at the very threshold; for the inference from a given existence in general to an absolutely necessary existence, seems to be correct and unavoidable, while the conditions of the *understanding* refuse to aid us in forming any conception of such a being.

Philosophers have always talked of an *absolutely necessary* being, and have nevertheless declined to take the trouble of conceiving, whether—and how—a being of this nature is even cogitable, not to mention that its existence is actually demonstrable. A verbal definition of the conception is certainly easy enough; it is something, the non-existence of which is impossible. But does this definition throw any light upon the conditions which render it impossible to cogitate the non-existence of a thing—conditions which we wish to ascertain, that we may discover whether we think anything in the conception of such a being or not? For the mere fact that I throw away, by means of the word *Unconditioned*, all the conditions which the understanding habitually requires in order to regard anything as necessary, is very far from making clear whether by means of the conception of the unconditionally necessary I think of something, or really of nothing at all.

Nay, more, this chance-conception, now become so current, many have endeavored to explain by examples, which seemed to render any inquiries regarding its intelligibility quite needless. Every geometrical proposition—a triangle has three angles—it was said, is absolutely necessary; and thus people talked of an object which lay out of the sphere of our understanding as if it were perfectly plain what the conception of such a being meant.

All the examples adduced have been drawn, without exception, from *judgments,* and not from *things.* But the unconditioned necessity of a judgment does not form the absolute necessity of a thing. On the contrary, the absolute necessity of a judgment is only a conditioned necessity of a thing, or of the predicate in a judgment. The proposition above-mentioned, does not enounce that three angles necessarily exist, but, upon condition that a triangle exists, three angles must necessarily exist—in it. And thus this logical necessity has been the source of the greatest delusions. Having formed an *à priori* conception of a thing, the content of which was made to embrace existence, we believed ourselves safe in concluding that, because existence belongs necessarily to the object of the conception (that is, under the condition of my positing this thing as given), the existence of the thing is also posited necessarily, and that it is therefore absolutely necessary—merely because its existence has been cogitated in the conception.

If, in an identical judgment, I annihilate the predicate in thought, and retain the subject, a contradiction is the result; and hence I say, the former belongs necessarily to the latter. But if I suppress both subject and predicate in thought, no contradiction arises; for there *is nothing* at all, and therefore no means of forming a contradiction. To suppose the existence of a triangle and not that of its three angles, is self-contradictory; but to suppose the non-existence of both triangle and angles is perfectly admissible. And so is it with the conception of an absolutely necessary being. Annihilate its existence in thought, and you annihilate the thing itself with all its predicates; how then can there be any room for contradiction? Externally, there is nothing to give rise to a contradiction, for a thing cannot be necessary externally; nor internally, for, by the annihilation or suppression of the thing itself, its internal properties are also annihilated. God is omnipotent—that is a necessary judgment. His omnipotence cannot be denied, if the existence of a Deity is posited—the existence, that is, of an infinite being, the two conceptions being identical. But when you say, *God does not exist*, neither omnipotence nor any other predicate is affirmed; they must all disappear with the subject, and in this judgment there cannot exist the least self-contradiction.

You have thus seen, that when the predicate of a judgment is annihilated in thought along with the subject, no internal contradiction can arise, be the predicate what it may. There is no possibility of evading the conclusion—you find yourselves compelled to declare: There are certain subjects which cannot be annihilated in thought. But this is nothing more than saying: There exist subjects which are absolutely necessary—the very hypothesis which you are called upon to establish. For I find myself unable to form the slightest conception of a thing which, when annihilated in thought with all its predicates, leaves behind a contradiction; and contradiction is the only criterion of impossibility, in the sphere of pure *à priori* conceptions.

Against these general considerations, the justice of which no one can dispute, one argument is adduced, which is regarded as furnishing a satisfactory demonstration from the fact. It is affirmed, that there is one and only one conception, in which the non-being or annihilation of the object is self-contradictory, and this is the conception of an *ens realissimum*. It possesses, you say, all reality, and you feel yourselves justified in admitting the possibility of such a being. (This I am willing to grant for the present, although the existence of a conception which is not self-contradictory, is far from being sufficient to prove the possibility of an object.*) Now the notion of all reality embraces in it that of existence; the notion of existence lies, therefore, in the conception of this possible thing. If this thing is annihilated in thought, the internal possibility of the thing is also annihilated, which is self-contradictory.

I answer: It is absurd to introduce—under whatever term disguised—into

---

*A conception is always possible, if it is not self-contradictory. This is the logical criterion of possibility, distinguishing the object of such a conception from the *nihil negativum*. But it may be, notwithstanding, an empty conception, unless the objective reality of this synthesis, by which it is generated, is demonstrated; and a proof of this kind must be based upon principles of possible experience, and not upon the principle of analysis or contradiction. This remark may be serviceable as a warning against concluding, from the possibility of a conception—which is logical, the possibility of a thing—which is real.

the conception of a thing, which is to be cogitated solely in reference to its possibility, the conception of its existence. If this is admitted, you will have apparently gained the day, but in reality have enounced nothing but a mere tautology. I ask, is the proposition, *this or that thing* (which I am admitting to be possible) *exists*, an analytical or a synthetical proposition? If the former, there is no addition made to the subject of your thought by the affirmation of its existence; but then the conception in your minds is identical with the thing itself, or you have supposed the existence of a thing to be possible, and then inferred its existence from its internal possibility—which is but a miserable tautology. The word *reality* in the conception of the thing, and the word *existence* in the conception of the predicate, will not help you out of the difficulty. For, supposing you were to term all positing of a thing, reality, you have thereby posited the thing with all its predicates in the conception of the subject and assumed its actual existence, and this you merely repeat in the predicate. But if you confess, as every reasonable person must, that every existential proposition is synthetical, how can it be maintained that the predicate of existence cannot be denied without contradiction—a property which is the characteristic of analytical propositions, alone.

I should have a reasonable hope of putting an end forever to this sophistical mode of argumentation, by a strict definition of the conception of existence, did not my own experience teach me that the illusion arising from our confounding a logical with a real predicate (a predicate which aids in the determination of a thing) resists almost all the endeavors of explanation and illustration. A *logical predicate* may be what you please, even the subject may be predicated of itself; for logic pays no regard to the content of a judgment. But the determination of a conception is a predicate, which adds to and enlarges the conception. It must not, therefore, be contained in the conception.

Being is evidently not a real predicate, that is, a conception of something which is added to the conception of some other thing. It is merely the positing of a thing, or of certain determinations in it. Logically, it is merely the copula of a judgment. The proposition, *God is omnipotent*, contains two conceptions, which have a certain object or content; the word *is*, is no additional predicate—it merely indicates the relation of the predicate to the subject. Now, if I take the subject (God) with all its predicates (omnipotence being one), and say, *God is*, or, *There is a God*, I add no new predicate to the conception of God, I merely posit or affirm the existence of the subject with all its predicates—I posit the *object* in relation to my *conception*. The content of both is the same; and there is no addition made to the conception, which expresses merely the possibility of the object, by my cogitating the object—in the expression, it *is*—as absolutely given or existing. Thus the real contains no more than the possible. A hundred real dollars contain no more than a hundred possible dollars. For, as the latter indicate the conception, and the former the object, on the supposition that the content of the former was greater than that of the latter, my conception would not be an expression of the whole object, and would consequently be an inadequate conception of it. But in reckoning my wealth there may be said to be more in a hundred real dollars, than in a hundred possible dollars—that is, in the mere conception of them. For the real object—the dollars—is not analytically contained in my conception, but forms a synthetical addition to my conception (which is merely a determination of my mental state), although this objective reality—this existence—apart from my conception, does not in the least degree increase the aforesaid hundred dollars.

By whatever and by whatever number of predicates—even to the complete determination of it—I may cogitate a thing I do not in the least augment the object of my conception by the addition of the statement, this thing exists. Otherwise, not exactly the same, but something more than what was cogitated in my conception, would exist, and I could not affirm that the exact object of my conception had real existence. If I cogitate a thing as containing all modes of reality except one, the mode of reality which is absent is not added to the conception of the thing by the affirmation that the thing exists; on the contrary, the thing exists—if it exist at all—with the same defect as that cogitated in its conception; otherwise not that which was cogitated, but something different, exists. Now, if I cogitate a being as the highest reality, without defect or imperfection, the question still remains—whether this being exists or not? For although no element is wanting in the possible real content of my conception, there is a defect in its relation to my mental state, that is, I am ignorant whether the cognition of the object indicated by the conception is possible *à posteriori*. And here the cause of the present difficulty becomes apparent. If the question regarded an object of sense merely, it would be impossible for me to confound the conception with the existence of a thing. For the conception merely enables me to cogitate an object as according with the general conditions of experience; while the existence of the object permits me to cogitate it as contained in the sphere of actual experience. At the same time, this connection with the world of experience does not in the least augment the conception, although a possible perception has been added to the experience of the mind. But if we cogitate existence by the pure category alone, it is not to be wondered at, that we should find ourselves unable to present any criterion sufficient to distinguish it from mere possibility.

Whatever be the content of our conception of an object, it is necessary to go beyond it, if we wish to predicate existence of the object. In the case of sensuous objects, this is attained by their connection according to empirical laws with some one of my perceptions; but there is no means of cognizing the existence of objects of pure thought, because it must be cognized completely *à priori*. But all our knowledge of existence (be it immediately by perception, or by inferences connecting some object with a perception) belongs entirely to the sphere of experience—which is in perfect unity with itself—and although an existence out of this sphere cannot be absolutely declared to be impossible, it is a hypothesis the truth of which we have no means of ascertaining.

The notion of a supreme being is in many respects a highly useful idea; but for the very reason that it is an idea, it is incapable of enlarging our cognition with regard to the existence of things. It is not even sufficient to instruct us as to the possibility of a being which we do not know to exist. The analytical criterion of possibility, which consists in the absence of contradiction in propositions, cannot be denied it. But the connection of real properties in a thing is a synthesis of the possibility of which an *à priori* judgment cannot be formed, because these realities are not presented to us specifically; and even if this were to happen, a judgment would still be impossible, because the criterion of the possibility of synthetical cognitions must be sought for in the world of experience, to which the object of an idea cannot belong. And thus the celebrated Leibnitz has utterly failed in his attempt to establish upon *à priori* grounds the possibility of this sublime ideal being.

The celebrated ontological or Cartesian argument for the existence of a Supreme Being is therefore insufficient; and we may as well hope to increase our stock of knowledge by the aid of mere ideas, as the merchant to augment his wealth by the addition of noughts to his cash-account.

Contingency: The Cosmological Argument

18. Summa Theologica

SAINT THOMAS AQUINAS

THE FIVE WAYS

The existence of god can be proved in five ways.

The first and more manifest way is the argument from motion. It is certain, and evident to our senses, that in the world some things are in motion. Now whatever is in motion is put in motion by another, for nothing can be in motion except it is in potentiality to that towards which it is in motion; whereas a thing moves inasmuch as it is in act. For motion is nothing else than the reduction of something from potentiality to actuality. But nothing can be reduced from potentiality to actuality, except by something in a state of actuality. Thus that which is actually hot, as fire, makes wood, which is potentially hot, to be actually hot, and thereby moves and changes it. Now it is not possible that the same thing should be at once in actuality and potentiality in the same respect, but only in different respects. For what is actually hot cannot simultaneously be potentially hot; but it is simultaneously potentially cold. It is therefore impossible that in the same respect and in the same way a thing should be both mover and moved, i.e., that it should move itself. Therefore, whatever is in motion must be put in motion by another. If that by which it is put in motion be itself put in motion, then this also must needs be put in motion by another, and that by another again. But this cannot go on to infinity, because then there would be no first mover, and, consequently, no other mover; seeing that subsequent movers move only inasmuch as they are put in motion by the first mover; as the staff moves only because it is put in motion by the hand. Therefore it is necessary to arrive at a first mover, put in motion by no other; and this everyone understands to be God.

The second way is from the nature of the efficient cause. In the world of sense we find there is an order of efficient causes. There is no case known (neither is it, indeed, possible) in which a thing is found to be the efficient cause of itself; for so it would be prior to itself, which is impossible. Now in efficient causes it is not possible to go on to infinity, because in all efficient causes following in order, the first is the cause of the intermediate cause, and the intermediate is the cause of the ultimate cause, whether the intermediate cause be several or one only. Now to take away the cause is to take away the effect. Therefore, if there be no first cause among efficient causes, there will be no ultimate, nor any intermediate cause. But if in efficient causes it is possible to go on to infinity, there will be no first efficient cause, neither will there be an ultimate effect, nor any intermediate efficient causes; all of which is plainly false. Therefore it is necessary to admit a first efficient cause, to which everyone gives the name of God.

The third way is taken from possibility and necessity and runs thus. We find in nature things that are possible to be and not to be, since they are found to be generated, and to corrupt, and consequently, they are possible to be and not to be. But it is impossible for these always to exist, for that which is possible not to be at some time is not. Therefore, if everything is possible not to be, then at one time there could have been nothing in existence. Now if this were true, even now there would be nothing in existence, because that which does not exist only begins to exist by something already existing. Therefore, if at one time nothing was in existence, it would have been impossible for anything to have begun to exist; and thus even now nothing would be in existence—which is absurd. Therefore, not all beings are merely possible, but there must exist something the existence of which is necessary. But every necessary thing either has its necessity caused by another, or not. Now it is impossible to go on to infinity in necessary things which have their necessity caused by another, as has been already proved in regard to efficient causes. Therefore we cannot but postulate the existence of some being having of itself its own necessity, and not receiving it from another, but rather causing in others their necessity. This all men speak of as God.

The fourth way is taken from the gradation to be found in things. Among beings there are some more and some less good, true, noble, and the like. But "more" and "less" are predicated of different things, according as they resemble in their different ways something which is the maximum, as a thing is said to be hotter according as it more nearly resembles that which is hottest; so that there is something which is truest, something best, something noblest, and, consequently, something which is uttermost being; for those things that are greatest in truth are greatest in being, as it is written in *Metaph*. ii. Now the maximum in any genus is the cause of all in that genus; as fire, which is the maximum of heat, is the cause of all hot things. Therefore there must also be something which is to all beings the cause of their being, goodness, and every other perfection; and this we call God.

The fifth way is taken from the governance of the world. We see that things which lack intelligence, such as natural bodies, act for an end, and this is evident from their acting always, or nearly always, in the same way, so as to obtain the best result. Hence it is plain that not fortuitously, but designedly, do they achieve their end. Now whatever lacks intelligence cannot move towards an end, unless it be directed by some being endowed with knowledge and intelligence; as the arrow is shot to its mark by the archer. Therefore some intelligent being exists by whom all natural things are directed to their end; and this being we call God.

19. A Reformulation of the Argument from Contingency

RICHARD TAYLOR

An active, living, and religious belief in the gods has probably never arisen and been maintained on purely metaphysical grounds. Such beliefs are found in every civilized land and time, and are often virtually universal in a particular culture, yet relatively few men have much of a conception of metaphysics. There are in fact entire cultures, such as ancient Israel, to whom metaphysics is quite foreign, though these cultures may nevertheless be religious.

Belief in the gods seems to have its roots in human desires and fears, particularly those associated with self-preservation. Like all other creatures, men have a profound will to live, which is what mainly gives one's existence a meaning from one sunrise to the next. Unlike other creatures, however, men are capable of the full and terrible realization of their own inevitable decay. A man can bring before his mind the image of his own grave, and with it the complete certainty of its ultimate reality, and against this his will naturally recoils. It can hardly seem to him less than an absolute catastrophe, the very end, so far as he is concerned, of everything, though he has no difficulty viewing death, as it touches others more or less remote from himself, as a perhaps puzzling, occasionally distressing, but nonetheless necessary aspect of nature. It is probably partly in response to this fear that he turns to the gods, as those beings of such power that they can overturn this verdict of nature.

The sources of religious belief are doubtless much more complex than this, but they seem to lie in man's will rather than in his speculative intelligence, nevertheless. Men who possess such a belief seldom permit any metaphysical considerations to wrest it from them, while those who lack it are seldom turned toward it by other metaphysical considerations. Still, in every land in which philosophy has flourished, there have been profound thinkers who have sought to discover some metaphysical basis for a rational belief in the existence of some supreme being or beings. Even though religion may properly be a matter of faith rather than reason, still, a philosophical person can hardly help wondering whether it might, at least in part, be also a matter of reason, and whether, in particular, the existence of God might be something that can be not merely believed but shown. It is this question that we want now to consider; that is, we want to see whether there are not strong metaphysical considerations from which the existence of some supreme and supranatural being might reasonably be inferred.

THE PRINCIPLE OF SUFFICIENT REASON

Suppose you were strolling in the woods and, in addition to the sticks, stones, and other accustomed litter of the forest floor, you one day came upon some quite unaccustomed object, something not quite like what you had ever seen before and would never expect to find in such a place. Suppose, for example, that it is a large ball, about your own height, perfectly smooth and translucent. You would deem this puzzling and mysterious, certainly, but if one considers the matter, it is no more inherently mysterious that such a thing should exist than that anything else should exist. If you were quite accustomed to finding such objects of various sizes around you most of the time, but had never seen an ordinary rock, then upon finding a large rock in the woods one day you would be just as puzzled and mystified. This illustrates the fact that something that is mysterious ceases to seem so simply by its accustomed presence. It is strange indeed, for example, that a world such as ours should exist; yet few men are very often struck by this strangeness, but simply take it for granted.

Suppose, then, that you have found this translucent ball and are mystified by it. Now whatever else you might wonder about it, there is one thing you would hardly question; namely, that it did not appear there all by itself, that it owes its existence to something. You might not have the remotest idea whence and how it came to be there, but you would hardly doubt that there was an explanation. The idea that it might have come from nothing at all, that it might exist without there being any explanation of its existence, is one that few people would consider worthy of entertaining.

This illustrates a metaphysical belief that seems to be almost a part of reason itself, even though few men ever think upon it; the belief, namely, that there is some explanation for the existence of anything whatever, some reason why it should exist rather than not. The sheer nonexistence of anything, which is not to be confused with the passing out of existence of something, never requires a reason; but existence does. That there should never have been any such ball in the forest does not require any explanation or reason, but that there should ever be such a ball does. If one were to look upon a barren plain and ask why there is not and never has been any large translucent ball there, the natural response would be to ask why there should be; but if one finds such a ball, and wonders why it is there, it is not quite so natural to ask why it should *not* be, as though existence should simply be taken for granted. That anything should not exist, then, and that, for instance, no such ball should exist in the forest, or that there should be no forest for it to occupy, or no continent containing a forest, or no earth, nor any world at all, do not seem to be things for which there needs to be any explanation or reason; but that such things should be, does seem to require a reason.

The principle involved here has been called the principle of sufficient reason. Actually, it is a very general principle, and is best expressed by saying that, in the case of any positive truth, there is some sufficient reason for it, something which, in this sense, makes it true—in short, that there is some sort of explanation, known or unknown, for everything.

Now some truths depend on something else, and are accordingly called *contingent*, while others depend only upon themselves, that is, are true by their very natures and are accordingly called *necessary*. There is, for example, a reason why the stone on my window sill is warm; namely, that the sun is shining upon it. This happens to be true, but not by its very nature. Hence, it is contingent, and depends upon something other than itself. It is also true that all the points of a circle are equidistant from the center, but this truth depends upon nothing but itself. No matter what happens, nothing can make it false. Similarly, it is a truth, and a necessary one, that if the stone on my window sill is a body, as it is, then it has a form, since this fact depends upon nothing but itself for its confirmation. Untruths are also, of course, either contingent or necessary, it being contingently false, for example, that the stone on my window sill is cold, and necessarily false that it is both a body and formless, since this is by its very nature impossible.

The principle of sufficient reason can be illustrated in various ways, as we have done, and if one thinks about it, he is apt to find that he presupposes it in his thinking about reality, but it cannot be proved. It does not appear to be itself a necessary truth, and at the same time it would be most odd to say it is contingent. If one were to try proving it, he would sooner or later have to appeal to considerations that are less plausible than the principle itself. Indeed, it is hard to see how one could even make an argument for it, without already assuming it. For this reason it might properly be called a presupposition of reason itself. One can deny that it is true, without embarrassment or fear of refutation, but one is then apt to find that what he is denying is not really what the prinicple asserts. We shall, then, treat it here as a datum—not something that is probably true, but as something which all men, whether they ever reflect upon it or not, seem more or less to presuppose.

THE EXISTENCE OF A WORLD

It happens to be true that something exists, that there is, for example, a world, and while no one ever seriously supposes that this might not be so, that there might exist nothing at all, there still seems to be nothing the least necessary in this, considering it just by itself. That no world should ever exist at all is perfectly comprehensible and seems to express not the slightest absurdity. Considering any particular item in the world it seems not at all necessary in itself that it should ever have existed, nor does it appear any more necessary that the totality of these things, or any totality of things, should ever exist.

From the principle of sufficient reason it follows, of course, that there must be a reason, not only for the existence of everything in the world but for the world itself, meaning by "the world" simply everything that ever does exist, except God, in case there is a god. This principle does not imply that there must be some purpose or goal for everything, or for the totality of all things; for explanations need not be, and in fact seldom are, teleological or purposeful. All the principle requires is that there be some sort of reason for everything. And it would certainly be odd to maintain that everything in the world owes its existence to something, that nothing in the world is either purely accidental, or such that it just bestows its own being upon itself, and then to deny this of the world itself. One can indeed *say* that the world is in some sense a pure accident, that there simply is no reason at all why this or any world should exist, and one can equally say that the world exists by its very nature, or is an inherently necessary being. But it is at least very odd and arbitrary to deny of this existing world the need for any sufficient reason, whether independent of itself or not, while presupposing that there is a reason for every other thing that ever exists.

Consider again the strange ball that we imagine has been found in the forest. Now we can hardly doubt that there must be an explanation for the existence of such a thing, though we may have no notion what that explanation is. It is not, moreover, the fact of its having been found in the forest rather than elsewhere that renders an explanation necessary. It matters not in the least where it happens to be, for our question is not how it happens to be *there* but how it happens to exist at all. If we in our imagination annihilate the forest, leaving only this ball in an open field, our conviction that it is a contingent thing and owes its existence to something other than itself is not reduced in the least. If we now imagine the field to be annihilated, and in fact everything else as well to vanish into nothingness, leaving only this ball to constitute the entire physical universe, then we cannot for a moment suppose that its existence has thereby been explained, or the need of any explanation eliminated, or that its existence is suddenly rendered self-explanatory. If we now carry this thought one step further and suppose that no other reality ever has existed or ever will exist, that this ball forever constitutes the entire physical universe, then we must still insist on there being some reason independent of itself why it should exist rather than not. If there must be a reason for the existence of any particular thing, then the necessity of such a reason is not eliminated by the mere supposition that certain other things do *not* exist. And again, it matters not at all what the thing in question is, whether it be large and complex, such as the world we actually find ourselves in, or whether it be something small, simple and insignificant, such as a ball, a bacterium, or the merest grain of sand. We do not avoid the necessity of a reason for the existence of something merely by describing it in this way or that. And it would, in any event, seem quite plainly absurd to say that if the world were comprised entirely of a single ball about six feet in diameter, or of a single grain of sand, then it would be contingent and there would have to be some explanation other than itself why such a thing exists, but that, since the actual world is vastly more complex than this, there is no need for an explanation of its existence, independent of itself.

BEGINNINGLESS EXISTENCE

It should now be noted that it is no answer to the question, why a thing exists, to state *how long* it has existed. A geologist does not suppose that he has explained why there should be rivers and mountains merely by pointing out that they are old. Similarly, if one were to ask, concerning the ball of which we have spoken, for some sufficient reason for its being, he would not receive any answer upon being told that it had been there since yesterday. Nor would it be any better answer to say that it had existed since before anyone could remember, or even that it had always existed; for the question was not one concerning its age but its existence. If, to be sure, one were to ask where a given thing came from, or how it came into being, then upon learning that it had always existed he would learn that it never really *came* into being at all; but he could still reasonably wonder why it should exist at all. If, accordingly, the world—that is, the totality of all things excepting God, in case there is a god—had really no beginning at all, but has always existed in some form or other, then there is clearly no answer to the question, where it came from and when; it did not, on this supposition, *come* from anything at all, at any time. But still, it can be asked why there is a world, why indeed there is a beginningless world, why there should have perhaps always been something rather than nothing. And, if the principle of sufficient reason is a good principle, there must be an answer to that question, an answer that is by no means supplied by giving the world an age, or even an infinite age.

CREATION

This brings out an important point with respect to the concept of creation that is often misunderstood, particularly by those whose thinking has been influenced by Christian ideas. People tend to think that creation—for example, the creation of the world by God—*means* creation *in time,* from which it of course logically follows that if the world had no beginning in time, then it cannot be the creation of God. This, however, is erroneous, for creation means essentially *dependence,* even in Christian theology. If one thing is the creation of another, then it depends for its existence on that other, and this is perfectly consistent with saying that both are eternal, that neither ever came into being, and hence, that neither was ever created at any point of time. Perhaps an analogy will help convey this point. Consider, then, a flame that is casting beams of light. Now there seems to be a clear sense in which the beams of light are dependent for their existence upon the flame, which is their source, while the flame, on the other hand, is not similarly dependent for its existence upon them. The beams of light arise from the flame, but the flame does not arise from them. In this sense, they are the creation of the flame; they derive their existence from it. And none of this has any reference to time; the relationship of dependence in such a case would not be altered in the slightest if we supposed that the flame, and with it the beams of light, had always existed, that neither had ever *come* into being.

Now if the world is the creation of God, its relationship to God should be thought of in this fashion; namely, that the world depends for its existence upon God, and could not exist independently of God. If God is eternal, as those who believe in God generally assume, then the world may (though it need not) be eternal too, without that altering in the least its dependence upon God for its existence, and hence without altering its being the creation of God. The supposition of God's eternality, on the other hand, does not by itself imply that the world is eternal too; for there is not the least reason why something of finite duration might not depend for its existence upon something of infinite duration—though the reverse is, of course, impossible.

GOD

If we think of God as "the creator of heaven and earth," and if we consider heaven and earth to include everything that exists except God, then we appear to have, in the foregoing considerations, fairly strong reasons for asserting that God, as so conceived, exists. Now of course most people have much more in mind than this when they think of God, for religions have ascribed to God ever so many attributes that are not at all implied by describing him merely as the creator of the world; but that is not relevant here. Most religious persons do, in any case, think of God as being at least the creator, as that being upon which everything ultimately depends, no matter what else they may say about him in addition. It is, in fact, the first item in the creeds of Christianity that God is the "creator of heaven and earth." And, it seems, there are good metaphysical reasons, as distinguished from the persuasions of faith, for thinking that such a creative being exists.

If, as seems clearly implied by the principle of sufficient reason, there must be a reason for the existence of heaven and earth—i.e., for the world—then that reason must be found either in the world itself, or outside it, in something that is literally supranatural, or outside heaven and earth. Now if we suppose that the world—i.e., the totality of all things except God—contains within itself the reason for its existence, we are supposing that it exists by its very nature, that is, that it is a necessary being. In that case there would, of course, be no reason for saying that it must depend upon God or anything else for its existence; for if it exists by its very nature, then it depends upon nothing but itself, much as the sun depends upon nothing but itself for its heat. This, however, is implausible, for we find nothing about the world or anything in it to suggest that it exists by its own nature, and we do find, on the contrary, ever so many things to suggest that it does not. For in the first place, anything which exists by its very nature must necessarily be eternal and indestructible. It would be a self-contradiction to say of anything that it exists by its own nature, or is a necessarily existing thing, and at the same time to say that it comes into being or passes away, or that it ever could come into being or pass away. Nothing about the world seems at all like this, for concerning anything in the world, we can perfectly easily think of it as being annihilated, or as never having existed in the first place, without there being the slightest hint of any absurdity in such a supposition. Some of the things in the universe are, to be sure, very old; the moon, for example, or the stars and the planets. It is even possible to imagine that they have always existed. Yet it seems quite impossible to suppose that they owe their existence to nothing but themselves, that they bestow existence upon themselves by their very natures, or that they are in themselves things of such nature that it would be impossible for them not to exist. Even if we suppose that something, such as the sun, for instance, has existed forever, and will never cease, still we cannot conclude just from this that it exists by its own nature. If, as is of course very doubtful, the sun has existed forever and will never cease, then it is possible that its heat and light have also existed forever and will never cease; but that would not show that the heat and light of the sun exist by their own natures. They are obviously contingent and depend on the sun for their existence, whether they are beginningless and everlasting or not.

There seems to be nothing in the world, then, concerning which it is at all plausible to suppose that it exists by its own nature, or contains within itself the reason for its existence. In fact, everything in the world appears to be quite plainly the opposite, namely, something that not only need not exist, but at some time or other, past or future or both, does not in fact exist. Everything in the world seems to have a finite duration, whether long or short. Most things, such as ourselves, exist only for a short while; they come into being, then soon cease. Other things, like the heavenly bodies, last longer, but they are still corruptible, and from all that we can gather about them, they too seem destined eventually to perish. We arrive at the conclusion, then, that while the world may contain some things which have always existed and are destined never to perish, it is nevertheless doubtful that it contains any such thing and, in any case, everything in the world is capable of perishing, and nothing in it, however long it may already have existed and however long it may yet remain, exists by its own nature, but depends instead upon something else.

While this might be true of everything in the world, is it necessarily true of the world itself? That is, if we grant, as we seem forced to, that nothing in the world exists by its own nature, that everything in the world is contingent and perishable, must we also say that the world itself, or the totality of all these perishable things, is also contingent and perishable? Logically, we are not forced to, for it is logically possible that the totality of all perishable things might itself be imperishable, and hence, that the world might exist by its own nature, even though it is comprised exclusively of things which are contingent. It is not logically necessary that a totality should share the defects of its members. For example, even though every man is mortal, it does not follow from this that the human race, or the totality of all men, is also mortal; for it is possible that there will always be human beings, even though there are no human beings which will always exist. Similarly, it is possible that the world is in itself a necessary thing, even though it is comprised entirely of things that are contingent.

This is logically possible, but it is not plausible. For we find nothing whatever about the world, any more than in its parts, to suggest that it exists by its own nature. Concerning anything in the world, we have not the slightest difficulty in supposing that it should perish, or even, that it should never have existed in the first place. We have almost as little difficulty in supposing this of the world itself. It might be somewhat hard to think of everything as utterly perishing and leaving no trace whatever of its ever having been, but there seems to be not the slightest difficulty in imagining that the world should never have existed in the first place. We can, for instance, perfectly easily suppose that nothing in the world had ever existed except, let us suppose, a single grain of sand, and we can thus suppose that this grain of sand has forever constituted the whole universe. Now if we consider just this grain of sand, it is quite impossible for us to suppose that it exists by its very nature, and could never have failed to exist. It clearly depends for its existence upon something other than itself, if it depends on anything at all. The same will be true if we consider the world to consist, not of one grain of sand, but of two, or of a million, or, as we in fact find, of a vast number of stars and planets and all their minuter parts.

It would seem, then, that the world, in case it happens to exist at all— and this is quite beyond doubt—is contingent and thus dependent upon something other than itself for its existence, if it depends upon anything at all. And it must depend upon something, for otherwise there could be no reason why it exists in the first place. Now that upon which the world depends must be something that either exists by its own nature or does not. If it does not exist by its own nature, then it, in turn, depends for its existence upon something else, and so on. Now then, we can say either of two things; namely, (1) that the world depends for its existence upon something else, which in turn depends on still another thing, this depending upon still another, *ad infinitum;* or (2) that the world derives its existence from something that exists by its own nature and which is accordingly eternal and imperishable, and is the creator of heaven and earth. The first of these alternatives, however, is impossible, for it does not render a sufficient reason why anything should exist in the first place. Instead of supplying a reason why any world should exist, it repeatedly begs off giving a reason. It explains what is dependent and perishable in terms of what is itself dependent and perishable, leaving us still without a reason why perishable things should exist at all, which is what we are seeking. Ultimately, then, it would seem that the world, or the totality of contingent or perishable things, in case it exists at all, must depend upon something that is necessary and imperishable, and which accordingly exists, not in dependence upon something else, but by its own nature.

"SELF-CAUSED"

What has been said thus far gives some intimation of what meaning should be attached to the concept of a self-caused being, a concept that is quite generally misunderstood, sometimes even by scholars. To say that something—God, for example—is self-caused, or is the cause of its own existence, does not mean that this being brings itself into existence, which is a perfectly absurd idea. Nothing can *bring* itself into existence. To say that something is self-caused (*causa sui*) means only that it exists, not contingently or in dependence upon something else, but by its own nature, which is only to say that it is a being which is such that it can neither come into being nor perish. Now whether such a being in fact exists or not, there is in any case no absurdity in the idea. We have found, in fact, that the principle of sufficient reason seems to point to the existence of such a being, as that upon which the world, with everything in it, must ultimately depend for its existence.

"NECESSARY BEING"

A being that depends for its existence upon nothing but itself, and is in this sense self-caused, can equally be described as a necessary being; that is to say, a being that is not contingent, and hence not perishable. For in the case of anything which exists by its own nature, and is dependent upon nothing else, it is impossible that it should not exist, which is equivalent to saying that it is necessary. Many persons have professed to find the gravest difficulties in this concept, too, but that is partly because it has been confused with other notions. If it makes sense to speak of anything as an *impossible* being, or something which by its very nature does not exist, then it is hard to see why the idea of a necessary being, or something which in its very nature exists, should not be just as comprehensible. And of course, we have not the slightest difficulty in speaking of something, such as a square circle or a formless body, as an impossible being. And if it makes sense to speak of something as being perishable, contingent, and dependent upon something other than itself for its existence, as it surely does, then there seems to be no difficulty in thinking of something as imperishable and dependent upon nothing other than itself for its existence.

"FIRST CAUSE"

From these considerations we can see also what is properly meant by a first cause, an appellative that has often been applied to God by theologians, and which many persons have deemed an absurdity. It is a common criticism of this notion to say that there need not be any first cause, since the series of causes and effects which constitute the history of the universe might be infinite or beginningless and must, in fact, be infinite in case the universe itself had no beginning in time. This criticism, however, reflects a total misconception of what is meant by a first cause. *First* here does not mean first in time, and when God is spoken of as a first cause, he is not being described as a being which, at some time in the remote past, *started* everything. To describe God as a first cause is only to say that he is literally a *primary* rather than a secondary cause, an *ultimate* rather than a derived cause, or a being upon which all other things, heaven and earth, ultimately depend for their existence. It is, in short, only to say that God is the creator, in the sense of creation explained above. Now this, of course, is perfectly consistent with saying that the world is eternal or beginningless. As we have seen, one gives no reason for the existence of a world merely by giving it an age, even if it is supposed to have an infinite age. To use a helpful analogy, we can say that the sun is the first cause of daylight and, for that matter, of the moonlight of the night as well, which means only that daylight and moonlight ultimately depend upon the sun for their existence. The moon, on the other hand, is only a secondary or derivative cause of its light. This light would be no less dependent upon the sun if we affirmed that it had no beginning, for an ageless and beginningless light requires a source no less than an ephemeral one. If we supposed that the sun has always existed, and with it its light, then we would have to say that the sun has always been the first—i.e., the primary or ultimate—cause of its light. Such is precisely the manner in which God should be thought of, and is by theologians often thought of, as the first cause of heaven and earth.

Design: The Teleological Argument

20. Natural Theology or Evidences of the Existence and Attributes of the Deity

WILLIAM PALEY

In crossing a heath, suppose I pitched my foot against a *stone*, and were asked how the stone came to be there; I might possible answer, that, for anything I knew to the contrary, it had lain there forever: nor would it perhaps be very easy to show the absurdity of this answer. But suppose I had found a *watch* upon the ground, and it should be inquired how the watch happened to be in that place: I should hardly think of the answer which I had before given, that, for anything I knew, the watch might have always been there. Yet why should not this answer serve for the watch as well as for the stone? Why is it not as admissible in the second case, as in the first? For this reason, and for no other, viz. that, when we come to inspect the watch, we perceive (what we could not discover in the stone) that its several parts are framed and put together for a purpose, e.g., that they are so formed and adjusted as to produce motion, and that motion so regulated as to point out the hour of the day; that if the different parts had been differently shaped from what they are, of a different size from what they are, or placed after any other manner, or in any other order, than that in which they are placed, either no motion at all would have been carried on in the machine, or none which would have answered the use that is now served by it. . . . This mechanism being observed (it requires indeed an examination of the instrument, and perhaps some previous knowledge of the subject, to perceive and understand it; but being once, as we have said, observed and understood), the inference, we think, is inevitable; that the watch must have had a maker; that there must have existed, at sometime, and at some place or other, an artificer or artificers, who formed it for the purpose which we find it actually to answer; who comprehended its construction, and designed its use.

Nor would it, I apprehend, weaken the conclusion, that we had never seen a watch made, that we had never known an artist capable of making one; that we were altogether incapable of executing such a piece of workmanship ourselves, or of understanding in what manner it was performed; all this being no more than what is true of some exquisite remains of ancient art, of some lost arts, and, to the generality of mankind, of the more curious productions of modern manufacture. Does one man in a million know how oval frames are turned? Ignorance of this kind exalts our opinion of the artist's skill, if he be unseen and unknown, but raises no doubt in our minds of the existence and agency of such an artist, at some former time, and in some place or other. Nor can I perceive that it varies at all the inference, whether the question arises concerning a human agent, or concerning an agent of a different species, or an agent possessing, in some respects, a different nature.

Neither, secondly, would it invalidate our conclusion, that the watch sometimes went wrong, or that it seldom went exactly right. The purpose of the machinery, the design and the designer, might be evident, and in the case supposed would be evident, in whatever way we accounted for the irregularity of the movement, or whether we could account for it or not. It is not necessary that a machine be perfect, in order to show with what design it was made: still less necessary, where the only question is, whether it were made with any design at all.

Nor, thirdly, would it bring any uncertainty into the argument, if there were a few parts of the watch, concerning which we could not discover, or had not yet discovered, in what manner they conduced to the general effect; or even some parts, concerning which we could not ascertain whether they conduced to that effect in any manner whatever. For, as to the first branch of the case; if by the loss, or disorder, or decay of the parts in question, the movement of the watch were found in fact to be stopped, or disturbed, or retarded, no doubt would remain in our minds as to the utility or intention of these parts, although we should be unable to investigate the manner according to which, or the connexion by which, the ultimate effect depended upon their action or assistance; and the more complex is the machine, the more likely is this obscurity to arise. Then, as to the second thing supposed, namely, that there were parts which might be spared, without prejudice to the movement of the watch, and that we had proved this by experiment—these superfluous parts, even if we were completely assured that they were such, would not vacate the reasoning which we had instituted concerning other parts. The indication of contrivance remained, with respect to them, nearly as it was before.

Nor, fourthly, would any man in his senses think the existence of the watch, with its various machinery, accounted for, by being told that it was one out of possible combinations of material forms; that whatever he had found in the place where he found the watch, must have contained some internal configuration or other; and that this configuration might be the structure now exhibited, viz. of the works of a watch, as well as a different structure.

Nor, fifthly, would it yield to his inquiry more satisfaction to be answered, that there existed in things a principle of order, which had disposed the parts of the watch into their present form and situation. He never knew a watch made by the principle of order; nor can he even form to himself an idea of what is meant by a principle of order distinct from the intelligence of the watchmaker.

Sixthly, he would be surprised to hear that the mechanism of the watch was no proof of contrivance, only a motive to induce the mind to think so. . . .

Neither, lastly, would our observer be driven out of his conclusion, or from his confidence in its truth, by being told that he knew nothing at all about the matter. He knows enough for his argument. He knows the utility of the end: he knows the subserviency and adaptation of the means to the end. These points being known, his ignorance of other points, affect not the certainty of his reasoning. The consciousness of knowing little need not beget a distrust of that which he does know.

EVEN A "SELF-REPRODUCING" WATCH IMPLIES A WATCHMAKER

Suppose, in the next place, that the person who found the watch, should, after sometime, discover, that, in addition to all the properties which he had hitherto observed in it, it possessed the unexpected property of producing, in the course of its movement, another watch like itself (the thing is conceivable), that it contained within it a mechanism, a system of parts, a mould for instance, or a complex adjustment of lathes, files, and other tools, evidently and separately calculated for this purpose; let us inquire, what effect ought such a discovery to have upon his former conclusion.

The first effect would be to increase his admiration of the contrivance, and his conviction of the consummate skill of the contriver. Whether he regarded the object of the contrivance, the distinct apparatus, the intricate, yet in many parts intelligible mechanism, by which it was carried on, he would perceive in this new observation, nothing but an additional reason for doing what he had already done,—for referring the construction of the watch to design, and to supreme art. If that construction *without* this property, or which is the same thing, before this property had been noticed, proved intention and art to have been employed about it, still more strong would the proof appear, when he came to the knowledge of this farther property, the crown and perfection of all the rest.

He would reflect, that though the watch before him were, *in some sense,* the maker of the watch which was fabricated in the course of its movements, yet it was in a very different sense from that in which a carpenter, for instance, is the maker of a chair; the author of its contrivance, the cause of the relation of its parts to their use. With respect to these, the first watch was no cause at all to the second: in no such sense as this was it the author of the constitution and order, either of the parts which the new watch contained, or of the parts by the aid and instrumentality of which it was produced. We might possibly say, but with great latitude of expression, that a stream of water ground corn; but no latitude of expression would allow us to say, no stretch of conjecture could lead us to think, that the stream of water built the mill, though it were too ancient for us to know who the builder was. What the stream of water does in the affair, is neither more nor less than this; by the application of an unintelligent impulse to a mechanism previously arranged, arranged independently of it, and arranged by intelligence, an effect is produced, viz. the corn is ground. But the effect results from the arrangement. The force of the stream cannot be said to be the cause or author of the effect, still less of the arrangement. Understanding and plan in the formation of the mill were not the less necessary, for any share which the water has in grinding the corn; yet is this share the same as that which the watch would have contributed to the production of the new watch, upon the supposition assumed in the last section. Therefore:

Though it be now no longer probable, that the individual watch which our observer had found was made immediately by the hand of an artificer, yet doth not this alteration in anywise affect the inference, that an artificer had been originally employed and concerned in the production? The argument from design remains as it was. Marks of design and contrivance are no more accounted for now than they were before. In the same thing, we may ask for the cause of different properties. We may ask for the cause of the color of a body, of its hardness, of its heat; and these causes may be all different. We are now asking for the cause of that subserviency to a case, that relation to an end, which we have remarked in the watch before us. No answer is given to this question by telling us that a preceding watch produced it. There cannot be design without a designer; contrivance, without a contriver; order, without choice; arrangement, without anything capable of arranging; subserviency and relation to a purpose, without that which could intend a purpose; means suitable to an end, and executing their office in accomplishing that end, without the end ever having been contemplated, or the means accommodated to it. Arrangement, disposition of parts, subserviency of means to an end, relation of instruments to a use, imply the presence of intelligence and mind. No one, therefore, can rationally believe, that the insensible, inanimate watch, from which the watch before us issued, was the proper cause of the mechanism we so much admire in it;—could be truly said to have constructed the instrument, disposed its parts, assigned their office, determined their order, action, and mutual dependency, combined their several motions into one result, and that also a result connected with the utilities of other beings. All these properties, therefore, are as much unaccounted for as they were before.

IMPOSSIBILITY OF AN INFINITE REGRESS

Nor is anything gained by running the difficulty farther back, i.e., by supposing the watch before us to have been produced from another watch, that from a former, and so on indefinitely. Our going back ever so far brings us no nearer to the last degree of satisfaction upon the subject. Contrivance is still unaccounted for. We still want a contriver. A designing mind is neither supplied by this supposition, nor dispensed with. If the difficulty were diminished the farther we went back, by going back indefinitely we might exhaust it. And this is the only case to which this sort of reasoning applies. Where there is a tendency, or, as we increase the number of terms, a continual approach towards a limit, *there,* by supposing the number of terms to be what is called infinite, we may conceive the limit to be attained: but where there is no such tendency, or approach, nothing is effected by lengthening the series. There is no difference, as to the point in question (whatever there may be as to many points), between one series and another; between a series which is finite, and a series which is infinite. A chain, composed of an infinite number of links, can no more support itself, than a chain composed of a finite number of links. And of this we are assured (though we never *can* have tried the experiment), because, by increasing the number of links, from ten, for instance, to a hundred, from a hundred to a thousand, etc., we make not the smallest approach, we observe not the smallest tendency, towards self-support. There is no difference in this respect (yet there may be a great difference in several respects) between a chain of a greater or less length, between one chain and another, between one that is finite and one that is infinite. This very much resembles the case before us. The machine which we are inspecting demonstrates, by its construction, contrivance and design. Contrivance must have had a contriver; design, a designer; whether the machine immediately proceeded from another machine or not. That circumstance alters not the case. That other machine may, in like manner, have proceeded from a former machine: nor does that alter the case; contrivance must have had a contriver. That former one from one preceding it: no alteration still; a contriver is still necessary. No tendency is perceived, no approach towards a diminution of this necessity. It is the same with any and every succession of these machines; a succession of ten, of a hundred, of a thousand; with one series as with another; a series which is finite, as with a series which is infinite. In whatever other respects they may differ, in this they do not. In all, equally, contrivance and design are unaccounted for.

The question is not simply, How came the first watch into existence? which question, it may be pretended, is done away by supposing the series of watches thus produced from one another to have been infinite, and consequently to have had no such *first,* for which it was necessary to provide a cause. This, perhaps, would have been nearly the state of the question, if nothing had been before us but an unorganized, unmechanized substance, without mark or indication of contrivance. It might be difficult to show that such substance could not have existed from eternity, either in succession (if it were possible, which I think it is not, for unorganized bodies to spring from one another) or by individual perpetuity. But that is not the question now. To suppose it to be so, is to suppose that it made no difference whether we had found a watch or a stone. As it is, the metaphysics of that question have no place; for, in the watch which we are examining, are seen contrivance, design; an end, a purpose; means for the end, adaptation to the purpose. And the question which irresistibly presses upon our thoughts, is, whence this contrivance and design? The thing required is the intending mind, the adapting hand, the intelligence by which the hand was directed. This question, this demand, is not shaken off, by increasing a number or succession of substances, destitute of these properties; nor the more, by increasing that number to infinity. If it be said, that upon the supposition of one watch being produced from another in the course of that other's movements, and by means of the mechanism within it, we have a cause for the watch in my hand, viz. the watch from which it proceeded: I deny, that for the design, the contrivance, the suitableness of means to an end, the adaptation of instruments to a use (all means which we discover in a watch), we have any cause whatever. It is in vain, therefore, to assign a series of such causes, or to allege that a series may be carried back to infinity; for I do not admit that we have yet any cause at all of the phenomena, still less any series of causes either finite or infinite. Here is contrivance, but no contriver: proofs of design, but no designer.

Our observer would farther also reflect, that the maker of the watch before him, was, in truth and reality, the maker of every watch produced from it; there being no difference (except that the latter manifests a more exquisite skill) between the making of another watch with his own hands, by the mediation of files, lathes, chisels, etc., and the disposing, fixing, and inserting of these instruments, or of others equivalent to them, in the body of the watch already made, in such a manner as to form a new watch in the course of the movements which he had given to the old one. It is only working by one set of tools instead of another.

The conclusion which the *first* examination of the watch, of its works, construction, and movement, suggested, was, that it must have had, for the cause and author of that construction, an artificer, who understood its mechanism, and designed its use. This conclusion is invincible. A *second* examination presents us with a new discovery. The watch is found, in the course of its movement, to produce another watch, similar to itself: and not only so, but we perceive in it a system or organization, separately calculated for that purpose. What effect would this discovery have or ought it to have, upon our former inference? What, as hath already been said, but to increase, beyond measure, our admiration of the skill which had been employed in the formation of such a machine! Or shall it, instead of this, all at once turn us round to an opposite conclusion, viz. that no art or skill whatever has been concerned in the business, although all other evidences of art and skill remain as they were, and this last and supreme piece of art be now added to the rest? Can this be maintained without absurdity? Yet this is atheism.

This is atheism: for every indication of contrivance, every manifestation of design, which existed in the watch, exists in the works of nature; with the difference, on the side of nature, of being greater and more, and that in a degree which exceeds all computation. I mean, that the contrivances of nature surpass the contrivances of art, in the complexity, subtlety, and curiosity of the mechanism; and still more, if possible, do they go beyond them in number and variety: yet, in a multitude of cases, are not less evidently mechanical, not less evidently contrivances, not less evidently accommodated to their end, or suited to their office, than are the most perfect productions of human ingenuity. . . .

21. Dialogues concerning Natural Religion

DAVID HUME

PART II

Not to lose any time in circumlocutions, said Cleanthes, addressing himself to Demea, much less in replying to the pious declamations of Philo, I shall briefly explain how I conceive this matter. Look round the world, contemplate the whole and every part of it: you will find it to be nothing but one great machine, subdivided into an infinite number of lesser machines, which again admit of subdivisions to a degree beyond what human senses and faculties can trace and explain. All these various machines, and even their most minute parts, are adjusted to each other with an accuracy which ravishes into admiration all men who have ever contemplated them. The curious adapting of means to ends, throughout all nature, resembles exactly, though it much exceeds, the productions of human contrivance—of human design, thought, wisdom, and intelligence. Since therefore the effects resemble each other, we are led to infer, by all the rules of analogy, that the causes also resemble, and that the Author of nature is somewhat similar to the mind of man, though possessed of much larger faculties, proportioned to the grandeur of the work which he has executed. By this argument *a posteriori,* and by this argument alone, do we prove at once the existence of a Deity and his similarity to human mind and intelligence.

I shall be so free, Cleanthes, said Demea, as to tell you that from the beginning I could not approve of your conclusion concerning the similarity of the Deity to men, still less can I approve of the mediums by which you endeavour to establish it. What! No demonstration of the Being of God! No abstract arguments! No proofs *a priori!* Are these which have hitherto been so much insisted on by philosophers all fallacy, all sophism? Can we reach no farther in this subject than experience and probability? I will not say that this is betraying the cause of a Deity; but surely, by this affected candour, you give advantages to atheists which they never could obtain by the mere dint of argument and reasoning.

What I chiefly scruple in this subject, said Philo, is not so much that all religious arguments are by Cleanthes reduced to experience, as that they appear not to be even the most certain and irrefragable of that inferior kind. That a stone will fall, that fire will burn, that the earth has solidity, we have observed a thousand and a thousand times; and when any new instance of this nature is presented, we draw without hesitation the accustomed inference. The exact similarity of the cases gives us a perfect assurance of a similar event, and a stronger evidence is never desired nor sought after. But wherever you depart, in the least, from the similarity of the cases, you diminish proportionably the evidence, and may at last bring it to a very weak *analogy,* which is confessedly liable to error and uncertainty. After having experienced the circulation of the blood in human creatures, we make no doubt that it takes place in Titius and Maevius; but from its circulation in frogs and fishes it is only a presumption, though a strong one, from analogy that it takes place in men and other animals. The analogical reasoning is much weaker when we infer the circulation of the sap in vegetables from our experience that the blood circulates in animals; and those who hastily followed that imperfect analogy are found, by more accurate experiments, to have been mistaken.

If we see a house, Cleanthes, we conclude, with the greatest certainty, that it had an architect or builder because this is precisely that species of effect which we have experienced to proceed from that species of cause. But surely you will not affirm that the universe bears such a resemblance to a house that we can with the same certainty infer a similar cause, or that the analogy is here entire and perfect. The dissimilitude is so striking that the utmost you can here pretend to is a guess, a conjecture, a presumption concerning a similar cause; and how that pretension will be received in the world, I leave you to consider.

It would surely be very ill received, replied Cleanthes; and I should be deservedly blamed and detested did I allow that the proofs of a Deity amounted to no more than a guess or conjecture. But is the whole adjustment of means to ends in a house and in the universe so slight a resemblance? the economy of final causes? the order, proportion, and arrangement of every part? Steps of a stair are plainly contrived that human legs may use them in mounting; and this inference is certain and infallible. Human legs are also contrived for walking and mounting; and this inference, I allow, is not altogether so certain because of the dissimilarity which you remark; but does it, therefore, deserve the name only of presumption or conjecture?

Good God! cried Demea, interrupting him, where are we? Zealous defenders of religion allow that the proofs of a Deity fall short of perfect evidence! And you, Philo, on whose assistance I depended in proving the adorable mysteriousness of the Divine Nature, do you assent to all these extravagant opinions of Cleanthes? For what other name can I give them? or, why spare my censure when such principles are advanced, supported by such an authority, before so young a man as Pamphilus?

You seem not to apprehend, replied Philo, that I argue with Cleanthes in his own way, and, by showing him the dangerous consequences of his tenets, hope at last to reduce him to our opinion. But what sticks most with you, I observe, is the representation which Cleanthes has made of the argument *a posteriori;* and, finding that that argument is likely to escape your hold and vanish into air, you think it so disguised that you can scarcely believe it to be set in its true light. Now, however much I may dissent, in other respects, from the dangerous principle of Cleanthes, I must allow that he has fairly represented that argument, and I shall endeavour so to state the matter to you that you will entertain no further scruples with regard to it.

Were a man to abstract from everything which he knows or has seen, he would be altogether incapable, merely from his own ideas, to determine what kind of scene the universe must be, or to give the preference to one state or situation of things above another. For as nothing which he clearly conceives could be esteemed impossible or implying a contradiction, every chimera of his fancy would be upon an equal footing; nor could he assign any just reason why he adheres to one idea or system, and rejects the others which are equally possible.

Again, after he opens his eyes and contemplates the world as it really is, it would be impossible for him at first to assign the cause of any one event, much less of the whole of things, or of the universe. He might set his fancy a rambling, and she might bring him in an infinite variety of reports and representations. These would all be possible, but, being all equally possible, he would never of himself give a satisfactory account for his preferring one of them to the rest. Experience alone can point out to him the true cause of any phenomenon.

Now, according to this method of reasoning, Demea, it follows (and is, indeed, tacitly allowed by Cleanthes himself) that order, arrangement, or the adjustment of final causes, is not of itself any proof of design, but only so far as it has been experienced to proceed from that principle. For aught we can know *a priori*, matter may contain the source or spring of order originally within itself, as well as mind does; and there is no more difficulty in conceiving that the several elements, from an internal unknown cause, may fall into the most exquisite arrangement, than to conceive that their ideas, in the great universal mind, from a like internal unknown cause, fall into that arrangement. The equal possibility of both these suppositions is allowed. But, by experience, we find (according to Cleanthes) that there is a difference between them. Throw several pieces of steel together, without shape or form, they will never arrange themselves so as to compose a watch. Stone and mortar and wood, without an architect, never erect a house. But the ideas in a human mind, we see, by an unknown, inexplicable economy, arrange themselves so as to form the plan of a watch or house. Experience, therefore, proves that there is an original principle of order in mind, not in matter. From similar effects we infer similar causes. The adjustment of means to ends is alike in the universe, as in a machine of human contrivance. The causes, therefore, must be resembling.

I was from the beginning scandalized, I must own, with this resemblance which is asserted between the Deity and human creatures, and must conceive it to imply such a degradation of the Supreme Being as no sound theist could endure. With your assistance, therefore, Demea, I shall endeavour to defend what you justly call the adorable mysteriousness of the Divine Nature, and shall refute this reasoning of Cleanthes, provided he allows that I have made a fair representation of it.

When Cleanthes had assented, Philo, after a short pause, proceeded in the following manner.

That all inferences, Cleanthes, concerning fact are founded on experience, and that all experimental reasonings are founded on the supposition that similar causes prove similar effects, and similar effects similar causes, I shall not at present much dispute with you. But observe, I entreat you, with what extreme caution all just reasoners proceed in the transferring of experiments to similar cases. Unless the cases be exactly similar, they repose no perfect confidence in applying their past observation to any particular phenomenon. Every alteration of circumstances occasions a doubt concerning the event; and it requires new experiments to prove certainly that the new circumstances are of no moment or importance. A change in bulk, situation, arrangement, age, disposition of the air, or surrounding bodies—any of these particulars may be attended with the most unexpected consequences. And unless the objects be quite familiar to us, it is the highest temerity to expect with assurance, after any of these changes, an event similar to that which before fell under our observation. The slow and deliberate steps of philosophers here, if anywhere, are distinguished from the precipitate march of the vulgar, who, hurried on by the smallest similitude, are incapable of all discernment or consideration.

But can you think, Cleanthes, that your usual phlegm and philosophy have been preserved in so wide a step as you have taken when you compared to the universe houses, ships, furniture, machines, and, from their similarity in some circumstances, inferred a similarity in their causes? Thought, design, intelligence, such as we discover in men and other animals, is no more than one of the springs and principles of the universe, as well as heat or cold, attraction or repulsion, and a hundred others which fall under daily observation. It is an active cause by which some particular parts of nature, we find, produce alterations on other parts. But can a conclusion, with any propriety, be transferred from parts to the whole? Does not the great disproportion bar all comparison and inference? From observing the growth of a hair, can we learn anything concerning the generation of a man? Would the manner of a leaf's blowing, even though perfectly known, afford us any instruction concerning the vegetation of a tree?

But allowing that we were to take the *operations* of one part of nature upon another for the foundation of our judgment concerning the *origin* of the whole (which never can be admitted), yet why select so minute, so weak, so bounded a principle as the reason and design of animals is found to be upon this planet? What peculiar privilege has this little agitation of the brain which we call *thought*, that we must thus make it the model of the whole universe? Our partiality in our own favour does indeed present it on all occasions, but sound philosophy ought carefully to guard against so natural an illusion. . . .

PART V

But to show you still more inconveniences, continued Philo, in your anthropomorphism, please to take a new survey of your principles. *Like effects prove like causes.* This is the experimental argument; and this, you say too, is the sole theological argument. Now it is certain that the liker the effects are which are seen and the liker the causes which are inferred, the stronger is the argument. Every departure on either side diminishes the probability and renders the experiment less conclusive. You cannot doubt of the principle; neither ought you to reject its consequences.

All the new discoveries in astronomy which prove the immense grandeur and magnificence of the works of nature are so many additional arguments for a Deity, according to the true system of theism; but, according to your hypothesis of experimental theism, they become so many objections, by removing the effect still farther from all resemblance to the effects of human art and contrivance. . . . If this argument, I say, had any force in former ages, how much greater must it have at present when the bounds of Nature are so infinitely enlarged and such a magnificent scene is opened to us? It is still more unreasonable to form our idea of so unlimited a cause from our experience of the narrow productions of human design and invention.

The discoveries by microscopes, as they open a new universe in miniature, are still objections, according to you, arguments, according to me. The further we push our researches of this kind, we are still led to infer the universal cause of all to be vastly different from mankind, or from any object of human experience and observation.

And what say you to the discoveries in anatomy, chemistry, botany? . . . These surely are no objections, replied Cleanthes; they only discover new instances of art and contrivance. It is still the image of mind reflected on us from innumerable objects. Add a mind *like the human,* said Philo. I know of no other, replied Cleanthes. And the liker, the better, insisted Philo. To be sure, said Cleanthes.

Now, Cleanthes, said Philo, with an air of alacrity and triumph, mark the consequences. *First,* by this method of reasoning you renounce all claim to infinity in any of the attributes of the Deity. For, as the cause ought only to be proportioned to the effect, and the effect, so far as it falls under our cognizance, is not infinite, what pretensions have we, upon your suppositions, to ascribe that attribute to the Divine Being? You will still insist that, by removing him so much from all similarity to human creatures, we give in to the most arbitrary hypothesis, and at the same time weaken all proofs of his existence.

Secondly, you have no reason, on your theory, for ascribing perfection to the Deity, even in his finite capacity, or for supposing him free from every error, mistake, or incoherence, in his undertakings. There are many inexplicable difficulties in the works of nature which, if we allow a perfect author to be proved *a priori,* are easily solved, and become only seeming difficulties from the narrow capacity of man, who cannot trace infinite relations. But according to your method of reasoning, these difficulties become all real, and, perhaps, will be insisted on as new instances of likeness to human art and contrivance. At least, you must acknowledge that it is impossible for us to tell, from our limited views, whether this system contains any great faults or deserves any considerable praise if compared to other possible and even real systems. Could a peasant, if the *Æneid* were read to him, pronounce that poem to be absolutely faultless, or even assign to it its proper rank among the productions of human wit, he who had never seen any other production?

But were this world ever so perfect a production, it must still remain uncertain whether all the excellences of the work can justly be ascribed to the workman. If we survey a ship, what an exalted idea must we form of the ingenuity of the carpenter who framed so complicated, useful, and beautiful a machine? And what surprise must we feel when we find him a stupid mechanic who imitated others, and copied an art which, through a long succession of ages, after multiplied trials, mistakes, corrections, deliberations, and controversies, had been gradually improving? Many worlds might have been botched and bungled, throughout an eternity, ere this system was struck out; much labour lost, many fruitless trials made, and a slow but continued improvement carried on during infinite ages in the art of world-making. In such subjects, who can determine where the truth, nay, who can conjecture where the probability lies, amidst a great number of hypotheses which may be proposed, and a still greater which may be imagined?

And what shadow of an argument, continued Philo, can you produce from your hypothesis to prove the unity of the Deity? A great number of men join in building a house or ship, in rearing a city, in framing a commonwealth; why may not several deities combine in contriving and framing a world? This is only so much greater similarity to human affairs. By sharing the work among several, we may so much further limit the attributes of each, and get rid of that extensive power and knowledge which must be supposed in one deity, and which, according to you, can only serve to weaken the proof of his existence. And if such foolish, such vicious creatures as man can yet often unite in framing and executing one plan, how much more those deities or demons, whom we may suppose several degrees more perfect!

To multiply causes without necessity is indeed contrary to true philosophy, but this principle applies not to the present case. Were one deity antecedently proved by your theory who were possessed of every attribute requisite to the production of the universe, it would be needless, I own, (though not absurd) to suppose any other deity existent. But while it is still a question whether all these attributes are united in one subject or dispersed among several independent beings, by what phenomena in nature can we pretend to decide the controversy? Where we see a body raised in a scale, we are sure that there is in the opposite scale, however concealed from sight, some counterpoising weight equal to it; but it is still allowed to doubt whether that weight be an aggregate of several distinct bodies or one uniform united mass. And if the weight requisite very much exceeds anything which we have ever seen conjoined in any single body, the former supposition becomes still more probable and natural. An intelligent being of such vast power and capacity as is necessary to produce the universe, or, to speak in the language of ancient philosophy, so prodigious an animal exceeds all analogy and even comprehension.

But further, Cleanthes: Men are mortal, and renew their species by generation; and this is common to all living creatures. The two great sexes of male and female, says Milton, animate the world. Why must this circumstance, so universal, so essential, be excluded from those numerous and limited deities? Behold, then, the theogony of ancient times brought back upon us.

And why not become a perfect anthropomorphite? Why not assert the deity or deities to be corporeal, and to have eyes, a nose, mouth, ears, etc.? Epicurus maintained that no man had ever seen reason but in a human figure; therefore, the gods must have a human figure. And this argument, which is deservedly so much ridiculed by Cicero, becomes, according to you, solid and philosophical.

In a word, Cleanthes, a man who follows your hypothesis is able, perhaps, to assert or conjecture that the universe sometime arose from something like design; but beyond that position he cannot ascertain one single circumstance, and is left afterwards to fix every point of his theology by the utmost license of fancy and hypothesis. This world, for aught he knows, is very faulty and imperfect, compared to a superior standard, and was only the first rude essay of some infant deity who afterwards abandoned it, ashamed of his lame performance; it is the work only of some dependent, inferior deity, and is the object of derision to his superiors; it is the production of old age and dotage in some superannuated deity, and ever since his death has run on at adventures, from the first impulse and active force which it received from him. You justly give signs of horror, Demea, at these strange suppositions; but these, and a thousand more of the same kind, are Cleanthes' suppositions, not mine. From the moment the attributes of the Deity are supposed finite, all these have place. And I cannot, for my part, think that so wild and unsettled a system of theology is, in any respect, preferable to none at all.

22. The Existence of God

RICHARD SWINBURNE

The teleological argument, whether from temporal or spatial order, is, I believe, a codification by philosophers of a reaction to the world deeply embedded in the human consciousness. Men see the comprehensibility of the world as evidence of a comprehending creator. The prophet Jeremiah lived in an age in which the existence of a creator-god of some sort was taken for granted. What was at stake was the extent of his goodness, knowledge, and power. Jeremiah argued from the order of the world that he was a powerful and reliable god, that god was God. He argued to the power of the creator from the extent of the creation—"The host of heaven cannot be numbered, neither the sand of the sea measured"; and he argued that its regular behaviour showed the reliability of the creator, and he spoke of the "covenant of the day and night" whereby they follow each other regularly, and "the ordinances of heaven and earth,"[1] and he used their existence as an argument for the trustworthiness of the God of Jacob. The argument from temporal order has been with us ever since.

You get the argument from temporal order also in Aquinas's fifth way, which runs as follows:

> The fifth way is based on the guidedness of nature. An orderedness of actions to an end is observed in all bodies obeying natural laws, even when they lack awareness. For their behaviour hardly ever varies, and will practically always turn out well; which shows that they truly tend to a goal, and do not merely hit it by accident. Nothing however that lacks awareness tends to a goal, except under the direction of someone with awareness and with understanding; the arrow, for example requires an archer. Everything in nature, therefore is directed to its goal by someone with understanding and this we call "God."[2]

Aquinas argues that the regular behaviour of each inanimate thing shows that some animate being is directing it (making it move to achieve some purpose, attain some goal); and from that he comes—rather quickly—to the conclusion that one "being with understanding" is responsible for the behaviour of all inanimate things.

It seems to me fairly clear that no argument from temporal order—whether Aquinas's fifth way or any other argument can be a good deductive argument. For although the premiss is undoubtedly correct—a vast pervasive order characterizes the world—the step from premiss to conclusion is not a valid deductive one. Although the existence of order may be good evidence of a designer, it is surely compatible with the non-existence of one—it is hardly a logically necessary truth that all order is brought about by a person. And although, as I have urged, the supposition that one person is responsible for the orderliness of the world is much simpler and so more probable than the supposition that many persons are, nevertheless, the latter supposition seems logically compatible with the data—so

[1] Jer. 33: 20f. and 25f.
[2] St. Thomas Aquinas, *Summa Theologiae*, Ia, 2.3, trans. T. McDermott, OP (London, 1964).

we must turn to the more substantial issue of whether the argument from the temporal order of the world to God is a good inductive argument. We had reached the conclusion that either the vast uniformity in the powers and liabilities of bodies was where explanation stopped, or that God brings this about by his continuous action, through an intention constant over time.

Let us represent by *e* this conformity of the world to order, and let *h* be the hypothesis of theism. It is not possible to treat a teleological argument in complete isolation from the cosmological argument. We cannot ask how probable the premiss of the teleological argument makes theism, independently of the premiss of the cosmological argument, for the premiss of the teleological argument entails in part the premiss of the cosmological argument. That there is order of the kind described entails at least that there is a physical universe. So let *k* be now, not mere tautological evidence, but the existence of a complex physical universe (the premiss of the version of the cosmological argument to which I devoted most attention). Let us ask how much more probable does the orderliness of such a universe make the existence of God than does the mere existence of the universe.

With these fillings, we ask whether $P(h/e.k) > P(h/k)$ and by how much. As we have seen $P(h/e.k)$ will exceed $P(h/k)$ if and only if $P(e/h.k) > P(e/ \sim h.k)$. Put in words with our current fillings for *h*, *e*, and *k*, the existence of order in the world confirms the existence of God if and only if the existence of this order in the world is more probable if there is a God than if there is not. We saw in [an earlier chapter] that where *h* is the hypothesis that there is a God $P(e/h.k)$ may exceed $P(e/ \sim h.k)$, either because *e* cannot be explained in any other way and is very unlikely to occur uncaused or because God has a character such that he is more likely to bring about *e* than alternative states. With respect to the cosmological argument, I suggested that its case rested solely on the first consideration. Here I shall suggest that again the first consideration is dominant, but that the second has considerable significance also.

Let us start with the first consideration. *e* is the vast uniformity in the powers and liabilities possessed by material objects—$P(e/ \sim h.k)$ is the probability that there should be that amount of uniformity in a God-less world, that this uniform distribution of the powers of things should be where explanation terminates, that they be further inexplicable. That there should be material bodies is strange enough; but that they should all have such similar powers which they inevitably exercise, seems passing strange. It is strange enough that physical objects should have powers at all—why should they not just be, without being able to make a difference to the world? But that they should all, throughout infinite time and space, have some general powers identical to those of all other objects (and they all be made of components of very few fundamental kinds, each component of a given kind being identical in all characteristics with each other such component) and yet there be no cause of this at all seems incredible. The universe is complex . . . in that there are so many bodies of different shapes, etc., and now we find an underlying orderliness in the identity of powers and paucity of kinds of components of bodies. Yet this orderliness, if there is no explanation of it in terms of the action of God, is the orderliness of coincidence—the fact that one body has certain powers does not explain the fact that a second body has—not the simplicity of a common underlying explanation. The basic complexity remains in the vast number of different bodies in which the orderliness of identical powers and components is embodied. It is a complexity too striking to occur unexplained. It cries out for explanation in terms of some single common source with the power to produce it. Just as we would seek to explain all the coins of the realm having an identical pattern in terms of their origin from a common mould, or all of many pictures' having a common style in terms of their being painted by the same painter, so too should we seek to explain all physical objects' having the same powers in terms of their deriving them from a common source. On these grounds alone $P(e/h.k) \gg P(e/k)$, and so $P(h/e.k) \gg P(h/k)$.[3]

I think, however, that we can go further by bringing in considerations from God's character—we saw in [an earlier chapter] that God will bring about a state of affairs if it is over all a good thing that he should, he will not bring about a state of affairs if it is over all a bad thing that he should, and that he will only bring about a state of affairs if it is in some way a good thing that he should. Put in terms of reasons—he will always act on overriding reasons and cannot act except for a reason. Now there are two reasons why human beings produce order. One is aesthetic—beauty comes in the patterns of things, such as dances and songs. Some sort of order is a necessary condition of phenomena having beauty; complete chaos is just ugly—although of course not any order is beautiful. The second reason why a human being produces order is that when there is order he or other rational agents can perceive that order and utilize it to achieve ends. If we see that there is a certain pattern of order in phenomena we can then justifiably predict that that order will continue, and that enables us to make predictions about the future on which we can rely. A librarian puts books in an alphabetical order of authors in order that he and users of the library who come to know that the order is there may subsequently be able to find any book in the library very quickly (because, given knowledge of the order, we can predict whereabouts in the library any given book will be).

God has similar reasons for producing an orderly, as opposed to a chaotic universe. In so far as some sort of order is a necessary condition of beauty, and it is a good thing—as it surely is—that the world be beautiful rather than ugly, God has reason for creating an orderly universe. Secondly, I shall argue . . . that it is good that God should make finite creatures with the opportunity to grow in knowledge and power. Now if creatures are going consciously to extend their control of the world, they will need to know how to do so. There will need to be some procedures which they can find out, such that if they follow those procedures, certain events will occur. This entails the existence of temporal order. There can only be such procedures if the world is orderly, and, I should add, there can only be such procedures ascertainable by men if the order of the world is such as to be discernible by men. To take a simple example, if hitting things leads to them breaking or penetrating other things, and heating things leads to them melting, men can discover these regularities and utilize them to make artefacts such as houses, tables, and chairs. They can heat iron ore to melt it to make nails, hammers, and axes, and use the latter to break wood into the right shapes to hammer together with nails to make the artefacts. Or, if light and other electro-

---

[3] "$\gg$" means "is much greater than." "$\ll$" means "is much less than."

magnetic radiation behave in predictable ways comprehensible by men, men can discover those ways and build telescopes and radio and television receivers and transmitters. A world must evince the temporal order exhibited by laws of nature if men are to be able to extrapolate from how things have behaved in the past, to how they will behave in the future, which extrapolation is necessary if men are to have the knowledge of how things will behave in the future, which they must have in order to be able to extend their control over the world. (There would not need to be complete determinism—agents themselves could be exempt from the full rigours of determinism, and there might be violations of natural laws from time to time. But basically the world has to be governed by laws of nature if agents are consciously to extend their control of the world.) If I am right in supposing that God has reason to create finite creatures with the opportunity to grow in knowledge and power, then he has reason to create temporal order. So I suggest that God has at least these two reasons for producing an orderly world. Maybe God has reasons for not making creatures with the opportunity to grow in knowledge and power, and so the second reason for his creating an orderly universe does not apply. But with one possible, and, I shall show, irrelevant qualification, the first surely does. God may choose whether or not to make a physical universe, but if he does, he has reason for making a beautiful and so an orderly one. God has reason, if he does make a physical universe, not to make a chaotic or botched-up one. The only reason of which I can think why God should make the universe in some respects ugly would be to give to creatures the opportunity to discover the aesthetic merits of different states of affairs and through cooperative effort to make the world beautiful for themselves. But then the other argument shows that if they are to be able to exercise such an opportunity the world will need to be orderly in some respects. (There will have to be predictable regularities which creatures may utilize in order to produce beautiful states of affairs.) So, either way, the world will need to be orderly. It rather looks as if God has overriding reason to make an orderly universe if he makes a universe at all. However, as I emphasized, human inquiry into divine reasons is a highly speculative matter. But it is nevertheless one in which men are justified in reaching tentative conclusions. For God is postulated to be an agent like ourselves in having knowledge, power, and freedom, although to an infinitely greater degree than we have. The existence of the analogy legitimizes us in reaching conclusions about his purposes, conclusions which must allow for the quantitative difference, as I have tried to do.

So I suggest that the order of the world is evidence of the existence of God both because its occurrence would be very improbable *a priori* and also because, in virtue of his postulated character, he has very good, apparently overriding, reason for making an orderly universe, if he makes a universe at all. It looks as if $P(e/h.k)$ equals I. For both reasons $P(e/h.k) \gg P(e/ \sim h.k)$ and so $P(h/e.k) \gg P(h/k)$. I conclude that the teleological argument from temporal order is a good C-inductive argument to the existence of God. *

---

*Earlier in the book Swinburne distinguishes a P-inductive argument from a C-inductive argument. A P-inductive argument is one in which the premises make the conclusion probable. A C-inductive argument is one in which the premises *add* to the probability of the conclusion (i.e., make it more probable than it would otherwise be).

Let us look at the argument from a slightly different angle. It is basically an argument by analogy, an analogy between the order in the natural world (the temporal order codified in laws of nature) and the patterns of order which men often produce (the ordered books on library shelves, or the temporal order in the movements of a dancer or the notes of a song). It argues from similarity between phenomena of two kinds B and B^* to similarity between their causes A and A^*. In view of the similarities between the two kinds of order B and B^*, the theist postulates a cause (A^*) in some respects similar to A (men); yet in view of the dissimilarities the theist must postulate a cause in other respects different. All arguments by analogy do and must proceed in this way. They cannot postulate a cause in all respects similar. They postulate a cause who is such that one would expect him to produce phenomena similar to B in the respects in which B^* are similar to B and different from B in the respects in which B^* are different from B.

All argument from analogy works like this. Thus various properties of light and sound were known in the nineteenth century, among them that both light and sound are reflected, refracted, diffracted, and show interference phenomena. In the case of sound these were known to be due to disturbance of the medium, air, in which it is transmitted. What could one conclude by analogy about the cause of the reflection, etc., of light? One could conclude that the propagation of light was, like the propagation of sound, the propagation of a wave-like disturbance in a medium. But one could not conclude that it was the propagation of a disturbance in the same medium—air, since light passed through space empty of air. Scientists had to postulate a separate medium—aether, the disturbance of which was responsible for the reflection, etc., of light. And not merely does all argument by analogy proceed like this, but all inductive inference can be represented as argument by analogy. For all inductive inference depends on the assumption that in certain respects things continue the same and in other respects they differ. Thus that crude inference from a number of observed swans all having been white to the next swan's being white is an argument by analogy. For it claims that the next swan will be like the observed swans in one respect—colour, while being unlike them in other respects.

In our case the similarities between the temporal order which men produce and the temporal order in nature codified in scientific laws mean postulating as cause of the latter a person who acts intentionally. The dissimilarities between the kinds of order include the world-wide extent of the order in nature in comparison with the very narrow range of order which men produce. This means postulating as cause of the former a person of enormous power and knowledge. Now, . . . a person has a body if there is a region of the world under his direct control and if he controls other regions of the world only by controlling the former and by its movements having predictable effects on the outside world. Likewise he learns about the world only by the world having effects on this region. If these conditions are satisfied, the person has a body, and the stated region is that body. But if a person brings about directly the connections between things, including the predictable connections between the bodies of other persons and the world, there is no region of the world, goings-on in which bring about those connections. The person must bring about those connections as a basic action. His control of the world must be immediate, not mediated by a body. So the dissimilarities between the two kinds of order necessarily lead to the postulation of a non-embodied person (rather than an embodied person) as cause of the temporal order in nature.

These considerations should suffice to rebut that persistent criticism of the argument from design which we have heard ever since Hume that, taken seriously, the argument ought to be postulating an embodied god, a giant of a man. "Why not," wrote Hume, "become a perfect anthropomorphite? Why not assert the deity or deities to be corporeal, and, to have eyes, a nose, mouth, ears, etc.?" The answer is the simple one that dissimilarities between effects lead the rational man to postulate dissimilarities between causes, and that this procedure is basic to inductive inference.

It is true that the greater the dissimilarities between effects, the weaker is the argument to the existence of a similar cause; and it has been a traditional criticism of the argument from design represented as an argument by analogy that the analogy is weak. The dissimilarities between the natural world and the effects which men produce are indeed striking; but the similarities between these are also, I have been suggesting, striking—in both there is the conformity of phenomena to a simple pattern of order detectable by men. But although the dissimilarities are perhaps sufficiently great to make the argument not a good P-inductive argument, this chapter suggests that it remains a good C-inductive argument. The existence of order in the universe increases significantly the probability that there is a God, even if it does not by itself render it probable.

THE ARGUMENT FROM BEAUTY

We saw that God has reason, apparently overriding reason, for making, not merely any orderly world (which we have been considering so far) but a beautiful world— at any rate to the extent to which it lies outside the control of creatures. (And he has reason too, I would suggest, even in whatever respects the world does lie within the control of creatures, to give them experience of beauty to develop, and perhaps also some ugliness to annihilate.) So God has reason to make a basically beautiful world, although also reason to leave some of the beauty or ugliness of the world within the power of creatures to determine; but he would seem to have overriding reason not to make a basically ugly world beyond the powers of crea- tures to improve. Hence, if there is a God there is more reason to expect a basically beautiful world than a basically ugly one. . . . *A priori,* however, there is no particular reason for expecting a basically beautiful rather than a basically ugly world. In consequence, if the world is beautiful, that fact would be evidence for God's existence. For, in this case, if we let k be "there is an orderly physical universe," e be "there is a beautiful universe," and h be "there is a God," $P(e/h.k)$ will be greater than $P(e/k)$; and so by our previous principles the argument from e to h will be another good C-inductive argument.

Few, however, would deny that our universe (apart from its animal and human inhabitants, and aspects subect to their immediate control) has that beauty. Poets and painters and ordinary men down the centuries have long admired the beauty of the orderly procession of the heavenly bodies, the scattering of the galaxies through the heavens (in some ways random, in some ways orderly), and the rocks, sea, and wind interacting on earth, "The spacious firmament on high, and all the blue aethereal sky," the water lapping against "the old eternal rocks," and the plants of the jungle and of temperate climates, contrasting with the desert and the Arctic wastes. Who in his senses would deny that here is beauty in abundance? If we confine ourselves to the argument from the beauty of the inanimate and plant worlds, the argument surely works.

Bibliography

Adams, Marilyn McCord. *William Ockham.* Notre Dame, Ind.: Notre Dame University Press, 1987.

Anselm, Saint. *Basic Writings (Proslogium, Monologium, Gaunilon's On Behalf of the Fool, Cur Deus Homo)* 2d ed. La Salle, Ill.: Open Court, 1962.

Ball, Stephen W. "Hegel on Proving the Existence of God." *International Journal for Philosophy of Religion* 10 (1979): 173–200.

Barnes, Jonathan. *The Ontological Argument.* London: Macmillan; New York: St. Martin's Press, 1972.

Bobik, Joseph. *Aquinas on Being and Essence.* Notre Dame, Ind.: Notre Dame University Press, 1965.

Bonansea, Bernardino M. *God and Atheism.* Washington, D.C.: Catholic University Press, 1979.

Bouwsma, O. K. "Anselm's Argument." In *The Nature of Philosophical Inquiry,* edited by J. Bobik. Notre Dame, Ind.: University of Notre Dame Press, 1970.

Burrill, Donald R., ed. *The Cosmological Arguments, A Spectrum of Opinion.* Garden City, N.Y.: Doubleday/Anchor Books, 1967.

Caputo, John D. "Kant's Refutation of the Cosmological Argument." *Journal of the American Academy of Religion* 42 (December 1974): 686–91.

Charlesworth, M. J. *St. Anselm's Proslogion: A Reply on Behalf of the Fool, by Gaunilo; and the Author's Reply to Gaunilo.* Oxford: Clarendon Press, 1965.

Copleston, F. C. *Aquinas.* Baltimore: Penguin, 1955.

Craft, J. L., and Ronald E. Hustwit, eds. *Without Proof or Evidence: Essays of O. K. Bouwsma.* Lincoln: University of Nebraska Press, 1984.

Craig, William. *The Cosmological Argument from Plato to Leibniz.* New York: Barnes and Noble, 1980.

Delahunty, Robert. "Descartes' Cosmological Argument." *Philosophical Quarterly* 30 (January 1980): 34–46.

Descartes, René. (Meditation V) *Discourse on Method and Meditations on First Philosophy.* Translated by Donald A. Cress. Indianapolis, Ind.: Hackett, 1980.

Donceel, Joseph F. *The Searching Mind: An Introduction to a Philosophy of God.* Notre Dame, Ind.: Notre Dame University Press, 1979.

Doney, Willis. "Spinoza's Ontological Proof." In *The Philosophy of Baruch Spinoza,* edited by Richard Kennington. Washington, D.C.: Catholic University of America Press, 1980.

Donnelly, John, ed. *Logical Analysis and Contemporary Theism*. New York: Fordham University Press, 1972.

Ebersole, Frank B. "Everyman's Ontological Argument." *Philosophical Investigations* 1 (Fall 1978): 1–15.

Farrer, Austin. *Faith and Speculation*. London: Black, 1967.

Ferre, Frederick, Joseph J. Kockelmans, and John E. Smith, eds. *The Challenge of Religion: Contemporary Readings in Philosophy of Religion*. New York: Seabury Press, 1982.

Flemming, Arthur. "Omnibenevolence and Evil." *Ethics* 96 (January 1986): 261–81.

Flew, Anthony. *God and Philosophy*. New York: Dell, 1966.

———. "Hume's Philosophy of Religion." *Philosophy* 20 (1986 supplement): 129–46.

Gamwell, Franklin I. *The Divine Good: Modern Moral Theory and the Necessity of God*. San Francisco: Harper & Row, 1990.

Geach, P. "Causality and Creation." *Sophia* 1 (1962).

Gilson, Etienne. *The Christian Philosophy of St. Thomas, Part 1*. London: Gollancz, 1957.

———. *Elements of Christian Philosophy*. Garden City, N.Y.: Doubleday, 1960.

Grim, Patrick. "Plantinga's God and Other Monstrosities." *Religious Studies* 15 (March 1979): 91–97.

Grisez, Germain. *Beyond the New Theism: A Philosophy of Religion*. Notre Dame, Ind.: Notre Dame University Press, 1975.

Hartshorne, Charles. *Natural Theology for Our Time*. La Salle, Ill.: Open Court, 1950.

———. *The Logic of Perfection*. La Salle, Ill.: Open Court, 1962.

———. *Anselm's Discovery: A Re-examination of the Ontological Proof for God's Existence*. La Salle, Ill.: Open Court, 1965.

Hawkins, D. J. B. *The Essentials of Theism*. London: Sheed and Ward, 1949.

Hebblethwaite, Brian, and Stewart Sutherland, eds. *The Philosophical Frontiers of Christian Theology: Essays Presented to D. M. MacKinnon*. New York: Cambridge University Press, 1982.

Hick, John. "God as Necessary Being." *Journal of Philosophy* 57 (1960).

———. *Philosophy of Religion*. Englewood Cliffs, N.J.: Prentice-Hall, 1963.

———. *A Proof of God's Existence: Recent Essays on the Ontological Argument*. New York: Macmillan, 1965.

———. *Evil and the God of Love*. New York: Harper & Row, 1966.

———. *Arguments for the Existence of God*. New York: Herder and Herder, 1971.

Hick, J., and A. McGill, eds. *The Many-Faced Argument*. New York: Macmillan, 1965.

Hintinka, Jaakko. "Kant on Existence, Predication, and the Ontological Argument." *Dialectica* 35 (1981): 128–46.

Hume, David. *Dialogues concerning Natural Religion*. Indianapolis, Ind.: Bobbs-Merrill, 1970.

Jacobson, John R., and Robert Lloyd Mitchell, eds. *Existence of God: Essays from the Basic Issues Forum*. Lewiston, N.Y.: Mellen Press, 1988.

Kant, Immanuel. *Critique of Pure Reason*. Translated by Norman Kemp Smith. London: Macmillan, 1956.

Kenny, A. *The Five Ways*. London: Routledge and Kegan Paul, 1968.

LeMahieu, D. L. *The Mind of William Paley: A Philosopher and His Age*. Lincoln: University of Nebraska Press, 1976.

Leslie, John. *Universes*. New York: Routledge, 1989.

Loux, Michael J. *Substance and Attribute: A Study in Ontology.* Dordrecht, The Netherlands: Reidel, 1978.

Mackie, John L. *The Miracle of Theism: Arguments for and against the Existence of God.* Oxford: Clarendon Press, 1982.

MacQuarrie, John. *In Search of Deity: An Essay in Dialectical Theism.* New York: Crossroad, 1985.

Malcolm, N. "Anselm's Ontological Arguments." *Philosophical Review* 69 (January 1960): 35–62.

Mascall, E. L. *He Who Is a Study in Traditional Theism.* London: Longmans, Green, 1943.

Matson, Wallace I. *The Existence of God.* Ithaca, N.Y.: Cornell University Press, 1965.

McPherson, Thomas. *The Argument from Design.* London: Macmillan, 1972; New York: St. Martin's Press, 1972.

Meynell, Hugo Anthony. *The Intelligible Universe: A Cosmological Argument.* Totowa, N.J.: Barnes and Noble, 1982.

Miller, Eddie L. *God and Reason: A Historical Approach to Philosophical Theology.* New York: Macmillan, 1972.

Morewedge, Parviz, ed. *Islamic Philosophical Theology.* Albany: State University of New York Press, 1979.

Munitz, Milton Karl. *The Mystery of Existence: An Essay in Philosophical Cosmology.* New York: Appleton-Century-Crofts, 1965.

Neville, Robert C. *God the Creator: On the Transcendence and Presence of God.* Chicago: University of Chicago Press, 1968.

Paley, William. *Natural Theology: Selections.* Indianapolis, Ind.: Bobbs-Merrill, 1963.

Parsons, Keith M. *God and the Burden of Proof: Plantinga, Swinburne, and the Analytic Defense of Theism.* Buffalo, N.Y.: Prometheus, 1989.

Pegis, Anton C., ed. *Basic Writings of Saint Thomas Aquinas.* New York: Random House, 1945.

Plantinga, Alvin. *The Ontological Argument: From St. Anselm to Contemporary Philosophers.* Garden City, N.Y.: Doubleday/Anchor Books, 1965.

———. "Kant's Objections to the Ontological Argument." *Journal of Philosophy* 63 (October 13, 1966): 537–46.

———. *God and Other Minds.* Ithaca, N.Y.: Cornell University Press, 1967.

———. *The Nature of Necessity.* Oxford: Clarendon Press, 1974.

———. *God, Freedom and Evil.* London: Allen and Unwin, 1975.

Pottinger, Garrell. "A Formal Analysis of the Ontological Argument." *American Philosophical Quarterly* 20 (January 1983): 37–46.

Reichenbach, Bruce R. *The Cosmological Argument: A Reassessment.* Springfield, Ill.: Thomas, 1972.

Ross, James. *Philosophical Theology.* New York: Bobbs-Merrill, 1969.

Rouner, Leroy S., ed. *On Nature.* Notre Dame, Ind.: University of Notre Dame Press, 1984.

Rowe, William L. "Cosmological Argument." *Nous* 5 (Fall 1971): 49–62.

———. *The Cosmological Argument.* Princeton, N.J.: Princeton University Press, 1975.

Salmon, Wesley. "Religion and Science: A New Look at Hume's Dialogue." *Philosophical Studies* 33 (1978): 145.

Schufreider, Gregory. *An Introduction to Anslem's Argument.* Philadelphia: Temple University Press, 1978.

Shaffer, Jerome. "Existence, Predication, and the Ontological Argument." *Mind* 71 (July 1962): 307–25.

Slote, Michael A. *Reason and Scepticism.* New York: Humanities Press, 1970.

Smart, J. J. C. "Laws of Nature and Cosmic Coincidences." *Philosophic Quarterly* 35 (July 1985): 272–80.

Stark, Elizabeth. "Shifting Images of the Almighty." *Psychology Today* 19 (June 1985): 12.

Swinburne, Richard. "The Argument from Design." *Philosophy* 43 (1968): 199–212.

———. "The Problem of Evil." In *Reason and Religion,* edited by Stuart C. Brown. Ithaca, N.Y.: Cornell University Press, 1977.

———. *The Existence of God.* Oxford: Oxford University Press, 1979.

———. *The Cosmological Argument from Plato to Leibniz.* New York: Barnes and Noble, 1980.

———. "Arguments for the Existence of God." *Philosophy* 24 (1988 supplement): 121–33.

Taylor, A. E. *Does God Exist?* London: Macmillan, 1945.

Taylor, Richard. *Metaphysics.* Englewood Cliffs, N.J.: Prentice-Hall, 1963.

Tennant, F. R. *Philosophical Theology,* vol. 2. Cambridge: Cambridge University Press, 1930.

Viney, Donald Wayne. *Charles Hartshorne and the Existence of God.* Albany, N.Y.: Suny Press, 1984.

Wood, Rega. "Scotus's Argument for the Existence of God." *Franciscan Studies* 47 (1987): 257–77.

CHAPTER *4*

Further Justifications for Belief

In addition to the classic and major "proofs" for the existence of God several secondary arguments have been made that are nevertheless considered quite significant: the pragmatic arguments of Blaise Pascal, the seventeenth-century French philosopher and mathematician, and of William James, the nineteenth-century American philosopher; the argument from religious experience that has been presented by mystics throughout human history; and the moral argument, including that of the eighteenth-century German philosopher Immanuel Kant. None possess quite the stature and rational force of the medieval arguments, yet they are oddly persuasive, with an immediate appeal and unusual staying power.

Pascal's wager, a highly practical argument, aims at convincing us that belief in God is a much better bet than disbelief. Since we are thought to possess free will and have the option to be theists or atheists, we ought to follow the way of faith as the more sensible and beneficial path.

Specifically, Pascal argues that if we do not believe in God and we are wrong, then damnation awaits us, and if we do not believe and we are right, we still have a hellish existence on earth, deprived of the support that religious belief provides. On the other hand, if we do believe in God and we are wrong, we still have a happy life this side of the grave, secure in the knowledge that our divine creator provides for us. And if we believe and we are right, then we enjoy the greatest reward, eternal beatitude in heaven.

Pascal's argument seems eminently reasonable, trading on the fact that, true or false, faith is the prudent wager. Even if the worst happens and we have made a mistake in believing, it is still better than the insecurity of atheism. What's more, by opting for belief, we might just win paradise. Since no one can prove the case one way or the other—yet we have to decide the issue—it makes much more sense to believe in God.

Upon analysis, however, we wonder whether belief based on self-interest would be an acceptable form of faith. If we believe in God for our own sake—that is, because of self-love, not love of God—it is not genuine belief at all. At the very least it is un-Christian because we are only trying to save ourselves. Some theologians have also wondered about the acceptability of a God who would condemn people to hell for nonbelief. Whether or not that is consistent with the Christian deity, surely those who profess belief in God in order to win heaven would not be allowed into heaven.

Pascal has also been criticized for assuming that a theist's life is happy and an atheist's, unhappy. This is not at all certain, because theism can carry with it an oppressive quality. Theists can cower before a God of judgment, fearing divine wrath and condemnation, and never enjoy a sense of privacy or solitude. They can feel constrained by rules about sin and virtue, and be made solemn, severe, and morbid by concern with the afterlife. Atheists, on the other hand, can experience greater control over their existence since they do not have to answer to an all-seeing, all-knowing, providential God. They can satisfy their desires without guilt or shame, create their own standard of values, and determine their life purposes for themselves. Not expecting immortality, they can make the most of their time on earth, using the brevity of their existence as a catalyst to more intense living. In other words, religion has a distinctly negative side and atheism, a definitely positive one; so it is an open question as to which offers greater happiness.

Even if belief were of greater benefit, it is hard to accept something as true just because it would be good for us if we did so. We need *good reasons* as a basis for faith, or we cannot maintain any self-respect. Some truths are bitter truths, some are happy ones; but an idea does not become true because it makes us happy. Therefore, knowing how wonderful it would be if God were real is not enough. In fact, it is virtually impossible to convince ourselves that an idea is true on these grounds; it smacks too much of wishful thinking.

In the last analysis, Pascal's wager is an argument not for the existence of God but for belief in God—belief that is recommended so that we cover all options. This is not a sound basis for faith and certainly does not constitute proof of God's existence.

William James's pragmatic argument is similar, claiming that we are justified in our "will to believe" because of the positive effects that flow from that commitment—it is the most workable and expedient choice. But James's argument suffers from the same defects as that of Pascal, as the readings will reveal.

A second and highly persuasive argument in this group of selections trades on the evidence supplied by *mystical experience*. A huge body of literature exists consisting of statements by individuals who claim to have been in contact with supernatural powers. These testimonials come from different periods of history and various countries, and from people of diverse religions and individual temperaments, but they all make the same claim: that they personally experienced the presence of a spiritual force in their lives, particularly the presence of God.

The classic mystics, who have thought and written most profoundly about their religious experiences, are people such as Jacob Boehme, Emanuel Swedenborg, Jan van Ruysbroeck, Johannes Tauler, Saint Theresa, and Saint John of the

Cross. They and many quite ordinary people have referred to visions and voices of a uniquely spiritual kind, sometimes to a radiant light suffusing all objects, the blurring of the distinction between subject and object, or a universal goodness permeating themselves and others. They may have practiced automatic writing, gripped by a force that dictated the words or moved the pen in their hand. Whether exhilarated or weakened by such experiences, they all have been so deeply affected by what they have seen, heard, or felt that their lives have been transformed.

William James, the nineteenth-century American philosopher, identifies four marks of the mystic state: transiency, meaning that the experience is fleeting and ephemeral; passivity, that the person is acted upon rather than being an active seeker; noetic quality, that some previously hidden knowledge is revealed; and ineffability, that nothing of what transpired can be verbalized or communicated to those who have not had the experience themselves. This is generally taken as a definitive list of characteristics; some might be added (in particular cases), but none taken away.

The crucial question, of course, has to do with the content of the religious experience: Is it proof of a supernatural reality, most particularly, does it show evidence of the existence of God?

Many critics have pointed out that each mystic tends to bring his or her religious ideas to the experience rather than deriving them from it. Nothing new is transmitted, but the person's previous beliefs are confirmed by the unusual events. The Hindu may see Brahma, and the Christian may see Saint Paul, which suggests that there was a predisposition to interpret the experience in a particular way. Obviously, evidence of this kind is highly questionable, for self-deception is extremely probable under such conditions.

However, couldn't it be argued that, although the form of the experience is dictated by one's background, the experience is authentic nonetheless? This may be true, but it might also be the case that the individual is merely projecting his or her own expectations. If the experience were to transcend the person's culture—for example, if a Hindu or Christian should see Mohammed—then the claim of authenticity would be more convincing; but that does not happen.

Even if the experiences are genuine, how do we know which of the various accounts of God that the mystics report is the one to be trusted? There is little agreement as to the nature of the reality experienced, and although that reality could be one God revealed through the forms and images of different religions, it could also be different conceptions of God. We cannot worship an amorphous notion of the godhead but only a being of particular character, and mysticism does not tell us which specific version of God is real.

In the same vein, mysticism is also criticized because it is impossible to determine whether a genuine religious experience has occurred or simply a hallucination, symptomatic of psychosis. If people report hearing unusual voices or seeing strange shapes, we do not know whether to canonize them or institutionalize them. Because the experience is private and incommunicable, it cannot be verified empirically, and we take a great risk in trusting people who are in an extraordinary state of mind. What they experienced could be either a unique revelation or a mere delusion. As Bertrand Russell has pointed out, "We can make no distinction between the man who eats little and sees heaven and the man who drinks much and sees snakes."

Obviously, the reports of mystics cannot be entirely dismissed with these arguments. The mystic is overwhelmingly convinced of the reality of his experience, and it functions as the central event in his life. Furthermore, a large number of people who would not regard themselves as mystics in the classic sense claim to have undergone similar experiences. Despite these considerations, however, the problem of verifying the genuineness of the experience remains intractable. How does one differentiate between "God spoke to me in a dream" and "I dreamt that God spoke to me"?

A third argument that has been offered in various forms is based on the connection between *ethics and religion.* The reasoning generally runs that if we accept the genuineness of moral values as to the rightness and wrongness of conduct, then we must believe in a divine being who created these values. For example, if we think that it is right to save life and wrong to take it, we must acknowledge the existence of a God who decreed "Thou shalt not kill." In other words, if such judgments are valid, then something must validate them, and that foundation can only be God.

By arguing that a moral law implies a moral lawgiver, this argument is similar to the teleological argument that design implies designer, but it is somewhat mystical in character also. Our moral "sense" of right and wrong is said to imply a God who implanted that conscience within us, in somewhat the same way as our awareness of our soul within our body suggests the existence of a spiritual being within the physical world.

Of course, for those who do not accept the objectivity of values, this argument has no force. That is, if you think that society makes up the moral rules—for example, that life is valuable because people say so, and not that people say so because it is valuable—then there is no need to assume a God behind morality. But if you believe that whatever is right is really right, at all times and all places, then you might accept God as the basis of these objective moral values. You would then argue that taking life is wrong because there is a God who prohibited it in the Ten Commandments.

Immanuel Kant presented an interesting variation on this theme when he argued that moral goodness or virtue should be rewarded with happiness. It is offensive, Kant maintained, to see people happy who have awful characters and do not deserve their happiness. More importantly, we sometimes see virtuous people who have not been made happy in life. Here we feel frustrated in our duty to produce the "best state of the world," which includes having virtue rewarded with happiness.

To remedy the situation, we have to postulate the existence of a God powerful enough to ensure that those with good moral character do, in fact, receive happiness. Given the way the world operates, there is no guarantee of this, but the two ought to coincide. Therefore, a God must exist to provide happiness to the virtuous. The demands of morality require the assumption of a divine being who will bring justice of this kind to humanity.

Kant's theory has been criticized on the grounds that there is no *necessity* for the union of virtue and happiness to be brought about, and to postulate a God who will effect this moral ideal is more of a high-minded wish than a proof of such a God's existence. That which ought to be sometimes can be, but there is no law in the universe that declares it must be. If God existed, the virtuous would be made happy, but we cannot argue in reverse—that since there should be justice of this kind, therefore God exists to bring it about.

As for the general position that values must ultimately come from God, we are not sure that this is true. Our sense of right and wrong may not have to be derived from God's word *or,* on the other hand, be a product of our upbringing. A secular ethic that reflects objective values is logically possible.

In fact, it may be impossible to base values on the commands of God because, presumably, God would issue commands for some reason, not just arbitrarily. In other words, there must be a basis for commanding certain actions, namely, that the actions are right; and this rightness would be recognized, not created, by God. The rightness of an act would not be due to its having been commanded by God; it would exist independent of God's will altogether.

If this conclusion is true, then the acceptance of moral values does not entail belief in God. Values lie in a separate realm altogether, so that even if there were no God, one could still affirm the rightness of preserving life, keeping promises, respecting property, telling the truth, and so forth. (Chapter 6 contains a more complete treatment of this point.)

In the selections that follow we will see the complete argument used by Pascal in his wager and by William James in *The Will to Believe.* The arguments spring from an overall philosophy of pragmatism, but the specific approach that they use here is often labeled *fideism,* the view that our knowledge begins with a faith commitment and that everything depends on the strength of our initial cognitive belief (a view also held by Tertullian, Kierkegaard, and Wittgenstein). Then W. K. Clifford presents an argument against the fideistic approach, stressing the importance of intellectual integrity. Clifford's approach is *evidentialism,* the position that we should not believe anything unless it has been rationally proven—that, in fact, ethics requires that all beliefs be criticized, compared, and tested (also the view of René Descartes, John Locke, David Hume, and Bertrand Russell, who talk about having to establish a "right to believe").

In the following sections, the "marks" of the mystic state are defined by William James, and Rudolf Otto describes the nature of the holy. A skeptical attitude toward mysticism is then presented by Bertrand Russell, who argues that, although mysticism offers "breadth and calm and profundity," there is no reason to believe the assertions of the mystics to be true. In the final section the moral argument is presented by Immanuel Kant, followed by a sympathetic but critical evaluation by A. E. Taylor.

Pragmatic Reasons

23. Pensées

BLAISE PASCAL

The metaphysical proofs of God are so remote from the reasoning of men, and so complicated, that they make little impression; and if they should be of service to some, it would be only during the moment that they see such demonstration; but an hour afterwards they fear they have been mistaken. . . .

The heart has its reasons, which reason does not know. . . . It is the heart which experiences God, and not the reason. This, then is faith: God felt by the heart, not by the reason. . . .

There are only three kinds of persons: those who serve God, having found Him; others who are occupied in seeking Him, not having found Him; while the remainder live without seeking Him, and without having found Him. The first are reasonable and happy, the last are foolish and unhappy; those between are unhappy and reasonable.

MAN'S DISPROPORTION

. . . Let man then contemplate the whole of nature in her full and grand majesty, and turn his vision from the low objects which surround him. . . . The whole visible world is only an imperceptible atom in the ample bosom of nature. No idea approaches it. . . . It is an infinite sphere, the centre of which is everywhere, the circumference nowhere. In short it is the greatest sensible mark of the almighty power of God, that imagination loses itself in that thought.

Returning to himself, let man consider what he is in comparison with all existence; let him regard himself as lost in this remote corner of nature; and from the little cell in which he finds himself lodged, I mean the universe, let him estimate at their true value the earth, kingdoms, cities and himself. What is a man in the Infinite?

But to show him another prodigy equally astonishing, let him examine the most delicate things he knows. Let a mite be given him, with its minute body and parts incomparably more minute, limbs with their joints, veins in the limbs, blood in the veins, humours in the blood, drops in the humours, vapours in the drops. Dividing these last things again, let him exhaust his powers of conception, and let the last object at which he can arrive be now that of our discourse. Perhaps he will think that here is the smallest point in nature. I will let him see therein a new abyss. I will paint for him not only the visible universe, but all that he can conceive of nature's immensity in the womb of this abridged atom. Let him see therein an infinity of universes, each of which has its firmament, its planets, its earth, in the same proportion as in the visible world; in each earth animals, and in the last mites, in which he will find again all that the first had, finding still in these others the same thing without end and without cessation. Let him lose himself in wonders as amazing in their littleness as the others in their vastness. For who will not be astounded at the fact that our body, which a little while ago was imperceptible in the universe, itself imperceptible in the bosom of the whole, is now a colossus, a world, or rather a whole, in respect of the nothingness which we cannot reach? He who regards himself in this light will be afraid of himself, and observing himself sustained in the body given him by nature between those two abysses of the Infinite and Nothing, will tremble at the sight of these marvels; and I think that, as his curiosity changes into admiration, he will be more disposed to contemplate them in silence than to examine them with presumption.

For in fact what is man in nature? A Nothing in comparison with the Infinite, an All in comparison with the Nothing, a mean between nothing and everything. Since he is infinitely removed from comprehending the extremes, the end of things and their beginning are hopelessly hidden from him in an impenetrable secret; he is equally incapable of seeing the Nothing from which he was made, and the Infinite in which he is swallowed up.

Let us then take our compass; we are something, and we are not everything. The nature of our existence hides from us the knowledge of first beginnings which are born of the Nothing; and the littleness of our being conceals from us the sight of the Infinite.

Our intellect holds the same position in the world of thought as our body occupies in the expanse of nature.

Limited as we are in every way, this state which holds the mean between two extremes is present in all our impotence. Our senses perceive no extreme. Too much sound deafens us; too much light dazzles us; too great distance or proximity hinders our view. . . . First principles are too self-evident for us; too much pleasure disagrees with us. . . . We feel neither extreme heat nor extreme cold. Excessive qualities are prejudicial to us and not perceptible by the senses; we do not feel but suffer them. Extreme youth and extreme age hinder the mind, as also too much and too little education. In short, extremes are for us as though they were not, and we are not within their notice. They escape us, or we them.

This is our true state; this is what makes us incapable of certain knowledge and of absolute ignorance. We sail within a vast sphere, ever drifting in uncertainty, driven from end to end. When we think to attach ourselves to any point and to fasten to it, it wavers and leaves us; and if we follow it, it eludes our grasp, slips past us, and vanishes for ever. Nothing stays for us. . . .

Let us therefore not look for certainty and stability. Our reason is always deceived by fickle shadows; nothing can fix the finite between the two Infinites, which both enclose and fly from it.

And what completes our incapability of knowing things, is the fact that they are simple, and that we are composed of two opposite natures, different in kind, soul and body. For it is impossible that our rational part should be other than spiritual; and if any one maintain that we are simply corporeal, this would far more exclude us from the knowledge of things, there being nothing so inconceivable as to say that matter knows itself. It is impossible to imagine how it should know itself.

So if we are simply material, we can know nothing at all; and if we are composed of mind and matter, we cannot know perfectly things which are simple, whether spiritual or corporeal. Hence it comes that almost all philosophers have confused ideas of things, and speak of material things in spiritual terms, and of spiritual things in material terms. For they say boldly that bodies have a tendency to fall, that they seek after their centre, that they fly from destruction, that they fear the void, that they have inclinations, sympathies, antipathies, all of which attributes pertain only to mind. And in speaking of minds, they consider them as in a place, and attribute to them movement from one place to another; and these are qualities which belong only to bodies.

What then shall man do in this state? Shall he doubt everything? Shall he doubt whether he is awake, whether he is being pinched, or whether he is being burned? Shall he doubt whether he doubts? Shall he doubt whether he exists? We cannot go so far as that; and I lay it down as a fact that there never has been a real complete sceptic. Nature sustains our feeble reason, and prevents it raving to this extent.

Shall he then say, on the contrary, that he certainly possessed truth—he who, when pressed ever so little, can show no title to it, and is forced to let go his hold?

What a chimera then is man! What a novelty! What a monster, what a chaos, what a contradiction, what a prodigy! Judge of all things, imbecile worm of the earth; depositary of truth, a sink of uncertainty and error; the pride and refuse of the universe!

Who will unravel this tangle? Nature confutes the sceptics, and reason confutes the dogmatists. What then will you become, O men! who try to find out by your natural reason what is your true condition? You cannot avoid one of these sects, nor adhere to one of them.

Know then, proud man, what a paradox you are to yourself. Humble yourself, weak reason; be silent, foolish nature; learn that man infinitely transcends man, and learn from your Master your true condition, of which you are ignorant. Hear God.

For in fact, if man had never been corrupt, he would enjoy in his innocence both truth and happiness with assurance; and if man had always been corrupt, he would have no idea of truth or bliss. But, wretched as we are, and more so than if there were no greatness in our condition, we have an idea of happiness, and cannot reach it. We perceive an image of truth, and possess only a lie. Incapable of absolute ignorance and of certain knowledge, we have thus been manifestly in a degree of perfection from which we have unhappily fallen.

Surely then it is a great evil thus to be in doubt, but it is at least an indispensable duty to seek when we are in such doubt; and thus the doubter who does not seek is altogether completely unhappy and completely wrong. And if besides this he is easy and content, professes to be so, and indeed boasts of it; if it is this state itself which is the subject of his joy and vanity, I have no words to describe so silly a creature.

How can people hold these opinions? What joy can we find in the expectation of nothing but hopeless misery? What reason for boasting that we are in impenetrable darkness? And how can it happen that the following argument occur to a reasonable man?

"I know not who put me into the world, nor what the world is, nor what I myself am. I am in terrible ignorance of everything. I know not what my body is, nor my senses, nor my soul, not even that part of me which thinks what I say, which reflects on all and on itself, and knows itself no more than the rest. I see those frightful spaces of the universe which surround me, and I find myself tied to one corner of this vast expanse, without knowing why I am put in this place rather than in another, nor why the short time which is given to me to live is assigned to me at this point rather than at another of the whole eternity which was before me or which shall come after. . . ."

Man is only a reed, the feeblest thing in nature; but he is a thinking reed. It is not necessary for the entire universe to take up arms in order to crush him: a vapour, a drop of water is sufficient to kill him. But if the universe crushed him, man would still be nobler than the thing which destroys him because he knows that he is dying; and the universe which has him at its mercy, is unaware of it.

All our dignity therefore lies in thought. It is by thought that we must raise ourselves, and not by space or time, which we could never fill. Let us apply ourselves then to thinking well: that is the first principle of morality.

The eternal silence of these infinite spaces terrifies me. . . .

THE WAGER

Let us now speak according to natural lights.

If there is a God, He is infinitely incomprehensible, since, having neither parts nor limits, He has no affinity to us. We are then incapable of knowing either what He is or if He is. This being so, who will dare to undertake the decision of the question? Not we, who have no affinity to Him.

Who then will blame Christians for not being able to give a reason for their belief, since they profess a religion for which they cannot give a reason? They declare, in expounding it to the world, that it is a foolishness, *stultitiam:* and then you complain that they do not prove it! If they proved it, they would not keep their word; it is in lacking proofs that they are not lacking in sense. "Yes, but although this excuses those who offer it as such, and takes away from them the blame of putting it forward without reason, it does not excuse those who receive." Let us then examine this point, and say, "God is, or He is not." But to which side shall we incline? Reason can decide nothing here. There is an infinite chaos which separates us. A game is being played at the extremity of this infinite distance where heads or tails will turn up. What will you wager? According to reason, you can do neither the one thing nor the other; according to reason, you can defend neither of the propositions.

Do not then reprove for error those who have made a choice; for you know nothing about it. "No, but I blame them for having made, not this choice, but a choice, for again both he who chooses heads and he who chooses tails are equally at fault, they are both in the wrong. The true course is not to wager at all."

Yes; but you must wager. It is not optional. You are embarked. Which will you choose then? Let us see. Since you must choose, let us see which interests you least. You have two things to lose, the true and the good; and two things to stake, your reason and your will, your knowledge and your happiness; and your nature has two things to shun, error and misery. Your reason is no more shocked in choosing one rather than the other, since you must of necessity choose. This is one point settled. But your happiness? Let us weigh the gain and the loss in wagering that God is. Let us estimate these two chances. If you gain, you gain all; if you lose, you lose nothing. Wager, then, without hesitation that He is.—"That is very fine. Yes, I must wager; but I may perhaps wager too much."—Let us see. Since there is an equal risk of gain and of loss, if you had only to gain two lives, instead of one, you might still wager. But if there were three lives to gain, you would have to play (since you are under the necessity of playing), and you would be imprudent, when you are forced to play, not to chance your life to gain three at a game where there is an equal risk of loss and gain. But there is an eternity of life and happiness. And this being so, if there were an infinity of chances, of which one only would be for you, you would still be right in wagering one to win two, and you would act stupidly, being obliged to play, by refusing to stake one life against three at a game in which out of an infinity of chances there is one for you, if there were an infinity of an infinitely happy life to gain. But there is here an infinity of an infinitely happy life to gain, a chance of gain against a finite number of chances of loss, and what you stake is finite. It is all divided; wherever the infinite is and there is not an infinity of chances of loss against that of gain, there is no time to hesitate, you must give all. And thus, when one is forced to play, he must renounce reason to preserve his life, rather than risk it for infinite gain, as likely to happen as the loss of nothingness.

For it is no use to say it is uncertain if we will gain, and it is certain that we risk, and that the infinite distance between the *certainty* of what is staked and the *uncertainty* of what will be gained, equals the finite good which is certainly staked against the uncertain infinite. It is not so, as every player stakes a certainty to gain an uncertainty, and yet he stakes a finite certainty to gain a finite uncertainty, without transgressing against reason. There is not an infinite distance between the certainty staked and the uncertainty of the gain; that is untrue. In truth, there is an infinity between the certainty of gain and the certainty of loss. But the uncertainty of the gain is proportioned to the certainty of the stake according to the proportion of the chances of gain and loss. Hence it comes that, if there are as many risks on one side as on the other, the course is to play even; and then the certainty of the stake is equal to the uncertainty of the gain, so far is it from fact that there is an infinite distance between them. And so our proposition is of infinite force, when there is the finite to stake in a game where there are equal risks of gain and of loss, and the infinite to gain. This is demonstrable; and if men are capable of any truths, this is one.

"I confess it, I admit it. But, still, is there no means of seeing the faces of the cards?"—Yes, Scripture and the rest, etc. "Yes, but I have my hands tied and my mouth closed; I am forced to wager, and am not free. I am not released, and am so made that I cannot believe. What, then would you have me do?"

True. But at least learn your inability to believe, since reason brings you to this, and yet you cannot believe. Endeavor then to convince yourself, not by increase of proofs of God, but by the abatement of your passions. You would like to attain faith, and do not know the way; you would like to cure yourself of unbelief, and ask the remedy for it. Learn of those who have been bound like you, and who now stake all their possessions. These are people who know the way which you would follow, and who are cured of an ill of which you would be cured. Follow the way by which they began; by acting as if they believed, taking the holy water, having masses said, etc. Even this will naturally make you believe, and deaden your acuteness.—"But this is what I am afraid of."—And why? What have you to lose?

. . . Now, what harm will befall you in taking this side? You will be faithful, honest, humble, grateful, generous, a sincere friend, truthful. Certainly you will not have those poisonous pleasures, glory and luxury; but will you have not others? I will tell you that you will thereby gain in this life, and that, at each step you take on this road, you will see so great certainty of gain, so much nothingness in what you risk, that you will at last recognize that you have wagered for something certain and infinite, for which you have given nothing.

If this discourse pleases you and seems impressive, know that it is made by a man who has knelt, both before and after it, in prayer to that Being, infinite and without parts, before whom he lays all he has, for you also to lay before Him all you have for your own good and for His glory, that so strength may be given to lowliness.

24. The Will to Believe

WILLIAM JAMES

In the recently published Life by Leslie Stephen of his brother, Fitzjames, there is an account of a school to which the latter went when he was a boy. The teacher, a certain Mr. Guest, used to converse with his pupils in this way:

"Gurney, what is the difference between justification and sanctification?—Stephen, prove the omnipotence of God!" etc. In the midst of our Harvard freethinking and indifference we are prone to imagine that here at your good old orthodox College conversation continues to be somewhat upon this order; and to show you that we at Harvard have not lost all interest in these vital subjects, I have brought with me to-night something like a sermon on justification by faith to read to you,—I mean an essay in justification *of* faith, a defence of our right to adopt a believing attitude in religious matters, in spite of the fact that our merely logical intellect may not have been coerced. "The Will to Believe," accordingly, is the title of my paper.

I have long defended to my own students the lawfulness of voluntarily adopted faith; but as soon as they have got well imbued with the logical spirit, they have as a rule refused to admit my contention to be lawful philosophically, even though in point of fact they were personally all the time chock-full of some faith or other themselves. I am all the while, however, so profoundly convinced that my own position is correct, that your invitation has seemed to me a good occasion to make my statements more clear. Perhaps your minds will be more open than those with which I have hitherto had to deal. I will be as little technical as I can, though I must begin by setting up some technical distinctions that will help us in the end.

I

Let us give the name of *hypothesis* to anything that may be proposed to our belief; and just as the electricians speak of live and dead wires, let us speak of any hypothesis as either *live* or *dead*. A live hypothesis is one which appeals as a real possibility to him to whom it is proposed. If I ask you to believe in the Mahdi, the notion makes no electric connection with your nature,—it refuses to scintillate with any credibility at all. As an hypothesis it is completely dead. To an Arab, however (even if he be not one of the Mahdi's followers), the hypothesis is among the mind's possibilities: it is alive. This shows that deadness and liveness in an hypothesis are not intrinsic properties, but relations to the individual thinker. They are measured by his willingness to act. The maximum of liveness in an hypothesis means willingness to act irrevocably. Practically, that means belief; but there is some believing tendency wherever there is willingness to act at all.

Next, let us call the decision between two hypotheses an *option*. Options may be of several kinds. They may be—1, *living* or *dead*; 2, *forced* or *avoidable*; 3, *momentous* or *trivial*; and for our purposes we may call an option a *genuine* option when it is of the forced, living, and momentous kind.

1. A living option is one in which both hypotheses are live ones. If I say to you: "Be a theosophist or be a Mohammedan," it is probably a dead option, because for you neither hypothesis is likely to be alive. But if I say: "Be an agnostic or be a Christian," it is otherwise: trained as you are, each hypothesis makes some appeal, however small, to your belief.

2. Next, if I say to you: "Choose between going out with your umbrella or without it," I do not offer you a genuine option, for it is not forced. You can easily

avoid it by not going out at all. Similarly, if I say, "Either love me or hate me," "Either call my theory true or call it false," your option is avoidable. You may remain indifferent to me, neither loving nor hating, and you may decline to offer any judgment as to my theory. But if I say, "Either accept this truth or go without it," I put on you a forced option, for there is no standing place outside of the alternative. Every dilemma based on a complete logical disjunction, with no possibility of not choosing, is an option of this forced kind.

3. Finally, if I were Dr. [Fridtjof] Nansen and proposed to you to join my North Pole expedition, your option would be momentous; for this would probably be your only similar opportunity, and your choice now would either exclude you from the North Pole sort of immortality altogether or put at least the chance of it into your hands. He who refuses to embrace a unique opportunity loses the prize as surely as if he tried and failed. *Per contra,* the option is trivial when the opportunity is not unique, when the stake is insignificant, or when the decision is reversible if it later prove unwise. Such trivial options abound in the scientific life. A chemist finds an hypothesis live enough to spend a year in its verification: he believes in it to that extent. But if his experiments prove inconclusive either way, he is quit for his loss of time, no vital harm being done.

It will facilitate our discussion if we keep all these distinctions well in mind.

II

The next matter to consider is the actual psychology of human opinion. When we look at certain facts, it seems as if our passional and volitional nature lay at the root of all our convictions. When we look at others, it seems as if they could do nothing when the intellect had once said its say. Let us take the latter facts up first.

Does it not seem preposterous on the very face of it to talk of our opinions being modifiable at will? Can our will either help or hinder our intellect in its perceptions of truth? Can we, by just willing it, believe that Abraham Lincoln's existence is a myth, and that the portraits of him in McClure's Magazine are all of some one else? Can we, by any effort of our will, or by any strength of wish that it were true, believe ourselves well and about when we are roaring with rheumatism in bed, or feel certain that the sum of the two one-dollar bills in our pocket must be a hundred dollars? We can *say* any of these things, but we are absolutely impotent to believe them; and of just such things is the whole fabric of the truths that we do believe in made up,—matters of fact, immediate or remote, as Hume said, and relations between ideas, which are either there or not there for us if we see them so, and which if not there cannot be put there by any action of our own.

In Pascal's *Thoughts* there is a celebrated passage known in literature as Pascal's wager. In it he tries to force us into Christianity by reasoning as if our concern with truth resembled our concern with the stakes in a game of chance. Translated freely his words are these: You must either believe or not believe that

God is—which will you do? Your human reason cannot say. A game is going on between you and the nature of things which at the day of judgment will bring out either heads or tails. Weigh what your gains and your losses would be if you should stake all you have on heads, or God's existence: if you win in such case, you gain eternal beatitude; if you lose, you lose nothing at all. If there were an infinity of chances, and only one for God in this wager, still you ought to stake your all on God; for though you surely risk a finite loss by this procedure, any finite loss is reasonable, even a certain one is reasonable, if there is but the possibility of infinite gain. Go, then, and take holy water, and have masses said; belief will come and stupefy your scruples,—*Cela vous fera croire et vous abêtira.* Why should you not? At bottom, what have you to lose?

You probably feel that when religious faith expresses itself thus, in the language of the gaming-table, it is put to its last trumps. Surely Pascal's own personal belief in masses and holy water had far other springs; and this celebrated page of his is but an argument for others, a last desperate snatch at a weapon against the hardness of the unbelieving heart. We feel that a faith in masses and holy water adopted wilfully after such a mechanical calculation would lack the inner soul of faith's reality; and if we were ourselves in the place of the Deity, we should probably take particular pleasure in cutting off believers of this pattern from their infinite reward. It is evident that unless there be some pre-existing tendency to believe in masses and holy water, the option offered to the will by Pascal is not a living option. Certainly no Turk ever took to masses and holy water on its account; and even to us Protestants these means of salvation seem such foregone impossibilities that Pascal's logic, invoked for them specifically, leaves us unmoved. As well might the Mahdi write to us, saying, "I am the Expected One whom God has created in his effulgence. You shall be infinitely happy if you confess me; otherwise you shall be cut off from the light of the sun. Weigh, then, your infinite gain if I am genuine against your finite sacrifice if I am not!" His logic would be that of Pascal; but he would vainly use it on us, for the hypothesis he offers us is dead. No tendency to act on it exists in us to any degree.

The talk of believing by our volition seems, then, from one point of view, simply silly. From another point of view it is worse than silly, it is vile. When one turns to the magnificent edifice of the physical sciences, and sees how it was reared; what thousands of disinterested moral lives of men lie buried in its mere foundations; what patience and postponement, what choking down of preference, what submission to the icy laws of outer fact are wrought into its very stones and mortar; how absolutely impersonal it stands in its vast augustness,—then how besotted and contemptible seems every little sentimentalist who comes blowing his voluntary smoke-wreaths, and pretending to decide things from out of his private dream! Can we wonder if those bred in the rugged and manly school of science should feel like spewing such subjectivism out of their mouths? The whole system of loyalties which grow up in the schools of science go dead against its toleration; so that it is only natural that those who have caught the scientific fever should pass over to the opposite extreme, and write sometimes as if the incorruptibly truthful intellect ought positively to prefer bitterness and unacceptableness to the heart in its cup.

> *It fortifies my soul to know*
> *That, though I perish, Truth is so—*

sings Clough, while Huxley exclaims:

> My only consolation lies in the reflection that, however bad our posterity may
> become, so far as they hold by the plain rule of not pretending to believe
> what they have no reason to believe, because it may be to their advantage so
> to pretend [the word "pretend" is surely here redundant], they will not have
> reached the lowest depth of immorality.

And that delicious *enfant terrible* Clifford writes:

> Belief is desecrated when given to unproved and unquestioned statements for the
> solace and private pleasure of the believer. . . . Whoso would deserve well of his
> fellows in this matter will guard the purity of his belief with a very fanaticism of
> jealous care, lest at any time it should rest on an unworthy object, and catch a
> stain which can never be wiped away. . . . If [a] belief has been accepted on
> insufficient evidence [even though the belief be true, as Clifford on the same page
> explains] the pleasure is a stolen one. . . . It is sinful because it is stolen in
> defiance of our duty to mankind. That duty is to guard ourselves from such beliefs
> as from a pestilence which may shortly master our own body and then spread to
> the rest of the town. . . . It is wrong always, everywhere, and for every one, to
> believe anything upon insufficient evidence.

III

All this strikes one as healthy, even when expressed, as by Clifford, with somewhat
too much of robustious pathos in the voice. Free-will and simple wishing do seem, in
the matter of our credences, to be only fifth wheels to the coach. Yet if any one
should thereupon assume that intellectual insight is what remains after wish and will
and sentimental preference have taken wing, or that pure reason is what then settles
our opinions, he would fly quite as directly in the teeth of the facts.

It is only our already dead hypotheses that our willing nature is unable to
bring to life again. But what has made them dead for us is for the most part a
previous action of our willing nature of an antagonistic kind. When I say "willing
nature," I do not mean only such deliberate volitions as may have set up habits of
belief that we cannot now escape from,—I mean all such factors of belief as fear
and hope, prejudice and passion, imitation and partisanship, the circumpressure of
our caste and set. As a matter of fact we find ourselves believing, we hardly know
how or why. Mr. Balfour gives the name of "authority" to all those influences, born
of the intellectual climate, that make hypotheses possible or impossible for us,
alive or dead. Here in this room, we all of us believe in molecules and the
conservation of energy, in democracy and necessary progress, in Protestant Christianity and the duty of fighting for "the doctrine of the immortal Monroe," all for
no reasons worthy of the name. We see into these matters with no more inner
clearness, and probably with much less, than any disbeliever in them might
possess. His unconventionality would probably have some grounds to show for its

conclusions; but for us, not insight, but the *prestige* of the opinions, is what makes the spark shoot from them and light up our sleeping magazines of faith. Our reason is quite satisfied, in nine hundred and ninety-nine cases out of every thousand of us, if it can find a few arguments that will do to recite in case our credulity is criticised by some one else. Our faith is faith in some one else's faith, and in the greatest matters this is most the case. Our belief in truth itself, for instance, that there is a truth, and that our minds and it are made for each other,—what is it but a passionate affirmation of desire, in which our social system backs us up? We want to have a truth; we want to believe that our experiments and studies and discussions must put us in a continually better and better position towards it; and on this line we agree to fight out our thinking lives. But if a Pyrrhonistic sceptic asks us *how we know* all this, can our logic find a reply? No! certainly it cannot. It is just one volition against another,—we willing to go in for life upon a trust or assumption which he, for his part, does not care to make.

As a rule we disbelieve all facts and theories for which we have no use. Clifford's cosmic emotions find no use for Christian feelings. Huxley belabors the bishops because there is no use for sacerdotalism in his scheme of life. Newman, on the contrary, goes over to Romanism, and finds all sorts of reasons good for staying there, because a priestly system is for him an organic need and delight. Why do so few "scientists" even look at the evidence for telepathy, so called? Because they think, as a leading biologist, now dead, once said to me, that even if such a thing were true, scientists ought to band together to keep it suppressed and concealed. It would undo the uniformity of Nature and all sorts of other things without which scientists cannot carry on their pursuits. But if this very man had been shown something which as a scientist he might *do* with telepathy, he might not only have examined the evidence, but even have found it good enough. This very law which the logicians would impose upon us—if I may give the name of logicians to those who would rule out our willing nature here—is based on nothing but their own natural wish to exclude all elements for which they, in their professional quality of logicians, can find no use.

Evidently, then, our non-intellectual nature does influence our convictions. There are passional tendencies and volitions which run before and others which come after belief, and it is only the latter that are too late for the fair; and they are not too late when the previous passional work has been already in their own direction. Pascal's argument, instead of being powerless, then seems a regular clincher, and is the last stroke needed to make our faith in masses and holy water complete. The state of things is evidently far from simple; and pure insight and logic, whatever they might do ideally, are not the only things that really do produce our creeds.

IV

Our next duty, having recognized this mixed-up state of affairs, is to ask whether it be simply reprehensible and pathological, or whether, on the contrary, we must treat it as a normal element in making up our minds. The thesis I defend is, briefly stated, this: *Our passional nature not only lawfully may, but must, decide an option between propositions, whenever it is a genuine option that cannot by its nature be decided on intellectual grounds; for to say, under such circumstances, "Do not decide, but leave the question open," is itself a passional decision,—just like deciding yes or no,—and is attended with the same risk of losing the truth.* The thesis thus abstractly expressed will, I trust, soon become quite clear. But I must first indulge in a bit more of preliminary work. . . .

X

In truths dependent on our personal action, then, faith based on desire is certainly a lawful and possibly an indispensable thing.

But now, it will be said, these are all childish human cases, and have nothing to do with great cosmical matters, like the question of religious faith. Let us then pass on to that. Religions differ so much in their accidents that in discussing the religious question we must make it very generic and broad. What then do we now mean by the religious hypothesis? Science says things are; morality says some things are better than other things; and religion says essentially two things.

First, she says that the best things are the more eternal things, the overlapping things, the things in the universe that throw the last stone, so to speak, and say the final word. "Perfection is eternal,"—this phrase of Charles Secretan seems a good way of putting this first affirmation of religion, an affirmation which obviously cannot yet be verified scientifically at all.

The second affirmation of religion is that we are better off even now if we believe her first affirmation to be true.

Now, let us consider what the logical elements of this situation are *in case the religious hypothesis in both its branches be really true.* (Of course, we must admit that possibility at the outset. If we are to discuss the question at all, it must involve a living option. If for any of you religion be a hypothesis that cannot, by any living possibility be true, then you need to go no farther. I speak to the "saving remnant" alone.) So proceeding, we see, first, that religion offers itself as a *momentous* option. We are supposed to gain, even now, by our belief, and to lose by our non-belief, a certain vital good. Secondly, religion is a *forced* option, so far as that good goes. We cannot escape the issue by remaining sceptical and waiting for more light, because, although we do avoid error in that way *if religion be untrue,* we lose the good, *if it be true,* just as certainly as if we positively chose to disbelieve. It is as if a man should hesitate indefinitely to ask a certain woman to marry him because he was not perfectly sure that she would prove an angel after he brought her home. Would he not cut himself off from that particular angel-possibility as decisively as if he went and married some one else? Scepticism, then, is not avoidance of option; it is option of a certain particular kind of risk. *Better risk loss of truth than chance of error,*—that is your faith-vetoer's exact position. He is actively playing his stake as much as the believer is; he is backing the field against the religious hypothesis, just as the believer is backing the religious hypothesis against the field. To preach scepticism to us as a duty until "sufficient evidence" for religion be found, is tantamount therefore to telling us, when in presence of the religious hypothesis, that to yield to our fear of its being error is wiser and better than to yield to our hope that it may be true. It is not intellect against all passions, then; it is only intellect with one passion laying down its law. And by what, forsooth, is the supreme wisdom of this passion warranted? Dupery for dupery, what proof is there that dupery through hope is so much worse than dupery through fear? I, for one, can see no proof; and I simply refuse obedience to the scientist's command to imitate his kind of option, in a case where my own stake is important enough to give me the right to choose my own form of risk. If religion be true and the evidence for it be still insufficient, I do not wish, by putting your extinguisher upon my nature (which feels to me as if it had after all some business in this matter), to forfeit my sole chance in life of getting upon the winning side,—that chance depending, of course, on my willingness to run the risk of acting as if my passional need of taking the world religiously might be prophetic and right.

All this is on the supposition that it really may be prophetic and right, and that, even to us who are discussing the matter, religion is a live hypothesis which may be true. Now, to most of us religion comes in a still further way that makes a veto on our active faith even more illogical. The more perfect and more eternal aspect of the universe is represented in our religions as having personal form. The universe is no longer a mere *It* to us, but a *Thou*, if we are religious; and any relation that may be possible from person to person might be possible here. For instance, although in one sense we are passive portions of the universe, in another we show a curious autonomy, as if we were small active centres on our own account. We feel, too, as if the appeal of religion to us were made to our own active good-will, as if evidence might be forever withheld from us unless we met the hypothesis half-way. To take a trivial illustration: just as a man who in a company of gentlemen made no advances, asked a warrant for every concession, and believed no one's word without proof, would cut himself off by such churlishness from all the social rewards that a more trusting spirit would earn,—so here, one who should shut himself up in snarling logicality and try to make the gods extort his recognition willy-nilly, or not get it at all, might cut himself off forever from his only opportunity of making the gods' acquaintance. This feeling, forced on us we know not whence, that by obstinately believing that there are gods (although not to do so would be so easy both for our logic and our life) we are doing the universe the deepest service we can, seems part of the living essence of the religious hypothesis. If the hypothesis *were* true in all its parts, including this one, then pure intellectualism, with its veto on our making willing advances, would be an absurdity; and some participation of our sympathetic nature would be logically required. I, therefore, for one, cannot see my way to accepting the agnostic rules for truth-seeking, or wilfully agree to keep my willing nature out of the game. I cannot do so for this plain reason, that *a rule of thinking which would absolutely prevent me from acknowledging certain kinds of truth if those kinds of truth were really there, would be an irrational rule.* That for me is the long and short of the formal logic of the situation, no matter what the kinds of truth might materially be.

I confess I do not see how this logic can be escaped. But sad experience makes me fear that some of you may still shrink from radically saying with me, *in abstracto*, that we have the right to believe at our own risk any hypothesis that is live enough to tempt our will. I suspect, however, that if this is so, it is because you have got away from the abstract logical point of view altogether, and are thinking (perhaps without realizing it) of some particular religious hypothesis which for you is dead. The freedom to "believe what we will" you apply to the case of some patent superstition; and the faith you think of is the faith defined by the schoolboy when he said, "Faith is when you believe something that you know ain't true." I can only repeat that this is misapprehension. *In concreto*, the freedom to believe can only cover living options which the intellect of the individual cannot by itself resolve; and living options never seem absurdities to him who has them to consider. When I look at the religious question as it really puts itself to concrete men, and when I think of all the possibilities which both practically and theoretically it involves, then this command that we shall put a stopper on our heart, instincts, and courage, and *wait*—acting of course meanwhile more or less as if religion were *not* true[1]—till doomsday, or till such time as our intellect and senses working together may have raked in evidence enough,—this command, I say, seems to me the queerest idol ever manufactured in the philosophic cave. Were we scholastic absolutists, there might be more excuse. If we had an infallible intellect with its objective certitudes, we might feel ourselves disloyal to such a perfect organ of knowledge in not trusting to it exclusively, in not waiting for its releasing word. But if we are empiricists, if we believe that no bell in us tolls to let us know for certain when truth is in our grasp, then it seems a piece of idle fantasticality to preach so solemnly our duty of waiting for the bell. Indeed we *may* wait if we will,—I hope you do not think that I am denying that,—but if we do so, we do so at our peril as much as if we believed. In either case we *act*, taking our life in our hands. No one of us ought to issue vetoes to the other, nor should we bandy words of abuse. We ought, on the contrary, delicately and profoundly to respect one another's mental freedom: then only shall we bring about the intellectual republic; then only shall we have that spirit of inner tolerance without which all our outer tolerance is soulless, and which is empiricism's glory; then only shall we live and let live, in speculative as well as in practical things.

I began by a reference to Fitzjames Stephen; let me end by a quotation from him.

> What do you think of yourself? What do you think of the world? . . . These are questions with which all must deal as it seems good to them. They are riddles of the Sphinx, and in some way or other we must deal with them. . . . In all important transactions of life we have to take a leap in the dark. . . . If we decide to leave the riddles unanswered, that is a choice; if we waver in our answer, that, too, is a choice: but whatever choice we make, we make it at our peril. If a man chooses to

---

[1] Since belief is measured by action, he who forbids us to believe religion to be true, necessarily also forbids us to act as we should if we did believe it to be true. The whole defence of religious faith hinges upon action. If the action required or inspired by the religious hypothesis is in no way different from that dictated by the naturalistic hypothesis, then religious faith is a pure superfluity, better pruned away, and controversy about its legitimacy is a piece of idle trifling, unworthy of serious minds. I myself believe, of course, that the religious hypothesis gives to the world an expression which specifically determines our reactions, and makes them in a large part unlike what they might be on a purely naturalistic scheme of belief.

turn his back altogether on God and the future, no one can prevent him; no one can show beyond reasonable doubt that he is mistaken. If a man thinks otherwise and acts as he thinks, I do not see that any one can prove that *he* is mistaken. Each must act as he thinks best; and if he is wrong, so much the worse for him. We stand on a mountain pass in the midst of whirling snow and blinding mist, through which we get glimpses now and then of paths which may be deceptive. If we stand still we shall be frozen to death. If we take the wrong road we shall be dashed to pieces. We do not certainly know whether there is any right one. What must we do? "Be strong and of a good courage." Act for the best, hope for the best, and take what comes. . . . If death ends all, we cannot meet death better.[2]

25. The Ethics of Belief

W. K. CLIFFORD

A shipowner was about to send to sea an emigrant ship. He knew that she was old, and not over-well built at the first; that she had seen many seas and climes, and often had needed repairs. Doubts had been suggested to him that possibly she was not seaworthy. These doubts preyed upon his mind and made him unhappy; he thought that perhaps he ought to have her thoroughly overhauled and refitted, even though this should put him to great expense. Before the ship sailed, however, he succeeded in overcoming these melancholy reflections. He said to himself that she had gone safely through so many voyages and weathered so many storms that it was idle to suppose she would not come safely home from this trip also. He would put his trust in Providence, which could hardly fail to protect all these unhappy families that were leaving their fatherland to seek for better times elsewhere. He would dismiss from his mind all ungenerous suspicions about the honesty of builders and contractors. In such ways he acquired a sincere and comfortable conviction that his vessel was thoroughly safe and seaworthy; he watched her departure with a light heart, and benevolent wishes for the success of the exiles in their strange new home that was to be; and he got his insurance money when she went down in midocean and told no tales.

What shall we say of him? Surely this, that he was verily guilty of the death of those men. It is admitted that he did sincerely believe in the soundness of his ship; but the sincerity of his conviction can in no wise help him, because he had no right to believe on such evidence as was before him. He had acquired his belief not by honestly earning it in patient investigation, but by stifling his doubts. And although in the end he may have felt so sure about it that he could not think otherwise, yet inasmuch as he had knowingly and willing worked himself into that frame of mind, he must be held responsible for it.

Let us alter the case a little, and suppose that the ship was not unsound after all; that she made her voyage safely, and many others after it. Will that diminish the

[2] Liberty, Equality, Fraternity, p. 353, 2d edition. London, 1874.

guilt of her owner? Not one jot. When an action is once done, it is right or wrong forever; no accidental failure of its good or evil fruits can possibly alter that. The man would not have been innocent, he would only have been not found out. The question of right or wrong has to do with the origin of his belief, not the matter of it; not what it was, but how he got it; not whether it turned out to be true or false, but whether he had a right to belive on such evidence as was before him.

There was once an island in which some of the inhabitants professed a religion teaching neither the doctrine of original sin nor that of eternal punishment. A suspicion got abroad that the professors of this religion had made use of unfair means to get their doctrines taught to children. They were accused of wresting the laws of their country in such a way as to remove children from the care of their natural and legal guardians; and even of stealing them away and keeping them concealed from their friends and relations. A certain number of men formed themselves into a society for the purpose of agitating the public about this matter. They published grave accusations against individual citizens of the highest position and character, and did all in their power to injure those citizens in the exercise of their professions. So great was the noise they made, that a Commission was appointed to investigate the facts; but after the Commission had carefully inquired into all the evidence that could be got, it appeared that the accused were innocent. Not only had they been accused on insufficient evidence, but the evidence of their innocence was such as the agitators might easily have obtained, if they had attempted a fair inquiry. After these disclosures the inhabitants of that country looked upon the members of the agitating society, not only as persons whose judgment was to be distrusted, but also as no longer to be counted honorable men. For although they had sincerely and conscientiously believed in the charges they had made, yet they had no right to believe on such evidence as was before them. Their sincere convictions, instead of being honestly earned by patient inquiring, were stolen by listening to the voice of prejudice and passion.

Let us vary this case also, and suppose, other things remaining as before, that a still more accurate investigation proved the accused to have been really guilty. Would this make any difference in the guilt of the accusers? Clearly not; the question is not whether their belief was true or false, but whether they entertained it on wrong grounds. They would no doubt say, "Now you see that we were right after all; next time perhaps you will believe us." And they might be believed, but they would not thereby become honorable men. They would not be innocent, they would only be not found out. Every one of them, if he chose to examine himself *in foro conscientiae*, would know that he had acquired and nourished a belief, when he had no right to believe on such evidence as was before him; and therein he would know that he had done a wrong thing.

It may be said, however, that in both of these supposed cases it is not the belief which is judged to be wrong, but the action following upon it. The shipowner might say, "I am perfectly certain that my ship is sound, but still I feel it my duty to have her examined, before trusting the lives of so many people to her." And it might be said to the agitator, "However convinced you were of the justice of your cause and the truth of your convictions, you ought not to have made a public attack upon any man's character until you had examined the evidence on both sides with the utmost patience and care."

In the first place, let us admit that, so far as it goes, this view of the case is right and necessary; right, because even when a man's belief is so fixed that he cannot think otherwise, he still has a choice in regard to the action suggested by it, and so cannot escape the duty of investigating on the ground of the strength of his convictions; and necessary, because those who are not yet capable of controlling their feelings and thoughts must have a plain rule dealing with overt acts.

But this being premised as necessary, it becomes clear that it is not sufficient, and that our previous judgment is required to supplement it. For it is not possible so to sever the belief from the action it suggests as to condemn the one without condemning the other. No man holding a strong belief on one side of a question, or even wishing to hold a belief on one side, can investigate it with such fairness and completeness as if he were really in doubt and unbiassed; so that the existence of a belief not founded on fair inquiry unfits a man for the performance of this necessary duty.

Nor is that truly a belief at all which has not some influence upon the actions of him who holds it. He who truly believes that which prompts him to an action has looked upon the action to lust after it, he has committed it already in his heart. If a belief is not realized immediately in open deeds, it is stored up for the guidance of the future. It goes to make a part of that aggregate of beliefs which is the link between sensation and action at every moment of all our lives, and which is so organized and compacted together that no part of it can be isolated from the rest, but every new addition modifies the structure of the whole. No real belief, however trifling and fragmentary it may seem, is ever truly insignificant; it prepares us to receive more of its like, confirms those which resembled it before, and weakens others; and so gradually it lays a stealthy train in our inmost thoughts, which may some day explode into overt action, and leave its stamp upon our character forever.

And no man's belief is in any case a private matter which concerns himself alone. Our lives are guided by that general conception of the course of things which has been created by society for social purposes. Our words, our phrases, our forms and processes and modes of thought, are common property, fashioned and perfected from age to age; an heirloom which every succeeding generation inherits as a precious deposit and a sacred trust to be handed on to the next one, not unchanged but enlarged and purified, with some clear marks of its proper handiwork. Into this, for good or ill, is woven every belief of every man who has speech of his fellows. An awful privilege, and an awful responsibility, that we should help to create the world in which posterity will live.

In the two supposed cases which have been considered, it has been judged wrong to believe on insufficient evidence, or to nourish belief by suppressing doubts and avoiding investigation. The reason of this judgment is not far to seek: it is that in both these cases the belief held by one man was of great importance to other men. But for as much as no belief held by one man, however seemingly trivial the belief, and however obscure the believer, is ever actually insignificant or without its effect on the fate of mankind, we have no choice but to extend our judgment to all cases of belief whatever. Belief, that sacred faculty which prompts the decisions of our will, and knits into harmonious working all the compacted energies of our being, is ours not for ourselves, but for humanity. It is rightly used on truths which have been established by long experience and waiting toil, and which have stood in the fierce light of free and fearless questioning. Then it helps to bind men together, and to strengthen and direct their common action. It is desecrated when given to unproved and unquestioned statements, for the solace and private pleasure of the believer; to add a tinsel splendor to the plain straight road of our life and display a bright mirage beyond it; or even to drown the common sorrows of our kind by a self-deception which allows them not only to cast down, but also to degrade us. Whoso would deserve well of his fellows in this matter will guard the purity of his belief with a very fanaticism of jealous care, lest at any time it should rest on an unworthy object, and catch a stain which can never be wiped away.

It is not only the leader of men, statesman, philosopher, or poet, that owes this bounden duty to mankind. Every rustic who delivers in the village alehouse his slow, infrequent sentences, may help to kill or keep alive the fatal superstitions which clog his race. Every hard-worked wife of an artisan may transmit to her children beliefs which shall knit society together, or rend it in pieces. No simplicity of mind, no obscurity of station, can escape the universal duty of questioning all that we believe.

It is true that this duty is a hard one, and the doubt which comes out of it is often a very bitter thing. It leaves us bare and powerless where we thought that we were safe and strong. To know all about anything is to know how to deal with it under all circumstances. We feel much happier and more secure when we think we know precisely what to do, no matter what happens, than when we have lost our way and do not know where to turn. And if we have supposed ourselves to know all about anything, and to be capable of doing what is fit in regard to it, we naturally do not like to find that we are really ignorant and powerless, that we have to begin again at the beginning, and try to learn what the thing is and how it is to be dealt with—if indeed anything can be learned about it. It is the sense of power attached to a sense of knowledge that makes men desirous of believing, and afraid of doubting.

This sense of power is the highest and best of pleasures when the belief on which it is founded is a true belief, and has been fairly earned by investigation. For then we may justly feel that it is common property, and holds good for others as well as for ourselves. Then we may be glad, not that I have learned secrets by which I am safer and stronger, but that we men have got mastery over more of the world; and we shall be strong, not for ourselves, but in the name of Man and in his strength. But if the belief has been accepted on insufficient evidence, the pleasure is a stolen one. Not only does it deceive ourselves by giving us a sense of power which we do not really possess, but it is sinful, because it is stolen in defiance of our duty to mankind. That duty is to guard ourselves from such beliefs as from a pestilence, which may shortly master our own body and then spread to the rest of the town. What would be thought of one who, for the sake of a sweet fruit, should deliberately run the risk of bringing a plague upon his family and his neighbors?

And, as in other such cases, it is not the risk only which has to be considered; for a bad action is always bad at the time when it is done, no matter what happens afterwards. Every time we let ourselves believe for unworthy reasons, we weaken our powers of self-control, of doubting, of judicially and fairly weighing evidence. We all suffer severely enough from the maintenance and support of false beliefs and the fatally wrong actions which they lead to, and the evil born when one such belief is entertained is great and wide. But a greater and wider evil arises when the credulous character is maintained and supported, when a habit of believing for unworthy reasons is fostered and made permanent. If I steal money from any person, there may be no harm done by the mere transfer of possession; he may not feel the loss, or it may prevent him from using the money badly. But I cannot help doing this great wrong towards Man, that I make myself dishonest. What hurts society is not that it should lose its property, but that it should become a den of thieves; for then it must cease to be society. This is why we ought not to do evil that good may come; for at any rate this great evil has come, that we have done evil and are made wicked thereby. In like manner, if I let myself believe anything on insufficient evidence, there may be no great harm done by the mere belief; it may be true after all, or I may never have occasion to exhibit it in outward acts. But I cannot help doing this great wrong toward Man, that I make myself credulous. The danger to society is not merely that it should believe wrong things, though that is great enough; but that it should become credulous, and lose the habit of testing things and inquiring into them; for then it must sink back into savagery.

The harm which is done by credulity in a man is not confined to the fostering of a credulous character in others, and consequent support of false beliefs. Habitual want of care about what I believe leads to habitual want of care in others about the truth of what is told to me. Men speak the truth to one another when each reveres the truth in his own mind and in the other's mind; but how shall my friend revere the truth in my mind when I myself am careless about it, when I believe things because I want to believe them, and because they are comforting and pleasant? Will he not learn to cry, "Peace," to me, when there is no peace? By such a course I shall surround myself with a thick atmosphere of falsehood and fraud, and in that I must live. It may matter little to me, in my cloud-castle of sweet illusions and darling lies; but it matters much to Man that I have made my neighbors ready to deceive. The credulous man is father to the liar and the cheat; he lives in the bosom of this his family, and it is no marvel if he should become even as they are. So closely are our duties knit together, that whoso shall keep the whole law, and yet offend in one point, he is guilty of all.

To sum up: it is wrong always, everywhere, and for anyone, to believe anything upon insufficient evidence.

If a man, holding a belief which he was taught in childhood or persuaded of afterwards, keeps down and pushes away any doubts which arise about it in his mind, purposely avoids the reading of books and the company of men that call in question or discuss it, and regards as impious those questions which cannot easily be asked without disturbing it—the life of that man is one long sin against mankind. . . .

Mystical and Religious Experience

26. The Varieties of Religious Experience

WILLIAM JAMES

Over and over again in these lectures I have raised points and left them open and unfinished until we should have come to the subject of Mysticism. Some of you, I fear, may have smiled as you noted my reiterated postponements. But now the hour has come when mysticism must be faced in good earnest, and those broken threads wound up together. One may say truly, I think, that personal religious experience has its root and centre in mystical states of consciousness; so for us, who in these lectures are treating personal experience as the exclusive subject of our study, such states of consciousness ought to form the vital chapter from which the other chapters get their light. Whether my treatment of mystical states will shed more light or darkness, I do not know, for my own constitution shuts me out from their enjoyment almost entirely, and I can speak of them only at second hand. But though forced to look upon the subject so externally, I will be as objective and receptive as I can; and I think I shall at least succeed in convincing you of the reality of the states in question, and of the paramount importance of their function.

First of all, then, I ask, What does the expression "mystical states of consciousness" mean? How do we part off mystical states from other states?

The words "mysticism" and "mystical" are often used as terms of mere reproach, to throw at any opinion which we regard as vague and vast and sentimental, and without a base in either facts or logic. For some writers a "mystic" is any person who believes in thought-transference, or spirit-return. Employed in this way the word has little value: there are too many less ambiguous synonyms. So, to keep it useful by restricting it, I will do what I did in the case of the word "religion," and simply propose to you four marks which, when an experience has them, may justify us in calling it mystical for the purpose of the present lectures. In this way we shall save verbal disputation, and the recriminations that generally go therewith.

1. *Ineffability.* The handiest of the marks by which I classify a state of mind as mystical is negative. The subject of it immediately says that it defies expression, that no adequate report of its contents can be given in words. It follows from this

that its quality must be directly experienced; it cannot be imparted or transferred to others. In this peculiarity mystical states are more like states of feeling than like states of intellect. No one can make clear to another who has never had a certain feeling, in what the quality or worth of it consists. One must have musical ears to know the value of a symphony; one must have been in love one's self to understand a lover's state of mind. Lacking the heart or ear, we cannot interpret the musician or the lover justly, and are even likely to consider him weak-minded or absurd. The mystic finds that most of us accord to his experiences an equally incompetent treatment.

2. *Noetic quality.* Although so similar to states of feeling, mystical states seem to those who experience them to be also states of knowledge. They are states of insight into depths of truth unplumbed by the discursive intellect. They are illuminations, revelations, full of significance and importance, all inarticulate though they remain; and as a rule they carry with them a curious sense of authority for after-time.

These two characters will entitle any state to be called mystical, in the sense in which I use the word. Two other qualities are less sharply marked, but are usually found. These are:—

3. *Transiency.* Mystical states cannot be sustained for long. Except in rare instances, half an hour, or at most an hour or two, seems to be the limit beyond which they fade into the light of common day. Often, when faded, their quality can but imperfectly be reproduced in memory; but when they recur it is recognized; and from one recurrence to another it is susceptible of continuous development in what is felt as inner richness and importance.

4. *Passivity.* Although the oncoming of mystical states may be facilitated by preliminary voluntary operations, as by fixing the attention, or going through certain bodily performances, or in other ways which manuals of mysticism prescribe; yet when the characteristic sort of consciousness once has set in, the mystic feels as if his own will were in abeyance, and indeed sometimes as if he were grasped and held by a superior power. This latter peculiarity connects mystical states with certain definite phenomena of secondary or alternative personality, such as prophetic speech, automatic writing, or the mediumistic trance. When these latter conditions are well pronounced, however, there may be no recollection whatever of the phenomenon, and it may have no significance for the subject's usual inner life, to which, as it were, it makes a mere interruption. Mystical states strictly so called are never merely interruptive. Some memory of their content always remains, and a profound sense of their importance. They modify the inner life of the subject between the times of their recurrence. Sharp divisions in this region are, however, difficult to make, and we find all sorts of gradations and mixtures.

These four characteristics are sufficient to mark out a group of states of consciousness peculiar enough to deserve a special name and to call for careful study. Let it then be called the mystical group.

Our next step should be to gain acquaintance with some typical examples. Professional mystics at the height of their development have often elaborately organized experiences and a philosophy based thereupon. But you remember what I said in my first lecture: phenomena are best understood when placed within their series, studied in their germ and in their over-ripe decay, and compared with their exaggerated and degenerated kindred. The range of mystical experience is very wide, much too wide for us to cover in the time at our disposal. Yet the method of serial study is so essential for interpretation that if we really wish to reach conclusions we must use it. I will begin, therefore, with phenomena which claim no special religious significance, and end with those of which the religious pretensions are extreme.

The simplest rudiment of mystical experience would seem to be that deepened sense of the significance of a maxim or formula which occasionally sweeps over one. "I've heard that said all my life," we exclaim, "but I never realized its full meaning until now." "When a fellow-monk," said Luther, "one day repeated the words of the Creed: 'I believe in the forgiveness of sins,' I saw the Scripture in an entirely new light; and straightway I felt as if I were born anew. It was as if I had found the door of paradise thrown wide open."[1]

This sense of deeper significance is not confined to rational propositions. Single words,[2] and conjunctions of words, effects of light on land and sea, odors and musical sounds, all bring it when the mind is tuned aright. Most of us can remember the strangely moving power of passages in certain poems read when we were young, irrational doorways as they were through which the mystery of fact, the wildness and the pang of life, stole into our hearts and thrilled them. The words have now perhaps become mere polished surfaces for us; but lyric poetry and music are alive and significant only in proportion as they fetch these vague vistas of a life continuous with our own, beckoning and inviting, yet ever eluding our pursuit. We are alive or dead to the eternal inner message of the arts according as we have kept or lost this mystical susceptibility.

A more pronounced step forward on the mystical ladder is found in an extremely frequent phenomenon, that sudden feeling, namely, which sometimes sweeps over us, of having "been here before," as if at some indefinite past time, in just this place, with just these people, we were already saying just these things. As Tennyson writes:

> Moreover, something is or seems,
> That touches me with mystic gleams,
> Like glimpses of forgotten dreams—
>
> Of something felt, like something here;
> Of something done, I know not where;
> Such as no language may declare.[3]

---

[1] Newman's *Securus judicat orbis terrarum* is another instance.

[2] "Mesopotamia" is the stock comic instance. —An excellent old German lady, who had done some traveling in her day, used to describe to me her *Sehnsucht* that she might yet visit "Phīladelphiā," whose wondrous name had always haunted her imagination. Of John Foster it is said that "single words (as *chalcedony*), or the names of ancient heroes, had a mighty fascination over him. 'At any time the word *hermit* was enough to transport him.' The words *woods* and *forests* would produce the most powerful emotion." Foster's Life, by Ryland, New York, 1846, p. 3.

[3] The Two Voices. In a letter to Mr. B. P. Blood, Tennyson reports of himself as follows:—

> "I have never had any revelations through anaesthetics, but a kind of waking trance— this for lack of a better word—I have frequently had, quite up from boyhood, when I have been all

Sir James Crichton-Browne has given the technical name of "dreamy states" to these sudden invasions of vaguely reminiscent consciousness. They bring a sense of mystery and of the metaphysical duality of things, and the feeling of an enlargement of perception which seems imminent but which never completes itself.

27. The Idea of the Holy
RUDOLF OTTO

THE ELEMENTS IN THE "NUMINOUS"

Creature-Feeling

The reader is invited to direct his mind to a moment of deeply-felt religious experience, as little as possible qualified by other forms of consciousness. Whoever cannot do this, whoever knows no such moments in his experience, is requested to read no further; for it is not easy to discuss questions of religious psychology with one who can recollect the emotions of his adolescence, the discomforts of indigestion, or, say, social feelings, but cannot recall any intrinsically religious feelings. We do not blame such a one, when he tries for himself to advance as far as he can with the help of such principles of explanation as he knows, interpreting "Aesthetics" in terms of sensuous pleasure, and "Religion" as a function of the gregarious instinct and social standards, or as something more primitive still. But the artist, who for his part has an intimate personal knowledge of the distinctive element in the aesthetic experience, will decline his theories with thanks, and the religious man will reject them even more uncompromisingly.

　　Next, in the probing and analysis of such states of the soul as that of solemn worship, it will be well if regard be paid to what is unique in them rather than to what they have in common with other similar states. To be *rapt* in worship is one thing; to be morally *uplifted* by the contemplation of a good deed is another; and it is not to their common features, but to those elements of emotional content peculiar to the first that we would have attention directed as precisely as possible. As Christians we undoubtedly here first meet with feelings familiar enough in a weaker form in other departments of experience, such as feelings of gratitude, trust, love, reliance, humble submission, and dedication. But this does not by any means exhaust the content of religious worship. Not in any of these have we got

---

alone. This has come upon me through repeating my own name to myself silently, till all at once, as it were out of the intensity of the consciousness of individuality, individuality itself seemed to dissolve and fade away into boundless being, and this not a confused state but the clearest, the surest of the surest, utterly beyond words—where death was an almost laughable impossibility—the loss of personality (if so it were) seeming no extinction, but the only true life. I am ashamed of my feeble description. Have I not said the state is utterly beyond words?"

　　Professor Tyndall, in a letter, recalls Tennyson saying of this condition: "By God Almighty! there is no delusion in the matter! It is no nebulous ecstasy, but a state of transcendent wonder, associated with absolute clearness of mind." Memoirs of Alfred Tennyson, ii. 473.

the special features of the quite unique and incomparable experience of solemn worship. In what does this consist?

Schleiermacher has the credit of isolating a very important element in such an experience. This is the "feeling of dependence." But this important discovery of Schleiermacher is open to criticism in more than one respect.

In the first place, the feeling or emotion which he really has in mind in this phrase is in its specific quality not a "feeling of dependence" in the "natural" sense of the word. As such, other domains of life and other regions of experience than the religious occasion the feeling, as a sense of personal insufficiency and impotence, a consciousness of being determined by circumstances and environment. The feeling of which Schleiermacher wrote has an undeniable analogy with these states of mind: they serve as an indication to it, and its nature may be elucidated by them, so that, by following the direction in which they point, the feeling itself may be spontaneously felt. But the feeling is at the same time also qualitatively different from such analogous states of mind. Schleiermacher himself, in a way, recognizes this by distinguishing the feeling of pious or religious dependence from all other feelings of dependence. His mistake is in making the distinction merely that between "absolute" and "relative" dependence, and therefore a difference of degree and not of intrinsic quality. What he overlooks is that, in giving the feeling the name "feeling of dependence" at all, we are really employing what is no more than a very close analogy. Any one who compares and contrasts the two states of mind introspectively will find out, I think, what I mean. It cannot be expressed by means of anything else, just because it is so primary and elementary a datum in our psychical life, and therefore only definable through itself. It may perhaps help him if I cite a well-known example, in which the precise "moment" or element of religious feeling of which we are speaking is most actively present. When Abraham ventures to plead with God for the men of Sodom, he says (Genesis xviii. 27): "Behold now, I have taken upon me to speak unto the Lord, which am but dust and ashes." There you have a self-confessed "feeling of dependence," which is yet at the same time far more than, and something other than, *merely* a feeling of dependence. Desiring to give it a name of its own, I propose to call it "creature-consciousness" or creature-feeling. It is the emotion of a creature, abased and overwhelmed by its own nothingness in contrast to that which is supreme above all creatures. . . .

MYSTERIUM TREMENDUM

The Analysis of "Tremendum"

We said above that the nature of the numinous can only be suggested by means of the special way in which it is reflected in the mind in terms of feeling. "Its nature is such that it grips or stirs the human mind with this and that determinate affective state." We have now to attempt to give a further indication of these determinate states. We must once again endeavour, by adducing feelings akin to them for the purpose of analogy or contrast, and by the use of metaphor and symbolic expres-

0743

BUSINESS REPLY MAIL
FIRST CLASS MAIL PERMIT NO. 100, PARSIPPANY NJ

POSTAGE WILL BE PAID BY ADDRESSEE

TIME COLLEGE BUREAU
PO BOX 5148
PARSIPPANY NJ 07054-9929

NO POSTAGE
NECESSARY
IF MAILED
IN THE
UNITED STATES

sions, to make the states of mind we are investigating ring out, as it were, of themselves.

Let us consider the deepest and most fundamental element in all strong and sincerely felt religious emotion. Faith unto Salvation, Trust, Love—all these are there. But over and above these is an element which may also on occasion, quite apart from them, profoundly affect us and occupy the mind with a wellnigh bewildering strength. Let us follow it up with every effort of sympathy and imaginative intuition wherever it is to be found, in the lives of those around us, in sudden, strong ebullitions of personal piety and the frames of mind such ebullitions evince, in the fixed and ordered solemnities of rites and liturgies, and again in the atmosphere that clings to old religious monuments and buildings, to temples and to churches. If we do so we shall find we are dealing with something for which there is only one appropriate expression, *mysterium tremendum.* The feeling of it may at times come sweeping like a gentle tide, pervading the mind with a tranquil mood of deepest worship. It may pass over into a more set and lasting attitude of the soul, continuing, as it were, thrillingly vibrant and resonant, until at last it dies away and the soul resumes its "profane," non-religious mood of everyday experience. It may burst in sudden eruption up from the depths of the soul with spasms and convulsions, or lead to the strangest excitements, to intoxicated frenzy, to transport, and to ecstasy. It has its wild and demonic forms and can sink to an almost grisly horror and shuddering. It has its crude, barbaric antecedents and early manifestations, and again it may be developed into something beautiful and pure and glorious. It may become the hushed, trembling, and speechless humility of the creature in the presence of—whom or what? In the presence of that which is a *Mystery* inexpressible and above all creatures.

It is again evident at once that here too our attempted formulation by means of a concept is once more a merely negative one. Conceptually "mysterium" denotes merely that before which the eyes are held closed, that which is hidden and esoteric, that which is beyond conception or understanding, extraordinary and unfamiliar. The term does not define the object more positively in its qualitative character. But though what is enunciated in the word is negative, what is meant is something absolutely and intensely positive. This pure positive we can experience in feelings, feelings which our discussion can help to make clear to us, in so far as it arouses them actually in our hearts.

1. *The Element of Awefulness.*   To get light upon the positive "quale" of the object of these feelings, we must analyse more closely our phrase *mysterium tremendum,* and we will begin first with the adjective.

"Tremor" is in itself merely the perfectly familiar and "natural" emotion of *fear.* But here the term is taken, aptly enough but still only by analogy, to denote a quite specific kind of emotional response, wholly distinct from that of being afraid, though it so far resembles it that the analogy of fear may be used to throw light upon its nature. There are in some languages special expressions which denote, either exclusively or in the first instance, this "fear" that is more than fear proper. The Hebrew *hiqdīsh* (hallow) is an example. To "keep a thing holy in the heart" means to mark it off by a feeling of peculiar dread, not to be mistaken for any ordinary dread, that is, to appraise it by the category of the numinous. But the Old Testament throughout is rich in parallel expressions for this feeling. Specially noticeable is the emāt of Yahweh ("fear of God"), which Yahweh can pour forth, dispatching almost like a daemon, and which seizes upon a man with paralysing effect. It is closely related to the δεῖμα πανικόν of the Greeks. Compare Exodus xxiii. 27: "I will send my fear before thee and will destroy all the people to whom thou shalt come . . ."; also Job ix. 34; xiii. 21 ("Let not his fear terrify me"; "Let not thy dread make me afraid"). Here we have a terror fraught with an inward shuddering such as not even the most menacing and overpowering created thing can instil. It has something spectral in it. . . .

2. The Element of "Overpoweringness" ("Majestas").   We have been attempting to unfold the implications of that aspect of the "mysterium tremendum" indicated by the adjective, and the result so far may be summarized in two words, constituting, as before, what may be called an "ideogram," rather than a concept proper, viz. "absolute unapproachability."

It will be felt at once that there is yet a further element which must be added, that, namely, of "might," "power," "absolute overpoweringness." We will take to represent this the term "majestas," majesty—the more readily because any one with a feeling for language must detect a last faint trace of the numinous still clinging to the word. The "tremendum" may then be rendered more adequately "tremenda majestas," or "aweful majesty." This second element of majesty may continue to be vividly perserved, where the first, that of unapproachability, recedes and dies away, as may be seen, for example, in Mysticism. It is especially in relation to this element of majesty or absolute overpoweringness that the creature-consciousness, of which we have already spoken, comes upon the scene, as a sort of shadow or subjective reflection of it. Thus, in contrast to "the overpowering" of which we are conscious as an object over against the self, there is the feeling of one's own abasement, of being but "dust and ashes" and nothingness. And this forms the numinous raw material for the feeling of religious humility. . . .

These are the characteristic notes of Mysticism in all its forms, however otherwise various in content. For one of the chiefest and most general features of Mysticism is just this *self-depreciation* (so plainly parallel to the case of Abraham), the estimation of the self, of the personal "I," as something not perfectly or essentially real, or even as mere nullity, a self-depreciation which comes to demand its own fulfillment in practice in rejecting the delusion of selfhood, and so makes for the annihilation of the self. And on the other hand Mysticism leads to a valuation of the transcendent object of its reference as that which through plenitude of being stands supreme and absolute, so that the finite self contrasted with it becomes conscious even in its nullity that "I am nought, Thou art all." There is no thought in this of any causal relation between God, the creator, and the self, the creature. The point from which speculation starts is not a "consciousness of absolute dependence"—of myself as result and effect of a divine cause—for that would in point of fact lead to insistence upon the reality of the self; it starts from a consciousness of the absolute superiority or supremacy of a power other than myself, and it is only as it falls back upon ontological terms to achieve its end—terms generally borrowed from natural science—that that element of the "tremendum," originally apprehended as "plenitude of power," becomes transmuted into "plenitude of being."

This leads again to the mention of Mysticism. No mere inquiry into the genesis of a thing can throw any light upon its essential nature, and it is hence immaterial to us how Mysticism historically arose. But essentially Mysticism is the stressing to a very high degree, indeed the overstressing, of the non-rational or supra-rational elements in religion; and it is only intelligible when so understood. The various phases and factors of the non-rational may receive varying emphasis, and the type of Mysticism will differ according as some or others fall into the background. What we have been analysing, however, is a feature that recurs in all forms of Mysticism everywhere, and it is nothing but the "creature-consciousness" stressed to the utmost and to excess, the expression meaning, if we may repeat the contrast already made, not "feeling of our createdness" but "feeling of our creaturehood," that is, the consciousness of the littleness of every creature in face of that which is above all creatures.

A characteristic common to all types of Mysticism is the *Identification*, in different degrees of completeness, of the personal self with the transcendant Reality. This identification has a source of its own, with which we are not here concerned, and springs from "moments" of religious experience which would require separate treatment. "Identification" alone, however, is not enough for Mysticism; it must be Identification with the Something that is at once absolutely supreme in power and reality and wholly non-rational. And it is among the mystics that we most encounter this element of religious consciousness. Récéjac has noticed this in his *Essai sur les fondements de la connaissance mystique* (Paris, 1897). He writes (p. 90):

> "Le mysticisme commence par la crainte, par le sentiment d'une *domination* universelle, *invincible*, et devient plus tard un désir d'union avec ce qui domine ainsi."

And some very clear examples of this taken from the religious experience of the present day are to be found in W. James (*Varieties of Religious Experience*, p. 66):

> "The perfect stillness of the night was thrilled by a more solemn silence. The darkness held a presence that was all the more felt because it was not seen. I could not any more have doubted that *He* was there than that I was. Indeed, I felt myself to be, if possible, the less real of the two."

This example is particularly instructive as to the relation of Mysticism to the "feelings of Identification," for the experience here recounted was on the point of passing into it.

3. *The Element of "Energy" or Urgency.* There is, finally, a third element comprised in those of "tremendum" and "majestas," awefulness and majesty, and this I venture to call the *urgency* or *energy* of the numinous object. It is particularly vividly perceptible in the "ὀργή" or "Wrath"; and it everywhere clothes itself in symbolic expressions—vitality, passion, emotional temper, will, force, move-

ment, excitement, activity, violence. These features are typical and recur again and again from the daemonic level up to the idea of the "living" God. We have here the factor that has everywhere more than any other prompted the fiercest opposition to the "philosophic" God of mere rational speculation, who can be put into a definition. And for their part the philosophers have condemned these expressions of the energy of the numen, whenever they are brought on to the scene, as sheer anthropomorphism. In so far as their opponents have for the most part themselves failed to recognize that the terms they have borrowed from the sphere of human conative and affective life have merely value as analogies, the philosophers are right to condemn them. But they are wrong, in so far as, this error notwithstanding, these terms stood for a genuine aspect of the divine nature—its non-rational aspect—a due consciousness of which served to protect religion itself from being "rationalized" away.

For wherever men have been contending for the "living" God and for voluntarism there, we may be sure, have been non-rationalists fighting rationalists and rationalism. It was so with Luther in his controversy with Erasmus; and Luther's "omnipotentia Dei" in his *De Servo Arbitrio* is nothing but the union of "majesty"—in the sense of absolute supremacy—with this "energy," in the sense of a force that knows not stint nor stay, which is urgent, active, compelling, and alive. In Mysticism, too, this element of "energy" is a very living and vigorous factor, at any rate in the "voluntaristic" Mysticism, the Mysticism of love, where it is very forcibly seen in that "consuming fire" of love whose burning strength the mystic can hardly bear, but begs that the heat that has scorched him may be mitigated, lest he be himself destroyed by it. And in this urgency and pressure the mystic's "love" claims a perceptible kinship with the ὀργή itself, the scorching and consuming wrath of God; it is the same "energy," only differently directed. "Love," says one of the mystics, "is nothing else than quenched Wrath."

THE ANALYSIS OF "MYSTERIUM"

Ein begriffener Gott ist kein Gott.
"A God comprehended is no God."

(*Tersteegen.*)

We gave to the object to which the numinous consciousness is directed the name "mysterium tremendum," and we then set ourselves first to determine the meaning of the adjective "tremendum"—which we found to be itself only justified by analogy—because it is more easily analysed than the substantive idea "mysterium." We have now to turn to this, and try, as best we may, by hint and suggestion, to get to a clearer apprehension of what it implies.

4. *The "Wholly Other".* It might be thought that the adjective itself gives an explanation of the substantive; but this is not so. It is not merely analytical; it is a synthetic attribute to it; i.e. "tremendum" adds something not necessarily inherent

in "mysterium." It is true that the reactions in consciousness that correspond to the one readily and spontaneously overflow into those that correspond to the other; in fact, any one sensitive to the use of words would commonly feel that the idea of "mystery" (*mysterium*) is so closely bound up with its synthetic qualifying attribute "aweful" (*tremendum*) that one can hardly say the former without catching an echo of the latter, "mystery" almost of itself becoming "aweful mystery" to us. But the passage from the one idea to the other need not by any means be always so easy. The elements of meaning implied in "awefulness" and "mysteriousness" are in themselves definitely different. The latter may so far preponderate in the religious consciousness, may stand out so vividly, that in comparison with it the former almost sinks out of sight; a case which again could be clearly exemplified from some forms of Mysticism. Occasionally, on the other hand, the reverse happens, and the "tremendum" may in turn occupy the mind without the "mysterium."

This latter, then, needs special consideration on its own account. We need an expression for the mental reaction peculiar to it; and here, too, only one word seems appropriate though, as it is strictly applicable only to a "natural" state of mind, it has here meaning only by analogy: it is the word "stupor." *Stupor* is plainly a different thing from *tremor*; it signifies blank wonder, an astonishment that strikes us dumb, amazement absolute. Taken, indeed, in its purely natural sense, "mysterium" would first mean merely a secret or a mystery in the sense of that which is alien to us, uncomprehended and unexplained; and so far "mysterium" is itself merely an ideogram, an analogical notion taken from the natural sphere, illustrating, but incapable of exhaustively rendering, our real meaning. Taken in the religious sense, that which is "mysterious" is—to give it perhaps the most striking expression—the "wholly other" (θάτερον, *anyad, alienum*), that which is quite beyond the sphere of the usual, the intelligible, and the familiar, which therefore falls quite outside the limits of the "canny," and is contrasted with it, filling the mind with blank wonder and astonishment.

This is already to be observed on the lowest and earliest level of the religion of primitive man, where the numinous consciousness is but an inchoate stirring of the feelings. What is really characteristic of this stage is *not*—as the theory of Animism would have us believe—that men are here concerned with curious entities, called "souls" or "spirits," which happen to be invisible. Representations of spirits and similar conceptions are rather one and all early modes of "rationalizing" a precedent experience, to which they are subsidiary. They are attempts in some way or other, it little matters how, to guess the riddle it propounds, and their effect is at the same time always to weaken and deaden the experience itself. They are the source from which springs, not religion, but the rationalization of religion, which often ends by constructing such a massive structure of theory and such a plausible fabric of interpretation, that the "mystery" is frankly excluded. Both imaginative "Myth," when developed into a system, and intellectualist Scholasticism, when worked out to its completion, are methods by which the fundamental fact of religious experience is, as it were, simply rolled out so thin and flat as to be finally eliminated altogether.

Even on the lowest level of religious development the essential characteristic is therefore to be sought elsewhere than in the appearance of "spirit" representa-tions. It lies rather, we repeat, in a peculiar "moment" of consciousness, to wit, the *stupor* before something "wholly other," whether such an other be named "spirit" or "daemon" or "deva," or be left without any name.

28. Mysticism

BERTRAND RUSSELL

Ought we to admit that there is available, in support of religion, a source of knowledge which lies outside science and may properly be described as "revela-tion"? This is a difficult question to argue, because those who believe that truths have been revealed to them profess the same kind of certainty in regard to them that we have in regard to objects of sense. We believe the man who has seen things through the telescope that we have never seen; why, then, they ask, should we not believe them when they report things that are to them equally unquestionable?

It is, perhaps, useless to attempt an argument such as will appeal to the man who has himself enjoyed mystic illumination. But something can be said as to whether we others should accept this testimony. In the first place, it is not subject to the ordinary tests. When a man of science tells us the result of an experiment, he also tells us how the experiment was performed; others can repeat it, and if the result is not confirmed it is not accepted as true; but many men might put them-selves into the situation in which the mystic's vision occurred without obtaining the same revelation. To this it may be answered that a man must use the appropri-ate sense: a telescope is useless to a man who keeps his eyes shut. The argument as to the credibility of the mystic's testimony may be prolonged almost indefinitely. Science should be neutral, since the argument is a scientific one, to be conducted exactly as an argument would be conducted about an uncertain experiment. Sci-ence depends upon perception and inference; its credibility is due to the fact that the perceptions are such as any observer can test. The mystic himself may be certain that he *knows*, and has no need of scientific tests; but those who are asked to accept his testimony will subject it to the same kind of scientific tests as those applied to men who say they have been to the North Pole. Science, as such, should have no expectation, positive or negative, as to the result.

The chief argument in favour of the mystics is their agreement with each other. "I know nothing more remarkable," says Dean Inge, "than the unanimity of the mystics, ancient, mediaeval, and modern; Protestant, Catholic, and even Bud-dhist or Mohammedan, though the Christian mystics are the most trustworthy." I do not wish to underrate the force of this argument, which I acknowledged long ago in a book called *Mysticism and Logic*. The mystics vary greatly in their capacity for giving verbal expression to their expriences, but I think we may take it that those who succeeded best all maintain: (1) that all division and separateness is unreal, and that the universe is a single indivisible unity; (2) that evil is illusory, and that the illusion arises through falsely regarding a part as self-subsistent; (3) that time is unreal, and that reality is eternal, not in the sense of being everlasting, but in the sense of being wholly outside time. I do not pretend that this is a complete account of the matters on which all mystics concur, but the three propositions that I have mentioned may serve as representatives of the whole. Let us now imagine ourselves a jury in a law-court, whose business it is to decide on the credibility of the witnesses who make these three somewhat surprising assertions.

We shall find, in the first place, that, while the witnesses agree up to a point, they disagree totally when that point is passed, although they are just as certain as when they agree. Catholics, but not Protestants, may have visions in which the Virgin appears; Christians and Mohammedans, but not Buddhists, may have great truths revealed to them by the Archangel Gabriel; the Chinese mystics of the Tao tell us, as a direct result of their central doctrine, that all government is bad, whereas most European and Mohammedan mystics, with equal confidence, urge submission to constituted authority. As regards the points where they differ, each group will argue that the other groups are untrustworthy; we might, there-fore, if we were content with a mere forensic triumph, point out that most mystics think most other mystics mistaken on most points. They might, however, make this only half a triumph by agreeing on the greater importance of the matters about which they are at one, as compared with those as to which their opinions differ. We will, in any case, assume that they have composed their differences, and concentrated the defence at these three points—namely, the unity of the world, the illusory nature of evil, and the unreality of time. What test can we, as impartial outsiders, apply to their unanimous evidence?

As men of scientific temper, we shall naturally first ask whether there is any way by which we can ourselves obtain the same evidence at first hand. To this we shall receive various answers. We may be told that we are obviously not in a receptive frame of mind, and that we lack the requisite humility; or that fasting and religious meditation are necessary; or (if our witness is Indian or Chinese) that the essential prerequisite is a course of breathing exercises. I think we shall find that the weight of experimental evidence is in favour of this last view, though fasting also has been frequently found effective. As a matter of fact, there is a definite physical discipline, called yoga, which is practised in order to produce the mystic's certainty, and which is recommended with much confidence by those who have tried it.[1] Breathing exercises are its most essential feature, and for our purposes we may ignore the rest.

In order to see how we could test the assertion that yoga gives insight, let us artificially simplify this assertion. Let us suppose that a number of people assure us that if, *for a certain time*, we breathe in a certain way, we shall become con-vinced that time is unreal. Let us go further, and suppose that, having tried their recipe, we have ourselves experienced a state of mind such as they describe. But now, having returned to our normal mode of respiration, we are not quite sure whether the vision was to be believed. How shall we investigate this question?

First of all, what can be meant by saying that time is unreal? If we really

---

[1] As regards yoga in China, see Waley, *The Way and its Power*, pp. 117–18.

mean what we say, we must mean that such statements as "this is before that" are mere empty noise, like "twas brillig." If we suppose anything less than this—as, for example, that there is a relation between events which puts them in the same order as the relation of earlier and later, but that it is a different relation—we shall not have made any assertion that makes any real change in our outlook. It will be merely like supposing that the Iliad was not written by Homer, but by another man of the same name. We have to suppose that there are no "events" at all; there must be only the one vast whole of the universe, embracing whatever is real in the misleading appearance of a temporal procession. There must be nothing in reality corresponding to the apparent distinction between earlier and later events. To say that we are born, and then grow, and then die, must be just as false as to say that we die, then grow small, and finally are born. The truth of what seems an individual life is merely the illusory isolation of one element in the timeless and indivisible being of the universe. There is no distinction between improvement and deterioration, no difference between sorrows that end in happiness and happiness that ends in sorrow. If you find a corpse with a dagger in it, it makes no difference whether the man died of the wound or the dagger was plunged in after death. Such a view, if true, puts an end, not only to science, but to prudence, hope, and effort; it is incompatible with worldly wisdom, and—what is more important to religion—with morality.

Most mystics, of course, do not accept these conclusions in their entirety, but they urge doctrines from which these conclusions inevitably follow. Thus Dean Inge rejects the kind of religion that appeals to evolution, because it lays too much stress upon a temporal process. "There is no law of progress, and there is no universal progress," he says. And again: "The doctrine of automatic and universal progress, the lay religion of many Victorians, labours under the disadvantage of being almost the only philosophical theory which can be definitely disproved." On this matter, which I shall discuss at a later stage, I find myself in agreement with the Dean, for whom, on many grounds, I have a very high respect. But he naturally does not draw from his premises all the inferences which seem to me to be warranted.

It is important not to caricature the doctrine of mysticism, in which there is, I think, a core of wisdom. Let us see how it seeks to avoid the extreme consequences which seem to follow from the denial of time.

The philosophy based upon mysticism has a great tradition, from Parmenides to Hegel. Parmenides says: "What is, is uncreated and indestructible; for it is complete, immovable, and without end. Nor was it ever, nor will it be; for now *it is*, all at once, a continuous one."[2] He introduced into metaphysics the distinction between reality and appearance, or the way of truth and the way of opinion, as he calls them. It is clear that whoever denies the reality of time must introduce some such distinction, since obviously the world *appears* to be in time. It is also clear that, if everyday experience is not to be *wholly* illusory, there must be some relation between appearance and the reality behind it. It is at this point, however, that the greatest difficulties arise: if the relation between appearance and

---

[2] Quoted from Burnet's *Early Greek Philosophy*, p. 199.

reality is made too intimate, all the unpleasant features of appearance will have their unpleasant counterparts in reality, while if the relation is made too remote, we shall be unable to make inferences from the character of appearance to that of reality, and reality will be left a vague Unknowable, as with Herbert Spencer. For Christians, there is the related difficulty of avoiding pantheism: if the world is *only* apparent, God created nothing, and the reality corresponding to the world is a part of God; but if the world is in any degree real and distinct from God, we abandon the wholeness of everything, which is an essential doctrine of mysticism, and we are compelled to suppose that, in so far as the world is real, the evil which it contains is also real. Such difficulties make thorough-going mysticism very difficult for an orthodox Christian. As the Bishop of Birmingham says: "All forms of pantheism . . . as it seems to me, must be rejected because, if man is actually a part of God, the evil in man is also in God."

All this time I have been supposing that we are a jury, listening to the testimony of the mystics, and trying to decide whether to accept or reject it. If, when they deny the reality of the world of sense, we took them to mean "reality" in the ordinary sense of the law-courts, we should have no hesitation in rejecting what they say, since we should find that it runs counter to all other testimony, and even to their own in their mundane moments. We must therefore look for some other sense. I believe that, when the mystics contrast "reality" with "appearance," the word "reality" has not a logical, but an emotional, significance: it means what is, in some sense, important. When it is said that time is "unreal," what should be said is that, in some sense and on some occasions, it is important to conceive the universe as a whole, as the Creator, if He existed, must have conceived it in deciding to create it. When so conceived, all process is within one completed whole; past, present, and future, all exist, in some sense, together, and the present does not have that pre-eminent reality which it has to our usual ways of apprehending the world. If this interpretation is accepted, mysticism expresses an emotion, not a fact; it does not assert anything, and therefore can be neither confirmed nor contradicted by science. The fact that mystics do make assertions is owing to their inability to separate emotional importance from scientific validity. It is, of course, not to be expected that they will accept this view, but it is the only one, so far as I can see, which, while admitting something of their claim, is not repugnant to the scientific intelligence.

The certainty and partial unanimity of mystics is no conclusive reason for accepting their testimony on a matter of fact. The man of science, when he wishes others to see what he has seen, arranges his microscope or telescope; that is to say, he makes changes in the external world, but demands of the observer only normal eyesight. The mystic, on the other hand, demands changes in the observer, by fasting, by breathing exercises, and by a careful abstention from external observation. (Some object to such discipline, and think that the mystic illumination cannot be artificially achieved; from a scientific point of view, this makes their case more difficult to test than that of those who rely on yoga. But nearly all agree that fasting and an ascetic life are helpful.) We all know that opium, hashish, and alcohol produce certain effects on the observer, but as we do not think these effects admirable we take no account of them in our theory of the universe. They may even, sometimes, reveal fragments of truth; but we do not regard them as sources of general wisdom. The drunkard who sees snakes does not imagine, afterwards, that he has had a revelation of a reality hidden from others, though some not wholly dissimilar belief must have given rise to the worship of Bacchus. In our own day, as William James related,[3] there have been people who considered that the intoxication produced by laughing-gas revealed truths which are hidden at normal times. From a scientific point of view, we can make no distinction between the man who eats little and sees heaven and the man who drinks much and see snakes. Each is in an abnormal physical condition, and therefore has abnormal perceptions. Normal perceptions, since they have to be useful in the struggle for life, must have some correspondence with fact; but in abnormal perceptions there is no reason to expect such correspondence, and their testimony, therefore, cannot outweigh that of normal perception.

The mystic emotion, if it is freed from unwarranted beliefs, and not so overwhelming as to remove a man wholly from the ordinary business of life, may give something of very great value—the same kind of thing, though in a heightened form, that is given by contemplation. Breadth and calm and profundity may all have their source in this emotion, in which, for the moment, all self-centred desire is dead, and the mind becomes a mirror for the vastness of the universe. Those who have had this experience, and believe it to be bound up unavoidably with assertions about the nature of the universe, naturally cling to these assertions. I believe myself that the assertions are inessential, and that there is no reason to believe them true. I cannot admit any method of arriving at truth except that of science, but in the realm of the emotions I do not deny the value of the experiences which have given rise to religion. Through association with false beliefs, they have led to much evil as well as good; freed from this association, it may be hoped that the good alone will remain.

---

[3] See his *Varieties of Religious Experience.*

The Moral Argument

29. God and Immortality as Postulates of Practical Reason

IMMANUEL KANT

The concept of the "highest" contains an ambiguity which, if not attended to, can occasion unnecessary disputes. The "highest" can mean the "supreme" (*supremum*) or the "perfect" (*consummatum*). The former is the unconditional condition, i.e., the condition which is subordinate to no other (*originarium*); the latter is that whole which is no part of a yet larger whole of the same kind (*perfectissimum*). That virtue (as the worthiness to be happy) is the supreme condition of whatever appears to us to be desirable and thus of all our pursuit of happiness and, consequently, that it is the supreme good have been proved in the Analytic. But these truths do not imply that virtue is the entire and perfect good as the object of the faculty of desire of rational finite beings. For this, happiness is also required, and indeed not merely in the partial eyes of a person who makes himself his end but even in the judgment of an impartial reason, which impartially regards persons in the world as ends-in-themselves. For to be in need of happiness and also worthy of it and yet not to partake of it could not be in accordance with the complete volition of an omnipotent rational being, if we assume such only for the sake of the argument. Inasmuch as virtue and happiness together constitute the possession of the highest good for one person, and happiness in exact proportion to morality (as the worth of a person and his worthiness to be happy) constitutes that of a possible world, the highest good means the whole, the perfect good, wherein virtue is always the supreme good, being the condition having no condition superior to it, while happiness, though something always pleasant to him who possesses it, is not of itself absolutely good in every respect but always presupposes conduct in accordance with the moral law as its condition. . . .

THE IMMORTALITY OF THE SOUL AS A POSTULATE OF
PURE PRACTICAL REASON

The achievement of the highest good in the world is the necessary object of a will determinable by the moral law. In such a will, however, the complete fitness of intentions to the moral law is the supreme condition of the highest good. This fitness, therefore, must be just as possible as its object, because it is contained in the command that requires us to promote the latter. But complete fitness of the will to the moral law is holiness, which is a perfection of which no rational being in the world of sense is at any time capable. But since it is required as practically necessary, it can be found only in an endless progress to that complete fitness; on principles of pure practical reason, it is necessary to assume such a practical progress as the real object of our will.

This infinite progress is possible, however, only under the presupposition of an infinitely enduring existence and personality of the same rational being; this is called the immortality of the soul. Thus the highest good is practically possible only on the supposition of the immortality of the soul, and the latter, as insepara-bly bound to the moral law, is a postulate of pure practical reason. By a postulate of pure practical reason, I understand a theoretical proposition which is not as such demonstrable, but which is an inseparable corollary of an a priori unconditionally valid practical law.

The thesis of the moral destiny of our nature, viz., that it is able only in an infinite progress toward complete fitness to the moral law, is of great use, not merely for the present purpose of supplementing the impotence of speculative reason, but also with respect to religion. Without it, either the moral law is completely degraded from its holiness, by being made out as lenient (indulgent) and thus compliant to our convenience, or its call and its demands are strained to an unattainable destina-tion, i.e., a hoped-for complete attainment of holiness of will, and are lost in fanatical theosophical dreams which completely contradict our knowledge of our-selves. In either case, we are only hindered in the unceasing striving toward the precise and persistent obedience to a command of reason which is stern, unindulgent, truly commanding, really and not just ideally possible.

Only endless progress from lower to higher stages of moral perfection is possible to a rational but finite being. The Infinite Being, to whom the temporal condition is nothing, sees in this series, which is for us without end, a whole conformable to the moral law; holiness, which His law inexorably commands in order to be true to His justice in the share He assigns to each in the highest good, is to be found in a single intellectual intuition of the existence of rational beings. All that can be granted to a creature with respect to hope for this share is consciousness of his tried character. And on the basis of his previous progress from the worse to the morally better, and of the immutability of intention which thus becomes known to him, he may hope for a further uninterrupted continuance of this progress, however long his existence may last, even beyond this life.[1] But he

---

[1] The conviction of the immutability of character in progress toward the good may appear to be impossible for a creature. For this reason, Christian doctrine lets it derive from the same Spirit which works sanctifica-

cannot hope here or at any foreseeable point of his future existence to be fully adequate to God's will, without indulgence or remission which would not harmonize with justice. This he can do only in the infinity of his duration which God alone can survey.

THE EXISTENCE OF GOD AS A POSTULATE OF PURE PRACTICAL REASON

The moral law led, in the foregoing analysis, to a practical problem which is assigned solely by pure reason and without any concurrence of sensuous incentives. It is the problem of the completeness of the first and principal part of the highest good, viz., morality; since this problem can be solved only in eternity, it led to the postulate of immortality. The same law must also lead us to affirm the possibility of the second element of the highest good, i.e., happiness proportional to that morality; it must do so just as disinterestedly as heretofore, by a purely impartial reason. This it can do on the supposition of the existence of a cause adequate to this effect, i.e., it must postulate the existence of God as necessarily belonging to the possibility of the highest good (the object of our will which is necessarily connected with the moral legislation of pure reason). We proceed to exhibit this connection in a convincing manner.

Happiness is the condition of a rational being in the world, in whose whole existence everything goes according to wish and will. It thus rests on the harmony of nature with his entire end and with the essential determining ground of his will. But the moral law commands as a law of freedom through motives wholly independent of nature and of its harmony with our faculty of desire (as incentives). Still, the acting rational being in the world is not at the same time the cause of the world and of nature itself. Hence there is not the slightest ground in the moral law for a necessary connection between the morality and proportionate happiness of a being which belongs to the world as one of its parts and as thus dependent on it. Not being nature's cause, his will cannot by its own strength bring nature, as it touches on his happiness, into complete harmony with his practical principles. Nevertheless, in the practical task of pure reason, i.e., in the necessary endeavor after the highest good, such a connection is postulated as necessary: we *should* seek to further the highest good (which therefore must be at least possible). Therefore also the existence is postulated of a cause of the whole of nature, itself distinct from nature, which contains the ground of the exact coincidence of happiness with morality. This supreme cause, however, must contain the

---

tion, i.e., this firm intention and therewith the consciousness of steadfastness in moral progress. But naturally one who is conscious of having persisted, from legitimate moral motives, to the end of a long life in a progress to the better may very well have the comforting hope, though not the certainty, that he will be steadfast in these principles in an existence continuing beyond this life. Though he can never be justified in his own eyes either here or in the hoped-for increase of natural perfection together with an increase of his duties, nevertheless in this progress toward a goal infinitely remote (a progress which in God's sight is regarded as equivalent to possession) he can have prospect of a blessed future. For "blessed" is the word which reason uses to designate a perfect well-being independent of all contingent causes in the world. Like holiness, it is an idea which can be contained only in an infinite progress and its totality and thus is never fully reached by any creature.

ground of the agreement of nature not merely with a law of the will of rational beings but with the idea of this law so far as they make it the supreme ground of determination of the will. Thus it contains the ground of the agreement of nature not merely with actions moral in their form but also with their morality as the motives to such actions, i.e., with their moral intention. Therefore, the highest good is possible in the world only on the supposition of a supreme cause of nature which has a causality corresponding to the moral intention. Now a being which is capable of actions by the idea of laws is an intelligence (a rational being), and the causality of such a being according to this idea of laws is his will. Therefore, the supreme cause of nature, insofar as it must be presupposed for the highest good, is a being which is the cause (and consequently the author) of nature through understanding and will, i.e., God. As a consequence, the postulate of the possibility of a highest derived good (the best world) is at the same time the postulate of the reality of a highest original good, namely, the existence of God. Now it was our duty to promote the highest good; and it is not merely our privilege but a necessity connected with duty as a requisite to presuppose the possibility of this highest good. This presupposition is made only under the condition of the existence of God, and this condition inseparably connects this supposition with duty. Therefore, it is morally necessary to assume the existence of God.

It is well to notice here that this moral necessity is subjective, i.e., a need, and not objective, i.e., duty itself. For there cannot be any duty to assume the existence of a thing, because such a supposition concerns only the theoretical use of reason. It is also not to be understood that the assumption of the existence of God is necessary as a ground of all obligation in general (for this rests, as has been fully shown, solely on the autonomy of reason itself). All that here belongs to duty is the endeavor to produce and to further the highest good in the world, the existence of which may thus be postulated though our reason cannot conceive it except by presupposing a highest intelligence. To assume its existence is thus connected with the consciousness of our duty, though this assumption itself belongs to the realm of theoretical reason. Considered only in reference to the latter, it is a hypothesis, i.e., a ground of explanation. But in reference to the comprehensibility of an object (the highest good) placed before us by the moral law, and thus as a practical need, it can be called *faith* and even pure *rational faith,* because pure reason alone (by its theoretical as well as practical employment) is the source from which it springs.

From this deduction it now becomes clear why the Greek schools could never succeed in solving their problem of the practical possibility of the highest good. It was because they made the rule of the use which the human will makes of its freedom the sole and self-sufficient ground of its possibility, thinking that they had no need of the existence of God for this purpose. They were certainly correct in establishing the principle of morals by itself, independently of this postulate and merely from the relation of reason to the will, thus making the principle of morality the *supreme* practical condition of the highest good; but this principle was not the *entire* condition of its possibility. The Epicureans had indeed raised a wholly false principle of morality, i.e., that of happiness, into the supreme one, and for law had substituted a maxim of arbitrary choice of each according to his inclination. But they proceeded consistently enough, in that they degraded their highest good in proportion to the baseness of their principle and expected no greater happiness than that which could be attained through human prudence (wherein both temperance and the moderation of inclinations belong), though everyone knows prudence to be scarce enough and to produce diverse results according to circumstances, not to mention the exceptions which their maxims continually had to admit and which made them worthless as laws. The Stoics, on the other hand, had chosen their supreme practical principle, virtue, quite cor-rectly as the condition of the highest good. But as they imagined the degree of virtue which is required for its pure law as completely attainable in this life, they not only exaggerated the moral capacity of man, under the name of "sage," beyond all the limits of his nature, making it into something which is contradicted by all our knowledge of men; they also refused to accept the second component of the highest good, i.e., happiness, as a special object of human desire. Rather, they made their sage like a god in the consciousness of the excellence of his person, wholly independent of nature (as regards his own contentment), exposing him to the evils of life but not subjecting him to them. (They also represented him as free from everything morally evil.) Thus they really left out of the highest good the second element (personal happiness), since they placed the highest good only in acting and in contentment with one's own personal worth, including it in the consciousness of moral character. But the voice of their own nature could have sufficiently refuted this.

The doctrine of Christianity,[2] even when not regarded as a religious doctrine, gives at this point a concept of the highest good (the Kingdom of God) which is alone sufficient to the strictest demand of practical reason. The moral law is holy (unyielding) and demands holiness of morals, although all moral perfection to which man can attain is only virtue, i.e., a law-abiding disposition resulting

---

[2] The view is commonly held that the Christian precept of morals has no advantage over the moral concept of the Stoics in respect to its purity; but the difference between them is nevertheless obvious. The Stoic system makes the consciousness of strength of mind the pivot around which all moral intentions should turn; and, if the followers of this system spoke of duties and even defined them accurately, they neverthe-less placed the incentives and the real determining ground of the will in an elevation of character above the base incentives of the senses which have their power only through weakness of the mind. Virtue was, therefore, for them a certain heroism of the sage who, raising himself above the animal nature of man, was sufficient to himself, subject to no temptation to transgress the moral law, and elevated above duties though he propounded duties to others. But all this they could not have done had they conceived this law in the same purity and rigor as does the precept of the Gospel. If I understand by "idea" a perfection to which the senses can give nothing adequate, the moral ideas are not transcendent, i.e., of such a kind that we cannot even sufficiently define the concept or of which we are uncertain whether there is a correspond-ing object (as are the ideas of speculative reason); rather, they serve as models of practical perfection, as an indispensable rule of moral conduct, and as a standard for comparison. If I now regard Christian morals from their philosophical side, it appears in comparison with the ideas of the Greek schools as follows: the ideas of the Cynics, Epicureans, Stoics, and Christians are, respectively, the simplicity of nature, prudence, wisdom, and holiness. In respect to the way they achieve them, the Greek schools differ in that the Cynics found common sense sufficient, while the others found it in the path of science, and thus all held it to lie in the mere use of man's natural powers. Christian ethics, because it formulated its precept as pure and uncompromising (as befits a moral precept), destroyed man's confidence of being wholly adequate to it, at least in this life; but it re-established it by enabling us to hope that, if we act as well as lies in our power, what is not in our power will come to our aid from another source, whether we know in what way or not. Aristotle and Plato differed only as to the origin of our moral concepts.

from respect for the law and thus implying consciousness of a continuous propensity to transgress it or at least to a defilement, i.e., to an admixture of many spurious (not moral) motives to obedience to the law; consequently, man can achieve only a self-esteem combined with humility. And thus with respect to the holiness required by the Christian law, nothing remains to the creature but endless progress, though for the same reason hope of endless duration is justified. The worth of a character completely accordant with the moral law is infinite, because all possible happiness in the judgment of a wise and omnipotent dispenser of happiness has no other limitation than the lack of fitness of rational beings to their duty. But the moral law does not of itself promise happiness, for the latter is not, according to concepts of any order of nature, necessarily connected with obedience to the law. Christian ethics supplies this defect of the second indispensable component of the highest good by presenting a world wherein reasonable beings single-mindedly devote themselves to the moral law; this is the Kingdom of God, in which nature and morality come into a harmony, which is foreign to each as such, through a holy Author of the world, who makes possible the derived highest good. The holiness of morals is prescribed to them even in this life as a guide to conduct, but the well-being proportionate to this, which is bliss, is thought of as attainable only in eternity. This is due to the fact that the former must always be the pattern of their conduct in every state, and progressing toward it is even in this life possible and necessary, whereas the latter, under the name of happiness, cannot (as far as our own capacity is concerned) be reached in this life and therefore is made only an object of hope. Nevertheless, the Christian principle of morality is not theological and thus heteronomous, being rather the autonomy of pure practical reason itself, because it does not make the knowledge of God and His will the basis of these laws but makes such knowledge the basis only of succeeding to the highest good on condition of obedience to these laws; it places the real incentive for obedience to the law not in the desired consequences of obedience but in the conception of duty alone, in true observance of which the worthiness to attain the latter alone consists.

In this manner, through the concept of the highest good as the object and final end of pure practical reason, the moral law leads to religion. Religion is the recognition of all duties as divine commands, not as sanctions, i.e., arbitrary and contingent ordinances of a foreign will, but as essential laws of any free will as such. Even as such, they must be regarded as commands of the Supreme Being because we can hope for the highest good (to strive for which is our duty under the moral law) only from a morally perfect (holy and beneficent) and omnipotent will; and, therefore, we can hope to attain it only through harmony with this will. But here again everything remains disinterested and based only on duty, without being based on fear or hope as incentives, which, if they became principles, would destroy the entire moral worth of the actions. The moral law commands us to make the highest possible good in a world the final object of all our conduct. This I cannot hope to effect except through the agreement of my will with that of a holy and beneficent Author of the world. And although my own happiness is included in the concept of the highest good as a whole wherein the greatest happiness is thought of as connected in exact proportion to the greatest degree of moral perfection possible to creatures, still it is not happiness but the moral law (which, in fact, sternly places restricting conditions upon my boundless longing for happiness) which is proved to be the ground determining the will to further the highest good.

Therefore, morals is not really the doctrine of how to make ourselves happy but of how we are to be *worthy* of happiness. Only if religion is added to it can the hope arise of someday participating in happiness in proportion as we endeavored not to be unworthy of it.

One is worthy of possessing a thing or state when his possession is harmonious with the highest good. We can easily see now that all worthiness is a matter of moral conduct, because this constitutes the condition of everything else (which belongs to one's state) in the concept of the highest good, i.e., participation in happiness. From this there follows that one must never consider morals itself as a doctrine of happiness, i.e., as an instruction in how to acquire happiness. For morals has to do only with the rational condition (*conditio sine qua non*) of happiness and not with means of achieving it. But when morals (which imposes only duties instead of providing rules for selfish wishes) is completely expounded, and a moral wish has been awakened to promote the highest good (to bring the Kingdom of God to us), which is a wish based on law and one to which no selfish mind could have aspired, and when for the sake of this wish the step to religion has been taken—then only can ethics be called a doctrine of happiness, because the *hope* for it first arises with religion.

From this it can also be seen that, if we inquire into God's final end in creating the world, we must name not the happiness of rational beings in the world but the highest good, which adds a further condition to the wish of rational beings to be happy, viz., the condition of being worthy of happiness, which is the morality of these beings, for this alone contains the standard by which they can hope to participate in happiness at the hand of a *wise* creator. For since wisdom, theoretically regarded, means the knowledge of the highest good and, practically, the suitability of the will to the highest good, one cannot ascribe to a supreme independent wisdom an end based merely on benevolence. For we cannot conceive the action of this benevolence (with respect to the happiness of rational beings) except as conformable to the restrictive conditions of harmony with the holiness[3] of His will as the highest original good. Then perhaps those who have placed the end of creation in the glory of God, provided this is not thought of anthropomorphically as an inclination to be esteemed, have found the best term. For nothing glorifies God more than what is the most estimable thing in the world, namely, respect for His command, the observance of sacred duty which His law

---

[3] Incidentally, and in order to make the peculiarity of this concept clear, I make the following remark. Since we ascribe various attributes to God, whose quality we find suitable also to creatures (e.g., power, knowledge, presence, goodness, etc.), though in God they are present in a higher degree under such names as omnipotence, omniscience, omnipresence, and perfect goodness, etc., there are three which exclusively and without qualification of magnitude are ascribed to God, and they are all moral. He is the only holy, the only blessed, and the only wise being, because these concepts of themselves imply unlimitedness. By the arrangement of these He is thus the holy lawgiver (and creator), the beneficient ruler (and sustainer), and the just judge. These three attributes contain everything whereby God is the object of religion, and in conformity to them the metaphysical perfections of themselves arise in reason.

imposes on us, when there is added to this His glorious plan of crowning such an excellent order with corresponding happiness. If the latter, to speak in human terms, makes Him worthy of love, by the former He is an object of adoration. Human beings can win love by doing good, but by this alone even they never win respect; the greatest well-doing does them honor only by being exercised according to worthiness.

It follows of itself that, in the order of ends, man (and every rational being) is an end-in-himself, i.e., he is never to be used merely as a means for someone (even for God) without at the same time being himself an end, and that thus the humanity in our person must itself be holy to us, because man is subject to the moral law and therefore subject to that which is of itself holy, and it is only on account of this and in agreement with this that anything can be called holy. For this moral law is founded on the autonomy of his will as a free will, which by its universal laws must necessarily be able to agree with that to which it subjects itself.

30. Does God Exist?

A. E. TAYLOR

THE MORAL ARGUMENT

As far as I can see, the systematic disregard of all "moral" arguments would only be possible to one who frankly takes the line that there *are* no moral facts, that is, that right and wrong are pure illusions; there are no such differences *in rerum natura*. But even those who in theory profess to hold this view always reveal to a little inspection that, being human, they do not really mean what they say. The denial that our accepted moral distinctions have any "objective validity" is alleged as a reason why we *ought* to be tolerant of violation of the current model code. I am told that I *ought* to make no complaint of a wife's infidelity because it is a baseless "superstition" to fancy that adultery—or anything else—is *wrong;* so *because* nothing whatever is wrong, *therefore* something—my moral disapproval of adultery, or untruthfulness, or ingratitude—*is* wrong. On the face of it this is self-contradictory—the man who says it really believes all the time in the existence of the distinction between right and wrong. Where he differs from the rest of us is only in holding that we put many things which are right in the class of wrong things, and put the thing he regards as particularly wrong—moral disapproval of conduct which he himself thinks right—in the class of right things. On his own showing there is at least one genuine moral fact, the fact that "intolerance" is wrong.[1]

---

[1] It would be no real reply to say that when the professed disbeliever in the reality of moral distinctions calls intolerance *wrong*, he is using the word *wrong* in a non-ethical sense of his own, and only means *e.g.* "not conducive to survival." The intolerance of a group with the will and the power to "eliminate" all who disagree with it may be highly conducive to the survival of the group, and the propagandist methods of our totalitarian dictators show that they are alive to the fact. Alternately the immoralist who calls intolerance *wrong* might conceivably only mean that it is a thing which he personally dislikes. But if he means no more

We may safely take it, then, that there are moral facts. They can be left out of account for the special purposes of the biologist, just as the fact that there are living organisms may be left unmentioned in a work on mechanics or physics. But life is as much a fact as gravitation, though the physicist cannot avoid talking about gravitation but need never mention life. Similarly the biologist is concerned with the fact that there is a distinction between the living and the lifeless, but never need refer to any distinction between right and wrong. Yet the two facts are equally facts, and any general theory about the universe which is to do justice to the "facts" must take both into account. It is as much the "nature of man" to be conscious of a difference between right and wrong as it is to be alive to a difference between male and female.[2]

Now what does this consciousness of a difference between right and wrong imply whenever it is felt? Plainly it implies that there is a way of living—the doing of the things we ought to do and the refusal to do the things we ought not to do—which is, in its own nature, the life we ought to lead, or the life which it is good to lead, as distinguished from other ways of life which are those which ought not to be followed, or which are bad. And in the end there is no reason why we ought to lead the life we ought to lead, or why it is good to lead that kind of life other than that this *is* how we ought to live, or how it *is* good to live. We cannot say "the reason why we ought to live thus, or why this kind of life is good is that it is a *means* to something else," because to say this raises the question "And why ought I to take the means to this result, or why is it good to take those means, rather than to take the quite different means to a quite different result?" Thus we are back again at the point from which we started, that there is something which ought to be done, or which it is good to do, *because* it ought to be done or is good to do. There is no getting away from "you ought simply because you ought."

This is just as true on a utilitarian theory of morality as on any other. If a man has persuaded himself that the only reason why he ought to be honest, truthful, chaste is that honesty, veracity, chastity are means to the promotion of human happiness, and that they have no value except as means to this result, the question still recurs, "But why ought I to promote human happiness, when I perhaps should prefer to go as I please without bothering about the effects of my conduct on the general happiness?" and to that question the Utilitarian can really only reply, "You ought to promote the general happiness because you ought, because it is the highest good." Even a *morality* of pure self-seeking is faced by the same problem. If you tell me that in the end the only reason why it is right for me to do some things and to avoid doing others is that by acting thus I shall secure my own happiness, it is open to me to retort that I do not set all this store by my own

---

than this, it is ridiculous in him to call on the rest of us to agree with him that it is wrong, that is, that *we* also dislike it. It will always be a complete answer to him to say "but *I* like intolerance quite well, and *de gustibus non est disputandum.*"

[2] It may be said that the first difference is perhaps only imagined, whereas the other is manifest to sight and touch. This would not be wholly true. The differences between man and woman are not confined to those glaring differences in configuration which can be directly detected by the senses; they extend to characteristic ways of thinking and feeling which do not disclose themselves thus grossly to the senses. We should rightly find fault with the "psychology" of a novelist whose women, though having the outward appearance of women, were made to feel and think like so many unbearded "men in women's clothes."

happiness—as R. L. Stevenson wrote, that mankind are partial to happiness is a statement which may be doubted—and that I do not see why I should. My egoistic Mentor could only give me the answer, "If you do not care about your own happiness, you *ought* to care about it." Kant's own account of the principle of morality may be open to criticism on more grounds than one, but on one fundamental point he is clearly right; any coherent theory of morality must presuppose what he calls a categorical imperative. It must assume that there is *something* which ought to be done for no other reason than that it ought to be done. To deny this would be tantamount to denying that there is any distinction whatever between right and wrong, and if you deny this, you can no longer have any theory of morality good or bad; you can only have a theory about the way in which the illusion that there is such a thing as morality has arisen. (Just as a man who denies that there can be such a thing as a witch can have no theory of witchcraft, or as one who denied that there is any sun or planets could have no theory of the solar system, though either might have theories about the way in which men have been deluded into fancying that there are witches or that there is a sun.)

What the sense of the difference between right and wrong implies, then, unless it is a pure delusion, is that there is something—the existence of persons living the life they ought to lead—which is of absolute worth, a good in itself and on its own account, and not merely as conducive to some further result whereto it is a mere means. And if this is true, an answer is suggested to our question whether there is anything to which the whole course of nature may stand as means to end. It would be a rational way of thinking to conceive of the whole system of nature as the means to a single end, the development and maintenance of intelligent and moral personalities, the only things known to us which have a worth which is both inherent and absolute.[3] If we can think thus of nature rightly, the singleness of the end to which the whole infinite complex of nature's processes are directed will be proof of the singleness of the directing intelligence they presuppose, and the coincidence of that end with the end of all moral action will be our warrant for ascribing goodness to that intelligence. We shall have replaced the plurality of possibly competing "departmental deities," which is perhaps all that the argument for "design in nature," taken by itself, would permit us to assert, by the "one God" of the great monotheistic religions.

To set the matter in the clearest light, let us consider two of the distinctive characteristics of our sense of right and wrong. (1) In the first place, the distinction between right and wrong is—if it exists at all—what the moralists of the seventeenth and eighteenth centuries called it—*immutable and eternal*. This does not mean that it may not be wrong for one man in one set of circumstances to

---

[3] It might be asked whether life itself, or at least sentient life, apart from intelligence or moral character, may not be the thing of inherent and absolute value, and the end of nature, if nature has an end. But the answer must pretty clearly be, NO. We are not destroying a thing of absolute value when we make a region of the earth a safe home for human beings by exterminating wild beasts and other "pests." To clear the country of wolves is no crime, though it would be a crime to make room for the civilized population by clearing the district in the same way of "savages." It is a crime to have extirpated the Tasmanians: it would not be one to have extinguished the "Tasmanian devil." It is one thing to treat rattlesnakes as "pizun," quite another to treat "Injuns" in the same fashion.

do what it would be equally wrong for another man in different circumstances not to do; it may be wrong for A, who has a family to support by his own exertions, to contribute to public charities sums it would be wrong in B, who has ample "private means" and only himself to support, not to contribute; it may be wrong for the magistrate dealing with a rebellion against his necessary and legitimate authority, to treat the principal instigator of trouble with a lenience which it is no more than a duty to show to the rank and file of those whom the "rebel" has led astray. There may perhaps be no hard-and-fast rule which we can trust unreservedly to show us what line of action would certainly be right in the particular case; it is at least possible that *every* case may have unique features which make it necessary to consider it on "its own merits." At least, we may concede so much for the purposes of our present argument. But when all this has been granted, it remains an integral part of what we mean by distinction between right and wrong, that the distinction is valid independently of the thoughts and wishes of any of us. If a man asks me now—I having the resources I have, and the claims on me being what they are, and he being in the situation in which he actually is and intending to apply the gift as he does intend—for a gift of a certain sum of money; it may be right to grant his request, or it may not; but if it is right, then it remains right whether I happen to think it so or not. If it is wrong for me to do a certain act, I may be a morally indifferent person and so never reflect that the act is wrong, or I may be mistaken and actually believe that the act in question is right, but my ignorance or my error makes no difference to the fact that what I am doing is really wrong. Still less do my wishes affect the moral character of the act. If it is right, no wish of mine to the contrary could make it wrong; and if it is wrong, no wishing that it were not wrong will make it anything but wrong. Just so, if a certain line is crooked, it is crooked, and though I may very possibly not remark this, or may even think that the line is straight, or may wish that it were straight, it is none the less crooked for all that.

(2) Again, it is universally characteristic of the sense of right and wrong that it is attended, as Butler puts it, with a consciousness of good or ill *desert*, merit or demerit. There are, indeed, difficult problems connected with this notion of *desert* which I must be content here merely to indicate without any attempt to solve them. It is hard sometimes to say of the "deserving" exactly what they deserve and at whose hands they deserve it. We commonly say that a man who is in business and is habitually industrious, honest and obliging "deserves to get on." Yet an undertaker carrying on business in a district where the inhabitants are healthy and long-lived may be "deserving" on all these grounds, but is not likely to make much of a living by his profession, and we should hesitate to say that he "deserves" a rise in the local mortality from disease or accident, though it may well be that his prosperity depends on it. No degree of honesty, industry, ability is likely to make the legal profession a source of prosperity anywhere where the public at large are so honest that neighbors make no attempt to take advantage of one another, so intelligent that when conflicts of interest arise, they readily see for themselves what arrangement will be fair to all parties, and so fraternal that they prefer amicable settlement of disputes, even with some personal loss, to resort to the courts. Yet we can hardly suggest that the deserving man of law deserves that his neighbours shall be stupid, grasping and litigious. I could not with a straight

face tell a healthy and peaceable man, "A. B. the undertaker deserves that you should die this winter," or "C.D. the barrister that you should start a long and expensive suit against E. F." If a man is deserving, there must be something in particular which he deserves and someone at whose hands he deserves it, and yet it seems plain that it would often be hard to say what is that *something* or who is that *somebody*.

Yet these difficulties do not affect the main point which Butler has in mind in what he says about desert.[4] It is true, as he says, that in our judgements upon ourselves we do pronounce ourselves to have in some way deserved ill when we have done ill. If the consequences of our misdeeds are calamitous, we recognize that we are not entitled to complain, or to look for the same sympathy we might reasonably expect if the same misfortune had befallen us without any contributory fault of our own. To expand one of Butler's own remarks, if one man is disinherited by some senile freak of the relative who had encouraged him to expect an inheritance, and a second as the consequence of folly, dissipation or ingratitude persisted in after due warning, the same pinch of need may be equally felt by both, but only the second has the added and peculiar bitterness of knowing that he has brought the need on himself by his own misdoing. Nor, as it is important to add, is there any necessary connection between this "sense of ill-desert" which attends conscious wrong-doing and the spirit of vindictiveness towards themselves, but it is just in the case of my own misdeeds that my sense of ill-desert is keenest: it is much easier to persuade myself about some other offender that he does not deserve all that his misconduct has brought upon him. At bottom what we all feel is, I take it, this: there is one source of pain of which we can always say that it is merited by a morally evil will; the man who wills evil always deserves that his evil will should be in the end frustrated, whereas the man who wills what is morally right, though he may not deserve to be rewarded with length of days or wealth, always deserves that his rightful will, because it is rightful, shall in the end take effect. It would not, so far as I can see, offend our moral sense that the course of history is not so controlled that every morally evil volition shall "get its due" in the shape of so much torture by fire and brimstone, or the like; indeed, we may perhaps think that the whole conception of an equivalence of so much discomfort to just such-and-such a degree of moral obliquity is preposterous. But it would, I believe, shock any man's moral sense to find that the world is so constituted that the man who wills evil in the end "gets his wicked will." What is "due" to the morally bad will is frustration, and frustration more or less complete as the volition itself is more or less perverted. And similarly, what is due to the good will is fulfilment more or less complete as the volition is itself more or less good. And these are the purposes

---

[4] "This approbation and disapprobation are altogether different from mere desire of our own, or of their happiness, and from sorrow upon missing it. For the object or occasion of this last kind of perception is satisfaction or uneasiness, whereas the object of the first is active behaviour. In one case, what our thoughts fix upon is our own condition; in the other, our conduct." " . . . men often say of themselves with remorse, and of others with some indignation, that they deserve to suffer for such calamities, because they brought them upon themselves, and would not take warning. Particularly when persons come to poverty and distress by a long course of extravagance . . . we plainly do not regard such people as a like object of compassion with those, who are brought into the same condition by unavoidable accident."—"Dissertation upon the Nature of Virtue" appended to the *Analogy*.

which we should count on finding fulfilled in the history of the universe, if nature itself has an end, and that end is the personal good life.

If so much is true, consider what follows. The law of right, we say, is eternally valid, unless our moral convictions are founded on mere illusion. But can a law be valid except by reference to an intelligence which recognizes and upholds it? Yet the human intelligences which are the only intelligences with which we are directly acquainted have taken a long time to reach such apprehension of the moral law as they possess; its leading principles have only dawned upon them very gradually and are still far from being universally recognized, and even those of us who admit them in theory in moments of calm are constantly disregarding them in practice, when our passions are stirred, or what we think to be our interest is at stake. As we know that there are many moral obligations to which our own society has only become alive in our own lifetime, so I suppose, we all hope that our successors will be conscious of obligations which have not yet dawned on our-selves, and sensible of faults which we perpetrate to-day without any consciousness that they are faults. Yet those demands of the law of right which we have not yet discovered are none the less requirements and our neglect of them none the less a fault because of our blindness. And a law cannot hold *in vacuo*. There could be no law of gravitation and no laws of motion if there were nothing which gravitated or moved, no laws of chemical combination if there were not a plurality of chemical elements. So there could be no law for the right direction of the will if there were no wills to direct. But were there no will in existence except the wills of human beings, who are so often ignorant of the law of right and so often defy it, it is not apparent what the *validity* of the law could mean. Recognition of the validity of the law thus seems to carry with it a reference to an intelligence which has not, like our own, to make acquaintance with it piecemeal, slowly and with difficulty, but has always been in full and clear possession of it, and a will which does not, like our own, often set it at nought, but is guided by it in all its operations.

Consider again that if reflection on the character of the moral law leads us to believe that nature as a whole serves a moral purpose (the development of moral personalities) and that purpose is one that is attained, we may fairly draw some important conclusions about the knowledge and power of the intelligence whose purpose this is. It, or He, as you will, must from the first know the whole system of nature in its minutest detail, so that nothing can take Him by surprise, and He must also, since the end is the fulfilment or frustration of every volition of every one of us according to its moral worth, be able directly to read the inmost secrets of all hearts; He must know not only what I do or say, but what I will, or even wish, to do or say, even though the actual speech or deed does not follow. And He must have such sovereign control of all that happens in nature that every detail contrib-utes to the realization of the supreme purpose. There must be no possibility that anything in nature can deflect the achievement of this purpose by a hair's breadth; so much follows at once from the admission that this is *the* purpose for which nature exists. It follows, does it not, that the supreme moral intelligence must be not merely in sovereign control of the course of nature, but must be the actual originator of nature and everything that nature contains, author, as the scholastic phrase ran, of form and matter alike? For to say less than this amounts to saying not that nature *exists* for this end, but only that it is an end to which a nature which exists for some other end, or for none at all, has been put. Hence if the implications of the moral law are what Kant, and though less explicitly Butler, take them to be, consideration of it leads us not merely to an acknowledgement of "one God" but of "one God . . . almighty, creator of heaven and earth and of all things visible and invisible."

Bibliography

Ahern, Dennis M. "Hume on the Evidential Impossibility of Miracles." In *Studies in Epistemology*, American Philosophical Quarterly Monograph no. 9, pp. 1–31. Oxford: Basil Blackwell, 1975.

Appleby, Peter C. "Mysticism and Ineffability." *International Journal of Philosophy and Religion* 11 (Fall 1980): 143–66.

Armstrong, Christopher, Jr. *Evelyn Underhill*. London: Eeromans and Mowbra, 1975.

Asin Palacios, Miguel. *Saint John of the Cross and Islam*. New York: Vantage Press, 1981.

Audi, Robert, and William J. Wainwright, eds. "The Migration of the Theistic Arguments: From Natural Theology to Evidentialist Apologetics." *Rationality, Religious Belief and Moral Commitment*. Ithaca, N.Y.: Cornell University Press, 1986.

Ayer, Alfred Jules. *The Origins of Pragmatism*. San Francisco: Freeman, Cooper, 1968.

Baillie, D. M. *Faith in God*. Edinburgh: Clark, 1927.

Baillie, John. *The Interpretation of Religion*. Edinburgh: Clark, 1929.

———. *The Idea of Revelation in Recent Thought*. New York: Columbia University Press, 1956.

———. *Our Knowledge of God*. New York: Scribner's, 1962.

———. *The Sense of the Presence of God*. London: Oxford University Press, 1962.

Basinger, David. "Christian Theism and the Concept of Miracle: Some Epistemological Perplexities." *Southeastern Journal of Philosophy* 18 (1980): 137–50.

Baumgardt, David. *Great Western Mystics: Their Lasting Significance*. New York: Columbia University Press, 1961.

Bayles, Ernest Edward. *Pragmatism in Education*. New York: Harper and Row, 1966.

Beattie, Paul H. "The Will to Believe in William James and His Father," part 1. *Religious Humanism* 21 (Spring 1987): 81–90.

Beck, L. W. *A Commentary on Kant's Critique of Practical Reason*. Chicago: University of Chicago Press, 1960.

Bennett, Charles A. *A Philosophical Study of Mysticism, an Essay*. New Haven, Conn.: Yale University Press, 1923.

Bergson, Henri. *The Two Sources of Morality and Religion*. Garden City, N.Y.: Doubleday, 1954.

Bolle, Kees W. *The Freedom of Man in Myth*. Nashville, Tenn.: Vanderbilt University Press, 1968.

Bowman, Mary Ann. *Western Mysticism: A Guide to the Basic Works*. Chicago: American Library Association, 1978.

Briggs, Thomas H. *Pragmatism and Pedagogy*. New York: Macmillan, 1940.

Broad, C. D. "Arguments for the Existence of God, II." *Journal of Theological Studies* 40 (1939): 161.

———. *Religion, Philosophy and Psychical Research.* London: Routledge and Kegan Paul, 1953; New York: Hillary House, 1953.

———. *Religion, Philosophy and Psychical Research.* New York: Humanities Press, 1969.

Butler, James D. *Four Philosophies and Their Practice in Education and Religion.* New York: Harper, 1957.

Cheney, Sheldon. *Men Who Have Walked with God.* New York: Knopf, 1945.

Clark, Walter H. *The Psychology of Religion.* New York: Macmillan, 1958.

Colledge, Eric. *The Medieval Mystics of England.* New York: Scribner's, 1961.

Conway, David Alton. "Mavrodes, Martin, and the Verification of Religious Experience". *International Journal of Philosophy and Religion* 2 (1971): 156–71.

Danto, Arthur. *Mysticism and Morality: Oriental Thought and Moral Philosophy.* New York: Basic Books, 1972.

Davies, Oliver. *God Within: The Mystical Tradition of Northern Europe.* New York: Paulist Press, 1988.

Dunbar, Helen F. *Symbolism in Medieval Thought and Its Consummation in the "Divine Comedy."* New York: Russell and Russell, 1961.

Edwards, Jonathan. *Religious Affections.* Edited by J. E. Smith. New Haven, Conn.: Yale University Press, 1959.

Erlandson, Douglas K. "A New Look at Miracles." *Religious Studies* 13 (1977): 417–28.

Ewing, Alfred G. "Awareness of God." *Philosophy* 40 (1965): 1–17.

Farmer, H. H. *Revelation and Religion.* London: Nisbet, 1954.

Flew, Antony. *God and Philosophy.* New York: Dell, 1966.

Freeman, Eugene, ed. *The Relevance of Charles Peirce.* La Salle, Ill.: Hegeler Institute, 1983.

Freemantle, Anne, ed. *The Protestant Mystics.* Boston: Little, Brown, 1964.

Freud, Sigmund. *The Future of an Illusion.* New York: Norton, 1961.

Friedman, M. S. *Martin Buber, the Life of Dialogue.* New York: Harper and Row, 1960.

Gale, Richard. "Mysticism and Philosophy." *Journal of Philosophy* 57 (1960): 471–80.

Garnett, A. C. *Religion and the Moral Life.* New York: Ronald Press, 1955.

Gaskin, J. C. A. "Miracles and the Religiously Significant Coincidence." *Ratio* 16 (1975): 72–81.

Gavin, William J. "The Will to Believe in Science and Religion." *International Journal of Philosophy and Religion* 15 (1984): 139–48.

Hambourger, Robert. "Belief in Miracles and Hume's Essay." NOUS 14 (1980): 587–604.

Happold, F. D. *Mysticism, a Study and an Anthology.* Baltimore: Penguin, 1963.

Helm, Paul. "Religious Experience." *Sophia* 16 (1977): 1–6.

Henning, James. *Instead of God: A Pragmatic Reconsideration of Beliefs and Values.* London: Boyars, 1985.

Hepburn, Ronald. *Christianity and Paradox.* London: Watts, 1958.

Hick, John. *Faith and Knowledge.* Ithaca, N.Y.: Cornell University Press, 1957.

———. *Arguments for the Existence of God.* New York: Herder and Herder, 1971.

Hobhouse, Stephen, ed. *Selected Mystical Writings.* New York: Harper, 1948.

Holland, R. F. "The Miraculous." *American Philosophical Quarterly* 2 (1965): 43–51.

Hook, Sidney, ed. *Religious Experience and Truth*. New York: New York University Press, 1961.

Idel, Moshe, and Bernard McGinn, eds. *Mystical Union and Monotheistic Faith*. New York: Macmillan, 1987.

Inge, William R. *Christian Mysticism*. London: Methuen, 1899.

———. *Mysticism in Religion*. Chicago: University of Chicago Press, 1948.

———. *Christian Mysticism*, 7th ed. New York: Meridan Books, 1956.

James, Joseph. *The Way of Mysticism, an Anthology*. London: Jonathan Cape, 1950.

James, William. *The Varieties of Religious Experience*. New York: Longmans, Green, 1902.

———. *The Meaning of Truth, a Sequel to "Pragmatism."* NY: Longmans, Green, 1909.

———. *Essays in Radical Empiricism and a Pluralistic Universe*. Gloucester, Mass.: Smith, 1967.

———. *Pragmatism*. Cambridge, Mass.: Harvard University Press, 1975.

Johann, Robert O. *The Pragmatic Meaning of God*. Milwaukee, Wisc.: Marquette University Press, 1966.

Kant, Immanuel. *Critique of Practical Reason*, part 2. New York: Liberal Arts Press, 1956.

Katz, Stephen. *Mysticism and Religious Traditions*. New York: Oxford University Press, 1983.

——— ed. *Mysticism and Philosophical Analysis*. New York: Oxford University Press, 1978.

Kellenberger, J. "The Ineffabilities of Mysticism," *American Philosophical Quarterly* 16 (1979): 307–15.

———. "Miracles." *International Journal of Philosophy and Religion* 10 (1979): 155–62.

Kennedy, Gail. *Pragmatism and American Culture*. Boston: Heath, 1950.

Kepler, Thomas S., ed. *The Fellowship of the Saints*. New York: Abingdon Press, 1958.

Kolenda, Konst Antin, and Bernard K. Duffy. "The Religious Humanism of American Pragmatism." *Religious Humanism* 18 (Summer 1984): 120–26.

Konvitz, Milton R. *The American Pragmatists: Selected Writings*. New York: Meridian Books, 1960.

Lafferty, Theodore T. *Nature and Values: Pragmatic Essays in Metaphysics*. Columbia, South Carolina: University of South Carolina Press, 1976.

Lassalle, Hugo. *Zen Meditation for Christians*. La Salle, Ill.: Open Court, 1974.

Levinson, Henry Samuel. *The Religious Investigations of William James*. Chapel Hill, North Carolina: University of North Carolina Press, 1981.

Lewis, H. D. *Our Experience of God*. New York: Macmillan, 1959.

Lovejoy, Arthur D. *The Thirteen Pragmatisms and Other Essays*. Baltimore: Johns Hopkins, 1963.

MacKinnon, Alastair. "Miracle and Paradox." *American Philosophical Quarterly* 4 (1967): 308–14.

Maclagen, William G. *The Theological Frontier of Ethics*. London: Allen and Unwin, 1961.

Martin, C. B. *Religious Belief*. Ithaca, N.Y.: Cornell University Press, 1959.

Matson, Wallace. *The Existence of God*. Ithaca, N.Y.: Cornell University Press, 1965.

Mavrodes, George I. *Belief in God: A Study in the Epistemology of Religion*. New York: Random House, 1970.

McCarthy, Gerald D., ed. *The Ethics of Belief Debate*. Atlanta: Scholars Press, 1986.

Merton, Thomas. *Mystics and Zen Masters*. New York: Dell, 1967.

Miles, T. R. *Religious Experience*. New York: St. Martin's Press, 1972.

Mills, Charles W. *Sociology and Pragmatism: The Higher Learning in America.* New York: Oxford University Press, 1966.

Mitchell, Basil. "The Grace of God." *Faith and Logic.* London: Allen and Unwin, 1957.

———. *The Justification of Religious Belief.* Macmillan, 1973.

Moore, Edward C. *American Pragmatism: Pierce, James and Dewey.* New York: Columbia University Press, 1961.

Niebuhr, H. Richard. *The Meaning of Revelation.* New York: Macmillan, 1959.

Oakes, Robert A. "Mediation, Encounters, and God." *International Journal of Philosophy and Religion* 2 (1971): 148–55.

O'Brien, Elmer. *Varieties of Mystical Experience.* New York: New American Library, 1964.

Oman, John. *The Natural and the Supernatural.* Cambridge: Cambridge University Press, 1931.

Orange, Donna M. *Peirce's Conception of God: A Developmental Study.* Lubbock, Tex.: Institute for Studies in Pragmaticism, 1984.

Organ, Troy. "The Language of Mysticism." *Monist* 47 (Spring 1963): 417–43.

Otto, Rudolf. *Mysticism, East and West.* New York: Macmillan, 1932.

———. *The Idea of the Holy.* London: Oxford University Press, 1923, 1950; Harmondsworth: Penguin, 1959.

Owen, H. P. *The Moral Argument for Christian Theism.* London: Allen and Unwin, 1965.

Paton, H. J. *The Modern Predicament.* London: Allen and Unwin; New York: Macmillan, 1955.

Penelhum, Terence. "Pascal's Wager." *Journal of Religion* 44 (July 1964): 201–9.

———. *Religion and Rationality.* New York: Random House, 1971.

———. *God and Skepticism.* Dordrecht, The Netherlands: Reidel, 1983.

Petry, Ray C. *Late Medieval Mysticism.* Philadelphia: Westminster Press, 1957.

Phillips, Stephen H. "Mysticism and Metaphor." *International Journal of Philosophy and Religion* 23 (1988): 17–41.

Pletcher, Galen. "Agreement among Mystics." *Sophia* 11 (1972): 5–15.

Potter, Charles F. *Creative Personality, the Next Step in Evolution.* New York: Funk and Wagnalls, 1950.

Proudfoot, Wayne. *Religious Experience.* Berkeley: University of California Press, 1985.

Raschke, Carl A. *Moral Action, God, and History in the Thought of Immanuel Kant.* Tallahassee, Fla.: American Academy of Religion; Missoula, Mont.: Scholars Press, University of Montana, 1975.

Rescher, Nicholas. *Pascal's Wager.* Notre Dame, Ind.: University of Notre Dame Press, 1985.

Robbins, J. Wesley. "John Hick on Religious Experience and Perception." *International Journal of Philosophy and Religion* 5 (1974): 108–18.

Robinson, Guy. "Miracles." *Ratio* 9 (1967): 155–66.

Rochberg-Halton, Eugene. *Meaning and Modernity: Social Theory in the Pragmatic Attitude.* Chicago: University of Chicago Press, 1986.

Rowe, William. *Philosophy of Religion.* Belmont, Calif.: Wadsworth, 1978.

Rucker, Egbert D. *The Chicago Pragmatists.* Minneapolis: University of Minnesota Press, 1969.

Runzo, Joseph, and Craig K. Ihara, eds. *Religious Experience and Religious Belief: Essays in the Epistemology of Religion.* Lanham, Md.: University Press of America, 1986.

Scheffler, Israel. *Four Pragmatists: A Critical Introduction to Peirce, James, Mead, and Dewey.* New York: Humanities Press, 1974.

Schleiermacher, Friedrich. *The Christian Faith.* Edinburgh: Clark, 1956.

———. *On Religion: Speeches to Its Cultured Despisers.* New York: Harper, 1958.

Schlesinger, George N. *Religion and Scientific Method.* Dordrecht, The Netherlands: Reidel, 1977.

Schweitzer, Albert. *The Mysticism of Paul the Apostle.* New York: Macmillan, 1955.

Shiner, Roger. "A Defence of Encounters." *Sophia* 12 (1973): 1–6.

Smart, Ninian. "Interpretations of Mystical Experience," *Religious Studies* 1 (1965): 75–87.

———. *Philosophers and Religious Truth,* 2d ed. New York: Macmillan, 1969.

Smith, John E. *Experience and God.* New York: Oxford University Press, 1968.

Sorley, W. R. *Moral Values and the Idea of God.* Cambridge: Cambridge University Press, 1918.

Stace, W. T. *Time and Eternity.* Princeton, N.J.: Princeton University Press, 1952.

———. *Mysticism and Philosophy.* Philadelphia: Lippincott, 1960; London: Macmillan, 1961.

———. *Stace's Teachings of the Mystics.* New York: New American Library, 1960.

Summers, Montague. *Essays in Petto.* London: Fortune Press, 1928.

Sumner, L. W, John G. Slater, and Fred Wilson, eds. *Pragmatism and Purpose: Essays Presented to Thomas A. Goudge.* Toronto: University of Toronto Press, 1981.

Suzuki, Daisetz J. *Mysticism: Christian and Buddhist.* New York: Harper, 1957.

Swinburne, Richard. *The Concept of Miracle.* New York: St. Martin's Press, 1970.

———. *The Existence of God.* Oxford: Clarendon Press, 1979.

Taylor, A. E. "The Vindication of Religion." In *Essays Catholic and Critical,* edited by Elgar Selwyn, 70–80. New York: Macmillan, 1926.

Teilhard de Chardin, Pierre. *Hymn of the Universe.* New York: Harper and Row, 1965.

Thayer, Horace S. *Meaning and Action: A Critical History of Pragmatism.* Indianapolis, Ind.: Bobbs-Merrill, 1968.

Thomas, George F. *Philosophy and Religious Belief.* New York: Scribner's, 1970.

Underhill, E. *Mysticism.* New York: Macmillan, 1930.

Van Wosep, Hendrikus B. *Seven Sages; The Story of American Philosophy: Franklin, Emerson, James, Dewey, Santayana, Peirce and Whitehead.* New York: Longmans, Green, 1960.

Von Hugel, Baron F. *The Mystical Element of Religion,* 2 vols., 2d ed. London: Dent, 1923.

Wainwright, William J. "Stace and Mysticism." *Journal of Religion* 50 (1970): 139–54.

———. "Mysticism and Sense Perception." *Religious Studies* 9 (1973):

———. "Morality and Mysticism." *Journal of Religion and Ethics* 4 (Spring 1976): 29–36.

———. *Mysticism: A Study of Its Nature, Cognitive Value and Moral Implications.* Madison: University of Wisconsin Press, 1981.

Walsh, David. *The Mysticism of Innerworldly Fulfillment: A Study of Jacob Boehme.* Gainesville, Fla.: University of Florida Press, 1983.

Webb, C. C. J. *Religious Experience.* Pound Ridge, N.Y.: Milford, 1945; London: Oxford University Press, 1945.

Wernham, James C. S. *James's Will-to-Believe Doctrine: A Heretical View.* Toronto: McGill-Queen's, 1987.

Wiener, Philip D. *Evolution and the Founders of Pragmatism, with a Forward by John Dewey.* New York: Harper and Row, 1949, 1965.

Yandell, Keith. "Miracles, Epistemology, and Hume's Barrier." *International Journal of Philosophy and Religion* 7 (1976): 391–417.

———. "The Ineffability Theme." *International Journal of Philosophy and Religion* 10 (1979): 209–31.

Young, Robert. "Miracles and Epistemology." *Religious Studies* 8 (1972): 115–26.

Zaehner, Robert Charles. *Mysticism, Sacred and Profane.* Oxford: Clarendon Press, 1957.

———. "Religious Faith as Experiencing-As." *Talk of God,* Royal Institute of Philosophy Lectures, 2, edited by G. N. A. Vesey, 20–35. London: Macmillan, 1968.

———. *Philosophers and Religious Truth,* 2d ed. New York: Macmillan, 1969.

———. "Mysticism, Contradiction, and Ineffability." *American Philosophical Quarterly* 10 (1973): 201–11.

———. *Zen, Drugs, and Mysticism.* New York: Pantheon Books, 1973.

———. ed. *The Teaching of the Mystics.* New York: New American Library, 1960.

———. *Faith and Knowledge,* 2d ed. Ithaca, N.Y.: Cornell University Press.

CHAPTER 5

Explanations for Natural Evil

*H*aving looked at arguments for the existence of God, we should now examine questions concerning the nature, and especially the character, of God. The major problem here is how to reconcile the natural evil that exists on earth and that causes human suffering, with the assumption of a wholly loving God who is omnipotent and omniscient. As the ancient Greek philosopher Epicurus put it, "Is he willing to prevent evil, but not able? Then he is impotent. Is he able but not willing? Then he is malevolent. Is he both able and willing? Whence then is evil?"

In dealing with natural evil we are not concerned with "man's inhumanity to man," that is, the awful things human beings do to one another out of malice, greed, revenge, or even patriotism and religion. God cannot be held accountable for such actions; people are responsible for their own behavior. According to scripture, human beings were blessed with free will, making them almost gods themselves, which they can use for good or ill. If they choose to abuse this gift by harming one another, that is not God's fault.

We are concerned instead with naturally existing evil, the evil that is part of the given environment on earth and that is experienced as pain and suffering by human beings. At least four categories of natural evil can be distinguished:

1. *Disasters and catastrophes,* including floods, fires, earthquakes, cyclones, volcanic eruptions, tidal waves, hurricanes, and perhaps droughts, blights, frosts, plagues ("pestilences"), and so on.

2. *Hostile environments,* such as deserts, wastelands, jungles, rain forests, arctic tundras, swamps, snow-covered mountains, and the seas and oceans which (unaccountably) make up two-thirds of the planet.

3. *Dangerous animals,* such as bears and cougars, lions and panthers, cobras and rattlesnakes, and poisonous insects such as tarantulas and scorpions as well as savage fish such as sharks and barracuda.

4. *Sickness, disease, and death.* This includes various cancers, tuberculosis, cerebral palsy, heart disease, leprosy, multiple sclerosis, and so on, as well as aging and death itself, the ultimate evils, usually accompanied by anguish and physical pain.

We wonder especially why innocent children should suffer—the baby born with sickle-cell anemia, a child crippled by poliomyelitis—and why there should be genetic defects and childhood diseases. We ask why Monet had to go blind or Beethoven go deaf. We even wonder why we live such a short time, and have to spend a third of our lives sleeping, another third working in order to stay alive.

To explain the presence of such evils in a world governed by a benevolent God, theologians and philosophers have offered a variety of theories. One of these theories claims that human beings suffer so that their character can be developed, or simply that *suffering builds character.* If the world were completely comfortable, there would be no incentive to develop ourselves into better people. We need trials and challenges that we can meet and master, thereby becoming stronger and finer human beings. Soft conditions tend to produce soft people, but with obstacles to overcome our souls can be improved. Stumbling blocks become stepping stones, and the development of our higher nature becomes possible.

Countless cases can be cited of individuals who would not have become outstanding in their field if it were not for their physical problems. For example, some people who had polio as children have become famous swimmers; some who were unable to walk have become concert violinists or pianists. The most famous example, perhaps, is Helen Keller, who was left deaf and blind by illness as an infant and became a remarkable human being because of it.

As the contemporary philosopher John Hick states in *Evil and the God of Love:*

> The world is not intended to be a paradise, but rather the scene of a history in which the human personality may be formed towards the pattern of Christ. Men are not to be thought of on the analogy of animal pets, whose life is to be made as agreeable as possible, but rather on the analogy of human children, who are to grow to adulthood in an environment whose primary and overriding purpose is not immediate pleasure but the realizing of the most valuable potentialities of human personality.

To Hick, the earth is a place of soul making.

Persuasive as this might sound, it may not be an adequate explanation. People struck by lightning are in no position to have their character improved, and that holds true of all those who die instantly from some natural disaster as well as babies who die at birth.

As for those who suffer, some certainly do become better people for having had a terrible experience, but some become much worse. Suffering can traumatize people and break their spirit, filling them with resentment, anger, and bitterness at being victimized. In fact, more people are demoralized by suffering than elevated by it, so a God concerned with improving human character would hardly use natural evil as a means. For every Helen Keller there are thousands who have been demeaned by their disabilities. The success won through adversity may be sweetest, but that is partly due to the fact that it happens so rarely.

It has also been pointed out that some people develop good character without suffering, and if that is the case, then it is not necessary to have evil in the world in order to build character. Even if it were necessary, we certainly do not need quite so much, or evil that is so awful. An occasional cold would do, perhaps influenza, but not widespread occurrences of cancer and heart disease. Or a few cold days might suffice to harden us, but we do not need ice storms, blizzards, and the Arctic.

Finally, some philosophers have noted that a good God, who could have chosen to design people in any number of ways, would not have designed them so that suffering was required for good character. A God who loves humanity would have formed human psychology in a very different way.

For the reasons described, the suffering-builds-character explanation for natural evil is difficult to accept.

Another explanation that has been proposed has strong biblical roots and maintains that *evil is punishment for sin.* Beginning with Adam and Eve, who were expelled from the Garden of Eden for disobedience to God's commands, the Bible is full of references to those who suffered because of moral transgressions. For example, Sodom and Gomorrah were destroyed because of the sinfulness of the people, and God sent the Flood because all of humanity, except for Noah and his wife, had become sinners.

Within Christianity it is assumed that people continue to violate God's laws because of original sin inherited from Adam, and therefore they must be punished through natural evils. We possess free will and can obey God's laws, but we are inherently depraved and have a propensity toward committing selfish and immoral acts ("In Adam's fall / We sinned all"). These unrighteous acts bring punishment down upon our heads in the form of disease, disasters, and a hostile environment.

As Eden, the earth was ideal, but we lost that paradise through our own willfulness. Now we must endure a world of mixed pleasures and pains, including those punishments that we receive (and deserve) by continuing to sin. Paradise may be regained, but only in the life to come; then, if we accept Christ as our savior, we can enter heaven where death and suffering are no more.

Behind this explanation lies the assumption that God is just, so that the good people are rewarded with blessings and the evil are punished with pain. If God did not operate this way, then the world would not be fair. This is what the seventeenth-century philosopher Gottfried W. Leibniz meant in saying that this is the best of all possible worlds: It is the most ideal world consistent with principles of justice.

In our everyday lives, we often assume that a just system of rewards and punishments does in fact operate. If we have an accident or contract some illness, it seems natural to ask, Why me? What have I done to deserve this? We then search our conscience to see what we did wrong to merit this penalty. And as children, if we catch cold after being in the snow without our boots or winter coat, we feel that (poetic) justice was done: it was our fault, and we got what we deserved.

The connection between wrongdoing and suffering is therefore commonly made, and it seems quite reasonable to attribute this just scheme to God's plan. The pain that people experience from natural causes is easily interpreted as punishment for sinful behavior and, therefore, perfectly justified. As fallen creatures who continually perform awful actions, we richly deserve the earth we inhabit: "As ye sow, so shall ye reap" (Galatians 6:7).

Again, the argument seems eminently sensible until we start analyzing it. If a just scheme were in operation, we would expect sinful people to suffer and saintly people to prosper, but no such reality can be found. Rather, people who are generally good sometimes experience a string of misfortunes while some terrible people get through life unscathed. Certainly, the amount of suffering is not proportional to the degree of sinfulness, and even the distribution seems very much askew. The conclusion must be that there is no correlation between what people receive and what they earn—between their character, on the one hand, and the pain and pleasure they experience, on the other. The next life may have justice in terms of heaven and hell (although we cannot know that), but this life certainly does not.

In this explanation and the previous one, the problem is that the wrong people suffer. Those who need or deserve suffering do not always receive it, while those who neither need nor deserve it sometimes suffer intensely.

Some philosophers have also pointed out that a loving God would not use a retributive system of justice but would practice the virtues of compassion and forgiveness. Particularly in the New Testament, God is presented not as a being of wrath and vengeance but one of kindness and mercy. A God of this character would not punish people for their mistakes and certainly would not seek revenge for any wrongdoing. Such a God would not make people pay but would try to make them better, not point a finger but extend a hand, and not get even but help people to improve. In other words, the concept of an infinitely loving God is incompatible with a scheme of punishment and retribution.

Finally, criticisms have been leveled at the idea of original sin, which is said to be responsible for the earth no longer being a paradise. The main question is why all the descendents of Adam and Eve—that is, the rest of the human race—should have to suffer for their mistake. The notion that all humanity carries some kind of "collective guilt" is highly questionable. We do not hold today's German people responsible for the Nazism of their forebears any more than we try people in a court of law for crimes their ancestors committed. Why, then, should all people be punished for Adam and Eve's sin and be born inherently depraved, in a world full of pain?

A number of other explanations could also be mentioned. For instance, it has been argued that *free will requires evil as a choice*. That is, for free will to be meaningful, we must have a choice between good and bad. If there were only good things to choose, or if we were so constituted that we could only choose good things, there would be no genuine choice.

The objections to this theory, however, are that if a range and variety of good things existed, that would certainly give us choice, and forming us so that we could only choose the good would not be a problem if a spectrum of good choices were available. Besides, in cases of natural evil, choice is seldom possible: the avalanche overwhelms its victims; the lava engulfs the town. Free will can hardly be exercised.

Another explanation is that *contrasts are necessary for appreciation:* unless we had the bad, we could not appreciate the good. We need sickness to make us grateful for our health, storms to make us value beautiful days, and deserts to help us appreciate lush farmland. Without contrasts, life could be good, but we would never realize that it is good, thus rendering our blessings utterly pointless.

Again, though, various shades of good would provide sufficient contrast to enable appreciation to occur. We do not need the opposite, that of bad, but only contrasts among degrees of good. (The least good, incidentally, would not then become bad; it would simply be the lowest in the category of good things. Chopped steak is not as good as filet mignon, but it isn't bad.) It would seem, then, that bad or evil is not necessary for appreciation.

Some critics have also noted that even if evil were necessary, there is far more of it and it is far more serious than is necessary for appreciation to occur. To relish fine health, we might need to compare it with having a virus, but we do not need a cholera epidemic. It has even been suggested that contrasts, good or bad, are not always necessary for appreciation; the baby seems to enjoy milk from the first without having tasted water, much less castor oil.

Still another explanation is to claim that *God is finite.* Here the original premises of the dilemma are changed so that God is not considered omnipotent and omniscient but limited in power or knowledge. God may want to create an ideal world but cannot do so. Perhaps God must contend with given conditions or an opposing power of evil such as the Devil. Or God may want what is best for human beings but simply not know everything needed to provide it. Perhaps, when first formulating natural laws, God could not foresee how those laws would unfold.

This explanation does protect God's goodness, but at the expense of affirming a less than perfect being. Most theologians are unwilling to pay that price; they seek an explanation that accounts for natural evil while retaining the concept of a God who is omnipotent, omniscient, and wholly good.

At this point, some people may want to throw up their hands and declare the issue to be a mystery far beyond the human intellect. This may be true, for as Shakespeare says in *Hamlet,* "There are more things in heaven and earth, Horatio, than are dreamt of in your philosophy." However, such people are then open to the charge of intellectual dishonesty, for it is rather like kicking over the chess-board when your opponent puts you in check.

Other people may feel that the failure to find a definitive solution to the problem of evil brings into question the very reality of God. Robert Browning wrote "God's in his heaven— / All's right with the world"; but if all's not right with the world, then perhaps God isn't in his heaven. The enormous suffering of the human race can certainly be an obstacle to belief in a loving God, and perhaps in God altogether.

Still others argue that although no one explanation accounts for all evil, the combination of theories constitutes a sufficient explanation. That is, in some cases evil is sent to improve a person's character, in other cases to punish people, in still others to enhance someone's appreciation of the good in life. The claim is that although the various theories do not completely explain human suffering, they offer a sufficient justification for it; the remainder can be taken on faith. Whether that is a defensible position is for the reader to judge.

In the following selections, John Stuart Mill describes the range and severity of natural evil, and John Hick offers his answer that suffering is character building. Then Moses Maimonides and G. W. Leibniz present their explanations of evil as punishment for sin.

Finally, the free-will defense is discussed by David Hume, who concludes that such an overabundance of evil is not needed in order to have choice, and John Stuart Mill then offers reasons for declaring that God must be limited.

Suffering Builds Character

31. Nature

JOHN STUART MILL

In sober truth, nearly all the things which men are hanged or imprisoned for doing to one another are nature's everyday performances. Killing, the most criminal act recognized by human laws, nature does once to every being that lives, and in a large proportion of cases after protracted tortures such as only the greatest monsters whom we read of ever purposely inflicted on their living fellow creatures. If by an arbitrary reservation we refuse to account anything murder but what abridges a certain term supposed to be allotted to human life, nature also does this to all but a small percentage of lives, and does it in all the modes, violent or insidious, in which the worst human beings take the lives of one another. Nature impales men, breaks them as if on the wheel, casts them to be devoured by wild beasts, burns them to death, crushes them with stones like the first Christian martyr, starves them with hunger, freezes them with cold, poisons them by the quick or slow venom of her exhalations, and has hundreds of other hideous deaths in reserve such as the ingenious cruelty of a Nabis or a Domitian[1] never surpassed. All this nature does with the most supercilious disregard both of mercy and of justice, emptying her shafts upon the best and noblest indifferently with the meanest and worst; upon those who are engaged in the highest and worthiest enterprises, and often as the direct consequence of the noblest acts; and it might almost be imagined as a punishment for them. She mows down those on whose existence hangs the well-being of a whole people,

---

[1] [Mill refers to Nabis, tyrant of Sparta, who seized power in 207 B.C., after Sparta's defeat by the Achaean League. His reputation as a "cruel monster" is based mostly on Polybius' statements, and not wholly confirmed by other writers, e.g., Livy and Plutarch.

Domitian was a Roman emperor, Titus Flavius Domitianus (A.D. 81–96). Mill refers to the later period of his reign when, in defense against the growing opposition and above all after the short-lived rebellion by Saturninus, he became unstable, ruthless, and revengeful. In constant fear of assassination, he condemned to death everybody he distrusted or disliked. His wife, Domitia, apparently out of fear for her own safety, became involved in the successful conspiracy to kill him. He was stabbed by a former slave who avenged the death of the master who had freed him.]

perhaps the prospects of the human race for generations to come, with as little compunction as those whose death is a relief to themselves or a blessing to those under their noxious influence. Such are nature's dealings with life. Even when she does not intend to kill, she inflicts the same tortures in apparent wantonness. In the clumsy provision which she has made for that perpetual renewal of animal life, rendered necessary by the prompt termination she puts to it in every individual instance, no human being ever comes into the world but another human being is literally stretched on the rack for hours or days, not unfrequently issuing in death. Next to taking life (equal to it, according to a high authority) is taking the means by which we live; and nature does this, too, on the largest scale and with the most callous indifference. A single hurricane destroys the hopes of a season; a flight of locusts, or an inundation, desolates a district; a trifling chemical change in an edible root starves a million of people. The waves of the sea, like banditti, seize and appropriate the wealth of the rich and the little all of the poor with the same accompaniments of stripping, wounding, and killing as their human antitypes. Everything, in short, which the worst men commit either against life or property is perpetrated on a larger scale by natural agents. Nature has noyades more fatal than those of Carrier;[2] her explosions of firedamp are as destructive as human artillery; her plague and cholera far surpass the poison cups of the Borgias.[3] Even the love of "order" which is thought to be a following of the ways of nature is in fact a contradiction of them. All which people are accustomed to deprecate as "disorder" and its consequences is precisely a counterpart of nature's ways. Anarchy and the Reign of Terror[4] are overmatched in injustice, ruin, and death by a hurricane and a pestilence.

But, it is said, all these things are for wise and good ends. On this I must first remark that whether they are so or not is altogether beside the point. Supposing it true that, contrary to appearances, these horrors when perpetrated by nature promote good ends, still, as no one believes that good ends would be promoted by our following the example, the course of nature cannot be a proper model for us to imitate. Either it is right that we should kill because nature kills, torture because nature tortures, ruin and devastate because nature does the like, or we ought not to consider at all what nature does, but what it is good to do. If there is such a thing as a *reductio ad absurdum*,[5] this surely amounts to one. If it is a sufficient reason for doing one thing that nature does it, why not another thing? If not all things, why any thing? The physical government of the world being full of the things which when done by men are deemed the greatest enormities, it cannot be religious or moral in us to guide our actions by the analogy of the course of nature.

---

[2] [Mill compares natural catastrophes with the "Noyades of Nantes" perpetrated by Jean Baptiste Carrier (1756–94), a notorious terrorist of the French Revolution. Prisoners involved, or allegedly involved, in the unsuccessful uprising at Nantes (1793) were forced to board vessels fitted with trapdoors. Without trial, they were then summarily drowned in the Loire.]

[3] [The Borgias were Cesare (1476–1507) and his sister Lucrezia (1480–1519) who, together with their father, Cardinal Rodrigo Borgia (later Pope Alexander VI), became notorious for their unscrupulous tactics and many murders either by poison or by dagger.]

[4] [An obvious reference to the Jacobin terror during the French Revolution.]

[5] [An indirect proof by arguing the impossibility of the contrary.]

This proposition remains true whatever occult quality of producing good may reside in those facts of nature which to our perceptions are most noxious, and which no one considers it other than a crime to produce artificially.

But, in reality, no one consistently believes in any such occult quality. The phrases which ascribe perfection to the course of nature can only be considered as the exaggerations of poetic or devotional feeling, not intended to stand the test of a sober examination. No one, either religious or irreligious, believes that the hurtful agencies of nature, considered as a whole, promote good purposes in any other way than by inciting human rational creatures to rise up and struggle against them. If we believed that those agencies were appointed by a benevolent Providence as the means of accomplishing wise purposes which could not be compassed if they did not exist, then everything done by mankind which tends to chain up these natural agencies or to restrict their mischievous operation, from draining a pestilential marsh down to curing the toothache or putting up an umbrella, ought to be accounted impious; which assuredly nobody does account them, notwithstanding an undercurrent of sentiment setting in that direction which is occasionally perceptible. On the contrary, the improvements on which the civilized part of mankind most pride themselves consist in more successfully warding off those natural calamities which, if we really believed what most people profess to believe, we should cherish as medicines provided for our earthly state by infinite wisdom. Inasmuch, too, as each generation greatly surpasses its predecessors in the amount of natural evil which it succeeds in averting, our condition, if the theory were true, ought by this time to have become a terrible manifestation of some tremendous calamity against which the physical evils we have learned to overmaster had previously operated as a preservative. Anyone, however, who acted as if he supposed this to be the case would be more likely, I think, to be confined as a lunatic than reverenced as a saint.

It is undoubtedly a very common fact that good comes out of evil, and, when it does occur, it is far too agreeable not to find people eager to dilate on it. But in the first place, it is quite as often true of human crimes as of natural calamities. The fire of London, which is believed to have had so salutary an effect on the healthiness of the city, would have produced that effect just as much if it had been really the work of the *furor papisticus* so long commemorated on the monument. The deaths of those whom tyrants or persecutors have made martyrs in any noble cause have done a service to mankind which would not have been obtained if they had died by accident or disease. Yet whatever incidental and unexpected benefits may result from crimes, they are crimes nevertheless. In the second place, if good frequently comes out of evil, the converse fact, evil coming out of good, is equally common. Every event, public or private, which, regretted on its occurrence, was declared providential at a later period on account of some unforeseen good consequence, might be matched by some other event, deemed fortunate at the time, but which proved calamitous or fatal to those whom it appeared to benefit. Such conflicts between the beginning and the end, or between the event and the expectation, are not only as frequent but are often held up to notice in the painful cases as in the agreeable, but there is not the same inclination to generalize on them or at all events they are not regarded by the moderns (though they were by the ancients) as similarly an indication of the divine purposes: men satisfy themselves with moralizing on the imperfect nature of our foresight, the uncertainty of events, and the vanity of human expectations. The simple fact is, human interests are so complicated, and the effects of any incident whatever so multitudinous, that if it touches mankind at all its influence on them is, in the great majority of cases, both good and bad. If the greater number of personal misfortunes have their good side, hardly any good fortune ever befell anyone which did not give either to the same or to some other person something to regret; and unhappily there are many misfortunes so overwhelming that their favorable side, if it exists, is entirely overshadowed and made insignificant, while the corresponding statement can seldom be made concerning blessings. The effects, too, of every cause depend so much on the circumstances which accidentally accompany it that many cases are sure to occur in which even the total result is markedly opposed to the predominant tendency; and thus not only evil has its good and good its evil side, but good often produces an overbalance of evil and evil an overbalance of good. This, however, is by no means the general tendency of either phenomenon. On the contrary, both good and evil naturally tend to fructify, each in its own kind, good producing good, and evil, evil. It is one of nature's general rules and part of her habitual injustice that "to him that hath shall be given, but from him that hath not shall be taken even that which he hath."[6] The ordinary and predominant tendency of good is toward more good. Health, strength, wealth, knowledge, virtue are not only good in themselves but facilitate and promote the acquisition of good, both of the same and of other kinds. The person who can learn easily is he who already knows much; it is the strong and not the sickly person who can do everything which most conduces to health; those who find it easy to gain money are not the poor but the rich; while health, strength, knowledge, talents are all means of acquiring riches, and riches are often an indispensable means of acquiring these. Again, *e converso*, whatever may be said of evil turning into good, the general tendency of evil is toward further evil. Bodily illness renders the body more susceptible of disease; it produces incapacity of exertion, sometimes debility of mind, and often the loss of means of subsistence. All severe pain, either bodily or mental, tends to increase the susceptibilities of pain forever after. Poverty is the parent of a thousand mental and moral evils. What is still worse, to be injured or oppressed, when habitual, lowers the whole tone of the character. One bad action leads to others, both in the agent himself, in the bystanders, and in the sufferers. All bad qualities are strengthened by habit, and all vices and follies tend to spread. Intellectual defects generate moral, and moral, intellectual; and every intellectual or moral defect generates others, and so on without end.

The much-applauded class of authors, the writers on natural theology, have, I venture to think, entirely lost their way and missed the sole line of argument which could have made their speculations acceptable to anyone who can perceive when two propositions contradict one another. They have exhausted the resources of sophistry to make it appear that all the suffering in the world exists to

---

[6] [Matt. 25. 29.]

prevent greater—that misery exists for fear lest there should be misery: a thesis which, if ever so well maintained, could only avail to explain and justify the works of limited beings, compelled to labor under conditions independent of their own will, but can have no application to a Creator assumed to be omnipotent who, if he bends to a supposed necessity, himself makes the necessity which he bends to. If the maker of the world *can* all that he will, he wills misery, and there is no escape from the conclusion. The more consistent of those who have deemed themselves qualified to "vindicate the ways of God to man" have endeavored to avoid the alternative by hardening their hearts and denying that misery is an evil. The goodness of God, they say, does not consist in willing the happiness of his creatures but their virtue; and the universe, if not a happy, is a just universe. But waiving the objections to this scheme of ethics, it does not at all get rid of the difficulty. If the Creator of mankind willed that they should all be virtuous, his designs are as completely baffled as if he had willed that they should all be happy; and the order of nature is constructed with even less regard to the requirements of justice than to those of benevolence. If the law of all creation were justice and the Creator omnipotent, then, in whatever amount suffering and happiness might be dispensed to the world, each person's share of them would be exactly proportioned to that person's good or evil deeds; no human being would have a worse lot than another without worse deserts; accident or favoritism would have no part in such a world, but every human life would be the playing out of a drama constructed like a perfect moral tale. No one is able to blind himself to the fact that the world we live in is totally different from this, insomuch that the necessity of redressing the balance has been deemed one of the strongest arguments for another life after death, which amounts to an admission that the order of things in this life is often an example of injustice, not justice. If it be said that God does not take sufficient account of pleasure and pain to make them the reward or punishment of the good or the wicked, but that virtue is itself the greatest good and vice the greatest evil, then these at least ought to be dispensed to all according to what they have done to deserve them; instead of which every kind of moral depravity is entailed upon multitudes by the fatality of their birth, through the fault of their parents, of society, or of uncontrollable circumstances, certainly through no fault of their own. Not even on the most distorted and contracted theory of good which ever was framed by religious or philosophical fanaticism can the government of nature be made to resemble the work of a being at once good and omnipotent.

The only admissible moral theory of Creation is that the Principle of Good *cannot* at once and altogether subdue the powers of evil, either physical or moral; could not place mankind in a world free from the necessity of an incessant struggle with the maleficent powers, or make them always victorious in that struggle, but could and did make them capable of carrying on the fight with vigor and with progressively increasing success. Of all the religious explanations of the order of nature, this alone is neither contradictory to itself nor to the facts for which it attempts to account. According to it, man's duty would consist, not in simply taking care of his own interests by obeying irresistible power, but in standing forward a not ineffectual auxiliary to a Being of perfect beneficence—a faith which seems much better adapted for nerving him to exertion than a vague and inconsistent reliance on an Author of Good who is supposed to be also the author of evil. And I venture to assert that such has really been, though often unconsciously, the faith of all who have drawn strength and support of any worthy kind from trust in a superintending Providence. There is no subject on which men's practical belief is more incorrectly indicated by the words they use to express it than religion. Many have derived a base confidence from imagining themselves to be favorites of an omnipotent but capricious and despotic Deity. But those who have been strengthened in goodness by relying on the sympathizing support of a powerful and good Governor of the world have, I am satisfied, never really believed that Governor to be, in the strict sense of the term, omnipotent. They have always saved his goodness at the expense of his power. They have believed, perhaps, that he could, if he willed, remove all the thorns from their individual path, but not without causing greater harm to someone else, or frustrating some purpose of greater importance to the general well-being. They have believed that he could do any one thing, but not any combination of things; that his government, like human government, was a system of adjustments and compromises; that the world is inevitably imperfect, contrary to his intention. And since the exertion of all his power to make it as little imperfect as possible leaves it no better than it is, they cannot but regard that power, though vastly beyond human estimate, yet as in itself not merely finite but extremely limited. They are bound, for example, to suppose that the best he could do for his human creatures was to make an immense majority of all who have yet existed be born (without any fault of their own) Patagonians, or Eskimos, or something nearly as brutal and degraded, but to give them capacities which, by being cultivated for very many centuries in toil and suffering and after many of the best specimens of the race have sacrificed their lives for the purpose, have at last enabled some chosen portions of the species to grow into something better, capable of being improved in centuries more into something really good, of which hitherto there are only to be found individual instances. It may be possible to believe with Plato that perfect goodness, limited and thwarted in every direction by the intractableness of the material, has done this because it could do no better. But that the same perfectly wise and good Being had absolute power over the material and made it, by voluntary choice, what it is—to admit this might have been supposed impossible to anyone who has the simplest notions of moral good and evil. Nor can any such person, whatever kind of religious phrases he may use, fail to believe that if Nature and Man are both the works of a Being of perfect goodness, that Being intended Nature as a scheme to be amended, not imitated by Man.

32. The Problem of Evil
JOHN HICK

To many, the most powerful positive objection to belief in God is the fact of evil. Probably for most agnostics it is the appalling depth and extent of human suffering, more than anything else, that makes the idea of a loving Creator seem so implausible and disposes them toward one or another of the various naturalistic theories of religion.

As a challenge to theism, the problem of evil has traditionally been posed in the form of a dilemma: if God is perfectly loving, he must wish to abolish evil; and if he is all-powerful, he must be able to abolish evil. But evil exists; therefore God cannot be both omnipotent and perfectly loving.

Certain solutions, which at once suggest themselves, have to be ruled out so far as the Judaic-Christian faith is concerned.

To say, for example (with contemporary Christian Science), that evil is an illusion of the human mind, is impossible within a religion based upon the stark realism of the Bible. Its pages faithfully reflect the characteristic mixture of good and evil in human experience. They record every kind of sorrow and suffering, every mode of man's inhumanity to man and of his painfully insecure existence in the world. There is no attempt to regard evil as anything but dark, menacingly ugly, heart-rending, and crushing. In the Christian scriptures, the climax of this history of evil is the crucifixion of Jesus, which is presented not only as a case of utterly unjust suffering, but as the violent and murderous rejection of God's Messiah. There can be no doubt, then, that for biblical faith, evil is unambiguously evil, and stands in direct opposition to God's will.

Again, to solve the problem of evil by means of the theory (sponsored, for example, by the Boston "Personalist" School)[1] of a finite deity who does the best he can with a material, intractable and co-eternal with himself, is to have abandoned the basic premise of Hebrew-Christian monotheism; for the theory amounts to rejecting belief in the infinity and sovereignty of God.

Indeed, any theory which would avoid the problem of the origin of evil by depicting it as an ultimate constituent of the universe, coordinate with good, has been repudiated in advance by the classic Christian teaching, first developed by Augustine, that evil represents the going wrong of something which in itself is good.[2] Augustine holds firmly to the Hebrew-Christian conviction that the universe is *good*—that is to say, it is the creation of a good God for a good purpose. He completely rejects the ancient prejudice, widespread in his day, that matter is evil. There are, according to Augustine, higher and lower, greater and lesser goods in immense abundance and variety; but everything which has being is good in its own way and degree, except in so far as it may have become spoiled or corrupted. Evil—whether it be an evil will, an instance of pain, or some disorder or decay in nature—has not been set there by God, but represents the distortion of something that is inherently valuable. Whatever exists is, as such, and in its proper place, good; evil is essentially parasitic upon good, being disorder and perversion in a fundamentally good creation. This understanding of evil as something negative means that it is not willed and created by God; but it does not mean (as some have supposed) that evil is unreal and can be disregarded. Clearly, the first effect of this doctrine is to accentuate even more the question of the origin of evil.

---

[1] Edgar Brightman's A *Philosophy of Religion* (Englewood Cliffs, N.J.: Prentice-Hall, Inc., 1940), Chaps. 8–10, is a classic exposition of one form of this view.
[2] See Augustine's *Confessions*, Book VII, Chap. 12; *City of God*, Book XII, Chap. 3; *Enchiridion*, Chap. 4.

Theodicy,[3] as many modern Christian thinkers see it, is a modest enterprise, negative rather than positive in its conclusions. It does not claim to explain, nor to explain away, every instance of evil in human experience, but only to point to certain considerations which prevent the fact of evil (largely incomprehensible though it remains) from constituting a final and insuperable bar to rational belief in God.

In indicating these considerations it will be useful to follow the traditional division of the subject. There is the problem of *moral evil* or wickedness: why does an all-good and all-powerful God permit this? And there is the problem of the *nonmoral evil* of suffering or pain, both physical and mental: why has an all-good and all-powerful God created a world in which this occurs?

Christian thought has always considered moral evil in its relation to human freedom and responsibility. To be a person is to be a finite center of freedom, a (relatively) free and self-directing agent responsible for one's own decisions. This involves being free to act wrongly as well as to act rightly. The idea of a person who can be infallibly guaranteed always to act rightly is self-contradictory. There can be no guarantee in advance that a genuinely free moral agent will never choose amiss. Consequently, the possibility of wrongdoing or sin is logically inseparable from the creation of finite persons, and to say that God should not have created beings who might sin amounts to saying that he should not have created people.

This thesis has been challenged in some recent philosophical discussions of the problem of evil, in which it is claimed that no contradiction is involved in saying that God might have made people who would be genuinely free and who could yet be guaranteed always to act rightly. A quotation from one of these discussions follows:

> If there is no logical impossibility in a man's freely choosing the good on one, or on several occasions, there cannot be a logical impossibility in his freely choosing the good on every occasion. God was not, then, faced with a choice between making innocent automata and making beings who, in acting freely, would sometimes go wrong: there was open to him the obviously better possibility of making beings who would act freely but always go right. Clearly, his failure to avail himself of this possibility is inconsistent with his being both omnipotent and wholly good.[4]

A reply to this argument is suggested in another recent contribution to the discussion.[5] If by a free action we mean an action which is not externally compelled but which flows from the nature of the agent as he reacts to the circumstances in which he finds himself, there is, indeed, no contradiction between our being free and our actions being "caused" (by our own nature) and

---

[3] The word "theodicy" from the Greek *theos* (God) and *dike* (righteous) means the justification of God's goodness in face of the fact of evil.

[4] J. L. Mackie, "Evil and Omnipotence," *Mind* (April, 1955), p. 209. A similar point is made by Antony Flew in "Divine Omnipotence and Human Freedom," *New Essays in Philosophical Theology*. An important critical comment on these arguments is offered by Ninian Smart in "Omnipotence, Evil and Supermen," *Philosophy* (April, 1961), with replies by Flew (January, 1962) and Mackie (April, 1962).

[5] Flew, in *New Essays in Philosophical Theology.*

therefore being in principle predictable. There is a contradiction, however, in saying that God is the cause of our acting as we do but that we are free beings in relation to God. There is, in other words, a contradiction in saying that God has made us so that we shall of necessity act in a certain way, and that we are genuinely independent persons in relation to him. If all our thoughts and actions are divinely predestined, however free and morally responsible we may seem to be to ourselves, we cannot be free and morally responsible in the sight of God, but must instead be his helpless puppets. Such "freedom" is like that of a patient acting out a series of posthypnotic suggestions: he appears, even to himself, to be free, but his volitions have actually been predetermined by another will, that of the hypnotist, in relation to whom the patient is not a free agent.

A different objector might raise the question of whether or not we deny God's omnipotence if we admit that he is unable to create persons who are free from the risks inherent in personal freedom. The answer that has always been given is that to create such beings is logically impossible. It is no limitation upon God's power that he cannot accomplish the logically impossible, since there is nothing here to accomplish, but only a meaningless conjunction of words[6]—in this case "person who is not a person." God is able to create beings of any and every conceivable kind; but creatures who lack moral freedom, however superior they might be to human beings in other respects, would not be what we mean by persons. They would constitute a different form of life which God might have brought into existence instead of persons. When we ask why God did not create such beings in place of persons, the traditional answer is that only persons could, in any meaningful sense, become "children of God," capable of entering into a personal relationship with their Creator by a free and uncompelled response to his love.

When we turn from the possibility of moral evil as a correlate of man's personal freedom to its actuality, we face something which must remain inexplicable even when it can be seen to be possible. For we can never provide a complete causal explanation of a free act; if we could, it would not be a free act. The origin of moral evil lies forever concealed within the mystery of human freedom.

The necessary connection between moral freedom and the possibility, now actualized, of sin throws light upon a great deal of the suffering which afflicts mankind. For an enormous amount of human pain arises either from the inhumanity or the culpable incompetence of mankind. This includes such major scourges as poverty, oppression and persecution, war, and all the injustice, indignity, and inequity which occur even in the most advanced societies. These evils are manifestations of human sin. Even disease is fostered to an extent, the limits of which have not yet been determined by psychosomatic medicine, by moral and emotional factors seated both in the individual and in his social environment. To the extent that all of these evils stem from human failures and wrong decisions, their possibility is inherent in the creation of free persons inhabiting a world which presents them with real choices which are followed by real consequences.

---

[6] As Aquinas said, " . . . nothing that implies a contradiction falls under the scope of God's omnipotence." *Summa Theologica*, Part I, Question 25, article 4.

We may now turn more directly to the problem of suffering. Even though the major bulk of actual human pain is traceable to man's misused freedom as a sole or part cause, there remain other sources of pain which are entirely independent of the human will, for example, earthquake, hurricane, storm, flood, drought, and blight. In practice, it is often impossible to trace a boundary between the suffering which results from human wickedness and folly and that which falls upon mankind from without. Both kinds of suffering are inextricably mingled together in human experience. For our present purpose, however, it is important to note that the latter category does exist and that it seems to be built into the very structure of our world. In response to it, theodicy, if it is wisely conducted, follows a negative path. It is not possible to show positively that each item of human pain serves the divine purpose of good; but, on the other hand, it does seem possible to show that the divine purpose as it is understood in Judaism and Christianity could not be forwarded in a world which was designed as a permanent hedonistic paradise.

An essential premise of this argument concerns the nature of the divine purpose in creating the world. The skeptic's assumption is that man is to be viewed as a completed creation and that God's purpose in making the world was to provide a suitable dwelling-place for this fully-formed creature. Since God is good and loving, the environment which he has created for human life to inhabit is naturally as pleasant and comfortable as possible. The problem is essentially similar to that of a man who builds a cage for some pet animal. Since our world, in fact, contains sources of hardship, inconvenience, and danger of innumerable kinds, the conclusion follows that this world cannot have been created by a perfectly benevolent and all-powerful deity.[7]

Christianity, however, has never supposed that God's purpose in the creation of the world was to construct a paradise whose inhabitants would experience a maximum of pleasure and a minimum of pain. The world is seen, instead, as a place of "soul-making" in which free beings grappling with the tasks and challenges of their existence in a common environment, may become "children of God" and "heirs of eternal life." A way of thinking theologically of God's continuing creative purpose for man was suggested by some of the early Hellenistic Fathers of the Christian Church, especially Irenaeus. Following hints from St. Paul, Irenaeus taught that man has been made as a person in the image of God but has not yet been brought as a free and responsible agent into the finite likeness of God, which is revealed in Christ.[8] Our world, with all its rough edges, is the sphere in which this second and harder stage of the creative process is taking place.

This conception of the world (whether or not set in Irenaeus' theological framework) can be supported by the method of negative theodicy. Suppose, contrary to fact, that this world were a paradise from which all possibility of pain and suffering were excluded. The consequences would be very far-reaching. For example, no one could ever injure anyone else: the murderer's knife would turn to paper or his bullets to thin air; the bank safe, robbed of a million dollars, would miracu-

---

[7] This is the nature of David Hume's argument in his discussion of the problem of evil in his *Dialogues*, Part XI.

[8] See Irenaeus' *Against Heresies*, Book IV, Chaps. 37 and 38.

lously become filled with another million dollars (without this device, on however large a scale, proving inflationary); fraud, deceit, conspiracy, and treason would somehow always leave the fabric of society undamaged. Again, no one would ever be injured by accident: the mountain-climber, steeplejack, or playing child falling from a height would float unharmed to the ground; the reckless driver would never meet with disaster. There would be no need to work, since no harm could result from avoiding work; there would be no call to be concerned for others in time of need or danger, for in such a world there could be no real needs or dangers.

To make possible this continual series of individual adjustments, nature would have to work by "special providences" instead of running according to general laws which men must learn to respect on penalty of pain or death. The laws of nature would have to be extremely flexible: sometimes gravity would operate, sometimes not; sometimes an object would be hard and solid, sometimes soft. There could be no sciences, for there would be no enduring world structure to investigate. In eliminating the problems and hardships of an objective environ-ment, with its own laws, life would become like a dream in which, delightfully but aimlessly, we would float and drift at ease.

One can at least begin to imagine such a world. It is evident that our present ethical concepts would have no meaning in it. If, for example, the notion of harming someone is an essential element in the concept of a wrong action, in our hedonistic paradise there could be no wrong actions—nor any right actions in distinction from wrong. Courage and fortitude would have no point in an environ-ment in which there is, by definition, no danger or difficulty. Generosity, kind-ness, the *agape* aspect of love, prudence, unselfishness, and all other ethical notions which presuppose life in a stable environment, could not even be formed. Consequently, such a world, however well it might promote pleasure, would be very ill adapted for the development of the moral qualities of human personality. In relation to this purpose it would be the worst of all possible worlds.

It would seem, then, that an environment intended to make possible the growth in free beings of the finest characteristics of personal life, must have a good deal in common with our present world. It must operate according to general and dependable laws; and it must involve real dangers, difficulties, problems, obsta-cles, and possibilities of pain, failure, sorrow, frustration, and defeat. If it did not contain the particular trials and perils which—subtracting man's own very consid-erable contribution—our world contains, it would have to contain others instead.

To realize this is not, by any means, to be in possession of a detailed theodicy. It is to understand that this world, with all its "heartaches and the thousand natural shocks that flesh is heir to," an environment so manifestly not designed for the maximization of human pleasure and the minimization of human pain, may be rather well adapted to the quite different purpose of "soul-making."[9]

These considerations are related to theism as such. Specifically, Christian

---

[9] This brief discussion has been confined to the problem of human suffering. The large and intractable problem of animal pain is not taken up here. For a discussion of it, see, for example, Nels Ferré, *Evil and the Christian Faith* (New York: Harper & Row, Publishers, Inc., 1947), Chap. 7; and Austin Farrer, *Love Almighty and Ills Unlimited* (New York: Doubleday & Company, Inc., 1961), Chap. 5.

theism goes further in the light of the death of Christ, which is seen paradoxically both (as the murder of the divine Son) as the worst thing that has ever happened and (as the occasion of man's salvation) as the best thing that has ever happened. As the supreme evil turned to supreme good, it provides the paradigm for the distinctively Christian reaction to evil. Viewed from the standpoint of Christian faith, evils do not cease to be evils; and certainly, in view of Christ's healing work, they cannot be said to have been sent by God. Yet, it has been the persistent claim of those seriously and wholeheartedly committed to Christian discipleship that tragedy, though truly tragic, may nevertheless be turned, through a man's reaction to it, from a cause of despair and alienation from God to a stage in the fulfillment of God's loving purpose for that individual. As the greatest of all evils, the crucifixion of Christ, was made the occasion of man's redemption, so good can be won from other evils. As Jesus saw his execution by the Romans as an experience which God desired him to accept, an experience which was to be brought within the sphere of the divine purpose and made to serve the divine ends, so the Christian response to calamity is to accept the adversities, pains, and afflictions which life brings, in order that they can be turned to a positive spiritual use.[10]

At this point, theodicy points forward in two ways to the subject of life after death.

First, although there are many striking instances of good being triumphantly brought out of evil through a man's or a woman's reaction to it, there are many other cases in which the opposite has happened. Sometimes obstacles breed strength of character, dangers evoke courage and unselfishness, and calamities produce patience and moral steadfastness. But sometimes they lead, instead, to resentment, fear, grasping selfishness, and disintegration of character. Therefore, it would seem that any divine purpose of soul-making which is at work in earthly history must continue beyond this life if it is ever to achieve more than a very partial and fragmentary success.

Second, if we ask whether the business of soul-making is worth all the toil and sorrow of human life, the Christian answer must be in terms of a future good which is great enough to justify all that has happened on the way to it.

---

[10] This conception of providence is stated more fully in John Hick, *Faith and Knowledge* (Ithaca: Cornell University Press, 1957), Chap. 7, from which some sentences are incorporated in this paragraph.

Evil as Punishment for Sin

33. Guide for the Perplexed

MOSES MAIMONIDES

Men frequently think that the evils in the world are more numerous than
the good things; many sayings and songs of the nations dwell on this idea. They
say that a good thing is found only exceptionally, whilst evil things are numerous
and lasting. Not only common people make this mistake, but even many who
believe that they are wise. Al-Razi wrote a well-known book *On Metaphysics* [or
Theology]. Among other mad and foolish things, it contains also the idea discovered by him that there exists more evil than good. For if the happiness of man and
his pleasure in the times of prosperity be compared with the mishaps that befall
him—such as grief, acute pain, defects, paralysis of the limbs, fears, anxieties, and
troubles—it would seem as if the existence of man is a punishment and a great evil
for him. This author commenced to verify his opinion by counting all the evils one
by one; by this means he opposed those who hold the correct view of the benefits
bestowed by God and His evident kindness, viz., that God is perfect goodness, and
that all that comes from Him is absolutely good. The origin of the error is to be
found in the circumstance that this ignorant man, and his party among the
common people, judge the whole universe by examining one single person. For an
ignorant man believes that the whole universe only exists for him; as if nothing
else required any consideration. If, therefore, anything happens to him contrary to
his expectation, he at once concludes that the whole universe is evil. If, however,
he would take into consideration the whole universe, form an idea of it, and
comprehend what a small portion he is of the universe, he will find the truth. For
it is clear that persons who have fallen into this wide-spread error as regards the
multitude of evils in the world, do not find the evils among the angels, the spheres
and stars, the elements, and that which is formed of them, viz., minerals and
plants, or in the various species of living beings, but only in some individual
instances of mankind. They wonder that a person, who became leprous in consequence of bad food, should be afflicted with so great an illness and suffer such a
misfortune; or that he who indulges so much in sensuality as to weaken his sight,
should be struck with blindness! and the like. What we have, in truth, to consider
is this:—The whole mankind at present in existence, and a fortiori, every other

species of animals, for an infinitesimal portion of the permanent universe. Comp. "Man is like to vanity" (Ps. cxliv. 4) "How much less man, that is a worm; and the son of man, which is a worm" (Job xxv. 6); "How much less in them who dwell in houses of clay" (ibid. iv. 19) "Behold, the nations are as a drop of the bucket" (Isa. xl. 15). There are many other passages in the books of the prophets expressing the same idea. It is of great advantage that man should know his station, and not erroneously imagine that the whole universe exists only for him. We hold that the universe exists because the Creator wills it so; that mankind is low in rank as compared with the uppermost portion of the universe, viz, with the spheres and the stars; but, as regards the angels, there cannot be any real comparison between man and angels, although man is the highest of all beings on earth; i.e., of all beings formed of the four elements. Man's existence is nevertheless a great boon to him, and his distinction and perfection is a divine gift. The numerous evils to which individual persons are exposed are due to the defects existing in the persons themselves. We complain and seek relief from our own faults; we suffer from the evils which we, by our own free will, inflict on ourselves and ascribe them to God, who is far from being connected with them! Comp. "Is destruction His (work)? No. Ye (who call yourselves) wrongly His sons, you are a perverse and crooked generation" (Deut. xxxii. 5). This is explained by Solomon, who says, "The foolishness of man perverteth his way, and his heart fretteth against the Lord" (Prov. xix. 3).

I explain this theory in the following manner. The evils that befall man are of three kinds:—

(1) The first kind of evil is that which is caused to man by the circumstance that he is subject to genesis and destruction, or that he possesses a body. It is on account of the body that some persons happen to have great deformities or paralysis of some of the organs. This evil may be part of the natural constitution of these persons, or may have developed subsequently in consequence of changes in the elements, e.g., through bad air, or thunderstorms, or landslips. We have already shown that, in accordance with the divine wisdom, genesis can only take place through destruction, and without the destruction of the individual members of the species the species themselves would not exist permanently. Thus the true kindness, and beneficence, and goodness of God is clear. He who thinks that he can have flesh and bones without being subject to any external influence, or any of the accidents of matter, unconsciously wishes to reconcile two opposites, viz., to be at the same time subject and not subject to change. If man were never subject to change there could be no generation; there would be one single being, but no individuals forming a species. Galen, in the third section of his book, "The Use of the Limbs," says correctly that it would be in vain to expect to see living beings formed of the blood of menstruous women and the semen virile, who will not die, will never feel pain, or will move perpetually, or shine like the sun. This dictum of Galen is part of the following more general proposition:—Whatever is formed of any matter receives the most perfect form possible in that species of matter; in each individual case the defects are in accordance with the defects of that individual matter. The best and most perfect being that can be formed of the blood and the semen is the species of man, for as far as man's nature is known, he is living,

reasonable, and mortal. It is therefore impossible that man should be free from this species of evil. You will, nevertheless, find that the evils of the above kind which befall man are very few and rare; for you find countries that have not been flooded or burned for thousands of years; there are thousands of men in perfect health, deformed individuals are a strange and exceptional occurrence, or say few in number if you object to the term exceptional,—they are not one-hundredth, not even one-thousandth part of those that are perfectly normal.

(2) The second class of evil comprises such evils as people cause to each other, when, e.g., some of them use their strength against others. These evils are more numerous than those of the first kind; their causes are numerous and known; they likewise originate in ourselves, though the sufferer himself cannot avert them. This kind of evil is nevertheless not widespread in any country of the whole world. It is of rare occurrence that a man plans to kill his neighbour or to rob him of his property by night. Many persons are, however, afflicted with this kind of evil in great wars; but these are not frequent, if the whole inhabited part of the earth is taken into consideration.

(3) The third class of evils comprises those which every one causes to himself by his own action. This is the largest class, and is far more numerous than the second class. It is especially of these evils that all men complain,—only few men are found that do not sin against themselves by this kind of evil. Those that are afflicted with it are therefore justly blamed in the words of the prophet, "This hath been by your means" (Mal. i. 9); the same is expressed in the following passage, "He that doeth it destroyeth his own soul" (Prov. vi. 32). In reference to this kind of evil, Solomon says, "The foolishness of man perverteth his way" (ibid. xix. 3). In the following passage he explains also that this kind of evil is man's own work, "Lo, this only have I found, that God hath made man upright, but they have thought out many inventions" (Eccles. vii. 29), and these inventions bring the evils upon him. The same subject is referred to in Job (v. 6), "For affliction cometh not forth of the dust, neither doth trouble spring out of the ground." These words are immediately followed by the explanation that man himself is the author of this class of evils, "But man is born unto trouble." This class of evils originates in man's vices, such as excessive desire for eating, drinking, and love; indulgence in these things in undue measure, or in improper manner, or partaking of bad food. This course brings diseases and afflictions upon body and soul alike. The sufferings of the body in consequence of these evils are well known; those of the soul are twofold:—First, such evils of the soul as are the necessary consequence of changes in the body, in so far as the soul is a force residing in the body; it has therefore been said that the properties of the soul depend on the condition of the body. Secondly, the soul, when accustomed to superfluous things, acquires a strong habit of desiring things which are neither necessary for the preservation of the individual nor for that of the species. This desire is without a limit, whilst things which are necessary are few in number and restricted within certain limits; but what is superfluous is without end—e.g., you desire to have your vessels of silver, but golden vessels are still better: others have even vessels of sapphire, or perhaps they can be made of emerald or rubies, or any other substance that could be suggested. Those who are ignorant and perverse in their thought are constantly

in trouble and pain, because they cannot get as much of superfluous things as a certain other person possesses. They as a rule expose themselves to great dangers, e.g., by sea-voyage, or service of kings, and all this for the purpose of obtaining that which is superfluous and not necessary. When they thus meet with the consequences of the course which they adopt, they complain of the decrees and judgments of God; they begin to blame the time, and wonder at the want of justice in its changes; that it has not enabled them to acquire great riches, with which they could buy large quantities of wine for the purpose of making themselves drunk, and numerous concubines adorned with various kind of ornaments of gold, embroidery, and jewels, for the purpose of driving themselves to voluptuousness beyond their capacities, as if the whole Universe existed exclusively for the purpose of giving pleasure to these low people. The error of the ignorant goes so far as to say that God's power is insufficient, because He has given to this Universe the properties which they imagine cause these great evils, and which do not help all evil-disposed persons to obtain the evils which they seek, and to bring their evil souls to the aim of their desires, though these, as we have shown, are really without limit. The virtuous and wise, however, see and comprehend the wisdom of God displayed in the Universe. Thus David says, "All the paths of the Lord are mercy and truth unto such as keep His covenant and His testimonies" (Ps. xxv. 10). For those who observe the nature of the Universe and the commandments of the Law, and know their purpose, see clearly God's mercy and truth in everything; they seek, therefore, that which the Creator intended to be the aim of man, viz., comprehension. Forced by the claims of the body, they seek also that which is necessary for the preservation of the body, "bread to eat and garment to clothe," and this is very little; but they seek nothing superfluous; with very slight exertion man can obtain it, so long as he is contented with that which is indispensable. All the difficulties and troubles we meet in this respect are due to the desire for superfluous things; when we seek unnecessary things, we have difficulty even in finding that which is indispensable. For the more we desire for that which is superfluous, the more we meet with difficulties; our strength and possessions are spent in unnecessary things, and are wanting when required for that which is necessary. Observe how Nature proves the correctness of this assertion. The more necessary a thing is for living beings, the more easily it is found and the cheaper it is; the less necessary it is, the rarer and dearer it is. E.g., air, water, and food are indispensable to man: air is most necessary, for if man is without air a short time he dies; whilst he can be without water a day or two. Air is also undoubtedly found more easily and cheaper (than water). Water is more necessary than food; for some people can be four or five days without food, provided they have water; water also exists in every country in larger quantities than food, and is also cheaper. The same proportion can be noticed in the different kinds of food; that which is more necessary in a certain place exists there in larger quantities and is cheaper than that which is less necessary. No intelligent person, I think, considers musk, amber, rubies, and emerald as very necessary for man except as medicines; and they as well as other like substances, can be replaced for this purpose by herbs and minerals. This shows the kindness of God to His creatures, even to us weak beings. His righteousness and justice as regards all animals are well known; for in the transient world there is among the various kinds of animals no individual being distinguished from the rest of the same species by a peculiar property or an additional limb. On the contrary, all physical, psychical, and vital forces and organs that are possessed by one individual are found also in the other individuals. If any one is somehow different it is by accident, in consequence of some exception, and not by a natural property; it is also a rare occurrence. There is no difference between individuals of a species in the due course of Nature; the difference originates in the various dispositions of their substances. This is the necessary consequence of the nature of the substance of that species; the nature of the species is not more favourable to one individual than to the other. It is no wrong or injustice that one has many bags of finest myrrh and garments embroidered with gold, while another has not those things, which are not necessary for our maintenance; he who has them has not thereby obtained control over anything that could be an essential addition to his nature, but has only obtained something illusory or deceptive. The other, who does not possess that which is not wanted for his maintenance, does not miss anything indispensable: "He that gathered much had nothing over, and he that gathered little had no lack: they gathered every man according to his eating" (Exod. xvi. 18). This is the rule at all times and in all places; no notice should be taken of exceptional cases, as we have explained.

In these two ways you will see the mercy of God toward His creatures, how He has provided that which is required, in proper proportions, and treated all individual beings of the same species with perfect equality. In accordance with this correct reflection the chief of the wise men says, "All His ways are judgment" (Deut. xxxii. 4): David likewise says: "All the paths of the Lord are mercy and truth" (Ps. xxv. 10); he also says expressly, "The Lord is good to all; and His tender mercies are over all His works" (ibid. cxlv. 9); for it is an act of great and perfect goodness that He gave us existence; and the creation of the controlling faculty in animals is a proof of His mercy towards them, as has been shown by us.

34. Theodicy

G. W. LEIBNIZ

The ancients had puny ideas on the works of God, and St. Augustine, for want of knowing modern discoveries, was at a loss when there was question of explaining the prevalence of evil. It seemed to the ancients that there was only one earth inhabited, and even of that men held the antipodes in dread: the remainder of the world was, according to them, a few shining globes and a few crystalline spheres. To-day, whatever bounds are given or not given to the universe, it must be acknowledged that there is an infinite number of globes, as great as and greater than ours, which have as much right as it to hold rational inhabitants, though it follows not at all that they are human. It is only one planet, that is to say one of the six principal satellites of our sun; and as all fixed stars are suns also, we see how small a thing our earth is in relation to visible things, since it is only an appendix of one amongst them. It may be that all suns are peopled only by blessed creatures, and nothing constrains us to think that many are damned, for few instances or few samples suffice to show the advantage which good extracts from evil. Moreover, since there is no reason for the belief that there are stars everywhere, is it not possible that there may be a great space beyond the region of the stars? Whether it be the Empyrean Heaven, or not, this immense space encircling all this region may in any case be filled with happiness and glory. It can be imagined as like the Ocean, whither flow the rivers of all blessed creatures, when they shall have reached their perfection in the system of the stars. What will become of the consideration of our globe and its inhabitants? Will it not be something incomparably less than a physical point, since our earth is as a point in comparison with the distance of some fixed stars? Thus since the proportion of that part of the universe which we know is almost lost in nothingness compared with that which is unknown, and which we yet have cause to assume, and since all the evils that may be raised in objection before us are in this near nothingness, haply it may be that all evils are almost nothingness in comparison with the good things which are in the universe.

But it is necessary also to meet the more speculative and metaphysical difficulties which have been mentioned, and which concern the cause of evil. The question is asked first of all, whence does evil come? *Si Deus est, unde malum? Si non est, unde bonum?* The ancients attributed the cause of evil to *matter*, which they believed uncreated and independent of God: but we, who derive all being from God, where shall we find the source of evil? The answer is, that it must be sought in the ideal nature of the creature, in so far as this nature is contained in the eternal verities which are in the understanding of God, independently of his will. For we must consider that there is an *original imperfection in the creature* before sin, because the creature is limited in its essence; whence ensues that it cannot know all, and that it can deceive itself and commit other errors. Plato said in *Timaeus* that the world originated in Understanding united to Necessity. Others have united God and Nature. This can be given a reasonable meaning. God will be the Understanding; and the Necessity, that is, the essential nature of things, will be the object of the understanding, in so far as this object consists in the eternal verities. But this object is inward and abides in the divine understanding. And therein is found not only the primitive form of good, but also the origin of evil: the Region of the Eternal Verities must be substituted for matter when we are concerned with seeking out the source of things.

This region is the ideal cause of evil (as it were) as well as of good: but, properly speaking, the formal character of evil has no *efficient* cause, for it consists in privation, as we shall see, namely, in that which the efficient cause does not bring about. That is why the Schoolmen are wont to call the cause of evil *deficient*.

Evil may be taken metaphysically, physically and morally. *Metaphysical evil* consists in mere imperfection, *physical evil* in suffering, and *moral evil* in sin. Now although physical evil and moral evil be not necessary, it is enough that by virtue of the eternal verities they be possible. And as this vast Region of Verities contains all possibilities it is necessary that there be an infinitude of possible worlds, that evil enter into divers of them, and that even the best of all contain a measure thereof. Thus has God been induced to permit evil.

But someone will say to me: why speak you to us of "permitting"? Is it not God that doeth the evil and that willeth it? Here it will be necessary to explain what "permission" is, so that it may be seen how this term is not employed without reason. But before that one must explain the nature of will, which has its own degrees. Taking it in the general sense, one may say that *will* consists in the inclination to do something in proportion to the good it contains. This will is called *antecedent* when it is detached, and considers each good separately in the capacity of a good. In this sense it may be said that God tends to all good, as good, *ad perfectionem simpliciter simplicem,* to speak like the Schoolmen, and that by an antecedent will. He is earnestly disposed to sanctify and to save all men, to exclude sin, and to prevent damnation. It may even be said that this will is efficacious *of itself* (*per se*), that is, in such sort that the effect would ensue if there were not some stronger reason to prevent it: for this will does not pass into final exercise (*ad summum conatum*), else it would never fail to produce its full effect, God being the master of all things. Success entire and infallible belongs only to the *consequent will,* as it is called. This it is which is complete; and in regard to it this rule obtains, that one never fails to do what one wills, when one has the power. Now this consequent will, final and decisive, results from the conflict of all the antecedent wills, of those which tend towards good, even as of those which repel evil; and from the concurrence of all these particular wills comes the total will. So in mechanics compound movement results from all the tendencies that concur in one and the same moving body, and satisfies each one equally, in so far as it is possible to do all at one time. It is as if the moving body took equal account of these tendencies, as I once showed in one of the Paris Journals (7 Sept. 1693), when giving the general law of the compositions of movement. In this sense also it may be said that the antecedent will is efficacious in a sense and even effective with success.

Thence it follows that God wills *antecedently* the good and *consequently* the best. And as for evil, God wills moral evil not at all, and physical evil or suffering he does not will absolutely. Thus it is that there is no absolute predestination to damnation; and one may say of physical evil, that God wills it often as a penalty owing to guilt, and often also as a means to an end, that is, to prevent greater evils or to obtain greater good. The penalty serves also for amendment and example. Evil often serves to make us savour good the more; sometimes too it contributes to a greater perfection in him who suffers it, as the seed that one sows is subject to a kind of corruption before it can germinate: this is a beautiful similitude, which Jesus Christ himself used.

Concerning sin or moral evil, although it happens very often that it may serve as a means of obtaining good or of preventing another evil, it is not this that renders it a sufficient object of the divine will or a legitimate object of a created will. It must only be admitted or *permitted* in so far as it is considered to be a certain consequence of an indispensable duty: as for instance if a man who was determined not to permit another's sin were to fail of his own duty, or as if an officer on guard at an important post were to leave it, especially in time of danger, in order to prevent a quarrel in the town between two soldiers of the garrison who wanted to kill each other.

The rule which states, *non esse facienda mala, ut eveniant bona,* and which even forbids the permission of a moral evil with the end of obtaining a physical good, far from being violated, is here proved, and its source and its reason are demonstrated. One will not approve the action of a queen who, under the pretext of saving the State, commits or even permits a crime. The crime is certain and the evil for the State is open to question. Moreover, this manner of giving sanction to crimes, if it were accepted, would be worse than a disruption of some one country, which is liable enough to happen in any case, and would perchance happen all the more by reason of such means chosen to prevent it. But in relation to God nothing is open to question, nothing can be opposed to *the rule of the best,* which suffers neither exception nor dispensation. It is in this sense that God permits sin: for he would fail in what he owes to himself, in what he owes to his wisdom, his goodness, his perfection, if he followed not the grand result of all his tendencies to good, and if he chose not that which is absolutely the best, notwithstanding the evil of guilt, which is involved therein by the supreme necessity of the eternal verities. Hence the conclusion that God wills all good *in himself antecedently,* that he wills the best *consequently* as an *end,* that he wills what is indifferent, and physical evil, sometimes as a *means,* but that he will only permit moral evil as the *sine qua non* or as a hypothetical necessity which connects it with the best. Therefore the *consequent will* of God, which has sin for its object, is only *permissive.*

It is again well to consider that moral evil is an evil so great only because it is a source of physical evils, a source existing in one of the most powerful of creatures, who is also most capable of causing those evils. For an evil will is in its department what the evil principle of the Manichaeans would be in the universe; and reason, which is an image of the Divinity, provides for evil souls great means of causing much evil. One single Caligula, one Nero, has caused more evil than an earthquake. An evil man takes pleasure in causing suffering and destruction, and for that there are only too many opportunities. But God being inclined to produce as much good as possible, and having all the knowledge and all the power necessary for that, it is impossible that in him there be fault, or guilt, or sin; and when he permits sin, it is wisdom, it is virtue.

It is indeed beyond question that we must refrain from preventing the sin of others when we cannot prevent their sin without sinning ourselves. But someone will perhaps bring up the objection that it is God himself who acts and who effects all that is real in the sin of the creature. This objection leads us to consider the *physical co-operation* of God with the creature, after we have examined the *moral co-operation,* which was the more perplexing. Some have believed, with the celebrated Durand de Saint-Pourçain and Cardinal Aureolus, the famous Schoolman, that the co-operation of God with the creature (I mean the physical co-operation) is only general and mediate, and that God creates substances and gives them the force they need; and that thereafter he leaves them to themselves, and does naught but conserve them, without aiding them in their actions. This opinion has been refuted by the greater number of Scholastic theologians, and it appears that in the past it met with disapproval in the writings of Pelagius.

Nevertheless a Capuchin named Louis Pereir of Dole, about the year 1630, wrote a book expressly to revive it, at least in relation to free actions. Some moderns incline thereto, and M. Bernier supports it in a little book on freedom and freewill. But one cannot say in relation to God what "to conserve" is, without reverting to the general opinion. Also it must be taken into account that the action of God in conserving should have some reference to that which is conserved, according to what it is and to the state wherein it is; thus his action cannot be general or indeterminate. These generalities are abstractions not to be found in the truth of individual things, and the conservation of a man standing is different from the conservation of a man seated. This would not be so if conservation consisted only in the act of preventing and warding off some foreign cause which could destroy that which one wishes to conserve; as often happens when men conserve something. But apart from the fact that we are obliged ourselves sometimes to maintain that which we conserve, we must bear in mind that conservation by God consists in the perpetual immediate influence which the dependence of creatures demands. This dependence attaches not only to the substance but also to the action, and one can perhaps not explain it better than by saying, with theologians and philosophers in general, that it is a continued creation.

The objection will be made that God therefore now creates man a sinner, he that in the beginning created him innocent. But here it must be said, with regard to the moral aspect, that God being supremely wise cannot fail to observe certain laws, and to act according to the rules, as well physical as moral, that wisdom has made him choose. And the same reason that has made him create man innocent, but liable to fall, makes him re-create man when he falls; for God's knowledge causes the future to be for him as the present, and prevents him from rescinding the resolutions made.

As for physical co-operation, here one must consider the truth which has made already so much stir in the Schools since St. Augustine declared it, that evil is a privation of being, whereas the action of God tends to the positive. This answer is accounted a quibble, and even something chimerical in the minds of many people. But here is an instance somewhat similar, which will serve to disabuse them.

The celebrated Kepler and R. Descartes (in his letters) after him have spoken of the "natural inertia of bodies"; and it is something which may be regarded as a perfect image and even as a sample of the original limitation of creatures, to show that privation constitutes the formal character of the imperfections and disadvantages that are in substance as well as in its actions. Let us suppose that the current of one and the same river carried along with it various boats, which differ among themselves only in the cargo, some being laden with wood, others with stone, and some more, the others less. That being so, it will come about that the boats most heavily laden will go more slowly than the others, provided it be assumed that the wind or the oar, or some other similar means, assist them not at all. It is not, properly speaking, weight which is the cause of this retardation, since the boats are going down and not upwards; but it is the same cause which also increases the weight in bodies that have greater density, which are, that is to say, less porous and more charged with matter that is proper to them: for the matter which passes through the pores, not receiving the same movement, must not be taken into account. It is therefore matter itself which originally is inclined to slowness or privation of speed; not indeed of itself to lessen this speed, having once received it, since that would be action, but to moderate by its receptivity the effect of the impression when it is to receive it. Consequently, since more matter is moved by the same force of the current when the boat is more laden, it is necessary that it go more slowly; and experiments on the impact of bodies, as well as reason, show that twice as much force must be employed to give equal speed to a body of the same matter but of twice the size. But that indeed would not be necessary if the matter were absolutely indifferent to repose and to movement, and if it had not this natural inertia whereof we have just spoken to give it a kind of repugnance to being moved. Let us now compare the force which the current exercises on boats, and communicates to them, with the action of God, who produces and conserves whatever is positive in creatures, and gives them perfection, being and force: let us compare, I say, the inertia of matter with the natural imperfection of creatures, and the slowness of the laden boat with the defects to be found in the qualities and the action of the creature; and we shall find that there is nothing so just as this comparison. The current is the cause of the boat's movement, but not of its retardation; God is the cause of perfection in the nature and the actions of the creature, but the limitation of the receptivity of the creature is the cause of the defects there are in its action. Thus the Platonists, St. Augustine and the Schoolmen were right to say that God is the cause of the material element of evil which lies in the positive, and not of the formal element, which lies in privation. Even so one may say that the current is the cause of the material element of the retardation, but not of the formal: that is, it is the cause of the boat's speed without being the cause of the limits to this speed. And God is no more the cause of sin than the river's current is the cause of the retardation of the boat. Force also in relation to matter is as the spirit in relation to the flesh; the spirit is willing and the flesh is weak, and spirits act . . .

The Free-Will and Finiteness Arguments

35. Dialogues concerning Natural Religion

DAVID HUME

. . . The whole earth, believe me, Philo, is cursed and polluted. A perpetual war is kindled amongst all living creatures. Necessity, hunger, want stimulate the strong and courageous; fear, anxiety, terror agitate the weak and infirm. The first entrance into life gives anguish to the new-born infant and to its wretched parent; weakness, impotence, distress attend each stage of that life, and it is, at last, finished in agony and horror.

Observe, too, says Philo, the curious artifices of nature in order to embitter the life of every living being. The stronger prey upon the weaker and keep them in perpetual terror and anxiety. The weaker, too, in their turn, often prey upon the stronger, and vex and molest them without relaxation. Consider that innumerable race of insects, which either are bred on the body of each animal or, flying about, infix their stings in him. These insects have others still less than themselves which torment them. And thus on each hand, before and behind, above and below, every animal is surrounded with enemies which incessantly seek his misery and destruction.

Man alone, said Demea, seems to be, in part, an exception to this rule. For by combination in society he can easily master lions, tigers, and bears, whose greater strength and agility naturally enable them to prey upon him.

On the contrary, it is here chiefly, cried Philo, that the uniform and equal maxims of nature are most apparent. Man, it is true, can, by combination, surmount all his *real* enemies and become master of the whole animal creation; but does he not immediately raise up to himself *imaginary* enemies, the demons of his fancy, who haunt him with superstitious terrors and blast every enjoyment of life? His pleasure, as he imagines, becomes in their eyes a crime; his food and repose give them umbrage and offence; his very sleep and dreams furnish new materials to anxious fear; and even death, his refuge from every other ill, presents only the dread of endless and innumerable woes. Nor does the wolf molest more the timid flock than superstition does the anxious breast of wretched mortals.

Besides, consider, Demea: This very society by which we surmount those wild beasts, our natural enemies, what new enemies does it not raise to us? What woe and misery does it not occasion? Man is the greatest enemy of man. Oppression, injustice, contempt, contumely, violence, sedition, war, calumny, treachery, fraud—by these they mutually torment each other, and they would soon dissolve that society which they had formed were it not for the dread of still greater ills which must attend their separation.

But though these external insults, said Demea, from animals, from men, from all the elements, which assault us form a frightful catalogue of woes, they are nothing in comparison of those which arise within ourselves, from the distempered condition of our mind and body. How many lie under the lingering torment of diseases? Hear the pathetic enumeration of the great poet.

> *Intestine stone and ulcer, colic-pangs,*
> *Demoniac frenzy, moping melancholy,*
> *And moon-struck madness, pining atrophy,*
> *Marasmus, and wide-wasting pestilence.*
> *Dire was the tossing, deep the groans: Despair*
> *Tended the sick, busiest from couch to couch.*
> *And over them triumphant Death his dart*
> *Shook: but delay'd to strike, though oft invok'd*
> *With vows, as their chief good and final hope.* [1]

The disorders of the mind, continued Demea, though more secret, are not perhaps less dismal and vexatious. Remorse, shame, anguish, rage, disappointment, anxiety, fear, dejection, despair—who has ever passed through life without cruel inroads from these tormentors? How many have scarcely ever felt any better sensations? Labour and poverty, so abhorred by everyone, are the certain lot of the far greater number; and those few privileged persons who enjoy ease and opulence never reach contentment or true felicity. All the goods of life united would not make a very happy man, but all the ills united would make a wretch indeed; and any one of them almost (and who can be free from every one?), nay, often the absence of one good (and who can possess all?) is sufficient to render life ineligible.

Were a stranger to drop on a sudden into this world, I would show him, as a specimen of its ills, an hospital full of diseases, a prison crowded with malefactors and debtors, a field of battle strewed with carcasses, a fleet floundering in the ocean, a nation languishing under tyranny, famine, or pestilence. To turn the gay side of life to him and give him a notion of its pleasures—whither should I conduct him? To a ball, to an opera, to court? He might justly think that I was only showing him a diversity of distress and sorrow.

There is no evading such striking instances, said Philo, but by apologies which still further aggravate the charge. Why have all men, I ask, in all ages, complained incessantly of the miseries of life? . . . They have no just reason, says one: these complaints proceed only from their discontented, repining, anxious

---

[1] Milton, *Paradise Lost*, Bk. XI.

disposition. . . . And can there possibly, I reply, be a more certain foundation of misery than such a wretched temper?

But if they were really as unhappy as they pretend, says my antagonist, why do they remain in life? . . .

Not satisfied with life, afraid of death—

this is the secret chain, say I, that holds us. We are terrified, not bribed to the continuance of our existence.

It is only a false delicacy, he may insist, which a few refined spirits indulge, and which has spread these complaints among the whole race of mankind. . . . And what is this delicacy, I ask, which you blame? Is it anything but a greater sensibility to all the pleasures and pains of life? And if the man of a delicate, refined temper, by being so much more alive than the rest of the world, is only so much more unhappy, what judgment must we form in general of human life?

Let men remain at rest, says our adversary, and they will be easy. They are willing artificers of their own misery. . . . No! reply I: an anxious languor follows their repose: disappointment, vexation, trouble, their activity and ambition.

I can observe something like what you mention in some others, replied Cleanthes, but I confess I feel little or nothing of it in myself, and hope that it is not so common as you represent it.

If you feel not human misery yourself, cried Demea, I congratulate you on so happy a singularity. Others, seemingly the most prosperous, have not been ashamed to vent their complaints in the most melancholy strains. Let us attend to the great, the fortunate emperor, Charles V, when, tired with human grandeur, he resigned all his extensive dominions into the hands of his son. In the last harangue which he made on that memorable occasion, he publicly avowed *that the greatest prosperities which he had ever enjoyed had been mixed with so many adversities that he might truly say he had never enjoyed any satisfaction or contentment.* But did the retired life in which he sought for shelter afford him any greater happiness? If we may credit his son's account, his repentance commenced the very day of his resignation.

Cicero's fortune, from small beginnings, rose to the greatest lustre and renown; yet what pathetic complaints of the ills of life do his familiar letters, as well as philosophical discourses, contain? And suitably to his own experience, he introduces Cato, the great, the fortunate Cato protesting in his old age that had he a new life in his offer he would reject the present.

Ask yourself, ask any of your acquaintance, whether they would live over again the last ten or twenty years of their life. No! but the next twenty, they say, will be better:

> And from the dregs of life, hope to receive
> What the first sprightly running could not give. [2]

---

[2] John Dryden, *Aureng-Zebe*, Act IV, sc. 1.

Thus, at last, they find (such is the greatness of human misery, it reconciles even contradictions) that they complain at once of the shortness of life and of its vanity and sorrow.

And is it possible, Cleanthes, said Philo, that after all these reflections, and infinitely more which might be suggested, you can still persevere in your anthropomorphism, and assert the moral attributes of the Deity, his justice, benevolence, mercy, and rectitude, to be of the same nature with these virtues in human creatures? His power, we allow, is infinite; whatever he wills is executed; but neither man nor any other animal is happy; therefore, he does not will their happiness. His wisdom is infinite; he is never mistaken in choosing the means to any end; but the course of nature tends not to human or animal felicity; therefore, it is not established for that purpose. Through the whole compass of human knowledge there are no inferences more certain and infallible than these. In what respect, then, do his benevolence and mercy resemble the benevolence and mercy of men?

Epicurus' old questions are yet unanswered.

Is he willing to prevent evil, but not able? then is he impotent. Is he able, but not willing? then is he malevolent. Is he both able and willing? whence then is evil?

You ascribe, Cleanthes, (and I believe justly) a purpose and intention to nature. But what, I beseech you, is the object of that curious artifice and machinery which she has displayed in all animals—the preservation alone of individuals, and propagation of the species? It seems enough for her purpose, if such a rank be barely upheld in the universe, without any care or concern for the happiness of the members that compose it. No resource for this purpose: no machinery in order merely to give pleasure or ease; no fund of pure joy and contentment; no indulgence without some want or necessity accompanying it. At least, the few phenomena of this nature are overbalanced by opposite phenomena of still greater importance.

Our sense of music, harmony, and indeed beauty of all kinds, gives satisfaction, without being absolutely necessary to the preservation and propagation of the species. But what racking pains, on the other hand, arise from gouts, gravels, megrims, toothaches, rheumatisms, where the injury to the animal machinery is either small or incurable? Mirth, laughter, play, frolic seem gratuitous satisfactions which have no further tendency; spleen, melancholy, discontent, superstition are pains of the same nature. How then does the Divine benevolence display itself, in the sense of you anthropomorphites? None but we mystics, as you were pleased to call us, can account for this strange mixture of phenomena, by deriving it from attributes infinitely perfect but incomprehensible.

And have you, at last, said Cleanthes smiling, betrayed your intentions, Philo? Your long agreement with Demea did indeed a little surprise me, but I find you were all the while erecting a concealed battery against me. And I must confess that you have now fallen upon a subject worthy of your noble spirit of opposition and controversy. If you can make out the present point, and prove mankind to be unhappy or corrupted, there is an end at once of all religion. For to what purpose establish the natural attributes of the Deity, while the moral are still doubtful and uncertain?

You take umbrage very easily, replied Demea, at opinions the most innocent and the most generally received, even amongst the religious and devout
themselves; and nothing can be more surprising than to find a topic like this—
concerning the wickedness and misery of man—charged with no less than atheism
and profaneness. Have not all pious divines and preachers who have indulged their
rhetoric on so fertile a subject, have they not easily, I say, given a solution of any
difficulties which may attend it? This world is but a point in comparison of the
universe; this life but a moment in comparison of eternity. The present evil
phenomena, therefore, are rectified in other regions, and in some future period of
existence. And the eyes of men, being then opened to larger views of things, see
the whole connection of general laws, and trace, with adoration, the benevolence
and rectitude of the Deity through all the mazes and intricacies of his providence.

No! replied Cleanthes, no! These arbitrary suppositions can never be
admitted, contrary to matter of fact, visible and uncontroverted. Whence can any
cause be known but from its known effects? Whence can any hypothesis be proved
but from the apparent phenomena? To establish one hypothesis upon another is
building entirely in the air; and the utmost we ever attain by these conjectures and
fictions is to ascertain the bare possibility of our opinion, but never can we, upon
such terms, establish its reality.

The only method of supporting Divine benevolence—and it is what I
willingly embrace—is to deny absolutely the misery and wickedness of man. Your
representations are exaggerated; your melancholy views mostly fictitious; your
inferences contrary to fact and experience. Health is more common than sickness;
pleasure than pain; happiness than misery. And for one vexation which we meet
with, we attain, upon computation, a hundred enjoyments.

Admitting your position, replied Philo, which yet is extremely doubtful,
you must at the same time allow that, if pain be less frequent than pleasure, it is
infinitely more violent and durable. One hour of it is often able to outweigh a day,
a week, a month of our common insipid enjoyments; and how many days, weeks,
and months are passed by several in the most acute torments? Pleasure, scarcely in
one instance, is ever able to reach ecstasy and rapture; and in no one instance can
it continue for any time at its highest pitch and altitude. The spirits evaporate, the
nerves relax, the fabric is disordered, and the enjoyment quickly degenerates into
fatigue and uneasiness. But pain often, good God, how often! rises to torture and
agony; and the longer it continues, it becomes still more genuine agony and
torture. Patience is exhausted, courage languishes, melancholy seizes us, and
nothing terminates our misery but the removal of its cause or another event which
is the sole cure of all evil, but which, from our natural folly, we regard with still
greater horror and consternation.

But not to insist upon these topics, continued Philo, though most obvious, certain, and important, I must use the freedom to admonish you, Cleanthes,
that you have put the controversy upon a most dangerous issue, and are unawares
introducing a total scepticism into the most essential articles of natural and revealed theology. What! no method of fixing a just foundation for religion unless
we allow the happiness of human life, and maintain a continued existence even in
this world, with all our present pains, infirmities, vexations, and follies, to be

eligible and desirable! But this is contrary to everyone's feeling and experience; it is contrary to an authority so established as nothing can subvert. No decisive proofs can ever be produced against this authority; nor is it possible for you to compute, estimate, and compare all the pains and all the pleasures in the lives of all men and of all animals; and thus, by your resting the whole system of religion on a point which, from its very nature, must for ever be uncertain, you tacitly confess that that system is equally uncertain.

But allowing you what never will be believed, at least, what you never possibly can prove, that animal or, at least, human happiness in this life exceeds its misery, you have yet done nothing; for this is not, by any means, what we expect from infinite power, infinite wisdom, and infinite goodness. Why is there any misery at all in the world? Not by chance, surely. From some cause then. Is it from the intention of the Deity? But he is perfectly benevolent. Is it contrary to his intention? But he is almighty. Nothing can shake the solidity of this reasoning, so short, so clear, so decisive, except we assert that these subjects exceed all human capacity, and that our common measures of truth and falsehood are not applicable to them—a topic which I have all along insisted on, but which you have, from the beginning, rejected with scorn and indignation.

But I will be contented to retire still from this intrenchment, for I deny that you can ever force me in it. I will allow that pain or misery in man is *compatible* with infinite power and goodness in the Deity, even in your sense of these attributes: what are you advanced by all these concessions? A mere possible compatibility is not sufficient. You must *prove* these pure, unmixed, and uncontrollable attributes from the present mixed and confused phenomena, and from these alone. A hopeful undertaking! Were the phenomena ever so pure and unmixed, yet, being finite, they would be insufficient for that purpose. How much more, where they are also so jarring and discordant!

Here, Cleanthes, I find myself at ease in my argument. Here I triumph. Formerly, when we argued concerning the natural attributes of intelligence and design, I needed all my sceptical and metaphysical subtilty to elude your grasp. In many views of the universe and of its parts, particularly the latter, the beauty and fitness of final causes strike us with such irresistible force that all objections appear (what I believe they really are) mere cavils and sophisms; nor can we then imagine how it was ever possible for us to repose any weight on them. But there is no view of human life or of the condition of mankind from which, without the greatest violence, we can infer the moral attributes or learn that infinite benevolence, conjoined with infinite power and infinite wisdom, which we must discover by the eyes of faith alone. It is your turn now to tug the labouring oar, and to support your philosophical subtilties against the dictates of plain reason and experience.

I scruple not to allow, said Cleanthes, that I have been apt to suspect the frequent repetition of the word *infinite*, which we meet with in all theological writers, to savour more of panegyric than of philosophy, and that any purposes of reasoning, and even of religion, would be better served were we to rest contented with more accurate and more moderate expressions. The terms *admirable, excellent, superlatively great, wise,* and *holy*—these sufficiently fill the imaginations of men, and anything beyond, besides that it leads into absurdities, has no influence on the affections or sentiments. Thus, in the present subject, if we abandon all human analogy, as seems your intention, Demea, I am afraid we abandon all religion and retain no conception of the great object of our adoration. If we preserve human analogy, we must forever find it impossible to reconcile any mixture of evil in the universe with infinite attributes; much less can we ever prove the latter from the former. But supposing the Author of nature to be finitely perfect, though far exceeding mankind, a satisfactory account may then be given of natural and moral evil, and every untoward phenomenon be explained and adjusted. A less evil may then be chosen in order to avoid a greater; inconveniences be submitted to in order to reach a desirable end; and, in a word, benevolence, regulated by wisdom and limited by necessity, may produce just such a world as the present. You, Philo, who are so prompt at starting views and reflections and analogies, I would gladly hear, at length, without interruption, your opinion of this new theory; and if it deserve our attention, we may afterwards at more leisure, reduce it into form.

My sentiments, replied Philo, are not worth being made a mystery of; and, therefore, without any ceremony, I shall deliver what occurs to me with regard to the present subject. It must, I think, be allowed that, if a very limited intelligence whom we shall suppose utterly unacquainted with the universe were assured that it were the production of a very good, wise, and powerful Being, however finite, he would, from his conjectures, form *beforehand* a different notion of it from what we find it to be by experience; nor would he ever imagine, merely from these attributes of the cause of which he is informed, that the effect could be so full of vice and misery and disorder, as it appears in this life. Supposing now that this person were brought into the world, still assured that it was the workmanship of such a sublime and benevolent Being, he might, perhaps, be surprised at the disappointment, but would never retract his former belief if founded on any very solid argument, since such a limited intelligence must be sensible of his own blindness and ignorance, and must allow that there may be many solutions of those phenomena which will for ever escape his comprehension. But supposing, which is the real case with regard to man, that this creature is not antecedently convinced of a supreme intelligence, benevolent, and powerful, but is left to gather such a belief from the appearances of things—this entirely alters the case, nor will he ever find any reason for such a conclusion. He may be fully convinced of the narrow limits of his understanding, but this will not help him in forming an inference concerning the goodness of superior powers, since he must form that inference from what he knows, not from what he is ignorant of. The more you exaggerate his weakness and ignorance, the more difficult you render him, and give him the greater suspicion that such subjects are beyond the reach of his faculties. You are obliged, therefore, to reason with him merely from the known phenomena, and to drop every arbitrary supposition or conjecture.

Did I show you a house or palace where there was not one apartment convenient or agreeable, where the windows, doors, fires, passages, stairs, and the whole economy of the building were the source of noise, confusion, fatigue, darkness, and the extremes of heat and cold, you would certainly blame the contrivance, without any further examination. The architect would in vain display his subtilty, and prove to you that, if this door or that window were altered, greater ills would ensue. What he says may be strictly true: the alteration of one particular, while the other parts of the building remain, may only augment the inconveniences. But still you would assert in general that, if the architect had had skill and good intentions, he might have formed such a plan of the whole, and might have adjusted the parts in such a manner as would have remedied all or most of the inconveniences. His ignorance, or even your own ignorance of such a plan, will never convince you of the impossibility of it. If you find any inconveniences and deformities in the building, you will always, without entering into any details, condemn the architect.

In short, I repeat the question: Is the world, considered in general and as it appears to us in this life, different from what a man or such a limited being would, *beforehand,* expect from a very powerful, wise, and benevolent Deity? It must be strange prejudice to assert the contrary. And from thence I conclude that, however consistent the world may be, allowing certain suppositions and conjectures with the idea of such a Deity, it can never afford us an inference concerning his existence. The consistency is not absolutely denied, only the inference. Conjectures, especially where infinity is excluded from the Divine attributes, may perhaps be sufficient to prove a consistency, but can never be foundations for any inference.

There seem to be *four* circumstances on which depend all or the greatest part of the ills that molest sensible creatures; and it is not impossible but all these circumstances may be necessary and unavoidable. We know so little beyond common life, or even of common life, that, with regard to the economy of a universe, there is no conjecture, however wild, which may not be just, nor any one, however plausible, which may not be erroneous. All that belongs to human understanding, in this deep ignorance and obscurity, is to be sceptical or at least cautious, and not to admit of any hypothesis whatever, much less of any which is supported by no appearance of probability. Now this I assert to be the case with regard to all the causes of evil and the circumstances on which it depends. None of them appear to human reason in the least degree necessary or unavoidable, nor can we suppose them such, without the utmost license of imagination.

The *first* circumstance which introduces evil is that contrivance or economy of the animal creation by which pains, as well as pleasures, are employed to excite all creatures to action, and make them vigilant in the great work of self-preservation. Now pleasure alone, in its various degrees, seems to human understanding sufficient for this purpose. All animals might be constantly in a state of enjoyment; but when urged by any of the necessities of nature, such as thirst, hunger, weariness, instead of pain, they might feel a diminution of pleasure by which they might be prompted to seek that object which is necessary to their subsistence. Men pursue pleasure as eagerly as they avoid pain; at least, they might have been so constituted. It seems, therefore, plainly possible to carry on the business of life without any pain. Why then is any animal ever rendered susceptible of such a sensation? If animals can be free from it an hour, they might enjoy a perpetual exemption from it, and it required as particular a contrivance of their organs to produce that feeling as to endow them with sight, hearing, or any of the senses. Shall we conjecture that such a contrivance was necessary, without any appearance of reason, and shall we build on that conjecture as on the most certain truth?

But a capacity of pain would not alone produce pain were it not for the *second* circumstance, viz., the conducting of the world by general laws; and this seems nowise necessary to a very perfect Being. It is true, if everything were conducted by particular volitions, the course of nature would be perpetually broken, and no man could employ his reason in the conduct of life. But might not other particular volitions remedy this inconvenience? In short, might not the Deity exterminate all ill, wherever it were to be found, and produce all good, without any preparation or long progress of causes and effects?

Besides, we must consider that, according to the present economy of the world, the course of nature, though supposed exactly regular, yet to us appears not so, and many events are uncertain, and many disappoint our expectations. Health and sickness, calm and tempest, with an infinite number of other accidents whose causes are unknown and variable, have a great influence both on the fortunes of particular persons and on the prosperity of public societies; and indeed all human life, in a manner, depends on such accidents. A being, therefore, who knows the secret springs of the universe might easily, by particular volitions, turn all these accidents to the good of mankind and render the whole world happy, without discovering himself in any operation. A fleet whose purposes were salutary to society might always meet with a fair wind. Good princes enjoy sound health and long life. Persons born to power and authority be framed with good tempers and virtuous dispositions. A few such events as these, regularly and wisely conducted, would change the face of the world, and yet would no more seem to disturb the course of nature or confound human conduct than the present economy of things where the causes are secret and variable and compounded. Some small touches given to Caligula's brain in his infancy might have converted him into a Trajan. One wave, a little higher than the rest, by burying Caesar and his fortune in the bottom of the ocean, might have restored liberty to a considerable part of mankind. There may, for aught we know, be good reasons why Providence interposes not in this manner, but they are unknown to us; and, though the mere supposition that such reasons exist may be sufficient to *save* the conclusion concerning the Divine attributes, yet surely it can never be sufficient to *establish* that conclusion.

If everything in the universe be conducted by general laws, and if animals be rendered susceptible to pain, it scarcely seems possible but some ill must arise in the various shocks of matter and the various concurrence and opposition of general laws; but this ill would be very rare were it not for the *third* circumstance which I proposed to mention, viz., the great frugality with which all powers and faculties are distributed to every particular being. So well adjusted are the organs and capacities of all animals, and so well fitted to their preservation, that, as far as history or tradition reaches, there appears not to be any single species which has yet been extinguished in the universe. Every animal has the requisite endowments, but these endowments are bestowed with so scrupulous an economy that any considerable diminution must entirely destroy the creature. Wherever one power is increased, there is a proportional abatement in the others. Animals which excel in swiftness are commonly defective in force. Those which possess both are either imperfect in some of their senses or are oppressed with the most craving wants. The human species, whose chief excellence is reason and sagacity, is of all others the most necessitous, and the most deficient in bodily advantages, without clothes, without arms, without food, without lodging, without any convenience of life, except what they owe to their own skill and industry. In short, nature seems to have formed an exact calculation of the necessities of her creatures, and, like a *rigid master,* has afforded them little more powers or endowments than what are strictly sufficient to supply those necessities. An *indulgent parent* would have bestowed a large stock in order to guard against accidents, and secure the happiness and welfare of the creature in the most unfortunate concurrence of circumstances. Every course of life would not have been so surrounded with precipices that the least departure from the true path, by mistake or necessity, must involve us in misery and ruin. Some reserve, some fund, would have been provided to ensure happiness, nor would the powers and the necessities have been adjusted with so rigid an economy. The Author of nature is inconceivably powerful; his force is supposed great, if not altogether inexhaustible, nor is there any reason, as far as we can judge, to make him observe this strict frugality in his dealings with his creatures. It would have been better, were his power extremely limited, to have created fewer animals, and to have endowed these with more faculties for their happiness and preservation. A builder is never esteemed prudent who undertakes a plan beyond what his stock will enable him to finish.

In order to cure most of the ills of human life, I require not that man should have the wings of the eagle, the swiftness of the stag, the force of the ox, the arms of the lion, the scales of the crocodile or rhinoceros; much less do I demand the sagacity of an angel or cherubim. I am contented to take an increase in one single power or faculty of his soul. Let him be endowed with a greater propensity to industry and labour, a more vigorous spring and activity of mind, a more constant bent to business and application. Let the whole species possess naturally an equal diligence with that which many individuals are able to attain by habit and reflection, and the most beneficial consequences, without any allay of ill, is the immediate and necessary result of this endowment. Almost all the moral as well as natural evils of human life arise from idleness; and were our species, by the original constitution of their frame, exempt from this vice or infirmity, the perfect cultivation of land, the improvement of arts and manufactures, the exact execution of every office and duty, immediately follow; and men at once may fully reach that state of society which is so imperfectly attained by the best regulated government. But as industry is a power, and the most valuable of any, nature seems determined, suitably to her usual maxims, to bestow it on man with a very sparing hand, and rather to punish him severely for his deficiency in it than to reward him for his attainments. She has so contrived his frame that nothing but the most violent necessity can oblige him to labour; and she employs all his other wants to overcome, at least in part, the want of diligence, and to endow him with some share of a faculty of which she has thought fit naturally to bereave him. Here our demands may be allowed very humble, and therefore the more reasonable. If we required the endowments of superior penetration and judgment, of a more delicate taste of beauty, of a nicer sensibility to benevolence and friendship, we might be told that we impiously pretend to break the order of nature, that we want to exalt ourselves into a higher rank of being, that the presents which we require, not being suitable to our state and condition, would only be pernicious to us. But it is hard, I dare to repeat it, it is hard that, being placed in a world so full of wants and necessities, where almost every being and element is either our foe or refuses its assistance . . . we should also have our own temper to struggle with, and should be deprived of that faculty which can alone fence against these multiplied evils.

The *fourth* circumstance whence arises the misery and ill of the universe is the inaccurate workmanship of all the springs and principles of the great machine of nature. It must be acknowledged that there are few parts of the universe which seem not to serve some purpose, and whose removal would not produce a visible defect and disorder in the whole. The parts hang all together, nor can one be touched without affecting the rest, in a greater or less degree. But at the same time, it must be observed that none of these parts or principles, however useful, are so accurately adjusted as to keep precisely within those bounds in which their utility consists; but they are, all of them, apt, on every occasion, to run into the one extreme or the other. One would imagine that this grand production had not received the last hand of the maker—so little finished is every part, and so coarse are the strokes with which it is executed. Thus the winds are requisite to convey the vapours along the surface of the globe, and to assist men in navigation; but how often, rising up to tempests and hurricanes, do they become pernicious? Rains are necessary to nourish all the plants and animals of the earth; but how often are they defective? how often excessive? Heat is requisite to all life and vegetation, but is not always found in the due proportion. On the mixture and secretion of the humours and juices of the body depend the health and prosperity of the animal; but the parts perform not regularly their proper function. What more useful than all the passions of the mind, ambition, vanity, love, anger? But how often do they break their bounds and cause the greatest convulsions in society? There is nothing so advantageous in the universe but what frequently becomes pernicious, by its excess or defect; nor has nature guarded, with the requisite accuracy, against all disorder or confusion. The irregularity is never perhaps so great as to destroy any species, but is often sufficient to involve the individuals in ruin and misery.

On the concurrence, then, of these *four* circumstances does all or the greatest part of natural evil depend. Were all living creatures incapable of pain, or were the world administered by particular volitions, evil never could have found access into the universe; and were animals endowed with a large stock of powers and faculties, beyond what strict necessity requires, or were the several springs and principles of the universe so accurately framed as to preserve always the just temperament and medium, there must have been very little ill in comparison of what we feel at present. What then shall we pronounce on this occasion? Shall we say that these circumstances are not necessary, and that they might easily have been altered in the contrivance of the universe? This decision seems too presumptuous for creatures so blind and ignorant. Let us be more modest in our conclusions. Let us allow that, if the goodness of the Deity (I mean a goodness like the human) could be established on any tolerable reasons a priori, these phenomena, however untoward, would not be sufficient to subvert that principle, but might easily, in some unknown manner, be reconcilable to it. But let us still assert that, as this goodness is not antecedently established but must be inferred from the phenomena, there can be no grounds for such an inference while there are so many ills in the universe, and while these ills might so easily have been remedied, as far as human understanding can be allowed to judge on such a subject. I am sceptic enough to allow that the bad appearances, notwithstanding all my reasonings, may be compatible with such attributes as you suppose, but surely they can never prove these attributes. Such a conclusion cannot result from scepticism, but must arise from the phenomena, and from our confidence in the reasonings which we deduce from these phenomena. . . .

36. Three Essays on Religion

JOHN STUART MILL

ATTRIBUTES

. . . Given the indications of a Deity, what *sort* of a Deity do they point to? What attributes are we warranted, by the evidence which nature affords of a creative mind, in assigning to that mind?

It needs no showing that the power, if not the intelligence, must be so far superior to that of man, as to surpass all human estimate. But from this to omnipotence and omniscience there is a wide interval. And the distinction is of immense practical importance.

It is not too much to say that every indication of design in the cosmos is so much evidence against the omnipotence of the Designer. For what is meant by design? Contrivance: the adaptation of means to an end. But the necessity for contrivance—the need of employing means—is a consequence of the limitation of power. Who would have recourse to means if to attain his end his mere word was sufficient? They very idea of means implies that the means have an efficacy which the direct action of the being who employs them has not. Otherwise they are not means, but an incumbrance. A man does not use machinery to move his arms. If he did, it could only be when paralysis had deprived him of the power of moving them by volition. But if the employment of contrivance is in itself a sign of limited power, how much more so is the careful and skilful choice of contrivances? Can any wisdom be shown in the selection of means, when the means have no efficacy but what is given them by the will of him who employs them, and when his will could have bestowed the same efficacy on any other means? Wisdom and contrivance are shown in overcoming difficulties, and there is no room for them in a Being for whom no difficulties exist. The evidences, therefore, of natural theology distinctly imply that the author of the cosmos worked under limitations; that he was obliged to adapt himself to conditions independent of his will, and to attain his ends by such arrangements as those conditions admitted of.

And this hypothesis agrees with what we have seen to be the tendency of the evidences in another respect. We found that the appearances in nature point indeed to an origin of the cosmos, or order in nature, and indicate that origin to be design but do not point to any commencement, still less creation, of the two great elements of the universe, the passive element and the active element, matter and force. There is in nature no reason whatever to suppose that either matter or force, or any of their properties, were made by the Being who was the author of the collocations by which the world is adapted to what we consider as its purposes; or that he has power to alter any of those properties. It is only when we consent to entertain this negative supposition that there arises a need for wisdom and contrivance in the order of the universe. The Deity had on this hypothesis to work out his ends by combining materials of a given nature and properties. Out of these materials he had to construct a world in which his designs should be carried into effect through given properties of matter and force, working together and fitting into one another. This did require skill and contrivance, and the means by which it is effected are often such as justly excite our wonder and admiration: but exactly because it requires wisdom, it implies limitation of power, or rather the two phrases express different sides of the same fact.

If it be said that an omnipotent Creator, though under no necessity of employing contrivances such as man must use, thought fit to do so in order to leave traces by which man might recognize his creative hand, the answer is that this equally supposes a limit to his omnipotence. For if it was his will that men should know that they themselves and the world are his work, he, being omnipotent, had only to will that they should be aware of it. Ingenious men have sought for reasons why God might choose to leave his existence so far a matter of doubt that men should not be under an absolute necessity of knowing it, as they are of knowing that three and two make five. These imagined reasons are very unfortunate specimens of casuistry; but even did we admit their validity, they are of no avail on the supposition of omnipotence, since if it did not please God to implant in man a complete conviction of his existence, nothing hindered him from making the conviction fall short of completeness by any margin he chose to leave. It is usual to dispose of arguments of this description by the easy answer, that we do not know what wise reasons the Omniscient may have had for leaving undone things which he had the power to do. It is not perceived that this plea itself implies a limit to omnipotence. When a thing is obviously good and obviously in accordance with what all the evidences of creation imply to have been the Creator's design, and we say we do not know what good reason he may have had for not doing it, we mean that we do not know to what other, still better object—to what object still more completely in the line of his purposes—he may have seen fit to postpone it. But the necessity of postponing one thing to another belongs only to limited power. Omnipotence could have made the objects compatible. Omnipotence does not need to weigh one consideration against another. If the Creator, like a human ruler, had to adapt himself to a set of conditions which he did not make, it is as unphilosophical as presumptuous in us to call him to account for any imperfections in his work; to complain that he left anything in it contrary to what, if the indications of design prove anything, he must have intended. He must at least know more than we know, and we cannot judge what greater good would have had to be sacrificed, or what greater evil incurred, if he had decided to remove this particular blot. Not so if he be omnipotent. If he be that, he must himself have willed that the two desirable objects should be incompatible; he must himself have willed that the obstacle to his supposed design should be insuperable. It cannot therefore *be* his design. It will not do to say that it was, but that he had other designs which interfered with it; for no one purpose imposes necessary limitations on another in the case of a Being not restricted by conditions of possibility.

Omnipotence, therefore, cannot be predicated of the Creator on grounds of natural theology. The fundamental principles of natural religion as deduced from the facts of the universe, negate his omnipotence. They do not, in the same manner, exclude omniscience: if we suppose limitation of power, there is nothing to contradict the supposition of perfect knowledge and absolute wisdom. But neither is there anything to prove it. The knowledge of the powers and properties of things necessary for planning and executing the arrangements of the cosmos is no doubt as much in excess of human knowledge as the power implied in creation is in excess of human power. And the skill, the subtlety of contrivance, the ingenuity as it would be called in the case of a human work, is often marvellous. But nothing obliges us to suppose that either the knowledge or the skill is infinite. We are not even compelled to suppose that the contrivances were always the best possible. If we venture to judge them as we judge the works of human artificers, we find abundant defects. The human body, for example, is one of the most striking instances of artful and ingenious contrivance which nature offers, but we may well ask whether so complicated a machine could not have been made to last longer, and not to get so easily and frequently out of order. We may ask why the human race should have been so constituted as to grovel in wretchedness and degradation for countless ages before a small portion of it was enabled to lift itself into the very imperfect state of intelligence, goodness and happiness which we enjoy. The divine power may not have been equal to doing more; the obstacles to a better arrangement of things may have been insuperable. But it is also possible that they were not. The skill of the Demiurge was sufficient to produce what we see; but we cannot tell that this skill reached the extreme limit of perfection compatible with the material it employed and the forces it had to work with. I know not how we can even satisfy ourselves on grounds of natural theology, that the Creator foresees all the future; that he foreknows all the effects that will issue from his own contrivances. There may be great wisdom without the power of foreseeing and calculating everything: and human workmanship teaches us the possibility that the workman's knowledge of the properties of the things he works on may enable him to make arrangements admirably fitted to produce a given result, while he may have very little power of foreseeing the agencies of another kind which may modify or counteract the operation of the machinery he has made. Perhaps a knowledge of the laws of nature on which organic life depends, not much more perfect than the knowledge which man even now possesses of some other natural laws, would enable man, if he had the same power over the materials and the forces concerned which he has over some of those of inanimate nature, to create

organized beings not less wonderful nor less adapted to their conditions of existence than those in nature.

Assuming then that while we confine ourselves to natural religion we
must rest content with a Creator less than Almighty; the question presents itself,
of what nature is the limitation of his power? Does the obstacle at which the power
of the Creator stops, which says to it: Thus far shalt thou go and no further, lie in
the power of other intelligent beings; or in the insufficiency and refractoriness of
the materials of the universe; or must we resign ourselves to admitting the hypothesis that the author of the cosmos, though wise and knowing, was not all-wise and
all-knowing, and may not always have done the best that was possible under the
conditions of the problem?

The first of these suppositions has until a very recent period been and in
many quarters still is, the prevalent theory even of Christianity. Though attributing,
and in a certain sense sincerely, omnipotence to the Creator, the received religion
represents him as for some inscrutable reason tolerating the perpetual counteraction
of his purposes by the will of another being of opposite character and of great though
inferior power, the Devil. The only difference on this matter between popular
Christianity and the religion of Ormuzd and Ahriman, is that the former pays its
good Creator the bad compliment of having been the maker of the Devil and of
being at all times able to crush and annihilate him and his evil deeds and counsels,
which nevertheless he does not do. But, as I have already remarked, all forms of
polytheism, and this among the rest, are with difficulty reconcileable with a universe governed by general laws. Obedience to law is the note of a settled government, and not of a conflict always going on. When powers are at war with one
another for the rule of the world, the boundary between them is not fixed but
constantly fluctuating. This may seem to be the case on our planet as between the
powers of good and evil when we look only at the results; but when we consider the
inner springs, we find that both the good and the evil take place in the common
course of nature, by virtue of the same general laws originally impressed—the same
machinery turning out now good, now evil things, and oftener still, the two combined. The division of power is only apparently variable, but really so regular that,
were we speaking of human potentates, we should declare without hesitation that
the share of each must have been fixed by previous consent. Upon that supposition
indeed, the result of the combination of antagonist forces might be much the same
as on that of a single creator with divided purposes.

But when we come to consider, not what hypothesis may be conceived, and
possibly reconciled with known facts, but what supposition is pointed to by the
evidences of natural religion; the case is different. The indications of design point
strongly in one direction, the preservation of the creatures in whose structure the
indications are found. Along with the preserving agencies there are destroying
agencies, which we might be tempted to ascribe to the will of a different Creator: but
there are rarely appearances of the recondite contrivance of means of destruction,
except when the destruction of one creature is the means of preservation to others.
Nor can it be supposed that the preserving agencies are wielded by one Being, the
destroying agencies by another. The destroying agencies are a necessary part of the
preserving agencies: the chemical compositions by which life is carried on could not

take place without a parallel series of decompositions. The great agent of decay in both organic and inorganic substances is oxidation, and it is only by oxidation that life is continued for even the length of a minute. The imperfections in the attainment of the purposes which the appearances indicate, have not the air of having been designed. They are like the unintended results of accidents insufficiently guarded against, or of a little excess or deficiency in the quantity of some of the agencies by which the good purpose is carried on, or else they are consequences of the wearing out of a machinery not made to last forever: they point either to shortcomings in the workmanship as regards its intended purpose, or to external forces not under the control of the workman, but which forces bear no mark of being wielded and aimed by any other and rival intelligence.

We may conclude, then, that there is no ground in natural theology for attributing intelligence or personality to the obstacles which partially thwart what seem the purposes of the Creator. The limitation of his power more probably results either from the qualities of the material—the substances and forces of which the universe is composed not admitting of any arrangements by which his purposes could be more completely fulfilled—or else, the purposes might have been more fully attained, but the Creator did not know how to do it; creative skill, wonderful as it is, was not sufficiently perfect to accomplish his purposes more thoroughly.

Bibliography

Ahern, M. B. *The Problem of Evil.* New York: Schocken Books, 1971.

Allen, Diogenes. "Natural Evil and the Love of God." *Religious Studies* 16 (1980): 439–56.

Beaty, Michael. "The Problem of Evil: The Unanswered Questions Argument." *Southwestern Philosophic Review* 4 (1988): 57–64.

Bennett, Philip W. "Evil, God and the Free Will Defense." *Australian Journal of Philosophy* 51 (1973): 39–50.

Bible, Book of Job.

Brightman, E. S. *The Problem of God.* Nashville, Tenn.: Abingdon Press, 1930.

Bowker, John. *Problems of Suffering in Religions of the World.* London: Cambridge University Press, 1970.

Buber, Martin. *Images of Good and Evil.* London: Routledge and Kegan Paul, 1952.

Burgess-Jackson, Keith. "Free Will, Omnipotence and the Problem of Evil." *American Journal of Theology and Philosophy* 9 (1988): 175–85.

Cahn, Steven M. "The Book of Job: The Great Dissent." *The Reconstructionist* 31 (1965): 14–19.

Chopp, Rebecca. "The Praxis of Suffering: An Interpretation of Liberation and Political Theologies." *Science and Society* 54 (1990): 119–22.

Chryssides, George D. "Evil and the Problem of God." *Religious Studies* 23 (1987): 467–75.

Conway, David A. "The Philosophical Problem of Evil." *International Journal of Philosophy and Religion* 24 (1988): 35–66.

Coughlan, Michael J. "The Free Will Defense and Natural Evil." *International Journal of Philosophy and Religion* 20 (1986): 93–108.

Cox, Harvey G. "Complaining to God." *Archiviodi Filosofia* 56 (1988): 311–25.

DeBurgh, W. G. *From Morality to Religion*. Bedford-Row, England: MacDonald and Evans, 1938.

DeVilliers, Peiter G. R., ed. *Like a Roaring Lion: Essays on the Bible, the Church and Demonic Powers*. Pretoria: University of South Africa, 1987.

Dore, Clement. "An Examination of the 'Soul-Making' Theodicy." *American Philosophical Quarterly* 7 (1970): 119–30.

Farrer, Austin. *Love Almighty and Ills Unlimited*. New York: Doubleday, 1961.

Feinberg, John S. *Theologies and Evil*. Washington D.C.: University Press of America, 1979.

Ferre, Nels. *Evil and the Christian Faith*. New York: Harper and Row, 1947.

Fitch, William. *God and Evil*. London: Pickering and Inglise, 1967.

Flew, Antony. "Divine Omnipotence and Human Freedom." *New Essays in Philosophical Theology*. London: Student Christian Movement Press; New York: The Macmillan Company, 1955.

————. *The Presumption of Atheism*. New York: Harper and Row, 1976.

Friedman, R. Z. "Evil and Moral Agency." *International Journal of Philosophy and Religion* 24 (1988): 3–20.

Geach, Peter. *Providence and Evil*. Cambridge: Cambridge University Press, 1977.

Griffin, David. *God, Power, and Evil: A Process Theodicy*. Philadelphia: Westminster Press, 1976.

Hare, Peter H., and Edward H. Madden. *Evil and the Concept of God*. Springfield, Ill.: Thomas, 1968.

Hasker, William. "Suffering, Soul-Making, and Salvation." *International Philosophical Quarterly* 28 (1988): 3–19.

Hick, John. *Evil and the God of Love*. New York: Harper and Row. 1978.

Hume, David. *Dialogues concerning Natural Religion*. Indianapolis, Ind.: Bobbs-Merrill, 1947.

Joad, Cyril E. *God and Evil*. New York: Philosophy Library, 1941.

Journet, Charles. *The Meaning of Evil*. New York: Kennedy, 1963.

Keller, James A. "The Problem of Evil and the Attributes of God." *International Journal of Philosophy and Religion* 26 (1989): 155–71.

Kropf, Richard W. *Evil and Evolution: A Theodicy*. Rutherford, N.J.: Fairleigh Dickinson University Press, 1984.

Kushner, Harold S. *When Bad Things Happen to Good People*. New York: Schocken Books, 1981.

Leibniz, Gottfried Wilhelm. *Theodicy: Essays on the Goodness of God, the Freedom of Man, and the Origin of Evil*. New Haven, Conn.: Yale University Press, 1952.

Lewis, C. S. *The Problem of Pain*. London: Bles, 1940.

Mackie, John Leslie. "Evil and Omnipotence." *Mind* 64 (1955): 200–212.

————. *The Miracle of Theism: Arguments for and against the Existence of God*. Oxford: Clarendon Press, 1982.

Martin, Michael. *Atheism: A Philosophical Analysis*. Philadelphia: Temple University Press, 1990.

Mather, Cotton. *Fair Weather, or, Considerations to Dispel the Clouds and Allay the Storms of Discontent . . . 1692*. Ann Arbor, Mich.: University Microfilms International, 1984.

Mavrodes, George, ed. *The Rationality of Belief in God.* Englewood Cliffs, N.J.: Prentice-Hall, 1970.

McCloskey, H. J. "God and Evil." *Philosophical Quarterly* 10 (1960): 97–114.

Metz, Johannes B., ed. *Moral Evil under Challenge.* New York: Herder and Herder, 1970.

Moser, Paul K. "Natural Evil and the Free Will Defense." *International Journal of Philosophy and Religion* 15 (1984): 49–56.

Myers, C. Mason. "Job and the Problem of Evil." *Philosophy and Literature* 11 (October 87): 226–41.

Niebuhr, Reinhold. *Moral Man and Immoral Society.* New York: Scribner's, 1932.

O'Connor, David. "On the Problem of Evil's Still Not Being What It Seems." *Philosophical Quarterly* 40 (1990): 72–78.

Ormsby, Eric L. *Theodicy in Islamic Thought.* Princeton, N.J.: Princeton University Press, 1984.

Penelhum, Terence. "Divine Goodness and the Problem of Evil." *Religious Studies* 2 (1966): 95–108.

Peterson, Michael L. "Recent Work on the Problem of Evil." *American Philosophical Quarterly* 20 (1983): 321–40.

Petit, Francois. *The Problem of Evil.* New York: Hawthorn Books, 1959.

Pike, N., ed. *God and Evil: Readings on the Theological Problem of Evil.* London: Prentice-Hall, 1964.

Plato, *Euthyphro.* New York: Random House, 1948.

Rashdall, Hastings. *The Theory of Good and Evil,* vol. 2, 2d ed. London: Oxford University Press, 1924.

Reichenbach, Bruce R. "Must God Create the Best Possible World?" *International Philosophical Quarterly* 19 (1979): 203–12.

———. *Evil and a Good God.* New York: Fordham University Press, 1982.

Rowe, William. "The Empirical Argument from Evil." In *Rationality, Religious Belief and Moral Commitment,* edited by Robert Audi and William J. Wainwright. Ithaca, N.Y.: Cornell University Press, 1986.

Russell, Bruce. "The Persistent Problem of Evil." *Faith and Philosophy* 6 (1989): 121–39.

Schulweis, Harold M. *Evil and the Morality of God.* Cincinnati, Ohio: Hebrew Union College Press, 1984.

Seeskin, Kenneth. "Job and the Problem of Evil." *Philosophy and Literature* 11 (1987): 226–41.

Sharma, R. P. "The Problem of Evil in Buddhism." *Journal of Dharma* 2 (1977): 307–11.

Smart, Ninian. "Omnipotence, Evil and Superman." *Philosophy* 36 (April/July, 1961).

Smith, Michael P. "What's So Good about Feeling Bad." *Faith and Philosophy* 2 (1985): 424–29.

Spinoza, Benedict. "Of Human Bondage," part 4 of *Ethics.* New York: Tudor.

Surin, Kenneth. *Theology and the Problem of Evil.* Oxford: Blackwell, 1986.

Swinburne, Richard. "Natural Evil." *American Philosophical Quarterly* 15 (1978): 295–301.

———. *The Existence of God.* Oxford: Clarendon Press, 1979.

Tsanoff, Radaslav. *The Nature of Evil.* New York: Macmillan, 1931.

Wainwright, William J. "God and the Necessity of Physical Evils." *Sophia* 11 (1972): 16–19.

Wall, George. "A New Solution to an Old Problem." *Religious Studies* 15 (1979): 511–30.

Walsh, James, and P. G. Walsh. *Divine Providence and Human Suffering.* Wilmington, Del:
    Glazier, 1985.
Whale, J. S. *The Christian Answer to the Problem of Evil,* 4th ed. London: Student Christian
    Movement Press, 1957.
Whitney, Barry L. *Evil and the Process God.* New York: Mellen Press, 1985.
Wilcox, John T. *The Bitterness of Job: A Philosophical Reading.* Ann Arbor, Mich.: Univer-
    sity of Michigan Press, 1989.
Williams, N. P. *The Ideas of the Fall and of Original Sin.* London: Longmans, Green, 1927.

CHAPTER 6

The Divine–Human Relationship

N umerous points of interaction can be specified between God and human beings. In the Judeo-Christian tradition God is said to have given the Bible to humans by inspiring the writing, including the writing of the Ten Commandments and the Sermon on the Mount—the supreme guides for human conduct. The Bible also contains the Gospels describing the life of Christ, writings which are sacred to Christians, and the sayings of the prophets such as Moses, Amos, and Isaiah, which are especially revered by Jews.

God is also attributed with performing miracles that entail the suspension of natural law, including parting the Red Sea, speaking from a burning bush, walking on water, making the blind see, feeding a multitude with a small amount of food, turning water into wine, and so on. He is also believed to respond to petitionary prayers, especially unselfish ones, and to communicate with people through visions and voices. He interacts with human beings on earth to protect them from danger and to cure them when they become ill. He offers signs, inspirations, and revelations. He creates each life for a purpose and shapes human history to some predetermined end.

Furthermore, the fundamental article of the Christian faith is that God sacrificed his only begotten Son, Jesus Christ, to redeem humanity from sin and, through people's faith and repentance, award eternal life. God came to earth for humanity's salvation, and we can enter heaven if we accept the basic articles of faith—above all, the divinity of Jesus—and if we lead our lives in the light of his example. Just as Christ was resurrected following the crucifixion, we can hope for everlasting life with God.

In exploring the divine–human relationship a major issue is the connection between God and morality, or more broadly, *religion and ethics.* The Bible offers numerous commandments, rules, and examples for righteous living, and many thinkers maintain that the biblical prescriptions and prohibitions are the basis for Western ethics. We have the values we do because God presented the Ten

Commandments to Moses on Mount Sinai, and because Jesus preached the Sermon on the Mount.

In philosophic terms the primary question is whether ethics depends on religion, that is, whether our principles are a result of God's revelation of values. Dostoyevski writes that if God were dead, everything would be permissible, but that may not be true.

The key discussion of this question occurs in a Platonic dialogue called the *Euthyphro*. In this dialogue Socrates asks Euthyphro to define the nature of piety. Socrates is about to face a charge of impiety in the Athenian court, and Euthyphro, by contrast, is bringing a charge of impiety against his own father—an act that implies strong knowledge of the subject. After some initial sparring, Euthyphro defines piety as "that which all the gods love."

Socrates then asks the question which is key to the issue: whether "the pious or holy is beloved by the gods because it is holy, or holy because it is beloved of the gods." To paraphrase and modernize this question, Is an act approved by God because it is right, or is it right because God approves of it? In the first case, God recognizes the rightness of an act and for that reason wills it; in the second case, God makes an act right by willing it.

As the dialogue develops, Euthyphro is forced to the conclusion that piety "is loved because it is holy, not holy because it is loved." The gods recognize what is holy, they do not create it. In other words, God commands various actions for a reason, that is, because they are right; God does not arbitrarily make actions right by commanding them. God could not, for instance, make the right wrong or the wrong right simply by saying so. Even if God were to change his mind and to tell us to steal from others or bear false witness, that would not make stealing or lying acceptable. Presumably, God's mind would rarely (if ever) be changed, even in response to petitionary prayers; but the point is that even God could not turn values upside down. Right and wrong cannot be inverted and therefore are independent of God's word.

We are also precluded from simply trusting the authority of God as contained in the Bible, for as the twentieth-century philosopher P. Nowell-Smith remarks, "We must judge for ourselves whether the Bible is the inspired word of a just and benevolent God or a curious amalgam of profound wisdom and gross superstition. To judge this is to make a moral decision, so that in the end, so far from morality being based on religion, religion is based on morality."

When we come to the area of *miracles* in the divine–human relationship, we are on very boggy ground. Just as with morality, this too depends in part on whether we can trust our understanding of the Bible, which contains numerous accounts of the miraculous. This immediately presents a problem. For even if we claim that the Bible is infallible (inerrant), that does not mean we are able to interpret it infallibly. In fact, it would be odd if we did, because human beings are always being described as limited and prone to error, particularly by religious thinkers contrasting fallible human knowledge with that of God's perfect understanding.

Not only is interpretation a problem, but the Bible sometimes presents conflicting testimonies on events, including miraculous occurrences. There are discrepancies over when and how Christ's healing miracles occurred, whether he carried his own cross, whether he was born of the Virgin Mary or had forebears traceable through Joseph, and so forth.

To take the example of the Resurrection, the Gospel of Mark mentions three women visitors who discover the empty tomb, Matthew cites two, and John one. Matthew and John say they arrived before dawn; Mark says after daybreak. Also, Matthew reports that the stone rolled away after they arrived; but Mark, Luke, and John say this happened after *their* arrival. Matthew, Mark, and Luke mention that angels were present, John does not, and Matthew and John have Jesus appearing first at the tomb, while Mark puts him elsewhere. In addition, Luke and John depict the risen Christ in graphic, physical terms, actually eating and inviting a doubting disciple to touch his wounds, but Saint Paul describes the risen Christ on the road to Damascus in spiritual, not physical, terms.

Discrepancies of this kind make it difficult to understand the nature of the miracle one is asked to accept. However, with the discovery of the Dead Sea Scrolls some forty years ago and the recently increased access to them, perhaps scholars will reconcile the problem of differing biblical accounts.

Apart from the Bible, we wonder whether miracles can be accepted as a concept. Can there be such a thing as the suspension of the laws of natural science?

It seems reasonable to assume that God, who made the laws, can suspend them. The real question is how to determine when an authentic miracle has taken place as distinguished from a mistaken hypothesis, a perceptual illusion, or a cognitive delusion. Miracle cures in medicine can simply be misdiagnosed or psychosomatic illnesses. They might even testify to the power of the mind over the body, apart from spiritual intervention. Superstition and mass hysteria can account for numerous miracles, as can psychological projection of our wishes and the reconstruction of events after the fact to fit our presuppositions.

At the same time, we must allow for the possibility that miracles are genuine phenomena in which God intervenes in human affairs to bring about an uncanny and extraordinary result. The objection that Hume expresses in the selection included here has little force. He argues that since miracles, by their very nature, rarely occur, they are the most improbable events imaginable. However, unique events can occur; things that never took place before can happen. The fact that something has not been does not prove that it cannot be, so we must not rule out the possibility that God can work miracles.

This raises the more ultimate question of *faith and reason.* Should we simply have faith that miracles, revelations, visions, and other supernatural phenomena actually occur, or should we demand that all such events satisfy the test of reason and scientific proof? The debate as to which has a higher claim to truth has waged for hundreds of years, especially during the Middle Ages. Some theologians have declared that reason supports faith; others, that faith and reason are incompatible; still others, that reason carries us just so far, after which we must make a leap of faith. Most theologians maintain, of course, that if faith and reason conflict, so much the worse for reason.

At bottom the question is epistemological: it is a matter of how religious

knowledge is obtained. In order to know God and to comprehend divine interaction with human beings, we first need to understand how to gain this mode of
knowledge. Although some similarities can be found with aesthetic awareness,
moral intuition, and insight into oneself, religious knowledge seems quite unique.
In any case, we are unsure what criteria to use in separating genuine knowledge
from sham and bogus claims.

We do not know just how scientific any given religious assertions should
be in order to protect us from absurdities and self-deception. We also do not know
whether private knowledge can be considered legitimate—that is, something
personally understood, but beyond articulation or expression, or truth that is
known to the individual but, by its very nature, is incommunicable to others. How
can we tell whether we know something that is inexpressible, or whether the fact
of its being inexpressible means that we do not have any knowledge at all?
Determining what constitutes a sound basis for faith is probably the most vexing
problem in the philosophy of religion.

In the following selections Emil Brunner presents a case for basing moral
principles on the commands of God, while Kai Nielsen demonstrates the independence of morality from religion. Then David Hume offers a celebrated (if flawed)
criticism of miracles, and C. S. Lewis discusses the possibility of miracles in the
light of ancient and modern knowledge of the universe.

In the final section, John Locke distinguishes the provinces of faith and
reason, and Paul Tillich presents a reinterpretation of faith as "the state of being
ultimately concerned."

Religion and Ethics

37. The Divine Imperative

EMIL BRUNNER

THE DIVINE COMMAND AS GIFT AND DEMAND

PROPOSITION: *We know God's will only through His revelation, in His own Word. Therefore His Command is also primarily a gift, and as such a demand.*

There is no such thing as an "intrinsic Good". . . . The hypostatization of a human conception of the Good as the "Idea of the Good" is not only an abstraction in the logical sense; it is due to the fact that man has been severed from his Origin, to that original perversion of the meaning of existence, which consists in the fact that man attributes to himself and his ideas an independent existence—that is, that man makes himself God. This personal estrangement from God transforms personal union with Him into an impersonal abstract idea; thus "the Good," the "Idea of the Good," "the Law," becomes the principle of life, an abstract idea, which has no vital connexion with life and therefore does violence to life. For the *Idea* of the Good did not create life, it has no interest in life. It is an alien force which has invaded life; yet it is not a living force, it is merely the shadow of the real force, namely, the will of God. It is He who unites what is with what ought to be, He, the Creator of Nature and of the spirit, of all that exists and of ideas; His will is the source of that which is and the basis of that which ought to be. The fact that (as we all know only too well) a terrible gulf yawns between that which is and that which ought to be, that the relation between them is not merely that of the imperfect to the perfect, but that they are actually in opposition to one another, was not always so—it is the result of that original perversion of truth—of which we become aware in the sense of Fate and Guilt.

Therefore of ourselves we cannot know the Good or the Will of God. It is, of course, true that God manifests Himself as the incomprehensible One, mighty and wise in the works of His creation, with an impressiveness which, even in the most unseeing, awakens awe in the presence of the mystery of the universe, and fills with wonder everyone who has not entirely lost the child-spirit. But being what we are, with our limited vision, this manifestation is not enough to reveal to us the will of the mysterious power which rules in Nature.

It is His will to *give*. Therefore He can only be revealed in the reality of His giving. It is His will to give Himself, to give His life to man, and in so doing to give salvation, satisfaction, and blessedness. To the extent in which this act of self-giving is achieved, His will is accomplished, and this act of fulfilment also carries with it the restoration of the perverted order of existence. In this event the life of man is once again placed within the orbit of the Divine giving, and in this it becomes good. *The Good consists simply and solely in the fact* that man receives and deliberately accepts his life as a gift from God, as life dependent on "grace," as the state of "being justified" because it has been granted as a gift, as "justification by faith." Only thus can we know the Will of God, that is, in this revelation of Himself in which He manifests Himself as disinterested, generous Love.

But this Divine giving is not accomplished in any magical way; it simply takes place in the fact that God *"apprehends"* man; God *claims* us for His love, for His generous giving. But this means that He claims our whole existence for Himself, for this love of His; He gives us His love. He gives us His love in such a way that He captures us completely by the power of His love. *To belong* to Him, to this love, and through His love, means that we are the *bondslaves*[1] of this will. To believe means to become a captive, to become His property, or rather, to know that we are His property. The revelation which makes it plain that the will of God is lavish in giving *to* man, makes it equally clear that His will makes a demand *on* man. His will *for* us also means that He wants something *from* us. He claims us for His love. This is His Command. It is the *"new* commandment," because only now can man perceive that it is the command of One who gives before He demands, and who only demands something from us in the act of giving Himself to us.

He claims us for His love, for the love with which He loves the world and man, for His sovereign love, His purpose of absolute love. That God claims us for *Himself* means that He claims us for the *Kingdom of God*, for a love which is absolutely universal and unlimited. His "glory" means that we recognize Him as the Sole Giver, and as the Giver of all life. His "holiness" means that He alone is supreme, so that resistance to His will can only spell misery. But it is also His will to assert Himself and exercise His will as the Supreme Giver, and this is His "love." Apart from holiness the love of God would not be unlimited, it would not be the only ground of life, it would not be the love of God. But God possesses no other holiness than this: that He wills to be known absolutely in His real nature, namely, as the absolute Supreme Lord over His Kingdom, as the One who alone possesses life, and the Good, and gives it to man. Therefore the demands of love can never be separated from the claims of God Himself.

He claims us for *His* love, not for an *idea* of love—and not for a conception of the divine love which can be gained from merely reading the Bible. He claims us for His present, living activity of love, which can only be, and must always remain, His work. Therefore we can never know beforehand what God will

---

[1] The play on the words *gehören* (to belong) and *hörig* (to be bound to another, even to the point of serfdom) cannot be reproduced in English.—TR.

require. God's command can only be perceived at the actual moment of hearing it. It would denote a breaking away from obedience if we were to think of the Divine Command as one which had been enacted once for all, to be interpreted by us in particular instances. To take this line would mean reverting to the legalistic distortion of His love. Love would then have become a "principle." The *free* love of God requires us to remain *free*, that we may be freely at His disposal. *You* cannot say what it means to love here and now; *He* alone can tell you what this means for you at this moment.

The Good is simply what *God* wills that we should do, not that which we would do on the basis of a principle of love. God wills to do something quite definite and particular through us, here and now, something which no other person could do at any other time. Just as the commandment of love is absolutely universal so also it is absolutely individual. But just as it is absolutely individual so also it is absolutely devoid of all caprice. "I will guide thee with Mine eye."[2] No one can experience this "moment" save I myself. The Divine Command is made known to us "in the secret place." Therefore it is impossible for us to know it beforehand; to wish to know it beforehand—legalism—is an infringement of the divine honour. The fact that the holiness of God must be remembered when we dwell on His love[3] means that we cannot have His love at our disposal, that it cannot ever be perceived as a universal principle, but only in the act in which He speaks to us Himself; even in His love He remains our *Master* and Lord. But He is our "Lord" in the sense that He tells us Himself what it means to "love," here and now.

It is, of course, true that we know God's love in His Word which is also a *deed*, in the Holy Scriptures. But this Word which has actually occurred as an event can only be perceived as *His* word which is now living and active—Jesus can only be known as the Christ and as "my Lord"—through the Holy Spirit.[4] This applies not only to the knowledge of that which God wills *for* us, but also to that which He desires to have *from* us. There is no faith, as such, apart from conduct. Real faith always means obedience to God; it means a living obedience, offered here and now, at this actual moment of time, to His loving will, which has an absolute and special significance at this particular moment. If faith does not issue in such obedience it loses its meaning, and is perverted—it becomes a mere theory; obedience, too, becomes mere ethical legalism if it is not based on faith of this kind.

The fact that God claims us for Himself, is His love, His grace, but even so His claim is still His Command. In a Christian ethic we are not dealing with "counsels" nor with exhortations, nor with "values", with something which we "prefer"—no, here we are confronted by a Command which must be taken in dead earnest. The fact that the Apostles exhort rather than command—which, rightly, is regarded as a distinction between the Old Testament and the New—does not mean that the imperative character of the Divine claim has been in any way

---

[2] Psalm xxxii. 8.
[3] Cf. *The Mediator*, pp. 281 ff. and 467 ff. (Eng. trans.).
[4] I Cor. xii. 3.

modified. The form of the exhortation is simply intended to remind us of the ground on which the Divine claim is based; that is, that every believer can indeed know the will of God for himself, through his faith in Christ. The apostolic exhortation implies that the believer is no longer a minor, and it sweeps away all legalistic heteronomy. Not even an Apostle can tell you what you ought to do; God Himself is the only One who can tell you this. There is to be no intermediary between ourselves and the Divine Will. God wishes to deal with us "personally," not through any medium.

Similarly, the difference between a command and a prohibition is not a matter of great importance. Every command is a prohibition and *vice versa*. Indeed, we may say that the distinction is only important to the extent in which the positive form of the Command—which predominates in the New Testament— points to the fact that God's relation to the world, as its Creator, is primarily positive and creative, not negative; hence we too, in the obedience of faith, are absorbed into this positive action of God. As the will of the Creator God's will is essentially positive; He does not will nothingness, the All-One, or Nirvana, but the world. Even in the New Testament there are plenty of prohibitions, and it is precisely the "hymn of Love" (I Cor. xiii) which conceives the commandment of love in a remarkably negative way, because truly Divinely ordered action in love can only take place as it breaks the natural tendency of our will.

God's will controls absolutely *everything*. He claims us and our whole existence. Hence both these statements are true: there are *no* "Adiaphora", and— everything is "adiaphoron"—save love. *Dilige et fac quod vis.* Everything is mechanical and therefore neutral—save the ordering of this mechanical sphere by love. And nothing is merely mechanical, since everything, even the very smallest thing, is connected with the whole, and is impregnated with a certain spirit. The Divine Command is imposed on every moment; there are no moral holidays. All life, the "natural" or material, as well as the spiritual, comes under the sovereign sway of God; indeed even the suffering caused by something, which we cannot alter is not excepted from this sovereignty; for God also wishes us to offer Him our endurance and our patience, our grateful acceptance, our reverent longing and our requests for His help.

It is *His* will that God wills to accomplish in the world; He is not the servant of some purpose outside Himself. God Himself is His own End. In His love, however, He sets up an End outside Himself—without ceasing to be His own End; this "end" is the communion of the creature with Himself, the Creator. This Divine will for "community" is God's Sovereign Will. Therefore salvation, beatitude, the fulfilment of the purpose of life, both for humanity as a whole, and for the individual, is included in God's royal purpose. The tables of prohibition in the Bible may be compared with the notices on power circuits: Do Not Touch! Because God wills to control our life, He commands and He forbids. This is the "eudaemonism" of the Gospel, and at the same time its absolutely serious view of duty. God wills our true happiness; but *He* wills it, and He wills it in such a way that no one else knows what His will is. It remains outside our disposal, and indeed we do not know it. We never know what is right for us, nor what is best for the other person. We go astray when we think that we can deduce this from some principle or another, or from some experience, and we distort the thought of the divine love if we think that we know what He ought to do for us in accordance with His love. But of one thing we may be quite sure: His will is love, even when we do not understand it—when He commands as well as when He gives.

Therefore in His revelation God's will is expressed by His sanctions, by rewards and punishments. God alone gives life; to be with Him is life; to resist Him is ruin. It is impossible to exist apart from God; it is impossible to be neutral towards Him. He who is not for Him is against Him. God's Command means eternal life and God means nothing else than this. He is Love. But His will is utterly serious; it is the will of the Lord of Life and Death. Anyone who—finally—resists Him, will only dash himself to pieces against the rock of His Being. This is the holiness of the love of God. As the divine love cannot be separated from His gift of life, so the Holiness of God cannot be separated from His judicial wrath, the denial and destruction of life. To have a share in the will of God, in the sense of union with His will, means salvation; to resist Him spells utter disaster.

The abstract legalistic system of ethics, because ideas have no connexion with life, can only judge this connexion of the moral element with reward and punishment as heteronomy, as the perversion of the moral endeavour. "We ought to do the Good for the sake of the Good." It does not perceive that behind this phrase, "for the sake of the Good," there lies concealed, "for My sake." And it does not understand that the Good is done for the sake of the Good when it is done for the sake of God, in obedience to the Divine Command. We ought to obey God because He commands it, not because obedience means happiness and disobedience means unhappiness. Faith would not be faith, obedience would not be obedience, if things were otherwise. But obedience would not be obedience towards God, did we not know that His Command means life and His prohibition death. The primary concern is not that which refers to my Ego, to my life; no, the primary concern is this: that it is God's will, the will of Him to whom my life belongs. But that which refers to *me*, that which refers to *my* life, is the necessary second element for it concerns the will of Him who Himself is life—even *my* life. Obedience would be impure if this second element were made the first. But it would be unreal, and indeed impossible, if this second element, as the second, were not combined with the first. We cannot do anything good which has no significance for life, and we cannot avoid anything evil, unless at the same time we know it to be harmful. It is not the question whether all morality is not mingled with self-interest—without self-interest nothing would concern us at all—but the question is this: is this self-interest regarded as founded in God or in myself? To do the Good for the sake of the Good is only a pale reflection of the genuine Good; to do the Good for the sake of God means to do the Good not because my moral dignity requires it, but because it is that which is commanded by God.

38. Ethics without God

KAI NIELSEN

Let us first ask: "Is something good because God wills or commands it or does God command it because it is good?" If we say God commands it because it is good, this implies that something can be good independently of God. This is so because 'God commands it *because* it is good' implies that God apprehends it to be good or takes it to be good or in some way knows it to be good and then tells us to do it. But if God does this, then it is at least *logically* possible for us to come to see or in some way know or come to appreciate that it is good without God's telling us to do it or informing us that it is good. Moreover, on this alternative, its goodness does not depend on its being willed by God or even on there being a God.

The points made above need explanation and justification. In making those remarks, I am giving to understand that good is not a creation of God but rather that something is good is something which is itself apprehended by God or known by God. (If all that talk seems too "cognitive" a way to speak of moral notions, we can alternatively speak of God's appreciating something to be good.) If this is so, it is in some way there to be apprehended or known or appreciated and thus it is at least *logically* possible for us to apprehend it or know it or appreciate it without knowing anything of God. Furthermore, since God himself apprehends it to be good and since it doesn't, on this alternative, become good simply because he wills it or commands it, there can be this goodness even in a godless world. Translated into the concrete, this means that, at the very least, it could be correct to assert that even in a world without God, killing little children is evil and caring for them is good.

Someone might grant that there is this logical (conceptual) independence of morality from religion, but still argue that, given man's corrupt and vicious nature in his fallen state, he, as a matter of fact, needs God's help to understand what is good, to know what he ought to do, and to quite categorically bind himself to striving to act as morality requires.

Though there is indeed extensive corruption in the palace of justice, such a response is still confused. With or without a belief in God, we can recognize such corruption. In some concrete situations at least, we understand perfectly well what is good, what we ought to do, and what morality requires of us. Moreover, the corruption religious apologists have noted does not lie here. The corruption comes not principally in our knowledge or understanding but in our "weakness of will." We find it in our inability to do what in a cool hour, we acknowledge to be good—"the good I would do that I do not." Religion, for some people at any rate, may be of value in putting their *hearts* into virtue, but that religion is necessary for some in this way does not show us how it can provide us with a knowledge of good and evil or an ultimate criterion for making such judgments (Toulmin, 1950: 202–225). It does not provide us, even if we are believers, with an ultimate standard of goodness.

Suppose we say instead—as Emil Brunner (1945) or C. F. Henry (1957), for example, surely would—that an action or attitude is right or good simply because God *wills* it or *commands* it. Its goodness arises from Divine *fiat*. God makes something good simply by commanding it.

Can *anything* be good or become good simply by being commanded or willed? Can a fiat, command, or ban *create* goodness or moral obligation? I do not think so. To see that it cannot, consider first some ordinary, mundane examples of ordering or commanding. Suppose I tell my students in a class I am teaching, "You must get a loose leaf notebook for this class." My commanding it, my telling my class they must do it, does not *eo ipso* make it something they *ought* to do or even make doing it good, though it might make it a prudent thing for them to do. But, whether or not it is prudent for them to do it, given my position of authority *vis-à-vis* them, it is, if there are no reasons for it, a perfectly arbitrary injunction on my part and not something that could correctly be said to be good. . . .

To this it will surely be replied: "It is true that these moral concepts cannot be identified with just any old command, but it is their being *Divine* commands which makes all the difference. It is *God's* willing it, *God's* telling us to do it, that makes it good"(Falk 1956: 123–131).

It is indeed true, for the believer at least, that it is *God's* commanding it or God's willing it that makes all the difference. This is so because the believer assumes and indeed fervently believes that God is good. But how, it should be asked, does the believer *know* that God is good, except by what is in the end his own quite fallible moral judgment or, if you will, appreciation or perception, that God is good? We must, to know that God is good, see that his acts, his revelation, his commands, are good. It is through the majesty and the goodness of his revelation, the depth and extent of his love, as revealed in the Scriptures, that we come to understand that God is good, that—so the claim goes—God is in reality the ultimate criterion for all our moral actions and attitudes.

It could, of course, be denied that *all* the commands, all the attitudes, exhibited in the Bible are of the highest moral quality. The behavior of Lot's daughters and the damnation of unbelievers are cases in point. But let us assume that the moral insights revealed in our Scriptures are of the very highest and that through his acts God reveals his goodness to us. But here we have in effect conceded the critical point put by the secularist. We can see from the very argumentation here that we must quite unavoidably use our own moral insight to decide that God's acts are good. We finally, and quite unavoidably, to come to any conclusion here, must judge for ourselves the moral quality of the alleged revelation; or, if you will, it is finally by what is no doubt fallible human insight that we must judge that what *purports* to be revelation is *indeed* revelation. We cannot avoid using our own moral understanding, corruptible and deceitful though it be, if we are ever to know that God is good. Fallible or not, our own moral understanding and judgment here is the *logically* prior thing.

The believer might indeed concede that if we start to inquire into, to deliberate about, the goodness of God, we cannot but end up saying what I have just said. But my mistake, he could argue, is in ever starting this line of inquiry in the first place. Who is man to inquire into, to question, the goodness of God? Who is he to ask whether God should be obeyed? That is utter blasphemy and folly. No *genuine believer* thinks for one moment he can question God's goodness or the bindingness of

God's will. That God is good, that indeed God is the Perfect Good, is *a given* for the believer. 'God is good' or 'God is the perfect Good' are, in the technical jargon of philosophy, analytic. Given the believer's usage, it makes no sense to ask if what God commands is good or if God is good. Any being who was not good could not properly be called 'God', where what we are talking about is the God of the Judeo-Christian tradition. Similarly, we could not properly call anything that was not perfectly good God. A person who seriously queried "Should I do what God ordains?" could not possibly be a believer. Indeed, Jews and Christians do not mean by 'He should do x' that 'God ordains x'; and 'One should do what God ordains' is not equivalent to 'What God ordains God ordains'; but not all tautologies, or analytic propositions, are statements of identity. It is not only blasphemy, it is, as well, logically speaking *senseless to question* the goodness of God.

Whence then, one might ask, the ancient problem of evil? But let us, for the occasion, assume what it is at least reasonable to assume, namely, that in some way 'God is good' and 'God is the Perfect Good' are analytic or 'truths of reason'. Even if this is so, it still remains true—though now it is a little less easy to see this—that we can only come to know that anything is good or evil through our own moral insight.

Let us see how this is so. First it is important to see that 'God is good' is not an identity statement, e.g., 'God' is not equivalent to 'good'. "God spoke to Moses" makes sense. "Good spoke to Moses" is not even English. "The steak is good" and "Knowles's speech in Parliament was good" are both standard English sentences, but if 'God' replaced 'good' as the last word in these sentences we have gibberish. But, as I have just said, not all tautologies are statements of identity. 'Wives are women', 'Triangles are three-sided' are not statements of identity, but they are clear cases of analytic propositions. It is at least reasonable to argue 'God is good' has the same status, but, if it does, we still must independently understand what is meant by 'good' and thus the criterion of goodness remains *independent* of God.

As we could not apply the predicate 'women' to wives, if we did not first understand what women are, and the predicate 'three-sided' to triangles if we did not understand what it was for something to be three-sided, so we could not apply the predicate 'good' to God unless we already understood what it meant to say that something was good and unless we had some criterion of goodness. Furthermore, we can and do meaningfully apply the predicate 'good' to many things and attitudes that can be understood by a person who knows nothing of God. Even in a godless world, to relieve suffering would still be good.

But is not 'God is the Perfect Good' an identity statement? Do not 'God' and 'the Perfect Good' refer to and/or mean the same thing? The meaning of both of these terms is so very indefinite that it is hard to be sure, but it is plain enough that a believer cannot seriously question the truth of 'God is the Perfect Good' and still remain a Christian or Jewish believer. But granting that, we still must have a criterion for goodness that is independent of religion, that is, independent of a belief in God, for clearly we could not judge anything to be *perfectly* good unless we could judge that it was good, and we have already seen that our criterion for goodness must be at least logically independent of God.

Someone still might say: Something must have gone wrong somewhere.

No believer thinks he can question or presume to *judge* God. A devoutly religious person simply must use God as his *ultimate criterion* for moral behavior (Brown 1963: 235–244; and 1966–67: 269–276. But in response see Nielsen 1971a). If God wills it, he, as a "knight of faith," must do it!

Surely this is *in a way* so, but it is perfectly compatible with everything I have so far said. 'God' by *definition* is 'a being worthy of worship', 'wholly good', 'a being upon whom we are completely dependent'. These phrases partially define the God of Judaism and Christianity. This being so, it makes no sense at all to speak of *judging* God or deciding that God is good or worthy of worship. But the crucial point here is this: before we can make any judgments at all that any conceivable being, force, Ground of Being, transcendental reality, person or whatever could be *worthy* of worship, could be properly called 'good', let alone 'the Perfect Good', we must have a logically prior understanding of goodness (Nielsen 1964). That we could call anything, or any foundation of anything, 'God', presupposes we have a moral understanding and the ability to discern what would be *worthy* of worship or perfectly good. Morality does not presuppose religion; religion presupposes morality. Feuerbach was at least partially right: our very concept of God seems, in an essential part at least, a logical product of our moral categories. . . .

Suppose someone argues that it is a matter of *faith* with him that what God commands is what he ought to do; it is a matter of *faith* with him that God's willing it is his ultimate criterion for something's being good. He might say, "I see the force of your argument, but for me it remains a straight matter of faith that there can be no goodness without God. I do not *know* that this is so; I cannot give *grounds* for believing that this is so; I simply humbly accept it on faith that something is good simply because God says that it is. I have no independent moral criterion."

My answer to such a fideist—to fix him with a label—is that in the very way he reasons, in his very talk of God as a being *worthy* of worship, he shows, his protestations to the contrary notwithstanding, that he has such an independent criterion. He shows in his very behavior, including his linguistic behavior, that something being willed or commanded does not *eo ipso* make it good or make it something that he ought to do, but that its being willed by a being *he takes* to be superlatively *worthy* of worship does make it something he, morally speaking, must do. But we should also note that it is by his own reflective decisions, by his own honest avowals, that he takes some being or, if you will, some x to be so *worthy* of worship, and thus he shows, in his very behavior, including his linguistic behavior, though not in his talk *about* his behavior, that he does not even take anything to be properly called 'God' unless he has already made a moral judgment about that being. He *says* that he takes God as his ultimate criterion for good on faith, but his actions, including, of course, his everyday linguistic behavior and not just his talk about talk, speak louder than his words, and he shows by them that even his God is in part a product of his moral awareness. Only if he had such a moral awareness could he use the word 'God', as a Jew or Christian uses it. So that his protestations notwithstanding, he clearly has a criterion for good and evil that is *logically independent* of his belief in God. His talk of faith does not and cannot at all alter that. . . .

IV

There is a further stage in the dialectic of the argument about religion and ethics that I want now to consider. I have shown that in a purely logical sense moral notions cannot simply rest on the doctrinal cosmic claims of religion. In fact quite the reverse is the case, namely, that only if a human being has a concept of good and evil that is not religiously dependent can he even have the Jewish-Christian-Islamic conception of Deity? In this very fundamental sense, it is not morality that rests on religion but religion on morality. Note that this argument could be made out, even if we grant the theist his metaphysical claims about what there is. That is to say, the claims I have hitherto made are quite independent of skeptical arguments about the reliability or even the coherence of claims to the effect that God exists.

Some defenders of the faith will grant that there is indeed such a fundamental independence of ethical belief from religious belief, though very few would accept my last argument about the dependence of religious belief on human moral understanding. But what is important to see here is that they could accept at least part of my basic claim and still argue that to develop a *fully human and adequate normative* ethic one must make it a God-centered ethic (Hick 1959: 494–516. For a criticism of such views see Nielsen 1973). Here, in the arguments for and against, the intellectual reliability of religious claims will become relevant.

The claim that such a religious moralist wishes to make is that only with a God-centered morality could we get a morality that would be adequate, that would go beyond the relativities and formalisms of a nonreligious ethic. Only a God-centered and perhaps only a Christ-centered morality could meet our deepest and most persistent moral demands. People have certain desires and needs; they experience loneliness and despair; they create certain "images of excellence"; they seek happiness and love. If the human animal was not like this, if man were not this searching, anxiety-ridden creature with a thirst for happiness and with strong desires and aversions, there would be no good and evil, no morality at all. In short, our moralities are relative to our human natures. And given the human nature that we in fact have, we cannot be satisfied with any purely secular ethic. Nothing "the world" can give us will finally satisfy us. We thirst for a father who will protect us—who will not let life be just one damn thing after another until we die and rot; we long for a God who can offer us the promise of a blissful everlasting life with him. We need to love and obey such a father. Unless we can convincingly picture to ourselves that we are creatures of such a loving sovereign, our deepest moral hopes will be frustrated.

No purely secular ethic can—or indeed should—offer such a hope, a hope that is perhaps built on an illusion, but still a hope that is worth, the believer will claim, the full risk of faith. Whatever the rationality of such a faith, our very human nature, some Christian moralists maintain, makes us long for such assurances. Without it our lives will be without significance, without moral sense; morality finds its *psychologically realistic foundation* in certain human purposes. And given human beings with their nostalgia for the absolute, human life without God will be devoid of all purpose or at least devoid of everything but trivial purposes.

Thus without a belief in God, there could be no humanly satisfying morality. Secular humanism in any of its many varieties is in reality inhuman.

It is true that a secular morality can offer no hope for a blissful immortality or a bodily resurrection to a "new life," and it is also true that secular morality does not provide for a protecting, loving father or some over-arching purpose *to* life. But we have to balance this off against the fact that these religious concepts are myths—sources of illusion and self-deception. We human beings are helpless, utterly dependent creatures for years and years. Because of this long period of infancy, there develops in us a deep psychological need for an all protecting father; we thirst for such security, but there is not the slightest reason to think that there is *such* security. Moreover, that people have feelings of dependence does not mean that there is something on which they can depend. That we have such needs most certainly does not give us any reason at all to think that there is such a super-mundane prop for our feelings of dependence.

Furthermore, and more importantly, if there is no such architectonic purpose *to* life, as our religions claim, this does not mean that there is no purpose *in* life—that there is no way of living that is ultimately satisfying and significant. It indeed appears to be true that all small purposes, if pursued too relentlessly and exclusively, leave us with a sense of emptiness. Even Mozart quartets listened to endlessly become boring, but a varied life lived with verve and with a variety of conscious aims can survive the destruction of Valhalla. That there is no purpose *to* life does not imply that there is no purpose *in* life. Human beings may not have a function and if this is so, then, unlike a tape recorder or a pencil or even a kind of homunculus, we do not have a purpose. There is nothing we are made for. But even so, we can and do have purposes in the sense that we have aims, goals, and things we find worth seeking and admiring. There are indeed things we prize and admire; the achievement of these things and the realization of our aims and desires, including those we are most deeply committed to, give moral significance to our lives (Baier 1981; Nielsen 1986b). We do not need a God to *give* meaning to our lives by making us for his sovereign purpose and perhaps thereby robbing us of our freedom. We, by our deliberate acts and commitments, can give meaning to our own lives. Here man has that "dreadful freedom" that makes possible his human dignity; freedom will indeed bring him anxiety, but he will then be the *rider* and not the *ridden* and, by being able to choose, seek out, and sometimes realize those things he most deeply prizes and admires, his life will take on a significance (Berlin 1969). A life lived without purpose is indeed a most dreadful life—a life in which we might have what the existentialists rather pedantically call the experience of nothingness. But we do not need God or the gods to give purpose to our lives or to give the lie to this claim about nothingness. And we can grow into a fallibilism without a nostalgia for the absolute.

There are believers who would resist some of this and who would respond that these purely human purposes, forged in freedom and anguish, are not sufficient to meet our deepest moral needs. Beyond that, they argue, man needs very much to see himself as a creature with a purpose in a divinely ordered universe. He needs to find some *cosmic* significance for his ideals and commitments; he wants and needs the protection and certainty of having a function. This certainty, as the

Grand Inquisitor realized, is even more desirable than his freedom. He wants and needs to live and be guided by the utterly sovereign will of God.

If, after wrestling through the kind of philosophical considerations I have been concerned to set forth, a religious moralist still really wants this and would continue to want it after repeated careful reflection, after all the consequences of his view and the alternatives had been placed vividly before him, after logical confusions had been dispelled, and after he had taken the matter to heart, his secularist interlocutor may find that with him he is finally caught in some ultimate disagreement in attitude.[1] Even this is far from certain, however, for it is not at all clear that there are certain determinate places in such dubious battles where argument and the giving of reasons just must come to an end and we must instead resort to persuasion or some other nonrational methods if we are to resolve our fundamental disagreements (Stevenson 1944: Chapters VIII, IX, and XIII; Stevenson 1963: Chapters IV; Stevenson 1966: 197–217).[2] But even if we finally do end up in such "pure disagreements in attitude," before we get there, there is a good bit that can be said. How could his purposes really be *his* own purposes, if he were a creature made to serve God's sovereign purpose and to live under the sovereign will of God? In such a circumstance would his ends be something he had deliberately chosen or would they simply be something that he could not help realizing? Moreover, is it really compatible with human dignity to be *made* for something? We should reflect here that we cannot without insulting people ask what they are for. Finally, is it not *infantile* to go on looking for some father, some order, some absolute, that will lift all the burden of *decision* from us (Evans 1973)? Children follow rules blindly, but do we want to be children all our lives? Is it really *hubris* or arrogance or sin on our part to wish for a life where we make our own decisions, where we follow the rules we do because we see the *point* of them, and where we need not crucify our intellects by believing in some transcendent purpose whose very intelligibilty is seriously in question? Perhaps by saying this I am only exhibiting my own *hubris,* my own corruption of soul, but I cannot believe that to ask this question is to exhibit such arrogance.

References

Baier, Kurt. "The Meaning of Life." Pp. 156–172 in E. D. Klemke (ed.), *The Meaning of Life.* New York: Oxford University Press, 1981.
Berlin, Isaiah. *Four Essays on Liberty.* New York: Oxford University Press, 1969.
Braithwaite, R. B. "An empiricist's view of the nature of religious belief." Pp. 198–201 in John Hick (ed.), *The Existence of God.* New York: Macmillan, 1964.
Brown, Patterson. "Religious morality." *Mind* 72 (April) 1963: 235–244. "God and the good." *Religious Studies* 2/2 (April) 1966: 269–276.

[1] That there is still a lot of room for argument here is brought out by Findlay (1963: Chapters IV, VI, IX and XV; and Findlay, 1957:97–114).
[2] Even if as thoroughly as Alasdair MacIntyre we reject the "emotivism" of the "enlightenment project," we do not have a more objective basis for our moral claims if we follow MacIntyre's positive program (MacIntyre, 1980 and 1981).

Brown, Stuart. *Proof and the Existence of God.* London: The Open University Press, 1973.

Brunner, Emil. *The Divine Imperative.* Trans. O. Wyon. Philadelphia: Westminister Press, 1947.

Evans, Donald. "Does religious faith conflict with moral freedom?" Pp. 305–342 in Gene Outka and John P. Reeder, Jr. (eds.), *Religion and Morality.* Garden City, NY: Anchor Books, 1973.

Ewing, A. C. "The autonomy of ethics." Pp. 63–83 in I. T. Ramsey (ed.), *Prospects for Metaphysics.* London: George Allen and Unwin, 1957.

Falk, W. D. "Moral perplexity." *Ethics* 66 (January) 1956: 123–131.

Findlay, J. N. "The structure of the kingdom of ends." *Proceedings of the British Academy* 43:97–114, 1957.

———. *Language, Mind and Value.* London: George Allen and Unwin, 1963.

Hare, R. N. "The Simple believer." Pp. 294–304 in Gene Outka and John P. Reeder, Jr. (eds.), *Religion and Morality.* Garden City, NY: Anchor Books, 1973.

Henry, F. H. *Christian Personal Ethics.* Grand Rapids, MI: William B. Eardmans, 1957.

Hick, John. "Belief and life: the fundamental nature of the Christian ethic." *Encounter* 20/4 (January) 1959: 494–516.

Jaggar, Alison "It does not matter whether we can derive 'ought' from 'is'." *Canadian Journal of Philosophy* 3/3 (March) 1974: 373–379.

Miracles and Physical Law

39. Enquiry concerning Human Understanding

DAVID HUME

OF MIRACLES

Part I.

I flatter myself, that I have discovered an argument . . . which, if just, will, with the wise and learned, be an everlasting check to all kinds of superstitious delusion, and consequently, will be useful as long as the world endures. For so long, I presume, will the accounts of miracles and prodigies be found in all history, sacred and profane.

Though experience be our only guide in reasoning concerning matters of fact; it must be acknowledged, that this guide is not altogether infallible, but in some cases is apt to lead us into errors. One, who in our climate, should expect better weather in any week of June than in one of December, would reason justly, and conformably to experience; but it is certain, that he may happen, in the event, to find himself mistaken. However, we may observe, that, in such a case, he would have no cause to complain of experience; because it commonly informs us beforehand of the uncertainty, by that contrariety of events, which we may learn from a diligent observation. All effects follow not with like certainty from their supposed causes. Some events are found, in all countries and all ages, to have been constantly conjoined together: Others are found to have been more variable, and sometimes to disappoint our expectations; so that, in our reasonings concerning matter of fact, there are all imaginable degrees of assurance, from the highest certainty to the lowest species of moral evidence.

A wise man, therefore, proportions his belief to the evidence. In such conclusions as are founded on an infallible experience, he expects the event with the last degree of assurance, and regards his past experience as a full *proof* of the future existence of that event. In other cases, he proceeds with more caution: He weighs the opposite experiments: He considers which side is supported by the greater number of experiments: to that side he inclines, with doubt and hesitation;

and when at last he fixes his judgement, the evidence exceeds not what we properly call *probability*. All probability, then, supposes an opposition of experiments and observations, where the one side is found to overbalance the other, and to produce a degree of evidence, proportioned to the superiority. A hundred instances or experiments on one side, and fifty on another, afford a doubtful expectation of any event; though a hundred uniform experiments, with only one that is contradictory, reasonably beget a pretty strong degree of assurance. In all cases, we must balance the opposite experiments, where they are opposite, and deduct the smaller number from the greater, in order to know the exact force of the superior evidence.

To apply these principles to a particular instance; we may observe, that there is no species of reasoning more common, more useful, and even necessary to human life, than that which is derived from the testimony of men, and the reports of eye-witnesses and spectators. This species of reasoning, perhaps, one may deny to be founded on the relation of cause and effect. I shall not dispute about a word. It will be sufficient to observe that our assurance in any argument of this kind is derived from no other principle than our observation of the veracity of human testimony, and of the usual conformity of facts to the reports of witnesses. It being a general maxim, that no objects have any discoverable connexion together, and that all the inferences, which we can draw from one to another, are founded merely on our experience of their constant and regular conjunction; it is evident, that we ought not to make an exception to this maxim in favour of human testimony, whose connexion with any event seems, in itself, as little necessary as any other. Were not the memory tenacious to a certain degree; had not men commonly an inclination to truth and a principle of probity; were they not sensible to shame, when detected in a falsehood: Were not these, I say, discovered by *experience* to be qualities, inherent in human nature, we should never repose the least confidence in human testimony. A man delirious, or noted for falsehood and villany, has no manner of authority with us.

And as the evidence, derived from witnesses and human testimony, is founded on past experience, so it varies with the experience, and is regarded either as a *proof* or a *probability*, according at the conjunction between any particular kind of report and any kind of object has been found to be constant or variable. There are a number of circumstances to be taken into consideration in all judgements of this kind; and the ultimate standard, by which we determine all disputes, that may arise concerning them, is always derived from experience and observation. Where this experience is not entirely uniform on any side, it is attended with an unavoidable contrariety in our judgements, and with the same opposition and mutual destruction of argument as in every other kind of evidence. We frequently hesitate concerning the reports of others. We balance the opposite circumstances, which cause any doubt or uncertainty; and when we discover a superiority on any side, we incline to it; but still with a diminution of assurance, in proportion to the force of its antagonist.

This contrariety of evidence, in the present case, may be derived from several different causes; from the opposition of contrary testimony; from the character or number of the witnesses; from the manner of their delivering their testimony; or from the union of all these circumstances. We entertain a suspicion concerning any matter of fact, when the witnesses contradict each other; when they are but few, or of a doubtful character; when they have an interest in what they affirm; when they deliver their testimony with hesitation, or on the contrary, with too violent asseverations. There are many other particulars of the same kind, which may diminish or destroy the force of any argument, derived from human testimony.

Suppose, for instance, that the fact, which the testimony endeavors to establish, partakes of the extraordinary and the marvellous; in that case, the evidence, resulting from the testimony, admits of a diminution, greater or less, in proportion as the fact is more or less unusual. The reason why we place any credit in witnesses and historians, is not derived from any *connexion,* which we perceive *a priori,* between testimony and reality, but because we are accustomed to find a conformity between them. But when the fact attested is such a one as has seldom fallen under our observation, here is a contest of two opposite experiences; of which the one destroys the other, as far as its force goes, and the superior can only operate on the mind by the force, which remains. The very same principle of experience, which gives us a certain degree of assurance in the testimony of witnesses, gives us also, in this case, another degree of assurance against the fact, which they endeavour to establish; from which contradition there necessarily arises a counterpoize, and mutual destruction of belief and authority.

I should not believe such a story were it told me by Cato, was a proverbial saying in Rome, even during the lifetime of that philosophical patriot. The incredibility of a fact, it was allowed, might invalidate so great an authority.

The Indian prince, who refused to believe the first relations concerning the effects of frost, reasoned justly; and it naturally required very strong testimony to engage his assent to facts, that arose from a state of nature, with which he was unacquainted, and which bore so little analogy to those events, of which he had had constant and uniform experience. Though they were not contrary to his experience, they were not conformable to it.

But in order to encrease the probability against the testimony of witnesses, let us suppose, that the fact, which they affirm, instead of being only marvellous, is really miraculous; and suppose also, that the testimony considered apart and in itself, amounts to an entire proof; in that case, there is proof against proof, of which the strongest must prevail, but still with a diminution of its force, in proportion to that of its antagonist.

A miracle is a violation of the laws of nature; and as a firm and unalterable experience has established these laws, the proof against a miracle, from the very nature of the fact, is as entire as any argument from experience can possibly be imagined. Why is it more than probable, that all men must die; that lead cannot, of itself, remain suspended in the air; that fire consumes wood, and is extinguished by water; unless it be, that these events are found agreeable to the laws of nature, and there is required a violation of these laws, or in other words, a miracle to prevent them? Nothing is esteemed a miracle, if it ever happen in the common course of nature. It is no miracle that a man, seemingly in good health, should die on a sudden: because such a kind of death, though more unusual than any other, has yet been frequently observed to happen. But it is a miracle, that a dead man should come to life; because that has never been observed in any age or country. There must, therefore, be a uniform experience against every miraculous event, otherwise the event would not merit that appellation. And as a uniform experience amounts to a proof, there is here a direct and full *proof*, from the nature of the fact, against the existence of any miracle; nor can such a proof be destroyed, or the miracle rendered credible, but by an opposite proof, which is superior.

The plain consequence is (and it is a general maxim worthy of our attention), "That no testimony is sufficient to establish a miracle, unless the testimony be of such a kind, that its falsehood would be more miraculous, than the fact, which it endeavours to establish; and even in that case there is a mutual destruction of arguments, and the superior only gives us an assurance suitable to that degree of force, which remains, after deducting the inferior." When anyone tells me, that he saw a dead man restored to life, I immediately consider with myself, whether it be more probable, that this person should either deceive or be deceived, or that the fact, which he relates, should really have happened. I weigh the one miracle against the other; and according to the superiority, which I discover, I pronounce my decision, and always reject the greater miracle. If the falsehood of his testimony would be more miraculous, than the event which he relates; then, and not till then, can he pretend to command my belief or opinion.

Part II.

In the foregoing reasoning we have supposed, that the testimony, upon which a miracle is founded, may possibly amount to an entire proof, and that the falsehood of that testimony would be a real prodigy: But it is easy to shew, that we have been a great deal too liberal in our concession, and that there never was a miraculous event established on so full an evidence.

For *first*, there is not to be found, in all history, any miracle attested by a sufficient number of men, of such unquestioned good-sense, education, and learning, as to secure us against all delusion in themselves; of such undoubted integrity, as to place them beyond all suspicion of any design to deceive others; of such credit and reputation in the eyes of mankind, as to have a great deal to lose in case of their being detected in any falsehood; and at the same time, attesting facts performed in such a public manner and in so celebrated a part of the world, as to render the detection unavoidable: All which circumstances are requisite to give us a full assurance in the testimony of men.

Secondly. We may observe in human nature a principle which, if strictly examined, will be found to diminish extremely the assurance, which we might, from human testimony, have, in any kind of prodigy. The maxim, by which we commonly conduct ourselves in our reasonings, is, that the objects, of which we have no experience, resemble those, of which we have; that what we have found to be most usual is always most probable; and that where there is an opposition of arguments, we ought to give the preference to such as are founded on the greatest number of past observations. But though, in proceeding by this rule, we readily reject any fact which is unusual and incredible in an ordinary degree; yet in advancing farther, the mind observes not always the same rule; but when anything is affirmed utterly absurd and miraculous, it rather the more readily admits of such a fact, upon account of that very circumstance, which ought to destroy all its authority. The passion of *surprise* and *wonder*, arising from miracles, being an agreeable emotion, gives a sensible tendency towards the belief of those events, from which it is derived. And this goes so far, that even those who cannot enjoy this pleasure immediately, nor can believe those miraculous events, of which they are informed, yet love to partake of the satisfaction at second-hand or by rebound, and place a pride and delight in exciting the admiration of others.

With what greediness are the miraculous accounts of travellers received, their descriptions of sea and land monsters, their relations of wonderful adventures, strange men, and uncouth manners? But if the spirit of religion join itself to the love of wonder, there is an end of common sense; and human testimony, in these circumstances, loses all pretensions to authority. A religionist may be an enthusiast, and imagine he sees what has no reality: he may know his narrative to be false, and yet persevere in it, with the best intentions in the world, for the sake of promoting so holy a cause: or even where this delusion has not place, vanity, excited by so strong a temptation, operates on him more powerfully than on the rest of mankind in any other circumstances; and self-interest with equal force. His auditors may not have, and commonly have not, sufficient judgement to canvass his evidence: what judgement they have, they renounce by principle, in these sublime and mysterious subjects: or if they were ever so willing to employ it, passion and a heated imagination disturb the regularity of its operations. Their credulity increases his impudence: and his impudence overpowers their credulity.

Eloquence, when at its highest pitch, leaves little room for reason or reflection; but addressing itself entirely to the fancy or the affections, captivates the willing hearers, and subdues their understanding. Happily, this pitch it seldom attains. But what a Tully or a Demosthenes could scarcely effect over a Roman or Athenian audience, every *Capuchin*, every itinerant or stationary teacher can perform over the generality of mankind, and in a higher degree, by touching such gross and vulgar passions.

The many instances of forged miracles, and prophecies, and supernatural events, which, in all ages, have either been detected by contrary evidence, or which detect themselves by their absurdity, prove sufficiently the strong propensity of mankind to the extraordinary and the marvellous, and ought reasonably to beget a suspicion against all relations of this kind. This is our natural way of thinking, even with regard to the most common and most credible events. For instance: There is no kind of report which rises so easily, and spreads so quickly, especially in country places and provincial towns, as those concerning marriages; insomuch that two young persons of equal condition never see each other twice, but the whole neighborhood immediately join them together. The pleasure of telling a piece of news so interesting, of propagating it, and of being the first reporters of it, spreads the intelligence. And this is so well known, that no man of sense gives attention to these reports, till he find them confirmed by some greater evidence. Do not the same passions, and others still stronger, incline the generality of mankind to believe and report, with the greatest vehemence and assurance, all religious miracles?

Thirdly. It forms a strong presumption against all supernatural and miraculous relations, that they are observed chiefly to abound among ignorant and barbarous nations; or if a civilized people has ever given admission to any of them, that people will be found to have received them from ignorant and barbarous ancestors, who transmitted them with that inviolable sanction and authority, which always attend received opinions. When we peruse the first histories of all nations, we are apt to imagine ourselves transported into some new world; where the whole frame of nature is disjointed, and every element performs its operations in a different manner, from what it does at present. Battles, revolutions, pestilence, famine and death, are never the effect of those natural causes, which we experience. Prodigies, omens, oracles, judgements, quite obscure the few natural events, that are intermingled with them. But as the former grow thinner every page, in proportion as we advance nearer the enlightened ages, we soon learn, that there is nothing mysterious or supernatural in the case, but that all proceeds from the usual propensity of mankind towards the marvellous, and that, though this inclination may at intervals receive a check from sense and learning, it can never be thoroughly extirpated from human nature.

It is strange, a judicious reader is apt to say, upon the perusal of these wonderful historians, *that such prodigious events never happen in our days.* But it is nothing strange, I hope, that men should lie in all ages. You must surely have seen instances enough of that frailty. You have yourself heard many such marvellous relations started, which, being treated with scorn by all the wise and judicious, have at least been abandoned even by the vulgar. Be assured, that those renowned lies, which have spread and flourished to such a monstrous height, arose from like beginnings; but being sown in a more proper soil, shot up at last into prodigies almost equal to those which they relate. . . .

I may add as a *fourth* reason, which diminishes the authority of prodigies, that there is no testimony for any, even those which have not been expressly detected, that is not opposed by an infinite number of witnesses; so that not only the miracle destroys the credit of testimony, but the testimony destroys itself. To make this the better understood, let us consider, that, in matters of religion, whatever is different is contrary; and that it is impossible the religions of ancient Rome, of Turkey, of Siam, and of China should, all of them, be established on any solid foundation. Every miracle, therefore, pretended to have been wrought in any of these religions (and all of them abound in miracles), as its direct scope is to establish the particular system to which it is attributed; so has it the same force, though more indirectly, to overthrow every other system. In destroying a rival system, it likewise destroys the credit of those miracles, on which that system was established; so that all the prodigies of different religions are to be regarded as contrary facts, and the evidences of these prodigies, whether weak or strong, as opposite to each other. According to this method of reasoning, when we believe any miracle of Mahomet or his successors, we have for our warrant the testimony of a few barbarous Arabians: And on the other hand, we are to regard the authority of Titus Livius, Plutarch, Tacitus, and, in short, of all the authors and witnesses, Grecian, Chinese, and Roman Catholic, who have related any miracle in their particular religion; I say, we are to regard their testimony in the same light as if they had mentioned that Mahometan miracle, and had in express terms contradicted it, with the same certainty as they have for the miracle they relate. This argument may appear over subtile and refined; but is not in reality different from the reasoning of a judge, who supposes, that the credit of two witnesses, maintaining a crime against any one, is destroyed by the testimony of two others, who affirm him to have been two hundred leagues distant, at the same instant when the crime is said to have been committed. . . .

40. Miracles

C. S. LEWIS

From the admission that God exists and is the author of Nature, it by no means follows that miracles must, or even can, occur. God Himself might be a being of such a kind that it was contrary to His character to work miracles. Or again, He might have made Nature the sort of thing that cannot be added to, subtracted from, or modified. The case against Miracles accordingly relies on two different grounds. You either think that the character of God excludes them or that the character of Nature excludes them. We will begin with the second which is the more popular ground. In this chapter I shall consider forms of it which are, in my opinion, very superficial—which might even be called misunderstandings or Red Herrings.

The first Red Herring is this. Any day you may hear a man (and not necessarily a disbeliever in God) say of some alleged miracle, "No. Of course I don't believe that. We know it is contrary to the laws of Nature. People could believe it in olden times because they didn't know the laws of Nature. We know now that it is a scientific impossibility."

By the "laws of Nature" such a man means, I think, the observed course of Nature. If he means anything more than that he is not the plain man I take him for but a philosophic Naturalist. . . . The man I have in view believes that mere experience (and specially those artificially contrived experiences which we call Experiments) can tell us what regularly happens in Nature. And he thinks that what we have discovered excludes the possibility of Miracle. This is a confusion of mind.

Granted that miracles *can* occur, it is, of course, for experience to say whether one has done so on any given occasion. But mere experience, even if prolonged for a million years, cannot tell us whether the thing is possible. Experiment finds out what regularly happens in Nature: the norm or rule to which she works. Those who believe in miracles are not denying that there is such a norm or rule: they are only saying that it can be suspended. A miracle is by definition an exception. How can the discovery of the rule tell you whether, granted a sufficient cause, the rule can be suspended? If we said that the rule was A, then experience might refute us by discovering that it was B. If we said that there was no rule, then experience might refute us by observing that there is. But we are saying neither of these things. We agree that there is a rule and that the rule is B. What has that got to do with the question whether the rule can be suspended? You reply, "But experience shows that it never has." We reply, "Even if that were so, this would not prove that it never can. But does experience show that it never has? The world is full of stories of people who say they have experienced miracles. Perhaps the stories are false: perhaps they are true. But before you can decide on that historical question, you must first . . . discover whether the thing is possible, and if possible, how probable."

The idea that the progress of science has somehow altered this question is closely bound up with the idea that people "in olden times" believed in them "because they didn't know the laws of Nature." Thus you will hear people say, "The early Christians believed that Christ was the son of a virgin, but we know that this is a scientific impossibility." Such people seem to have an idea that belief in miracles arose at a period when men were so ignorant of the course of nature that they did not perceive a miracle to be contrary to it. A moment's thought shows this to be nonsense: and the story of the Virgin Birth is a particularly striking example. When St. Joseph discovered that his fiancée was going to have a baby, he not unnaturally decided to repudiate her. Why? Because he knew just as well as any modern gynaecologist that in the ordinary course of nature women do not have babies unless they have lain with men. No doubt the modern gynaecologist knows several things about birth and begetting which St. Joseph did not know. But those things do not concern the main point—that a virgin birth is contrary to the course of nature. And St. Joseph obviously knew *that*. In any sense in which it is true to say now, "The thing is scientifically impossible," he would have said the same: the thing always was, and was always known to be, impossible *unless* the regular processes of nature were, in this particular case, being over-ruled or supplemented by something from beyond nature. When St. Joseph finally accepted the view that his fiancée's pregnancy was due not to unchastity but to a miracle, he accepted the miracle as something contrary to the known order of nature. All records of miracles teach the same thing. In such stories the miracles excite fear and wonder (this is what the very word *miracle* implies) among the spectators, and are taken as evidence of supernatural power. If they were not known to be contrary to the laws of nature how could they suggest the presence of the supernatural? How could they be surprising unless they were seen to be exceptions to the rules? And how can anything be seen to be an exception till the rules are known? If there ever were men who did not know the laws of nature *at all*, they would have no idea of a miracle and feel no particular interest in one if it were performed before them. Nothing can seem extraordinary until you have discovered what is ordinary. Belief in miracles, far from depending on an ignorance of the laws of nature, is only possible in so far as those laws are known. We have already seen that if you begin by ruling out the supernatural you will perceive no miracles. We must now add that you will equally perceive no miracles until you believe that nature works according to regular laws. If you have not yet noticed that the sun always rises in the East you will see nothing miraculous about his rising one morning in the West.

If the miracles were offered us as events that normally occurred, then the progress of science, whose business is to tell us what normally occurs, would render belief in them gradually harder and finally impossible. The progress of science has in just this way (and greatly to our benefit) made all sorts of things incredible which our ancestors believed; man-eating ants and gryphons in Scythia, men with one single gigantic foot, magnetic islands that draw all ships towards them, mermaids and fire-breathing dragons. But those things were never put forward as supernatural interruptions of the course of nature. They were put forward as items within her ordinary course—in fact as "science." Later and better science has therefore rightly removed them. Miracles are in a wholly different position. If there were fire-breathing dragons our big-game hunters would find them: but no one ever pretended that the Virgin Birth or Christ's walking on the water could be reckoned on to recur. When a thing professes from the very outset to be a unique invasion of Nature by something from outside, increasing knowledge of Nature can never make it either more or less credible than it was at the beginning. In this sense it is mere confusion of thought to suppose that advancing science has made it harder for us to accept miracles. We always knew they were contrary to the natural course of events; we know still that if there is something beyond Nature, they are possible. Those are the bare bones of the question; time and progress and science and civilisation have not altered them in the least. The grounds for belief and disbelief are the same to-day as they were two thousand—or ten thousand—years ago. If St. Joseph had lacked faith to trust God or humility to perceive the holiness of his spouse, he could have disbelieved in the miraculous origin of her Son as easily as any modern man; and any modern man who believes in God can accept the miracle as easily as St. Joseph did. You and I may not agree . . . as to whether miracles happen or not. But at least let us not talk nonsense. Let us not allow vague rhetoric about the march of science to fool us into supposing that the most complicated account of birth, in terms of genes and spermatozoa, leaves us any more convinced than we were before that *nature* does not send babies to young women who "know not a man."

The second Red Herring is this. Many people say, "They could believe in miracles in olden times because they had a false conception of the universe. They thought the Earth was the largest thing in it and Man the most important creature. It therefore seemed reasonable to suppose that the Creator was specially interested in Man and might even interrupt the course of Nature for his benefit. But now that we know the real immensity of the universe—now that we perceive our own planet and even the whole Solar System to be only a speck—it becomes ludicrous to believe in them any longer. We have discovered our insignificance and can no longer suppose that God is so drastically concerned in our petty affairs."

Whatever its value may be as an argument, it may be stated at once that this view is quite wrong about facts. The immensity of the universe is not a recent discovery. More than seventeen hundred years ago Ptolemy taught that in relation to the distance of the fixed stars the whole Earth must be regarded as a point with no magnitude. His astronomical system was universally accepted in the Dark and Middle Ages. The insignificance of Earth was as much a commonplace to Boethius, King Alfred, Dante, and Chaucer as it is to Mr. H. G. Wells or Professor [J. B. J.] Haldane. Statements to the contrary in modern books are due to ignorance.

The real question is quite different from what we commonly suppose. The real question is why the spatial insignificance of Earth, after being asserted by Christian philosophers, sung by Christian poets, and commented on by Christian moralists for some fifteen centuries, without the slightest suspicion that it conflicted with their theology, should suddenly in quite modern times have been set up as a stock argument against Christianity and enjoyed, in that capacity, a brilliant career. I will offer a guess at the answer to this question presently. For the moment, let us consider the strength of this stock argument.

When the doctor at a *post-mortem* looks at the dead man's organs and diagnoses poison he has a clear idea of the different state in which the organs would have been if the man had died a natural death. If from the vastness of the universe and the smallness of Earth we diagnose that Christianity is false we ought to have a clear idea of the sort of universe we should have expected if it were true. But have we? Whatever space may really be, it is certain that our perceptions make it appear three dimensional; and to a three-dimensional space no boundaries are conceivable. By the very forms of our perceptions therefore we must feel as if we lived somewhere in infinite space: and whatever size the Earth happens to be, it must of course be very small in comparison with infinity. And this infinite space must either be empty or contain bodies. If it were empty, or if it contained nothing but our own Sun, then that vast vacancy would certainly be used as an argument against the very existence of God. Why, it would be asked, should He create one speck and leave all the rest of space to nonentity? If, on the other hand, we find (as we actually do) countless bodies floating in space, they must be either habitable or uninhabitable. Now the odd thing is that *both* alternatives are equally used as objections to Christianity. If the universe is teeming with life other than ours, then this, we are told, makes it quite ridiculous to believe that God could be so concerned with the human race as to "come down from Heaven" and be made man for its redemption. If, on the other hand, our planet is really unique in harbouring organic life, then this is thought to prove that life is only an accidental byeproduct in the universe and so again to disprove our religion. It seems that we are hard to please. We treat God as the police treat a man when he is arrested; whatever He does will be used in evidence against Him. This kind of objection to the Christian faith is not really based on the observed nature of the actual universe at all. You can make it without waiting to find out what the universe is like, for it will fit any kind of universe we choose to imagine. The doctor here can diagnose poison without looking at the corpse for he has a theory of poison which he will maintain *whatever* the state of the organs turns out to be.

The reason why we cannot even imagine a universe so built as to exclude these objections is, perhaps, as follows. Man is a finite creature who has sense enough to know that he is finite: therefore, on any conceivable view, he finds himself dwarfed by reality as a whole. He is also a derivative being: the cause of his existence lies not in himself but (immediately) in his parents and (ultimately) *either* in the character of Nature as a whole *or* (if there is a God) in God. But there must be something, whether it be God or the totality of Nature, which exists in its own right or goes on "of its own accord": not as the product of causes beyond itself, but simply because it does. In the face of that something, whichever it turns out to be, man must feel his own derived existence to be unimportant, irrelevant, almost accidental. There is no question of religious people fancying that all exists for man and scientific people discovering that it does not. Whether the ultimate and inexplicable being—that which simply *is*—turns out to be God or "the whole show," of course it does not exist for us. On either view we are faced with something which existed before the human race appeared and will exist after the Earth has become uninhabitable; which is utterly independent of us though we are totally dependent on it; and which, through vast ranges of its being, has no relevance to our own hopes and fears. For no man was, I suppose, ever so mad as to think that man, or all creation, *filled* the Divine Mind; if we are a small thing to space and time, space and time are a much smaller thing to God. It is a profound mistake to imagine that Christianity ever intended to dissipate the bewilderment and even the terror, the sense of our own nothingness, which come upon us when we think about the nature of things. It comes to intensify them. Without such sensations there is no religion. Many a man, brought up in the glib profession of some shallow form of Christianity, who comes through reading Astronomy to realise for the first time how majestically indifferent most reality is to man, and who perhaps abandons his religion on that account, may at the moment be having his first genuinely religious experience.

Christianity does not involve the belief that all things were made for man. It does involve the belief that God loves man and for his sake became man and died. I have not yet succeeded in seeing how what we know (and have known since the days of Ptolemy) about the size of the universe affects the credibility of this doctrine one way or the other.

The sceptic asks how we can believe that God so "came down" to this one tiny planet. The question would be embarrassing if we knew (1) that there are rational creatures on any of the other bodies that float in space; (2) that they have, like us, fallen and need redemption; (3) that their redemption must be in the same mode as ours; (4) that redemption in this mode has been withheld from them. But we know none of them. The universe may be full of happy lives that never needed redemption. It may be full of lives that have been redeemed in modes suitable to their condition, of which we can form no conception. It may be full of lives that have been redeemed in the very same mode as our own. It may be full of things quite other than life in which God is interested though we are not.

If it is maintained that anything so small as the Earth must, in any event, be too unimportant to merit the love of the Creator, we reply that no Christian ever supposed we did merit it. Christ did not die for men because they were intrinsically worth dying for, but because He is intrinsically love, and therefore loves infinitely. And what, after all, does the *size* of a world or a creature tell us about its "importance" or value?

Faith and Reason

41. Essay concerning Human Understanding

JOHN LOCKE

OF FAITH AND REASON, AND THEIR DISTINCT PROVINCES

[I have] shown, 1. That we are of necessity ignorant, and want knowledge of all sorts, where we want ideas. 2. That we are ignorant, and want rational knowledge, where we want proofs. 3. That we want certain knowledge and certainty, as far as we want clear and determined specific ideas. 4. That we want probability to direct our assent in matters where we have neither knowledge of our own, nor testimony of other men, to bottom our reason upon.

From these things thus premised, I think we may come to lay down the measures and boundaries between faith and reason; the want whereof many possibly have been the cause, if not of great disorders, yet at least of great disputes, and perhaps mistakes in the world. For till it be resolved how far we are to be guided by reason, and how far by faith, we shall in vain dispute, and endeavour to convince one another in matters of religion.

I find every sect, as far as reason will help them, make use of it gladly: and where it fails them they cry out, it is matter of faith, and above reason. And I do not see how they can argue with any one, or ever convince a gainsayer who makes use of the same plea, without setting down strict boundaries between faith and reason; which ought to be the first point established in all questions where faith has any thing to do.

Reason therefore here, as contradistinguished to faith, I take to be the discovery of the certainty or probability of such propositions or truths, which the mind arrives at by deduction made from such ideas which it has got by the use of its natural faculties, viz. by sensation or reflection.

Faith, on the other side, is the assent to any proposition, not thus made out by the deductions of reason; but upon the credit of the proposer, as coming from God, in some extraordinary way of communication. This way of discovering truths to men we call revelation.

First then I say, that no man inspired by God can by any revelation communicate to others any new simple ideas, which they had not before from sensation or reflection. For whatsoever impressions he himself may have from the immediate hand of God, this revelation, if it be of new simple ideas, cannot be conveyed to another, either by words or any other signs. Because words, by their immediate operation on us, cause no other ideas but of their natural sounds; and it is by the custom of using them for signs, that they excite and revive in our minds latent ideas; but yet only such ideas as were there before. For words seen or heard recall to our thoughts those ideas only which to us they have been wont to be signs of; but cannot introduce any perfectly new, and formerly unknown simple ideas. The same holds in all other signs, which cannot signify to us things of which we have before never had any idea at all.

Thus whatever things were discovered to St. Paul, when he was rapt up into the third heaven, whatever new ideas his mind there received, all the description he can make to others of that place is only this, that there are such things, "as eye hath not seen, nor ear heard, nor hath it entered into the heart of man to conceive." And supposing God should discover to any one, supernaturally, a species of creatures inhabiting, for example, Jupiter or Saturn, (for that it is possible there may be such nobody can deny) which had six senses; and imprint on his mind the ideas conveyed to theirs by that sixth sense; he could no more, by words, produce in the minds of other men those ideas, imprinted by that sixth sense, than one of us could convey the idea of any colour by the sounds of words into a man, who, having the other four senses perfect, had always totally wanted the fifth of seeing. For our simple ideas then, which are the foundation and sole matter of all our notions and knowledge, we must depend wholly on our reason, I mean our natural faculties; and can by no means receive them, or any of them, from traditional revelation; I say, traditional revelation, in distinction to original revelation. By the one, I mean that first impression, which is made immediately by God, on the mind of any man, to which we cannot set any bounds; and by the other, those impressions delivered over to others in words, and the ordinary ways of conveying our conceptions one to another.

Secondly, I say, that the same truths may be discovered, and conveyed down from revelation, which are discoverable to us by reason, and by those ideas we naturally may have. So God might, by revelation, discover the truth of any proposition in Euclid; as well as men, by the natural use of their faculties, come to make the discovery themselves. In all things of this kind, there is little need or use of revelation, God having furnished us with natural and surer means to arrive at the knowledge of them. For whatsoever truth we come to the clear discovery of, from the knowledge and contemplation of our own ideas, will always be certainer to us than those which are conveyed to us by traditional revelation. For the knowledge we have, that this revelation came at first from God, can never be so sure, as the knowledge we have from the clear and distinct perception of the agreement or disagreement of our own ideas; *v. g.* if it were revealed some ages since, that the three angles of a triangle were equal to two right ones, I might assent to the truth of that proposition, upon the credit of the tradition, that it was revealed; but that would never amount to so great a certainty as the knowledge of it, upon the comparing and measuring my own ideas of two right angles, and the three angles of a triangle. The like holds in matter of fact, knowable by our senses; *v. g.* the history of the deluge is conveyed to us by writings which had their original from revelation: and yet nobody, I think, will say he has as certain and clear a knowledge of the flood as Noah that saw it; or that he himself would have had, had he then been alive and seen it. For he has no greater assurance than that of his senses that it is writ in the book supposed writ by Moses inspired; but he has not so great an assurance that Moses writ that book as if he had seen Moses write it. So that the assurance of its being a revelation is less still than the assurance of his senses.

In propositions then, whose certainty is built upon the clear perception of the agreement or disagreement of our ideas, attained either by immediate intuition, as in self-evident propositions, or by evident deductions of reason in demonstrations, we need not the assistance of revelation, as necessary to gain our assent, and introduce them into our minds. Because the natural ways of knowledge could settle them there, or had done it already; which is the greatest assurance we can possibly have of any thing, unless where God immediately reveals it to us: and there too our assurance can be no greater than our knowledge is, that it is a revelation from God. But yet nothing, I think, can, under that title, shake or over-rule plain knowledge; or rationally prevail with any man to admit it for true, in a direct contradiction to the clear evidence of his own understanding. For since no evidence of our faculties, by which we receive such revelations, can exceed, if equal, the certainty of our intuitive knowledge, we can never receive for a truth any thing that is directly contrary to our clear and distinct knowledge: *v. g.* the ideas of one body, and one place, do so clearly agree, and the mind has so evident a perception of their agreement, that we can never assent to a proposition, that affirms the same body to be in two distant places at once, however it should pretend to the authority of a divine revelation: since the evidence, first, that we deceive not ourselves, in ascribing it to God; secondly, that we understand it right; can never be so great as the evidence of our own intuitive knowledge, whereby we discern it impossible for the same body to be in two places at once. And therefore no proposition can be received for divine revelation, or obtain the assent due to all such, if it be contradictory to our clear intuitive knowledge. Because this would be to subvert the principles and foundations of all knowledge, evidence, and assent whatsoever: and there would be left no difference between truth and falsehood, no measures of credible and incredible in the world, if doubtful propositions shall take place before self-evident, and what we certainly know give way to what we may possibly be mistaken in. In propositions therefore contrary to the clear perception of the agreement or disagreement of any of our ideas, it will be in vain to urge them as matters of faith. They cannot move our assent, under that or any other title whatsoever. For faith can never convince us of any thing that contradicts our knowledge. Because though faith be founded on the testimony of God (who cannot lie) revealing any proposition to us; yet we cannot have an assurance of the truth of its being a divine revelation greater than our own knowledge: since the whole strength of the certainty depends upon our knowledge that God revealed it;

which in this case, where the proposition supposed revealed contradicts our knowledge or reason, will always have this objection hanging to it, viz. that we cannot tell how to conceive that to come from God, the bountiful Author of our being, which, if received for true, must overturn all the principles and foundations of knowledge he has given us; render all our faculties useless; wholly destroy the most excellent part of his workmanship, our understandings; and put a man in a condition, wherein he will have less light, less conduct, than the beast that perisheth. For if the mind of man can never have a clearer (and perhaps not so clear) evidence of any thing to be a divine revelation, as it has of the principles of its own reason, it can never have a ground to quit the clear evidence of its reason, to give a place to a proposition, whose revelation has not a greater evidence than those principles have.

Thus far a man has use of reason, and ought to hearken to it, even in immediate and original revelation, where it is supposed to be made to himself: but to all those who pretend not to immediate revelation, but are required to pay obedience, and to receive the truths revealed to others, which by the tradition of writings, or word of mouth, are conveyed down to them; reason has a great deal more to do, and is that only which can induce us to receive them. For matter of faith being only divine revelation, and nothing else; faith, as we use the word, (called commonly divine faith) has to do with no propositions but those which are supposed to be divinely revealed. So that I do not see how those who make revelation alone the sole object of faith, can say, that it is a matter of faith, and not of reason, to believe that such or such a proposition, to be found in such or such a book, is of divine inspiration; unless it be revealed, that that proposition, or all in that book, was communicated by divine inspiration. Without such a revelation, the believing or not believing that proposition or book to be of divine authority can never be matter of faith, but matter of reason; and such as I must come to an assent to only by the use of my reason, which can never require or enable me to believe that which is contrary to itself: it being impossible for reason ever to procure any assent to that, which to itself appears unreasonable.

In all things, therefore, where we have clear evidence from our ideas, and those principles of knowledge I have above-mentioned, reason is the proper judge; and revelation, though it may in consenting with it confirm its dictates, yet cannot in such cases invalidate its decrees: nor can we be obliged, where we have the clear and evident sentence of reason, to quit it for the contrary opinion, under a pretence that it is matter of faith; which can have no authority against the plain and clear dictates of reason.

But, thirdly, there being many things, wherein we have very imperfect notions, or none at all; and other things, of whose parts, present, or future existence, by the natural use of our faculties, we can have no knowledge at all; these, as being beyond the discovery of our natural faculties, and above reason are, when revealed, the proper matter of faith. Thus, that part of the angels rebelled against God, and thereby lost their first happy state; and that the dead shall rise, and live again: these, and the like, being beyond the discovery of reason, are purely matters of faith with which reason has directly nothing to do.

But since God in giving us the light of reason has not thereby tied up his own hands from affording us, when he thinks fit, the light of revelation in any of those matters wherein our natural faculties are able to give a probable determination; revelation, where God has been pleased to give it, must carry it against the probable conjectures of reason. Because the mind not being certain of the truth of that it does not evidently know, but only yielding to the probability that appears in it, is bound to give up its assent to such a testimony; which, it is satisfied, comes from one who cannot err; and will not deceive. But yet it still belongs to reason to judge of the truth of its being a revelation, and of the signification of the words wherein it is delivered. Indeed, if any thing shall be thought revelation which is contrary to the plain principles of reason, and the evident knowledge the mind has of its own clear and distinct ideas; there reason must be hearkened to, as to a matter within its province: since a man can never have so certain a knowledge, that a proposition, which contradicts the clear principles and evidence of his own knowledge, was divinely revealed, or that he understands the words rightly wherein it is delivered; as he has, that the contrary is true: and so is bound to consider and judge of it as a matter of reason, and not swallow it, without examination, as a matter of faith.

First, whatever proposition is revealed, of whose truth our mind, by its natural faculties and notions, cannot judge; that is purely matter of faith, and above reason.

Secondly, all propositions, whereof the mind, by the use of its natural faculties, can come to determine and judge from naturally acquired ideas, are matter of reason; with this difference still, that in those concerning which it has but an uncertain evidence, and so is persuaded of their truth only upon probable grounds, which still admit a possibility of the contrary to be true, without doing violence to the certain evidence of its own knowledge, and overturning the principles of its own reason; in such probable propositions, I say, an evident revelation ought to determine our assent even against probability. For where the principles of reason have not evidenced a proposition to be certainly true or false, there clear revelation, as another principle of truth, and ground of assent, may determine: and so it may be matter of faith, and be also above reason. Because reason, in that particular matter, being able to reach no higher than probability, faith gave the determination, where reason came short; and revelation discovered on which side the truth lay.

Thus far the dominion of faith reaches, and that without any violence or hindrance to reason; which is not injured or disturbed, but assisted and improved, by new discoveries of truth coming from the eternal fountain of all knowledge. Whatever God hath revealed, is certainly true; no doubt can be made of it. This is the proper object of faith; but whether it be a divine revelation or no, reason must judge; which can never permit the mind to reject a greater evidence to embrace what is less evident, nor allow it to entertain probability in opposition to knowledge and certainty. There can be no evidence that any traditional revelation is of divine original, in the words we receive it, and in the sense we understand it, so clear and so certain as that of the principles of reason: and therefore nothing that is contrary to, and inconsistent with, the clear and self-evident dictates of reason, has a right to be urged or assented to as a matter of faith, wherein reason hath nothing to do. Whatsoever is divine revelation ought to over-rule all our opinions, prejudices, and interest, and hath a right to be received with full assent. Such a submission as this, of our reason to faith, takes not away the landmarks of knowledge; this shakes not the foundations of reason, but leaves us that use of our faculties for which they were given us.

If the provinces of faith and reason are not kept distinct by these boundaries, there will, in matters of religion, be no room for reason at all; and those extravagant opinions and ceremonies that are to be found in the several religions of the world will not deserve to be blamed. For to this crying up of faith, in opposition to reason, we may, I think, in good measure ascribe those absurdities that fill almost all the religions which possess and divide mankind. For men having been principled with an opinion, that they must not consult reason in the things of religion, however apparently contradictory to common sense, and the very principles of all their knowledge, have let loose their fancies and natural superstition; and have been by them led into so strange opinions, and extravagant practices in religion, that a considerate man cannot but stand amazed at their follies, and judge them so far from being acceptable to the great and wise God, that he cannot avoid thinking them ridiculous, and offensive to a sober good man. So that, in effect, religion, which should most distinguish us from beasts, and ought most peculiarly to elevate us, as rational creatures, above brutes, is that wherein men often appear most irrational and more senseless than beasts themselves. "Credo, quia impossibile est"; I believe, because it is impossible, might in a good man pass for a sally of zeal; but would prove a very ill rule for men to choose their opinions or religion by.

42. Dynamics of Faith

PAUL TILLICH

WHAT FAITH IS

I. Faith as Ultimate Concern

Faith is the state of being ultimately concerned: the dynamics of faith are the dynamics of man's ultimate concern. Man, like every living being, is concerned about many things, above all about those which condition his very existence, such as food and shelter. But man, in contrast to other living beings, has spiritual concerns—cognitive, aesthetic, social, political. Some of them are urgent, often extremely urgent, and each of them as well as the vital concerns can claim ultimacy for a human life or the life of a social group. If it claims ultimacy it demands the total surrender of him who accepts this claim, and it promises total fulfillment even if all other claims have to be subjected to it or rejected in its name. If a national group makes the life and growth of the nation its ultimate concern, it demands that all other concerns, economic well-being, health and life, family, aesthetic and cognitive truth, justice and humanity, be sacrificed. The extreme nationalisms of our century are laboratories for the study of what ultimate concern means in all aspects of human existence, including the smallest concern of one's daily life. Everything is centered in the only god, the nation—a god who certainly proves to be a demon, but who shows clearly the unconditional character of an ultimate concern.

But it is not only the unconditional demand made by that which is one's ultimate concern, it is also the promise of ultimate fulfillment which is accepted in the act of faith. The content of this promise is not necessarily defined. It can be expressed in indefinite symbols or in concrete symbols which cannot be taken literally, like the "greatness" of one's nation in which one participates even if one has died for it, or the conquest of mankind by the "saving race," etc. In each of these cases it is "ultimate fulfillment" that is promised, and it is exclusion from such fulfillment which is threatened if the unconditional demand is not obeyed.

An example—and more than an example—is the faith manifest in the religion of the Old Testament. It also has the character of ultimate concern in demand, threat and promise. The content of this concern is not the nation— although Jewish nationalism has sometimes tried to distort it into that—but the content is the God of justice, who, because he represents justice for everybody and every nation, is called the universal God, the God of the universe. He is the ultimate concern of every pious Jew, and therefore in his name the great commandment is given: "You shall love the Lord your God with all your heart, and with all your soul, and with all your might" (Deut 6:5). This is what ultimate concern means and from these words the term "ultimate concern" is derived. They state unambiguously the character of genuine faith, the demand of total surrender to the subject of ultimate concern. The Old Testament is full of commands which make the nature of this surrender concrete, and it is full of promises and threats in relation to it. Here also are the promises of symbolic indefiniteness, although they center around fulfillment of the national and individual life, and the threat is the exclusion from such fulfillment through national extinction and individual catastrophe. Faith, for the men of the Old Testament, is the state of being ultimately and unconditionally concerned about Jahweh and about what he represents in demand, threat and promise.

Another example—almost a counter-example, yet nevertheless equally revealing—is the ultimate concern with "success" and with social standing and economic power. It is the god of many people in the highly competitive Western culture and it does what every ultimate concern must do: it demands unconditional surrender to its laws even if the price is the sacrifice of genuine human relations, personal conviction, and creative *eros*. Its threat is social and economic defeat, and its promise—indefinite as all such promises—the fulfillment of one's being. It is the breakdown of this kind of faith which characterizes and makes religiously important most contemporary literature. Not false calculations but a misplaced faith is revealed in novels like *Point of No Return*. When fulfilled, the promise of this faith proves to be empty.

Faith is the state of being ultimately concerned. The content matters infinitely for the life of the believer, but it does not matter for the formal definition of faith. And this is the first step we have to make in order to understand the dynamics of faith.

2.   Faith as a Centered Act

Faith as ultimate concern is an act of the total personality. It happens in the center of the personal life and includes all its elements. Faith is the most centered act of the human mind. It is not a movement of a special section or a special function of man's total being. They all are united in the act of faith. But faith is not the sum total of their impacts. It transcends every special impact as well as the totality of them and it has itself a decisive impact on each of them.

Since faith is an act of the personality as a whole, it participates in the dynamics of personal life. These dynamics have been described in many ways, especially in the recent developments of analytic psychology. Thinking in polarities, their tensions and their possible conflicts, is a common characteristic of most of them. This makes the psychology of personality highly dynamic and requires a dynamic theory of faith as the most personal of all personal acts. The first and decisive polarity in analytic psychology is that between the so-called unconscious and the conscious. Faith as an act of the total personality is not imaginable without the participation of the unconscious elements in the personality structure. They are always present and decide largely about the content of faith. But, on the other hand, faith is a conscious act and the unconscious elements participate in the creation of faith only if they are taken into the personal center which transcends each of them. If this does not happen, if unconscious forces determine the mental status without a centered act, faith does not occur, and compulsions take its place. For faith is a matter of freedom. Freedom is nothing more than the possibility of centered personal acts. The frequent discussion in which faith and freedom are contrasted could be helped by the insight that faith is a free, namely, centered act of the personality. In this respect freedom and faith are identical.

Also important for the understanding of faith is the polarity between what Freud and his school call ego and superego. The concept of the superego is quite ambiguous. On the one hand, it is the basis of all cultural life because it restricts the uninhibited actualization of the always-driving libido; on the other hand, it cuts off man's vital forces, and produces disgust about the whole system of cultural restrictions, and brings about a neurotic state of mind. From this point of view, the symbols of faith are considered to be expressions of the superego or, more concretely, to be an expression of the father image which gives content to the superego. Responsible for this inadequate theory of the superego is Freud's naturalistic negation of norms and principles. If the superego is not established through valid principles, it becomes a suppressive tyrant. But real faith, even if it uses the father image for its expression, transforms this image into a principle of truth and justice to be defended even against the "father." Faith and culture can be affirmed only if the superego represents the norms and principles of reality.

This leads to the question of how faith as a personal, centered act is related to the rational structure of man's personality which is manifest in his meaningful language, in his ability to know the true and to do the good, in his sense of beauty and justice. All this, and not only his possibility to analyze, to calculate and to argue, makes him a rational being. But in spite of this larger concept of reason we must deny that man's essential nature is identical with the rational character of his mind. Man is able to decide for or against reason, he is able to create beyond reason or to destroy below reason. This power is the power of his self, the center of self-relatedness in which all elements of his being are united. Faith is not an act of any of his rational functions, as it is not an act of the unconscious, but it is an act in which both the rational and the nonrational elements of his being are transcended.

Faith as the embracing and centered act of the personality is "ecstatic." It transcends both the drives of the nonrational unconscious and the structures of the rational conscious. It transcends them, but it does not destroy them. The ecstatic character of faith does not exclude its rational character although it is not identical with it, and it includes nonrational strivings without being identical with them. In the ecstasy of faith there is an awareness of truth and of ethical value; there are also past loves and hates, conflicts and reunions, individual and collective influences. "Ecstasy" means "standing outside of oneself"—without ceasing to be oneself—with all the elements which are united in the personal center.

A further polarity in these elements, relevant for the understanding of faith, is the tension between the cognitive function of man's personal life, on the one hand, and emotion and will, on the other hand. . . . At this point it must be stated as sharply and insistently as possible that in every act of faith there is cognitive affirmation, not as the result of an independent process of inquiry but as an inseparable element in a total act of acceptance and surrender. This also excludes the idea that faith is the result of an independent act of "will to believe." There is certainly affirmation by the will of what concerns one ultimately, but faith is not a creation of the will. In the ecstasy of faith the will to accept and to surrender is an element, but not the cause. And this is true also of feeling. Faith is not an emotional outburst: this is not the meaning of ecstasy. Certainly, emotion is in it, as in every act of man's spiritual life. But emotion does not produce faith. Faith has a cognitive content and is an act of the will. It is the unity of every element in the centered self. Of course, the unity of all elements in the act of faith does not prevent one or the other element from dominating in a special form of faith. It dominates the character of faith but it does not create the act of faith.

This also answers the question of a possible psychology of faith. Everything that happens in man's personal being can become an object of psychology. And it is rather important for both the philosopher of religion and the practical minister to know how the act of faith is embedded in the totality of psychological processes. But in contrast to this justified and desirable form of a psychology of faith there is another one which tries to derive faith from something that is not faith but is most frequently fear. The presupposition of this method is that fear or something else from which faith is derived is more original and basic than faith. But this presupposition cannot be proved. On the contrary, one can prove that in the scientific method which leads to such consequences faith is already effective.

Faith precedes all attempts to derive it from something else, because these attempts are themselves based on faith.

3.   The Source of Faith

We have described the act of faith and its relation to the dynamics of personality. Faith is a total and centered act of the personal self, the act of unconditional, infinite and ultimate concern. The question now arises: what is the source of this all-embracing and all-transcending concern? The word "concern" points to two sides of a relationship, the relation between the one who is concerned and his concern. In both respects we have to imagine man's situation in itself and in his world. The reality of man's ultimate concern reveals something about his being, namely, that he is able to transcend the flux of relative and transitory experiences of his ordinary life. Man's experiences, feelings, thoughts are conditioned and finite. They not only come and go, but their content is of finite and conditional concern—unless they are elevated to unconditional validity. But this presupposes the general possibility of doing so; it presupposes the element of infinity in man. Man is able to understand in an immediate personal and central act the meaning of the ultimate, the unconditional, the absolute, the infinite. This alone makes faith a human potentiality.

Human potentialities are powers that drive toward actualization. Man is driven toward faith by his awareness of the infinite to which he belongs, but which he does not own like a possession. This is in abstract terms what concretely appears as the "restlessness of the heart" within the flux of life.

The unconditional concern which is faith is the concern about the unconditional. The infinite passion, as faith has been described, is the passion for the infinite. Or, to use our first term, the ultimate concern is concern about what is experienced as ultimate. In this way we have turned from the subjective meaning of faith as a centered act of the personality to its objective meaning, to what is meant in the act of faith. It would not help at this point of our analysis to call that which is meant in the act of faith "God" or "a god." For at this step we ask: What in the idea of God constitutes divinity? The answer is: It is the element of the unconditional and of ultimacy. This carries the quality of divinity. If this is seen, one can understand why almost everything "in heaven and on earth" has received ultimacy in the history of human religion. But we also can understand that a critical principle was and is at work in man's religious consciousness, namely, that which is really ultimate over against what claims to be ultimate but is only preliminary, transitory, finite.

The term "ultimate concern" unites the subjective and the objective side of the act of faith—the *fides qua creditur* (the faith through which one believes) and the *fides quae creditur* (the faith which is believed). The first is the classical term for the centered act of the personality, the ultimate concern. The second is the classical term for that toward which this act is directed, the ultimate itself, expressed in symbols of the divine. This distinction is very important, but not ultimately so, for the one side cannot be without the other. There is no faith without a content toward which it is directed. There is always something meant in the act of faith. And there is no way of having the content of faith except in the act of faith. All speaking about divine matters which is not done in the state of ultimate concern is meaningless. Because that which is meant in the act of faith cannot be approached in any other way than through an act of faith.

In terms like ultimate, unconditional, infinite, absolute, the difference between subjectivity and objectivity is overcome. The ultimate of the act of faith and the ultimate that is meant in the act of faith are one and the same. This is symbolically expressed by the mystics when they say that their knowledge of God is the knowledge God has of himself; and it is expressed by Paul when he says (I Cor. 13) that he will know as he is known, namely, by God. God never can be object without being at the same time subject. Even a successful prayer is, according to Paul (Rom. 8), not possible without God as Spirit praying within us. The same experience expressed in abstract language is the disappearance of the ordinary subject-object scheme in the experience of the ultimate, the unconditional. In the act of faith that which is the source of this act is present beyond the cleavage of subject and object. It is present as both and beyond both.

This character of faith gives an additional criterion for distinguishing true and false ultimacy. The finite which claims infinity without having it (as, e.g., a nation or success) is not able to transcend the subject-object scheme. It remains an object which the believer looks at as a subject. He can approach it with ordinary knowledge and subject it to ordinary handling. There are, of course, many degrees in the endless realm of false ultimacies. The nation is nearer to true ultimacy than is success. Nationalistic ecstasy can produce a state in which the subject is almost swallowed by the object. But after a period the subject emerges again, disappointed radically and totally, and by looking at the nation in a skeptical and calculating way does injustice even to its justified claims. The more idolatrous a faith the less it is able to overcome the cleavage between subject and object. For that is the difference between true and idolatrous faith. In true faith the ultimate concern is a concern about the truly ultimate; while in idolatrous faith preliminary, finite realities are elevated to the rank of ultimacy. The inescapable consequence of idolatrous faith is "existential disappointment," a disappointment which penetrates into the very existence of man! This is the dynamics of idolatrous faith that it is faith, and as such, the centered act of a personality that the centering point is something which is more or less on the periphery; and that, therefore, the act of faith leads to a loss of the center and to a disruption of the personality. The ecstatic character of even an idolatrous faith can hide this consequence only for a certain time. But finally it breaks into the open.

Bibliography

Abraham, William J. *Divine Revelation and the Limits of Historical Criticism.* New York: Oxford University Press, 1982.

Abraham, William J., and Steven W. Holtzer. *The Rationality of Religious Belief: Essays in Honor of Basil Mitchell.* Oxford: Clarendon Press; New York: Oxford University Press, 1987.

Ahern, Dennis M. "Miracles and Physical Impossibility." *Canadian Journal of Philosophy,* 7 (1977): 71–79.

Alston, William P. "Divine–Human Dialogue and the Nature of God." *Faith and Philosophy* 2 (1985): 5–20.

Aquinas, Thomas. *On the Truth of the Catholic Faith,* vol. 1. Garden City, N.Y.: Doubleday Image, 1955.

Audi, Robert, and William J. Wainwright, eds. *Rationality, Religious Belief, and Moral Commitment: New Essays in the Philosophy of Religion.* Ithaca, N.Y.: Cornell University Press, 1986.

Baillie, John. *The Idea of Revelation in Recent Thought.* New York: Columbia University Press, 1956.

Banner, Michael C. *The Justification of Science and the Rationality of Religious Belief.* Oxford: Clarendon Press; New York: Oxford University Press, 1990.

Basinger, David, and Randall Basinger. *Philosophy and Miracle: The Contemporary Debate.* Lewiston, N.Y.: Mellen Press, 1986.

Bennett, Jane. *Unthinking Faith and Enlightenment: Nature and the State in a Post-Hegelian Era.* New York: New York University Press, 1987.

Blanshard, Brand. "Catholicism and Revelation." *Humanist* 32 (1972): 25–26.

———. *Reason and Belief.* London: Allen and Unwin, 1974.

Brunner, Emil. *Revelation and Reason.* Philadelphia: Westminster Press, 1946.

Clark, Stephen R. L. *A Parliament of Souls.* Oxford: Clarendon Press; New York: Oxford University Press, 1990.

Collier, John. "Against Miracles." *Dialogue* 25 (Summer 1986): 349–52.

Cragg, Kenneth. *Alive to God, Muslim and Christian Prayer.* London: Oxford University Press, 1970.

Crossley, John P. "Theological Ethics and the Naturalistic Fallacy." *Journal of Religious Ethics* 6 (Spring 1978): 121–34.

Crosson, Frederick, ed. *The Autonomy of Religious Belief.* Notre Dame Ind.: University of Notre Dame Press, 1981.

Dalferth, Ingolf U. *Theology and Philosophy.* New York: Blackwell, 1988.

DeBurgh, W. G. *The Life of Reason.* London: MacDonald and Evans, 1949.

Delaney, C. F., ed. *Rationality and Religious Belief.* Notre Dame, Ind.: University of Notre Dame Press, 1978.

Dodd, C. H. *The Authority of the Bible.* Glasgow: Collins, 1978.

Farmer, H. H. *The World and God.* London: Nisbet, 1942.

Flew, Antony. *God and Philosophy.* London: Hutchinson, 1966.

Fitzer, Joseph, ed. *Romance and the Rock: Nineteenth-Century Catholics on Faith and Reason.* Minneapolis, Minn.: Fortress Press, 1989.

Frank, Erick. *Philosophical Understanding and Religious Truth.* New York: Oxford University Press, 1966.

Garavaso, Pieranna. "Taylor's Defenses of Two Traditional Arguments for the Existence of God." *Sophia* 29 (1990): 31–41.

Geisler, Norman L. *Miracles and Modern Thought.* Grand Rapids, Mich.: Zondervan, 1982.

Gill, Jerry H. *The Possibility of Religious Knowledge.* Grand Rapids, Mich.: Eerdmans, 1971.

Grant, Robert McQueen. *Miracle and Natural Law in Graeco-Roman and Early Christian Thought.* Amsterdam: North Holland, 1952.

Green, Ronald Michael. *Religion and Moral Reason: A New Method for Comparative Study.* New York: Oxford University Press, 1988.

Hegel, George Wilhelm Friedrich. *Faith and Knowledge.* Albany, N.Y.: State University of New York Press, 1977.

Helm, Paul, ed. *The Divine Command Theory of Ethics.* Oxford: Oxford University Press, 1979.

Hoffman, Joshua. "On Petitionary Prayer." *Faith and Philosophy* 2 (1985): 30–37.

Holland, R. F. "The Miraculous." *American Philosophical Quarterly* 2 (1965): 43–51.

Hooykaas, Reijer. *Natural Law and Divine Miracle.* Leiden, The Netherlands: Brill, 1959.

Jaeschke, Walter. *Reason in Religion: The Foundations of Hegel's Philosophy of Religion.* Berkeley: University of California Press, 1990.

Jaspers, Karl. *Philosophical Faith and Revelation.* New York: Harper and Row, 1967.

Kellenberger, J. *Religious Discovery, Faith and Knowledge.* Englewood Cliffs, N.J.: Prentice-Hall, 1972.

———. "Miracles." *International Journal of Philosophy and Religion* 10 (1979): 145–62.

Kenney, Anthony John Patrick. *Faith and Reason.* New York: Columbia University Press, 1983.

Kenny, Anthony. *The God of the Philosophers.* Oxford: Clarendon Press, 1979.

Kroner, Richard. *Between Faith and Thought: Reflections and Suggestions.* New York: Oxford University Press, 1966.

Lewis, C. S. *Miracles.* New York: Macmillan, 1947.

Lewis, H. D. "Revelation and Reason." *Hibbert Journal* 43: 194–97.

Lieb, Irwin C. *The Four Faces of Man: A Philosophical Study of Practice, Reason, Art, and Religion.* Philadelphia: University of Pennsylvania Press, 1971.

Lowe, E. J. "Miracles and Laws of Nature." *Religious Studies* 23 (1987): 263–78.

Mavrodes, George. "Miracles and the Laws of Nature." *Faith and Philosophy* 2 (1985): 333–46.

———. *Revelation in Religious Belief.* Philadelphia: Temple University Press, 1988.

———. "Revelation and the Bible." *Faith and Philosophy* 6 (1989): 398–411.

Mayberry, Thomas C. "God and Moral Authority." *Monist* 54 (1970): 106–23.

Miles, Thomas Richard. *Religion and the Scientific Outlook.* London: Allen and Unwin, 1959.

Miller, Ed L. *Classical Statements of Faith and Reason.* New York: Random House, 1970.

Mitchell, Basil. *Faith and Logic; Oxford Essays in Philosophical Theology.* London: Allen and Unwin, 1957.

———. *The Justification of Religious Belief.* London: Macmillan, 1973.

———. *Morality: Religious and Secular.* Oxford: Clarendon Press, 1980.

Moreno, Francisco Josie. *Between Faith and Reason: An Approach to Individual and Social Psychology.* New York: New York University Press, 1977.

Morrison, Roy D. "Theology and Ethics: The Perspective of Black Philosophy." *Philosophy of Religion and Theory* (1975): 123–38.

Nash, Ronald H. *Faith and Reason: Searching for a Rational Faith.* Grand Rapids, Mich.: Academic Books, 1988.

Nielsen, Kai. "On the Logic of 'Revelation'." *Sophia* 9 (1970): 8–13.

———. *Ethics without God.* London: Pemberton Books, 1973.

Nowell-Smith, Patrick. "Miracles—The Philosophical Approach." *Hibbert Journal* 48 354–60.

Outka, Gene, and J. P. Reeder, eds. *Religion and Morality: A Collection of Essays.* New York: Anchor Books, 1973.

Owen, Huw Parri. *The Moral Argument for Christian Theism.* London: Allen and Unwin, 1965.

Penelhum, Terence. *God and Skepticism: A Study in Skepticism and Fideism.* Dordrecht, The Netherlands: Reidel, 1983.

Phillips, D. Z. *The Concept of Prayer.* London: Routledge and Kegan Paul, 1965.

Pinnock, Clark H. *Biblical Revelation, the Foundation of Christian Theology.* Chicago: Moody Press, 1971.

Plantinga, Alvin. *Faith and Philosophy, Philosophical Studies in Religion and Ethics.* Grand Rapids, Mich.: Eerdmans, 1964.

Plantinga, Alvin, and Nicholas Wolterstorff, eds. *Faith and Rationality: Reason and Belief in God.* Notre Dame, Ind.: University of Notre Dame Press, 1983.

Purtill, Richard L. *C. S. Lewis's Case for the Christian Faith.* San Francisco: Harper and Row, 1981.

Quinn, Philip L. *Divine Commands and Moral Requirements.* Oxford: Clarendon Press, 1978.

Ranganathananda, Swami. *Science and Religion.* Calcutta: Advaita Ashrama, 1978.

Ro, Young-Chan. "The Place of Ethics in the Christian Tradition and the Confucian Tradition: A Methodological Prolegomenon." *Religious Studies* 22 (1986): 51–62.

Roberts, James Deotis. *Faith and Reason.* Boston: Christopher, 1962.

Ross, Steven L. "Another Look at God and Morality." *Ethics* 94 (1983): 87–98.

Rust, Eric Charles. *Science and Faith: Towards a Theological Understanding of Nature.* New York: Oxford University Press, 1967.

Schwartz, Charles, and Bertie G. Schwartz. *Faith through Reason; A Modern Interpretation of Judaism.* New York: Macmillan, 1946.

Sheperd, John J. "The Concept of Revelation." *Religious Studies* 16 (1980): 425–37.

Sherry, Patrick, ed. *Philosophers on Religion: A Historical Reader.* London: Chapman, 1987.

Shook, Glenn Alfred. *Mysticism, Science and Revelation.* Oxford: Ronald, 1953.

Smart, Ninian. *Philosophers and Religious Truth.* London: SCM, 1964.

Smith, George H. *Atheism: The Case against God.* Buffalo, N.Y.: Prometheus Books, 1979.

Smith, Steven G. "The Evidence of God Having Spoken." *Faith and Philosophy* 3 (1986): 68–77.

Sokolowski, Robert. *The God of Faith and Reason: Foundations of Christian Theology.* Notre Dame, Ind.: University of Notre Dame Press, 1982.

Stanesby, Derek. *Science, Reason and Religion.* London: Croom Helm, 1985.

Stein, Gordon, ed. *An Anthology of Atheism and Rationalism.* Buffalo, New York: Prometheus Books, 1980.

Stump, Eleonore. "Petitionary Prayer." *American Philosophical Quarterly* 16 (1979): 81–91.

Swinburne, Richard. *The Concept of Miracle.* London: Macmillan, 1970.

———. *Faith and Reason.* Oxford: Clarendon Press, 1981.

Trembath, Kem Tobert. *Evangelical Theories of Biblical Inspiration: A Review and Proposal.* New York: Oxford University Press, 1987.

Veldhuis, Ruurd, Andy F. Sanders, and Heine J. Siebrand, eds. *Belief in God and Intellectual Honesty: Essays*. Assen, The Netherlands: Van Gorcum, 1990.

Wallace, Gerry. "Moral and Religious Appraisals." *International Journal of Philosophy and Religion* 16 (1984): 263–70.

Whittaker, John H. *Matters of Faith and Matters of Principle: Religious Truth Claims and Their Logic*. San Antonio, Tex.: Trinity University Press, 1981.

CHAPTER *7*

The Question of Immortality

*T*he greatest yearning of human beings is to avoid death, to live forever with mind, soul, and body intact in a realm that is like earthly life at its best. We want to remain in being as ourselves, and not be extinguished when our body expires. The longing for religion may well express this desperation for a way to have prolonged, if not eternal, life together with those we love.

This desire is translated into academic terms when we inquire into the grounds for believing in immortality and the form that life after death might take. Some thinkers maintain that the promise of eternal life is peripheral to religion, and others, that it holds a central place; this too becomes a matter for speculation. In fact, belief in the immortality of the soul is even more widespread than belief in God, but is it essential? Is a religion inadequate if it does not offer its adherents the hope of a life to come?

Three forms of belief in immortality can be distinguished. First, the familiar idea of *life after death*, whereby the soul is said to continue in existence after the body has disintegrated, living on forever in some spiritual realm. This notion occurs preeminently in Christianity where the believers take as a fundamental principle of faith that their adherence to the religion will guarantee them eternal life in heaven.

Interpretations differ as to what is required to win this immortality. According to one view, the major requirement is to accept a *set of beliefs.* This means especially a belief in God the Father and in Jesus as the Christ, that is, the Son of God and the Saviour. However, other articles of faith are listed in the Nicene Creed, the official creed of Roman Catholicism, and the Apostles' Creed, extensively used by Protestants. For example, both creeds refer to belief in "God the Father Almighty, creator of heaven and earth . . . and in Jesus Christ," but they also specify beliefs, for instance, that Christ "descended into hell" (or darkness), that there was a "resurrection of the body" (or of the dead), and that there exists a "Holy Ghost . . . Who proceedeth from the Father and the Son."

324

According to a second view, the *Christian life* is stressed more than adherence to principles. On this reading, to achieve heaven, one must follow in the footsteps of Christ and try to emulate his morally perfect existence. Professing belief, but living in ways that Christ condemns, is sheer hypocrisy—"by their fruits ye shall know them" (Matthew 7:20). Specifically, leading a Christian life means practicing altruistic love (agape) toward all humanity, including one's enemies and the poor, the sick, and the lowly. It also means returning good for evil, turning the other cheek, and acting with humility, charity, patience, and grace. One should practice the cardinal virtues of prudence, fortitude, temperance, and justice and avoid the seven deadly sins of pride, covetousness, lust, anger, gluttony, envy, and sloth.

By a third interpretation, sheer *devotion* is needed to win salvation. This is the approach of monks in monasteries and nuns in convents who commit themselves to God by meditation, prayer, purity, and simplicity. They may not be concerned with doing Christian works at all but hope for God's grace and election to heaven by sacrificing their lives in complete devotion.

As to the nature of heaven and hell, the Bible has relatively little to say, which is rather surprising, since so much emphasis is placed on living in such a way that we receive our heavenly reward and avoid damnation.

Heaven is described as a state of bliss, called the Beatific Vision, in which God is seen face to face. "The souls of the good abide in heaven forever, and the glorified bodies shall be united in heaven to the souls after the general resurrection on Judgment Day" (The Islamic heaven is pictured as a garden of sensuous delights, although that may be an allegorical view.)

Hell, by contrast, is the eternal home of those damned by God, deprived of the sight of him forever. The physical punishment seems to consist of fire, and in extrabiblical sources such as Dante's *Divine Comedy* and the paintings of Hieronymous Bosch, to include various torments instigated by Lucifer, the ruler of hell. (The Islamic notion is much the same, and in Jewish thought a realm called Sheol or Tophet is identified where souls wander in gloom and misery.)

Obviously, in Christianity the goal is life after death in the realm of heaven, where the soul lives forever in the sight of God.

A second type of immortality consists of *reincarnation* and the eventual extinction of consciousness and individuality, final freedom from the wheel of rebirth. This version of immortality was described in the introduction to chapter 2 in the section concerning Hinduism.

To the Hindu and the Buddhist, life is a series of reincarnations; and according to the moral quality of one's life (karma), one is reborn at a specific level of existence. The Hindus believe they can inhabit higher or lower castes, which are rigid social classes usually connected with occupations and surrounded by rules governing the person's association with members of other castes. The lowest level is the Outcaste, with the Sudra (worker) above that, followed by the Vaisya (shopkeeper, businessperson), then the Kshatriya (nobleman), and finally the Brahmin (priest). The Buddhist, on the other hand, hopes to move from the position of Layman to that of Monk, and this can occur even within a lifetime.

In both cases, when the highest level is reached, the person can then be liberated from the round of rebirths and enter "Nirvana." Here the individual soul merges with the world soul, that is, the person is absorbed by the divine and becomes one with everything. All separateness, individuality, identity, and awareness is lost, and a transformation takes place from personal, temporal existence to a timeless mode of being.

To those in the West, the idea of losing one's self and dissolving into the divine, with no consciousness of being in existence, is not very appealing. We want to live on as ourselves and to know that we are alive. However, if life is considered a trial containing little but suffering and frustrated desire, then repeated lives can be considered a curse, and the highest blessing would be the absolute extinction of consciousness. That lies at the root of the Eastern notion that the ideal goal is the annihilation of the self.

A third type of immortality is *timelessness*, a state that can be attained this side of the grave. In ideal moments the individual has a sense of being outside the grip of time altogether in a state that is eternal, a feeling that forever is somehow present now. Time becomes irrelevant, stands still, has no power to compel us, and becomes suspended; we have a sense of experiencing eternity in the timeless instant.

Philosophers who endorse this version of immortality, such as George Santayana, maintain that it occurs when the objects of our thoughts are themselves timeless. For example, when we contemplate some perfect mathematical relation, appreciate a beautiful object, understand a scientific reality, or meditate on a spiritual or metaphysical truth, we exist timelessly. More sensual observers claim that such timelessness can occur in lovemaking or even under the influence of certain drugs or when we are drinking fine wine; romantics report a sense of the eternal in love or in the presence of the good.

Whatever the source, the claim is that no personal immortality can be expected in some other life but that immortality is a state of being that is realizable in the here and now. It may even be the real interpretation of Christianity, "eternal life in the midst of time," as Seth Pringle-Pattison says, "an all-satisfying present experience of the love of God in Christ."

Some writers, such as Henri Bergson, describe a biological immortality that we achieve through our descendents. Our stock is passed onto future generations who exhibit our physical and perhaps mental qualities. Bergson refers to a "germ-plasm" as the fundamental biological substance that takes the form of individuals and is perpetuated through reproduction. Some modern writers, such as sociobiologists, speak of the genes as maintaining themselves in being by using people to transmit them from parent to child. People are devices whereby genes create more genes, just as chickens are used by eggs to produce more eggs. But less exotic theories simply claim that part of our biological self is transmitted to future generations, so that our line continues in our children, grandchildren, and beyond.

Also, an immortality of influence can be described in which we realize our impact on succeeding generations. Writers, artists, and educators feel this strongly, as do scientists, politicians, soldiers, and statesmen. Quite simply, we realize that we can profoundly affect those who come after us and that we never know when that influence will end. We live on in the remembrance of others and through everyone whom we touch. Therefore, as Jean-Paul Sartre says, we are responsible not just for our own lives but for the effect of our actions on other people. He feels we should live in such a way that we exert a life-enhancing influence on the world and on the future. John Donne expressed a similar view when he wrote:

> No man is an island, entire of itself; every man is a piece of the continent, a part of the main; if a clod be washed away by the sea, Europe is the less, as well as if a promontory were, as well as if a manor of thy friends or of thine own were; any man's death diminishes me, because I am involved in mankind; and therefore never send to know for whom the bell tolls; it tolls for thee.

Although the different conceptions of immortality are interesting, all but the first—that of personal immortality—seem like ways of consoling ourselves. In the last analysis, they are rather cold comfort. We want to know that our soul—that is, we ourselves—will survive after death and live forever in a blessed state of consciousness.

Various philosophers have offered arguments attempting to prove this type of immortality, although no one argument is fully convincing. The group of American philosophers known as the pragmatists offered one "proof," and it centers around the factor of emotional satisfaction.

According to the *pragmatic argument,* most people want to continue to live on after death because they find life enjoyable. Therefore, the idea of immortality is not only emotionally satisfying but also psychologically constructive. It makes our present life more endurable, gives us hope and promise, and reduces our anxiety about the alternative of extinction or nothingness.

Now if a theory makes life more endurable and cannot be proven one way or the other by scientific evidence, then we are justified in believing it. To many pragmatists, reasoning is rationalization in any case—that is, finding "reasons for what the heart desires." Why not, then, allow ourselves the comfort of a conscious decision to believe in an afterlife?

Furthermore, the prospect of our own death is unimaginable. The seventeenth-century French writer François de La Rochefoucauld once remarked that we can no more look at death directly than at the sun. The English philosopher C. D. Broad has written, "It is easy enough to think of anyone else as having really ceased to exist; but it is almost impossible to give more than a cold intellectual assent to the same proposition about oneself." A commitment to belief, then—whether about the existence of God or a life to come—is pragmatically justified.

The obvious objection to this kind of argument, of course, is that it hardly proves immortality. It helps us understand both why the yearning for immortality is universal and why people would want to believe it to be true, but it does not demonstrate that the claim is justified. In this world, unfortunately, the wish does not prove the reality. In the absence of good evidence regarding life after death, we cannot categorically declare it must be so simply because we would find it comforting if it were.

Some pragmatists also claim that unless we believe in immortality, we would have no incentive for moral living. Here the assumption is that without the hope of eternal blessedness or the fear of eternal damnation, people would lead lives of self-gratification. A moral decline would ensue as people made the most of this life, expecting no other beyond the grave. However, we are not sure this is so, and even if it were, that would not prove that life after death is a reality. It would only show that certain negative results would follow if people did not believe in the life to come.

Similarly, a pragmatic argument has been offered that human existence would have no meaning unless we accepted the idea of immortality. The American philosopher William E. Hocking, for example, claims that our lives have purpose only in relation to the past and the future, which means we must assume "another world" that provides a context for the present one.

The same objections as mentioned earlier can be raised here. Human life can be meaningful without endless amounts of time. Even if it could not, that hardly shows we live forever. Just because the consequences of believing that life ends are undesirable, that does not prove that life continues endlessly.

In addition to pragmatic arguments, a host of *psychic arguments* have been offered by mystics such as Meister Eckhart and Jacob Boehme. These mystics claim to have had immediate experiences of the eternal that provide them with incontrovertible assurance that the human soul is eternal. Countless people have also reported that they have seen the ghosts of departed relatives in the family home or have spoken with the spirits of dead persons at a séance. Some people report out-of-body experiences, others a series of previous lives; some take dictation from people like Mozart; others claim they returned to life after having been declared dead and describe their state.

All of these reports are meant to prove that people continue to live in another realm after death. The main difficulty, of course, consists in verifying the authenticity of the communication. None of the claims have ever been shown to be legitimate; rather, each one can be explained away as self-deception or the deceitful practices of some charlatan. Ignorance, credulity, and superstition seem to lie behind our propensity to accept such accounts.

In the last analysis, it is the *religious argument* that believers in immortality use to support their contention. That is, people who believe in life after death do so as a consequence of their general faith. They argue that since there is a God who cares for us with absolute love, who created us as creatures of ultimate worth made in the divine image, we must continue to exist eternally. It would make no sense for God to create us only to destroy us. Rather, we must assume that an infinitely loving being would "call us to him at the last trumpet" so that we could enjoy the ultimate gift of eternal life.

Whether or not one believes in immortality, then, depends mainly on one's larger religious framework. The atheist finds the belief unconvincing, but to the religious person it makes perfect sense.

The following selections deal with the three meanings of immortality that have been described. Jacques Maritain and Miguel de Unamuno each discuss the sense of immortality as salvation, a life after death as contained within the Christian tradition. Maritain describes the human soul and its destiny; de Unamuno explains that the longing of the human soul for eternity is the essence of religion.

Plato in the *Phaedo* presents a particular argument for reincarnation based on his contention that knowledge is recollection. That is, if we learn nothing new but only remember that which we already know, then we must believe that the soul containing that knowledge has existed before. In the same section Joseph Campbell elaborates on the historical forms of the "myth of eternal return" and on the contrasting views of the ego in the East and the West.

In the last section, A. Seth Pringle-Pattison explains eternal life as "a quality of experience which transcends time altogether," and George Santayana discusses the role of intellect, truth, logic, and excellence in achieving immortality.

Salvation: Life after Death

43. The Immortality of the Soul

JACQUES MARITAIN

I.   THE EXISTENCE OF THE SOUL

It is of this immortality, and of the way in which the Scholastics established its rational certainty, that I should now like to speak.

We must of course realize that we have a soul before we can discuss whether it is immortal. How does St. Thomas Aquinas proceed in this matter?

He observes first that man has an activity, the activity of the intellect, which is in itself immaterial. The activity of the intellect is immaterial because the proportionate or "connatural" object of the human intellect is not, like the object of the senses, a particular and limited category of things, or rather a particular and limited category of the qualitative properties of things. The proportionate or "connatural" object of the intellect is the nature of the sense-perceivable things considered in an all-embracing manner, whatever the sense concerned may be. It is not only—as for sight—color or the colored thing (which absorbs and reflects such or such rays of light) nor—as for hearing—sound or the sound-source; it is the whole universe and texture of sense-perceivable reality which can be known by the intellect, because the intellect does not stop at qualities, but pierces beyond, and proceeds to look at essence (that which a thing *is*). This very fact is a proof of the spirituality, or complete immateriality of our intellect; for every activity in which matter plays an intrinsic part is limited to a given category of material objects, as is the case for the senses, which perceive only those properties which are able to act upon their physical organs.

There is already, in fact, a certain immateriality in sense-knowledge; knowledge, as such, is an immaterial activity, because when I am in the act of knowing, I become, or am, the very thing that I know, a thing other than myself, insofar as it is other than myself. And how can I be, or become, other than myself, if it is not in a supra-subjective, or immaterial manner? Sense-knowledge is a very poor kind of knowledge; insofar as it is knowledge, it is immaterial, but it is an immaterial activity intrinsically conditioned by, and dependent upon, the material functioning of the sense-organs. Sense-knowledge is the immaterial achievement, the immaterial actuation and product of a living bodily organ; and its very object is also something half material, half immaterial; I mean a physical quality *intentionally* or immaterially present in the medium by which it acts on the sense-organ (something comparable to the manner in which a painter's idea is immaterially present in his paint-brush).

But with intellectual knowledge we have to do with an activity which is in itself completely immaterial. The human intellect is able to know whatever participates in being and truth; the whole universe can be inscribed in it; this means that, in order to be known, the object known by the intellect has been stripped of any existential condition of materiality. This rose, which I see, has contours; but Being, of which I am thinking, is more spacious than space. The object of the intellect is universal, for instance that universal or de-individualized object which is apprehended in the idea of man, of animal, of atom; the object of the intellect is a universal which remains what it is while being identified with an infinity of individuals. And this is only possible because things, in order to become objects of the mind, have been entirely separated from their material existence. To this it must be added that the operation of our intellect does not stop at the knowledge of the nature of sense-perceivable things; it goes further; it knows by analogy the spiritual natures; it extends to the realm of merely possible things; its field has infinite magnitude.

Thus, the objects known by the human intellect, taken not as things existing in themselves, but precisely as objects determining the intellect and united with it, are purely immaterial.

Furthermore, just as the condition of the *object* is immaterial, so is the condition of the *act* which bears upon it, and is determined or specified by it. The object of the human intellect is, as such, purely immaterial; the act of the human intellect is also purely immaterial.

And, moreover, if the act of the intellectual power is purely immaterial, that *power* itself is also purely immaterial. In man, this thinking animal, the intellect is a purely spiritual power. Doubtless it depends upon the body, upon the conditions of the brain. Its activity can be disturbed or hindered by a physical disorder, by an outburst of anger, by a drink or a narcotic. But this dependence is an *extrinsic* one. It exists because our intelligence cannot act without the joint activity of the memory and the imagination, of the internal senses and external senses, all of which are organic powers residing in some material organ, in some special part of the body. As for the intellect itself, it is not *intrinsically* dependent upon the body since its activity is immaterial; the human intellect does not reside in any special part of the body. It is not contained by the body, but rather contains it. It uses the brain, since the organs of the internal senses are in the brain; yet the brain is not an organ of the intelligence; there is no part of the organism whose act is intellectual operation. The intellect has no organ.

Finally, since intellectual power is spiritual, or purely immaterial in itself, its *first substantial root*, the subsisting principle from which this power proceeds and which acts through its instrumentality, is also spiritual.

So much for the spirituality of the intellect. Now, thought or the operation of the intellect is an act and emanation of man as a unit; and when I think, it
is not only my intellect which thinks: it is *I*, my own self. And my own self is a
bodily self; it involves matter; it is not a spiritual or purely immaterial subject. The
body is an essential part of man. The intellect is not the whole man.

Therefore the intellect, or rather the substantial root of the intellect,
which must be as immaterial as the intellect, is only a part, albeit an essential part,
of man's substance.

But man is not an aggregate, a juxtaposition of two substances; man is a
natural whole, a single being, a single substance.

Consequently, we must conclude that the essence or substance of man is
single, but that this single substance itself is a compound, the components of
which are the body and the spiritual intellect: or rather matter, of which the body
is made, and the spiritual principle, one of the powers of which is the intellect.
Matter—in the Aristotelian sense of prime matter, or of that root potentiality
which is the common stuff of all corporeal substance—matter, substantially united
with the spiritual principle of the intellect, is ontologically molded, shaped from
within and in the innermost depths of being, by this spiritual principle as by a
substantial and vital impulse, in order to constitute that body of ours. In this
sense, Saint Thomas, after Aristotle, says that the intellect is the form, the
substantial form of the human body.

That is the Scholastic notion of the human soul. The human soul, which
is the root principle of the intellectual power, is the first principle of life of the
human body, and the substantial form, the *entelechy*, of that body. And the human
soul is not only a substantial form or entelechy, as are the souls of plants and
animals according to the biological philosophy of Aristotle; the human soul is also
a spirit, a spiritual substance able to exist apart from matter, since the human soul
is the root principle of a spiritual power, the act of which is intrinsically independent of matter. The human soul is both a soul and a spirit, and it is its very
substantiality, subsistence and existence, which are communicated to the whole
human substance, in order to make human substance be what it is, and to make it
subsist and exist. Each element of the human body is human, and exists as such, by
virtue of the immaterial existence of the human soul. Our body, our hands, our
eyes exist by virtue of the existence of our soul.

The immaterial soul is the first substantial root not only of the intellect,
but of all that which, in us, is spiritual activity; and it is also the first substantial
root of all our other living activities. It would be inconceivable that a non-spiritual
soul, that kind of soul which is not a spirit and cannot exist without informing
matter—namely, the souls of plants or animals in Aristotelian biology—should
possess a power or faculty *superior* to its own degree in being, that is, immaterial, or
act through a supra-material instrumentality independent of any corporeal organ
and physical structure. But when it is a question of a spirit which is a soul, or of a
spiritual soul, as the human soul is, then it is perfectly conceivable that such a soul
should have, aside from immaterial or spiritual faculties, other powers and activi-

ties which are organic and material, and which, relating to the union between soul and body, pertain to a level of being *inferior* to that of the spirit.

II. THE SPIRITUALITY OF THE HUMAN SOUL

Thus, the very way in which the Scholastics arrived at the existence of the human soul also established its spirituality. Just as the intellect is spiritual, that is to say intrinsically independent of matter in its operation and in its nature, so also, and for the same reason, the human soul, the substantial root of the intellect, is spiritual, that is, intrinsically independent of matter in its nature and in its existence; it does not live by the body, the body lives by it. The human soul is a spiritual substance which, by its substantial union with matter, gives existence and countenance to the body.

That is my second point. As we have seen, the Scholastics demonstrated it by a metaphysical analysis of the intellect's operation, carefully distinguished from the operation of the senses. They adduced, of course, much other evidence in support of their demonstration. In their consideration of the intellect, they observed, for instance, that the latter is capable of *perfect reflection*, that is, of coming back entirely upon itself—not in the manner of a sheet of paper, half of which can be folded on the other half, but in a complete manner, so that it can grasp its whole operation and penetrate it by knowledge, and can contain itself and its own principle, the existing self, in its own knowing activity, a perfect reflection or self-containing of which any material agent, extended in space and time, is essentially incapable. Here we are confronted with that phenomenon of self-knowledge, of *prise de conscience* or becoming aware of oneself, which is a privilege of the spirit, as Hegel (after St. Augustine) was to emphasize, and which plays so tremendous a part in the history of humanity and the development of its spiritual energies. . . .

III. THE IMMORTALITY OF THE HUMAN SOUL

The third point follows immediately from the second. The immortality of the human soul is an immediate corollary of its spirituality. A soul which is spiritual in itself, intrinsically independent of matter in its nature and existence, cannot cease existing. A spirit—that is, a "form" which needs nothing other than itself (save the influx of the Prime Cause) to exercise existence—once existing cannot cease existing. A spiritual soul cannot be corrupted, since it possesses no matter; it cannot be disintegrated, since it has no substantial parts; it cannot lose its individual unity, since it is self-subsisting, nor its internal energy, since it contains within itself all the sources of its energies. The human soul cannot die. Once it exists, it cannot disappear; it will necessarily exist forever, endure without end.

Thus, philosophic reason, put to work by a great metaphysician like Thomas Aquinas, is able to prove the immortality of the human soul in a demonstrative manner. Of course, this demonstration implies a vast and articulate network of metaphysical insights, notions and principles (relating to essence and nature, substance, act and potency, matter and form, operation, etc.) the validity of which is necessarily presupposed. We can appreciate fully the strength of the Scholastic demonstration only if we realize the significance and full validity of the metaphysical notions involved. If modern times feel at a loss in the face of metaphysical knowledge, I fancy that it is not metaphysical knowledge which is to blame, but rather modern times and the weakening of reason they have experienced.

It is not surprising, on the other hand, that the philosophical demonstration I have just summarized is an abstract and a difficult one. The great and fundamental truths which are spontaneously grasped by the natural instinct of the human mind are always the most arduous for philosophic reason to establish. . . .

IV.   THE CONDITION AND DESTINY OF THE IMMORTAL SOUL

What can philosophy tell us about the natural condition of the immortal soul after the death of its body? That is my fourth and last point. Philosophy can tell us very little indeed on this subject. Let us try to summarize the few indications there are. All the organic and sensuous powers of the human soul remain dormant in a separated soul, for they cannot be brought into play without the body. The separated soul is itself engulfed in a complete sleep with regard to the material world; the external senses and their perceptions have vanished; the images of memory and imagination, the impulses of instinct and passion have vanished. But this sleep is not like the sleep we know, obscure and filled with dreams; it is lucid and intelligent, alive to spiritual realities. For now light shines from within. The intellect and the spiritual powers are awake and active. From the very fact of its separation from the body, the soul now knows itself through itself; its very substance has become transparent to its intellect; it is intellectually penetrated to its innermost depths. The soul knows itself in an intuitive manner; it is dazzled by its own beauty, the beauty of a spiritual substance, and it knows other things through its own substance already known, in the measure in which other things resemble it. It knows God through that image of God which the soul itself is. And in accordance with its state of incorporeal existence, it receives from God, the sun of the spirits, certain ideas and inspirations which directly enlighten it, and help the natural light of the human intellect, of that intellect which is, as Saint Thomas Aquinas phrased it, the lowest in the hierarchy of spirits.

Saint Thomas teaches also that all that is of the intellect and the spirit, and especially the intellectual memory, which is but one with the intellect, keeps alive, in the separated soul, the whole treasure of knowledge acquired during our bodily life. The intellectual knowledge, the intellectual virtues acquired here below subsist in the separated soul. Whereas the images of the sense-memory, which had its seat in the brain, disappear, that which has penetrated into the intellectual memory is preserved. Thus, in an intellectual and spiritual manner, the separated soul ever knows those whom it loved. And it loves them spiritually. And it is able to converse with other spirits by opening to them what abides in its inner thoughts and is taken hold of by its free will.

We may thus imagine that, at the moment when it leaves the body, the soul is suddenly immersed into itself as into a shining abyss, where all that was buried within it, all its dead, rise up again in full light, insofar as all this was encompassed in the subconscious or supraconscious depths of the spiritual life of its intellect and will. Then all that is true and good in the soul becomes a blessing for it at the touch of this all-pervading revelatory light; all that is warped and evil becomes a torment for it under the effect of the very same light.

I do not believe that natural reason can go further in its understanding of the natural condition of the separated soul. What would be the life and happiness of souls if their state after death were a purely natural state? Their supreme good would consist in wisdom, untrammeled spiritual life, mutual friendship, and first and foremost in advancing constantly in their natural knowledge and love of God, Whom they would, however, never see face to face. It would be happiness in motion, never absolutely fulfilled—what Leibniz called *un chemin par des plaisirs,* "a road amidst spiritual pleasures."

But if we wish to know more, can we not go beyond philosophy? Philosophy itself will then entrust us to the guidance of a knowledge whose sources are superior to its own. Christians know that man does not live in a state of pure nature. They know that he was created in a state of grace, and that, after the first sin which wounded our race, he has been living in a state of fallen and redeemed nature; they know that he is made for supernatural blessedness. In answer to the question of the separated soul's destiny, the Scholastic doctors spoke not as philosophers, but as theologians whose knowledge rests on the data of Revelation.

Insofar as man participates in the metaphysical privileges of spirit and personality, he has aspirations which transcend human nature and its possibilities, and which consequently may be called transnatural aspirations: the longing for a state in which he would know things completely and without error, in which he would enjoy perfect communion with spirits, in which he would be free without being able to fail or to sin, in which he would inhabit a realm of unfading justice, in which he would have the intuitive knowledge of the First Cause of being.

Such a longing cannot be fulfilled by nature. It can be fulfilled by grace. The immortal soul is involved and engaged in the great drama of the Redemption. If, at the moment of its separation from the body, at the moment when its choice is immutably fixed forever, the immortal soul prefers its own will and self-love to the will and gift of God, if it prefers misery with pride to the blessing of grace, then it is granted what it has wished for. It has it, and it will never cease wanting and preferring it, for a free choice made in the condition of a *pure* spirit is an eternal choice. If the soul opens itself to the will and gift of God, Whom it loves more than its own existence, then it is granted what it has loved, it enters forever into the joy of the uncreated Being, it sees God face to face and knows Him as it is known by Him, intuitively. Thus, it becomes God by participation, as Saint John of the Cross phrased it, and, through grace, it attains that communion in divine life, that blessedness for the sake of which all things have been created. And the degree of its blessedness itself, the degree of its vision, will correspond to the degree of the inner impetus which projects it into God, in other words, to the degree of love to which it has attained in its life on earth. In the last analysis, therefore, we must say with Saint

John of the Cross: It is upon our love that we shall be judged. In its state of blessedness the immortal soul will know creation in the Creator, by that kind of knowledge which Saint Augustine called "matutinal" knowledge, because it is produced in the eternal morning of Creative Ideas; the immortal soul will be equal to the angels, and will communicate freely with the whole realm of spirits; it will love God, henceforth clearly seen, with a sovereign necessity; and it will exert free will with regard to all its actions concerning creatures, but its free will shall no longer be liable to failure and sin; the soul will inhabit the realm of unfading justice, that of the three divine Persons and of the blessed spirits; it will grasp and possess the divine Essence which, infinitely clearer and more intelligible than any of our ideas, will illumine the human intellect from within and will itself be the intelligible medium, the actuating form through which it will be known. According to a line of the Psalms which Saint Thomas loved and often quoted: "In Thy light shall we see light."

Such are the teachings of Saint Thomas, both as a philosopher and as a theologian, about the condition and destiny of the human soul. Immortality is not a more or less precarious, successful or unsuccessful survival in other men, or in the ideal waves of the universe. Immortality is a nature-given, inalienable property of the human soul as a spiritual substance. And grace makes eternal life possible to all, to the most destitute as well as to the most gifted. The eternal life of the immortal soul is its transforming union with God and His intimate life, a union which is to be accomplished inchoatively here below, by love and contemplation and, after the body's death, in a definite and perfect manner, by the beatific vision. For eternal life begins here upon earth, and the soul of man lives and breathes where it loves; and love, in living faith, has strength enough to make the soul of man experience unity with God—"two natures in a single spirit and love, *dos naturalezas en un espiritu y amor de Dios.*"

I do not believe that a philosopher can discuss the immortality of the soul without taking into consideration the complementary notions which religious thought adds to the true and inadequate answers which reason and philosophy can furnish by themselves.

44. The Tragic Sense of Life

MIGUEL DE UNAMUNO

IF YOU WERE TO DIE TOMORROW

Man is said to be a reasoning animal. I do not know why he has not been defined as an affective or feeling animal. Perhaps that which differentiates him from other animals is feeling rather than reason. More often I have seen a cat reason than laugh or weep. Perhaps it laughs or weeps inwardly—but then perhaps, also inwardly, the crab resolves equations of the second degree.

And thus, in a philosopher, what must needs most concern us is the man.

Take Kant, the man Immanuel Kant, who was born and lived at Königsberg, in the latter part of the eighteenth century and the beginning of the nineteenth. In the philosophy of this man Kant, a man of heart and head—that is to say, a man—there is a significant somersault, as Kierkegaard, another man—and what a man!—would have said, the somersault from the *Critique of Pure Reason* to the *Critique of Practical Reason*. He reconstructs in the latter what he destroyed in the former, in spite of what those may say who do not see the man himself. After having examined and pulverized with his analysis the traditional proofs of the existence of God, of the Aristotelian God, who is the God corresponding to the abstract God, the unmoved prime Mover, he reconstructs God anew; but the God of the conscience, the Author of the moral order—the Lutheran God, in short. This transition of Kant exists already in embryo in the Lutheran notion of faith.

Kant reconstructed with the heart that which with the head he had overthrown. And we know, from the testimony of those who knew him and from his testimony in his letters and private declarations, that the man Kant, the more or less selfish old bachelor who professed Philosophy at Königsberg at the end of the century of the Encyclopedia and the goddess of Reason, was a man much preoccupied with the problem—I mean with the only real vital problem, the problem that strikes at the very root of our being, the problem of our individual and personal destiny, of the immortality of the soul. The man Kant was not resigned to die utterly. And because he was not resigned to die utterly he made that leap, that immortal somersault, from the one Critique to the other.

Whosoever reads the *Critique of Practical Reason* carefully and without blinkers will see that, in strict fact, the existence of God is therein deduced from the immortality of the soul, and not the immortality of the soul from the existence of God. The categorical imperative leads us to a moral postulate which necessitates in its turn, in the teleological or rather eschatological order, the immortality of the soul, and in order to sustain this immortality God is introduced. All the rest is the jugglery of the professional of philosophy.

The man Kant felt that morality was the basis of eschatology, but the professor of philosophy inverted the terms.

Another professor, the professor and man William James, has somewhere said that for the generality of men God is the provider of immortality. Yes, for the generality of men, including the man Kant, the man James, and the man who writes these lines which you, reader, are reading.

Talking to a peasant one day, I proposed to him the hypothesis that there might indeed be a God who governs heaven and earth, a Consciousness of the Universe, but that for all that the soul of every man may not be immortal in the traditional and concrete sense. He replied: "Then wherefore God?" So answered, in the secret tribunal of their consciousness, the man Kant and the man James. Only in their capacities as professors they were compelled to justify rationally an attitude in itself so little rational. Which does not mean, of course, that the attitude is absurd.

The problem is tragic and eternal, and the more we seek to escape from it, the more it thrusts itself upon us. Four-and-twenty centuries ago, in his dialogue on the immortality of the soul, the serene Plato—but was he serene?—spoke of the uncertainty of our dream of being immortal and of the *risk* that the dream might be vain, and from his own soul there escaped this profound cry—Glorious is the risk! Glorious is the risk that we are able to run of our souls never dying—a sentence that was the germ of Pascal's famous argument of the wager.

Faced with this risk, I am presented with arguments designed to eliminate it, arguments demonstrating the absurdity of the belief in the immortality of the soul; but these arguments fail to make any impression upon me, for they are reasons and nothing more than reasons, and it is not with reasons that the heart is appeased. I do not want to die—no; I neither want to die nor do I want to want to die; I want to live for ever and ever and ever. I want this "I" to live—this poor "I" that I am and that I feel myself to be here and now, and therefore the problem of the duration of my soul, of my own soul, tortures me.

I am the centre of my universe, the centre of the universe, and in my supreme anguish I cry with Michelet, "Mon moi, ils m'arrachent mon moi!" What is a man profited if he shall gain the whole world and lose his own soul? (Matt. xvi. 26). Egoism, you say? There is nothing more universal than the individual, for what is the property of each is the property of all. Each man is worth more than the whole of humanity, nor will it do to sacrifice each to all save in so far as all sacrifice themselves to each. That which we call egoism is the principle of psychic gravity, the necessary postulate. "Love thy neighbour as thyself," we are told, the presupposition being that each man loves himself; and it is not said "love thyself." And, nevertheless, we do not know how to love ourselves.

Put aside the persistence of your own self and ponder what they tell you. Sacrifice yourself to your children! And sacrifice yourself to them because they are yours, part and prolongation of yourself, and they in their turn will sacrifice themselves to their children, and these children to theirs, and so it will go on without end, a sterile sacrifice by which nobody profits. I came into the world to create my self, and what is to become of all our selves? Live for the True, the Good, the Beautiful! We shall see presently the supreme vanity and the supreme insincerity of this hypocritical attitude.

"That art thou!" they tell me with the Upanishads. And I answer: Yes, I am that, if that is I and all is mine, and mine the totality of things. As mine I love the All, and I love my neighbour because he lives in me and is part of my consciousness, because he is like me, because he is mine.

Oh, to prolong this blissful moment, to sleep, to eternalize oneself in it! Here and now, in this discreet and diffused light, in this lake of quietude, the storm of the heart appeased and stilled the echoes of the world! Insatiable desire now sleeps and does not even dream; use and wont, blessed use and wont, are the rule of my eternity; my disillusions have died with my memories, and with my hopes my fears.

And they come seeking to deceive us with a deceit of deceits, telling us that nothing is lost, that everything is transformed, shifts and changes, that not the least particle of matter is annihilated, not the least impulse of energy is lost, and there are some who pretend to console us with this! Futile consolation! It is not my matter or my energy that is the cause of my disquiet, for they are not mine if I myself am not mine—that is, if I am not eternal. No, my longing is not to be submerged in the vast All, in an infinite and eternal Matter or Energy, or in God; not to be possessed by God, but to possess Him, to become myself God, yet without ceasing to be I myself, who am now speaking to you. Tricks of monism avail us nothing; we crave the substance and not the shadow of immortality.

Materialism, you say? Materialism? Without doubt; but either our spirit is likewise some kind of matter or it is nothing. I dread the idea of having to tear myself away from my flesh; I dread still more the idea of having to tear myself away from everything sensible and material, from all substance. Yes, perhaps this merits the name of materialism; and if I grapple myself to God with all my powers and all my senses, it is that He may carry me in His arms beyond death, looking into these eyes of mine with the light of His heaven when the light of earth is dimming in them for ever. Self-illusion? Talk not to me of illusion—let me live!

They also call this pride—"stinking pride" Leopardi called it—and they ask us who are we, vile earthworms, to pretend to immortality; in virtue of what? wherefore? by what right? "In virtue of what?" you ask; and I reply, In virtue of what do we now live? "Wherefore?"—and wherefore do we now exist? "By what right?"—and by what right are we? To exist is just as gratuitous as to go on existing for ever. Do not let us talk of merit or of right or of the wherefore of our longing, which is an end in itself, or we shall lose our reason in a vortex of absurdities. I do not claim any right or merit; it is only a necessity; I need it in order to live.

And you, who are you? you ask me; and I reply with Obermann, "For the universe, nothing; for myself, everything!" Pride? Is it pride to want to be immortal? Unhappy men that we are! 'Tis a tragic fate, without a doubt, to have to base the affirmation of immortality upon the insecure and slippery foundation of the desire for immortality; but to condemn this desire on the ground that we believe it to have been proved to be unattainable, without undertaking the proof, is merely supine. I am dreaming . . . ? Let me dream, if this dream is my life. Do not awaken me from it. I believe in the immortal origin of this yearning for immortality, which is the very substance of my soul. But do I really believe in it . . . ? And wherefore do you want to be immortal? you ask me, wherefore? Frankly, I do not understand the question, for it is to ask the reason of the reason, the end of the end, the principle of the principle.

But it is in our endeavour to represent to ourselves what the life of the soul after death really means that uncertainty finds its surest foundation. This it is that most shakes our vital desire and most intensifies the dissolvent efficacy of reason. For even if by a mighty effort of faith we overcome that reason which tells and teaches us that the soul is only a function of the physical organism, it yet remains for our imagination to conceive an image of the immortal and eternal life of the soul. This conception involves us in contradictions and absurdities, and it may be that we shall arrive with Kierkegaard at the conclusion that if the mortality of the soul is terrible, not less terrible is its immortality.

But when we have overcome the impediment of reason, when we have achieved the faith, however painful and involved in uncertainty it may be, that our personal consciousness shall continue after death, what difficulty, what impediment, lies in the way of our imagining to ourselves this persistence of self in harmony with our desire? Yes, we can imagine it as an eternal rejuvenescence, as an eternal growth of ourselves, and as a journeying towards God, towards the Universal Consciousness, without ever an arrival, we can imagine it as. . . . But who shall put fetters upon the imagination, once it has broken the chain of the rational?

Once again I must repeat that the longing for the immortality of the soul, for the permanence, in some form or another, of our personal and individual consciousness, is as much of the essence of religion as is the longing that there may be a God. The one does not exist apart from the other, the reason being that fundamentally they are one and the same thing. But as soon as we attempt to give a concrete and rational form to this longing for immortality and permanence, to define it to ourselves, we encounter even more difficulties than we encountered in our attempt to rationalize God.

The universal consent of mankind has again been invoked as a means of justifying this immortal longing for immortality to our own feeble reason. *Permanere animos arbitratur consensu nationum omnium*, said Cicero, echoing the opinion of the ancients (*Tuscul. quaest.*, xvi., 36). But this same recorder of his own feelings confessed that, although when he read the arguments in favour of the immortality of the soul in the *Phaedo* of Plato he was compelled to assent to them, as soon as he put the book aside and began to revolve the problem in his own mind, all his previous assent melted away, *assentio omnis illa illabitur* (*Cap.* xi. 25). And what happened to Cicero happens to us all, and it happened likewise to Swedenborg, the most daring visionary of the other world. Swedenborg admitted that he who discourses of life after death, putting aside all erudite notions concerning the soul and its mode of union with the body, believes that after death he shall live in a glorious joy and vision, as a man among angels; but when he begins to reflect upon the doctrine of the union of the soul with the body, or upon the hypothetical opinion concerning the soul, doubts arise in him as to whether the soul is thus or otherwise, and when these doubts arise, his former idea is dissipated (*De coelo et inferno*, § 183). Neverthe-less, as Cournot says, "it is the destiny that awaits me, *me* or my *person*, that moves, perturbs and consoles me, that makes me capable of abnegation and sacrifice, whatever be the origin, the nature or the essence of this inexplicable bond of union, in the absence of which the philosophers are pleased to determine that my person must disappear" (*Traité*, etc., § 297).

And the supreme commandment that arises out of love towards God, and the foundation of all morality, is this: Yield yourself up entirely, give your spirit to the end that you may save it, that you may eternalize it. Such is the sacrifice of life.

The individual *qua* individual, the wretched captive of the instinct of preservation and of the senses, cares only about preserving himself, and all his concern is that others should not force their way into his sphere, should not interrupt his idleness; and in return for their abstention or for the sake of example he refrains from forcing himself upon them, from interrupting their idleness, from disturbing them, from taking possession of them. "Do not do unto others what you would not have them do unto you," he translates thus: I do not interfere with others—let them not interfere with me. And he shrinks and pines and perishes in this spiritual avarice and this repellent ethic of anarchic individualism: each one for himself. And as each one is not himself, he can hardly live for himself.

But as soon as the individual feels himself in society, he feels himself in God, and kindled by the instinct of perpetuation he glows with love towards God, and with a dominating charity he seeks to perpetuate himself in others, to perennialize his spirit, to eternalize it, to unnail God, and his sole desire is to seal his spirit upon other spirits and to receive their impress in return. He has shaken off the yoke of his spiritual sloth and avarice.

What is our heart's truth, anti-rational though it be? The immortality of the human soul, the truth of the persistence of our consciousness without any termination whatsoever, the truth of the human finality of the Universe. And what is its moral proof? We may formulate it thus: Act so that in your own judgment and in the judgment of others you may merit eternity, act so that you may become irreplaceable, act so that you may not merit death. Or perhaps thus: Act as if you were to die to-morrow, but to die in order to survive and be eternalized. The end of morality is to give personal, human finality to the Universe; to discover the finality that belongs to it—if indeed it has any finality—and to discover it by acting.

More than a century ago, 1804, in Letter XC of that series that constitutes the immense monody of his *Obermann,* Sénancour wrote the words which I have put at the head of this chapter—and of all the spiritual descendants of the patriarchal Rousseau, Sénancour was the most profound and the most intense; of all the men of heart and feeling that France has produced, not excluding Pascal, he was the most tragic. "Man is perishable. That may be; but let us perish resisting, and if it is nothingness that awaits us, do not let us so act that it shall be a just fate." Change this sentence from its negative to the positive form—"And if it is nothingness that awaits us, let us so act that it shall be an unjust fate"—and you get the firmest basis of action for the man who cannot or will not be a dogmatist.

Reincarnation: The Wheel of Rebirth

45. Phaedo

PLATO

Cebes added: Your favourite doctrine, Socrates, that knowledge is simply recollection, if true, also necessarily implies a previous time in which we have learned that which we now recollect. But this would be impossible unless our soul had been in some place before existing in the form of man; here then is another proof of the soul's immortality.

But tell me, Cebes, said Simmias, interposing, what arguments are urged in favour of this doctrine of recollection. I am not very sure at the moment that I remember them.

One excellent proof, said Cebes, is afforded by questions. If you put a question to a person in a right way, he will give a true answer of himself, but how could he do this unless there were knowledge and right reason already in him? And this is most clearly shown when he is taken to a diagram or to anything of that sort.

But if, said Socrates, you are still incredulous, Simmias, I would ask you whether you may not agree with me when you look at the matter in another way;—I mean, if you are still incredulous as to whether knowledge is recollection?

Incredulous I am not, said Simmias; but I want to have this doctrine of recollection brought to my own recollection, and, from what Cebes has said, I am beginning to recollect and be convinced: but I should still like to hear what you were going to say.

This is what I would say, he replied:—We should agree, if I am not mistaken, that what a man recollects he must have known at some previous time.

Very true.

And what is the nature of this knowledge or recollection? I mean to ask, Whether a person who, having seen or heard or in any way perceived anything, knows not only that, but has a conception of something else which is the subject, not of the same but of some other kind of knowledge, may not be fairly said to recollect that of which he has the conception?

What do you mean?

I mean what I may illustrate by the following instance:—The knowledge of a lyre is not the same as the knowledge of a man?

True.

And yet what is the feeling of lovers when they recognize a lyre, or a garment, or anything else which the beloved has been in the habit of using? Do not they, from knowing the lyre, form in the mind's eye an image of the youth to whom the lyre belongs? And this is recollection. In like manner any one who sees Simmias may remember Cebes; and there are endless examples of the same thing.

Endless, indeed, replied Simmias.

And recollection is most commonly a process of recovering that which has been already forgotten through time and inattention.

Very true, he said.

Well; and may you not also from seeing the picture of a house or a lyre remember a man? and from the picture of Simmias, you may be led to remember Cebes;

True.

Or you may also be led to the recollection of Simmias himself?

Quite so.

And in all these cases, the recollection may be derived from things either like or unlike?

It may be.

And when the recollection is derived from like things, then another consideration is sure to arise, which is—whether the likeness in any degree falls short or not of that which is recollected?

Very true, he said.

And shall we proceed a step further, and affirm that there is such a thing as equality, not of one piece of wood or stone with another, but that, over and above this, there is absolute equality? Shall we say so?

Say so, yes, replied Simmias, and swear to it, with all the confidence in life.

And do we know the nature of this absolute essence?

To be sure, he said.

And whence did we obtain our knowledge? Did we not see equalities of material things, such as pieces of wood and stones, and gather from them the idea of an equality which is different from them? For you will acknowledge that there is a difference. Or look at the matter in another way:—Do not the same pieces of wood or stone appear at one time equal, and at another time unequal?

That is certain.

But are real equals ever unequal? or is the idea of equality the same as of inequality?

Impossible, Socrates.

Then these (so-called) equals are not the same with the idea of equality?

I should say, clearly not, Socrates.

And yet from these equals, although differing from the idea of equality, you conceived and attained that idea?

Very true, he said.

Which might be like, or might be unlike them?

Yes.

But that makes no difference: whenever from seeing one thing you conceived another, whether like or unlike, there must surely have been an act of recollection?

Very true.

But what would you say of equal portions of wood and stone, or other material equals? and what is the impression produced by them? Are they equals in the same sense in which absolute equality is equal? or do they fall short of this perfect equality in a measure?

Yes, he said, in a very great measure too.

And must we not allow, that when I or anyone, looking at any object, observes that the thing which he sees aims at being some other thing, but falls short of, and cannot be, that other thing, but is inferior, he who makes this observation must have had a previous knowledge of that to which the other, although similar, was inferior.

Certainly.

And has not this been our own case in the matter of equals and of absolute equality?

Precisely.

Then we must have known equality previously to the time when we first saw the material equals, and reflected that all these apparent equals strive to attain absolute equality, but fall short of it?

Very true.

And we recognize also that this absolute equality has only been known, and can only be known, through the medium of sight or touch, or of some other of the senses, which are all alike in this respect?

Yes, Socrates, as far as the argument is concerned, one of them is the same as the other.

From the senses then is derived the knowledge that all sensible things aim at an absolute equality of which they fall short?

Yes.

Then before we began to see or hear or perceive in any way, we must have had a knowledge of absolute equality, or we could not have referred to that standard the equals which are derived from the senses?—for to that they all aspire, and of that they fall short.

No other inference can be drawn from the previous statements.

And did we not see and hear and have the use of our other senses as soon as we were born?

Certainly.

Then we must have acquired the knowledge of equality at some previous time?

Yes.

That is to say, before we were born, I suppose?

True.

And if we acquired this knowledge before we were born, and were born having the use of it, then we also knew before we were born and at the instant of birth not only the equal or the greater or the less, but all other ideas; for we are not speaking only of equality, but of beauty, goodness, justice, holiness, and of all which we stamp with the name of essence in the dialectical process, both when we ask and when we answer questions. Of all this we may certainly affirm that we acquired the knowledge before birth?

We may.

But if, after having acquired, we have not forgotten what in each case we acquired, then we must always have come into life having knowledge, and shall always continue to know as long as life lasts—for knowing is the acquiring and retaining knowledge and not forgetting. Is not forgetting, Simmias, just the losing of knowledge?

Quite true, Socrates.

But if the knowledge which we acquired before birth was lost by us at birth, and if afterwards by the use of the senses we recovered what we previously knew, will not the process which we call learning be a recovering of the knowledge which is natural to us, and may not this be rightly termed recollection?

Very true.

So much is clear—that when we perceive something, either by the help of sight, or hearing, or some other sense, from that perception we are able to obtain a notion of some other thing like or unlike which is associated with it but has been forgotten. Whence, as I was saying, one of two alternatives follows:—either we had this knowledge at birth, and continued to know through life; or, after birth, those who are said to learn only remember, and learning is simply recollection.

Yes, that is quite true, Socrates.

And which alternative, Simmias, do you prefer? Had we the knowledge at our birth, or did we recollect the things which we knew previously to our birth?

I cannot decide at the moment.

At any rate you can decide whether he who has knowledge will or will not be able to render an account of his knowledge? What do you say?

Certainly, he will.

But do you think that every man is able to give an account of these very matters about which we are speaking?

Would that they could, Socrates, but I rather fear that tomorrow, at this time, there will no longer be anyone alive who is able to give an account of them such as ought to be given.

Then you are not of opinion, Simmias, that all men know these things?

Certainly not.

They are in process of recollecting that which they learned before?

Certainly.

But when did our souls acquire this knowledge?—not since we were born as men?

Certainly not.

And therefore, previously?

Yes.

Then, Simmias, our souls must also have existed without bodies before they were in the form of man, and must have had intelligence.

Unless indeed you suppose, Socrates, that these notions are given us at the very moment of birth; for this is the only time which remains.

Yes, my friend, but if so, when do we lose them? for they are not in us when we are born—that is admitted. Do we lose them at the moment of receiving them, or if not at what other time?

No, Socrates, I perceive that I was unconsciously talking nonsense.

Then may we not say, Simmias, that if, as we are always repeating, there is an absolute beauty, and goodness, and an absolute essence of all things; and if to this, which is now discovered to have existed in our former state, we refer all our sensations, and with this compare them, finding these ideas to be pre-existent and our inborn possession—then our souls must have had a prior existence, but if not, there would be no force in the argument? There is the same proof that these ideas must have existed before we were born, as that our souls existed before we were born; and if not the ideas, then not the souls.

Yes, Socrates; I am convinced that there is precisely the same necessity for the one as for the other; and the argument retreats successfully to the position that the existence of the soul before birth cannot be separated from the existence of the essence of which you speak. For there is nothing which to my mind is so patent as that beauty, goodness, and the other notions of which you were just now speaking, have a most real and absolute existence; and I am satisfied with the proof.

Well, but is Cebes equally satisfied? for I must convince him too.

I think, said Simmias, that Cebes is satisfied: although he is the most incredulous of mortals, yet I believe that he is sufficiently convinced of the existence of the soul before birth. But that after death the soul will continue to exist is not yet proven even to my own satisfaction. I cannot get rid of the feeling of the many to which Cebes was referring—the feeling that when the man dies the soul will be dispersed, and that this may be the extinction of her. For admitting that she may have been born elsewhere, and framed out of other elements, and was in existence before entering the human body, why after having entered in and gone out again may she not herself be destroyed and come to an end?

Very true, Simmias, said Cebes; about half of what was required has been proven; to wit, that our souls existed before we were born:—that the soul will exist after death as well as before birth is the other half of which the proof is still wanting, and has to be supplied; when that is given the demonstration will be complete.

But that proof, Simmias and Cebes, has been already given, said Socrates, if you put the two arguments together—I mean this and the former one, in which we admitted that everything living is born of the dead. For if the soul exists before birth, and in coming to life and being born can be born only from death and dying, must she not after death continue to exist, since she has to be born again?—Surely the proof which you desire has been already furnished. Still I suspect that you and Simmias would be glad to probe the argument further. Like children, you are haunted with a fear that when the soul leaves the body, the wind may really blow her away and scatter her; especially if a man should happen to die in a great storm and not when the sky is calm.

Cebes answered with a smile: Then, Socrates, you must argue us out of our fears—and yet, strictly speaking, they are not our fears, but there is a child within us to whom death is a sort of hobgoblin: him too we must persuade not to be afraid when he is alone in the dark.

Socrates said: Let the voice of the charmer be applied daily until you have charmed away the fear.

46. The Masks of God

JOSEPH CAMPBELL

The myth of eternal return, which is still basic to Oriental life, displays an order of fixed forms that appear and reappear through all time. The daily round of the sun, the waning and waxing moon, the cycle of the year, and the rhythm of organic birth, death, and new birth, represent a miracle of continous arising that is fundamental to the nature of the universe. We all know the archaic myth of the four ages of gold, silver, bronze, and iron, where the world is shown declining, growing ever worse. It will disintegrate presently in chaos, only to burst forth again, fresh as a flower, to recommence spontaneously the inevitable course. There never was a time when time was not. Nor will there be a time when this kaleidoscopic play of eternity in time will have ceased.

There is therefore nothing to be gained, either for the universe or for man, through individual originality and effort. Those who have identified themselves with the mortal body and its affections will necessarily find that all is painful, since everything—for them—must end. But for those who have found the still point of eternity, around which all—including themselves—revolves, everything is acceptable as it is; indeed, can even be experienced as glorious and wonderful. The first duty of the individual, consequently, is simply to play his given role—as do the sun and moon, the various animal and plant species, the waters, the rocks, and the stars—without resistance, without fault; and then, if possible, so to order his mind as to identify its consciousness with the inhabiting principle of the whole.

The dreamlike spell of this contemplative, metaphysically oriented tradition, where light and darkness dance together in a world-creating cosmic shadow play, carries into modern times an image that is of incalculable age. In its primitive form it is widely known among the jungle villages of the broad equatorial zone that extends from Africa eastward, through India, Southeast Asia, and Oceania, to Brazil, where the basic myth is of a dreamlike age of the beginning, when there was neither death nor birth, which, however, terminated when a murder was committed. The body of the victim was cut up and buried. And not only did the food plants on which the community lives arise from those buried parts, but on all who ate of their fruit the organs of reproduction appeared; so that death, which had come into the world through a killing, was countered by its opposite, generation, and the self-consuming thing that is life, which lives on life, began its interminable course.

Throughout the dark green jungles of the world there abound not only dreadful animal scenes of tooth and claw, but also terrible human rites of cannibal communion, dramatically representing—with the force of an initiatory shock—the murder scene, sexual act, and festival meal of the beginning, when life and death became two, which had been one, and the sexes became two, which also had been one. Creatures come into being, live on the death of others, die, and become the food of others, continuing, thus, into and through the transformations of time, the timeless archetype of the mythological beginning; and the individual matters no more than a fallen leaf. Psychologically, the effect of the enactment of such a rite is to shift the focus of the mind from the individual (who perishes) to the everlasting group. Magically, it is to reinforce the ever-living life in all lives, which appears to be many but is really one; so that the growth is stimulated of the yams, coconuts, pigs, moon, and breadfruits, and of the human community as well.[. . .]

For the West, however, the possibility of such an egoless return to a state of soul antecedent to the birth of individuality has long since passed away; and the first important stage in the branching off can be seen to have occurred in that very part of the nuclear Near East where the earliest god-kings and their courts had been for centuries ritually entombed: namely Sumer, where a new sense of the separation of the spheres of god and man began to be represented in myth and ritual about 2350 B.C. The king, then, was no longer a god, but a servant of the god, his Tenant Farmer, supervisor of the race of human slaves created to serve the gods with unremitting toil. And no longer identity, but relationship, was the paramount concern. Man had been made not to *be* God but to know, honor, and serve him; so that even the king, who, according to the earlier mythological view, had been the chief embodiment of divinity on earth, was now but a priest offering sacrifice in tendance to One above—not a god returning himself in a sacrifice to Himself.

In the course of the following centuries, the new sense of separation led to a counter-yearning for return—not to identity, for such was no longer possible of conception (creator and creature were not the same), but to the presence and vision of the forfeited god. Hence the new mythology brought forth, in due time, a development away from the earlier static view of returning cycles. A progressive, temporally oriented mythology arose, of a creation, once and for all, at the beginning of time, a subsequent fall, and a work of restoration, still in progress. The world no longer was to be known as a mere showing in time of the paradigms of eternity, but as a field of unprecedented cosmic conflict between two powers, one light and one dark.

The earliest prophet of this mythology of cosmic restoration was, apparently, the Persian Zoroaster, whose dates, however, have not been securely established. They have been variously placed between c. 1200 and c. 550 B.C., so that, like Homer (of about the same span of years), he should perhaps be regarded rather as symbolic of a tradition than as specifically, or solely, one man. The system associated with his name is based on the idea of a conflict between the wise lord, Ahura Mazda, "first father of the Righteous Order, who gave to the sun and stars their path," and an independent evil principle, Angra Mainyu, the Deceiver, principle of the lie, who, when all had been excellently made, entered into it in every particle. The world, consequently, is a compound wherein good and evil, light and dark, wisdom and violence, are contending for a victory. And the privilege and duty of each man—who, himself, as a part of creation, is a compound of good and evil—is to elect, voluntarily, to engage in the battle in the interest of the light. It is supposed that with the birth of Zoroaster, twelve thousand years following the creation of the world, a decisive turn was given the conflict in favor of the good, and that when he returns, after another twelve millennia, in the person of the messiah Saoshyant, there will take place a final battle and cosmic conflagration, through which the principle of darkness and the lie will be undone. Whereafter, all will be light, there will be no further history, and the Kingdom of God (Ahura Mazda) will have been established in its pristine form forever.

It is obvious that a potent mythical formula for the reorientation of the human spirit is here supplied—pitching it forward along the way of time, summoning man to an assumption of autonomous responsibility for the renovation of the universe in God's name, and thus fostering a new, potentially political (not finally contemplative) philosophy of holy war. "May we be such," runs a Persian prayer, "as those who bring on this renovation and make this world progressive, till its perfection shall have been achieved."

The first historic manifestation of the force of this new mythic view was in the Achaemenian empire of Cyrus the Great (died 529 B.C.) and Darius I (reigned c. 521–486 B.C.), which in a few decades extended its domain from India to Greece, and under the protection of which the post-exilic Hebrews both rebuilt their temple (Ezra 1:1–11) and reconstructed their traditional inheritance. The second historic manifestation was in the Hebrew application of its universal message to themselves; the next was in the world mission of Christianity; and the fourth, in that of Islam.

"Enlarge the place of your tent, and let the curtains of your habitations be stretched out; hold not back, lengthen your cords and strengthen your stakes. For you will spread abroad to the right and to the left, and your descendants will possess the nations and will people the desolate cities" (Isaiah 54:2–3; c. 546–536 B.C.).

"And this gospel of the kingdom will be preached throughout the whole world as a testimony to all nations; and then the end will come" (Matthew 24:14; c. 90 A.D.).

"And slay them wherever you catch them, and turn them out from where they have turned you out; for tumult and oppression are worse than slaughter. . . . And fight them on until there is no more tumult or oppression and there prevail justice and faith in Allah; but if they cease, let there be no hostility except to those who practice oppression" (Koran 2:191, 193; c. 632 A.D.).

Two completely opposed mythologies of the destiny and virtue of man, therefore, have come together in the modern world.[. . .]

The extent to which the mythologies—and therewith psychologies—of the Orient and Occident diverged in the course of the period between the dawn of civilization in the Near East and the present age of mutual rediscovery appears in their opposed versions of the shared mythological image of the first being, who was originally one but became two.

"In the beginning," states an Indian example of c. 700 B.C., preserved in the Brihadaranyaka Upanishad,

> this universe was nothing but the Self in the form of a man. It looked around and saw that there was nothing but itself, whereupon its first shout was, "It is I!"; whence the concept "I" arose. (And that is why, even now, when addressed, one answers first, "It is I!" only then giving the other name that one bears.)
>
> Then he was afraid. (That is why anyone alone is afraid.) But he considered: "Since there is no one here but myself, what is there to fear?" Whereupon the fear departed. (For what should have been feared? It is only to a second that fear refers.)
>
> However, he still lacked delight (therefore, we lack delight when alone) and desired a second. He was exactly as large as a man and woman embracing. This Self then divided itself in two parts; and with that, there were a master and a mistress. (Therefore this body, by itself, as the sage Yajnavalkya declares, is like half of a split pea. And that is why, indeed, this space is filled by a woman.)
>
> The male embraced the female, and from that the human race arose. She, however, reflected: "How can he unite with me, who am produced from himself? Well then, let me hide!" She became a cow, he a bull and united with her; and from that cattle arose. She became a mare, he a stallion; she an ass, he a donkey and united with her; and from that solid-hoofed animals arose. She became a goat, he a buck; she a sheep, he a ram and united with her; and from that goats and sheep arose. Thus he poured forth all pairing things, down to the ants. Then he realized: "I, actually, am creation; for I have poured forth all this." Whence arose the concept "Creation" [Sanskrit *sṛṣṭiḥ*: "what is poured forth"].
>
> Anyone understanding this becomes, truly, himself a creator in this creation.

The best-known Occidental example of this image of the first being, split in two, which seem to be two but are actually one, is, of course, that of the Book of Genesis, second chapter, where it is turned, however, to a different sense. For the couple is separated here by a superior being, who, as we are told, caused a deep sleep to fall upon the man and, while he slept, took one of his ribs. In the Indian version it is the god himself that divides and becomes not man alone but all creation; so that everything is a manifestation of that single inhabiting divine substance: there is no other; whereas in the Bible, God and man, from the beginning, are distinct. Man is made in the image of God, indeed, and the breath of God has been breathed into his nostrils; yet his being, his self, is not that of God, nor is it one with the universe. The fashioning of the world, of the animals, and of Adam (who then became Adam and Eve) was accomplished not within the sphere of divinity but outside of it. There is, consequently, an *intrinsic*, not merely *formal,* separation. And the goal of knowledge cannot be to *see* God here and now in all things; for God is not in things. God is transcendent. God is beheld only by the dead. The goal of knowledge has to be, rather, to know the *relationship* of God to his creation, or, more specifically, to man, and through such knowledge, by God's grace, to link one's own will back to that of the Creator.

Moreover, according to the biblical version of this myth, it was only after creation that man fell, whereas in the Indian example creation itself was a fall— the fragmentation of a god. And the god is not condemned. Rather, his creation, his "pouring forth" (*sṛṣṭiḥ*), is described as an act of voluntary, dynamic will-to-be-more, which anteceded creation and has, therefore, a metaphysical, symbolical, not literal, historical meaning. The fall of Adam and Eve was an event within the already created frame of time and space, an accident that should not have taken place. The myth of the Self in the form of a man, on the other hand, who looked around and saw nothing but himself, said "I," felt fear, and then desired to be two, tells of an intrinsic, not errant, factor in the manifold of being, the correction or undoing of which would not improve, but dissolve, creation. The Indian point of view is metaphysical, poetical; the biblical, ethical and historical.

Adam's fall and exile from the garden was thus in no sense a metaphysical departure of divine substance from itself, but an event only in the history, or pre-history, of man. And this event in the created world has been followed throughout the remainder of the book by the record of man's linkage and failures of linkage back to God—again, historically conceived. For, as we next hear, God himself, at a certain point in the course of time, out of his own volition, moved toward man, instituting a new law in the form of a covenant with a certain people. And these became, therewith, a priestly race, unique in the world. God's reconciliation with man, of whose creation he had repented (Genesis 6:6), was to be achieved only by virtue of this particular community—in time: for in time there should take place the realization of the Lord God's kingdom on earth, when the heathen monarchies would crumble and Israel be saved, when men would "cast forth their idols of silver and their idols of gold, which they made to themselves to worship, to the moles and to the bats."

> *Be broken, you peoples, and be dismayed;*
> *give ear, all you far countries;*
> *gird yourselves and be dismayed;*
> *gird yourselves and be dismayed.*
> *Take counsel together, but it will come to nought;*
> *speak a word, but it will not stand,*
> *for God is with us.*

In the Indian view, on the contrary, what is divine here is divine there also; nor has anyone to wait—or even to hope—for a "day of the Lord." For what has been lost is in each his very self (*ātman*), here and now, requiring only to be sought. Or, as they say: "Only when men shall roll up space like a piece of leather will there be an end of sorrow apart from knowing God."

The question arises (again historical) in the world dominated by the Bible, as to the identity of the favored community, and three are well known to have developed claims: the Jewish, the Christian, and the Moslem, each supposing itself to have been authorized by a particular revelation. God, that is to say, though conceived as outside of history and not himself its substance (transcendent: not immanent), is supposed to have engaged himself miraculously in the enterprise of restoring fallen man through a covenant, sacrament, or revealed book, with a view to a general, communal experience of fulfillment yet to come. The world is corrupt and man a sinner; the individual, however, through engagement along with God in the destiny of the only authorized community, participates in the coming glory of the kingdom of righteousness, when "the glory of the Lord shall be revealed, and all flesh shall see it together."

In the experience and vision of India, on the other hand, although the holy mystery and power have been understood to be indeed transcendent ("other than the known; moreover, above the unknown"), they are also, at the same time, immanent ("like a razor in a razorcase, like fire in tinder"). It is not that the divine is every*where*: it is that the divine is every*thing*. So that one does not require any outside reference, revelation, sacrament, or authorized community to return to it. One has but to alter one's psychological orientation and recognize (re-cognize) what is within. Deprived of this recognition, we are removed from our own reality by a cerebral shortsightedness which is called in Sanskrit *māyā*, "delusion" (from the verbal root *mā*, "measure, measure out, to form, to build," denoting, in the first place, the power of a god or demon to produce illusory effects, to change form, and to appear under the deceiving masks; in the second place, "magic," the production of illusions and, in warfare, camouflage, deceptive tactics; and finally, in philosophical discourse, the illusion superimposed upon reality as an effect of ignorance). Instead of the biblical exile from a geographically, historically conceived garden wherein God walked in the cool of the day, we have in India, therefore, already c. 700 B.C. (some three hundred years before the putting together of the Pentateuch), a *psychological* reading of the great theme.

The shared myth of the primal androgyne is applied in the two traditions to the same task—the exposition of man's distance, in his normal secular life, from the divine Alpha and Omega. Yet the arguments radically differ, and therefore support two radically different civilizations. For, if man has been removed from the divine through a historical event, it will be a historical event that leads him back, whereas if it has been by some sort of psychological displacement that he has been blocked, psychology will be his vehicle of return. And so it is that in India the final focus of concern is not the community (though, as we shall see, the idea of the holy community plays a formidable role as a disciplinary force), but yoga.

THE TWO VIEWS OF EGO

The Indian term *yoga* is derived from the Sanskrit verbal root *yuj*, "to link, join, or unite," which is related etymologically to "yoke," a yoke of oxen, and is in sense analogous to the word "religion" "to link back, or bind." Man, the creature, is by religion bound back to God. However, religion, *religio*, refers to a linking historically conditioned by way of a covenant, sacrament, or Koran, whereas yoga is the psychological linking of the mind to that superordinated principle "by which the mind knows." Furthermore, in yoga what is linked is finally the self to itself, consciousness to consciousness, for what had seemed, through *māyā*, to be two are in reality not so; whereas in religion what are linked are God and man, which are not the same.

It is of course true that in the popular religions of the Orient the Gods are worshiped as though external to their devotees, and all the rules and rites of a covenanted relationship are observed. Nevertheless, the ultimate realization, which the sages have celebrated, is that the god worshiped as though without is in reality a reflex of the same mystery as oneself. As long as an illusion of ego remains, the commensurate illusion of a separate deity also will be there; and vice versa, as long as the idea of a separate deity is cherished, an illusion of ego, related to it in love, fear, worship, exile, or atonement, will also be there. But precisely that illusion of duality is the trick of *māyā*. "Thou art that" (*tat tvam asi*) is the proper thought for the first step to wisdom.

In the beginning, as we have read, there was only the Self; but it said "I" (Sanskrit, *aham*) and immediately felt fear, after which, desire.

It is to be remarked that in this view of the instant of creation (presented from within the sphere of the psyche of the creative being itself) the same two basic motivations are identified as the leading modern schools of depth analysis have indicated for the *human* psyche: aggression and desire. Carl G. Jung, in his early paper on *The Unconscious in Normal and Pathological Psychology* (1916), wrote of two psychological types: the introvert, harried by fear, and the extrovert, driven by desire. Sigmund Freud also, in his *Beyond the Pleasure Principle* (1920), wrote of "the death wish" and "the life wish": on the one hand, the will to violence and the fear of it (*thanatos, destrudo*), and, on the other hand, the need and desire to love and be loved (*eros, libido*). Both spring spontaneously from the deep dark source of the energies of the psyche, the *id*, and are governed, therefore, by the self-centered "pleasure principle": *I* want: *I* am afraid. Comparably, in the Indian myth, as soon as the self said "I" (*aham*), it knew first fear, and then desire.

But now—and here, I believe, is a point of fundamental importance for our reading of the basic difference between the Oriental and Occidental approaches to the cultivation of the soul—in the Indian myth the principle of ego, "I" (*aham*), is identified completely with the pleasure principle, whereas in the psychologies of both Freud and Jung its proper function is to know and relate to external reality (Freud's "reality principle"): not the reality of the metaphysical but that of the physical, empirical sphere of time and space. In other words, spiritual maturity, as understood in the modern Occident, requires a differentiation of *ego* from *id*, whereas in the Orient, throughout the history at least of every teaching that has stemmed from India, ego (*aham-kāra*: "the making of the sound 'I' ") is impugned as the principle of libidinous delusion, to be dissolved.[. . .]

Now it is to be observed that in the version [. . .] of the temptation of the Buddha, the Antagonist represents all three of the first triad of ends (the so-called *trivarga*: "aggregate of three"); for in his character as the Lord Desire he personifies the first; as the Lord Death, the aggressive force of the second; while in his summons to the meditating sage to arise and return to the duties of his station in society, he promotes the third. And, indeed, as a manifestation of that Self which not only poured forth but permanently supports the universe, he is the proper incarnation of these ends. For they do, in fact, support the world. And in most of the rites of all religions, this triune god, we may say, in one aspect or another, is the one and only god adored.

However, in the name and achievement of the Buddha, the "Illuminated One," the fourth end is announced: release from delusion. And to the attainment of this, the others are impediments, difficult to remove, yet, for one of purpose, not invincible. Sitting at the world navel, pressing back through the welling creative force that was surging into and through his own being, the Buddha actually broke back into the void beyond, and—ironically—the universe immediately burst into bloom. Such an act of self-noughting is one of individual effort. There can be no question about that. However, an Occidental eye cannot but observe that there is no requirement or expectation anywhere in this Indian system of four ends—neither in the primary two of the natural organism and the impressed third of society, nor in the exalted fourth of release—for a maturation of the personality through intelligent, fresh, individual adjustment to the time-space world round about, creative experimentation with unexplored possibilities, and the assumption of personal responsibility for unprecedented acts performed within the context of the social order. In the Indian tradition all has been perfectly arranged from all eternity. There can be nothing new, nothing to be learned but what the sages have taught from of yore. And finally, when the boredom of this nursery horizon of "I want" against "thou shalt" has become insufferable, the fourth and final aim is all that is offered—of an extinction of the infantile ego altogether: disengagement or release (*moksha*) from both "I" and "thou."

In the European West, on the other hand, where the fundamental doctrine of the freedom of the will essentially dissociates each individual from every other, as well as from both the will in nature and the will of God, there is placed upon each the responsibility of coming intelligently, out of his own experience and volition, to some sort of relationship with—not identity with or extinction in—the all, the void, the suchness, the absolute, or whatever the proper term may be for that which is beyond terms. And, in the secular sphere likewise, it is normally expected that an educated ego should have developed away from the simple infantile polarity of the pleasure and obedience principles toward a personal, uncompulsive, sensitive relationship to empirical reality, a certain adventurous attitude toward the unpredictable, and a sense of personal responsibility for decisions. Not life as a good soldier, but life as a developed, unique individual, is the ideal. And we shall search the Orient in vain for anything quite comparable. There the ideal, on the contrary, is the quenching, not development, of ego. That is the formula turned this way and that, up and down the line, throughout the literature: a systematic, steady, continually drumming devaluation of the "I" principle, the reality function—which has remained, consequently, undeveloped, and so, wide open to the seizures of completely uncritical mythic identifications.

47. Eternal Life

A. SETH PRINGLE-PATTISON

. . . We (often) find both theologians and philosophers insisting on the idea of an "eternal life," not as something in the future, a continuance of existence after our earthly life is ended, but as an experience, a state of being, to be enjoyed here and now. So, for example, in Schleiermacher's famous declaration: "The goal and the character of the religious life is not the immortality desired and believed in by many. . . . It is not the immortality that is outside of time, behind it or rather after it, and which still is in time. It is the immortality which we can have now in this temporal life. In the midst of finitude to be one with the Infinite, and in every moment to be eternal, that is the immortality of religion." The idea is very commonly put forward, as it is in this passage of Schleiermacher's, in opposition to banal and selfishly personal conceptions of a future life, which have nothing religious about them; and hence such statements are often interpreted as implying that the enjoyment of the eternal life described is limited to the opportunities afforded by the present life. They are taken as definitely negating the idea of personal immortality in any ordinary sense of the term. This negative attitude is, no doubt, adopted by many: they put forward the possibility of realizing eternal life here and now *in place of* the further life which we ordinarily mean by immortality. Schleiermacher himself, at least during the earlier part of his career, seems to have held such a view. There is recounted in Dr. Martineau's *Study of Religion* the touching story of his ineffectual efforts to console a young widow whose husband, according to Schleiermacher's teaching, had "melted away into the great All." But eternity and immortality are by no means necessarily exclusive terms: on the contrary, our experience here and now may carry in it "the power of an endless life," and be in truth the only earnest or guarantee of such a life.

It is a commonplace of philosophical criticism that the term "eternal," when strictly and properly used, does not mean endless continuance *in* time, but a quality of experience which transcends time altogether. Thus in Spinoza, where the contrast is specially emphasized, eternity means rational necessity. We know things "under a certain form of eternity" when we see them not as isolated contin-

gent events, but as necessary parts of a single system, each integral to the whole. It
is of the nature of reason (*de natura rationis*) so to regard things, and the perception
of this timeless necessity is a very real experience. Mr. Bertrand Russell has told
our own generation afresh, in this connexion, that "mathematics [is] . . . capable
of a stern perfection such as only the greatest art can show. The true spirit of
delight, the exaltation, the sense of being more than man, which is the touch-
stone of the highest excellence, is to be found in mathematics as surely as in
poetry." (*Philosophical Essays.*) For Spinoza the necessity of reason is not divorced,
as with Mr. Russell, from actual existence. It is Spinoza's vision of the universe as
in all its parts a system of divine necessity which creates in him "the intellectual
love of God," that supreme emotion which expels lower or merely selfish desires,
because it is itself joy and peace, the perfect satisfaction of the mind (*vera mentis
acquiescentia*). "All our happiness or unhappiness," he tells us, "depends solely on
the quality of the object on which our love is fixed. . . . But love towards an
object eternal and infinite feeds the mind with a joy that is pure with no tinge of
sadness." (*De Intellectus Emendatione.*) Such is the life of "thoughts immortal and
divine" of which we found Plato and Aristotle also speaking as opening up to the
thinker a present immortality. For Spinoza this "eternal life" is realized in the
intellectual vision of truth and harmony; and, as he twice over reminds us in the
Short Treatise, Truth—the ultimate or all-embracing Truth—is God Himself. This
is the "intuition (*scientia intuitiva*) in which knowledge culminates.

But Art, or, to put it more widely, the perception of Beauty, also yields us
experiences under a similar "form of eternity."

> *A thing of beauty is a joy for ever:*
> *Its loveliness increases; it will never*
> *Pass into nothingness.*

Art, it has been said, is the wide world's memory of things. Think only of some of
the great stories which have delighted generation after generation, the tale of
Troy, the wanderings of Odysseus, the history of Don Quixote. Think of the figures
of drama, every turn of whose fate is graven upon our mind and heart, "forms more
real than living man," who trod the boards centuries before our coming, and on
whom the curtain will rise as many ages after we have gone. Or take the forms
bequeathed to us by the sculptor's art, or some melody of immortal loveliness.
Perhaps this sense of bodiless immortality is most vividly realized by the ordinary
person in the case of a musical work, as the sounds fill the air and the instruments
give its harmonies and sequences once more a brief existence for the bodily ear.

In Art, as Schopenhauer loved to insist, the objects we contemplate have
the eternity and universality of the Platonic Ideas. They are lifted out of the
stream of becoming which constitutes individual existence; and in contemplating
them we are emancipated from the tyranny of the Will, that is to say, of selfish
desire. In aesthetic perception our knowledge is pure and disinterested; our objectivity is complete. "The subject and the object mutually fill and penetrate each
other completely." Science, based on the principle of causality, is constantly
investigating the relations of its object to other things, and is involved, thereby, in
an endless quest. "Art is everywhere at its goal, for it plucks the object of its

contemplation out of the world's course, and has it isolated before it. And this particular thing, which in that stream was a small perishing part, becomes to art the representative of the whole, an equivalent of the endless multitude in space and time. The course of time stops; relations vanish for it; only the essential, the Idea, is its object." Our individuality has fallen from us: "we are only that *one* eye of the world which looks out from all knowing creatures, but only in man can become perfectly free from the service of the will." "Then all at once the peace which we were always seeking, but which fled from us on the former path of the desires, comes to us of its own accord and it is well with us: we keep a Sabbath from the penal slavery of the will; the wheel of Ixion stands still." Many, accordingly, have celebrated Art in this strain, as the only refuge of the spirit from the miseries and weariness of the actual world,

> *The weariness, the fever, and the fret,*
> *Here where men sit and hear each other groan.*

To such natures—to Keats, from whom I have quoted, to Goethe and Schiller at certain points in their career—Art thus becomes a religion, or at least is made to do duty for one. Such moments, however, of selfless contemplation and aesthetic enjoyment cannot be more than intermittent, Schopenhauer confesses, and therefore Art cannot achieve that perfect and final deliverance which we seek from the misery of existence. For that we must go, he teaches, to religion, to a religion like Buddhism, which inculcates the resolute extermination of the will to live.

It is in religion, after all, that the term "eternal life" is most familiar to us. It occurs constantly in the New Testament as the designation of a frame of mind or spiritual attitude which is intended to be realized here and now. The meaning of the phrase in early Christian usage can hardly be fully understood, however, without a glance at the Jewish apocalyptic beliefs, so prominent in men's minds at the time, with which it was at first closely associated, but with which it comes to be in a sense contrasted. We have seen in a previous Lecture how slow was the growth of an effective doctrine of a future life among the Hebrews. When it did arise, it was associated with the national hope of a Messianic kingdom. "The day of Jahveh," originally conceived simply as a judgment on the enemies of Israel executed by the national god, and the inauguration of a new period of material prosperity under his protection, had been transformed by the prophets into the idea of a day of judgment upon Israel itself for the nation's sins; and with the rise of a true monotheism (from the seventh century onwards) this judgment was extended to include all the nations of the earth. The result of the prophesied judgment was to be the establishment of the righteous and penitent remnant of Israel under a prince of the house of David, or a dynasty of such warrior kings and righteous rulers. Other nations—the Gentiles— were either to be destroyed, according to the bitter nationalism of some of the prophets, or, according to the larger-hearted, brought into this divinely established kingdom by conversion. The kingdom was to be set up on this present earth and would last for ever, and the righteous dead of Israel were to be raised from Sheol to participate in its blessedness.

This was the first form of the apocalyptic idea, but in course of time— about the close of the second century B.C.—it came to be realized that the earth (whether as we know it or as transformed into "a new heaven and a new earth") was unfit to be the scene of such an eternal kingdom: the Kingdom of God could be realized only in a spiritual world to come. The idea of a Messianic reign of the saints upon earth was not abandoned, but it was conceived as temporary in duration (sometimes as lasting a thousand years), and as a prelude to the final judgment which inaugurates the eternal kingdom of God. The important point, however, remains the same, namely, the sharp distinction drawn between "the present age," in which the powers of wickedness hold sway, and "the coming age," when the divine kingdom will be realized. The appearance of the Messiah, now conceived as a supernatural being—"the Son of man" or "the Son of God"—is the event which is to mark the advent, or at least the near approach, of the new age. Such were the convictions of the religious part of the Jewish nation in the time of Jesus, and this eschatology meets us everywhere in the New Testament. The sense of the imminence of the coming of the Kingdom is universal. "The Kingdom of Heaven is at hand" was the text of John the Baptist's preaching, and the phrase was appropriated and applied by Jesus in his own way. The first idea which the words roused in the minds of his hearers was the thought of this future dispensation, to be ushered in catastrophically by the appearance of the Messiah on the clouds of heaven to judge the world. Jesus himself appears to have shared the general belief that this event would take place within the life-time of those whom he was addressing: "There be some standing here which shall not taste of death, till they see the Son of man coming in his Kingdom." (Matt. xvi. 28.) "This generation shall not pass, till all these things be fulfilled." (Matt. xxiv. 34.) When he sent out the Twelve on their preaching mission, he is represented as saying that, before their return, the expected event would have taken place: "Verily I say unto you, Ye shall not have gone over the cities of Israel, till the Son of man be come." (Matt. x. 23.) We need not wonder, therefore, if, in spite of the rest of their Master's teaching about the spiritual nature of the Kingdom, the disciples continued to give his sayings about it this future reference, and had to be rebuked for the thoroughly mundane hopes of reward and distinction which they linked with its establishment.

Yet, from the beginning of his teaching, Jesus made the inheritance of this kingdom dependent on purely spiritual conditions. He taught not simply, like John the Baptist or the prophets before him, that the kingdom of heaven was at hand, but that it was already a present fact—"in their midst" or "within them"; and, in so doing, he stepped out of the ranks of the Hebrew prophets and came forward as the bearer of a new message from God to man. And the gospel he proclaimed was not a promise of future reward for certain beliefs about himself, but, as every genuinely religious message must be, a gospel of deliverance, a message of present salvation: "Come unto me, all ye that labour and are heavy laden, and *I will give you rest. Take my yoke upon you and learn of me; for I am meek and lowly in heart: and ye shall find rest unto your souls.*" (Matt. xi. 28–9.) It is an insight which changes the face of the world and "makes all things new." Above all it is an insight into what salvation really means. Not a password enabling a man to escape dire penalties in the future or admitting him to great rewards, but a change of the inner man, the adoption of a new attitude towards life and its happenings. The changed attitude is not to be understood as the condition of salvation, in the sense that salvation is something different from the spiritual state and externally added to it. As St. Paul says, "To be spiritually minded *is* life and peace." (Rom. viii. 6.) This, then, is the salvation of the soul, the only salvation that matters, as the Platonic Socrates had already so impressively insisted: and when Jesus says "A man's *life* consisteth not in the abundance of the things which he possesseth" (Luke xii. 15), or "What shall it profit a man if he shall gain the whole world and lose his own *soul?*" (Mark viii. 36), the words "life" and "soul" are clearly used in the Platonic sense and not in an eschatological reference. Hence we have the antithesis of "life" and "death," so recurrent in the New Testament, both terms being used to signify a present spiritual state. The message of the Gospel is continually referred to as a message of "life," and the change it effects is described as a passage from "death unto life." The antithesis is equated by St. Paul with his own favourite contrast between the flesh and the spirit. "To be carnally minded is death; but to be spiritually minded is life and peace." "The law of the spirit of life in Christ Jesus hath made me free from the law of sin and death . . . The body is dead because of sin, but the spirit is life because of righteousness." (Rom. viii. 1–10.) He also inweaves with his statement that other sense of "death," contained in the most characteristic teaching of Jesus, that "whosoever will save his life shall lose it: and whosoever will lose his life for my sake shall find it." (Matt. xvi. 25.) This is, in his own emphatic phrase, the very "word of the cross" (I Cor. i. 18), life through death. We must die to self—to selfish desires and egoistic cravings—before we can find our true self in that wider life which is at once the love of the brethren and the love of God. In this sense, St. Paul protests, he dies daily: only by dying with Christ, "crucifying the flesh with the passions and the lusts thereof" (Gal. v. 24, Revised Version), can we share with him the higher life to which he showed the way. As sharing that life, "walking in Him," "complete in Him," St. Paul describes believers as already "risen with Christ." Thus the death and resurrection of Jesus, which he accepted (we know) as historical facts, and his own resurrection, to which he undoubtedly looked forward as a future event, became for the Apostle, as a religious thinker, a description of the eternal nature of the spiritual life, symbols of an experience daily realized. It is in this sense that Christ is said to have brought *life and immortality* to light through the gospel (2 Tim. i. 10). "This gift to men" (I purposely quote a strictly orthodox commentator) "is not the inculcation of the truth of an endless existence, nor any dogma of the soul's deathless perpetuity, but the revelation of a higher life."

Life, in the mystical sense indicated, often more specifically "eternal life," is the very burden of the Fourth Gospel and the Johannine Epistles. "I am come," says the Johannine Christ, "that they might have life, and that they might have it more abundantly." (John x. 10.) "He that eateth my flesh and drinketh my blood hath eternal life." (John vi. 54.). This spiritual sense both of life and of resurrection forms the kernel of the Lazarus story, where it expressly emphasized against the literalism of Martha. "Martha saith unto him, I know that he shall rise again in the resurrection at the last day. Jesus said unto her, I am the resurrection and the life: he that believeth in me, though he were dead, yet shall he live: and whosoever liveth and believeth in me shall never die." (John xi. 24–6.) So again: "The hour cometh *and now is,* when the dead shall hear the voice of the Son of God, and they that hear shall live." (John v. 25.) This is the same spiritual sense of life and resurrection as an accomplished fact that we have in St. Paul. The dead here are the spiritually dead who are to be quickened or made alive. "This is life eternal, that they should know thee, the only true God, and Jesus Christ whom thou hast sent." (John xvii. 3.) Similary in the Epistles: "God hath given to us eternal life, and this life is in his Son. He that hath the Son hath life." (I John v. 11–12.) "We know that we have passed from death unto life, because we love the brethren. He that loveth not his brother abideth in death." (I John iii. 14.) "He that loveth not, knoweth not God; for God is love. . . . If we love one another, God abideth in us, and his love is perfected in us." (I John iv. 8–12.) "This is the true God, and eternal life." (I John v. 20.)

The emphatic present tense throughout these passages is evidence sufficient of the writer's meaning. Eternal life is not a state of existence to follow upon physical death, but an all-satisfying present experience of the love of God in Christ. It is, as the theologians say, "participation in the being of the spiritual Christ." The fruit of such an experience (to quote St. Paul's list) is "love, joy, peace." (Gal. v. 22.) "My peace I give unto you," says the Johannine Christ. (John xiv. 27.) "These things have I spoken unto you, that your joy might be full." (John xv. 11.) "And ye shall know the truth, and the truth shall make you free." (John viii. 32.) This is the eternal life in the midst of time which is claimed by the saints as an immediate experience, one which time can neither increase nor diminish, one to which considerations of time are, in fact, indifferent, because we are at rest in the present.

48. Ideal Immortality

GEORGE SANTAYANA

INTELLECTUAL VICTORY OVER CHANGE

The more we reflect, the more we live in memory and idea, the more convinced and penetrated we shall be by the experience of death; yet, without our knowing it, perhaps, this very conviction and experience will have raised us, in a way, above mortality. That was a heroic and divine oracle which, in informing us of our decay, made us partners of the gods' eternity, and by giving us knowledge poured into us, to that extent, the serenity and balm of truth. As it is memory that enables us to feel that we are dying and to know that everything actual is in flux, so it is memory that opens to us an ideal immortality, unacceptable and meaningless to the old Adam, but genuine in its own way and undeniably true. It is an immortality in representation—a representation which envisages things in their truth as they have in their own day possessed themselves in reality. It is no subterfuge or superstitious effrontery, called to disguise or throw off the lessons of experience; on the contrary, it is experience itself, reflection itself, and knowledge of mortality. Memory does not reprieve or postpone the changes which it registers, nor does it itself possess a permanent duration; it is, if possible, less stable and more mobile than primary sensation. It is, in point of existence, only an internal and complex kind of sensibility. But in intent and by its significance it plunges to the depths of time; it looks still on the departed and bears witness to the truth that, though absent from this part of experience, and incapable of returning to life, they nevertheless existed once in their own right, were as living and actual as experience is to-day, and still help to make up, in company with all past, present, and future mortals, the filling and value of the world.

As the pathos and heroism of life consists in accepting as an opportunity the fate that makes our own death, partial or total, serviceable to others, so the glory of life consists in accepting the knowledge of natural death as an opportunity to live in the spirit. The sacrifice, the self-surrender, remains real; for, though the compensation is real, too, and at moments, perhaps, apparently overwhelming, it is always incomplete and leaves beneath an incurable sorrow. Yet life can never contradict its basis or reach satisfactions essentially excluded by its own conditions. Progress lies in moving forward from the given situation, and satisfying as well as may be the interests that exist. And if some initial demand has proved hopeless, there is the greater reason for cultivating other sources of satisfaction, possibly more abundant and lasting. Now, reflection is a vital function; memory and imagination have to the full the rhythm and force of life.

THE GLORY OF IT

But these faculties, in envisaging the past or the ideal, envisage the eternal, and the man in whose mind they predominate is to that extent detached in his affections from the world of flux, from himself, and from his personal destiny. This detachment will not make him infinitely long-lived, nor absolutely happy, but it may render him intelligent and just, and may open to him all intellectual pleasures and all human sympathies.

There is accordingly an escape from death open to man; one not found by circumventing nature, but by making use of her own expedients in circumventing her imperfections. Memory, nay, perception itself, is a first stage in this escape, which coincides with the acquisition and possession of reason. When the meaning of successive perceptions is recovered with the last of them, when a survey is made of objects whose constitutive sensations first arose independently, this synthetic moment contains an object raised above time on a pedestal of reflection, a thought indefeasibly true in its ideal deliverance, though of course fleeting in its psychic existence. Existence is essentially temporal and life foredoomed to be mortal, since its basis is a process and an opposition; it floats in the stream of time, never to return, never to be recovered or repossessed. But ever since substance became at some sensitive point intelligent and reflective, ever since time made room and pause for memory, for history, for the consciousness of time, a god, as it were, became incarnate in mortality and some vision of truth, some self-forgetful satisfaction, became a heritage that moment could transmit to moment and man to man.

This heritage is humanity itself, the presence of immortal reason in creatures that perish. Apprehension, which makes man so like a god, makes him in one respect immortal; it quickens his numbered moments with a vision of what never dies, the truth of those moments and their inalienable values.

REASON MAKES MAN'S DIVINITY

To participate in this vision is to participate at once in humanity and in divinity, since all other bonds are material and perishable, but the bond between two thoughts that have grasped the same truth, of two instants that have caught the same beauty, is a spiritual and imperishable bond. It is imperishable simply because it is ideal and resident merely in import and intent. The two thoughts, the two instants, remain existentially different; were they not two they could not come from different quarters to unite in one meaning and to behold one object in distinct and conspiring acts of apprehension. Being independent in existence, they can be united by the identity of their burden, by the common worship, so to speak, of the same god. Were this ideal goal itself an existence, it would be incapable of uniting anything; for the same gulf which separated the two original minds would open between them and their common object. But being, as it is, purely ideal, it can become the meeting-ground of intelligences and render their union ideally eternal. Among the physical instruments of thought there may be rivalry and impact—the two thinkers may compete and clash—but this is because each seeks his own physical survival and does not love the truth stripped of its accidental associations and provincial accent. Doctors disagree in so far as they are not truly doctors, but, as Plato would say, seek, like sophists, and wage-earners, to circumvent and defeat one another. The conflict is physical and can extend to the subject-matter only in so far as this is tainted by individual prejudice and not wholly lifted from the sensuous to the intellectual plane. In the ether there are no winds of doctrine. The intellect, being the organ and source of the divine, is divine and single; if there were many sorts of intellect, many principles of perspective, they would fix and create incomparable and irrelevant worlds. Reason is one in that it gravitates toward an object, called truth, which could not have the function it has, of being a focus for mental activities, if it were not one in reference to the operations which converge upon it.

This unity in truth, as in reason, is of course functional only, not physical or existential. The beats of thought and the thinkers are innumerable; indefinite, too, the variations to which their endowment and habits may be subjected. But the condition of spiritual communion or ideal relevance in these intelligences is their possession of a method and grammar essentially identical. Language, for example, is significant in proportion to the constancy in meaning which words and locutions preserve in a speaker's mind at various times, or in the minds of various persons. This constancy is never absolute. Therefore language is never wholly significant, never exhaustively intelligible. There is always mud in the well, if we have drawn up enough water. Yet in peaceful rivers, though they flow, there is an appreciable degree of translucency. So, from moment to moment, and from man to man, there is an appreciable element of unanimity, of constancy and congruity of intent. On this abstract and perfectly identical function science rests together with every rational formation.

AND HIS IMMORTALITY

The same function is the seat of human immortality. Reason lifts a larger or smaller element in each man to the plane of ideality according as reason more or less thoroughly leavens and permeates the lump. No man is wholly immortal, as no philosophy is wholly true and no language wholly intelligible; but only in so far as intelligible is a language a language rather than a noise, only in so far as true is a philosophy more than a vent for cerebral humours, and only in so far as a man is rational and immortal is he a man and not a sensorium.

It is hard to convince people that they have such a gift as intelligence. If they perceive its animal basis they cannot conceive its ideal affinities or under-stand what is meant by calling it divine; if they perceive its ideality and see the immortal essences that swim into its ken, they hotly deny that it is an animal faculty, and invent ultramundane places and bodiless persons in which it is to reside; as if those celestial substances could be, in respect to thought, any less material than matter or, in respect to vision and life, any less instrumental than bodily organs. It never occurs to them that if nature has added intelligence to animal life it is because they belong together. Intelligence is a natural emanation of vitality. If eternity could exist otherwise than as a vision in time, eternity would have no meaning for men in the world, while the world, men, and time would have no vocation or status in eternity. The travail of existence would be without excuse, without issue or consummation, while the conceptions of truth and of perfection would be without application to experience, pure dreams about things preternatural and unreal, vacantly conceived, and illogically supposed to have something to do with living issues. But truth and perfection, for the very reason that they are not problematic existences but inherent ideals, cannot be banished from discourse. Experience may lose any of its data; it cannot lose, while it endures, the terms with which it operates in becoming experience. Now, truth is relevant to every opinion which looks to truth for its standard, and perfection is envisaged in every cry for relief, in every effort at betterment. Opinions, volitions, and passionate refusals fill human life. So that when the existence of truth is denied, truth is given the only status which it ever required—it is conceived.

IT IS THE LOCUS OF ALL TRUTHS

Nor can any better defense be found for the denial that nature and her life have a status in eternity. This statement may not be understood, but if grasped at all it will not be questioned. By having a status in eternity is not meant being parts of an eternal existence, petrified or congealed into something real but motionless. What is meant is only that whatever exists in time, when bathed in the light of reflec-tion, acquires an indelible character and discloses irreversible relations; every fact, in being recognised, takes its place in the universe of discourse, in that ideal sphere of truth which is the common and unchanging standard for all assertions. Language, science, art, religion, and all ambitious dreams are compacted of ideas. Life is as much a mosaic of notions as the firmament is of stars; and these ideal and transpersonal objects, bridging time, fixing standards, establishing values, constituting the natural rewards of all living, are the very furniture of eternity, the goals and playthings of that reason which is an instinct in the heart as vital and spontaneous as any other. Or rather, perhaps, reason is a supervening instinct by which all other instincts are interpreted, just as the *sensus communis* or transcendental unit of psychology is a faculty by which all perceptions are brought face to face and compared. So that immortality is not a privilege reserved for a part only of experience, but rather a relation pervading every part in varying measure. We may, in leaving the subject, mark the degrees and phases of this idealisation.

EPICUREAN IMMORTALITY, THROUGH THE TRUTH OF EXISTENCE

Animal sensation is related to eternity only by the truth that it has taken place. The fact, fleeting as it is, is registered in ideal history, and no inventory of the world's riches, no true confession of its crimes, would ever be complete that ignored that incident. This indefeasible character in experience makes a first sort of ideal immortality, one on which those rational philosophers like to dwell who have not speculation enough to feel quite certain of any other. It was a consolation to the Epicurean to remember that, however brief and uncertain might be his tenure of delight, the past was safe and the present sure. "He lives happy," says Horace, "and master over himself, who can say daily, I have lived. To-morrow let Jove cover the sky with black clouds or flood it with sunshine; he shall not thereby render vain what lies behind, he shall not delete and make never to have existed what once the hour has brought in its flight." Such self-concentration and hugging of the facts has no power to improve them; it gives to pleasure and pain an impartial eternity, and rather tends to intrench in sensuous and selfish satisfactions a mind that has lost faith in reason and that deliberately ignores the difference in scope and dignity which exists among various pursuits. Yet the reflection is staunch and in its way heroic; it meets a vague and feeble aspiration, that looks to the infinite, with a just rebuke; it points to real satisfactions, experienced successes, and asks us to be content with the fulfilment of our own wills. If you have seen the world, if you have played your game and won it, what more would you ask for? If you have tasted the sweets of existence, you should be satisfied; if the experience has been bitter, you should be glad that it comes to an end.

Of course, as we have seen, there is a primary demand in man which death and mutation contradict flatly, so that no summons to cease can ever be obeyed with complete willingness. Even the suicide trembles and the ascetic feels the stings of the flesh. It is the part of philosophy, however, to pass over those natural repugnances and overlay them with as much countervailing rationality as can find lodgment in a particular mind. The Epicurean, having abandoned politics and religion and being afraid of any far-reaching ambition, applied philosophy honestly enough to what remained. Simple and healthy pleasures are the reward of simple and healthy pursuits; to chafe against them because they are limited is to import a foreign and disruptive element into the case; a healthy hunger has its limit, and its satisfaction reaches a natural term. Philosophy, far from alienating us from those values, should teach us to see their perfection and to maintain them in our ideal. In other words, the happy filling of a single hour is so much gained for the universe at large, and to find joy and sufficiency in the flying moment is perhaps the only means open to us for increasing the glory of eternity.

LOGICAL IMMORTALITY, THROUGH OBJECTS OF THOUGHT

Moving events, while remaining enshrined in this fashion in their permanent setting, may contain other and less external relations to the immutable. They may represent it. If the pleasures of sense are not cancelled when they cease, but continue to satisfy reason in that they once satisfied natural desires, much more will the pleasures of reflection retain their worth, when we consider that what they aspired to and reached was no momentary physical equilibrium but a permanent truth. As Archimedes, measuring the hypotenuse, was lost to events, being engaged in an event of much greater transcendence, so art and science interrupt the sense for change by engrossing attention in its issues and its laws. Old age often turns pious to look away from ruins to some world where youth endures and where what ought to have been is not overtaken by decay before it has quite come to maturity. Lost in such abstract contemplations, the mind is weaned from mortal concerns. It forgets for a few moments a world in which it has so little more to do and so much, perhaps, still to suffer. As a sensation of pure light would not be distinguishable from light itself, so a contemplation of things not implicating time in their structure becomes, so far as its own deliverance goes, a timeless existence. Unconsciousness of temporal conditions and of the very flight of time makes the thinker sink for a moment into identity with timeless objects. And so immortality, in a second ideal sense, touches the mind.

ETHICAL IMMORTALITY, THROUGH TYPES OF EXCELLENCE

The transitive phases of consciousness, however, have themselves a reference to eternal things. They yield a generous enthusiasm and love of good which is richer in consolation than either Epicurean self-concentration or mathematical ecstasy. Events are more interesting than the terms we abstract from them, and the forward movement of the will is something more intimately real than is the catalogue of our past experiences. Now the forward movement of the will is an avenue to the eternal. What would you have? What is the goal of your endeavour? It must be some success, the establishment of some order, the expression of some experience. These points once reached, we are not left merely with the satisfaction of abstract success or the consciousness of ideal immortality. Being natural goals, these ideals are related to natural functions. Their attainment does not exhaust but merely liberates, in this instance, the function concerned, and so marks the perpetual point of reference common to that function in all its fluctuations. Every attainment of perfection in an art—as for instance in government—makes a return to perfection easier for posterity, since there remains an enlightening example, together with faculties predisposed by discipline to recover their ancient virtue. The better a man evokes and realises the ideal the more he leads the life that all others, in proportion to their worth, will seek to live after him, and the more he helps them to live in that nobler fashion. His presence in the society of immortals thus becomes, so to speak, more pervasive. He not only vanquishes time by his own rationality, living now in the eternal, but he continually lives again in all rational beings.

Since the ideal has this perpetual pertinence to mortal struggles, he who lives in the ideal and leaves it expressed in society or in art enjoys a double immortality. The eternal has absorbed him while he lived, and when he is dead his influence brings others to the same absorption, making them, through that ideal identity with the best in him, reincarnations and perennial seats of all in him which he could rationally hope to rescue from destruction. He can say, without any subterfuge or desire to delude himself, that he shall not wholly die; for he will have a better notion than the vulgar of what constitutes his being. By becoming the spectator and confessor of his own death and of universal mutation, he will have identified himself with what is spiritual in all spirits and masterful in all apprehension; and so conceiving himself, he may truly feel and know that he is eternal.

Bibliography

Abhedananda, Swami. *Mystery of Death: Philosophy and Religion of the Kathaup Anishad.* London: Luzac, 1953.
Baillie, John. *And the Life Everlasting.* London: Oxford University Press, 1934.
Bedham, Paul, and Linda Bedham, eds. *Death and Immortality in the Religions of the World.* New York: Paragon House, 1987.
Bloch, Maurice, and Jonathan Parry, eds. *Death and the Regeneration of Life.* New York: Cambridge University Press, 1982.
Broad, C. D. *Lectures on Psychical Research.* New York: Humanity Press, 1962.
Chidester, David. *Patterns of Transcendence: Religion, Death and Dying.* Belmont, Calif.: Wadsworth, 1990.
Crombie, I. M. *An Examination of Plato's Doctrines,* vol. 1. New York: Humanities Press, 1962.
Davidson, Herbert A. *Proofs for Eternity, Creation and the Existence of God in Medieval Islamic and Jewish Philosophy.* New York: Oxford, 1987.
Dickinson, G. Lowes. *Is Immortality Desirable?* Boston: Houghton Mifflin, 1909.
Ducasse, C. J. *Nature, Mind and Death.* La Salle, Ill.: Open Court, 1951.
———. *The Belief in a Life after Death.* London: Blackwell, 1961.

———. *A Critical Examination of the Belief in a Life after Death.* Springfield, Ill.: Thomas, 1961.

Edwards, Paul. "The Case against Reincarnation (Part 1)." *Free Inquiry* 6 (1986): 24–34.

———. "The Case against Reincarnation (Part 2)." *Free Inquiry* 7 (1986–87): 38–48.

Finkelstein, Louis. "The Beginnings of the Jewish Doctrine of Immortality." *Freedom and Reason,* edited by Salo W. Baron, Ernest Nagel, and Koppel S. Pinson. New York: Free Press, 1951.

Flew, Antony. "Immortality." In *Encyclopedia of Philosophy,* edited by Paul Edwards, New York: Free Press, 1965.

———. *The Presumption of Atheism,* part 3. New York: Harper and Row, 1976.

———. *God, Freedom, and Immortality: A Critical Analysis.* Buffalo: Prometheus, 1984.

Fontinell, Eugene. *Self, God, and Immortality: A Jamesian Investigation.* Philadelphia: Temple University Press, 1986.

Frazer, J. G. *The Belief in Immortality.* London: Macmillan, 1913.

Geach, Peter. *God and the Soul.* London: Routledge and Kegan Paul, 1969.

Gowen, Julie. "God and Timelessness: Everlasting or Eternal?" *Sophia* 26 (1987): 15–29.

Hick, John. *Death and Eternal Life.* New York: Harper and Row, 1976.

———. "Religious Pluralism and Salvation." *Faith and Philosophy* 5 (1988): 365–77.

Holmes, John Haynes. *Is Death the End?* New York: Putnam, 1915.

Hume, David. *Of the Immortality of the Soul,* vol. 4 of *The Philosophical Works of David Hume.* London: Longmans, 1882.

Jaeger, Werner W. "The Greek Ideas of Immortality." 53 *Harvard Theological Review* (1959): 135–48.

James, William. *Human Immortality.* Boston: Houghton Mifflin, 1898.

Jantzen, Grace M. "Do We Need Immortality?" *Modern Theology* 1 (1984): 33–44.

Kant, Immanuel. *Critique of Practical Reason,* 6th ed. London: Longmans, Green, 1909.

Keller, Edmund B. "Hebrew Thoughts on Immortality and Resurrection." *International Journal of Philosophy and Religion* 5 (1974): 16–44.

Kenny, Anthony. *The God of the Philosophers.* Oxford: Clarendon Press, 1979.

Kolb, David A. "Forever?" *Philosophical Quarterly* 24 (1974): 1–16.

Kolenda, Konstantin. *Religion without God.* Buffalo, N.Y.: Prometheus Books, 1976.

Küng, Hans. *Eternal Life.* New York: Doubleday, 1984.

Lamont, Corliss. *The Illusion of Immortality.* New York: Wisdom Library, 1959.

Leuba, James H. *The Belief in God and Immortality.* Chicago: Open Court, 1921.

Lewis, Hywel D. *The Self and Immortality.* London: Macmillan, 1973.

———. *Persons and Life after Death: Essays by Hywel D. Lewis and Some of His Critics.* New York: Harper and Row, 1978.

Lindsay, Ronald A. "Thomas Aquinas's Complete Guide to Heaven and Hell." *Free Inquiry* 10 (Summer 1990): 38–39.

Lodge, Oliver. *Why I Believe in Personal Immortality.* Cassell, 1939.

Loy, David. "The Difference between 'Samsara' and 'Nirvana'." *Philosophy East and West* 33 (1983): 355–66.

McTaggart, J. M. E. *Some Dogmas of Religion.* London: Arnold, 1906.

Mill, John Stuart. "The Utility of Religion," and "Theism," part 3, *Three Essays on Religion.* New York: Longmans, Green, 1923.

Mohr, Richard D. "Plato on Time and Eternity." *Ancient Philosophy* 6 (1986): 39–46.

Myers, F. W. H. *Human Personality and Its Survival of Bodily Death*. London: Longmans, Green, 1903.

Nelson, Herbert J. "Time(s), Eternity, and Duration." *International Journal of Philosophy and Religion* 22 (1987): 3–19.

Neufeldt, Ronald W., ed. *Karma and Rebirth: Post-Classical Developments*. Albany, N.Y.: State University of New York Press, 1986.

O'Flaherty, Wendy Doniger, ed. *Karma and Rebirth in Classical Indian Traditions*. Berkeley: University of California Press, 1980.

Penelhum, Terence. *Survival and Disembodied Existence*. London: Routledge and Kegan Paul, 1970.

———, ed. *Immortality*. Belmont, Calif.: Wadsworth, 1973.

Perrett, Roy W. *Death and Immortality*. Dordrecht, The Netherlands: Nijhoff, 1986.

Perry, John. *Personal Identity and Immortality*. Indianapolis, Ind.: Hackett, 1979.

Perry, Ralph B. *The Hope for Immortality*. New York: Vanguard Press, 1945.

Phillips, D. Z. *Death and Immortality*. New York: St. Martin's Press, 1970.

Plotinus. *The Essence of Plotinus*. New York: Oxford University Press, 1934.

Price, Henry Habberley. *Essays in the Philosophy of Religion*. Oxford: Clarendon Press, 1972.

Purtill, Richard. *Thinking about Religion*. Englewood Cliffs, N.J.: Prentice-Hall, 1978.

Quinton, Anthony. "The Soul." *Journal of Philosophy* 59 (1962): 393–409.

Ramsey, Ian. *Freedom and Immortality*. London: SCM Press, 1960.

Reichenbach, Bruce. *Is Man the Phoenix? A Study of Immortality*. Grand Rapids, Mich.: Eerdmans, 1978.

Royce, Josiah. *The Conception of Immortality*. Boston: Houghton Mifflin, 1900.

Santayana, George. *Reason in Religion*. New York: Dover, 1982.

Sherry, Patrick, ed. *Philosophers on Religion: A Historical Reader*. London: Chapman, 1987.

Smart, Ninian. "Nirvana and Timelessness." *Journal of Dharma* 1 (1976): 318–23.

Smith, Jame Idleman, and Yvonne Yazbeck Haddad. *The Islamic Understanding of Death and Resurrection*. Albany: State University of New York Press, 1981.

Stein, Gordon. *Survival and Disembodied Existence*. New York: Humanities Press, 1970.

———, ed. *A Second Anthology of Atheism and Rationalism*. Buffalo, N.Y.: Prometheus, 1987.

Suzuki, Daisetz Teitaro. *Mysticism: Christian and Buddhist*. New York: Harper, 1957.

Swinburne, Richard. *The Coherence of Theism*. Oxford: Oxford University Press, 1977.

Taliaferro, Charles. "Why We Need Immortality." *Modern Theology* 6 J190, 367–77.

Taylor, A. E. *The Christian Hope of Immortality*. London: Centenary Press, 1938.

Toynbee, Arnold Joseph, and Arthur Koestler. *Life after Death*. London: Weidenfeld and Nichol, 1976.

Tyrrell, G. N. M. *The Personality of Man*. N.Y.: Penquin Books, 1946.

Van Inwagen, Peter. "The Possibility of Resurrection." *International Journal of Philosophy and Religion* (1978): 114–21.

von Hugel, Baron F. *Eternal Life*, 2d ed. Edinburgh: Clark, 1913.

PART III

The Modern
Perspective

CHAPTER 8

Obstacles to Religious Belief

A variety of dynamic intellectual movements have arisen in the modern age, many directly concerned with religion, others having strong religious implications. They range from psychology to political theory, and from science to linguistics. They include French existentialism, American humanism, and black activism, as well as liberation theology, "God-is-dead" theology, and feminist theory. Out of this intellectual ferment have come fresh perspectives and new interpretations of religion, together with a number of severe criticisms of traditional religious beliefs.

Freudian psychology is one such criticism, for Freud regarded religion as an "infantile neurosis" that needs to be cured if we are to become mature, healthy adults. Freud's general position is that the motive for religion lies in the human need for emotional comfort, especially for relief from the disasters, accidents, sickness, and other natural evils that surround us. In response to this threat, people "humanized" nature, imbuing it with character and personality. If nature is impersonal, we remain unprotected, but if events are caused by personalized deities, then we can work on the disposition of these deities and thus gain a certain measure of control. (In fact, when the gods are constructed so as to resemble our fathers, we are able to cajole, appease, bribe, and otherwise manipulate them so that they are robbed of some of their power.) Once human beings achieve maturity as a race, they no longer need to personalize nature and invent notions of spirits who can be made merciful; they shed such fictions and face the reality of an impersonal and sometimes brutal world.

A more specific theory of Freud's is that as children we idolize our father as the epitome of all virtues. However, as we grow older, we detect numerous flaws in this supposedly model being. We realize that he has shortcomings and limitations; he cannot protect us from everything or give us all that we want. At that critical point, the healthy response is to accept that reality and move forward. We realize that our father is very much the same as everyone else; with his own faults and strong points, he tries and sometimes fails, but overall is probably a decent enough human being. In other words, if we are strong and honest enough, we do not deny the truth, and this enables us to progress toward adulthood.

However, the unhealthy response at that juncture is to project the image of our lost ideal onto a spirit, which we then reify, or regard as real. Because of our disappointment in our earthly father—coupled with our desperate need for him to be what we imagined—we create a cosmic father who is perfect in all respects. Furthermore, we imagine that this all-knowing and all-powerful father can give us everything we desire, including the ultimate gift of eternal life. He only requires that we believe in him implicitly and obey his rules. If we humble ourselves before him, ask for his mercy and kindness, and confess our wrongdoings, he will then grant us forgiveness and a place with him in heaven forever.

Religion is therefore an illusion arising from psychological needs and sanctioned by those needs. Mature persons resolve their conflicts effectively by being realistic and assuming personal responsibility in the world; immature people cling to religion as an obsessional neurosis. When we are psychologically healthy, religion disappears.

Oddly enough, one of Freud's followers, Carl Jung, reached an opposite conclusion. He agreed with Freud that religion is based on emotional needs, but he thought these needs so basic to human nature that they could not be denied without inducing neurosis. Religion appeals to our "fictional and imaginative processes," and the theorems of mathematics or the findings of science never replace something so fundamental.

Those who disagree entirely with Freud charge that he may be showing why we believe in God—that is, our motivation in doing so—but that he has not proven that God is a fiction. In fact, God may use devices such as inducing a propensity toward animism or filling us with a natural disappointment in our earthly father in order to bring human beings to himself. If God "created man in his own image," it would be appropriate to think of God in human terms, including that of a Father with children on earth (and a Son in heaven).

Equally critical of religious belief is the political philosopher Karl Marx, who called religion the "opiate of the masses." On his reading, religion is "parson-power," a way of suppressing people's desire to improve the economic and political conditions of their lives. Although most people lead a miserable existence of hardship and deprivation, they are held down by religion which preaches acceptance of one's lot in life and champions the virtues of patience, humility, and self-denial.

Christianity in particular collaborates with rulers in keeping citizens passive by telling them to trust in God for help and not return injury for injury: "If we are struck, we should turn the other cheek; if someone asks for our coat, we should give him our cloak also." We are told that the meek shall inherit the earth, and the last shall be first; that the poor are blessed, and a rich man can no more get into heaven than a camel can pass through the eye of a needle (see, for example, Luke 6:20–38 and Mark 10:25). With such messages, Marx feels, people will never revolt against injustice, assume political power, and improve the economic conditions of their lives.

Marx's contention that religion is an instrument manipulated by political schemers is reinforced by the seventeenth-century English philosopher Thomas Hobbes, who recommended religion to monarchs as a way of controlling subjects. Hobbes wrote that rulers should be careful to fulfill three ends: (1) to impress upon the people that the decrees do not proceed from the monarch's fancy but are the will of God; (2) to promote the idea that whatever is prohibited by law is also prohibited by God; and (3) to encourage religious ceremonies, sacrifices, and festivals so people think that disasters such as famines or failures in war are due to God's wrath.

Machiavelli, the sixteenth-century Italian political philosopher, also recommended that shrewd leaders use religion for their own purposes. Machiavelli, in the *Discourses*, wrote that it is "the duty of princes and heads of republics to uphold the foundations of the religions of their countries, for then it is easy to keep their people religious, and consequently well conducted and united. And therefore everything that tends to favor religion (even though it were believed to be false) should be received and availed of to strengthen it."

Although Hobbes and Machiavelli favored religion in society and Marx opposed it, they all maintained that it functions to maintain social order. Marx was against religion because he did not want order but revolution that would bring about social justice and greater economic well-being for the people.

Those who criticize this analysis first point out that religion can be a force for social change, not just an instrument for maintaining the status quo. Christianity in particular has been a revolutionary force, for just as Christ whipped the moneylenders out of the temple, Christians have banded together as the church militants, whether fighting in the armies of the Crusades or violently opposing fascism. Some also argue that although political expediency may account for the maintenance of religion, it hardly accounts for its origin. Even though unscrupulous rulers have used religion for their own ends, that does not mean religion is not the product of revelation. Instead of explaining away the religious phenomenon it only shows how God has been sullied.

Attacks against religion have come not only from psychology and political philosophy but also from science, both in its early development and in its recent forms. When scientists began to explain in naturalistic terms phenomena that had been treated as supernatural in origin, such efforts posed a distinct threat to religion.

For example, scientists described solar eclipses not as miracles but as partial or complete blockages of the sun's light by the moon in its orbit. Rainbows were no longer viewed as benedictions but as optical events caused by the refraction and reflection of the sun's rays in raindrops or mist. Earthquakes and volcanic eruptions were not signs from God but the result of tectonic shifts or the release of high temperatures and pressures in the earth's core. And lightning and thunder did not show the wrath of heaven but were due to a discharge of atmospheric electricity, which caused a flash and an explosive sound as the air suddenly expanded.

Religious leaders in turn considered the study of anatomy a threat, not only because it desecrated the body, which was the temple of the soul, but because it violated certain doctrines about the body's makeup. It revealed, for example, that men had the same number of ribs on each side; had woman been made from one of man's ribs, there should have been fewer on one side. In the same way, insanity was attributed to demonic possession, which meant that exorcism was needed to cast out devils, not psychiatry to cure psychosis. And disease was thought to be produced by the displeasure of God and cured by miracles, or as Saint Augustine wrote, "All diseases of Christians are to be ascribed to three demons." When medical science posited natural causes for physical or mental disease, this view was treated as heresy.

The most famous example of the ancient conflict was, of course, the seventeenth-century dispute over whether the astronomical theory of Ptolemy or that of Copernicus was correct. Ptolemy had maintained that the sun revolved around the earth—the geocentric view—and this position was accepted by Saint Thomas Aquinas and Christianity in general. (It was also popularized by Dante.) Copernicus, on the other hand, claimed that the earth revolved around the sun— a heliocentric position championed by Galileo. The empirical evidence notwithstanding, Galileo was made to publicly and officially recant his "error." In fact, church officials refused to look through Galileo's telescope for fear that they would be convinced by faulty reason and fallible senses of something that they knew by faith to be untrue.

The conflict escalated, especially following the discoveries of Newton, who offered a mechanical explanation for the world in place of claims of moral order, and Darwin, who developed a naturalistic theory of evolution that challenged the idea of supernatural purpose.

Religion has responded in various ways, arguing, for example, that a great deal of scripture is metaphor, allegory, or myth that stands for profound truth. Nevertheless, the scientific revolution has substantially undermined belief in God. A direct correlation can be found between the rise of science and the rise of religious skepticism throughout the world.

Still another attack against religion was launched in the twentieth century by philosophers who approached the religious question from the perspective of language. One group, who were labeled the *logical positivists*, began by asking how sentences become meaningful. That is, they took as their primary problem how to differentiate between meaningful and meaningless assertions, and they devised a principle of verification for distinguishing the two.

According to the *verification principle* as articulated by its principal proponent A. J. Ayer, a sentence is meaningful to a person "if, and only if, he knows how to verify the proposition which it purports to express—that is, if he knows what observations would lead him, under certain conditions, to accept the proposition as being true, or reject it as being false." In other words, if we can specify the tests or operations that are relevant to establishing the truth or falsity of an assertion, then that assertion is meaningful. We can then go on to decide whether it is true or false, for at least it makes sense. However, if we cannot specify any empirical factors that apply to an assertion's truth or falsity, then it must be declared meaningless. To then wonder about its truth would be like asking whether Lewis Carroll's sentence " 'Twas brillig, and the slithy toves / Did gyre and gimble in the wabe" ("Jabberwocky") is true or false. Obviously, it is neither because it is meaningless.

The positivists maintained that certain sentences seem to make sense because the grammar of the sentence is familiar, but they are actually non-sense. For example, moral judgments such as "Return good for evil" cannot be verified empirically and so are absurd. The same would be true of the poet Shelley's aesthetic assertion that "Life, like a dome of many-colored glass, / Stains the white radiance of eternity," or of the philosopher Hegel's contention that "the Absolute enters into but is itself incapable of evolution and progress." How would one test the truth or falsity of such claims?

Most significant for our purposes, the positivists also maintained that religious assertions are meaningless for the same reason. Again, they did not call such statements false. Their charge was even more devastating: they claimed the statements were senseless, in fact, not genuine statements at all. Since no factual verification is possible for the sentence "God is in heaven," we need not even consider the truth of such a claim. As A. J. Ayer wrote, "The assertion that there is a god is nonsensical" and "the atheist's assertion that there is no god is equally nonsensical."

A group of philosophers who followed them called the *linguistic analysts* did not take such an extreme position, but they did challenge religious assertions from a somewhat different perspective. The analysts maintained that there were different categories of discourse, each with its own mode of verification and each meaningful in its own way. All sentences did not have to pass the test of empirical verification; each had its particular type of proof. Assertions that could be classified as moral, aesthetic, historical, metaphysical, and so forth needed to be established by methods unique and separate to each one. Similarly, religious claims did not have to pass scientific tests but standards of verification distinctive to religion.

The problem came, however, in deciding whether religious claims met even those internal standards. By this approach a key question is, What would have to happen to make one withdraw a given assertion? If nothing at all would ever count against a religious assertion, even using the standards appropriate to the category of religious discourse, then that claim could not be taken seriously. A claim that is compatible with everything really asserts nothing.

For example, what would count against the proposition that "God is good"? Pain, including the suffering of children, is discounted by the believer; so is the imperfection of the world and the various injustices that God allows. They are all treated as consistent with God's love for humanity. What, then, would have to happen, even theoretically, to justify the conclusion that the proposition is false?

Using their particular linguistic approach, then, the analysts also undermined religious belief. They found that religion had great difficulty in satisfying even a minimalist standard of verification.

Logical positivism has lost a considerable amount of credibility in recent years, mainly because the standard of verification appears arbitrary. Why should only empirically verifiable propositions be considered meaningful? Furthermore, the verification principle itself does not seem empirically verifiable, which means that, by its own criteria, it is a meaningless assertion.

The criticism of linguistic analysis is more difficult to refute, although many philosophers do question whether language should be accorded so much importance in religious matters. The analysts have sometimes been charged with fiddling with words while the world burns.

In the selections that follow, Ludwig Feuerbach presents his theory of God as a projection of the human psyche, although to him that does not mean religion should be rejected in all of its aspects. Karl Marx then elaborates his idea that "Die religion . . . ist das Opium des Volkes," (Religion is the opiate of the masses) and Freud offers his analysis of religion as a psychological illusion developed by the human mind to make life tolerable.

The next writer, Albert Einstein, has sometimes been considered religious (he said, for example, "God does not play dice"), but in this selection he clearly states that God has no place in his conception of the universe. H. J. Paton then describes in detail the conflicts between science and religion in modern times, considering especially the engulfing effects of physics, biology, and psychology.

In the final section, A. J. Ayer lays out the tenets of logical positivism and its consequences for the meaningfulness of religious discourse. This is followed by a discussion of verification and religious language by Antony Flew, R. M. Hare, and Basil Mitchell, three prominent linguistic analysts.

Feuerbach, Marx, and Freud

49. The Essence of Christianity

LUDWIG FEUERBACH

Religion is the dream of the human mind. But even in dreams we do not find ourselves in emptiness or in heaven, but on earth, in the realm of reality; we only see real things in the entrancing splendour of imagination and caprice, instead of in the simple daylight of reality and necessity. Hence I do nothing more to religion—and to speculative philosophy and theology also—than to open its eyes, or rather to turn its gaze from the internal towards the external, i.e., I change the object as it is in the imagination into the object as it is in reality.

INTRODUCTION

The Essence of Religion Considered Generally

In the perceptions of the senses consciousness of the object is distinguishable from consciousness of self; but in religion, consciousness of the object and self-consciousness coincide. The object of the senses is out of man, the religious object is within him, and therefore as little forsakes him as his self-consciousness or his conscience; it is the intimate, the closest object. "God," says Augustine, for example, "is nearer, more related to us, and therefore more easily known by us, than sensible, corporeal things" (*De Genesi ad litteram*, 1. v. c. 16). The object of the senses is in itself indifferent—independent of the disposition or of the judgment; but the object of religion is a selected object; the most excellent, the first, the supreme being; it essentially presupposes a critical judgment, a discrimination between the divine and the non-divine, between that which is worthy of adoration and that which is not worthy. And here may be applied, without any limitation, the proposition: the object of any subject is nothing else than the subject's own nature taken objectively. Such as are a man's thoughts and dispositions, such is his God; so much worth as a man has, so much and no more has his God. Consciousness of God is self-consciousness, knowledge of God is self-knowledge. By his God thou knowest the man, and by the man, his God; the two are

377

identical. Whatever is God to a man, that is his heart and soul; and conversely, God is the manifested inward nature, the expressed self of a man,—religion the solemn unveiling of a man's hidden treasures, the revelation of his intimate thoughts, the open confession of his lovesecrets.

But when religion—consciousness of God—is designated as the self-consciousness of man, this is not to be understood as affirming that the religious man is directly aware of this identity; for, on the contrary, ignorance of it is fundamental to the peculiar nature of religion. To preclude this misconception, it is better to say, religion is man's earliest and also indirect form of self-knowledge. Hence, religion everywhere precedes philosophy, as in the history of the race, so also in that of the individual. Man first of all sees his nature as if *out of* himself, before he finds it in himself. His own nature is in the first instance contemplated by him as that of another being. Religion is the childlike condition of humanity; but the child sees his nature—man—out of himself; in childhood a man is an object to himself, under the form of another man. Hence the historical progress of religion consists in this; that what by an earlier religion was regarded as objective, is now recognized as subjective; that is, what was formerly contemplated and worshipped as God is now perceived to be something *human.* What was at first religion becomes at a later period idolatry; man is seen to have adored his own nature. Man has given objectivity to himself, but has not recognized the object as his own nature: a later religion takes this forward step; every advance in religion is therefore a deeper self-knowledge. But every particular religion, while it pronounces its predecessors idolatrous, excepts itself— and necessarily so, otherwise it would no longer be religion—from the fate, the common nature of all religions: it imputes only to other religions what is the fault, if fault it be, of religion in general. Because it has a different object, a different tenor, because it has transcended the ideas of preceding religions, it erroneously supposes itself exalted above the necessary eternal laws which constitute the essence of religion—it fancies its objects, its ideas, to be superhuman. But the essence of religion, thus hidden from the religious, is evident to the thinker, by whom religion is viewed objectively, which it cannot be by its votaries. And it is our task to show that the antithesis of divine and human is altogether illusory, that it is nothing else than the antithesis between the human nature in general and the human individual; that, consequently, the object and contents of the Christian religion are altogether human.

Religion, at least the Christian, is the relation of man to himself, or more correctly to his own nature (i.e., his subjective nature); but a relation to it, viewed as a nature apart from his own. The divine being is nothing else than the human being, or, rather, the human nature purified, freed from the limits of the individual man, made objective—i.e., contemplated and revered as another, a distinct being. All the attributes of the divine nature are, therefore, attributes of the human nature.

In relation to the attributes, the predicates of the Divine Being, this is admitted without hesitation, but by no means in relation to the subject of these predicates. The negation of the subject is held to be irreligion, nay, atheism; though not so the negation of the predicates. But that which has no predicates or qualities, has no effect upon me; that which has no effect upon me has no existence for me. To deny all the qualities of a being is equivalent to denying the being himself. A being without qualities is one which cannot become an object to the mind, and such a being is virtually non-existent. Where man deprives God of all qualities, God is no longer anything more to him than a negative being. To the truly religious man, God is not a being without qualities, because to him he is a positive, real being. The theory that God cannot be defined, and consequently cannot be known by man, is therefore the offspring of recent times, a product of modern unbelief. . . . On the ground that God is unknowable, man excuses himself to what is yet remaining of his religious conscience for his forgetfulness of God, his absorption in the world: he denies God practically by his conduct,—the world has possession of all his thoughts and inclinations,—but he does not deny him theoretically, he does not attack his existence; he lets that rest. But this existence does not affect or incommode him; it is merely negative existence, an existence without existence, a self-contradictory existence,—a state of being which, as to its effects, is not distinguishable from non-being. The denial of determinate, positive predicates concerning the divine nature is nothing else than a denial of religion, with, however, an appearance of religion in its favor, so that it is not recognized as a denial; it is simply a subtle, disguised atheism. The alleged religious horror of limiting God by positive predicates is only the irreligious wish to know nothing more of God, to banish God from the mind. Dread of limitation is dread of existence.

There is, however, a still milder way of denying the divine predicates than the direct one just described. It is admitted that the predicates of the divine nature are finite, and more particularly, human qualities, but their rejection is rejected; they are even taken under protection, because it is necessary to man to have a definite conception of God, and since he is man he can form no other than a human conception of him. In relation to God, it is said, these predicates are certainly without any objective validity; but to me, if he is to exist for me, he cannot appear otherwise than as he does appear to me, namely, as a being with attributes analogous to the human. But this distinction between what God is in himself, and what he is for me destroys the peace of religion, and is besides in itself an unfounded and untenable distinction. I cannot know whether God is something else in himself or for himself than he is for me; what he is to me is to me all that he is. . . . In the distinction above stated, man takes a point of view above himself, i.e., above his nature, the absolute measure of his being; but this transcendentalism is only an illusion; for I can make the distinction between the object as it is in itself, and the object as it is for me, only where an object can really appear otherwise to me, not where it appears to me such as the absolute measure of my nature determines it to appear—such as it must appear to me.

Scepticism is the arch-enemy of religion; but the distinction between object and conception—between God as he is in himself, and God as he is for me—is a sceptical distinction, and therefore an irreligious one.

Wherever, therefore, this idea, that the religious predicates are only anthropomorphisms, has taken possession of a man, there has doubt, has unbelief, obtained the mastery of faith. And it is only the inconsequence of faint-heartedness and intellectual imbecility which does not proceed from this idea to the formal negation of the predicates, and from thence to the negation of the subject to which they relate. If thou doubtest the objective truth of the predicates, thou must also doubt the objective truth of the subject whose predicates they are. If thy predicates are anthropomorphisms, the subject of them is an anthropomorphism, too. If love, goodness, personality, etc., are human attributes, so also is the subject which thou presupposest, the existence of God, the belief that there is a God, an anthropomorphism—a presupposition purely human. Whence knowest thou that the belief in a God at all is not a limitation of man's mode of conception? . . .

Thou believest in love as a divine attribute because thou thyself lovest; thou believest that God is a wise, benevolent being because thou knowest nothing better in thyself than benevolence and wisdom; and thou believest that God exists, that therefore he is a subject—whatever exists is a subject, whether it be defined as substance, person, essence, or otherwise—because thou thyself existed, art thyself a subject. Thou knowest no higher human good than to love, than to be good and wise; and even so thou knowest no higher happiness than to exist, to be a subject; for the consciousness of all reality, of all bliss, is for thee bound up in the consciousness of being a subject, of existing. God is an existence, a subject to thee, for the same reason that he is to thee a wise, a blessed, a personal being. The distinction between the divine predicates and the divine subject is only this, that to thee the subject, the existence, does not appear an anthropomorphism, because the conception of it is necessarily involved in thy own existence as a subject, whereas the predicates do appear anthropomorphisms, because their necessity—the necessity that God should be conscious, wise, good, etc.,—is not an immediate necessity, identical with the being of man, but is evolved by his self-consciousness, by the activity of his thought. I am a subject, I exist, whether I be wise or unwise, good or bad. To exist is to man the first datum; it constitutes the very idea of the subject; it is presupposed by the predicates. Hence man relinquishes the predicates, but the existence of God is to him a settled, irrefragable, absolutely certain, objective truth. But, nevertheless, this distinction is merely an apparent one. The necessity of the subject lies only in the necessity of the predicate. Thou art a subject only in so far as thou art a human subject; the certainty and reality of thy existence lie only in the certainty and reality of thy human attributes. What the subject is lies only in the predicate; the predicate is the *truth* of the subject—the subject only the personified, existing predicate, the predicate conceived as existing. Subject and predicate are distinguished only as existence and essence. The negation of the predicates is therefore the negation of the subject. What remains of the human subject when abstracted from the human attributes? Even in the language of common life the divine predicates—Providence, Omniscience, Omnipotence—are put for the divine subject. . . .

Religion is that conception of the nature of the world and of man which is essential to, i.e., identical with, a man's nature. But man does not stand above this his necessary conception; on the contrary, it stands above him; it animates, determines, governs him. The necessity of a proof, of a middle term to unite qualities with existence, the possibility of a doubt, is abolished. Only that which is apart from my own being is capable of being doubted by me. How then can I doubt of God, who is my being? To doubt of God is to doubt of myself. Only when God is thought of abstractly, when his predicates are the result of philosophic abstraction, arises the distinction or separation between subject and predicate, existence and nature—arises the fiction that the existence of the subject is something else than the predicate, something immediate, indubitable, in distinction from the predicate, which is held to be doubtful. But this is only a fiction. A God who has abstract predicates has also an abstract existence. Existence, being, varies with varying qualities.

Thus what theology and philosophy have held to be God, the Absolute, the Infinite, is not God; but that which they have held not to be God is God: namely, the attribute, the quality, whatever has reality. Hence he alone is the true atheist to whom the predicates of the Divine Being,—for example, love, wisdom, justice,—are nothing; not he to whom merely the subject of these predicates is nothing. And in no wise is the negation of the subject necessarily also a negation of the predicates considered in themselves. These have an intrinsic, independent reality; they force their recognition upon man by their very nature; they are self-evident truths to him; they prove, they attest themselves. It does not follow that goodness, justice, wisdom, are chimeras because the existence of God is a chimera, nor truths because this is a truth. The idea of God is dependent on the idea of justice, of benevolence; a God who is not benevolent, not just, not wise, is no God; but the converse does not hold. The fact is not that a quality is divine because God has it, but that God has it because it is in itself divine; because without it God would be a defective being. Justice, wisdom, in general every quality which constitutes the divinity of God, is determined and known by itself independently, but the idea of God is determined by the qualities which have thus been previously judged to be worthy of the divine nature; only in the case in which I identify God and justice, in which I think of God immediately as the reality of the idea of justice, is the idea of God self-determined. But if God as a subject is the determined, while the quality, the predicate, is the determining, then in truth the rank of the godhead is due not to the subject, but to the predicate.

Now, when it is shown that what the subject is lies entirely in the attributes of the subject; that is, that the predicate is the true subject; it is also proved that if the divine predicates are attributes of the human nature, the subject of those predicates is also of the human nature. But the divine predicates are partly general, partly personal. The general predicates are the metaphysical, but these serve only as external points of support to religion; they are not the characteristic definitions of religion. It is the personal predicates alone which constitute the essence of religion—in which the Divine Being is the object of religion. Such are, for example, that God is a Person, that he is the moral Lawgiver, the Father of mankind, the Holy One, the Just, the Good, the Merciful. It is, however, at once, clear, or it will at least be clear in the sequel, with regard to these and other definitions, that, especially as applied to a personality, they are purely human definitions, and that consequently man in religion—in his relation to God—is in relation to his own nature; for to the religious sentiment these predicates are not mere conceptions, mere images, which man forms of God, to be distinguished from that which God is in himself, but truths, facts, realities. Religion knows nothing of anthropomorphisms; to it they are not anthropomorphisms. It is the very essence of religion, that to it these definitions express the nature of God. They are pronounced to be images only by the understanding, which reflects on religion, and which while defending them yet before its own tribunal denies them. But to the religious sentiment God is a real Father, real Love and Mercy; for to it he is a real, living, personal being, and therefore his attributes are also living and personal. Nay, the definitions which are the most sufficing to the religious senti-ment are precisely those which give the most offence to the understanding, and which in the process of reflection on religion it denies. Religion is essentially emotion; hence, objectively also, emotion is to it necessarily of a divine nature. Even anger appears to it an emotion not unworthy of God, provided only there be a religious motive at the foundation of this anger.

But here it is also essential to observe, and this phenomenon is an ex-tremely remarkable one, characterizing the very core of religion, that in propor-tion as the divine subject is in reality human, the greater is the apparent difference between God and man; that is, the more, by reflection on religion, by theology, is the identity of the divine and human denied, and the human, considered as such, is depreciated. The reason of this is, that as what is positive in the conception of the divine being can only be human, the conception of man, as an object of consciousness, can only be negative. To enrich God, man must become poor; that God may be all, man must be nothing. But he desires to be nothing in himself, because what he takes from himself is not lost to him, since it is preserved in God. Man has his being in God; why then should he have it in himself? Where is the necessity of positing the same thing twice, of having it twice? What man with-draws from himself, what he renounces in himself, he only enjoys in an incompara-bly higher and fuller measure in God. . . .

In brief, man in relation to God denies his own knowledge, his own thoughts, that he may place them in God. Man gives up his personality; but in return, God, the Almighty, infinite, unlimited being, is a person; he denies human dignity, the human *ego*; but in return God is to him a selfish, egotistical being, who in all things seeks only himself, his own honor, his own ends, he represents God as simply seeking the satisfaction of his own selfishness, while yet he frowns on that of every other being; his God is the very luxury of egoism. Religion further denies goodness as a quality of human nature; man is wicked, corrupt, incapable of good; but, on the other hand, God is only good—the Good Being. Man's nature demands as an object goodness, personified as God; but is it not hereby declared that goodness is an essential tendency of man? If my heart is wicked, my understanding perverted, how can I perceive and feel the holy to be holy, the good to be good? . . . Either goodness does not exist at all for man, or, if it does exist, therein is revealed to the individual man the holiness and goodness of human nature.

Man—this is the mystery of religion—projects his being into objectivity, and then again makes himself an object to this projected image of himself thus converted into a subject; he thinks of himself as an object to himself, but as the object of an object, of another being than himself. Thus here. Man is an object to God. That man is good or evil is not indifferent to God; no! He has a lively, profound interest in man's being good; he wills that man should be good, happy— for without goodness there is no happiness. Thus the religious man virtually retracts the nothingness of human activity, by making his dispositions and actions an object to God, by making man the end of God—for that which is an object to the mind is an end in action; by making the divine activity a means of human salvation. God acts, that man may be good and happy. Thus man, while he is apparently humiliated to the lowest degree, is in truth exalted to the highest. Thus, in and through God, man has in view himself alone. It is true that man places the aim of his action in God, but God has no other aim of action than the moral and eternal salvation of man; thus man has in fact no other aim than himself. The divine activity is not distinct from the human.

APPENDIX

Man has his highest being, his God, in himself; not in himself as an individual, but in his essential nature, his species. No individual is an adequate representation of his species, but only the human individual is conscious of the distinction between the species and the individual; in the sense of this distinction lies the root of religion. The yearning of man after something above himself is nothing else than the longing after the perfect type of his nature, the yearning to be free from himself, i.e., from the limits and defects of his individuality. Individuality is the self-conditioning, the self-limitation of the species. Thus man has cognizance of nothing above himself, of nothing beyond the nature of humanity; but to the individual man this nature presents itself under the form of an individual man. Thus, for example, the child sees the nature of man *above itself* in the form of its parents, the pupil in the form of his tutor. But all feelings which man experiences toward a superior man, nay, in general, all moral feelings which man has towards man, are of a religious nature. *Man feels nothing towards God which he does not also feel toward man. Homo homini deus est.* Want teaches prayer; but in misfortune, in sorrow, man kneels to entreat help of man also. Feeling makes God a man, but for the same reason it makes man a God. How often in deep emotion, which alone speaks genuine truth, man exclaims to man: Thou art, thou hast been my re-deemer, my saviour, my protecting spirit, my God! We feel awe, reverence, humil-ity, devout admiration, in thinking of a truly great, noble man; we feel ourselves worthless, we sink into nothing, even in the presence of human greatness. The purely, truly human emotions are religious; but for that reason the religious emo-tions are purely human; the only difference is that the religious emotions are vague, indefinite; but even this is only the case when the object of them is indefinite. Where God is positively defined, is the object of positive religion, there God is also the object of positive, definite human feelings, the object of fear and love, and therefore he is a positively human being; for there is nothing more in God than what lies in feeling. If in the heart there is fear and terror, in God there is anger; if in the heart there is joy, hope, confidence, in God there is love. . . . Thus even in religion man bows before the nature of man under the form of a personal human being; religion itself expressly declares—and all anthropomorphisms declare this in opposition to Pantheism,—*quod supra nos nihil ad nos;* that is, a God who inspires us with no human emotions, who does not reflect our own emotions, in a word, who is not a man—such a God is nothing to us, has no interest for us, does not concern us.

It is clear from what has been said, that only where in truth, if not according to the subjective conception, the distinction between the divine and human being is abolished, is the objective existence of God, the existence of God as an objective, distinct being abolished—only there, I say, is religion made a mere matter of feeling or conversely, feeling the chief point in religion. The last refuge of theology therefore is feeling. God is renounced by the understanding; he has no longer the dignity of a real object, of a reality which imposes itself on the understanding; hence he is transferred to feeling: in feeling his existence is thought to be secure. And doubtless this is the safest refuge; for to make feeling the essence of religion is nothing else than to make feeling the essence of God. And as certainly as I exist, so certainly does my God exist. The certainty of God is here nothing else than the self-certainty of human-feeling, the yearning after God is the yearning after unlimited, uninterrupted, pure feeling. In life the feelings are interrupted; they collapse; they are followed by a state of void, of insensibility. The religious problem, therefore, is to give fixity to feeling in spite of the vicissitudes of life, and to separate it from repugnant disturbances and limitations: God himself is nothing else than undisturbed, uninterrupted feeling, feeling for which there exists no limits, no opposite. If God were a being distinct from thy feeling, he would be known to thee in some other way than simply in feeling; but just because thou perceivest him only by feeling, he exists only in feeling—he is himself only feeling.

50. On Religion

KARL MARX

The chief defect of all hitherto existing materialism—that of Feuerbach included—is that the thing [*Gegenstand*], reality, sensuousness, is conceived only in the form of the *object* [*Objekt*] or of *contemplation* [*Anschauung*], but not as *human sensuous activity, practice,* not subjectively. Hence it happened that the *active* side, in contradistinction to materialism, was developed by idealism—but only abstractly, since, of course, idealism does not know real, sensuous activity as such.

Feuerbach wants sensuous objects, really differentiated from the thought-objects, but he does not conceive human activity itself *as objective [gegenständliche]* activity. Hence, in the *Essence of Christianity,* he regards the theoretical attitude as the only genuinely human attitude, while practice is conceived and fixed only in its dirty-judaical form of appearance. Hence he does not grasp the significance of "revolutionary," of "practical-critical," activity.

The question whether objective [*gegenständliche*] truth can be attributed to human thinking is not a question of theory but a *practical* question. In practice man must prove the truth, that is, the reality and power, the this-sidedness [*Diesseitigkeit*] of his thinking. The dispute over the reality or non-reality of thinking which is isolated from practice is a purely *scholastic* question.

The materialist doctrine that men are products of circumstances and upbringing, and that, therefore, changed men are products of other circumstances and changed upbringing, forgets that it is men that change circumstances and that the educator himself needs educating. Hence, this doctrine necessarily arrives at dividing society into two parts, of which one is superior to society (in Robert Owen, for example).

The coincidence of the changing of circumstances and of human activity can be conceived and rationally understood only as *revolutionizing practice.*

Feuerbach starts out from the fact of religious self-alienation, the duplication of the world into a religious, imaginary world and a real one. His work consists in the dissolution of the religious world into its secular basis. He overlooks the fact that after this work is completed the chief thing still remains to be done. For the fact that the secular foundation detaches itself from itself and establishes itself in the clouds as an independent realm is really only to be explained by the self-cleavage and self-contradictoriness of this secular basis. The latter must itself, therefore, first be understood in its contradiction, and then revolutionized in practice by the removal of the contradiction. Thus, for instance, once the earthly family is discovered to be the secret of the holy family, the former must then itself be criticized in theory and revolutionized in practice.

Feuerbach, not satisfied with *abstract thinking,* appeals to *sensuous contemplation;* but he does not conceive sensuousness as *practical,* human-sensuous activity.

Feuerbach resolves the religious essence into the *human* essence. But the human essence is no abstraction inherent in each single individual. In its reality it is the ensemble of the social relations.

Feuerbach, who does not enter upon a criticism of this real essence, is consequently compelled:

1. To abstract from the historical process and to fix the religious sentiment [*Gemüt*] as something by itself and to presuppose an abstract—*isolated*—human individual.
2. The human essence, therefore, can with him be comprehended only as "genius," as an internal, dumb generality which merely *naturally* unites the many individuals.

Feuerbach, consequently, does not see that the "religious sentiment" is itself a *social product,* and that the abstract individual whom he analyzes belongs in reality to a particular form of society.

Social life is essentially *practical.* All mysteries which mislead theory to mysticism find their rational solution in human practice and in the comprehension of this practice.

The highest point attained by *contemplative* materialism, that is, materialism which does not understand sensuousness as practical activity, is the contemplation of single individuals in "civil society."

The standpoint of the old materialism is "civil" society; the standpoint of the new is *human* society, or socialized humanity.

The philosophers have only *interpreted* the world, in various ways; the point, however, is to *change* it.

For Germany the *criticism of religion* is in the main complete, and criticism of religion is the premise of all criticism.

The *profane* existence of error, is discredited after its *heavenly oratio pro aris et focis*[1] has been rejected. Man, who looked for a superman in the fantastic reality of heaven and found nothing there but the *reflexion* of himself, will no longer be disposed to find but the *semblance* of himself, the non-human [*Unmensch*] where he seeks and must seek his true reality.

The basis of irreligious criticism is: Man *makes religion,* religion does not make man. In other words, religion is the self-consciousness and self-feeling of man who has either not yet found himself or has already lost himself again. But *man* is no abstract being squatting outside the world. Man is *the world of man,* the state, society. This state, this society, produce religion, *a reversed world-consciousness,* because they are a *reversed world.* Religion is the general theory of that world, its encyclopaedic compendium, its logic in a popular form, its spiritualistic *point d'honneur,* its enthusiasm, its moral sanction, its solemn completion, its universal ground for consolation and justification. It is the *fantastic realization* of the human essence because the *human essence* has no true reality. The struggle against religion is therefore mediately the fight against *the other world,* of which religion is the spiritual aroma.

Religious distress is at the same time the *expression* of real distress and the *protest* against real distress. Religion is the sigh of the oppressed creature, the heart of a heartless world, just as it is the spirit of a spiritless situation. It is the *opium* of the people.

The abolition of religion as the *illusory* happiness of the people is required for their *real* happiness. The demand to give up the illusions about its condition is the *demand to give up a condition which needs illusions.* The criticism of religion is therefore *in embryo the criticism of the vale of woe,* the *halo* of which is religion.

Criticism has plucked the imaginary flowers from the chain not so that

---

[1] Speech for the altars and hearths.—Ed.

man will wear the chain without any fantasy or consolation but so that he will shake off the chain and cull the living flower. The criticism of religion disillusions man to make him think and act and shape his reality like a man who has been disillusioned and has come to reason, so that he will revolve round himself and therefore round his true sun. Religion is only the illusory sun which revolves round man as long as he does not revolve round himself.

The task of history, therefore, once the *world beyond the truth* has disappeared, is to establish the *truth of this world*. The immediate *task of philosophy*, which is at the service of history, once the *saintly form* of human self-alienation has been unmasked, is to unmask self-alienation in its *unholy forms*. Thus the criticism of heaven turns into the criticism of the earth, the *criticism of religion* into the *criticism of right* and the *criticism of theology* into the *criticism of politics*. . . .

The weapon of criticism cannot, of course, replace criticism of the weapon, material force must be overthrown by material force; but theory also becomes a material force as soon as it has gripped the masses. Theory is capable of gripping the masses as soon as it demonstrates *ad hominem,* and it demonstrates *ad hominem* as soon as it becomes radical. To be radical is to grasp the root of the matter. But for the man the root is man himself. The evident proof of the radicalism of German theory, and hence of its practical energy, is that it proceeds from a resolute *positive* abolition of religion. The criticism of religion ends with the teaching that *man is the highest essence for man,* hence with the *categoric imperative to overthrow all relations* in which man is a debased, enslaved, abandoned, despicable essence, relations which cannot be better described than by the cry of a Frenchman when it was planned to introduce a tax on dogs: Poor dogs! They want to treat you as human beings!

Even historically, theoretical emancipation has specific practical significance for Germany. For Germany's *revolutionary* past is theoretical, it is the *Reformation.* As the revolution then began in the brain of the *monk,* so now it begins in the brain of the *philosopher.*

Luther, we grant, overcame bondage out of *devotion* by replacing it by bondage out of *conviction.* He shattered faith in authority because he restored the authority of faith. He turned priests into laymen because he turned laymen into priests. He freed man from outer religiosity because he made religiosity the inner man. He freed the body from chains because he enchained the heart.

But if Protestantism was not the true solution of the problem it was at least the true setting of it. It was no longer a case of the layman's struggle against the *priest outside himself* but of his struggle against *his own priest inside himself,* his *priestly nature.* And if the Protestant transformation of the German laymen into priests emancipated the lay popes, the *princes,* with the whole of their priestly clique, the privileged and philistines, the philosophical transformation of priestly Germans into men will emancipate the *people.* But *secularization* will not stop at the *confiscation of church estates* set in motion mainly by hypocritical Prussia any more than emancipation stops at princes. The Peasant War, the most radical fact of German history, came to grief because of theology. Today, when theology itself has come to grief, the most unfree fact of German history, our *status quo,* will be shattered against philosophy. On the eve of the Reformation official Germany was the most unconditional slave of Rome. On the eve of its revolution it is the unconditional slave of less than Rome, of Prussia and Austria, of country junkers and philistines.

Meanwhile, a major difficulty seems to stand in the way of a *radical* German revolution.

For revolutions require a *passive* element, a *material* basis. Theory is fulfilled in a people only insofar as it is the fulfilment of the needs of that people. But will the monstrous discrepancy between the demands of German thought and the answers of German reality find a corresponding discrepancy between civil society and the state and between civil society and itself? Will the theoretical needs be immediate practical needs? It is not enough for thought to strive for realization, reality must itself strive towards thought.

But Germany did not rise to the intermediary stage of political emancipation at the same time as the modern nations. It has not yet reached in practice the stages which it has surpassed in theory. How can it do a *somersault*, not only over its own limitations, but at the same time over the limitations of the modern nations, over limitations which it must in reality feel and strive for as for emancipation from its real limitations? Only a revolution of radical needs can be a radical revolution and it seems that precisely the preconditions and ground for such needs are lacking.

If Germany has accompanied the development of the modern nations only with the abstract activity of thought without taking an effective share in the real struggle of that development, it has, on the other hand, shared the *sufferings* of that development, without sharing in its enjoyment or its partial satisfaction. To the abstract activity on the one hand corresponds the abstract suffering on the other. That is why Germany will one day find itself on the level of European decadence before ever having been on the level of European emancipation. It will be comparable to a *fetish worshipper* pining away with the diseases of Christianity.

51. The Future of an Illusion

SIGMUND FREUD

We know already how the individual reacts to the injuries that culture and other men inflict on him: he develops a corresponding degree of resistance against the institutions of this culture, of hostility towards it. But how does he defend himself against the supremacy of nature, of fate, which threatens him, as it threatens all?

Culture relieves him of this task: it performs it in the same way for everyone. (It is also noteworthy that pretty well all cultures are the same in this respect.) It does not cry a halt, as it were, in its task of defending man against nature; it merely pursues it by other methods. This is a complex business; man's seriously menaced self-esteem craves for consolation, life and the universe must be rid of their terrors, and incidentally man's curiosity, reinforced, it is true, by the strongest practical motives, demands an answer.

With the first step, which is the humanization of nature, much is already won. Nothing can be made of impersonal forces and fates; they remain eternally remote. But if the elements have passions that rage like those in our own souls, if death itself is not something spontaneous, but the violent act of an evil Will, if everywhere in nature we have about us beings who resemble those of our own environment, then indeed we can breathe freely, we can feel at home in face of the supernatural, and we can deal psychically with our frantic anxiety. We are perhaps still defenceless, but no longer helplessly paralysed; we can at least react; perhaps indeed we are not even defenceless, we can have recourse to the same methods against these violent supermen of the beyond that we make use of in our own community; we can try to exorcise them, to appease them, to bribe them, and so rob them of part of their power by thus influencing them. Such a substitution of psychology for natural science provides not merely immediate relief, it also points the way to a further mastery of the situation.

For there is nothing new in this situation. It has an infantile prototype, and is really only the continuation of this. For once before one has been in such a state of helplessness: as a little child in one's relationship to one's parents. For one had reason to fear them, especially the father, though at the same time one was sure of his protection against the dangers then known to one. And so it was natural to assimilate and combine the two situations. Here, too, as in dream-life, the wish came into its own. The sleeper is seized by a presentiment of death, which seeks to carry him to the grave. But the dream-work knows how to select a condition that will turn even this dreaded event into a wish-fulfilment: the dreamer sees himself in an ancient Etruscan grave, into which he has descended, happy in the satisfaction it has given to his archæological interests. Similarly man makes the forces of nature not simply in the image of men with whom he can associate as his equals—that would not do justice to the overpowering impression they make on him—but he gives them the characteristics of the father, makes them into gods, thereby following not only an infantile, but also, as I have tried to show, a phylogenetic prototype.

In the course of time the first observations of law and order in natural phenomena are made, and therewith the forces of nature lose their human traits. But men's helplessness remains, and with it their father-longing and the gods. The gods retain their threefold task: they must exorcise the terrors of nature, they must reconcile one to the cruelty of fate, particularly as shown in death, and they must make amends for the sufferings and privations that the communal life of culture has imposed on man.

But within these there is a gradual shifting of the accent. It is observed that natural phenomena develop of themselves from inward necessity; without doubt the gods are the lords of nature: they have arranged it thus and now they can leave it to itself. Only occasionally, in the so-called miracles, do they intervene in its course, as if to protest that they have surrendered nothing of their original sphere of power. As far as the vicissitudes of fate are concerned, an unpleasant suspicion persists that the perplexity and helplessness of the human race cannot be remedied. This is where the gods are most apt to fail us; if they themselves make fate, then their ways must be deemed inscrutable. The most gifted people of the ancient world dimly surmised that above the gods stands Destiny and that the gods themselves have their destinies. And the more autonomous nature becomes and the more the gods withdraw from her, the more earnestly are all expectations concentrated on the third task assigned to them and the more does morality become their real domain. It now becomes the business of the gods to adjust the defects and evils of culture, to attend to the sufferings that men inflict on each other in their communal life, and to see that the laws of culture, which men obey so ill, are carried out. The laws of culture themselves are claimed to be of divine origin, they are elevated to a position above human society, and they are extended over nature and the universe.

And so a rich store of ideas is formed, born of the need to make tolerable the helplessness of man, and built out of the material offered by memories of the helplessness of his own childhood and the childhood of the human race. It is easy to see that these ideas protect man in two directions; against the dangers of nature and fate, and against the evils of human society itself. What it amounts to is this: life in this world serves a higher purpose; true, it is not easy to guess the nature of this purpose, but certainly a perfecting of human existence is implied. Probably the spiritual part of man, the soul, which in the course of time has so slowly and unwillingly detached itself from the body, is to be regarded as the object of this elevation and exaltation. Everything that takes place in this world expresses the intentions of an Intelligence, superior to us, which in the end, though its devious ways may be difficult to follow, orders everything for good, that is, to our advantage. Over each one of us watches a benevolent, and only apparently severe, Providence, which will not suffer us to become the plaything of the stark and pitiless forces of nature; death itself is not annihilation, not a return to inorganic lifelessness, but the beginning of a new kind of existence, which lies on the road of development to something higher. And to turn to the other side of the question, the moral laws that have formed our culture govern also the whole universe, only they are upheld with incomparably more force and consistency by a supreme judicial court. In the end all good is rewarded, all evil punished, if not actually in this life, then in the further existences that begin after death. And thus all the terrors, the sufferings, and the hardships of life are destined to be obliterated; the life after death, which continues our earthly existence as the invisible part of the spectrum adjoins the visible, brings all the perfection that perhaps we have missed here. And the superior wisdom that directs this issue, the supreme goodness that expresses itself thus, the justice that thus achieves its aim—these are the qualities of the divine beings who have fashioned us and the world in general; or rather of the one divine being into which in our culture all the gods of antiquity have been condensed. The race that first succeeded in thus concentrating the divine qualities was not a little proud of this advance. It had revealed the father nucleus which had always lain hidden behind every divine figure; fundamentally it was a return to the historical beginnings of the idea of God. Now that God was a single person, man's relations to him could recover the intimacy and intensity of the child's relation to the father. If one had done so much for the father, then surely one would be rewarded . . .

Empirical Science

52. Science and Religion

ALBERT EINSTEIN

It would not be difficult to come to an agreement as to what we understand by science. Science is the century-old endeavor to bring together by means of systematic thought the perceptible phenomena of this world into as thoroughgoing an association as possible. To put it boldly, it is the attempt at the posterior reconstruction of existence by the process of conceptualization. But when asking myself what religion is, I cannot think of an answer so easily. And even after finding an answer which may satisfy me at this particular moment, I still remain convinced that I can never under any circumstances bring together, even to a slight extent, all those who have given this question serious consideration.

At first, then, instead of asking what religion is, I should prefer to ask what characterizes the aspirations of a person who gives me the impression of being religious: a person who is religiously enlightened appears to me to be one who has, to the best of his ability, liberated himself from the fetters of his selfish desires and is preoccupied with thoughts, feelings, and aspirations to which he clings because of their super-personal value. It seems to me that what is important is the force of this super-personal content and the depth of the conviction concerning its overpowering meaningfulness, regardless of whether any attempt is made to unite this content with a Divine Being, for otherwise it would not be possible to count Buddha and Spinoza as religious personalities. Accordingly, a religious person is devout in the sense that he has no doubt of the significance and loftiness of those super-personal objects and goals which neither require nor are capable of rational foundation. They exist with the same necessity and matter-of-factness as he himself. In this sense religion is the age-old endeavor of mankind to become clearly and completely conscious of these values and goals and constantly to strengthen and extend their effects. If one conceives of religion and science according to these definitions then a conflict between them appears impossible. For science can only ascertain what *is*, but not what should be, and outside of its domain value judgments of all kinds remain necessary. Religion, on the other hand, deals only with evaluations of human thought and action; it cannot justifiably speak of facts and relationships between facts. According to this interpretation, the well-known conflicts between religion and science in the past must all be ascribed to a misapprehension of the situation which has been described.

For example, a conflict arises when a religious community insists on the absolute truthfulness of all statements recorded in the Bible. This means an intervention on the part of religion into the sphere of science; this is where the struggle of the Church against the doctrines of Galileo and Darwin belongs. On the other hand, representatives of science have often made an attempt to arrive at fundamental judgments with respect to values and ends on the basis of scientific method, and in this way have set themselves in opposition to religion. These conflicts have all sprung from fatal errors.

Now, even though the realms of religion and science in themselves are clearly marked off from each other, nevertheless there exist between the two, strong reciprocal relationships and dependencies. Though religion may be that which determines the goal, it has, nevertheless, learned from science, in the broadest sense, what means will contribute to the attainment of the goals it has set up. But science can only be created by those who are thoroughly imbued with the aspiration towards truth and understanding. This source of feeling, however, springs from the sphere of religion. To this there also belongs the faith in the possibility that the regulations valid for the world of existence are rational, that is comprehensible to reason. I cannot conceive of a genuine scientist without that profound faith. The situation may be expressed by an image: science without religion is lame, religion without science is blind.

Though I have asserted above, that in truth a legitimate conflict between religion and science cannot exist, I must nevertheless qualify this assertion once again on an essential point, with reference to the actual content of historical religions. This qualification has to do with the concept of God. During the youthful period of mankind's spiritual evolution, human fantasy created gods in man's own image, who, by the operations of their will were supposed to determine, or at any rate to influence, the phenomenal world. Man sought to alter the disposition of these gods in his own favor by means of magic and prayer. The idea of God in the religions taught at present is a sublimation of that old conception of the gods. Its anthropomorphic character is shown, for instance, by the fact that men appeal to the Divine Being in prayers and plead for the fulfillment of their wishes.

Nobody, certainly, will deny that the idea of the existence of an omnipotent, just and omnibeneficent personal God is able to accord men solace, help and guidance; also, by virtue of its simplicity the concept is accessible to the most undeveloped mind. But, on the other hand, there are decisive weaknesses attached to this idea in itself, which have been painfully felt since the beginning of history. That is, if this Being is omnipotent, then every occurrence, including every human action, every human thought, and every human feeling and aspiration is also His work; how is it possible to think of holding men responsible for their deeds and thoughts before such an Almighty Being? In giving out punishment and rewards He would to a certain extent be passing judgment on Himself. How can this be combined with the goodness and righteousness ascribed to Him?

The main source of the present-day conflicts between the spheres of religion and science lies in this concept of a personal God. It is the aim of science to establish general rules which determine the reciprocal connection of objects and events in time and space. For these rules, or laws of nature, absolutely general validity is required—not proven. It is mainly a program, and faith in the possibility of its accomplishment in principle is only founded on partial success. But hardly anyone could be found who would deny these partial successes and ascribe them to human self-deception. The fact that on the basis of such laws we are able to predict the temporal behavior of phenomena in certain domains with great precision and certainty, is deeply embedded in the consciousness of the modern man, even though he may have grasped very little of the contents of those laws. He need only consider that planetary courses within the solar system may be calculated in advance with great exactitude on the basis of a limited number of simple laws. In a similar way, though not with the same precision, it is possible to calculate in advance the mode of operation of an electric motor, a transmission system, or of a wireless apparatus, even when dealing with a novel development.

To be sure, when the number of factors coming into play in a phenomenological complex is too large, scientific method in most cases fails us. One need only think of the weather, in which case prediction even for a few days ahead is impossible. Nevertheless no one doubts that we are confronted with a causal connection whose causal components are in the main known to us. Occurrences in this domain are beyond the reach of exact prediction because of the variety of factors in operation, not because of any lack of order in nature.

We have penetrated far less deeply into the regularities obtaining within the realm of living things, but deeply enough nevertheless to sense at least the rule of fixed necessity. One need only think of the systematic order in heredity, and in the effect of poisons, as for instance alcohol, on the behavior of organic beings. What is still lacking here is a grasp of connections of profound generality, but not a knowledge of order in itself.

The more a man is imbued with the ordered regularity of all events, the firmer becomes his conviction that there is no room left by the side of this ordered regularity for causes of a different nature. For him neither the rule of human nor the rule of divine will exists as an independent cause of natural events. To be sure, the doctrine of a personal God interfering with natural events could never be refuted, in the real sense, by science, for this doctrine can always take refuge in those domains in which scientific knowledge has not yet been able to set foot.

But I am persuaded that such behavior on the part of the representatives of religion would not only be unworthy but also fatal. For a doctrine which is able to maintain itself not in clear light but only in the dark, will of necessity lose its effect on mankind, with incalculable harm to human progress. In their struggle for the ethical good, teachers of religion must have the stature to give up the doctrine of a personal God, that is, give up that source of fear and hope which in the past placed such vast power in the hands of priests. In their labors they will have to avail themselves of those forces which are capable of cultivating the Good, the True, and the Beautiful in humanity itself. This is, to be sure, a more difficult but an incomparably more worthy task.[1] After religious teachers accomplish the refining process indicated, they will surely recognize with joy that true religion has been ennobled and made more profound by scientific knowledge.

If it is one of the goals of religion to liberate mankind as far as possible from the bondage of egocentric cravings, desires, and fears, scientific reasoning can aid religion in yet another sense. Although it is true that it is the goal of science to discover rules which permit the association and foretelling of facts, this is not its only aim. It also seeks to reduce the connections discovered to the smallest possible number of mutually independent conceptual elements. It is in this striving after the rational unification of the manifold that it encounters its greatest successes, even though it is precisely this attempt which causes it to run the greatest risk of falling a prey to illusions. But whoever has undergone the intense experience of successful advances made in this domain, is moved by profound reverence for the rationality made manifest in existence. By way of the understanding he achieves a far-reaching emancipation from the shackles of personal hopes and desires, and thereby attains that humble attitude of mind towards the grandeur of reason incarnate in existence, which, in its profoundest depths, is inaccessible to man. This attitude, however, appears to me to be religious, in the highest sense of the word. And so it seems to me that science not only purifies the religious impulse of the dross of its anthropomorphism, but also contributes to a religious spiritualization of our understanding of life.

The further the spiritual evolution of mankind advances, the more certain it seems to me that the path to genuine religiosity does not lie through the fear of life, and the fear of death, and blind faith, but through striving after rational knowledge. In this sense I believe that the priest must become a teacher if he wishes to do justice to his lofty educational mission.

53. Intellectual Impediments to Religious Belief

H. J. PATON

RELIGION AND SCIENCE

Intellectual impediments to religion are made possible by the intellectual element in religion itself. Every religion, and certainly every developed religion, offers us a doctrine of man, a doctrine of history, a doctrine of the universe, and a doctrine of God. The exact status of such doctrines may be difficult to determine, and obsession with theory may be one of the major religious aberrations. Nevertheless religion cannot get on without some sort of doctrine, even if this can be reduced to the barest minimum.

---

[1] This thought is convincingly presented in Herbert Samuel's book, "Belief and Action."

Doctrine necessarily claims to be true, and this means that it enters into competition with other doctrines also claiming to be true. We may hold that one doctrine is true from one point of view and another from another; but ultimately there can be only one truth, or one comprehensive system of truths, in which divergent points of view are reconciled. We may not be able to effect this reconciliation, but to abandon the belief that such a reconciliation is possible is to abandon reason altogether and to have no defence against lunacy.

What are the doctrines with which religion, so far as it is doctrinal, may, and does, come into conflict? They can all be summed up in one word—science. But this bald statement is in need of some further elucidation.

In the first place, science has to be interpreted widely. It includes, not only the natural sciences, but also the mental and social sciences, such as psychology and anthropology. It covers also the modern methods of historical and literary criticism. The development of all these disciplines in the last four hundred years has brought religion face to face with a situation very different from any that existed before.

In the second place, it may be objected that there is no such thing as science—there are only sciences in the plural—and that all this talk about a conflict between religion and science is too vague to be profitable.

In such an objection there is some truth, and we ought always to be chary of those who are in the habit of telling us that Science (with a capital S) teaches us this or that and admits of no further argument. Assertions of this kind often spring, not directly from science, but from semi-popular philosophy, and some of the impediments to religion may fall under this description. Nevertheless we are blind if we fail to see that in method, in outlook, and in what can be described as atmosphere, science—all science—may be opposed to religion. Even if scientific knowledge is ultimately compatible with religion, it does not appear to be so at first sight; and indeed it seems to contradict a great deal formerly considered by theologians to be necessary for a saving faith. Furthermore, whatever may be true as regards logical compatibility, there is at least a psychological opposition between the scientific and the religious attitude. The gradual spread of the scientific outlook—and we are all affected by it even if the scientists say we are not nearly as much affected as we ought to be—has tended, not so much to refute religious belief, but rather to make it fade and wither. To quote Professor [H. H.] Price: "it has led to that inner emptiness and lack of faith . . . which is our fundamental and, as it seems, incurable disease."

It may be replied that all this is very much out of date—a mere survival of Victorian rationalism long ago abandoned. Those who comfort themselves thus are, I am afraid, deceived. It is true that science to-day—apart from the followers of Karl Marx, who was more of a prophet than a scientist—is not so cocksure as it once was about the finality of its teaching and is more prepared for revolutionary discoveries. It is also true that the note of hostility to religion is often, though by no means always, less strident than it was in the past. All this is to the good, but the main reason for the lesser stridency is that the modern rationalist no longer considers himself to be battling for victory: he supposes that the victory is already won. The greater amiability of present-day discussions is no doubt a straw that can help to show which way the wind is blowing; but those who clutch at that straw may only give the impression that they are drowning men.

RELIGION AND PHYSICS

The tide of science which threatens to submerge religion began to flow when Copernicus discovered that the earth was not the centre of the physical universe, but only one of the planets revolving round the sun. This tidal movement became more perceptible when Galileo confirmed his discovery and began to develop the modern methods of observation and measurement which have led to such astonishing triumphs. As if aware of the impending danger, the Church reacted violently, and condemned these doctrines as incompatible with Holy Scripture. Yet in spite of its utmost endeavours the tide has flowed relentlessly for more than four hundred years. Its rise has continuously accelerated and is certain—unless there is a world catastrophe—to accelerate more and more. During the whole of this period—if we may change the metaphor—religion has been fighting a rearguard action, abandoning one position after another till it is uncertain how much is left.

Why is it that the amazing achievements of modern physics and astronomy have seemed so inimical to religion? It is not merely that they overthrow primitive Biblical speculations about the physical universe—although, when a book has been regarded as divinely inspired throughout, to contradict the least part of it may seem to destroy the authority of the whole. Nor is it merely that man is seen as the creature of a day, clinging precariously to a whirling planet in a solar system which is itself utterly insignificant amid the vast reaches of interstellar space and astronomical time. These and many other considerations all play their part; but perhaps the main impediments to religion arise from two things—from the character of scientific method and from the conception of the world as governed throughout by unvarying law.

On scientific method little need here be said, although psychologically it may be the strongest influence of all. A scientific training makes it difficult or impossible to accept statements on authority, to be satisfied with second- or third-hand evidence, to believe in marvels which cannot be experimentally repeated, or to adopt theories which cannot be verified by empirical observation. There may be exceptions to this rule; for some scientists seem to lose their critical power once they stray beyond the narrow limits of their own subject. But there can be no doubt that in this respect the influence of science is both powerful and pervasive, and that it is unfavourable to much that passes for religion. How far that influence may in its turn lead to error or extravagance it is not here necessary to enquire. For our present purpose it is enough to recognize that the whole attitude, not merely of scientists, but of thoughtful men brought up in a scientific age, towards all the problems of life, whether secular or sacred, has been affected to an extent which it is almost impossible to exaggerate. Here may be found perhaps the greatest impediment to the unquestioning acceptance of any simple and traditional religious faith.

It is more difficult to gauge the effects which follow from conceiving the physical universe as subject to laws which admit of no exceptions. As late as the eighteenth century many thinkers regarded the discovery of physical laws as a revelation of the divine plan by which the universe is governed; and the very simplicity and comprehensiveness of the plan was taken to be a proof of divine benevolence and wisdom. Yet at least as early as Descartes it was already realized that physical laws were independent of, if not opposed to, the idea of purpose in the universe. It is this second interpretation which has prevailed. When Laplace, speaking of the existence of God, said "I have no need of that hypothesis," he meant that the conception of God's activity or purpose played no part in his formulation of scientific law, as it had done in the work of other thinkers, including the great Isaac Newton himself. In that specific sense the dictum of Laplace is the universal assumption of science to-day.

If modern physics is unfavourable to belief in a divine purpose or plan, it is still more unfavourable to belief in miracles. So far as these are considered to be breaches of physical laws, they cannot be accepted without rejecting the most fundamental presuppositions of science. Hence it is not surprising that they have become somewhat of an embarrassment to religion. At one time they were invoked to guarantee the truth of revelation. Now, if they are defended at all, it is revelation that is invoked to guarantee the truth of miracles, and their occurrence is explained as the manifestation of some higher law.

So far as physics is incompatible with miracles and has no use for a divine purpose in the universe, it is hard to see how we can retain the idea of providence in general and of special providences in particular. But this is not the worst. The character of scientific law appears to require a universal determinism which applies to the movements of human bodies as much as to the movement of the smallest electron or the remotest star. This cuts at the roots of all morality and so of religion as well.

There are some who seek to escape from this gloomy situation by reminding us that the old-fashioned mechanical views of physics are now abandoned. The concepts of mechanical cause and effect have been given up, and in place of causal laws we are left only with statistical averages. Physics itself even recognizes a principle of indeterminacy and so leaves at least a chink for human freedom. Hence perhaps the future before religion is not quite so black as it has been painted.

Without any wish to be dogmatic on these difficult subjects we must still ask ourselves whether those who find comfort in such considerations may not also be clutching at straws. To abandon the old-fashioned view of causation is by no means to give up the universality of law: all it amounts to is that the laws have a different character. The microscopic space left open by the principle of indeterminacy is far too small for the exercise of human freedom—if indeed we can conceive human freedom at all as manifested only in the apparent chinks and interstices of the physical universe. The late Professor Susan Stebbing was right when she said "It cannot be maintained that all that is required for human freedom is some amount of uncertainty in the domain of microphysics." And if we wish to argue that the new physics is less unfavourable to religion than the old, we must take into our reckoning what is called the second law of thermodynamics, according to which the universe is steadily running down. It is hard to see how this can offer any ground either for moral optimism or for religious faith.

The general effect of the modern scientific outlook is summed up in the eloquent, and by now familiar, words of Mr. Bertrand Russell. "That man is the product of causes which had no prevision of the end they were achieving; that his origin, his growth, his hopes and fears, his loves and beliefs, are but the outcome of accidental collocations of atoms; that no fire, no heroism, no intensity of thought and feeling, can preserve an individual life beyond the grave; that all the labours of the ages, all the inspiration, all the noon-day brightness of human genius, are destined to extinction in the vast death of the solar system, and that the whole temple of man's achievement must inevitably be buried beneath the débris of a universe in ruins—all these things, if not quite beyond dispute, are yet so nearly certain, that no philosophy which rejects them can hope to stand. Only within the scaffolding of these truths, only on the firm foundations of unyielding despair, can the soul's habitation henceforth be safely built."

If Mr. Russell's views be regarded as suspect, let us listen to the less eloquent, but hardly less despairing, words of a deeply religious thinker—Dr. Albert Schweizer. "My solution of the problem," he says, "is that we must make up our minds to renounce completely the optimistic-ethical interpretation of the world. If we take the world as it is, it is impossible to attribute to it a meaning in which the aims and objects of mankind and of individual men have a meaning also."

RELIGION AND BIOLOGY

If the first great wave that threatened to engulf religion came from physics, the second came from biology. The Darwinian theory of evolution overthrew the belief that each species was the object of a special creation and possessed a fixed and unchanging character. This served to upset the authority alike of Aristotle and of the book of Genesis. But still worse than this, the process of evolution appeared to be mechanical rather than purposive, blind rather than intelligent, and so to render nugatory the argument from design, which was commonly regarded as the most cogent proof for the existence of God. Furthermore, from a human point of view evolution in its working seemed wasteful and even cruel, and the main qualities making for survival appeared to be lust and violence and deceit. It gave less than no support to belief in the wisdom and benevolence of the Creator or to the view that the end of creation was the furtherance of virtue. But perhaps the greatest shock of all came from the discovery that man, far from having been specially created in the image of God, was himself the product of this unintelligent process of evolution and must look back to a long line of ape-like ancestors. Nowadays we take all this calmly in our stride, partly perhaps through lack of imagination. We may even feel in a curious way that it unites us more intimately with the world of nature of which we form a part. But it should not cause us surprise if to our Victorian grandfathers it seemed that

> The pillar'd firmament is rott'nness,
> And earth's base built on stubble.

In comparison with this the other shocks from biology may seem unimportant, but we have to remember that the effect of scientific discoveries is cumulative. Of these further shocks we need mention only one.

It has always been recognized that the soul is in some ways dependent on the body; and we all know from ordinary experience how a minor indisposition, or even fatigue, may dull our mind and blunt our emotions and weaken our will. But the development of physiology began to show in ever minuter detail how close is the connexion between mind and body, and how utterly we depend on the structure of our brain and nervous system. The very existence of the soul began to be questioned. Why should we postulate a soul instead of recognizing that mental functions are completely dependent on bodily functions? Above all, why should we suppose, against all the empirical evidence, that the soul could exist as a separate entity after the death of the body? The belief in immortality, one of the strongholds of religion, or at least of many religions, was being steadily undermined. Conclusions based on these detailed discoveries were supported further by the general theory of evolution, which abolished the sharp separation of man from the other animals, as also by the general theory that physical laws govern the movements of all bodies, not excluding the organic bodies of plants and animals and men. Some philosophers and scientists hold it out as a possibility, and indeed as an ideal, that the laws of biology, and even of psychology, may one day be reduced to laws of physics.

One general result emerges from all this. Man displays his intelligence in discovering laws of nature and then awakes, perhaps with horror, to the fact that these laws apply to himself: for science he is only one object among many others and has to be understood in the same way as the rest. Thus man is finally entangled in the meshes of the net that he himself has woven; and when we say this, we must add that it is true, not merely of his body, but of his soul. Science is, as it were, a machine constructed by man in order to master the universe; but the machine has turned against its maker and seeks to master him as well.

RELIGION AND PSYCHOLOGY

The third great wave threatening religion comes from psychology, which is, at least etymologically, the science of the soul. This is a more recent wave; and as we disappear gasping under its onrush, we are hardly yet in a position to study its shape. Indeed its shape is perhaps not yet definitely formed. Its exponents at times contradict one another with a freedom ordinarily reserved for philosophers; and some of them indulge in a boldness of speculation from which a respectable philosopher would shrink. We are offered a choice between different schools of thought.

Thus there is a Behaviouristic school, which, as a further expansion of physiology, makes still more formidable the impediments already considered. The

Behaviourists ignore in practice, if they do not also deny in theory, the mental phenomena formerly considered open to introspection—our thoughts, our emotions, our volitions, and so on: they are content to study only the bodily behaviour of human and other animals, and so to blur still further the dividing line between man and the brutes. A very different method is adopted by the schools of psychoanalysis which originate from Freud, both by those which seek to carry further the work of the master and by those which attempt to modify and improve it. All of them start from an examination of human consciousness, especially of human dreams; and they claim on this basis to bring under scientific investigation the vast and obscure domain of the unconscious, whose existence had been merely suspected and whose character had not been seriously explored. According to them the human mind is like an iceberg, by far the greater part of which is under water and not amenable to direct observation. By means of inference they attempt to describe in detail these murky nether regions; and they have been able, as it were, to draw up from the ocean's depths many strange, and on the whole unpleasing, objects for our contemplation and instruction.

The schools which consider human consciousness to be worthy of scientific attention take up different attitudes to religion. As we have seen, they may regard it as a harmful illusion or as a healing and even "real" illusion, whatever that may be. But, broadly speaking, even at the best they offer cold comfort to religion, and the attitude of Freud himself is conspicuously hostile. Besides, they exhibit the general tendency to assume determinism in mental processes; they encourage the view that reason has little or no part to play in human behaviour; and even if they regard mind as a possible object of study, it is for them only one object among others and requires no special principles for its understanding. All psychology is an example of what I meant when I said that the soul is entangled in the meshes of the scientific net which man has devised for the better understanding of the physical world. And many psychologists believe that religious experience can be explained—or explained away—in accordance with the ordinary laws that have been found to account for other mental phenomena.

This third wave is perhaps logically less intimidating to religion than the other two, if only because psychology is not yet fully developed as a science. Psycho-analysis has called attention to mental phenomena hitherto neglected; it has thrown light on dark places; and it has done mental healing a service for which the world must be grateful. Whatever be its defects, it has opened up the way for fresh advances, but has it already advanced so far that even its fundamental concepts are firmly established? Sometimes it may seem not to have got much beyond a stage like that in chemistry when the phenomena of combustion were explained by postulating a hypothetical substance, now forgotten, which was known as "phlogiston"; or at least—if this is too depreciatory—not beyond the comparatively recent stage in physics when "ether" had to be postulated as an elastic substance permeating all space and forming a medium through which rays of light were propagated. It may be heretical to say so, but it seems to me rather improbable that our old friends, the Ego, the Super-Ego, and the Id, will occupy permanent niches in the scientific pantheon.

Nevertheless, even if this third wave may not yet be so very imposing logically, psychologically—partly perhaps by its very vagueness—it is to-day al-most the most formidable of the three, at least as far as popular or semi-popular thinking is concerned. In spite of attempts to make use of it in the interests of religion, it produces an emotional and intellectual background so different from that of religious tradition that the combination of the two becomes very difficult. What is sometimes said of philosophies is even more true of religious beliefs—they are usually not refuted, but merely abandoned. When the spiritual climate has altered, they may simply fade away; and we seem to be witnessing something rather like this at the present crisis of our civilization.

RELIGION AND HISTORY

There are other human sciences besides psychology, and their influence has also tended to be psychologically, if not logically, unfavourable to religion. Anthropol-ogy, for example, tends on the whole to blur sharp distinctions between the primitive and the developed, and among heathen superstitions it finds parallels even for the most sacred mysteries of the higher religions. It suggests that religion is a survival of something primitive in the experience of the race, just as psychol-ogy suggests it is a survival of something primitive in the experience of the child. Even economics takes a hand in the unholy assault. The classical economists may have been tempted at times to suppose that the "economic man" was, not a mere useful abstraction, but the only kind of man there is; and this tendency has been hardened into a dogma by the Marxists. They tell us that our bourgeois religion, like our bourgeois morality, is only an ideology—that is, an illusory "rationaliza-tion" of purely economic factors—and one of the main impediments to human progress. All these human sciences, among which sociology also may be included, have the common characteristic of treating man as one object among other ob-jects: they tend to explain his thoughts, his actions, and his emotions as the effect of forces outside himself—forces whose influence can be determined, and even controlled, in accordance with ascertainable scientific laws.

Here then we have a whole series of little wavelets, not perhaps very impressive in isolation and colliding at times with one another, yet all driving inexorably in the same general direction. But belonging to the same series there is one special wave so menacing that we may be inclined to call it the fourth great wave—the wave of historical method and historical criticism.

The modern development of the historical method is particularly menac-ing to Christianity, since of all the great religions Christianity has laid most stress on history—the history of the Jews, the history of the Founder, and the history of the Church. Modern criticism has undermined first the authority of the Old Testament and then the authority of the New in such a way that the traditional belief in an infallible Book, written down by God's penmen at His dictation, can no longer be accepted by any intelligent man of independent judgement who has given serious consideration to the subject. We have instead a most fallible human record compiled by mortal men, who, even if they were gifted with a special religious insight, were unacquainted with the canons of historical evidence and unfamiliar with the ideals of historical accuracy. Christian thinkers have made great and creditable efforts to adjust themselves to this new situation—the other world-religions are probably not even yet fully awake to their danger. The methods of modern scholarship may be able to sort out what is reasonably certain from what is at least doubtful as well as from what is in all probability fictitious. On these points there are, and are bound to be, differences among scholars, and it is only experts who can profitably form an opinion. Hence it is always possible, and it may often be justifiable, to dismiss the arguments of laymen in these subjects as ignorant or exaggerated. Nevertheless the plain man used to be faced with a plain situation which he could understand. He was told that every historical statement in the Bible, or at least in the New Testament, was true. He has now to be told that while the religious teaching in the Bible retains its unique value, some of its historical statements are true, while some are untrue, and others have been traditionally misunderstood. Even if he is sensible enough not to hold that if anything goes, the whole thing goes, he yet feels that he does not know where he stands, and that he is ill-equipped to come to a decision in matters about which the doctors differ. This is a new impediment to the simplicity of religious faith. . . .

THE PREDICAMENT OF RELIGION

. . . There are doubtless many other reasons, some of them less creditable, for the growing indifference to religion; but reasons of the type I have described are worthy of special consideration since they spring, not from human wickedness and folly, but from the highest achievements of human thought. They affect, not only the intellectuals, but also, through them, the immense mass of men who take their opinions at second and third and fourth hand. The whole spiritual atmosphere is altered, and even the ordinary religious man speaks today in a different tone about special providences and the hope of immortality, if he speaks of them at all.

In such circumstances it is unconvincing to tell us that the conflict of religion and science is now happily out-moded, that so and so has put forward new theories about scientific methodology and somebody else has confirmed some statement in the Biblical record from a newly-discovered papyrus or from some archaeological remains. This is mere tinkering with the subject; and we should not be surprised if those who have been brought up in the new atmosphere and have little or no experience of religion are apt to dismiss the easy optimism of some religious teachers as springing from blindness or ignorance, if not from hypocrisy. Nor can it be denied that they sometimes have ample excuse. The situation to be faced is one unknown to St. Paul and St. Augustine, to Aquinas and Duns Scotus, to Luther and Calvin; and it can be met, if it is to be met at all, only by a new effort of thinking at least as great as any of theirs. So long as this is lacking, the modern world is bound to suffer from a divided mind and from a conflict between the heart and the head. If religion has to satisfy the whole man, its demand is that the men who follow it must be whole-minded as well as whole-hearted. The very wholeness at which religion aims is impossible unless the spiritual disease caused by the fatal rift between science and religion can receive its own specific intellectual cure.

Linguistic Philosophy

54. Language, Truth and Logic

A. J. AYER

The traditional disputes of philosophers are, for the most part, as unwarranted as they are unfruitful. The surest way to end them is to establish beyond question what should be the purpose and method of a philosophical enquiry. And this is by no means so difficult a task as the history of philosophy would lead one to suppose. For if there are any questions which science leaves it to philosophy to answer, a straightforward process of elimination must lead to their discovery.

We may begin by criticising the metaphysical thesis that philosophy affords us knowledge of a reality transcending the world of science and common sense. Later on, when we come to define metaphysics and account for its existence, we shall find that it is possible to be a metaphysician without believing in a transcendent reality; for we shall see that many metaphysical utterances are due to the commission of logical errors, rather than to a conscious desire on the part of their authors to go beyond the limits of experience. But it is convenient for us to take the case of those who believe that it is possible to have knowledge of a transcendent reality as a starting-point for our discussion. The arguments which we use to refute them will subsequently be found to apply to the whole of metaphysics.

One way of attacking a metaphysician who claimed to have knowledge of a reality which transcended the phenomenal world would be to enquire from what premises his propositions were deduced. Must he not begin, as other men do, with the evidence of his senses? And if so, what valid process of reasoning can possibly lead him to the conception of a transcendent reality? Surely from empirical premises nothing whatsoever concerning the properties, or even the existence, of anything super-empirical can legitimately be inferred. But this objection would be met by a denial on the part of the metaphysician that his assertions were ultimately based on the evidence of his senses. He would say that he was endowed with a faculty of intellectual intuition which enabled him to know facts that could not be known through sense-experience. And even if it could be shown that he was relying on empirical premises, and that his venture into a non-empirical world was therefore logically unjustified, it would not follow that the assertions which he made concerning this non-empirical world could not be true. For the fact that a conclusion does not follow from its putative premise is not sufficient to show that it is false. Consequently, one cannot overthrow a system of transcendent metaphysics merely by criticising the way in which it comes into being. What is required is rather a criticism of the nature of the actual statements which comprise it. And this is the line of argument which we shall, in fact, pursue. For we shall maintain that no statement which refers to a "reality" transcending the limits of all possible sense-experience can possibly have any literal significance; from which it must follow that the labours of those who have striven to describe such a reality have all been devoted to the production of nonsense.

It may be suggested that this is a proposition which has already been proved by Kant. But although Kant also condemned transcendent metaphysics, he did so on different grounds. For he said that the human understanding was so constituted that it lost itself in contradictions when it ventured out beyond the limits of possible experience and attempted to deal with things in themselves. And thus he made the impossibility of a transcendent metaphysic not, as we do, a matter of logic, but a matter of fact. He asserted, not that our minds could not conceivably have had the power of penetrating beyond the phenomenal world, but merely that they were in fact devoid of it. And this leads the critic to ask how, if it is possible to know only what lies within the bounds of sense-experience, the author can be justified in asserting that real things do exist beyond, and how he can tell what are the boundaries beyond which the human understanding may not venture, unless he succeeds in passing them himself. As Wittgenstein says, "in order to draw a limit to thinking, we should have to think both sides of this limit,"[1] a truth to which Bradley gives a special twist in maintaining that the man who is ready to prove that metaphysics is impossible is a brother metaphysician with a rival theory of his own.[2]

Whatever force these objections may have against the Kantian doctrine, they have none whatsoever against the thesis that I am about to set forth. It cannot here be said that the author is himself overstepping the barrier he maintains to be impassable. For the fruitlessness of attempting to transcend the limits of possible sense-experience will be deduced, not from a psychological hypothesis concerning the actual constitution of the human mind, but from the rule which determines the literal significance of language. Our charge against the metaphysician is not that he attempts to employ the understanding in a field where it cannot profitably venture, but that he produces sentences which fail to conform to the conditions under which alone a sentence can be literally significant. Nor are we ourselves obliged to talk nonsense in order to show that all sentences of a certain type are necessarily devoid of literal significance. We need only formulate the criterion which enables us to test whether a sentence expresses a genuine proposition about a matter of fact, and then point out that the sentences under consideration fail to satisfy it. And this we shall now proceed to do. We shall first of all formulate the criterion in somewhat vague terms, and then give the explanations which are necessary to render it precise.

---

[1] *Tractatus Logico-Philosophicus*, Preface.
[2] Bradley, *Appearance and Reality*, 2nd ed., p. 1.

The criterion which we use to test the genuineness of apparent statements of fact is the criterion of verifiability. We say that a sentence is factually significant to any given person, if, and only if, he knows how to verify the proposition which it purports to express—that is, if he knows what observations would lead him, under certain conditions, to accept the proposition as being true, or reject it as being false. If, on the other hand, the putative proposition is of such a character that the assumption of its truth, or falsehood, is consistent with any assumption whatsoever concerning the nature of his future experience, then, as far as he is concerned, it is, if not a tautology, a mere pseudo-proposition. The sentence expressing it may be emotionally significant to him; but it is not literally significant. And with regard to questions the procedure is the same. We enquire in every case what observations would lead us to answer the question, one way or the other; and, if none can be discovered, we must conclude that the sentence under consideration does not, as far as we are concerned, express a genuine question, however strongly its grammatical appearance may suggest that it does.

As the adoption of this procedure is an essential factor in the argument of this book [Language, Truth and Logic], it needs to be examined in detail.

In the first place, it is necessary to draw a distinction between practical verifiability, and verifiability in principle. Plainly we all understand, in many cases believe, propositions which we have not in fact taken steps to verify. Many of these are propositions which we could verify if we took enough trouble. But there remain a number of significant propositions, concerning matters of fact, which we could not verify even if we chose; simply because we lack the practical means of placing ourselves in the situation where the relevant observations could be made. A simple and familiar example of such a proposition is the proposition that there are mountains on the farther side of the moon. No rocket has yet been invented which would enable me to go and look at the farther side of the moon, so that I am unable to decide the matter by actual observation. But I do know what observations would decide it for me, if, as is theoretically conceivable, I were once in a position to make them. And therefore I say that the proposition is verifiable in principle, if not in practice, and is accordingly significant. On the other hand, such a metaphysical pseudo-proposition as "the Absolute enters into, but is itself incapable of, evolution and progress," is not even in principle verifiable. For one cannot conceive of an observation which would enable one to determine whether the Absolute did, or did not, enter into evolution and progress. Of course it is possible that the author of such a remark [Hegel] is using English words in a way in which they are not commonly used by English-speaking people, and that he does, in fact, intend to assert something which could be empirically verified. But until he makes us understand how the proposition that he wishes to express would be verified, he fails to communicate anything to us. And if he admits, as I think the author of the remark in question would have admitted, that his words were not intended to express either a tautology or a proposition which was capable, at least in principle, of being verified, then it follows that he has made an utterance which has no literal significance even for himself. . . .

This . . . brings us to the question of the possibility of religious knowledge. We shall see that this possibility has already been ruled out by our treatment of metaphysics. But, as this is a point of considerable interest, we may be permitted to discuss it at some length.

It is now generally admitted, at any rate by philosophers, that the existence of a being having the attributes which define the god of any non-animistic religion cannot be demonstratively proved. To see that this is so, we have only to ask ourselves what are the premises from which the existence of such a god could be deduced. If the conclusion that a god exists is to be demonstratively certain, then these premises must be certain; for, as the conclusion of a deductive argument is already contained in the premises, any uncertainty there may be about the truth of the premises is necessarily shared by it. But we know that no empirical proposition can ever be anything more than probable. It is only *a priori* propositions that are logically certain. But we cannot deduce the existence of a god from an *a priori* proposition. For we know that the reason why *a priori* propositions are certain is that they are tautologies. And from a set of tautologies nothing but a further tautology can be validly deduced. It follows that there is no possibility of demonstrating the existence of a god.

What is not so generally recognised is that there can be no way of proving that the existence of a god, such as the God of Christianity, is even probable. Yet this also is easily shown. For if the existence of such a god were probable, then the proposition that he existed would be an empirical hypothesis. And in that case it would be possible to deduce from it, and other empirical hypotheses, certain experimental propositions which were not deducible from those other hypotheses alone. But in fact this is not possible. It is sometimes claimed, indeed, that the existence of a certain sort of regularity in nature constitutes sufficient evidence for the existence of a god. But if the sentence "God exists" entails no more than that certain types of phenomena occur in certain sequences, then to assert the existence of a god will be simply equivalent to asserting that there is the requisite regularity in nature; and no religious man would admit that this was all he intended to assert in asserting the existence of a god. He would say that in talking about God, he was talking about a transcendent being who might be known through certain empirical manifestations, but certainly could not be defined in terms of those manifestations. But in that case the term "god" is a metaphysical term. And if "god" is a metaphysical term, then it cannot be even probable that a god exists. For to say that "God exists" is to make a metaphysical utterance which cannot be either true or false. And by the same criterion, no sentence which purports to describe the nature of a transcendent god can possess any literal significance.

It is important not to confuse this view of religious assertions with the view that is adopted by atheists, or agnostics.[3] For it is characteristic of an agnostic to hold that the existence of a god is a possibility in which there is no good reason either to believe or disbelieve; and it is characteristic of an atheist to hold that it is at least probable that no god exists. And our view that all utterances about the nature of God are nonsensical, so far from being identical with, or even lending any support to, either of these familiar contentions, is actually incompatible with

---

[3] This point was suggested to me by Professor H. H. Price.

them. For if the assertion that there is a god is nonsensical, then the atheist's assertion that there is no god is equally nonsensical, since it is only a significant proposition that can be significantly contradicted. As for the agnostic, although he refrains from saying either that there is or that there is not a god, he does not deny that the question whether a transcendent god exists is a genuine question. He does not deny that the two sentences "There is a transcendent god" and "There is no transcendent god" express propositions one of which is actually true and the other false. All he says is that we have no means of telling which of them is true, and therefore ought not to commit ourselves to either. But we have seen that the sentences in question do not express propositions at all. And this means that agnosticism also is ruled out.

Thus we offer the theist the same comfort as we gave to the moralist. His assertions cannot possibly be valid, but they cannot be invalid either. As he says nothing at all about the world, he cannot justly be accused of saying anything false, or anything for which he has insufficient grounds. It is only when the theist claims that in asserting the existence of a transcendent god he is expressing a genuine proposition that we are entitled to disagree with him.

It is to be remarked that in cases where deities are identified with natural objects, assertions concerning them may be allowed to be significant. If, for example, a man tells me that the occurrence of thunder is alone both necessary and sufficient to establish the truth of the proposition that Jehovah is angry, I may conclude that, in his usage of words, the sentence "Jehovah is angry" is equivalent to "It is thundering." But in sophisticated religions, though they may be to some extent based on men's awe of natural process which they cannot sufficiently understand, the "person" who is supposed to control the empirical world is not himself located in it; he is held to be superior to the empirical world, and so outside it; and he is endowed with super-empirical attributes. But the notion of a person whose essential attributes are non-empirical is not an intelligible notion at all. We may have a word which is used as if it named this "person," but, unless the sentences in which it occurs express propositions which are empirically verifiable, it cannot be said to symbolize anything. And this is the case with regard to the word "god," in the usage in which it is intended to refer to a transcendent object. The mere existence of the noun is enough to foster the illusion that there is a real, or at any rate a possible entity corresponding to it. It is only when we enquire what God's attributes are that we discover that "God," in this usage, is not a genuine name.

It is common to find belief in a transcendent god conjoined with belief in an after-life. But, in the form which it usually takes, the content of this belief is not a genuine hypothesis. To say that men do not ever die, or that the state of death is merely a state of prolonged insensibility, is indeed to express a significant proposition, though all the available evidence goes to show that it is false. But to say that there is something imperceptible inside a man, which is his soul or his real self, and that it goes on living after he is dead, is to make a metaphysical assertion which has no more factual content than the assertion that there is a transcendent god.

It is worth mentioning that, according to the account which we have given of religious assertions, there is no logical ground for antagonism between religion and natural science. As far as the question of truth or falsehood is concerned, there is no opposition between the natural scientist and the theist who believes in a transcendent god. For since the religious utterances of the theist are not genuine propositions at all, they cannot stand in any logical relation to the propositions of science. Such antagonism as there is between religion and science appears to consist in the fact that science takes away one of the motives which make men religious. For it is acknowledged that one of the ultimate sources of religious feeling lies in the inability of men to determine their own destiny; and science tends to destroy the feeling of awe with which men regard an alien world, by making them believe that they can understand and anticipate the course of natural phenomena, and even to some extent control it. The fact that it has recently become fashionable for physicists themselves to be sympathetic towards religion is a point in favour of this hypothesis. For this sympathy towards religion marks the physicists' own lack of confidence in the validity of their hypotheses, which is a reaction on their part from the anti-religious dogmatism of nineteenth-century scientists, and a natural outcome of the crisis through which physics has just passed.

It is not within the scope of this enquiry to enter more deeply into the causes of religious feeling, or to discuss the probability of the continuance of religious belief. We are concerned only to answer those questions which arise out of our discussion of the possibility of religious knowledge. The point which we wish to establish is that there cannot be any transcendent truths of religion. For the sentences which the theist uses to express such "truths" are not literally significant.

An interesting feature of this conclusion is that it accords with what many theists are accustomed to say themselves. For we are often told that the nature of God is a mystery which transcends the human understanding. But to say that something transcends the human understanding is to say that it is unintelligible. And what is unintelligible cannot significantly be described. Again, we are told that God is not an object of reason but an object of faith. This may be nothing more than an admission that the existence of God must be taken on trust, since it cannot be proved. But it may also be an assertion that God is the object of a purely mystical intuition, and cannot therefore be defined in terms which are intelligible to the reason. And I think there are many theists who would assert this. But if one allows that it is impossible to define God in intelligible terms, then one is allowing that it is impossible for a sentence both to be significant and to be about God. If a mystic admits that the object of his vision is something which cannot be described, then he must also admit that he is bound to talk nonsense when he describes it.

For his part, the mystic may protest that his intuition does reveal truths to him, even though he cannot explain to others what these truths are; and that we who do not possess this faculty of intuition can have no ground for denying that it is a cognitive faculty. For we can hardly maintain *a priori* that there are no ways of discovering true propositions except those which we ourselves employ. The answer is that we set no limit to the number of ways in which one may come to formulate a true proposition. We do not in any way deny that a synthetic truth may be discovered by purely intuitive methods as well as by the rational method of induction. But we do say that every synthetic proposition, however it may have been arrived at, must be subject to the test of actual experience. We do not deny *a priori* that the mystic is able to discover truths by his own special methods. We wait to hear what are the propositions which embody his discoveries, in order to see whether they are verified or confuted by our empirical observations. But the mystic, so far from producing propositions which are empirically verified, is unable to produce any intelligible propositions at all. And therefore we say that his intuition has not revealed to him any facts. It is no use his saying that he has apprehended facts but is unable to express them. For we know that if he really had acquired any information, he would be able to express it. He would be able to indicate in some way or other how the genuineness of his discovery might be empirically determined. The fact that he cannot reveal what he "knows," or even himself devise an empirical test to validate his "knowledge," shows that his state of mystical intuition is not a genuinely cognitive state. So that in describing his vision the mystic does not give us any information about the external world; he merely gives us indirect information about the condition of his own mind.

These considerations dispose of the argument from religious experience, which many philosophers still regard as a valid argument in favour of the existence of a god. They say that it is logically possible for men to be immediately acquainted with God, as they are immediately acquainted with a sense-content, and that there is no reason why one should be prepared to believe a man when he says that he is seeing a yellow patch, and refuse to believe him when he says that he is seeing God. The answer to this is that if the man who asserts that he is seeing God is merely asserting that he is experiencing a peculiar kind of sense-content, then we do not for a moment deny that his assertion may be true. But, ordinarily, the man who says that he is seeing God is saying not merely that he is experiencing a religious emotion, but also that there exists a transcendent being who is the object of this emotion; just as the man who says that he sees a yellow patch is ordinarily saying not merely that his visual sense-field contains a yellow sense-content, but also that there exists a yellow object to which the sense-content belongs. And it is not irrational to be prepared to believe a man when he asserts the existence of a yellow object, and to refuse to believe him when he asserts the existence of a transcendent god. For whereas the sentence "There exists here a yellow-coloured material thing" expresses a genuine synthetic proposition which could be empirically verified, the sentence "There exists a transcendent god" has, as we have seen, no literal significance.

We conclude, therefore, that the argument from religious experience is altogether fallacious. The fact that people have religious experiences is interesting from the psychological point of view, but it does not in any way imply that there is such a thing as religious knowledge, any more than our having moral experiences implies that there is such a thing as moral knowledge. The theist, like the moralist, may believe that his experiences are cognitive experiences, but, unless he can formulate his "knowledge" in propositions that are empirically verifiable, we may be sure that he is deceiving himself. It follows that those philosophers who fill their books with assertions that they intuitively "know" this or that moral or religious "truth" are merely providing material for the psycho-analyst. For no act of intuition can be said to reveal a truth about any matter of fact unless it issues in verifiable propositions. And all such propositions are to be incorporated in the system of empirical propositions which constitutes science.

55. Theology and Falsification

ANTONY FLEW, R. M. HARE, AND BASIL MITCHELL

THEOLOGY AND FALSIFICATION

A
Antony Flew

Let us begin with a parable. It is a parable developed from a tale told by John Wisdom in his haunting and revelatory article "Gods."[1] Once upon a time two explorers came upon a clearing in the jungle. In the clearing were growing many flowers and many weeds. One explorer says, "Some gardener must tend this plot." The other disagrees, "There is no gardener." So they pitch their tents and set a watch. No gardener is ever seen. "But perhaps he is an invisible gardener." So they set up a barbed-wire fence. They electrify it. They patrol with bloodhounds. (For they remember how H. G. Wells's *The Invisible Man* could be both smelt and touched though he could not be seen.) But no shrieks ever suggest that some intruder has received a shock. No movements of the wire ever betray an invisible climber. The bloodhounds never give cry. Yet still the Believer is not convinced. "But there is a gardener, invisible, intangible, insensible to electric shocks, a gardener who has no scent and makes no sound, a gardener who comes secretly to look after the garden which he loves." At last the Sceptic despairs, "But what remains of your original assertion? Just how does what you call an invisible, intangible, eternally elusive gardener differ from an imaginary gardener or even from no gardener at all?"

In this parable we can see how what starts as an assertion, that something exists or that there is some analogy between certain complexes of phenomena, may be reduced step by step to an altogether different status, to an expression perhaps of a "picture preference."[2] The Sceptic says there is no gardener. The Believer says there is a gardener (but invisible, etc.). One man talks about sexual behaviour. Another man prefers to talk of Aphrodite (but knows that there is not really a superhuman person additional to, and somehow responsible for, all sexual

[1] P.A.S., 1944–5, reprinted as Ch. X of *Logic and Language*, Vol I (Blackwell, 1951), and in his *Philosophy and Psychoanalysis* (Blackwell, 1953).
[2] Cf. J. Wisdom, "Other Minds," *Mind*, 1940; reprinted in his *Other Minds* (Blackwell, 1952).

phenomena).[3] The process of qualification may be checked at any point before the original assertion is completely withdrawn and something of that first assertion will remain (Tautology). Mr. Wells's invisible man could not, admittedly, be seen, but in all other respects he was a man like the rest of us. But though the process of qualification may be, and of course usually is, checked in time, it is not always judiciously so halted. Someone may dissipate his assertion completely without noticing that he has done so. A fine brash hypothesis may thus be killed by inches, the death by a thousand qualifications.

And in this, it seems to me, lies the peculiar danger, the endemic evil, of theological utterance. Take such utterances as "God has a plan," "God created the world," "God loves us as a father loves his children." They look at first sight very much like assertions, vast cosmological assertions. Of course, this is no sure sign that they either are, or are intended to be, assertions. But let us confine ourselves to the cases where those who utter such sentences intend them to express assertions. (Merely remarking parenthetically that those who intend or interpret such utterances as crypto-commands, expressions of wishes, disguised ejaculations, concealed ethics, or as anything else but assertions, are unlikely to succeed in making them either properly orthodox or practically effective.)

Now to assert that such and such is the case is necessarily equivalent to denying that such and such is not the case.[4] Suppose then that we are in doubt as to what someone who gives vent to an utterance is asserting, or suppose that, more radically, we are sceptical as to whether he is really asserting anything at all, one way of trying to understand (or perhaps it will be to expose) his utterance is to attempt to find what he would regard as counting against, or as being incompatible with, its truth. For if the utterance is indeed an assertion, it will necessarily be equivalent to a denial of the negation of that assertion. And anything which would count against the assertion, or which would induce the speaker to withdraw it and to admit that it had been mistaken, must be part of (or the whole of) the meaning of the negation of that assertion. And to know the meaning of the negation of an assertion, is as near as makes no matter, to know the meaning of that assertion.[5] And if there is nothing which a putative assertion denies then there is nothing which it asserts either: and so it is not really an assertion. When the Sceptic in the parable asked the Believer, "Just how does what you call an invisible, intangible, eternally elusive gardener differ from an imaginary gardener or even from no gardener at all?" he was suggesting that the Believer's earlier statement had been so eroded by qualification that it was no longer an assertion at all.

Now it often seems to people who are not religious as if there was no conceivable event or series of events the occurrence of which would be admitted

---

[3] Cf. Lucretius, *De Rerum Natura*, II, 655–60,

> Hic siquis mare Neptunum Cereremque vocare
> Constituet fruges et Bacchi nomine abuti
> Mavolat quam laticis proprium proferre vocamen
> Concedamus ut hic terrarum dictitet orbem
> Esse deum matrem dum vera re tamen ipse
> Religione animum turpi contingere parcat.

[4] For those who prefer symbolism: $p \equiv \sim \sim p$.

[5] For by simply negating $\sim p$ we get p: $\sim \sim p \equiv p$.

by sophisticated religious people to be a sufficient reason for conceding "There wasn't a God after all" or "God does not really love us then." Someone tells us that God loves us as a father loves his children. We are reassured. But then we see a child dying of inoperable cancer of the throat. His earthly father is driven frantic in his efforts to help, but his Heavenly Father reveals no obvious sign of concern. Some qualification is made—God's love is "not a merely human love" or it is "an inscrutable love," perhaps—and we realize that such sufferings are quite compatible with the truth of the assertion that "God loves us as a father (but, of course, . . .)." We are reassured again. But then perhaps we ask: what is this assurance of God's (appropriately qualified) love worth, what is this apparent guarantee really a guarantee against? Just what would have to happen not merely (morally and wrongly) to tempt but also (logically and rightly) to entitle us to say "God does not love us" or even "God does not exist"? I therefore put to the succeeding symposiasts the simple central questions, "What would have to occur or to have occurred to constitute for you a disproof of the love of, or of the existence of, God?"

University College of North Staffordshire
England

B[6]

R. M. Hare

I wish to make it clear that I shall not try to defend Christianity in particular, but religion in general—not because I do not believe in Christianity, but because you cannot understand what Christianity is, until you have understood what religion is.

I must begin by confessing that, on the ground marked out by Flew, he seems to me to be completely victorious. I therefore shift my ground by relating another parable. A certain lunatic is convinced that all dons want to murder him. His friends introduce him to all the mildest and most respectable dons that they can find, and after each of them has retired, they say, "You see, he doesn't really want to murder you; he spoke to you in a most cordial manner; surely you are convinced now?" But the lunatic replies, "Yes, but that was only his diabolical cunning; he's really plotting against me the whole time, like the rest of them; I know it I tell you." However many kindly dons are produced, the reaction is still the same.

Now we say that such a person is deluded. But what is he deluded about? About the truth or falsity of an assertion? Let us apply Flew's test to him. There is no behaviour of dons that can be enacted which he will accept as counting against his theory; and therefore his theory, on this test, asserts nothing. But it does not follow that there is no difference between what he thinks about dons and what most of us think about them—otherwise we should not call him a lunatic and

---

[6] Some references to intervening discussion have been excised—Editors.

ourselves sane, and dons would have no reason to feel uneasy about his presence in Oxford.

Let us call that in which we differ from this lunatic, our respective *bliks*. He has an insane *blik* about dons; we have a sane one. It is important to realize that we have a sane one, not no *blik* at all; for there must be two sides to any argument—if he has a wrong *blik,* then those who are right about dons must have a right one. Flew has shown that a *blik* does not consist in an assertion or system of them; but nevertheless it is very important to have the right *blik.*

Let us try to imagine what it would be like to have different *bliks* about other things than dons. When I am driving my car, it sometimes occurs to me to wonder whether my movements of the steering-wheel will always continue to be followed by corresponding alterations in the direction of the car. I have never had a steering failure, though I have had skids, which must be similar. Moreover, I know enough about how the steering of my car is made, to know the sort of thing that would have to go wrong for the steering to fail—steel joints would have to part, or steel rods break, or something—but how do I know that this won't happen? The truth is, I don't know, I just have a *blik* about steel and its properties, so that normally I trust the steering of my car; but I find it not at all difficult to imagine what it would be like to lose this *blik* and acquire the opposite one. People would say I was silly about steel; but there would be no mistaking the reality of the difference between our respective *bliks*—for example, I should never go in a motor-car. Yet I should hesitate to say that the difference between us was the difference between contradictory assertions. No amount of safe arrivals or bench-tests will remove my *blik* and restore the normal one; for my *blik* is compatible with any finite number of such tests.

It was Hume who taught us that our whole commerce with the world depends upon our *blik* about the world; and that differences between *bliks* about the world cannot be settled by observation of what happens in the world. That was why, having performed the interesting experiment of doubting the ordinary man's *blik* about the world, and showing that no proof could be given to make us adopt one *blik* rather than another, he turned to backgammon to take his mind off the problem. It seems, indeed, to be impossible even to formulate as an assertion the normal *blik* about the world which makes me put my confidence in the future reliability of steel joints, in the continued ability of the road to support my car, and not gape beneath it revealing nothing below; in the general non-homicidal tendencies of dons; in my own continued well-being (in some sense of that word that I may not now fully understand) if I continue to do what is right according to my lights; in the general likelihood of people like Hitler coming to a bad end. But perhaps a formulation less inadequate than most is to be found in the Psalms: "The earth is weak and all the inhabiters thereof: I bear up the pillars of it."

The mistake of the position which Flew selects for attack is to regard this kind of talk as some sort of *explanation,* as scientists are accustomed to use the word. As such, it would obviously be ludicrous. We no longer believe in God as an Atlas—*nous n'avons pas besoin de cette hypothèse.* But it is nevertheless true to say that, as Hume saw, without a *blik* there can be no explanation; for it is by our *bliks* that we decide what is and what is not an explanation. Suppose we believed that everything that happened, happened by pure chance. This would not of course be an assertion; for it is compatible with anything happening or not happening, and so, incidentally, is its contradictory. But if we had this belief, we should not be able to explain or predict or plan anything. Thus, although we should not be *asserting* anything different from those of a more normal belief, there would be a great difference between us; and this is the sort of difference that there is between those who really believe in God and those who really disbelieve in him.

The word "really" is important, and may excite suspicion. I put it in, because when people have had a good Christian upbringing, as have most of those who now profess not to believe in any sort of religion, it is very hard to discover what they really believe. The reason why they find it so easy to think that they are not religious, is that they have never got into the frame of mind of one who suffers from the doubts to which religion is the answer. Not for them the terrors of the primitive jungle. Having abandoned some of the more picturesque fringes of religion, they think that they have abandoned the whole thing—whereas in fact they still have got, and could not live without, a religion of a comfortably substantial, albeit highly sophisticated, kind, which differs from that of many "religious people" in little more than this, that "religious people" like to sing Psalms about theirs—a very natural and proper thing to do. But nevertheless there may be a big difference lying behind—the difference between two people who, though side by side, are walking in different directions. I do not know in what direction Flew is walking; perhaps he does not know either. But we have had some examples recently of various ways in which one can walk away from Christianity, and there are any number of possibilities. After all, man has not changed biologically since primitive times; it is his religion that has changed, and it can easily change again. And if you do not think that such changes make a difference, get acquainted with some Sikhs and some Mussulmans of the same Punjabi stock; you will find them quite different sorts of people.

There is an important difference between Flew's parable and my own which we have not yet noticed. The explorers do not *mind* about their garden; they discuss it with interest, but not with concern. But my lunatic, poor fellow, minds about dons; and I mind about the steering of my car; it often has people in it that I care for. It is because I mind very much about what goes on in the garden in which I find myself, that I am unable to share the explorers' detachment.

Balliol College
Oxford

C

Basil Mitchell

Flew's article is searching and perceptive, but there is, I think, something odd about his conduct of the theologian's case. The theologian surely would not deny that the fact of pain counts against the assertion that God loves men. This very incompatibility generates the most intractable of theological problems—the problem of evil. So the theologian *does* recognize the fact of pain as counting against Christian doctrine. But it is true that he will not allow it—or anything—to count decisively against it; for he is committed by his faith to trust in God. His attitude is not that of the detached observer, but of the believer.

Perhaps this can be brought out by yet another parable. In time of war in an occupied country, a member of the resistance meets one night a stranger who deeply impresses him. They spend that night together in conversation. The Stranger tells the partisan that he himself is on the side of the resistance—indeed that he is in command of it, and urges the partisan to have faith in him no matter what happens. The partisan is utterly convinced at that meeting of the Stranger's sincerity and constancy and undertakes to trust him.

They never meet in conditions of intimacy again. But sometimes the Stranger is seen helping members of the resistance, and the partisan is grateful and says to his friends, "He is on our side."

Sometimes he is seen in the uniform of the police handing over patriots to the occupying power. On these occasions his friends murmur against him: but the partisan still says, "He is on our side." He still believes that, in spite of appearances, the Stranger did not deceive him. Sometimes he asks the Stranger for help and receives it. He is then thankful. Sometimes he asks and does not receive it. Then he says, "The Stranger knows best." Sometimes his friends, in exasperation, say, "Well, what *would* he have to do for you to admit that you were wrong and that he is not on our side?" But the partisan refuses to answer. He will not consent to put the Stranger to the test. And sometimes his friends complain, "Well, if *that's* what you mean by his being on our side, the sooner he goes over to the other side the better."

The partisan of the parable does not allow anything to count decisively against the proposition "The Stranger is on our side." This is because he has committed himself to trust the Stranger. But he of course recognizes that the Stranger's ambiguous behaviour *does* count against what he believes about him. It is precisely this situation which constitutes the trial of his faith.

When the partisan asks for help and doesn't get it, what can he do? He can (*a*) conclude that the stranger is not on our side or; (*b*) maintain that he is on our side, but that he has reasons for withholding help.

The first he will refuse to do. How long can he uphold the second position without its becoming just silly?

I don't think one can say in advance. It will depend on the nature of the impression created by the Stranger in the first place. It will depend, too, on the manner in which he takes the Stranger's behaviour. If he blandly dismisses it as of no consequence, as having no bearing upon his belief, it will be assumed that he is thoughtless or insane. And it quite obviously won't do for him to say easily, "Oh, when used of the Stranger the phrase "is on our side" *means* ambiguous behaviour of this sort." In that case he would be like the religious man who says blandly of a terrible disaster, "It is God's will." No, he will only be regarded as sane and reasonable in his belief, if he experiences in himself the full force of the conflict.

It is here that my parable differs from Hare's. The partisan admits that many things may and do count against his belief: whereas Hare's lunatic who has a *blik* about dons doesn't admit that anything counts against his *blik*. Nothing *can* count against *bliks*. Also the partisan has a reason for having in the first instance committed himself, viz. the character of the Stranger; whereas the lunatic has no reason for his *blik* about dons—because, of course, you can't have reasons for *bliks*.

This means that I agree with Flew that theological utterances must be assertions. The partisan is making an assertion when he says, "The Stranger is on our side."

Do I want to say that the partisan's belief about the Stranger is, in any sense, an explanation? I think I do. It explains and makes sense of the Stranger's behaviour: it helps to explain also the resistance movement in the context of which he appears. In each case it differs from the interpretation which the others put upon the same facts.

"God loves men" resembles "the Stranger is on our side" (and many other significant statements, e.g. historical ones) in not being conclusively falsifiable. They can both be treated in at least three different ways: (1) As provisional hypotheses to be discarded if experience tells against them; (2) As significant articles of faith; (3) As vacuous formulae (expressing, perhaps, a desire for reassurance) to which experience makes no difference and which make no difference to life.

The Christian, once he has committed himself, is precluded by his faith from taking up the first attitude: "Thou shalt not tempt the Lord thy God." He is in constant danger, as Flew has observed, of slipping into the third. But he need not; and, if he does, it is a failure in faith as well as in logic.

Keble College
Oxford

D

Antony Flew

It has been a good discussion: and I am glad to have helped to provoke it. But now—at least in *University*—it must come to an end: and the Editors of *University* have asked me to make some concluding remarks. Since it is impossible to deal with all the issues raised or to comment separately upon each contribution, I will concentrate on Mitchell and Hare, as representative of two very different kinds of response to the challenge made in "Theology and Falsification."

The challenge, it will be remembered, ran like this. Some theological utterances seem to, and are intended to, provide explanations or express assertions. Now an assertion, to be an assertion at all, must claim that things stand thus and thus; *and not otherwise*. Similarly an explanation, to be an explanation at all, must explain why this particular thing occurs; *and not something else*. Those last clauses are crucial. And yet sophisticated religious people—or so it seemed to me—are apt to overlook this, and tend to refuse to allow, not merely that anything actually does occur, but that anything conceivably could occur, which would count against their theological assertions and explanations. But in so far as they do this their supposed explanations are actually bogus, and their seeming assertions are really vacuous.

Mitchell's response to this challenge is admirably direct, straightforward, and understanding. He agrees "that theological utterances must be assertions." He agrees that if they are to be assertions, there must be something that would count against their truth. He agrees, too, that believers are in constant danger of transforming their would-be assertions into "vacuous formulae." But he takes me to task for an oddity in my "conduct of the theologian's case. The theologian surely would not deny that the fact of pain counts against the assertion that God loves men. This very incompatibility generates the most intractable of theological problems, the problem of evil." I think he is right. I should have made a distinction between two very different ways of dealing with what looks like evidence against the love of God: the way I stressed was the expedient of qualifying the original assertion; the way the theologian usually takes, at first, is to admit that it looks bad but to insist that there is—there must be—some explanation which will show that, in spite of appearances, there really is a God who loves us. His difficulty, it seems to me, is that he has given God attributes which rule out all possible saving explanations. In Mitchell's parable of the Stranger it is easy for the believer to find plausible excuses for ambiguous behavior: for the Stranger is a man. But suppose the Stranger is God. We cannot say that he would like to help but cannot: God is omnipotent. We cannot say that he would help if he only knew: God is omniscient. We cannot say that he is not responsible for the wickedness of others: God creates those others. Indeed an omnipotent, omniscient God must be an accessory before (and during) the fact to every human misdeed; as well as being responsible for every non-moral defect in the universe. So, though I entirely concede that Mitchell was absolutely right to insist against me that the theologian's first move is to look for an *explanation*, I still think that in the end, if relentlessly pursued, he will have to resort to the avoiding action of *qualification*. And there lies the danger of that death by a thousand qualifications, which would, I agree, constitute "a failure in faith as well as in logic."

Hare's approach is fresh and bold. He confesses that "on the ground marked out by Flew, he seems to me to be completely victorious." He therefore introduces the concept of *blik*. But while I think there is room for some such concept in philosophy, and that philosophers should be grateful to Hare for his invention, I nevertheless want to insist that any attempt to analyse Christian religious utterances as expressions or affirmations of a *blik* rather than as (at least would-be) assertions about the cosmos is fundamentally misguided. *First*, because thus interpreted they would be entirely unorthodox. If Hare's religion really is a *blik*, involving no cosmological assertions about the nature and activities of a supposed personal creator, then surely he is not a Christian at all? *Second*, because thus interpreted, they could scarcely do the job they do. If they were not even intended as assertions then many religious activities would become fraudulent, or merely silly. If "You ought *because* it is God's will" asserts no more than "You ought," then the person who prefers the former phraseology is not really giving a reason, but a fraudulent substitute for one, a dialectical dud cheque. If "My soul must be immortal *because* God loves his children, etc." asserts no more than "My soul must be immortal," then the man who reassures himself with theological arguments for immortality is being as silly as the man who tries to clear his overdraft by writing his bank a cheque on the same account. (Of course neither of these utterances would be distinctively Christian: but this discussion never pretended to be so confined.) Religious utterances may indeed express false or even bogus assertions: but I simply do not believe that they are not both intended and interpreted to be or at any rate to presuppose assertions, at least in the context of religious practice; whatever shifts may be demanded, in another context, by the exigencies of theological apologetic.

One final suggestion. The philosophers of religion might well draw upon George Orwell's last appalling nightmare *1984* for the concept of *doublethink.* "*Doublethink* means the power of holding two contradictory beliefs simultaneously, and accepting both of them. The party intellectual knows that he is playing tricks with reality, but by the exercise of *doublethink* he also satisfies himself that reality is not violated" (*1984,* p. 220). Perhaps religious intellectuals too are sometimes driven to doublethink in order to retain their faith in a loving God in the face of the reality of a heartless and indifferent world. But of this more another time, perhaps.

University College of North Staffordshire
England

Bibliography

Aman, Kenneth. "Using Marxism: A Philosophical Critique of Liberation Theology." *International Philosophical Quarterly* 25 (1985): 393–401.
Ayer, A. J. *Language, Truth and Logic.* New York: Dover, 1936.
———, ed. *Logical Positivism.* New York: Free Press, 1959.
Bancroft, Nancy. "Marxism Requires Atheism: Implications for Religious Believers (Christians)." *Journal of Ecumenical Studies* 22 (1985): 567–75.
Banner, Michael C. *The Justification of Science and the Rationality of Religious Belief.* Oxford: Clarendon Press; New York: Oxford University Press, 1990.
Barbour, Ian G. *Science and Religion: New Perspectives on the Dialogue.* New York: Harper and Row, 1968.
Bettelheim, Bruno. *Freud and Man's Soul.* New York: Knopf, 1982.
Blackstone, William T. *The Problem of Religious Language.* Englewood Cliffs, N.J.: Prentice-Hall, 1963.
Bonansea, Bernardino M. *God and Atheism.* Washington, D.C.: Catholic University Press, 1979.
Bridgman, Laird, and John D. Carter. "Christianity and Psychoanalysis: Original Sin—Oedipal or Preoedipal?" *Journal of Psychology and Theology,* 17 (1989): 3–8.
Brummer, Vincent. *Theology and Philosophical Inquiry: An Introduction.* London: Macmillan, 1981.
Cahn, Steven, and David Shatz, eds. *Contemporary Philosophy of Religion.* Oxford: Oxford University Press, 1982.

Carnap, Rudolf. "The Elimination of Metaphysics through Logical Analysis of Language." In *Logical Positivism*, edited by A. J. Ayer, 60–81. New York: Free Press, 1959.

Cohen, L. Jonathan. *The Dialogue of Reason: An Analysis of Analytical Philosophy*. Oxford: Clarendon Press; New York: Oxford University Press, 1986.

Coulson, Charles Alfred. *Science and the Idea of God*. Cambridge: Cambridge University Press, 1958.

Dampier, William Cecil. *A History of Science and Its Relations with Philosophy and Religion*. Cambridge, England: Cambridge University Press, 1948.

Donnelly, John, ed. *Logical Analysis and Contemporary Theism*. New York: Fordham University Press, 1972.

Ferre, Frederick. *Language, Logic and God*. New York: Harper and Row, 1969.

Feuerbach, Ludwig Andreas. *The Essence of Christianity*. New York: Harper, 1957.

———. *Lectures on the Essence of Religion*. New York: Harper and Row, 1967.

Flew, Antony, and Alasdair MacIntyre, eds. *New Essays in Philosophical Theology*. New York: Macmillan, 1964.

Freud, Sigmund. *Moses and Monotheism*. New York: Modern Library, 1938.

———. *Totem and Taboo*. New York: Norton, 1950.

———. *The Future of an Illusion*. New York: Norton, 1975.

Funkenstein, Amos. *Theology and the Scientific Imagination from the Middle Ages to the Seventeenth Century*. Princeton, N.J.: Princeton University Press, 1986.

Gay, Peter. *A Godless Jew: Freud, Atheism, and the Making of Psychoanalysis*. New Haven: Yale University Press; Cincinnati: Hebrew Union College Press, 1987.

Gay, Voleny Patrick. *Reading Freud: Psychology, Neurosis, and Religion*. Chico, Calif.: Scholars Press, 1983.

Guirdham, Arthur. *Christ and Freud: A Study of Religious Experience and Observance*. London: Allen and Unwin, 1959.

Hepburn, Ronald W. *Christianity and Paradox*. London: Watts, 1958.

Hick, John, ed. *The Existence of God*. New York: Macmillan, 1964.

High, D. M. *New Essays on Religious Language*. Oxford: Clarendon Press, 1969.

Hocking, William Ernest. *Science and the Idea of God*. Chapel Hill: University of North Carolina Press, 1944.

Hook, Sidney, ed. "The Meaning and Justification of Religious Symbols." In *Religious Experience and Truth*. New York: New York University Press, 1961.

Huxley, Julian. *What Dare I Think? The Challenge of Modern Science to Human Action and Belief, including the Henry LaBarre Jayne Foundation Lectures (Philadelphia) for 1931*. New York: Harper, 1931.

Jaki, Stanley L. *The Road of Science and the Ways to God*. Chicago: University of Chicago Press, 1978.

Kovel, Joel. "Beyond the Future of an Illusion: Further Reflections on Freud and Religion." *Psychoanalytic Review* 77 (1990): 69–87.

Marshall, Ronald F. "In Between Ayer and Adler: God in Contemporary Philosophy." *Word World* 2 (1982): 69–81.

Marx, Karl. *K. Marx and F. Engels on Religion*. Moscow: Foreign Languages, 1957.

———. *Selected Essays*. Freeport, NY: Books for Libraries Press, 1968.

———. *The Communist Manifesto*. New York: Norton, 1988.

Mascal, E. L. *Existence and Analogy*. New York: Longman, 1949.

———. *Words and Images.* New York: Ronald Press, 1957.

McGovern, Arthur F. "Atheism: Is It Essential to Marxism?" *Journal of Ecumenical Studies* 22 (1985): 487–589.

McKown, Delos B. *The Classical Marxist Critiques of Religion: Marx, Engels, Lenin, Kautsky.* The Hague: Nijhoff, 1975.

Miles, T. R. *Religion and the Scientific Outlook.* London: Allen and Unwin, 1959.

Mitchell, Basil, ed. *Faith and Logic.* London: Allen and Unwin, 1957.

Munz, Peter. *Problems of Religious Knowledge.* London: Student Christian Movement Press, 1959.

Murphy, James M. "Sex and Gender of God, Christ, and Humankind." *Journal of Psychology and Christianity* 7 (1988): 27–37.

Needham, Joseph. *Science, Religion and Reality.* New York: Braziller, 1955.

Nelson, Cary, and Lawrence Grossberg, eds. *Marxism and the Interpretation of Culture.* Urbana: University of Illinois Press, 1988.

Neusner, Ernest S. Frerichs, and Paul Virgil McCracken Flesher. *Religion, Science, and Magic: In Concert and in Conflict.* New York: Oxford University Press, 1989.

Peacocke, A. R. *Creation and the World of Science.* Oxford: Clarendon Press; New York: Oxford University Press, 1979.

———. *The Sciences and Theology in the Twentieth Century.* Notre Dame, Ind.: University of Notre Dame Press, 1981.

Plant, W. Gunther. *Judaism and the Scientific Spirit.* New York: Union of American Hebrew Congregations, 1962.

Preus, James S. *Explaining Religion: Criticism and Theory from Bodin to Freud.* New Haven, Conn.: Yale University Press, 1987.

Raines, John C., and Thomas Dean. *Marxism and Radical Religion, Essays toward a Revolutionary Humanism.* Philadelphia: Temple University Press, 1970.

Ramsey, Ian T. *Religious Language.* London: Student Christian Movement Press, 1957.

———. *Freedom and Immortality.* London: Student Christian Movement Press, 1960.

Rice, Emanuel. *Freud and Moses: The Long Journey Home.* Albany: State University of New York Press, 1990.

Rolston, Holmes. *Science and Religion: A Critical Survey.* Philadelphia: Temple University Press, 1987.

Ross, James F. *Philosophical Theology.* Indianapolis, Ind.: Bobbs-Merrill, 1969.

Russell, Bertrand. *Why I Am Not a Christian, and Other Essays on Religion and Related Subjects.* Edited by Paul Edwards. New York: Simon and Schuster, 1957.

———. *Religion and Science.* London: Oxford University Press, 1961.

———. *A Collection of Critical Essays.* Edited by D. F. Pears. Garden City, N.Y.: Anchor Books, 1972.

Ryle, Gilbert. "The Theory of Meaning." In *Philosophy and Ordinary Language,* edited by Charles E. Caton, 128–53. Urbana: University of Illinois Press, 1963.

Schlick, Moritz. "Meaning and Verification." *Philosophical Review* 45 (1936).

Schmidt, Paul F. *Religious Knowledge.* New York: Free Press of Glencoe, 1961.

Stuermann, Walter Earl. *Logic and Faith, a Study of the Relations between Science and Religion.* Philadelphia: Westminster Press, 1962.

Tillich, Paul. *Dynamics of Faith.* New York: Harper and Row, 1957.

Urmson, J. O. *Philosophical Analysis.* Oxford: Clarendon Press, 1956.

White, Andrew Dickson. *A History of the Warfare of Science with Theology in Christendom.* New York: Braziller, 1955.

Williams, Bernard Arthur Owen, and Alan Montefiore, eds. *British Analytical Philosophy.* New York: Humanities Press, 1971.

Wisdom, J. O. "Metamorphoses of the Verifiability Theory of Meaning." *Mind* 72 (1963): 335–47.

Zillboorg, Gregory. *Psychoanalysis and Religion.* London: Allen and Unwin, 1967.

Zurdeeg, Willem F. "The Future of Philosophy." *Publications in Philosophy.* Stockton, Calif.: College of the Pacific, 1932.

———. *An Analytical Philosophy of Religion.* Nashville, Tenn.: Abingdon Press, 1958.

———. *Science and Creationism: A View from the National Academy of Sciences/Committee on Science and Creationism.* Washington, D.C.: National Academy Press, 1984.

Twentieth-Century Movements

Apart from the criticisms of religion arising from psychology, political theory, science, and linguistic philosophy, various philosophic and theological movements have swept through the twentieth century with profound effects on religion. One such movement, *existentialism*, is identified with French thinkers such as Jean-Paul Sartre and Gabriel Marcel, and German philosophers such as Martin Heidegger and Karl Jaspers. Its origins can be traced to the nineteenth-century thought of Friedrich Nietzsche and Søren Kierkegaard, and it has been expressed in literary form in the works of Albert Camus, Franz Kafka, and Fyodor Dostoyevski. The Spanish writer Miguel de Unamuno can be included as an existentialist, as can the Russian thinker Nicholas Berdyaev, the Jewish theologian Martin Buber, and the Protestant theologian Paul Tillich.

The movement takes as its starting point the actual condition of human beings in the world. That is, existentialists begin at the level of our actual and concrete lives and then ask what it means to be a human being, especially in the present century. Further, they ask what is required to maximize our individual existence when faced with the truth of the human condition. We want to live authentically, not with comforting illusions but in the light of reality, to affirm our existence so that it is as rich and intense as possible. The answer as to how that should be done separates the various existentialists, but the sense that existence is the most important matter for human beings unites them all.

All of the existentialists agree that the human condition is extraordinarily difficult. We are prey to anxiety, dread, forlornness, alienation, anguish, and so forth, all of which we must transcend to lead satisfying lives. Anxiety, for example, is a generalized apprehension about our eventual nonbeing, the realization that we all face extinction or, at best, a radical transformation to another mode of being.

Anxiety is not the same as fear, which has a precise object. We are afraid of such things as heights or of being alone or a person threatening us with a knife.

In the case of anxiety, however, we cannot specify the locus of our uneasiness; in fact, we often say it is nothing. But that in itself is instructive. We are anxious, not about something but about nothing, about emptiness, the void, annihilation. We live in perpetual dread of the cessation of our lives. It is this reality, largely denied but lying within our understanding, that must be accepted into our conscious thoughts. Once faced, it can be overcome and can actually serve as a catalyst to a fuller existence in the time remaining to us.

All of the existentialists also agree that we are capable of overcoming such obstacles, whether of a debilitating psychological kind or of a physical kind, for as human beings, we are free in our choices and actions. In fact, reflection on our condition enables us to choose the sort of life we want to have. Animals or objects are not aware of their situation and actually have a fixed nature already when they come into existence, but we human beings are conscious of living our lives and can freely decide what we want to become.

For this reason the existentialists say that, in the case of human beings, *existence precedes essence,* whereas for animals or objects it is just the reverse. In other words, as human beings, we are first thrown into existence and then develop our essences or essential selves through the decisions that we make. We choose ourselves through our actions, which then define the kind of person we are to be; and we are always free to do otherwise, to become a different sort of person by making other choices in our lives. But having made our choices, we then must stand behind them, accepting responsibility for the individual that we are.

Religion is a significant factor in human existence, and our decision regarding it can either heighten or lessen the authenticity of our existence. To some existentialists, religion detracts from life because it is regarded as superstition; to accept the myth of God is an act of "bad faith," mental suicide. To others, it constitutes the only way of ridding ourselves of enervating anxiety, dread, forlornness, and so forth; it produces joy in life and a truly genuine existence.

The most famous passage in existential literature that deals with the response to religion comes from Friedrich Nietzsche, who wrote:

> *The Madman*   Have you not heard of that madman who lit a lantern in the bright morning hours, ran to the market place, and cried incessantly, "I seek God! I seek God!" As many of those who do not believe in God were standing around just then, he provoked much laughter. Why, did he get lost? said one. Did he lose his way like a child? said another. Or is he hiding? Is he afraid of us? Has he gone on a voyage? or emigrated? Thus they yelled and laughed. The madman jumped into their midst and pierced them with his glances.
>
> "Whither is God" he cried. "I shall tell you. *We have killed him*—you and I. All of us are his murderers. But how have we done this? How were we able to drink up the sea? Who gave us the sponge to wipe away the entire horizon? What did we do when we unchained this earth from its sun? Whither is it moving now? Whither are we moving now? Away from all suns? Are we not plunging continually? Backward, sideward, forward, in all directions? Is there any up or down left? Are we not straying as through an infinite nothing? Do we not feel the breath of empty space? Has it not become colder? Is not night and more night coming on all the while? Must not lanterns be lit in the morning? Do we not hear anything

yet of the noise of the grave-diggers who are burying God? Do we not smell anything yet of God's decomposition? Gods too decompose. God is dead. God remains dead. And we have killed him. How shall we, the murderers of all murderers, comfort ourselves? What was holiest and most powerful of all that the world has yet owned has bled to death under our knives. Who will wipe this blood off us? What water is there for us to clean ourselves? What festivals of atonement, what sacred games shall we have to invent? Is not the greatness of this deed too great for us? Must not we ourselves become gods simply to seem worthy of it? There has never been a greater deed; and whoever will be born after us—for the sake of this deed he will be part of a higher history than all history hitherto." (*The Gay Science*)

Notice that, although the Madman declares that "God is dead," he is not joyful at being liberated from an oppressive being. Rather, his words reflect desperation at the loss of moorings and purpose, and he realizes that human beings are alone, abandoned because of their own disbelief.

Nevertheless, despite our forlornness we must now become gods ourselves. We already possess the godlike ability to decide freely on the nature of our existence, both as individuals and as a race, and we are wholly accountable for the future we create. As Jean-Paul Sartre says, we are "condemned to be free," and so long as we are human beings there is no way of escaping the responsibility for choice. Once God is dead, "man is the future of man"; we must decide our own destiny and do so in the void.

The theistic response is quite different, of course. To an existentialist like Kierkegaard, God is very much alive, but the problem is in knowing the divine will with respect to human beings. Since God can do what is irrational and even immoral by our standards, we never know whether we really understand God's wishes. We could be acting as a saint or suffering the delusions of the insane.

However, we must make a commitment even in the absence of knowledge—and one that may defy logic or morality. That commitment, in the face of absurdity, could be our test of faith. We will never know with any degree of assurance, but we must listen to the voice of God as we hear it. We must do whatever God commands, exactly as Abraham did in being willing to sacrifice his son Isaac when he believed that God asked it of him.

In both theistic and atheistic existentialism, then, the responsibility for choice rests with us as individuals, and we have to decide on what would be the most meaningful existence for ourselves.

Another twentieth-century movement is that of *God-is-dead theology*, sometimes called radical theology. This rather shocking phrase comes from Nietzsche, but it does not signify an unabashed atheism. The meaning of "the death of God" among theologians such as Gilbert Vahanian, William Hamilton, Mark Van Buren, T. J. J. Altizer, and Joseph Fletcher has a religious sense and is rather complex in intension and connotation. The "slogan" can have a variety of closely connected meanings beside the atheistic one that the natural order is everything.

It might mean, for example, that there is a permanent death of the concept of God, that the traditional idea is now meaningless because the modern world finds it archaic and simplistic. If we are to reestablish contact with the living God, we cannot use the language of dead beliefs. On this reading, it is the concept of God that requires a radical redefinition to connect with the intellectual sophistication of our age.

Another meaning of the phrase is that all corrupted senses of God are now dead, including perhaps the God presented in the Bible. Here the emphasis is on destroying the false idols that have been erected in God's place, that is, eliminating all counterfeit notions of God. Along with this there is usually some opposition to the way God is portrayed in the language of worship. Praying to heathen images with supplication, dependency, and self-loathing must be eliminated because such practices are inconsistent with human dignity.

Dietrich Bonhoeffer (as well as the theologians Harvey Cox and John Robinson) uses the phrase "God is dead" to mean that people can be genuinely human only if God forsakes us and edges himself out of the world. We cannot appeal for outside help and remain self-respecting human beings. If human beings are to live, then God must die.

Still another interpretation is that Christianity has died in our culture. It has not been repudiated or disproven but has simply been abandoned and has perished of neglect. According to this view, Christianity no longer occupies a central place in our everyday affairs or informs any aspect of our society, whether in matters of art, literature, business, politics, or anything else. People no longer feel the force of God in their daily lives or appeal for divine help even in personal crises. Instead, experts now give us counseling to cope with our problems. What was at the heart of life in the Middle Ages is no longer meaningful in our time.

Perhaps the major meaning of the death of God, however, is that people today experience the absence, not the presence, of God. This is somewhat akin to the "dark night of the soul" of Christianity where believers felt that God had withdrawn from them, but it also carries a sense that the divine is absent from our consciousness. God hovers at the edge of reality—neither imminent nor transcendent, no longer a spirit resident within us or a distant father. The sense of awe, majesty, solemnity, and mystery that was a part of human life has been replaced by rationality, pleasure, and self-reliance. Our mood no longer tolerates spiritual emotions and supernatural beings.

Joseph Fletcher, for instance, says that once there existed a God to whom praise and adoration were appropriate, but that time is past. William Hamilton believes that faith in the human community is all that is left, and Mark Van Buren declares that we can only have faith in "this-worldly" procedures. T. J. J. Altizer feels that the sacred is absent today but that if we press unbelief far enough, it could possibly return.

They all treat God as a shadow rather than a substantial being, outmoded and absent from our emotional lives. Some even ask whether one can "make it as a Christian without God" and treat life as having a consecration of its own. But they all agree that God is dead in that, as the divine Father, he is not felt the way he had been before.

Humanism, a third twentieth-century movement, can be defined as the philosophy that human beings have developed to their present state through natural processes, not through divine will, and that the well-being of all human beings here on earth should be our principal concern.

To the humanist, human beings are biochemical organisms that have evolved from protoplasmic jelly to highly complex, thinking creatures. This development has occurred not through a cosmic plan but through chance variation among species and through natural selection—in short, by evolution. We are entirely a part of nature and can be explained not by theology but by the categories of science. There is no purpose behind our being, although, having developed consciousness, we can now set purposes of our own. Matter gave rise to mind, and this mind enables us to direct our energies toward the satisfaction of our individual and collective needs.

At this point in our history, we have not only physical needs but desires that are social, psychological, economic, political, and aesthetic in nature. We should use our rational intelligence and the methods of science to fulfill those desires. We have to create a social order that will foster the full development of the individual, a political structure that will allow maximum human freedom, and an economic system that will provide a comfortable standard of living for all. Instead of being distracted by an imaginary life to come, we must devote ourselves to the improvement of human life on earth.

We will, of course, never achieve all of our ideals, and the perfectibility of the human species is an impossibility, but we can reach some goals for our own and succeeding generations. Using reason and science, we have the means for achieving a degree of social harmony, creativity and productivity, moral purpose, growth, and fulfillment. We can make human life meaningful and satisfying even though no ultimate satisfactions exist and no cosmic meaning ennobles human life.

As for the values that should motivate us, here the humanists reject any final or transcendental source of ethics. They also see no grounding in nature, which is an impersonal and neutral force. The only sanction for values lies in human welfare. Whatever is conducive to the betterment of the human species is praiseworthy; whatever is harmful should be shunned. Human interests alone are important and should be addressed.

Generally, the humanists favor democracy as the best governmental form for promoting human welfare. With its emphasis on freedom and civil liberties, the dignity of the individual, equality and justice, scientific inquiry, and so forth, democracy seems more likely than fascism or communism to bring happiness to human society. Above all, the humanists affirm the dignity and worth of human life and our ability to achieve happiness and self-realization through reason and science.

One version of humanism does not, however, reject the supernatural in focusing on the welfare of humankind. Rather, it supports a human-centered religion in which God is thought to want perfect happiness to exist on earth. We therefore do the work of God by pursuing an ideal existence for human beings in this life.

In the following selections Friedrich Nietzsche presents his critique of Christianity as antithetical to full existence, while Søren Kierkegaard explains his existential view of faith and commitment through the biblical story of Abraham. To complete the section, Martin Buber describes the centrality of the I–Thou relation.

William Hamilton then explains the death-of-God idea, and Joseph Fletcher applies the concept to conduct, arguing that situation ethics is the only viable morality, with love as a sufficient foundation.

Finally, Corliss Lamont defines humanism in ten points, and Erich Fromm describes humanistic religion. This is not religious humanism but a related approach "centered around man and his strengths."

56. The Antichrist

FRIEDRICH NIETZSCHE

1

What is good? Everything that heightens the feeling of power in man, the will to power, power itself.

What is bad? Everything that is born of weakness.

What is happiness? The feeling that power is *growing*, that resistance is overcome.

Not contentedness but more power; not peace but war; not virtue but fitness (Renaissance virtue, *virtù*, virtue that is moraline-free).

The weak and the failures shall perish: first principle of *our* love of man. And they shall even be given every possible assistance.

What is more harmful than any vice? Active pity for all the failures and all the weak: Christianity.

2

The problem I thus pose is not what shall succeed mankind in the sequence of living beings (man is an *end*), but what type of man shall be *bred*, shall be *willed*, for being higher in value, worthier of life, more certain of a future.

Even in the past this higher type has appeared often—but as a fortunate accident, as an exception, never as something *willed*. In fact, this has been the type most dreaded—almost *the* dreadful—and from dread the opposite type was willed, bred, and *attained:* the domestic animal, the herd animal, the sick human animal—the Christian.

3

Mankind does *not* represent a development toward something better or stronger or higher in the sense accepted today. "Progress" is merely a modern idea, that is, a false idea. The European of today is vastly inferior in value to the European of the

Renaissance: further development is altogether *not* according to any necessity in the direction of elevation, enhancement, or strength.

In another sense, success in individual cases is constantly encountered in the most widely different places and cultures: here we really do find a *higher type*, which is, in relation to mankind as a whole, a kind of overman. Such fortunate accidents of great success have always been possible and *will* perhaps always be possible. And even whole families, tribes, or peoples may occasionally represent such a *bull's-eye*.

4

Christianity should not be beautified and embellished: it has waged deadly war against this higher type of man; it has placed all the basic instincts of this type under the ban; and out of these instincts it has distilled evil and the Evil One: the strong man as the typically reprehensible man, the "reprobate." Christianity has sided with all that is weak and base, with all failures; it has made an ideal of whatever *contradicts* the instinct of the strong life to preserve itself; it has corrupted the reason even of those strongest in spirit by teaching men to consider the supreme values of the spirit as something sinful, as something that leads into error—as temptations. The most pitiful example: the corruption of Pascal, who believed in the corruption of his reason through original sin when it had in fact been corrupted only by his Christianity.

5

It is a painful, horrible spectacle that has dawned on me: I have drawn back the curtain from the *corruption* of man. In my mouth, this word is at least free from one suspicion: that it might involve a moral accusation of man. It is meant—let me emphasize this once more—*moraline-free*. So much so that I experience this corruption most strongly precisely where men have so far aspired most deliberately to "virtue" and "godliness." I understand corruption, as you will guess, in the sense of decadence: it is my contention that all the values in which mankind now sums up its supreme desiderata are *decadence-values*.

I call an animal, a species, or an individual corrupt when it loses its instincts, when it chooses, when it prefers, what is disadvantageous for it. A history of "lofty sentiments," of the "ideals of mankind"—and it is possible that I shall have to write it—would almost explain too *why* man is so corrupt. Life itself is to my mind the instinct for growth, for durability, for an accumulation of forces, for *power*: where the will to power is lacking there is decline. It is my contention that all the supreme values of mankind *lack* this will—that the values which are symptomatic of decline, *nihilistic* values, are lording it under the holiest names.

6

Christianity is called the religion of *pity*. Pity stands opposed to the tonic emotions which heighten our vitality: it has a depressing effect. We are deprived of strength when we feel pity. That loss of strength which suffering as such inflicts on life is still further increased and multiplied by pity. Pity makes suffering contagious. Under certain circumstances, it may engender a total loss of life and vitality out of all proportion to the magnitude of the cause (as in the case of the death of the Nazarene). That is the first consideration, but there is a more important one.

Suppose we measure pity by the value of the reactions it usually produces; then its perilous nature appears in an even brighter light. Quite in general, pity crosses the law of development, which is the law of *selection*. It preserves what is ripe for destruction; it defends those who have been disinherited and condemned by life; and by the abundance of the failures of all kinds which it keeps alive, it gives life itself a gloomy and questionable aspect.

Some have dared to call pity a virtue (in every *noble* ethic it is considered a weakness); and as if this were not enough, it has been made *the* virtue, the basis and source of all virtues. To be sure—and one should always keep this in mind— this was done by a philosophy that was nihilistic and had inscribed the *negation of life* upon its shield. Schopenhauer was consistent enough: pity negates life and renders it *more deserving of negation*.

Pity is the *practice* of nihilism. To repeat: this depressive and contagious instinct crosses those instincts which aim at the preservation of life and at the enhancement of its value. It multiplies misery and conserves all that is miserable, and is thus a prime instrument of the advancement of decadence: pity persuades men to *nothingness!* Of course, one does not say "nothingness" but "beyond" or "God," or "*true* life," or Nirvana, salvation, blessedness.

This innocent rhetoric from the realm of the religious-moral idiosyncrasy appears much less innocent as soon as we realize which tendency it is that here shrouds itself in sublime words: *hostility against life*. Schopenhauer was hostile to life; therefore pity became a virtue for him.

Aristotle, as is well known, considered pity a pathological and dangerous condition, which one would be well advised to attack now and then with a purge: he understood tragedy as a purge. From the standpoint of the instinct of life, a remedy certainly seems necessary for such a pathological and dangerous accumulation of pity as is represented by the case of Schopenhauer (and unfortunately by our entire literary and artistic decadence from St. Petersburg to Paris, from Tolstoi to Wagner)—to puncture it and make it *burst*.

In our whole unhealthy modernity there is nothing more unhealthy than Christian pity. To be physicians *here*, to be inexorable *here*, to wield the scalpel *here*—that is *our* part, that is *our* love of man, that is how *we* are philosophers, we *Hyperboreans*.

7

It is necessary to say whom we consider our antithesis: it is the theologians and whatever has theologians' blood in its veins—and that includes our whole philosophy.

Whoever has seen this catastrophe at close range or, better yet, been subjected to it and almost perished of it, will no longer consider it a joking matter (the free-thinking of our honorable natural scientists and physiologists is, to my mind, a joke: they lack passion in these matters, they do not suffer them as their passion and martyrdom). This poisoning is much more extensive than is generally supposed: I have found the theologians' instinctive arrogance wherever anyone today considers himself an "idealist"—wherever a right is assumed, on the basis of some higher origin, to look at reality from a superior and foreign vantage point.

The idealist, exactly like the priest, holds all the great concepts in his hand (and not only in his hand!); he plays them out with a benevolent contempt for the "understanding," the "senses," "honors," "good living," and "science"; he considers all that *beneath* him, as so many harmful and seductive forces over which "the spirit" hovers in a state of pure for-itselfness—as if humility, chastity, poverty, or, in one word, *holiness*, had not harmed life immeasurably more than any horrors or vices. The pure spirit is the pure lie.

As long as the priest is considered a *higher* type of man—this *professional* negator, slanderer, and poisoner of life—there is no answer to the question: what *is* truth? For truth has been stood on its head when the conscious advocate of nothingness and negation is accepted as the representative of "truth." . . .

8

In Christianity neither morality nor religion has even a single point of contact with reality. Nothing but imaginary *causes* ("God," "soul," "ego," "spirit," "free will"—for that matter, "unfree will"), nothing but imaginary *effects* ("sin," "redemption," "grace," "punishment," "forgiveness of sins"). Intercourse between imaginary *beings* ("God," "spirits," "souls"); an imaginary *natural* science (anthropocentric; no trace of any concept of natural causes); an imaginary *psychology* (nothing but self-misunderstandings, interpretations of agreeable or disagreeable general feelings—for example, of the states of the *nervus sympathicus*—with the aid of the sign language of the religio-moral idiosyncrasy: "repentance," "pangs of conscience," "temptation by the devil," "the presence of God"); an imaginary *teleology* ("the kingdom of God," "the Last Judgment," "eternal life").

This *world of pure fiction* is vastly inferior to the world of dreams insofar as the latter *mirrors* reality, whereas the former falsifies, devalues, and negates reality. Once the concept of "nature" had been invented as the opposite of "God," "natural" had to become a synonym of "reprehensible": this whole world of fiction is rooted in *hatred* of the natural (of reality!); it is the expression of a profound vexation at the sight of reality.

But this explains everything. Who alone has good reason to lie his way out of reality? He who suffers from it. But to suffer from reality is to be a piece of reality that has come to grief. The preponderance of feelings of displeasure over feelings of pleasure is the cause of this fictitious morality and religion; but such a preponderance provides the very formula for decadence.

9

A critique of the *Christian conception of God* forces us to the same conclusion. A people that still believes in itself retains its own god. In him it reveres the conditions which let it prevail, its virtues: it projects its pleasure in itself, its feeling of power, into a being to whom one may offer thanks. Whoever is rich wants to give of his riches; a proud people needs a god: it wants to *sacrifice*. Under such conditions, religion is a form of thankfulness. Being thankful for himself, man needs a god. Such a god must be able to help and to harm, to be friend and enemy—he is admired whether good or destructive. The *anti-natural* castration of a god, to make him a god of the good alone, would here be contrary to everything desirable. The evil god is needed no less than the good god: after all, we do not owe our own existence to tolerance and humanitarianism.

What would be the point of a god who knew nothing of wrath, revenge, envy, scorn, cunning, and violence? who had perhaps never experienced the delightful *ardeurs* of victory and annihilation? No one would understand such a god: why have him then?

To be sure, when a people is perishing, when it feels how its faith in the future and its hope of freedom are waning irrevocably, when submission begins to appear to it as the prime necessity and it becomes aware of the virtues of the subjugated as the conditions of self-preservation, then its god *has* to change too. Now he becomes a sneak, timid and modest; he counsels "peace of soul," hate-no-more, forbearance, even "love" of friend and enemy. He moralizes constantly, he crawls into the cave of every private virtue, he becomes god for everyman, he becomes a private person, a cosmopolitan.

Formerly, he represented a people, the strength of a people, everything aggressive and power-thirsty in the soul of a people; now he is merely the good god.

Indeed, there is no other alternative for gods: *either* they are the will to power, and they remain a people's gods, *or* the incapacity for power, and then they necessarily become *good*. . . .

10

The Christian conception of God—God as god of the sick, God as a spider, God as spirit—is one of the most corrupt conceptions of the divine ever attained on earth. It may even represent the low-water mark in the descending development of divine types. God degenerated into the *contradiction* of life, instead of being its transfiguration and eternal Yes! God as the declaration of war against life, against nature, against the will to live! God—the formula for every slander against "this world," for every lie about the "beyond"! God—the deification of nothingness, the will to nothingness pronounced holy!

11

That the strong races of northern Europe did not reject the Christian God certainly does no credit to their religious genius—not to speak of their taste. There is no excuse whatever for their failure to dispose of such a sickly and senile product of decadence. But a curse lies upon them for this failure: they have absorbed sickness, old age, and contradiction into all their instincts—and since then they have not *created* another god. Almost two thousand years—and not a single new god! But still, as if his existence were justified, as if he represented the ultimate and the maximum of the god-creating power, of the *creator spiritus* in man, this pitiful god of Christian monotono-theism! This hybrid product of decay, this mixture of zero, concept, and contradiction, in which all the instincts of decadence, all cowardices and wearinesses of the soul, find their sanction!

57. Fear and Trembling

SØREN KIERKEGAARD

Faith is precisely this paradox, that the individual as the particular is higher than the universal, is justified over against it, is not subordinate but superior—yet in such a way, be it observed, that it is the particular individual who, after he has been subordinated as the particular to the universal, now through the universal becomes the individual who as the particular is superior to the universal, *inasmuch as the individual as the particular stands in an absolute relation to the absolute*. This position cannot be mediated, for all mediation comes about precisely by virtue of the universal; it is and remains to all eternity a paradox, inaccessible to thought. And yet faith is this paradox. . . .

That for the particular individual this paradox may easily be mistaken for a temptation (*Anfechtung*) is indeed true, but one ought not for this reason to conceal it. That the whole constitution of many persons may be such that this paradox repels them is indeed true, but one ought not for this reason to make faith something different in order to be able to possess it, but ought rather to admit that one does not possess it, whereas those who possess faith should take care to set up certain criteria so that one might distinguish the paradox from a temptation (*Anfechtung*).

Now the story of Abraham contains such a teleological suspension of the ethical. . . . Abraham's relation to Isaac, ethically speaking, is quite simply expressed by saying that a father shall love his son more dearly than himself. Yet within its own compass the ethical has various gradations. Let us see whether in this story there is to be found any higher expression for the ethical such as would ethically explain his conduct, ethically justify him in suspending the ethical obligation toward his son, without in this search going beyond the teleology of the ethical.

When an undertaking in which a whole nation is concerned is hindered, when such an enterprise is brought to a standstill by the disfavor of heaven, when the angry deity sends a calm which mocks all efforts, when the seer performs his heavy task and proclaims that the deity demands a young maiden as a sacrifice— then will the father heroically make the sacrifice. He will magnanimously conceal his pain, even though he might wish that he were "the lowly man who dares to weep," not the king who must act royally. And though solitary pain forces its way into his breast and he has only three confidants among the people, yet soon the whole nation will be cognizant of his pain, but also cognizant of his exploit, that for the welfare of the whole he was willing to sacrifice her, his daughter, the lovely young maiden. "O charming bosom! O beautiful cheeks! O bright golden hair!" (v. 687). And the daughter will affect him by her tears, and the father will turn his face away, but the hero will raise the knife.—When the report of this reaches the ancestral home, then will the beautiful maidens of Greece blush with enthusiasm, and if the daughter was betrothed, her true love will not be angry but be proud of sharing in the father's deed, because the maiden belonged to him more feelingly than to her father.

When the intrepid judge, who saved Israel in the hour of need, in one breath binds himself and God by the same vow, then heroically the young maiden's jubilation, the beloved daughter's joy, he will turn to sorrow, and with her all Israel will lament her maiden youth; but every free-born man will understand, and every stout-hearted woman will admire Jephtha, and every maiden in Israel will wish to act as did his daughter. For what good would it do if Jephtha were victorious by reason of his vow, if he did not keep it? Would not the victory again be taken from the nation?

When a son is forgetful of his duty, when the state entrusts the father with the sword of justice, when the laws require punishment at the hand of the father, then will the father heroically forget that the guilty one is his son, he will magnanimously conceal his pain, but there will not be a single one among the people, not even the son, who will not admire the father, and whenever the law of Rome is interpreted, it will be remembered that many interpreted it more learnedly, but none so gloriously as Brutus.

If, on the other hand, while a favorable wind bore the fleet on with swelling sails to its goal, Agamemnon had sent that messenger who fetched Iphigenia in order to be sacrificed; if Jephtha, without being bound by any vow which decided the fate of the nation, had said to his daughter, "Bewail now thy virginity for the space of two months, for I will sacrifice thee"; if Brutus had had a righteous son and yet would have ordered the lictors to execute him—who would have understood them? If these three men had replied to the query why they did it by saying, "It is a trial in which we are tested," would people have understood them better? . . .

The difference between the tragic hero and Abraham is clearly evident. The tragic hero still remains within the ethical. He lets one expression of the ethical find its *telos* in a higher expression of the ethical; the ethical relation between father and son, or daughter and father, he reduces to a sentiment which has its dialectic in the idea of morality. Here there can be no question of a teleological suspension of the ethical.

With Abraham the situation was different. By his act he overstepped the ethical entirely and possessed a higher *telos* outside of it, in relation to which he suspended the former. For I should very much like to know how one would bring Abraham's act into relation with the universal, and whether it is possible to discover any connection whatever between what Abraham did and the universal—except the fact that he transgressed it. It was not for the sake of saving a people, not to maintain the idea of the state, that Abraham did this, and not in order to reconcile angry deities. If there could be a question of the deity being angry, he was angry only with Abraham, and Abraham's whole action stands in no relation to the universal; it is a purely personal undertaking. Therefore, whereas the tragic hero is great by reason of his moral virtue, Abraham is great by reason of a personal virtue. In Abraham's life there is no higher expression for the ethical than this, that the father shall love his son. Of the ethical in the sense of morality there can be no question in this instance. Insofar as the universal was present, it was indeed cryptically present in Isaac, hidden as it were in Isaac's loins, and must therefore cry out with Isaac's mouth, "Do it not! Thou art bringing everything to naught."

Why then did Abraham do it? For God's sake, and (in complete identity with this) for his own sake. He did it for God's sake because God required this proof of his faith; for his own sake he did it in order that he might furnish the proof. The unity of these two points of view is perfectly expressed by the word which has always been used to characterize this situation: it is a trial, a temptation (*Fristelse*). A temptation—but what does that mean? What ordinarily tempts a man is that which would keep him from doing his duty, but in this case the temptation is itself the ethical—which would keep him from doing God's will.

Here is evident the necessity of a new category if one would understand Abraham. Such a relationship to the deity paganism did not know. The tragic hero does not enter into any private relationship with the deity, but for him the ethical is the divine, hence the paradox implied in his situation can be mediated in the universal.

Abraham cannot be mediated, and the same thing can be expressed also by saying that he cannot talk. As soon as I talk I express the universal, and if I do not do so, no one can understand me. Therefore if Abraham would express himself in terms of the universal, he must say that his situation is a temptation (*Anfechtung*), for he has no higher expression for that universal which stands above the universal which he transgresses.

Therefore, though Abraham arouses my admiration, he at the same time appalls me. He who denies himself and sacrifices himself for duty gives up the finite in order to grasp the infinite, and that man is secure enough. The tragic hero gives up the certain for the still more certain, and the eye of the beholder rests upon him confidently. But he who gives up the universal in order to grasp something still higher which is not the universal—what is he doing? Is it possible that this can be anything else but a temptation (*Anfechtung*)? And if it be possible, but the individual was mistaken—what can save him? He suffers all the pain of the tragic hero, he brings to naught his joy in the world, he renounces everything—and perhaps at the same instant debars himself from the sublime joy which to him was so precious that he would purchase it at any price. Him the beholder cannot understand nor let his eye rest confidently upon him. . . .

The story of Abraham contains therefore a teleological suspension of the ethical. As the individual he became higher than the universal: this is the paradox which does not permit of mediation. It is just as inexplicable how he got into it as it is inexplicable how he remained in it. If such is not the position of Abraham, then he is not even a tragic hero but a murderer. To want to continue to call him the father of faith, to talk of this to people who do not concern themselves with anything but words, is thoughtless. A man can become a tragic hero by his own powers—but not a knight of faith. When a man enters upon the way, in a certain sense the hard way of the tragic hero, many will be able to give him counsel; to him who follows the narrow way of faith no one can give counsel, him no one can understand. Faith is a miracle, and yet no man is excluded from it; for that in which all human life is unified is passion, and faith is a passion.

58. I and Thou

MARTIN BUBER

The life of human beings is not passed in the sphere of transitive verbs alone. It does not exist in virtue of activities alone which have some *thing* for their object.

I perceive something. I am sensible of something. I imagine something. I will something. I feel something. I think something. The life of human beings does not consist of all this and the like alone.

This and the like together establish the realm of *It*.

But the realm of *Thou* has a different basis.

When *Thou* is spoken, the speaker has no thing for his object. For where there is a thing there is another thing. Every *It* is bounded by others; *It* exists only through being bounded by others. But when *Thou* is spoken, there is no thing. *Thou* has no bounds.

When *Thou* is spoken, the speaker has no *thing*; he has indeed nothing. But he takes his stand in relation.

It is said that man experiences his world. What does that mean?

Man travels over the surface of things and experiences them. He extracts knowledge about their constitution from them: he wins an experience from them. He experiences what belongs to the things.

But the world is not presented to man by experiences alone. These present him only with a world composed of *It* and *He* and *She* and *It* again.

I experience something.—If we add "inner" to "outer" experiences, nothing in the situation is changed. We are merely following the uneternal division that springs from the lust of the human race to whittle away the secret of death. Inner things or outer things, what are they but things and things!

I experience something.—If we add "secret" to "open" experiences, nothing in the situation is changed. How self-confident is that wisdom which perceives a closed compartment in things, reserved for the initiate and manipulated only with the key. O secrecy without a secret! O accumulation of information! It, always It!

The man who experiences has not part in the world. For it is "in him" and not between him and the world that the experience arises.

The world has no part in the experience. It permits itself to be experienced, but has no concern in the matter. For it does nothing to the experience, and the experience does nothing to it.

As experience, the world belongs to the primary word *I–It*.

The primary word *I–Thou* establishes the world of relation.

The spheres in which the world of relation arises are three.

First, our life with nature. There the relation sways in gloom, beneath the level of speech. Creatures live and move over against us, but cannot come to us, and when we address them as *Thou*, our words cling to the threshold of speech.

Second, our life with men. There the relation is open and in the form of speech. We can give and accept the *Thou*.

Third, our life with spiritual beings. There the relation is clouded, yet it discloses itself; it does not use speech, yet begets it. We perceive no *Thou*, but nonetheless we feel we are addressed and we answer—forming, thinking, acting. We speak the primary word with our being, though we cannot utter *Thou* with our lips.

But with what right do we draw what lies outside speech into relation with the world of the primary word?

In every sphere in its own way, through each process of becoming that is present to us we look out toward the fringe of the eternal *Thou*; in each we are aware of a breath from the eternal *Thou*; in each *Thou* we address the eternal *Thou*.

I consider a tree.

I can look on it as a picture: stiff column in a shock of light, or splash of green shot with the delicate blue and silver of the background.

I can perceive it as movement: flowing veins on clinging, pressing pith, suck of the roots, breathing of the leaves, ceaseless commerce with earth and air—and the obscure growth itself.

I can classify it in a species and study it as a type in its structure and mode of life.

I can subdue its actual presence and form so sternly that I recognise it only as an expression of law—of the laws in accordance with which a constant opposition of forces is continually adjusted, or of those in accordance with which the component substances mingle and separate.

I can dissipate it and perpetuate it in number, in pure numerical relation.

In all this the tree remains my object, occupies space and time, and has its nature and constitution.

It can, however, also come about, if I have both will and grace, that in considering the tree I become bound up in relation to it. The tree is now no longer *It*. I have been seized by the power of exclusiveness.

To effect this it is not necessary for me to give up any of the ways in which I consider the tree. There is nothing from which I would have to turn my eyes away in order to see, and no knowledge that I would have to forget. Rather is everything, picture and movement, species and type, law and number, indivisibly united in this event.

Everything belonging to the tree is in this: its form and structure, its colours and chemical composition, its intercourse with the elements and with the stars, are all present in a single whole.

The tree is no impression, no play of my imagination, no value depending on my mood; but it is bodied over against me and has to do with me, as I with it— only in a different way.

Let no attempt be made to sap the strength from the meaning of the relation: relation is mutual.

The tree will have a consciousness, then, similar to our own? Of that I have no experience. But do you wish, through seeming to succeed in it with yourself, once again to disintegrate that which cannot be disintegrated? I encounter no soul or dryad of the tree, but the tree itself.

If I face a human being as my *Thou*, and say the primary word *I–Thou* to him, he is not a thing among things, and does not consist of things.

Thus human being is not *He* or *She*, bounded from every other *He* and *She*, a specific point in space and time within the net of the world; nor is he a nature able to be experienced and described, a loose bundle of named qualities. But with no neighbour, and whole in himself, he is *Thou* and fills the heavens. This does not mean that nothing exists except himself. But all else lives in *his* light.

Just as the melody is not made up of notes nor the verse of words nor the statue of lines, but they must be tugged and dragged till their unity has been scattered into these many pieces, so with the man to whom I say *Thou*. I can take out from him the colour of his hair, or of his speech, or of his goodness. I must continually do this. But each time I do it he ceases to be *Thou*.

And just as prayer is not in time but time in prayer, sacrifice not in space but space in sacrifice, and to reverse the relation is to abolish the reality, so with the man to whom I say *Thou*. I do not meet with him at some time and place or other. I can set him in a particular time and place; I must continually do it; but I set only a *He* or a *She*, that is an *It*, no longer my *Thou*.

So long as the heaven of *Thou* is spread out over me the winds of causality cower at my heels, and the whirlpool of fate stays its course.

I do not experience the man to whom I say *Thou*. But I take my stand in relation to him, in the sanctity of the primary word. Only when I step out of it do I experience him once more. In the act of experience *Thou* is far away.

Even if the man to whom I say *Thou* is not aware of it in the midst of his experience, yet relation may exist. For *Thou* is more than *It* realises. No deception penetrates here; here is the cradle of the Real Life.

This is the eternal source of art: a man is faced by a form which desires to be made through him into a work. This form is no offspring of his soul, but is an appearance which steps up to it and demands of it the effective power. The man is concerned with an act of his being. If he carries it through, if he speaks the primary word out of his being to the form which appears, then the effective power streams out, and the work arises.

The act includes a sacrifice and a risk. This is the sacrifice: the endless possibility that is offered up on the altar of the form. For everything which just this moment in play ran through the perspective must be obliterated; nothing of that may penetrate the work. The exclusiveness of what is facing it demands that it be so. This is the risk: the primary word can only be spoken with the whole being. He who gives himself to it may withhold nothing of himself. The work does not suffer me, as do the tree and the man, to turn aside and relax in the world of *It*; but it commands. If I do not serve it aright it is broken, or it breaks me.

I can neither experience nor describe the form which meets me, but only body it forth. And yet I behold it, splendid in the radiance of what confronts me, clearer than all the clearness of the world which is experienced. I do not behold it as a thing among the "inner" things nor as an image of my "fancy," but as that which exists in the present. If test is made of its objectivity the form is certainly not "there." Yet what is actually so much present as it is? And the relation in which I stand to it is real, for it affects me, as I affect it.

To produce is to draw forth, to invent is to find, to shape is to discover. In bodying forth I disclose. I lead the form across—into the world of *It*. The work produced is a thing among things, able to be experienced and described as a sum of qualities. But from time to time it can face the receptive beholder in its whole embodied form.

—What, then, do we experience of *Thou?*
　　　—Just nothing. For we do not experience it.
　　　—What, then, do we know of *Thou?*
　　　—Just everything. For we know nothing isolated about it any more.

The *Thou* meets me through grace—it is not found by seeking. But my speaking of the primary word to it is an act of my being, is indeed *the* act of my being.

The *Thou* meets me. But I step into direct relation with it. Hence the relation means being chosen and choosing, suffering and action in one; just as any action of the whole being, which means the suspension of all partial actions and consequently of all sensations of actions grounded only in their particular limitation, is bound to resemble suffering.

The primary word *I–Thou* can be spoken only with the whole being. Concentration and fusion into the whole being can never take place through my agency, nor can it ever take place without me. I become through my relation to the *Thou*; as I become *I*, I say *Thou*.

All real living is meeting. . . .

Every real relation with a being or life in the world is exclusive. Its *Thou* is freed, steps forth, is single, and confronts you. It fills the heavens. This does not mean that nothing else exists; but all else lives in *its* light. As long as the presence of the relation continues, this its cosmic range is inviolable. But as soon as a *Thou* becomes *It*, the cosmic range of the relation appears as an offence to the world, its exclusiveness as an exclusion of the universe.

In the relation with God unconditional exclusiveness and unconditional inclusiveness are one. He who enters on the absolute relation is concerned with nothing isolated any more, neither things nor beings, neither earth nor heaven; but everything is gathered up in the relation. For to step into pure relation is not to disregard everything but to see everything in the *Thou*, not to renounce the world but to establish it on its true basis. To look away from the world, or to stare at it, does not help a man to reach God; but he who sees the world in Him stands in His presence. "Here world, there God" is the language of *It*; "God in the world" is another language of *It*; but to eliminate or leave behind nothing at all, to include the whole world in the *Thou*, to give the world its due and its truth, to include nothing beside God but everything in him—this is full and complete relation.

Men do not find God if they stay in the world. They do not find Him if they leave the world. He who goes out with his whole being to meet his *Thou* and carries to it all being that is in the world, finds Him who cannot be sought.

Of course God is the "wholly Other"; but He is also the wholly Same, the wholly Present. Of course He is the *Mysterium Tremendum* that appears and over-throws; but He is also the mystery of the self-evident, nearer to me than my *I*.

If you explore the life of things and of conditioned being you come to the unfathomable, if you deny the life of things and of conditioned being you stand before nothingness, if you hallow this life you meet the living God.

"God-Is-Dead" Theology

59. The New Essence of Christianity

WILLIAM HAMILTON

BELIEF IN A TIME OF THE DEATH OF GOD

We cannot objectify God, but we must speak about him. So we get into trouble, our words become distorted, and we raise questions about his location and behavior that we cannot answer. If we objectify him, we make him part of the world, but a part we cannot see. We make him part of the causal sequences of the world, and try to fit him into the order and disorder that we see. But then we find that we must say that he made the world or that he caused the evil and suffering of the world, or we refuse to say this. And so we have on our hands either a capricious tyrant causing evil as well as good, or an ineffectual thing, impotent before evil and causing only the good. We seek for words that express God as something other than personal, and we fall into the danger of making him less than personal. The God seen as a person, making the world, manipulating some people towards good, condemning other people to damnation—the objectified God, in other words—this is the God many have declared to be dead today. This is the God who must disappear, so that we may remake our thinking and our speaking about him. "The courage to be," Dr. [Paul] Tillich writes in one of his most elusive and profound statements, "is rooted in the God who appears when God has disappeared in the anxiety of doubt."[1]

These two affirmations suggest the contours of the rediscovered Augustinian-Reformed portrait of God in our time. They point to what might be called a recovery of God's divinity, his holiness, his separateness from men. Each of the two basic statements we used to describe this portrait carried a positive and a negative component. The first declared that we cannot know God, but that he has made himself known to us. The second stated that God cannot be properly spoken of or treated as an object, but that we can still praise, adore, speak to him. Put technically, the generally received portrait of God today supports the Reformed insistence that the finite cannot contain the infinite (*finitum non capax infiniti*) and rejects the

---

[1] *The Courage to Be* (New Haven: Yale University Press, 1952), p. 190.

Lutheran tradition which declares that in the humanity of Jesus the finite has received, and thus can contain, the infinite (*finitum capax infiniti*).[2]

There is a great deal to be said for this rediscovery of the divinity of God, but it may be that we are beginning to pay too dear a price for it. Are we not, perhaps, beginning to lose the delicate balance between negation and affirmation that this position requires? We have come to find it far easier to say "we cannot know" than to say "he can make himself known." His holiness and separateness are beginning to look like an indifference. Now it comes as no great surprise to remind ourselves that the most scrupulously correct theological statements have their own built-in difficulties. One of the reasons why theological moods change is that men come to a time when they want to live with new kinds of difficulties. Theology is always like having six storm windows to cover eight windows. One is quite free to choose which six windows to keep the cold air from entering, and you can live pretty well for a while in the protected rooms. But the uncovered windows will let the cold air in sooner or later, and the whole house will feel it. This contemporary portrait of God is serving well at many points, but some leakage is beginning to be felt.

THE PROBLEM OF SUFFERING

I am convinced that the most serious leakage caused by this traditional and correct portrait of God today is at the point of the problem of suffering. There is something in this correct doctrine of God that keeps it from dealing responsibly with the problem, and therefore, because of this silence and carelessness, one can claim today that the problem of suffering has become a major barrier to faith for many sensitive unbelievers.[3]

It is not that the theology dominated by this doctrine of God does not mention the problem. It does, but when it does it is just not good enough. It may, for example, make much of the mystery of iniquity and ask us to shy away from questions about suffering on the grounds that we have no right to put impious questions to the holy God. It may speak of the ontological impossibility of evil; it may say that we are not asked to understand, but only to fight evil; it may say that God is the source of all, good and evil alike, and this is what it means to affirm the divinity of God, and if we don't like it we don't need to affirm him.

---

[2] Eberhard Bethge has recently noted that the Lutheran *finitum capax infiniti* was very close to the center of Bonhoeffer's thought:

> "While other dialectical theologians thought of the sovereignty of revelation as gloriously manifest in its freedom and its intangibility, Bonhoeffer, quite after Lutheran fashion, thought of it as apparent in its self-disclosure. Bonhoeffer differed from the other dialectical theologians of those years in his emphasis on the *finitum capax infiniti*." "The Editing and Publishing of the Bonhoeffer Papers," *The Andover Newton Bulletin*, LII, No. 2 (December, 1959), p. 20. See also Bonhoeffer, *Gesammelte Schriften*, II (Munich: Kaiser Verlag, 1959), p. 278.

[3] "The insurmountable barrier to Christianity does seem to me to be the problem of evil. But it is also a real obstacle for traditional humanism. There is the death of children, which means a divine reign of terror, but there is also the killing of children, which is an expression of a human reign of terror. We are wedged between two kinds of arbitrary law." Albert Camus, quoted by John Cruickshank, *Albert Camus and the Literature of Revolt* (New York: Galaxy Books, Oxford University Press, 1960), pp. xii–xiii.

Now this kind of evasion may be correct, may even be true, and is certainly very safe. But we miss something: we miss the curious fact that participation in the reality of suffering sometimes destroys the very possibility of faith. The special power of the problem of suffering is that it can really dry up in a man any capacity or wish to call out for the presence of God. If theology cannot reshape its statements about God to face this fact, many men will continue to prefer some sort of humanism without answers to a correct doctrine of God without answers. . . .

THE DEATH OF GOD

I am not here referring to a belief in the nonexistence of God.[4] I am talking about a growing sense, in both non-Christians and Christians, that God has withdrawn, that he is absent, even that he is somehow dead. Elijah taunted the false prophets and suggested that their god may have gone on a journey, since he could not be made to respond to their prayers.[5] Now, many seem to be standing with the false prophets, wondering if the true God has not withdrawn himself from his people. This feeling ranges from a sturdy unbelieving confidence in God's demise to the troubled believer's cry that he is no longer in a place where we can call upon him. Arthur Koestler represents the confident mood:

> God is dethroned; and although the incognisant masses are tardy in realising the event, they feel the icy draught caused by that vacancy. Man enters upon a spiritual ice age; the established churches can no longer provide more than Eskimo huts where their shivering flock huddles together.[6]

The patronizing and confident tone of this announcement reminds us of both Feuerbach and Nietzsche. In the famous passage in "The Gay Science" where the idea of the death of God is put forward by Nietzsche, a madman is portrayed as searching for God, calling out for him, and finally concluding that he and all men have killed him. The man's hearers do not understand his words, and he concludes that he has come with his message too early. He goes on to wander about the city's churches, calling out, "What are these churches now if they are not the tombs and sepulchers of God?" Koestler's igloos and Nietzsche's tombs are spiritually, if not architecturally, related. But in spite of Nietzsche's statement that the madman had come too soon, his declaration of God's death was heard and believed. And in the

---

[4] "The world has become an entity rounded off in itself, which is neither actually open at certain points where it merges into God, nor undergoes at certain observable points the causal impact of God . . . but it points to God as its presupposition only as a whole, and even so not very obviously. . . . We are experiencing today that we can make no image of God that is not carved from the wood of this world. The educated man of our time has the duty, painful though fruitful, to accept this experience. He is not to suppress it by a facile, anthropomorphic 'belief in God,' but interpret it correctly, realizing that, in fact, it has nothing in common with atheism." Karl Rahner, "Wissenschaft als Confession?" *Wort und Wahrheit*, November, 1954, pp. 812–13. Quoted by Hans Urs von Balthasar, *Science, Religion and Christianity* (London: Burns & Oates, 1958), p. 95. Published in America by the Newman Press, Westminster, Md.
[5] I Kings 18:27.
[6] "The Trail of the Dinosaur," *Encounter* (London), May, 1955. One should add that Koestler never seems to stand still, and that at the close of his recent book *The Lotus and the Robot* (London: Hutchinson & Co., Ltd., 1960), he has a very modest word of praise for Christianity, and, if not for dogma, at least for "the tenets of Judeo-Christian ethics."

nineteenth century, as De Lubac writes, "man is getting rid of God in order to regain possession of the human greatness which, it seems to him, is being unwarrantably withheld by another. In God he is overthrowing an obstacle in order to gain his freedom."[7] Freud shared something of this Nietzschean conviction that God must be dethroned and killed to make way for the proper evaluation and freedom of man. And of course, as against many forms of religion, even this strident cry bears some truth.

But Koestler's confident assurance of God's dethronement and death is not the only way modern man describes his sense of God's absence or disappearance. When Dr. Tillich refers to the death of God he usually means the abolition of the idea of God as one piece of being alongside others, of God as a big person. Death of God for him is thus the death of the idols, or the false gods. The novels of Albert Camus, on the other hand, portray not only a world from which the false gods, and the holy God of the theological revival, have departed, but a world from which any and all gods have silently withdrawn. The world of these novels is a world in which the word God simply refuses to have any meaning. This is not treated as a good thing or a terrible thing; it is just a fact that is ruefully assumed. It is the God described by the best and most sophisticated theologians of our time, who seems to many today to have withdrawn from his world. When we feel this, we do not feel free or strong, but weak, unprotected, and frightened.[8]

We seem to be those who are trying to believe in a time of the death of God. Just what do we mean when we say this? We mean that the Augustinian-Reformed portrait of God itself is a picture of a God we find more and more elusive, less and less for us or with us. And so we wonder if God himself is not absent. When we speak of the death of God, we speak not only of the death of the idols or the falsely objectivized Being in the sky; we speak, as well, of the death in us for any power to affirm any of the traditional images of God. We mean that the world is not God and that it does not point to God.[9] Since the supports men have always depended on to help them affirm God seem to be gone, little wonder that many take the next step and wonder whether God himself has gone. Little wonder that Lent is the only season when we are at home, and that that cry of dereliction from the cross is sometimes the only biblical word that can speak to us. If Jesus can wonder about being forsaken by God, are we to be blamed if we wonder?

---

[7] Henri de Lubac, *The Drama of Atheist Humanism* (New York: Sheed & Ward, 1949), p. 6.

[8] "Men are frightened at the absence of God from the world, they feel that they can no longer realize the Divine, they are terrified at God's silence, at his withdrawal into his own inaccessibility. . . . This experience which men think they must interpret theoretically as atheism, is yet a genuine experience of the most profound existence . . . with which popular Christian thought and speech will not have finished for a long time." Rahner, *op. cit.*, p. 812, quoted by Von Balthasar, *op. cit.*, p. 96.

[9] The classical Reformation conception of Providence depended for its formulation on the presence of a whole series of orders that were self-evident to sixteenth-century man: the order of the celestial bodies, the order of the political realm, the order and predictability of the natural world, the order and inner coherence of the self. Men as diverse as Calvin and Shakespeare drew on this experience of order in their own work. In the *Institutes*, I. 5., Calvin used this external orderliness as a means of illuminating the sovereign care of God over the world. Tragedy, for Shakespeare, was the unusual and odd breakdown of the natural order of human life. Hamlet's perception that "the time is out of joint" is a perception of a disorder that is the basis of Shakespeare's sense of tragedy. See also Ulysses' speech on order in *Troilus and Cressida*, Act I, Scene 3.

BEYOND THE DEATH OF GOD

Now, a believing Christian can face without distress any announcement about the disappearance of the idols from the religious world of man, but he cannot live as a Christian for long with the suspicion that God himself has withdrawn. How is it possible to turn this difficult corner, and to move from an acknowledgment of God's disappearance to a sense of some kind of reappearance and presence? This sense of the separation of God from the world, Ronald Gregor Smith writes,

> does not lead to mere or sheer undialectical atheism. Any assertion of the absence of God and even further of his nonexistence among the phenomena of the world is dialectically confronted by the equal assertion of his presence. I am sorry if this sounds like a mere verbal trick, but it cannot be helped.[10]

There is something disarming about Gregor Smith's unwillingness to look carefully at the connections between the sense of disappearance of God and the problem of his reappearance. But his way of putting it does indeed sound like a verbal trick, and we must try to discover if there are not ways of moving from the one state to the other.

One of the favorite contemporary attempts to do this might be called the Augustinian doubt maneuver. Augustine noted that he overcame his temptation toward skepticism by observing that even skepticism implied some affirmation of truth, the truth at least of the skeptical position.

> Everyone who knows that he is in doubt about something knows a truth, and in regard to this that he knows he is certain. Therefore he is certain about a truth. Consequently everyone who doubts if there be a truth has in himself a true thing on which he does not doubt.[11]

This may or may not be a convincing way to overcome radical skepticism. But it certainly cannot be used to mean that we can, by a kind of interior maneuver, affirm that we know the very thing we doubt. Augustine did not use it thus; we may doubt one truth, but that implies, he tells us, that we know another thing in our act of doubt, namely, that we are doubters. But some Christians have tried to claim that somehow doubt implies faith. God's existence, we are often told, is most profoundly proven in the very experience of doubting or denying him. Of course, passionate doubt has a resemblance to passionate faith. Both have a deep concern for the problem of truth; both real doubt and real faith deeply care. But it is not good enough to suggest that "There is no God" or "I cannot know that there is a God" really bears the same meaning as "Thou art my God." Let us continue to say that doubt is a necessary way for many of us to faith; that faith never overcomes doubt finally and completely; that lively faith can bear a good deal of doubt around the edges. But the depth of doubt is not the depth of faith; these are two places, not one, and a choice must finally be made between them. We cannot evade such a problem by a trick of redefinition.

This confusion of doubt and faith obscures the problem of moving from an

---

[10] "A Theological Perspective of the Secular," *The Christian Scholar,* XLIII, No. 1 (March, 1960), p. 22.
[11] *On True Religion,* XXIX. 73.

affirmation about the disappearance of God to an affirmation of his presence. I wonder if the following, and quite beautiful, passage from Dr. Tillich, is not also obscure in its apparent identification of having with not-having.

> To the man who longs for God and cannot find Him; to the man who wants to be acknowledged by God and cannot even believe that He is; to the man who is striving for a new and imperishable meaning of his life and cannot discover it—to this man Paul speaks. We are each such a man. Just in this situation, where the Spirit is far from our consciousness, where we are unable to pray or to experience any meaning in life, the Spirit is working quietly in the depth of our souls. In the moment when we feel separated from God, meaningless in our lives, and con-demned to despair, we are not left alone. The Spirit, sighing and longing in us and with us, represents us. It manifests what we really are. In feeling this against feeling, in believing this against belief, in knowing this against knowledge, we like Paul, possess all.[12]

Now this is less specious than the doubt-equals-faith position. And it points to a profound truth. Faith is never the claim to own or possess. God comes to us finally when we confess that we have nothing in our hands to bring. Our not-knowing alone leads to knowing; our not-having is the only way to possession. All this is true, and very close to the Protestant conviction that God's access is to sinners and not to saints. But it will not do. Such a word as Dr. Tillich's can do much. It can persuade the man who struggles for God that there is a sense in which he has been found. It can portray the Christian tradition attractively as one which knows, welcomes, and lives with the experience of struggle and not-knowing. But it will not serve to transform an experience of not-having into an experience of having. For all of our verbalizing, these remain two different experiences, and we are not finally helped by those who do not face openly the distinctions.

The curious thing about this matter of God's disappearance is that even in those moments when we are most keenly aware of God's absence we still, some-how, find it possible to pray for his return. Perhaps we ought to conclude that the special Christian burden of our time is the situation of being without God. There is, for some reason, no possession of God for us, but only a hope, only a waiting.[13] This is perhaps part of the truth: to be a Christian today is to stand, somehow, as a man without God but with hope. We know too little to know him now; we only know enough to be able to say that he will come, in his own time, to the broken and contrite heart, if we continue to offer that to him. Faith is, for many of us, we

---

[12] *The Shaking of the Foundations* (New York: Scribner's, 1958), p. 139.

[13] Perhaps one of the reasons why Samuel Beckett's *Waiting for Godot* has fascinated us is that Beckett has portrayed so many of the ambiguities in our feeling about God today. Godot, for whom Vladimir and Estragon wait, seems to stand for the traditional God for whom all of us think we are waiting. This Godot has a white beard (p. 59), he punishes those who reject him (p. 60), he saves (pp. 48, 61), he is the one to whom Vladimir and Estragon offer a "kind of prayer," a "vague supplication" (p. 13). In Godot there is a combination of absence and harshness. He is always postponing his visit; yet he is said to beat the young boy's brother (p. 34). Vladimir asks the boy, Godot's messenger, "What does he do, Mr. Godot?" And the boy replies, "He does nothing, Sir" (p. 59). At the close of the play, when Godot still has not arrived, Estragon asks if they should not drop Godot altogether. To this Vladimir replies, "He'd punish us" (p. 60). Finally, is the Christian critic being over-eager when he notes that the waiting takes place by a tree—the only part of the landscape that has not died (pp. 60–61)? (The page references are to the Grove Press edition, New York, 1954.)

might say, purely eschatological. It is a kind of trust that one day he will no longer be absent from us. Faith is a cry to the absent God; faith is hope.

An identification of faith with hope is possible, but a little more can be said. The absent one has a kind of presence; the one for whom the Christian man waits still makes an impact on us. W. H. Auden has described this presence very accurately.

> *In our anguish we struggle*
> *To elude Him, to lie to Him, yet His love observes*
> *His appalling promise; His predilection*
> *As we wander and weep is with us to the end.*
> *Minding our meanings, our least matter dear to Him. . . .*
> *It is where we are wounded that is when He speaks*
> *Our creaturely cry, concluding His children*
> *In their mad unbelief to have mercy on them all*
> *As they wait unawares for His world to come.* [14]

In this there is waiting, but also something else. God is also the one whom we struggle to elude; as Augustine says, "Thou never departest from us, and yet only with difficulty do we return to thee."[15] He speaks to us at the point where we are wounded. And even though our wound is our separation from him, the separation is not absolute. The reflections of Psalm 139 and Genesis 32:24–25 in this fragment from Auden remind us of part of our situation.

Thus, neither "death of God," "absence of God," nor "disappearance of God" is wholly adequate to describe the full meaning of our religious situation. Our experience of God is deeply dissatisfying to us, even when we are believers. In one sense God seems to have withdrawn from the world and its sufferings, and this leads us to accuse him of either irrelevance or cruelty. But in another sense, he is experienced as a pressure and a wounding from which we would love to be free. For many of us who call ourselves Christians, therefore, believing in the time of the "death of God" means that he is there when we do not want him, in ways we do not want him, and he is not there when we do want him.

The rediscovery of the divinity of God which we described at the start of this chapter seems defective on two counts. It gives us a portrait of God that does not seem able to receive honestly the threat posed by the problem of suffering, and it does not accurately enough describe the curious mixture of the disappearance and presence of God that is felt by many today. I am not sure just what ought to be our proper response to this curious mixture. There seems to be some ground for terror here, so that we can partly agree with Ingmar Bergmann when he said recently that "if God is not there, life is an outrageous terror." Yet in another sense we face the special texture of our unsatisfactory religious situation with calmness. Most of us are learning to accept these things: the disappearance of God from the world, the coming of age of the world, as it has been called, the disappearance of religion as a lively factor in modern life, the fact that there are men who can live

---

[14] From *The Age of Anxiety*, by W. H. Auden. Copyright 1946, 1947 by W. H. Auden. Reprinted by permission of Random House, Inc. Also with the permission of Faber and Faber, Ltd., publishers.

[15] *Confessions*, VIII. 8.

both without God and without despair. We are coming to accept these calmly as events not without their advantages. Perhaps our calmness will disappear when we face the possibility that God will even more decisively withdraw—that he will withdraw from our selves as he has already withdrawn from the world, that not only has the world become sheer world but that self will become sheer self. For if there are men today who can do without God, it still seems to be true that we cannot do so. We are afraid of ourselves without him, even though what we know of him may be only a pressure and a wounding. . . .

60. Situation Ethics

JOSEPH FLETCHER

LOVE ALONE IS ALWAYS GOOD

The First Proposition: "Only one 'thing' is intrinsically good; namely, love: nothing else at all."

The rock-bottom issue in all ethics is "value." Where is it, what is its locus? Is the worthiness or worthness of a thing inherent *in* it? Or is it contingent, *relative* to other things than itself? Is the good or evil of a thing, and the right or wrong of an action, intrinsic or extrinsic?

Nominal Good

The medieval realist-nominalist debate, in part carried on around this basic question of ethical understanding, is by no means merely archaic or an outworn argument. Everything hangs on it. . . . For an intelligent adult grasp of the problems of ethics it is *this* question which has to be settled first. It is a most pervasive issue in Christian ethics even if it lurks mostly beneath the surface, unrecognized by the simpleminded. Ockham and Scotus in the Middle Ages, and Descartes in modern times, postulated the view that any "good" is nominal, i.e., it is what it is only because God regards it as good. This was opposed to the "realist" view that God wills a thing because it *is* good. God finds "valuable" whatever suits his (love's) needs and purposes. Situation ethics, at the level of human value judgments, is likewise nominalistic. (A non-Christian version may be seen in Charles Stevenson's *Ethics and Language*.[1])

The whole mind-set of the modern man, *our* mind-set, is on the nominalists' side. No better example can be found than Brunner's flat assertion that there are no intrinsic values and that value exists only "in reference to persons."[2] Martin Buber is equally plain about it; he says that "value is always value for a

---

[1] *Yale University Press*, 1944, esp. ch. viii.
[2] *The Divine Imperative*, pp. 194–195.

person rather than something with an absolute, independent existence."[3] Another kind of personalist, a very metaphysical one, Edgar Brightman, argued that "in personality is the only true intrinsic value we know or could conceive; all values are but forms of personal experience."[4] There *are* no "values" at all; there are only things (material and nonmaterial) which *happen* to be valued by persons. This is the personalist view.

[William] Temple's way of putting it was that value, like revelation, "depends for its actuality upon the appreciating mind."[5] In another place he concludes: "Value, as it appears to me, consists in an interaction of mind and environment, but always of such a kind that the mind is finding in the environment the objective occasion for its own satisfaction."[6] In his attempt to define the good Christologically, Dietrich Bonhoeffer came close to seeing the "property versus predicate" issue, but he fell short, he missed it.[7] On this score, as on so many others, we see how he had to leave his ethic "half-baked" because of his early death and the privation of his heroic last years.

Hence it follows that in Christian situation ethics nothing is worth anything in and of itself. It gains or acquires its value only because it happens to help persons (thus being good) or hurt persons (thus being bad). The person who is "finding" the value may be either divine (God willing the good) or human (a man valuing something). Persons—God, self, neighbor—are both the subjects and objects of value; *they* determine it to be value, and they determine it to be value for some person's sake. It is a value because somebody decided it was worth something. Oscar Wilde was clever but not deep when he said, "A cynic is a man who knows the price of everything, and the value of nothing." There is no other way to set value but by price, even though *money* is not always the truest measure. Good and evil are extrinsic to the thing or the action. It all depends on the situation. What is right in one case, e.g., lending cash to a father who needs it for his hungry family, may be wrong in another case, e.g., lending cash to a father with hungry children when he is known to be a compulsive gambler or alcoholic.

Speaking more timidly than a situationist would, but solidly on the point, Temple says: "It is doubtful if any act is right 'in itself.' Every act is a link in a chain of causes and effects. It cannot be said that it is wrong to take away a man's possessions against his will, for that would condemn all taxation—or the removal of a revolver from a homicidal maniac; neither of these is stealing—which is always wrong; though high authority has held that a starving man may steal a loaf rather than die of hunger, because life is of more value than property and should be chosen first for preservation if both cannot be preserved together. The rightness of an act, then, nearly always and perhaps always, depends on the way in which the act is related to circumstances; this is what is meant by calling it relatively right;

---

[3] See Maurice B. Friedman, *Martin Buber: The Life of Dialogue* (The Chicago University Press, 1955), p. 20.
[4] *Nature and Values* (Henry Holt & Company, Inc., 1945), p. 62.
[5] *Nature, Man and God*, p. 211.
[6] *Christianity in Thought and Action* (The Macmillan Company, 1936), p. 26.
[7] *Ethics*, pp. 55–62.

but this does not in the least imply that it is only doubtfully right. It may be, in those circumstances, certainly and absolutely right."[8]

Love Is a Predicate

Apart from the helping or hurting of people, ethical judgments or evaluations are meaningless. Having as its supreme norm the neighbor love commanded of Christians, Christian situation ethics asserts firmly and definitely: *Value, worth, ethical quality, goodness or badness, right or wrong—these things are only predicates, they are not properties.* They are not "given" or objectively "real" or self-existent.[9] There is only one thing that is always good and right, intrinsically good regardless of the context, and that one thing is love. Yet we should not, perhaps, call love a "thing." Neutral as it is as a word, it may tend in the reader's mind to reify love, to suggest that it is a tangible, objective existent. (The New Testament sometimes speaks of love as if it were a property, sometimes as a predicate. Paul and the Gospel writers were entirely innocent of the problem we are discussing. It never occurred to them.)

But love is not a substantive—nothing of the kind. It is a principle, a "formal" principle, expressing what type of real actions Christians are to call good. (Exactly the same is true of justice.) It is the *only* principle that always obliges us in conscience. Unlike all other principles you might mention, love alone when well served is always good and right in every situation. Love is the only universal. But love is not something we *have* or *are*, it is something we *do*. Our task is to act so that more good (i.e., loving-kindness) will occur than any possible alternatives; we are to be "optimific," to seek an optimum of loving-kindness. It is an attitude, a disposition, a leaning, a preference, a purpose.

When we say that love is always good, what we mean is that whatever is loving in any *particular* situation is good! Love is a way of relating to persons, and of using things. As H. R. Niebuhr once said, "God nowhere commands love for its own sake."[10] It is for the sake of people and it is not a good-in-itself. Neither, of course, is it merely one "virtue" among others, as some pious moral manuals and Sunday school tracts make it out to be. It is not a virtue at all; it is the one and only *regulative principle* of Christian ethics.

Reinhold Niebuhr, who is closer to situationism than to any other ethical method, nevertheless held a sort of supernaturalistic notion of love as some "thing" or power that men lack except in a finite and insufficient measure. He saw love as an "absolute" property or capacity or state, rather than a predicate, a way of characterizing what we *do* when we actually *act* in a concrete situation. He spoke of love as something we *have* in one measure or another.

Therefore he could hold that Jesus' cross typified a "perfect love" which was unique, utter sacrificial unselfishness, beyond men except as approximated in

---

[8] *Religious Experience* (London: James Clarke & Company, Ltd., 1958), pp. 173–174.
[9] A philosophical defense of the predicative concept is in Stephen Toulmin, *An Examination of the Place of Reason in Ethics* (Cambridge: Cambridge University Press, 1950). He successfully attacks the "nonnatural" property thesis of G. E. Moore.
[10] *Christ and Culture* (Harper & Brothers, 1951), p. 15.

relative justice.[11] On the contrary, if love is to be understood situationally, as a predicate rather than a property, what we must understand is that Jesus' going to the cross was *his* role and vocation in *his* situation with *his* obligation as the Son of God. We cannot therefore speak with Niebuhr of the "impossibility" of love, even though we join him in speaking of its *relativity.* Love does not say to us, "*Be* like me." It says, "*Do* what you can where you are."

Karl Barth puts himself in an untenable corner with the intrinsic fallacy. On the subject of abortion he first says that an unformed, unborn embryo is a child and that to stop it is murder. Then he declares, uncomfortably, that although abortion is "absolutely" wrong, it can sometimes be excused and forgiven. Therefore he is in the intrinsic camp but merciful about it. Finally he blurts out: "Let us be quite frank and say that there are situations in which the killing of germinating life does not constitute murder *but is in fact commanded*" (italics added).[12] This puts Barth in the anomalous position of saying that to obey God's command (to act lovingly) is to do something absolutely wrong. Clearly this is theological-ethical nonsense. (It undermines his treatment of euthanasia, sterilization, and other questions for the same reason.)

Barth might have trusted Luther more. Said Luther: "Therefore, when the law impels one against love, it ceases and should *no longer be a law*; but where no obstacle is in the way, the keeping of the law is a proof of love, which lies hidden in the heart. Therefore you have need of the law, that love may be manifested; but if it cannot be kept without injury to the neighbor, God wants us to suspend and ignore the law."[13]

Only in the divine being, only in God, is love substantive. With men it is a formal principle, a predicate. Only with God is it a property. This is because God *is* love. Men, who are finite, only *do* love. That is, they try in obedience to obey love's command to be like God, to imitate him. The *imitatio Dei, imitatio Christi,* is to love the neighbor. Says Augustine, in order to know whether a man is a *good* man "one does not ask what he believes or what he hopes, but what he loves."[14] Love may only be "predicated" of human actions and relationships according to how they take shape in the situation. Men may be lovable and loving, but only God *is* love. And in the Bible the image of God, man's model, is not reason but love. "God is not reason but love, and he employs reason as the instrument of his love."[15] In the strict sense of the word, this is the theology of situation ethics.

The other side of the proposition that only love is intrinsically good is, of course, that only malice is intrinsically evil. If goodwill is the only thing we are always obliged to do, then ill will is the only thing we are always forbidden to do.

---

[11] *An Interpretation of Christian Ethics* (Harper & Brothers, 1935), passim. In 1956 he said, "I am not . . . able to defend, or interested in defending, any position I took [in that book]" (*Reinhold Niebuhr,* ed. by C. W. Kegley and R. W. Bretall [The Macmillan Company, 1956], p. 435).

[12] *Church Dogmatics,* Vol. III, Bk. 4, pp. 416–421.

[13] Sermon, Eighteenth Sunday After Trinity, in "The Church Postil," *Works,* ed. by J. N. Linker (Luther House, 1905), Vol. V, p. 175.

[14] "Enchiridion," Ch. 117, in *Works,* ed. by M. Dods (Edinburgh: T. & T. Clark, 1873), Vol. IX, p. 256.

[15] Martin Heinecken, *God in the Space Age* (Holt, Rinehart & Winston, Inc., 1959), p. 168.

A literal synonym for goodwill is "benevolence," but by usage the word now smacks of something far less intense and committed than the *agapē* of the New Testament! Even "goodwill" has acquired a connotation of *respectability*, as when it is paid for as an asset in the sale of a business.

The opposite of benevolence is "malevolence," but here again the word's use has given it a more direct and deliberate meaning than Christian situation ethics cares to adopt. Indeed, in any careful analysis it must be made quite clear that actually the true opposite of love is not hate but indifference. Hate, bad as it is, at least treats the neighbor as a *thou*, whereas indifference turns the neighbor into an *it*, a thing. This is why we may say that there is actually one thing worse than evil itself, and that is indifference to evil. In human relations the nadir of morality, the lowest point, as far as Christian ethics is concerned, is manifest in the phrase, "I couldn't care less." This is why we must not forget that the New Testament calls upon us to love people, not principles.

Kant's second maxim, to treat people as ends and never as means, is strictly parallel to the New Testament's "law of love." (The term actually never occurs, *ho nomos teis agapeis*, but it is substantially there in such passages as Rom. 13:10 and Gal. 5:14.) And Kant's contention that the only really good thing is a good will, which is what the New Testament means by *agapē* or "love," goes necessarily and logically with his second maxim. Whatever is benevolent is right; whatever is malevolent or indifferent is wrong. This is the radical simplicity of the Gospel's ethic, even though it can lead situationally to the most complicated, headaching, heartbreaking calculations and gray rather than black or white decisions.

Only Extrinsic

This posture or perspective sets us over against all "intrinsicalist" ethics, against all "given" or "natural" or "objectively valid" laws and maxims, whether of the natural law or the Scriptural law varieties. It means, too, that there are no universals of any kind. Only love is objectively valid, only love is universal. Therefore when John Bennett pleads, in the spirit of Luther's *pecca fortiter*, that "there are situations in which the best we can do is evil," we have to oppose what he says—much as we admire its spirit.[16] On Bennett's basis, if a small neighborhood merchant tells a lie to divert some "protection" racketeers from their victims, no matter how compassionately the lie is told, he has chosen to do *evil*. It is, of course, excused or forgiven or pardoned as a so-called "lesser evil." This has always been possible in the merciful casuistry of the ethical realists or intrinsicalists. But no matter how lovingly such "bad things" may be done they are still evil, still wrong, they still require repentance and forgiveness!

This confused assertion that the shopkeeper's lie is both loving and wrong is an obvious contradiction. It is due to the intrinsic doctrine of value. Because its starting point is an ontological rather than existential conception of right and wrong, it is compelled in this barbarous way to divorce what is right from what is

[16] *Christianity and the Contemporary Scene*, ed. by R. C. Miller and H. M. Shires (Morehouse-Gorman Company, Inc., 1942), p. 119.

good. It even opposes them to each other! . . . It causes, and always has caused, Christian ethicists to claim that what love requires is often not the "right" thing but nevertheless excusable because of conditions. But for the situationist what makes the lie right is its loving purpose; he is not hypnotized by some abstract law, "Thou shalt not lie." He refuses to evaluate "white lies" told out of pity and espionage in wartime as *ipso jure* wrong.

If a lie is told unlovingly it is wrong, evil; if it is told in love it is good, right. Kant's legalism produced a "universal"—that a lie is always wrong. But what if you have to tell a lie to keep a promised secret? Maybe you lie, and if so, good for you if you follow love's lead. Paul's "speaking the truth in love" (Eph. 4:15) illuminates the point: we are to tell the truth for love's sake, not for its own sake. If love vetoes the truth, so be it. Right and wrong, good and bad, are things that *happen* to what we say and do, whether they are "veracious" or not, depending upon how much love is served in the situation. The merchant chose to do a good thing, not an excusably bad thing. Love *made* it good. *The situationist holds that whatever is the most loving thing in the situation is the right and good thing.* It is not excusably evil, it is positively good. This is the fundamental point of the extrinsic position.

The intrinsicalists, i.e., the legalists, have always dominated Christian ethics. "It is," says Brunner, "the curse of 'Christian morality' that it always regards the most legalistic view as the 'most serious.' "[17] It is obvious to some of us at least that the positive, extrinsic view has never really even been glimpsed by them. They have therefore had, under the pressure of love, to develop the Lesser Evil (or its other side, the Greater Good). The backbone of all legalism is the notion that value (good or evil) is a property "in" our actions. The sway of this metaphysics in moral theology has forced such absurd positions as this: A captured soldier may not commit suicide out of sacrificial love, under overweening torture, to avoid betraying his comrades to the enemy; this is because of the evil of suicide itself, intrinsically.[18]

Bishop Pike tries to be a consistent situationist. He sets "existential" ethics over against "ontological" ethics in a very promising way. But it never really comes off! He says stoutly, "As St. Thomas Aquinas reminded us, a negative particular destroys an affirmative universal."[19] He says this in pointing out that even in the Apocrypha, Judith is praised for lying to Holofernes and using her sex (though she remained a *technical* virgin, according to the canonical story) whoringly in order to murder him. Yet for all this sturdy ethical evaluation of Judith's situational action "to save Israel," Pike ends with the opinion that a justifiable violation of a sound principle (e.g., homicide is wrong) is never *good*, however "right" situationally!

He cannot disentangle himself from the intrinsicalists' net. He *thinks* of right and wrong as real things, "ontologically," after all. He says, "What we have is not an exception to the rules which makes [the action] *good* or even neutral in character, but a balance of goods and evils and a resulting choice of the greater of

[17] *The Divine Imperative*, p. 355.
[18] See *The Clergy Review*, Vol. 40 (1955), pp. 170–174, 534–537.
[19] *Doing the Truth*, pp. 40–42, 142.

two goods, the lesser of two evils (though . . . the choice may be, in the situation, *the right thing*)" (his italics). This is the talk of ontological or intrinsic ethics, not of existential or extrinsic ethics!

But situation ethics, on the extrinsic view that right and wrong are only predicates, not properties, finds the locus of value in the circumstances of the soldier's suicide, and in what it means for people. It locates the evil in the multiple destruction of life and the betrayal of loyalty that results if the prisoner's willing sacrifice of his life, like Christ's on the cross, is forbidden by a law or principle. Extrinsicalism fights back at the unlovingness of law-bound conscience which reifies good and evil, treating value as if it were a thing-in-itself (Kant's *Ding-an-sich*), when in fact it is only a function of human decisions. Here is the normative relativism we espouse. It waves good-by to legalism and dogmatism.

For the classical moralists, therefore, suicide and lying are always wrong regardless of circumstances and relativities, even though loving concern might excuse such actions in the situation. Faced with the shocking possibility that law may have to condemn what love has done, the priests and preachers have worked out a false kind of casuistry that has grown up into a bewildering thicket of pilpul. Confused and contradictory and muddled as it is, it is after all a loving attempt to escape entrapment in its own metaphysic. It has to lie on a Procrustean bed of its own making. Having set out laws based on ethical absolutes and universals, love compels them to make more and more rules with which to break the rules. This is the ridiculous result when law ethics (as in the Christian tradition) tries to keep control, yet wants also to pay homage to love. It can't eat its cake and have it too.

But it is all wrong at the very start: the intrinsic theory of goodness is what the Greeks called the *prōton pseudon*—the basic mistake of the legalists. No law or principle or value is good as such—not life or truth or chastity or property or marriage or anything but love. *Only one thing is intrinsically good, namely, love: nothing else at all.*

Humanism—Secular and Religious

61. The Philosophy of Humanism

CORLISS LAMONT

HUMANISM DEFINED

Humanism has had a long and notable career, with roots reaching far back into the past and deep into the life of civilizations supreme in their day. It has had eminent representatives in all the great nations of the world. As the American historian Professor Edward P. Cheyney says, Humanism has meant many things: "It may be the reasonable balance of life that the early Humanists discovered in the Greeks; it may be merely the study of the humanities or polite letters; it may be the freedom from religiosity and the vivid interest in all sides of life of a Queen Elizabeth or a Benjamin Franklin; it may be the responsiveness to all human passions of a Shakespeare or a Goethe; or it may be a philosophy of which man is the center and sanction. It is in the last sense, elusive as it is, that Humanism has had perhaps its greatest significance since the sixteenth century."

It is with this last sense of Humanism that this book [*The Philosophy of Humanism*] is mainly concerned. And I shall endeavor to the best of my ability to remove any elusiveness or ambiguity from this meaning of the word. The philosophy of Humanism represents a specific and forthright view of the universe, the nature of man, and the treatment of human problems. The term *Humanist* first came into use in the early sixteenth century to designate the writers and scholars of the European Renaissance. Contemporary Humanism includes the most enduring values of Renaissance Humanism, but in philosophic scope and significance goes far beyond it.

To define twentieth-century humanism briefly, I would say that it is a philosophy of joyous service for the greater good of all humanity in this natural world and advocating the methods of reason, science, and democracy. While this statement has many profound implications, it is not difficult to grasp. Humanism in general is not a way of thinking merely for professional philosophers, but is also a credo for average men and women seeking to lead happy and useful lives. It does not try to appeal to intellectuals by laying claim to great originality, or to the multitude by promising the easy fulfillment of human desires either upon this earth or in some supernatural dream world. But Humanism does make room for the various aspects of human nature. Though it looks upon reason as the final arbiter of what is true and good and beautiful, it insists that reason should fully recognize the emotional side of man. Indeed, one of Humanism's main functions is to set free the emotions from cramping and irrational restrictions.

Humanism is a many-faceted philosophy, congenial to this modern age, yet fully aware of the lessons of history and the richness of the philosophic tradition. Its task is to organize into a consistent and intelligible whole the chief elements of philosophic truth and to make that synthesis a powerful force and reality in the minds and actions of living men. What, then, are the basic principles of Humanism that define its position and distinguish it from other philosophic viewpoints? There are, as I see it, ten central propositions in the Humanist philosophy:

First, Humanism believes in a naturalistic metaphysics or attitude toward the universe that considers all forms of the supernatural as myth; and that regards Nature as the totality of being and as a constantly changing system of matter and energy which exists independently of any mind or consciousness.

Second, Humanism, drawing especially upon the laws and facts of science, believes that man is an evolutionary product of the Nature of which he is part; that his mind is indivisibly conjoined with the functioning of his brain; and that as an inseparable unity of body and personality he can have no conscious survival after death.

Third, Humanism, having its ultimate faith in man, believes that human beings possess the power or potentiality of solving their own problems, through reliance primarily upon reason and scientific method applied with courage and vision.

Fourth, Humanism, in opposition to all theories of universal determinism, fatalism, or predestination, believes that human beings, while conditioned by the past, possess genuine freedom of creative choice and action, and are, within certain objective limits, the masters of their own destiny.

Fifth, Humanism believes in an ethics or morality that grounds all human values in this-earthly experiences and relationships and that holds as its highest goal the this-worldly happiness, freedom, and progress—economic, cultural, and ethical—of all mankind, irrespective of nation, race, or religion.

Sixth, Humanism believes that the individual attains the good life by harmoniously combining personal satisfactions and continuous self-development with significant work and other activities that contribute to the welfare of the community.

Seventh, Humanism believes in the widest possible development of art and the awareness of beauty, including the appreciation of Nature's loveliness and splendor, so that the aesthetic experience may become a pervasive reality in the life of men.

Eighth, Humanism believes in a far-reaching social program that stands for the establishment throughout the world of democracy, peace, and a high standard of living on the foundations of a flourishing economic order, both national and international.

Ninth, Humanism believes in the complete social implementation of reason and scientific method; and thereby in the use of democratic procedures, including full freedom of expression and civil liberties, throughout all areas of economic, political, and cultural life.

Tenth, Humanism, in accordance with scientific method, believes in the unending questioning of basic assumptions and convictions, including its own. Humanism is not a new dogma, but is a developing philosophy ever open to experimental testing, newly discovered facts, and more rigorous reasoning.

I think that these ten points embody Humanism in its most acceptable modern form. This philosophy can be more explicitly characterized as scientific Humanism, secular Humanism, naturalistic Humanism, or democratic Humanism, depending on the emphasis that one wishes to give. Whatever it be called, Humanism is the viewpoint that men have but one life to lead and should make the most of it in terms of creative work and happiness; that human happiness is its own justification and requires no sanction or support form supernatural sources; that in any case the supernatural, usually conceived of in the form of heavenly gods or immortal heavens, does not exist; and that human beings, using their own intelligence and cooperating liberally with one another, can build an enduring citadel of peace and beauty upon this earth.

It is true that no people has yet come near to establishing the ideal society. Yet Humanism asserts that man's own reason and efforts are man's best and, indeed, only hope; and that man's refusal to recognize this point is one of the chief causes of his failures throughout history. The Christian West has been confused and corrupted for almost 2,000 years by the idea so succinctly expressed by St. Augustine, "Cursed is everyone who places his hope in man."

In an era of continuing crisis and disintegration like that of the twentieth century, men face the temptation of fleeing to some compensatory realm of make-believe or supernatural solace. Humanism stands uncompromisingly against this tendency, which both expresses and encourages defeatism. The Humanist philosophy persistently strives to remind men that their only home is in this mundane world. There is no use in our searching elsewhere for happiness and fulfillment, for there is no place else to go. We human beings must find our destiny and our promised land in the here and now, or not at all. And Humanism is interested in a future life, not in the sense of some fabulous paradise in the skies, but as the ongoing enjoyment of earthly existence by generation after generation through eternities of time.

On the ethical and social side Humanism sets up service to one's fellowmen as the ultimate moral ideal. It holds that the individual can find his own highest good in working for the good of all, which of course includes himself and his family. In this sophisticated and disillusioned era Humanism emphatically rejects, as psychologically naïve and scientifically unsound, the widespread notion that human beings are moved merely by self-interest. It repudiates the constant rationalization of brute egoism into pretentious schemes on behalf of individuals or groups bent on self-aggrandizement. It refuses to accept the reduction of human motivation to economic terms, to sexual terms, to pleasure-seeking terms, or to *any* one limited set of human desires. It insists on the reailty of genuine altruism as one of the moving forces in the affairs of men.

Since we live during a time of nationalism run wild, of terrible world wars, of hate and misunderstanding between peoples and governments, I want to underscore at the start Humanism's goal of the welfare of *all* mankind. In its primary connotation Humanism means simply human-being-ism, that is, devotion to the interests of human beings, wherever they live and whatever their status. Though certain groups in certain countries have in the past put themselves beyond the pale of human decency, and though this could happen again, Humanism cannot tolerate discrimination against any people or nation as such. And it reaffirms the spirit of cosmopolitanism, of international friendship, and of the essential brotherhood of man. Humanists feel *compassionate concern* for their fellowmen throughout the globe.

An English bishop recently asserted that "50 per cent of the intelligent people of the modern world are Humanists." Most of the individuals to whom he refers probably do not call themselves Humanists and may never have taken the trouble to find out to what precise school of philosophy they belong. It is important, however, that all those who actually are Humanists should come to recognize in the word *Humanism* the symbol of their central purpose in life, their community of interests and their sense of fellowship. As Walter Lippmann has written in his Humanist book, *A Preface to Morals*, "If civilization is to be coherent and confident it must be *known* in that civilization what its ideals are." This implies that those ideals shall be given a habitation and a name in some philosophy.

Now much that is essentially Humanist in twentieth-century civilization is not openly acknowledged to be so. In the United States, where there is so much confusion of spirit and intellect, lip service to outworn religious concepts or their mere ceremonial use has steadily increased among those who profess some form of supernatural faith. No nation in the world is more secular and this-worldly in its predominant interests than America. These secular trends have extended to the Sabbath. Automobiles, the massive Sunday newspapers, golf and baseball, radio, television, and motion pictures have all made tremendous inroads on the day of worship.

In order to keep their following, the churches themselves have turned more and more to philanthropic activities and the Social Gospel, that is, away from concern with the future joys and punishments of the next world to a concern with the present needs of their parishioners and humanity in this world. Modern secularization has penetrated deep into the great organized religious bodies. In Protestant circles the Young Men's Christian Association and the Young Women's Christian Association have sought to attract youth into religious paths by providing facilities for social life, lodging, sports, and vocational training. Even the Catholic Church, which has retained with little compromise its traditional theology, has bowed to secular pressures by instituting organizations with a lay purpose and program, such as the Knights of Columbus and the National Catholic Welfare Conference.

America's belief in democracy and progress, its buoyant optimism and idealism, its reliance on science and invention, all fit into the Humanist pattern. Our increasing dependence on the machine and on scientific techniques tends to do away with old-time appeals to the supernatural. The stronghold of supernatural religion has always been in the country rather than in the city. But today the spread of urban culture generally and of scientific methods in agriculture has radically altered the outlook of the rural population. Modern farmers turn more and more to tractors, irrigation, flood control, and the rotation of crops to solve their problems, in place of last-minute prayers to supernatural forces.

There is a great deal in the American tradition that is fundamentally Humanist in character. In fact, our Declaration of Independence gave resounding affirmation to the social aims of Humanism when it proclaimed that "all men" have the inalienable right to "life, liberty and the pursuit of happiness." This generalization was clearly meant to apply to human beings everywhere and not just the inhabitants of the thirteen colonies. Accordingly, the famous document that launched the United States on its career as an independent nation makes a close approach to the cardinal Humanist doctrine that holds out the welfare of humanity at large as the final goal.

The author of the Declaration himself, Thomas Jefferson, described by Charles and Mary Beard as "the natural leader of a humanistic democracy," alluded to the Declaration in these words: "May it be to the world, what I believe it will be (to some parts sooner, to others later, but finally to all), the signal of arousing men to burst the chains under which monkish ignorance and superstition had persuaded them to bind themselves, and to assume the blessings and security of self-government."

Abraham Lincoln expanded on these Humanist sentiments in his Independence Hall speech of 1861 in which he defined the "great principle" that had held the United States together for so long: "It was not the mere matter of separation of the colonies from the motherland, but that sentiment in the Declaration of Independence which gave liberty not alone to the people of this country, but hope to all the world, for all future time. It was that which gave promise that in due time the weights would be lifted from the shoulders of all men, and that all should have an equal chance."

The Preamble to the American Constitution gives a significant summary of Humanist purposes limited to a national scale. Thus: "We, the people of the United States, in order to form a more perfect Union, establish justice, insure domestic tranquility, provide for the common defence, promote the general welfare and secure the blessings of liberty to ourselves and our posterity, do ordain and establish this Constitution for the United States of America." The specific concern here for future generations is unusual and is definitely an advanced Humanist idea. It is worthy of note, too, that both the Preamble and the Constitution itself omit all reference to Deity. The Bill of Rights further clears the way for secular interests by guaranteeing separation between the state and religion.

While the American people today do not yet recognize clearly the direction in which they are moving, their highest aims and much in their everyday pattern of existence implicitly embody the viewpoint of Humanism. As for the large social-economic programs of the contemporary world centering around such terms as capitalism, free enterprise, collectivism, socialism, and communism, Humanism should be able to illumine them to a considerable degree. But no matter what happens to these programs in the light of human events and the march of history, no matter which ones succeed or do not succeed, the philosophy of Humanism will always remain pertinent.

If this philosophy approximates the truth in its underlying generalizations, then it is a philosophy which, with some changes in phraseology, was appropriate to ancient times and which in the main will hold good for the shape of things to come. Economic and political systems will come and go, nations and empires and civilizations rise and fall, but Humanism, as a philosophic system in which mankind's interests upon this earth are the first word and the last word, is unlikely to become obsolete. Naturally, however, any particular expression of Humanism will eventually be superseded.

The humanistic spirit, then, while finding wider and more conscious formulation in the modern era and in the more developed nations, has been inherent and struggling for expression in the race of man since first he appeared upon this planet. So Humanism sums up not only the current tendencies of mankind to construct a more truly human world, but also the best in men's aspirations throughout the age-long history of human thought and endeavor.

62. What Is Humanistic Religion?

ERICH FROMM

It would far transcend the scope of this chapter to attempt a review of all types of religion. Even to discuss only those types which are relevant from the psychological standpoint cannot be undertaken here. I shall therefore deal with only one distinction, but one which in my opinion is the most important, and which cuts across nontheistic and theistic religions: that between *authoritarian* and *humanistic* religions.

What is the principle of authoritarian religion? The definition of religion given in the *Oxford Dictionary*, while attempting to define religion as such, is a rather accurate definition of authoritarian religion. It reads: "[Religion is] recognition on the part of man of some higher unseen power as having control of his destiny, and as being entitled to obedience, reverence, and worship."

Here the emphasis is on the recognition that man is controlled by a higher power outside of himself. But this alone does not constitute authoritarian religion. What makes it so is the idea that this power, because of the control it exercises, is *entitled* to "obedience, reverence and worship." I italicize the word "entitled" because it shows that the reason for worship, obedience, and reverence lies not in the moral qualities of the deity, not in love or justice, but in the fact that it has control, that is, has power over man. Furthermore it shows that the higher power has a right to force man to worship him and that lack of reverence and obedience constitutes sin.

The essential element in authoritarian religion and in the authoritarian religious experience is the surrender to a power transcending man. The main virtue of this type of religion is obedience, its cardinal sin is disobedience. Just as the deity is conceived as omnipotent or omniscient, man is conceived as being powerless and insignificant. Only as he can gain grace or help from the deity by complete surrender can he feel strength. Submission to a powerful authority is one of the avenues by which man escapes from his feeling of aloneness and limitation. In the act of surrender he loses his independence and integrity as an individual but he gains the feeling of being protected by an awe-inspiring power of which, as it were, he becomes a part.

In Calvin's theology we find a vivid picture of authoritarian, theistic thinking. "For I do not call it humility," says Calvin, "if you suppose that we have anything left. . . . We cannot think of ourselves as we ought to think without utterly despising everything that may be supposed an excellence in us. This humility is unfeigned submission of a mind overwhelmed with a weighty sense of its own misery and poverty; for such is the uniform description of it in the word of God."[1]

The experience which Calvin describes here, that of despising everything in oneself, of the submission of the mind overwhelmed by its own poverty, is the very essence of all authoritarian religions whether they are couched in secular or in theological language. In authoritarian religion God is a symbol of power and force, He is supreme because He has supreme power, and man in juxtaposition is utterly powerless.

Authoritarian secular religion follows the same principle. Here the Führer or the beloved "Father of His People" or the State or the Race or the Socialist Fatherland becomes the object of worship; the life of the individual becomes insignificant and man's worth consists in the very denial of his worth and strength. Frequently authoritarian religion postulates an ideal which is so abstract and so distant that it has hardly any connection with the real life of real people. To such ideals as "life after death" or "the future of mankind" the life and happiness of persons living here and now may be sacrificed; the alleged ends justify every means and become symbols in the names of which religious or secular "elites" control the lives of their fellow men.

Humanistic religion, on the contrary, is centered around man and his strength. Man must develop his power of reason in order to understand himself, his relationship to his fellow men and his position in the universe. He must recognize the truth, both with regard to his limitations and his potentialities. He must develop his powers of love for others as well as for himself and experience the solidarity of all living beings. He must have principles and norms to guide him in this aim. Religious experience in this kind of religion is the experience of oneness with the All, based on one's relatedness to the world as it is grasped with thought and with love. Man's aim in humanistic religion is to achieve the greatest

---

[1] Johannes Calvin, *Institutes of the Christian Religion* (Presbyterian Board of Christian Education, 1928), p. 681.

strength, not the greatest powerlessness; virtue is self-realization, not obedience. Faith is certainty of conviction based on one's experience of thought and feeling, not assent to propositions on credit of the proposer. The prevailing mood is that of joy, while the prevailing mood in authoritarian religion is that of sorrow and of guilt.

Inasmuch as humanistic religions are theistic, God is a symbol of *man's own powers* which he tries to realize in his life, and is not a symbol of force and domination, having *power over man.*

Illustrations of humanistic religions are early Buddhism, Taoism, the teachings of Isaiah, Jesus, Socrates, Spinoza, certain trends in the Jewish and Christian religions (particularly mysticism), the religion of Reason of the French Revolution. It is evident from these that the distinction between authoritarian and humanistic religion cuts across the distinction between theistic and nontheistic, and between religions in the narrow sense of the word and philosophical systems of religious character. What matters in all such systems is not the thought system as such but the human attitude underlying their doctrines.

One of the best examples of humanistic religions is early Buddhism. The Buddha is a great teacher, he is the "awakened one" who recognizes the truth about human existence. He does not speak in the name of a supernatural power but in the name of reason. He calls upon every man to make use of his own reason and to see the truth which he was only the first to find. Once man takes the first step in seeing the truth, he must apply his efforts to live in such a way that he develops his powers of reason and of love for all human creatures. Only to the degree to which he succeeds in this can he free himself from the bondage of irrational passions. While man must recognize his limitations according to Buddhistic teaching, he must also become aware of the powers in himself. The concept of Nirvana as the state of mind the fully awakened one can achieve is not one of man's helplessness and submission but on the contrary one of the development of the highest powers man possesses. . . .

Zen-Buddhism, a later sect within Buddhism, is expressive of an even more radical anti-authoritarian attitude. Zen proposes that no knowledge is of any value unless it grows out of ourselves; no authority, no teacher can really teach us anything except to arouse doubts in us; words and thought systems are dangerous because they easily turn into authorities whom we worship. Life itself must be grasped and experienced as it flows, and in this lies virtue. . . .

Another illustration of a humanistic religious system is to be found in Spinoza's religious thinking. While his language is that of medieval theology, his concept of God has no trace of authoritarianism. God could not have created the world different from what it is. He cannot change anything; in fact, God is identical with the totality of the universe. Man must see his own limitations and recognize that he is dependent on the totality of forces outside himself over which he has no control. Yet his are the powers of love and of reason. He can develop them and attain an optimum of freedom and of inner strength.

The distinction between authoritarian and humanistic religion not only cuts across various religions, it can exist within the same religion. Our own religious tradition is one of the best illustrations of this point. Since it is of fundamental importance to understand fully the distinction between authoritarian and humanistic religion I shall illustrate it further from a source with which every reader is more or less familiar, the Old Testament.

The beginning of the Old Testament[2] is written in the spirit of authoritarian religion. The picture of God is that of the absolute ruler of a patriarchal clan, who has created man at his pleasure and can destroy him at will. He has forbidden him to eat from the tree of knowledge of good and evil and has threatened him with death if he transgresses this order. But the serpent, "more clever than any animal," tells Eve, "Ye shall not surely die: For God doth know that in the day ye eat thereof, then your eyes shall be opened, and ye shall be as gods, knowing good and evil."[3] God proves the serpent to be right. When Adam and Eve have transgressed he punishes them by proclaiming enmity between man and nature, between man and the soil and animals, and between men and women. But man is not to die. However, "the man has become as one of us, to know good and evil: and now, lest he put forth his hand, and take also of the tree of life, and eat, and live for ever,"[4] God expels Adam and Eve from the garden of Eden and puts an angel with a flaming sword at the east "to keep the way of the tree of life."

The text makes very clear what man's sin is: it is rebellion against God's command; it is disobedience and not any inherent sinfulness in the act of eating from the tree of knowledge. On the contrary, further religious development has made the knowledge of good and evil the cardinal virtue to which man may aspire. The text also makes it plain what God's motive is: it is concern with his own superior role, the jealous fear of man's claim to become his equal. . . .

That early Christianity is humanistic and not authoritarian is evident from the spirit and text of all Jesus' teachings. Jesus' precept that "the kingdom of God is within you" is the simple and clear expression of nonauthoritarian thinking. But only a few hundred years later, after Christianity had ceased to be the religion of the poor and humble peasants, artisans, and slaves (the *Am haarez*) and had become the religion of those ruling the Roman Empire, the authoritarian trend in Christianity became dominant. Even so, the conflict between the authoritarian and humanistic principles in Christianity never ceased. It was the conflict between Augustine and Pelagius, between the Catholic Church and the many "heretic" groups and between various sects within Protestantism. The humanistic, democratic element was never subdued in Christian or in Jewish history, and this element found one of its most potent expressions in the mystic thinking within both religions. The mystics have been deeply imbued with the experience of man's strength, his likeness to God, and with the idea that God needs man as much as man needs God; they have understood the sentence that man is created in the image of God to mean the fundamental identity of God and man. Not fear and submission but love and the assertion of one's own powers are the basis of mystical experience. *God is not a symbol of power over man but of man's own powers.*

---

[2] The historical fact that the beginning of the Bible may not be its oldest part does not need to be considered here since we use the text as an illustration of two principles and not to establish a historical sequence.
[3] Genesis 3:4–5.
[4] *Ibid.* 3:22.

Thus far we have dealt with the distinctive features of authoritarian and humanistic religions mainly in descriptive terms. But the psychoanalyst must proceed from the description of attitudes to the analysis of their dynamics, and it is here that he can contribute to our discussion from an area not accessible to other fields of inquiry. The full understanding of an attitude requires an appreciation of those conscious and, in particular, unconscious processes occurring in the individual which provide the necessity for and the conditions of its development.

While in humanistic religion God is the image of man's higher self, a symbol of what man potentially is or ought to become, in authoritarian religion God becomes the sole possessor of what was originally man's: of his reason and his love. The more perfect God becomes, the more imperfect becomes man. He *projects* the best he has onto God and thus impoverishes himself. Now God has all love, all wisdom, all justice—and man is deprived of these qualities, he is empty and poor. He had begun with the feeling of smallness, but he now has become completely powerless and without strength; all his powers have been projected onto God. This mechanism of projection is the very same which can be observed in interpersonal relationships of a masochistic, submissive character, where one person is awed by another and attributes his own powers and aspirations to the other person. It is the same mechanism that makes people endow the leaders of even the most inhuman systems with qualities of superwisdom and kindness.[5]

When man has thus projected his own most valuable powers unto God, what of his relationship to his own powers? They have become separated from him and in this process he has become *alienated* from himself. Everything he has is now God's and nothing is left in him. *His only access to himself is through God.* In worshiping God he tries to get in touch with that part of himself which he has lost through projection. After having given God all he has, he begs God to return to him some of what originally was his own. But having lost his own he is completely at God's mercy. He necessarily feels like a "sinner" since he has deprived himself of everything that is good, and it is only through God's mercy or grace that he can regain that which alone makes him human. And in order to persuade God to give him some of his love, he must prove to him how utterly deprived he is of love; in order to persuade God to guide him by his superior wisdom he must prove to him how deprived he is of wisdom when he is left to himself.

But this alienation from his own powers not only makes man feel slavishly dependent on God, it makes him bad too. He becomes a man without faith in his fellow men or in himself, without the experience of his own love, of his own power of reason. As a result the separation between the "holy" and the "secular" occurs. In his worldly activities man acts without love, in that sector of his life which is reserved to religion he feels himself to be a sinner (which he actually is, since to live without love is to live in sin) and tries to recover some of his lost humanity by being in touch with God. Simultaneously, he tries to win forgiveness by emphasizing his own helplessness and worthlessness. Thus the attempt to obtain forgiveness results in the activation of the very attitude from which his sins stem. He is caught in a painful dilemma. The more he praises God, the emptier he becomes. The

---

[5] Cf. the discussion about symbiotic relationship in *Escape from Freedom*, pp. 158 ff.

emptier he becomes, the more sinful he feels. The more sinful he feels, the more he praises his God—and the less able is he to regain himself.

Analysis of religion must not stop at uncovering those psychological processes within man which underly his religious experience; it must proceed to discover the conditions which make for the development of the authoritarian and humanistic character structures, respectively, from which different kinds of religious experience stem. Such a sociopsychological analysis goes far beyond [this] context. . . . However, the principal point can be made briefly. What people think and feel is rooted in their character and their character is molded by the total configuration of their practice of life—more precisely, by the socioeconomic and political structure of their society. In societies ruled by a powerful minority which holds the masses in subjection, the individual will be so imbued with fear, so incapable of feeling strong or independent, that his religious experience will be authoritarian. Whether he worships a punishing, awesome God or a similarly conceived leader makes little difference. On the other hand, where the individual feels free and responsible for his own fate, or among minorities striving for freedom and independence, humanistic religious experience develops. The history of religion gives ample evidence of this correlation between social structure and kinds of religious experience. Early Christianity was a religion of the poor and downtrodden; the history of religious sects fighting against authoritarian political pressure shows the same principle again and again. Judaism, in which a strong antiauthoritarian tradition could grow up because secular authority never had much of a chance to govern and to build up a legend of its wisdom, therefore developed the humanistic aspect of religion to a remarkable degree. Whenever, on the other hand, religion allied itself with secular power, the religion had by necessity to become authoritarian. The real fall of man is his alienation from himself, his submission to power, his turning against himself even though under the guise of his worship of God.

From the spirit of authoritarian religion stem two fallacies of reasoning which have been used again and again as arguments for theistic religion. One argument runs as follows: How can you criticize the emphasis on dependence on a power transcending man; is not man dependent on forces outside himself which he cannot understand, much less control?

Indeed, man is dependent; he remains subject to death, age, illness, and even if he were to control nature and to make it wholly serviceable to him, he and his earth remain tiny specks in the universe. But it is one thing to recognize one's dependence and limitations, and it is something entirely different to indulge in this dependence, to worship the forces on which one depends. To understand realistically and soberly how limited our power is is an essential part of wisdom and of maturity; to worship it is masochistic and self-destructive. The one is humility, the other self-humiliation.

We can study the difference between the realistic recognition of our limitations and the indulgence in the experience of submission and powerlessness in the clinical examination of masochistic character traits. We find people who have a tendency to incur sickness, accidents, humiliating situations, who belittle and weaken themselves. They believe that they get into such situations against their will and intention, but a study of their unconscious motives shows that actually they are driven by one of the most irrational tendencies to be found in man, namely, by an unconscious desire to be weak and powerless; they tend to shift the center of their life to powers over which they feel no control, thus escaping from freedom and from personal responsibility. We find furthermore that this masochistic tendency is usually accompanied by its very opposite, the tendency to rule and to dominate others, and that the masochistic and the dominating tendencies form the two sides of the authoritarian character structure.[6] Such masochistic tendencies are not always unconscious. We find them overtly in the sexual masochistic perversion where the fulfillment of the wish to be hurt or humiliated is the condition for sexual excitement and satisfaction. We find it also in the relationship to the leader and the state in all authoritarian secular religions. Here the explicit aim is to give up one's own will and to experience submission under the leader or the state as profoundly rewarding.

Another fallacy of theological thinking is closely related to the one concerning dependence. I mean here the argument that there must be a power or being outside of man because we find that man has an ineradicable longing to relate himself to something beyond himself. Indeed, any sane human being has a need to relate himself to others; a person who has lost that capacity completely is insane. No wonder that man has created figures outside of himself to which he relates himself, which he loves and cherishes because they are not subject to the vacillations and inconsistencies of human objects. That God is a symbol of man's need to love is simple enough to understand. But does it follow from the existence and intensity of this human need that there exists an outer being who corresponds to this need? Obviously that follows as little as our strongest desire to love someone proves that there is a person with whom we are in love. All it proves is our need and perhaps our capacity.

The underlying theme [thus far] is the conviction that the problem of religion is not the problem of God but the problem of man; religious formulations and religious symbols are attempts to give expression to certain kinds of human experience. What matters is the nature of these experiences. The symbol system is only the cue from which we can infer the underlying human reality. Unfortunately the discussion centered around religion since the days of the Enlightenment has been largely concerned with the affirmation or negation of a belief in God rather than with the affirmation or negation of certain human attitudes. "Do you believe in the existence of God?" has been made the crucial question of religionists and the denial of God has been the position chosen by those fighting the church. It is easy to see that many who profess the belief in God are in their human attitude idol worshipers or men without faith, while some of the most ardent "atheists," devoting their lives to the betterment of mankind, to deeds of brotherliness and love, have exhibited faith and a profoundly religious attitude. Centering the religious discussion in the acceptance or deinal of the symbol God blocks the understanding of the religious problem as a human problem and prevents the development of that human attitude which can be called religious in a humanistic sense.

---

[6] See *Escape from Freedom*, pp. 141 ff.

Many attempts have been made to retain the symbol God but to give it a meaning different from the one which it has in the monotheistic tradition. One of the outstanding illustrations is Spinoza's theology. Using strictly theological language he gives a definition of God which amounts to saying there is no God in the sense of the Judaeo-Christian tradition. He was still so close to the spiritual atmosphere in which the symbol God seemed indispensable that he was not aware of the fact that he was negating the existence of God in the terms of his new definition.

In the writings of a number of theologians and philosophers in the nineteenth century and at present one can detect similar attempts to retain the word God but to give it a meaning fundamentally different from that which it had for the Prophets of the Bible or for the Christian and Jewish theologians of the Middle Ages. There need be no quarrel with those who retain the symbol God although it is questionable whether it is not a forced attempt to retain a symbol whose significance is essentially historical. However this may be, one thing is certain. The real conflict is not between belief in God and "atheism" but between a humanistic, religious attitude and an attitude which is equivalent to idolatry regardless of how this attitude is expressed—or disguised—in conscious thought.

Bibliography

Altizer, Thomas J. J. *History as Apocalypse.* Albany: State University of New York Press, 1985.

———, ed. *Toward a New Christianity, Readings in the Death of God Theology.* New York: Harcourt, Brace and World, 1967.

Altizer, Thomas J. J., et al. *Deconstruction and Theology.* New York: Crossroads, 1982.

Apostol, Robert Z., ed. *Human Values in a Secular World.* New York: Humanities Press, 1970.

Araya, Victorio. *God of the Poor: The Mystery of God in Latin American Liberation Theology.* Maryknoll, N.Y.: Orbis Books, 1987.

Ayers, Robert H. *Religious Language and Knowledge.* Athens, Ga.: University of Georgia Press, 1972.

Beckford, J. A., and T. Luckmann, eds. *The Changing Face of Religion.* Newbury Park, Calif.: Sage, 1989.

Bennett, Bill. "Secular Humanism: America's Most Dangerous Religion." *Humanist* 42 (1982): 42–45, 53.

Bernard, Walter. "Reflections on the Basic Idea of Religious Humanism." *Religious Humanism* 10 (1976): 2–9.

Berryman, Philip. *Liberation Theology: Essential Facts about the Revolutionary Movement in Latin America—and Beyond.* New York: Pantheon Books, 1987.

Boff, Leonardo. *Church, Charisma and Power: Liberation Theology and the Institutional Church.* New York: Crossroads, 1985.

———. *Introducing Liberation Theology.* Maryknoll, N.Y.: Orbis Books, 1987.

Bowden, Charles I. "Bertrand Russell: Liberalism, Science, and Religion." *Religious Humanism* 19 (1984): 36–40.

Buber, Martin. *I and Thou.* New York: Scribner's, 1970.

———. *Eclipse of God: Studies in the Relation between Religion and Philosophy.* Atlantic Highlands, N.Y.: Humanities Press International, 1988.

Campbell, Richard. "Existential Truth and the Limits of Discourse." In *Being and Truth,* edited by A. Kee and E. Long, 85–110. New York: Atheneum, 1986.

Castillo Cardenas, Gonzalo. *Liberation Theology from Below.* Maryknoll, N.Y.: Orbis Books, 1987.

Cone, James H. *A Black Theology of Liberation.* Maryknoll, N.Y.: Orbis Books, 1986.

Craighead, Houston. "Rudolf Bultmann and the Impossibility of God-Talk." *Faith and Philosophy* 1 (1984): 203–15.

Creegan, Charles L. *Wittgenstein and Kierkegaard: Religion, Individuality, and Philosophical Method.* London: Routledge and Kegan Paul, 1989.

Crites, Stephen. *In the Twilight of Christendom; Hegel versus Kierkegaard on Faith and History.* Chambersberg, Pa.: American Academy of Religion, 1972.

D'Arcy, Martin Cyril. *Humanism and Christianity.* New York: World, 1969.

Davis, George Washington. *Existentialism and Theology: An Investigation of the Contribution of Rudolf Bultmann to Theological Thought.* New York: Philosophical Library, 1957.

Dunning, Stephen N. *Kierkegaard's Dialectic of Inwardness: A Structural Analysis of the Theory of Stages.* Princeton, N.J.: Princeton University Press, 1985.

Durant, John, ed. *Darwinism and Divinity: Essays on Evolution and Religious Belief.* Oxford: Blackwell, 1985.

Evans, James H. *Black Theology: A Critical Assessment and Annotated Bibliography.* New York: Greenwood Press, 1987.

Ferm, Deane William. *Third World Liberation Theologies: An Introductory Survey.* Maryknoll, N.Y.: Orbis Books, 1986.

———, ed. *Third World Liberation Theologies: A Reader.* Maryknoll, N.Y.: Orbis Books, 1986.

Friedman, Maurice S. *Martin Buber and the Eternal.* New York: Human Sciences Press, 1986.

Gaskin, J. C. A., ed. *Varieties of Unbelief: From Epicurus to Sartre.* New York: Macmillan, 1989.

Geffre, Claude, and Jean P. Jossua, eds. *Nietzsche and Christianity.* New York: Seabury Press, 1981.

Glenn, Norval D., and Erin Gotard. "The Religion of Blacks in the United States: Some Recent Trends and Current Characteristics." *American Journal of Sociology* 83 (1977): 443–51.

Haring, Bernhard. *The Christian Existentialist: The Philosophy and Theology of Self-fulfillment in Modern Society.* New York: New York University Press, 1968.

Herberg, Will, ed. *Four Existentialist Theologians: A Reader from the Works of J. Maritain, N. Berdyeau, M. Buber and P. Tillich.* Garden City, N.Y.: Doubleday, 1958.

Hitchcock, James. *What Is Secular Humanism?* Ann Arbor, Mich.: Servant, 1982.

Hoffmann, R. Joseph, and Gerald A. Larue, eds. *Biblical versus Secular Ethics: The Conflict.* Buffalo, N.Y.: Prometheus Books, 1988.

Hook, Sidney. *The Quest for Being.* New York: St. Martin's Press, 1961.

Hubben, William. *Four Prophets of Our Destiny: Kierkegaard, Dostoevsky, Nietzsche and Kafka.* New York: Macmillan, 1952.

Hudelson, Richard. "Marxism and Liberation Theology." *Counseling and Values* 31 (1986): 64–76.

Hunnex, Milton DeVerne. *Existentialism and Christian Belief.* Chicago: Moody Press, 1969.

Imboden, Roberta. *From the Cross to the Kingdom: Sartrean Dialectics and Liberation Theology.* San Francisco: Harper and Row, 1987.

Jaspers, Karl. *Myth and Christianity: An Inquiry into the Possibility of Religion without Myth.* New York: Noonday Press, 1958.

———. *The Great Philosophers.* Edited by Hannah Arendt. New York: Harcourt, Brace and World, 1962.

Jolinet, Regis. *Sartre: The Theology of the Absurd.* Westminster, Md.: Newman Press, 1967.

Kamuyu-Wa-Kang'ethe. "The Death of God: An African Viewpoint." *Caribbean Journal of Religious Studies* 6 (1985): 1–23.

Kaufman, Walter Arnold. *Nietzsche: Philosopher, Psychologist, Antichrist.* Princeton, N.J.: Princeton University Press, 1969.

———. *Existentialism, Religion, and Death: Thirteen Essays.* New York: New American Library, 1976.

Keen, Sam. *Gabriel Marcel.* Richmond, Va.: John Knox Press, 1967.

Kierkegaard, Søren. *Fear and Trembling, and the Sickness unto Death.* Garden City, N.Y.: Doubleday, 1954.

———. *The Concept of Dread.* Princeton, N.J.: Princeton University Press, 1957.

Kurtz, Paul. *In Atheisme et Ognosticisme (Atheism and Agnosticism).* Edited by J. Marx. Brussels: Institute Press, 1987.

Mackintosh, Hugh Ross. *Types of Modern Theology; Schleiermacher to Barth.* New York: Scribner's, 1937.

Macquarie, John. *An Existentialist Theology; A Comparison of Heidegger and Bultmann.* New York: Harper and Row, 1965.

Marcel, Gabriel Honoré. *Creative Fidelity.* New York: Crossroad, 1982.

Michalson, Carl, ed. *Christianity and the Existentialists.* New York: Scribner's, 1956.

Miller, Ed L., ed. *Classical Statements on Faith and Reason.* New York: Random House, 1970.

Natoli, Charles M. *Nietzsche and Pascal on Christianity.* New York: Lang, 1985.

Nietzsche, Friedrich Wilhelm. *The Philosophy of Nietzsche.* New York: Modern Library, 1937.

———. *Thus Spake Zarathustra.* London: Dent; New York: Dutton, 1958.

———. *The Dawn of Day.* New York: Gordon Press, 1974.

O'Flaherty, James C., Timothy F. Sellner, and Robert M. Helm, eds. *Studies in Nietzsche and the Judaeo-Christian Tradition.* Chapel Hill: University of North Carolina Press, 1985.

Olson, Alan M. *Transcendence and Hermeneutics: An Interpretation of the Philosophy of Karl Jaspers.* Boston: Nijhoff, 1979.

Perkins, Robert L., ed. *The Concept of Anxiety.* Macon, Ga.: Mercer University Press, 1985.

Pitt, Jack. "Russell on Religion." *International Journal of Philosophy and Religion* 6 (1975): 40–53.

Plaskow, Judith. *Sex, Sin, and Grace: Women's Experience and the Theologies of Reinhold Niebuhr and Paul Tillich.* Washington, D.C.: University Press of America, 1980.

Roberts, David Everett. *Existentialism and Religious Belief.* New York: Oxford University Press, 1959.

Rogers, Carl R. *Carl Rogers—Dialogues: Conversations with Martin Buber, Paul Tillich, B. F. Skinner, Gregory Bateson, Michael Polanyi, Rollo May, and Others.* Edited by Howard Kirschenbaum and Valerie Land Henderson. Boston: Houghton Mifflin, 1989.

Rupp, George. *Beyond Existentialism and Zen: Religion in a Pluralistic World.* New York: Oxford University Press, 1979.

Sartre, Jean-Paul. *The Philosophy of J. P. Sartre.* Edited by Robert Denoon Cumming. New York: Random House, 1965.

Sobrino, Jon. *Christology at the Crossroads: A Latin American Approach.* Maryknoll, N.Y.: Orbis Books, 1978.

Tabb, William K., ed. *Churches in Struggle: Liberation Theologies and Social Change in North America.* New York: Monthly Review Press, 1986.

Thomte, Reidar. *Kierkegaard's Philosophy of Religion.* Princeton, N.J.: Princeton University Press, 1948.

Thulstrup, Niles, and Marie Mikulova Thulstrup, eds. *The Legacy and Interpretation of Kierkegaard.* Copenhagen: Reitzel, 1981.

Tillich, Paul. *What Is Religion?* Edited by James Luther Adams. New York: Harper and Row, 1969.

———. *The Spiritual Situation in Our Technical Society.* Edited by J. Mark Thomas. Macon, Ga.: Mercer University Press, 1988.

Williamson, Rene de Visme. *Politics and Protestant Theology: An Interpretation of Tillich, Barth, Bonhoeffer, and Brunner.* Baton Rouge: Louisiana State University Press, 1976.

Wingfield, Harold L. "The Historical and Changing Role of the Black Church: The Social and Political Implications." *Western Journal of Black Studies* 12 (1988): 127–34.

Witvliet, Theo. *The Way of the Black Messiah.* Oak Park, Ill.: Meyer-Stone Books, 1987.

CHAPTER 10

Religion and Politics

*I*n a well-known passage in the New Testament, Jesus distinguished between the things that are Caesar's and those that are God's (Mark 12:17). This is often interpreted to mean that politics and religion occupy different spheres, and that someone's religious convictions should not intrude into the realm of political behavior. Church and state must remain separate, and religion should affect neither a person's choice as to whom to elect nor the elected official's decisions about how to govern. A particular legislator's faith should not determine the laws that are enacted, any more than judges should decide cases in terms of their own religious beliefs.

However, in the history of religion a contrary view has also been held. Some religious figures have seen political action as a natural outgrowth of their faith—in fact, an obligation that follows from it. Jesus is also identified with this approach when he said: "The Spirit of the Lord is upon me, because he has annointed me to preach good tidings to the poor. He hath sent me to proclaim release to the captives, and recovery of sight to the blind, to set at liberty them that are bruised" (Luke 4:18). The thrust of "By their fruits ye shall know them" is that Christian action—not mere theological speculation or assent to a creed—will show whether one is a follower of Christ.

This faith-in-action approach has been followed increasingly in our own times, although it is fraught with questions about which political acts are religious. Were the Crusades a proper exercise of religious power? Should the massacres of the Reformation have taken place? Were the Salem witch-hunts justified, or the Spanish Inquisition? Should the German churches have refused communion to anti-Nazis? Should capitalism, with its emphasis on free-market forces and competition, be opposed on the grounds of its being incompatible with Christian communion, cooperation, and love? Should communism be resisted for its atheistic message or embraced because of its doctrine of universal brotherhood?

A significant portion of religious thinkers today maintain that religion should have a social conscience and work to bring about peace and justice. Furthermore, they believe that the spirit of religion, especially Christianity, is most closely allied with democracy. They accept the view of philosophers such as Jacques Maritain, who wrote:

> Not only does the democratic state of mind proceed from the inspiration of the Gospel, but it cannot exist without it. . . . To have faith in the dignity of the person and in common humanity, in human rights and in justice—that is, in essentially spiritual values; . . . to sustain and revive the sense of equality without sinking into a levelling equalitarianism; to respect authority, knowing that its wielders are only men, like those they rule, and derive their trust from the consent or the will of the people whose vicars and representatives they are; to believe in the sanctity of law . . . to have faith in liberty and in fraternity, an heroical inspiration and an heroical belief are needed which fortify and vivify reason, and which none other than Jesus of Nazareth brought forth in the world." (*Christianity and Democracy*)

One movement that takes its inspiration from such an identification is what can be called *black activism*. This is basically a political movement that seeks the liberation of people who are oppressed because of racial injustice. In the United States it has taken the form of protest movements against segregation and the prejudice that has kept African Americans from having equal status. In the mid-twentieth century, especially, protest marches, sit-ins, boycotts, demonstrations, and so forth erupted in a number of major cities in efforts to secure equal treatment of blacks in schools, public facilities, housing, and all other social realms. The results included integration, guarantees of blacks' right to vote, more equitable pay scales, and greater justice in the courts. Nevertheless, inequities persist and black activists continue to point up not only the systematic exclusion of blacks from the political life of the country and continual legal injustices but also their inferior economic position by virtue of being consigned to the lowest-paying jobs and being most vulnerable to unemployment.

In a number of African countries, most notably South Africa, black activism has been directed against the colonial rule that caused the oppression of black people. In Africa the native population was conquered or dominated by Europeans, and the countries were heavily exploited for their natural resources and cheap labor. Undoubtedly, colonial rule did a great deal of good by way of providing medical treatment, efficient communication, government, and transportation, and a general modernization of the infrastructure, but the wealth that was extracted did more for the Europeans than for the Africans.

As a result, political movements have gathered force in Africa over the last thirty years to establish self-rule by the black majority. The Africans have demanded the return of their countries from the white minority governments. At times the struggle has been extremely violent, but the consistent outcome has been the establishment of coalition governments or rule by the indigenous peoples. Even in South Africa, the country that has most staunchly resisted the black majority's demands (and therefore has faced censure by the world community), remarkable progress has now been made. At this point, racial injustice has been enormously reduced and the African countries are largely governed by the African peoples.

Behind the protest movements in the United States, and to a certain extent in Africa also, has been a social commitment based on religious convictions. Many of the leaders have found biblical mandates for their campaigns for equality and justice, and they have inspired their followers by citing the social gospel of Jesus. Although mainly Christian in nature, the protest movements have also found support from some Islamic elements, particularly in the United States, where many blacks have traced their heritage to North African religion.

The image of Jesus as a pale, Nordic type was dismissed as contrary to history, and the religious ideals of devotion, prayer, and meditation were also rejected in favor of religion as a doctrine of liberation. "Who keeps faith forever, / secures justice for the oppressed, gives food to the hungry. / The Lord sets captives free; / the Lord gives sight to the blind. / The Lord raises up those that were bowed down" (Psalm 146:6–8).

The feminist movement has paralleled black activism in struggling for social justice, and feminist theorists claim that the established form of religion suppresses women. Specifically, feminists argue that the concept of God as a man reflects the male domination of our culture and reinforces that image. Since the family, the society, and the state have been patriarchal in structure, God was depicted in the Bible as a divine father. Both Judaism and Christianity embrace this concept—Judaism with a stern male God, angry, jealous, and righteous; Christianity, with a loving Father who sacrificed his only Son.

Feminists claim that projecting God as male, rather than both male and female, has provided a model whereby men occupy a superior position in the society, and the subjugation of women is thereby justified. Women, left without a sense of the divine within themselves, must relate to a man in order to participate in the nature of God. Men, on the other hand, have a direct connection and relationship with God, since it is they who were made in his image. Women play a subservient role, serving God by being a servant to men. Male power is therefore legitimated, while women's self-image is demeaned.

Women are rarely allowed to be ordained, and in Catholicism they may become nuns, but not priests. They may be elevated as purity incarnate in the image of Ruth or the Virgin Mary, or they may be identified with Eve, the temptress, or with Mary Magdalene, the prostitute. But the Bible rarely presents complete women who seem fully human, rather than merely symbolic.

Nevertheless, when we engage in biblical exegesis, we discover that the feminine element is strongly present, although, the feminists claim, it has been systematically suppressed by male theologians. Numerous references are made to a female element or even to the deity as female in both Judeo-Christian scripture and in the sacred writings of other religions. Usually the female is associated with creation stories or with maternal warmth and wisdom. She is birth, absorption, carnality, youth, and life-giving power. Hinduism and Buddhism have numerous female divinities, and in the mythologies of Egypt, Greece, and Rome the image of the goddess is prominent as the earth, the sea, the moon, the hunt, and so forth.

Perhaps God should be viewed as androgynous, having the character of both male and female, or perhaps as a being devoid of sexual identity altogether. (Carl Jung, the Swiss psychologist, has suggested that Catholicism is superior to

Protestantism in that the female figure of Mary is given greater emphasis. He thinks that a religion is not psychologically satisfying unless it contains the "completion seeking female" as well as the "perfection seeking male.") Or maybe the female principle in religion should be recovered so that mutuality, engagement, relatedness, compassion, and grace are restored as religious values. Through such efforts women would then feel represented in the highest image that human beings have conceived and, as a consequence, might be given equal status in our culture.

Liberation theology complements this aspect of the women's movement in that it sees religion as an important part of the struggle for freedom. In fact, the liberation theologians validate their revolutionary efforts through a political interpretation of scripture, as does black activism.

A great deal of liberation theology is centered in Latin America and in Third World countries generally where the people feel oppressed by tyranny and dictatorship. It functions to reassure the disenfranchised first, that God is on their side and second, that they are on the side of God as they oppose despotic governments.

According to liberation theology, the spiritual life and the material life are not in opposition. Rather, adequate material conditions are essential for the good of our soul, and the desire for a decent standard of living is in accord with people's spiritual dignity. In the same way, we should not divide spiritual faith and physical existence, or contemplation and action, because life is a whole and our daily work is a part of our spirituality. Therefore, it is perfectly legitimate to insist on comforts of the flesh as well as satisfactions of the spirit. We are entitled to the abundance of the earth as well as freedom and peace, and we should not have to endure war, famine, displacement, and impoverishment.

Furthermore, we should not allow the exploitation of human beings (including our own exploitation), for then we are allowing sin to flourish on earth. When a few rich families own almost all the land (as in many Latin American countries), that cannot be pleasing to God. As a loving being, the Lord would not want his people to suffer starvation and personal indignities, whether from economic, political, or social measures. God is one with the poor, the lowly, and the downtrodden and wants them uplifted in their earthly existence, not only in the life to come.

Throughout liberation theology there is a strong sense of Jesus as the saviour of the rejected and despised people, not the privileged or the ruling class. For example, Richard Shaull writes:

> Like many of the prophets (Jesus) came from the lower classes. The accounts of his birth emphasize his humble origins. His family came from the 'hill country of Judea' (Luke 1:65); he was born in a stable because his parents could not afford a room at the inn. His birth was announced only to shepherds in the fields, and he spent his early years working as a carpenter.
>   When Jesus began his public ministry, he . . . spent his time with the sick and lowly, with sinners and foreigners. Most of those around him suffered from a lack of something: food, money, health, prospects, special abilities, prestige in the eyes of the righteous and the rich. From the beginning he addressed himself to the marginalized people." (*Heralds of a New Reformation*)

Similarly, in *Ethics and the Theology of Liberation,* Enrique Dussel writes: "Jesus is identified with the poor, and, listening to the poor who ask a new kingdom of him, he acts on behalf of those poor. In doing so, he subverts the established order. Therefore the order kills him." The message is that God knows our sufferings, because, as Jesus, he experienced them, and he approves of our refusal to submit to unjust and inhumane treatment. If we take our destiny in our hands and combat the perpetrators of evil, we have God's sanction and blessing we are fighting the food fight.

In the following selections Martin Luther King, Jr. describes his commitment to peace, love, and nonviolent methods of effecting change. Then Bishop Desmond Tutu explains the nature of black theology and the role of the church in South Africa.

In the next section, Rosemary Radford Reuther presents an account of the female nature of God, and Carol P. Christ describes the importance of the Goddess to women.

In the final section, Jon Sobrino writes about love and justice in liberation theology, and Gustavo Gutierrez explains his conception of the role of Christianity in South America.

Black Activism

63. The Trumpet of Conscience

MARTIN LUTHER KING, JR.

PEACE ON EARTH . . .

This Christmas season finds us a rather bewildered human race. We have neither peace within nor peace without. Everywhere paralyzing fears harrow people by day and haunt them by night. Our world is sick with war; everywhere we turn we see its ominous possibilities. And yet, my friends, the Christmas hope for peace and goodwill toward all men can no longer be dismissed as a kind of pious dream of some utopian. If we don't have goodwill toward men in this world, we will destroy ourselves by the misuse of our own instruments and our own power. Wisdom born of experience should tell us that war is obsolete. There may have been a time when war served as a negative good by preventing the spread and growth of an evil force, but the very destructive power of modern weapons of warfare eliminates even the possibility that war may any longer serve as a negative good. And so, if we assume that life is worth living, if we assume that mankind has a right to survive, then we must find an alternative to war—and so let us this morning explore the conditions for peace. Let us . . . think anew on the meaning of that Christmas hope: "Peace on Earth, Good Will toward Men." And as we explore these conditions, I would like to suggest that modern man really go all out to study the meaning of nonviolence, its philosophy and its strategy.

We have experimented with the meaning of nonviolence in our struggle for racial justice in the United States, but now the time has come for man to experiment with nonviolence in all areas of human conflict, and that means nonviolence on an international scale.

Now let me suggest first that if we are to have peace on earth, our loyalties must become ecumenical rather than sectional. Our loyalties must transcend our race, our tribe, our class, and our nation; and this means we must develop a world perspective. No individual can live alone; no nation can live alone, and as long as we try, the more we are going to have war in this world. Now the judgment of God is upon us, and we must either learn to live together as brothers or we are all going to perish together as fools.

Yes, as nations and individuals, we are interdependent. I have spoken to you before of our visit to India some years ago. It was a marvelous experience; but I say to you this morning that there were those depressing moments. How can one avoid being depressed when one sees with one's own eyes evidences of millions of people going to bed hungry at night? How can one avoid being depressed when one sees with one's own eyes thousands of people sleeping on the sidewalks at night? More than a million people sleep on the sidewalks of Bombay every night; more than half a million sleep on the sidewalks of Calcutta every night. They have no houses to go into. They have no beds to sleep in. As I beheld these conditions, something within me cried out: "Can we in America stand idly by and not be concerned?" And an answer came: "Oh, no!" And I started thinking about the fact that right here in our country we spend millions of dollars every day to store surplus food; and I said to myself: "I know where we can store that food free of charge—in the wrinkled stomachs of the millions of God's children in Asia, Africa, Latin America, and even in our own nation, who go to bed hungry at night."

It really boils down to this: that all life is interrelated. We are all caught in an inescapable network of mutuality, tied into a single garment of destiny. Whatever affects one directly, affects all indirectly. We are made to live together because of the interrelated structure of reality. Did you ever stop to think that you can't leave for your job in the morning without being dependent on most of the world? You get up in the morning and go to the bathroom and reach over for the sponge, and that's handed to you by a Pacific islander. You reach for a bar of soap, and that's given to you at the hands of a Frenchman. And then you go into the kitchen to drink your coffee for the morning, and that's poured into your cup by a South American. And maybe you want tea: that's poured into your cup by a Chinese. Or maybe you're desirous of having cocoa for breakfast, and that's poured into your cup by a West African. And then you reach over for your toast, and that's given to you at the hands of an English-speaking farmer, not to mention the baker. And before you finish eating breakfast in the morning, you've depended on more than half of the world. This is the way our universe is structured, this is its interrelated quality. We aren't going to have peace on earth until we recognize this basic fact of the interrelated structure of all reality.

Now let me say, secondly, that if we are to have peace in the world, men and nations must embrace the nonviolent affirmation that ends and means must cohere. One of the great philosophical debates of history has been over the whole question of means and ends. And there have always been those who argued that the end justifies the means, that the means really aren't important. The important thing is to get to the end, you see.

So, if you're seeking to develop a just society, they say, the important thing is to get there, and the means are really unimportant; any means will do so long as they get you there—they may be violent, they may be untruthful means; they may even be unjust means to a just end. There have been those who have argued this throughout history. But we will never have peace in the world until men everywhere recognize that ends are not cut off from means, because the means represent the ideal in the making, and the end in process, and ultimately you can't reach good ends through evil means, because the means represent the seed and the end represents the tree.

It's one of the strangest things that all the great military geniuses of the world have talked about peace. The conquerors of old who came killing in pursuit of peace, Alexander, Julius Caesar, Charlemagne, and Napoleon, were akin in seeking a peaceful world order. If you will read *Mein Kampf* closely enough, you will discover that Hitler contended that everything he did in Germany was for peace. And the leaders of the world today talk eloquently about peace. Every time we drop our bombs in North Vietnam, President Johnson talks eloquently about peace. What is the problem? They are talking about peace as a distant goal, as an end we seek, but one day we must come to see that peace is not merely a distant goal we seek, but that it is a means by which we arrive at that goal. We must pursue peaceful ends through peaceful means. All of this is saying that, in the final analysis, means and ends must cohere because the end is pre-existent in the means, and ultimately destructive means cannot bring about constructive ends.

Now let me say that the next thing we must be concerned about if we are to have peace on earth and goodwill toward men is the nonviolent affirmation of the sacredness of all human life. Every man is somebody because he is a child of God. And so when we say "Thou shalt not kill," we're really saying that human life is too sacred to be taken on the battlefields of the world. Man is more than a tiny vagary of whirling electrons or a wisp of smoke from a limitless smoldering. Man is a child of God, made in His image, and therefore must be respected as such. Until men see this everywhere, until nations see this everywhere, we will be fighting wars. One day somebody should remind us that, even though there may be political and ideological differences between us, the Vietnamese are our brothers, the Russians are our brothers, the Chinese are our brothers; and one day we've got to sit down together at the table of brotherhood. But in Christ there is neither Jew nor Gentile. In Christ there is neither male nor female. In Christ there is neither Communist nor capitalist. In Christ, somehow, there is neither bound nor free. We are all one in Christ Jesus. And when we truly believe in the sacredness of human personality, we won't exploit people, we won't trample over people with the iron feet of oppression, we won't kill anybody.

There are three words for "love" in the Greek New Testament; one is the word "*eros.*" Eros is a sort of aesthetic, romantic love. Plato used to talk about it a great deal in his dialogues, the yearning of the soul for the realm of the divine. And there is and can always be something beautiful about *eros,* even in its expressions of romance. Some of the most beautiful love in all of the world has been expressed this way.

Then the Greek language talks about "*philos,*" which is another word for love, and *philos* is a kind of intimate love between personal friends. This is the kind of love you have for those people that you get along with well, and those whom you like on this level you love because you are loved.

Then the Greek language has another word for love, and that is the word "*agapē.*" Agapē is more than romantic love, it is more than friendship. *Agapē* is understanding, creative, redemptive goodwill toward all men. *Agapē* is an overflowing love which seeks nothing in return. Theologians would say that it is the love of God operating in the human heart. When you rise to love on this level, you love all men not because you like them, not because their ways appeal to you, but you love them because God loves them. This is what Jesus meant when He said, "Love your enemies." And I'm happy that He didn't say, "Like your enemies," because there are some people that I find it pretty difficult to like. Liking is an affectionate emotion, and I can't like anybody who would bomb my home. I can't like anybody who would exploit me. I can't like anybody who would trample over me with injustices. I can't like them. I can't like anybody who threatens to kill me day in and day out. But Jesus reminds us that love is greater than liking. Love is understanding, creative, redemptive goodwill toward all men. And I think this is where we are, as a people, in our struggle for racial justice. We can't ever give up. We must work passionately and unrelentingly for first-class citizenship. We must never let up in our determination to remove every vestige of segregation and discrimination from our nation, but we shall not in the process relinquish our privilege to love.

I've seen too much hate to want to hate, myself, and I've seen hate on the faces of too many sheriffs, too many white citizens' councilors, and too many Klansmen of the South to want to hate, myself; and every time I see it, I say to myself, hate is too great a burden to bear. Somehow we must be able to stand up before our most bitter opponents and say: "We shall match your capacity to inflict suffering by our capacity to endure suffering. We will meet your physical force with soul force. Do to us what you will and we will still love you. We cannot in all good conscience obey your unjust laws and abide by the unjust system, because noncooperation with evil is as much a moral obligation as is cooperation with good, and so throw us in jail and we will still love you. Bomb our homes and threaten our children, and, as difficult as it is, we will still love you. Send your hooded perpetrators of violence into our communities at the midnight hour and drag us out on some wayside road and leave us half-dead as you beat us, and we will still love you. Send your propaganda agents around the country, and make it appear that we are not fit, culturally and otherwise, for integration, and we'll still love you. But be assured that we'll wear you down by our capacity to suffer, and one day we will win our freedom. We will not only win freedom for ourselves; we will so appeal to your heart and conscience that we will win you in the process, and our victory will be a double victory."

If there is to be peace on earth and goodwill toward men, we must finally believe in the ultimate morality of the universe, and believe that all reality hinges on moral foundations. Something must remind us of this as we once again stand in the Christmas season and think of the Easter season simultaneously, for the two somehow go together. Christ came to show us the way. Men love darkness rather than the light, and they crucified Him, and there on Good Friday on the Cross it was still dark, but then Easter came, and Easter is an eternal reminder of the fact that the truth-crushed earth will rise again. Easter justifies Carlyle in saying, "No lie can live for ever." And so this is our faith, as we continue to hope for peace on earth and goodwill toward men: let us know that in the process we have cosmic companionship.

In 1963, on a sweltering August afternoon, we stood in Washington,

D.C., and talked to the nation about many things. Toward the end of that afternoon, I tried to talk to the nation about a dream that I had had, and I must confess to you today that not long after talking about that dream I started seeing it turn into a nightmare. I remember the first time I saw that dream turn into a nightmare, just a few weeks after I had talked about it. It was when four beautiful, unoffending, innocent Negro girls were murdered in a church in Birmingham, Alabama. I watched that dream turn into a nightmare as I moved through the ghettos of the nation and saw my black brothers and sisters perishing on a lonely island of poverty in the midst of a vast ocean of material prosperity, and saw the nation doing nothing to grapple with the Negroes' problem of poverty. I saw that dream turn into a nightmare as I watched my black brothers and sisters in the midst of anger and understandable outrage, in the midst of their hurt, in the midst of their disappointment, turn to misguided riots to try to solve that problem. I saw that dream turn into a nightmare as I watched the war in Vietnam escalating, and as I saw so-called military advisers, 16,000 strong, turn into fighting soldiers until today over 500,000 American boys are fighting on Asian soil. Yes, I am personally the victim of deferred dreams, of blasted hopes, but in spite of that I close today by saying I still have a dream, because, you know, you can't give up in life. If you lose hope, somehow you lose that vitality that keeps life moving, you lose that courage to be, that quality that helps you to go on in spite of all. And so today I still have a dream.

      I have a dream that one day men will rise up and come to see that they are made to live together as brothers. I still have a dream this morning that one day every Negro in this country, every colored person in the world, will be judged on the basis of the content of his character rather than the color of his skin, and every man will respect the dignity and worth of human personality. I still have a dream today that one day the idle industries of Appalachia will be revitalized, and the empty stomachs of Mississippi will be filled, and brotherhood will be more than a few words at the end of a prayer, but rather the first order of business on every legislative agenda. I still have a dream today that one day justice will roll down like water, and righteousness like a mighty stream. I still have a dream today that in all of our state houses and city halls men will be elected to go there who will do justly and love mercy and walk humbly with their God. I still have a dream today that one day war will come to an end, that men will beat their swords into plowshares and their spears into pruning hooks, that nations will no longer rise up against nations, neither will they study war any more. I still have a dream today that one day the lamb and the lion will lie down together and every man will sit under his own vine and fig tree and none shall be afriad. I still have a dream today that one day every valley shall be exalted and every mountain and hill will be made low, the rough places will be made smooth and the crooked places straight, and the glory of the Lord shall be revealed, and all flesh shall see it together. I still have a dream that with this faith we will be able to adjourn the councils of despair and bring new light into the dark chambers of pessimism. With this faith we will be able to speed up the day when there will be peace on earth and goodwill toward men. It will be a glorious day, the morning stars will sing together, and the sons of God will shout for joy.

64. Hope and Suffering

DESMOND MPILO TUTU

THE ROLE OF THE CHURCH IN SOUTH AFRICA

Introduction—A Black Theology perspective

Before tackling the major subject, may I be permitted a few preliminary words on Black Theology which I wrote a few years ago.

"African and Black Theology are a sharp critique of how theology has tended to be done mostly in the North Atlantic world. Westerners usually call for an ecumenical, a universal theology, which they often identify with their brand of theologizing. Now this is thoroughly erroneous. Western theology is no more universal than another brand of theology can ever hope to be. For theology can never properly claim a universality which rightly belongs only to the eternal Gospel of Jesus Christ. Theology is a human activity possessing the limitations and the particularities of those who are theologizing. It can speak relevantly only when it speaks to a particular historically and spatio-temporally conditioned Christian community, and it must have the humility to accept the scandal of its particularity as well as its transience.

"Theology is not eternal nor can it ever hope to be perfect. There is no final theology. Of course, the true insights of each theology must have universal relevance, but theology gets distorted if it sets out from the very beginning to speak, or attempt to speak, universally. Christ is the universal man only because He is first and foremost a real and, therefore, a particular man. There must therefore of necessity be a diversity of theologies. And our unity arises because ultimately we all are reflecting on the one Divine activity which aims to set man free from all that enslaves him. There must be a plurality of theologies because we do not all apprehend the transcendent in exactly the same way, nor can we be expected to express our experience in the same way. On this point Maurice Wiles, Regius Professor of Divinity, University of Oxford, writes:

> Theology today is inductive and empirical in approach. It is the ever changing struggle to give expression to man's response to God. It is always inadequate and provisional. Variety is to be welcomed because no one approach can ever do justice to the transcendent reality of God. Our partial expressions need to be complemented by the different apprehensions of those whose traditions are other than our own. There are no fixed criteria for the determination of theological truth and error. We ought therefore to be ready to tolerate a considerable measure even of what seems to us to be error, for we cannot be certain that it is we who are right. On this view a wide range of theological difference (even including what we regard as error) is not in itself a barrier to unity. ("Theology and Unity" in *Theology*, Vol. 77, No. 643, January 1974).

"Dr. Ilogu can thus say there is 'a wrong premise that theology must remain an "unchanging doctrine".' Vital theology, as the reflection upon the world, man and his activities through the Word of God, is at its best when it becomes living theology by becoming relevant to the age and time and the men living in them. Theology therefore must change from epoch to epoch and even from place and time to place and time. The fact of God's activities in creation and redemption through Christ, and in the sanctification of man through the Holy Spirit, do not change, but their interpretation and their application to man's situation do change (Ibid, p. 148).

"African and Black Theology must be concerned—and vitally concerned—with liberation because, as we have shown, liberation is a serious preoccupation at the present time and it is not seen as being an alternative to personal salvation in Jesus Christ. No, it is seen in Africa as the inescapable consequence of taking the Gospel of Jesus Christ seriously. Only a spiritually, politically, socially and economically free Africa, where Christianity today is expanding faster than anywhere else in the world, can make a distinctive contribution to the life of the body of Jesus Christ and to the world community as a whole. Of course, there are differences between these two kinds of theology and there must be differences because in a sense these two kinds of theology develop from different contexts. African theology on the whole can afford to be a little more leisurely though I am not convinced of this, because Africa by and large is politically independent but there is not the same kind of oppression which is the result of White racism in South Africa.

"Black Theology arises in a context of Black suffering at the hands of rampant White racism. And consequently Black Theology is much concerned to make sense theologically of the Black Experience whose main ingredient is Black suffering, in the light of God's revelation of Himself in the Man, Jesus Christ. It is concerned with the significance of Black Existence, with liberation, with the meaning of reconciliation, with humanization, with forgiveness. It is much more aggressive and abrasive in its assertions, because of a burning and evangelistic zeal, as it must convert the Black man out of the stupor of his subservience and obsequiousness, to the acceptance of the thrilling and demanding responsibility of full human personhood, to make him reach out to the glorious liberty of the sons of God. It burns to awaken the White man to the degradation into which he has fallen by dehumanizing the Black man, and so it is concerned with the liberation of the oppressor equally as with that of the oppressed. It is not so naïve as to think that only economic or political oppression are what matter. But liberation must thus be understood in a total sense as removal of all that which keeps us in bondage, all that which makes us less than what God intended us to be." . . .

Some New Testament evidence of the liberation Exodus motif

In the gospel according to Matthew we are constantly made aware of the Old Testament parallels in the New Testament. In fact this gospel is divided into five parts to reflect the five-fold law—the Pentateuch. Jesus is the Greek form of Joshua and he led the Israelites across the Jordan into the Promised Land. This second Joshua will lead God's people out of the bondage and wilderness of sin and alienation, we are being told in a stylized way, into the Promised Land of Shalom, of wholeness, that characterizes the Kingdom of Heaven.

Matthew makes Jesus out to be the second Moses who also goes up a mountain to deliver His law—the Torah of the Sermon on the Mount. It is quite inconceivable that Matthew, writing in a Jewish milieu, could have depicted Jesus as Moses the law-giver and separated this totally from Moses of the Exodus—because the law and the deliverance from bondage have an organic relationship in Jewish thinking. In Luke's gospel, we are told that the subject about which Jesus spoke with Elijah and Moses at the transfiguration was "His departure, the destiny He was to fulfil in Jerusalem" (Luke 9:31). The Greek word Luke uses for this departure is *Exodos*. Is this a mere coincidence, or does the word chosen have a theological significance meant to evoke the deliverance God wrought in Egypt, as giving meaning to that which Jesus would effect in Jerusalem?

The imagery of deliverance, of rescuing, of being set free—this imagery forms an important, indeed a crucial part of how the New Testament describes the saving and atoning work of Jesus. He Himself, revealing the terrible cost of redeeming us and effecting reconciliation between God and us and between ourselves, as well as with the rest of creation, speaks of Himself and His later work on the cross as a ransom for many (Mark 10:45;11). He inaugurates the Kingdom of God, His Father, by taking on the forces of the evil one. His mighty works of healing the sick, exorcizing the demon-possessed, opening the eyes of the blind and the ears of the deaf—these are signs to those who have eyes to see that the Kingdom of God has broken into human affairs. God has intervened decisively on the side of man. So Jesus is the strong man who comes to snatch back the ill-gotten booty of Beelzebub (Matthew 12:29–31). Being a sinner is like being a slave to sin, to death, to the Devil (Romans 6:5–13; John 8:30–35). And the truth and the Son will set us free, and we will be really free. Indeed the whole creation is travailing in bondage, longing for its release as it looks for the revelation of the glorious liberty of the children of God (Romans 8:18–22). Jesus is then depicted as He who is setting God's children free—so that it is imperative for Him to heal the woman crippled for eighteen years even if it must happen on the Sabbath, because this daughter of Abraham has been kept a prisoner by Satan in her infirmity (Luke 13:10–17). Ephesians and Colossians delight in describing Our Lord and Saviour as a conquering general who has routed the powers of evil and is now leading them in a public spectacle in His conquering hero's procession—He leads captivity itself captive and so can give gifts to us human beings (Ephesians 4:7; Colossians 2:15); we have been bought with a price (1 Peter 1:18; Acts 20:28) so that we are no longer our own; we have been made free to be a royal house, serving God as priests (Revelation 1:5).

The crown of all the New Testament evidence occurs in Christ's characterization of His ministry in the words of Isaiah:

> The spirit of the Lord is upon me for he has anointed me. He has sent me to announce Good News to the poor, to proclaim release for prisoners and recovery of sight for the blind; to let the broken victims go free, to proclaim the acceptable Year of the Lord. (Isaiah 61:1–3)

And that acceptable year in the Old Testament was the Year of Jubilee, the year for setting slaves free (Leviticus 25).

In His ministry Jesus aroused the wrath of the religious establishment by hobnobbing with those who were called sinners, the prostitutes, the tax-collectors who collaborated with the hated Roman overlord and were despised for so doing (Mark 2:15–17). "He who has seen me has seen the Father" (John 14:7–10). He was revealing the self-same God who was biased in favour of the poor, the oppressed and the outcast, and Jesus ultimately died for being on that side.

I have demonstrated that the Exodus motif, the liberation motif, is deeply embedded in the biblical tradition. Then why are White Christians so flabbergasted when Black Christians invoke it?

Christian particularity

The reason in fact is quite simple. The Gospel of Jesus Christ is a many-splendoured thing, a jewel with several facets. In a situation such as in Ulster, the aspect of the Gospel that will be relevant there is the Gospel as reconciliation. If you are oppressed and the victim of exploitation then the Gospel for you will be liberation, and so on.

Black and White Christians look at Jesus Christ and they see a different reality. It is almost like beauty, which is said to be in the eye of the beholder. It depends on who and where you are, as to what is going to be pertinent for you. Then what is the role of the Church?

The role of the Church in South Africa

The Church exists primarily to worship and adore God. It must praise His most Holy Name. But it can never use this as a form of escapism. Precisely because it worships such a God it must take seriously the world He has created and which He loved so much that He gave His only begotten Son for it. Christians remember the strictures of the Old Testament prophets against an empty and formalistic worship. At the beginning of this paper we quoted examples of these prophetic denunciations. Jesus Himself reminded His followers that they could not offer an acceptable sacrifice on the altar if they had not been reconciled to their brother (Matthew 5:24), and the evangelist declares that anyone who claims to love God but hates his brother is a liar, because how can he love God whom he has not seen when he hates the brother whom he has? Our so-called vertical relationship with God is authenticated and expressed through our so-called horizontal relationship with our neighbour. Christianity knows nothing about pie in the sky when you die, or a concern for man's soul only. That would be a travesty of the religion of Jesus of Nazareth, who healed the sick, fed the hungry, etc. Christianity has been described as the most materialistic of the great religions. Jesus showed that for the spiritual God, His kingdom must have absolute centrality; but precisely because this was so, because He turned Godwards, He of necessity had to be turned manwards. He was the Man for others precisely because He was first and foremost the Man of God. If it must needs be so for the Son of God, it could not be otherwise for His Church.

The Church is constantly tempted to be conformed to the world, to want influence that comes from power, prestige and privilege, and it forgets all the while that its Lord and Master was born in a stable, that the message of the angels about His birth was announced first not to the high and mighty but to the simple rustic shepherds. The Church forgets that His solidarity was with the poor, the downtrodden, the sinners, the despised ones, the outcasts, the prostitutes, the very scum of society. These were His friends whom He said would go to heaven before the self-righteous ones, the Pharisees, the scribes, the religious leaders of His day. The Church thinks to its peril that it must sanctify any particular status quo, that it must identify with the powerful and uphold the system which will invariably be exploitative and oppressive to some extent. When it succumbs to the temptations of power and identifies with a powerful establishment, then woe betide that Church when that system is overthrown, when the powerless, the poor come into their own! It will go down with that system as happened especially to the Roman Catholics in Mozambique, and the Anglican Church in Zimbabwe and now the Roman Catholics in Zimbabwe.

The Church is always in the world but never of the world, and so must always maintain a critical distance from the political set-up so that it can exercise its prophetic ministry, "Thus saith the Lord," to denounce all that is contrary to the divine will whatever the cost. The Church has only one ultimate loyalty and that is to its Lord and Master Jesus Christ. The Church knows therefore that it will always have to say to worldly rulers whose laws are at variance with the laws of God that "We had much rather obey God than man" (Acts 4:19).

The Church must be ever ready to wash the disciples' feet, a serving Church, not a triumphalistic Church, biased in favour of the powerless to be their voice, to be in solidarity with the poor and oppressed, the marginalized ones—yes, preaching the Gospel of reconciliation but working for justice first, since there can never be real reconciliation without justice. It will demonstrate in its very life that Jesus has broken down the wall of partition, and so in its common life there will be no artificial barriers to any Christian being able to participate fully.

A Church that is in solidarity with the poor can never be a wealthy Church. It must sell all in a sense to follow its Master. It must sit loosely to the things of this world, using its wealth and resources for the sake of the least of Christ's brethren.

Such a Church will have to be a suffering Church, one which takes up its cross to follow Jesus. A Church that does not suffer is a contradiction in terms if it is not marked by the cross and inspired by the Holy Spirit. It must be ready to die, for only so can it share in Christ's passion so as to share His resurrection.

> A grain of wheat remains a solitary grain unless it falls into the ground and dies; but if it dies, it bears a rich harvest. The man who loves himself is lost, but he who hates himself in this world will be kept safe for eternal life. If anyone serves me, he must follow me; where I am, my servant will be. Whoever serves me will be honoured by my Father. (John 12:24–26)

I pray that for the sake of our children, for the sake of our land and for God's sake, the Dutch Reformed Church will be converted to its true vocation as the Church of God, because if that were to happen, if it were to stop giving spurious biblical support to the most vicious system—apartheid—since Nazism, if it were to become truly prophetic, if it were to be identified with the poor, the disadvantaged, the oppressed, if it were to work for the liberation of all God's children in this land, then, why, we would have the most wonderful country in the world. If it does not do these things and do them soon, then when liberation comes it will be consigned to the outer darkness for having retarded the liberation struggle and for misleading the Afrikaner. That is my fervent prayer for my fellow Christians in the Dutch Reformed Church. Woe betide all of us if the grace of God fails to move this great Church, and all churches, to be agents of the great God of the Exodus, the liberator God.

Pretoria University
March 1981

65. The Female Nature of God

ROSEMARY RADFORD REUTHER

The exclusively male image of God in the Judaeo-Christian tradition has become a critical issue of contemporary religious life. This question does not originate first of all in theology or in hermeneutics. It originates in the experience of alienation from this male image of God experienced by feminist women. It is only when this alienation is taken seriously that the theological and exegetical questions begin to be raised.

1. WHAT IS THE PROBLEM?

The problem of the male image of God cannot be treated as trivial or an accidental question of linguistics. It must be understood first of all as an ideological bias that reflects the sociology of patriarchal societies; that is, those societies dominated by male, property-holding heads of families. Although not all patriarchal societies have male monotheist religions, in those patriarchal societies which have this view of God, the God-image serves as the central reinforcement of the structure of patriarchal rule. The subordinate status of women in the social and legal order is reflected in the subordinate status of women in the cultus. The single male God is seen not only as creator and lawgiver of this secondary status of women. The very structure of spirituality in relation to this God enforces her secondary status.

What this means quite simply is the following. When God is projected in the image of one sex, rather than both sexes, and in the image of the ruling class of this sex, then this class of males is seen as consisting in the ones who possess the image of God primarily. Women are regarded as relating to God only secondarily and through inclusion in the male as their "head." This is stated very specifically by St. Augustine in his treatise *On the Trinity* (7, 7, 10).

The male monotheist image of God dictates a certain structure of divine-human relationship. God addresses directly only the patriarchal ruling class. All other groups—women, children, slaves—are addressed by God only indirectly and through the mediation of the patriarchal class. This hierarchal order of God/

Man/Woman appears throughout Hebrew law. But it also reappears as a theological principle in the New Testament. Thus Paul (despite Gal. 3:28) in I Cor. 11:3 and 7 reaffirms this patriarchal order of relationships:

> But I want you to understand that the head of every man is Christ, the head of a woman is her husband, and the head of Christ is God. . . . For a man ought not to cover his head, since he is the image and glory of God; but the woman is the glory of man.

Thus the woman is seen as lacking the image of God or direct relation to God, in herself, but only secondarily, as mediated through the male.

2. THE SUPPRESSED "FEMININE" IN PATRIARCHAL THEOLOGY

Recognising the fundamentally ideological, and even idolatrous, nature of this male-dominant image of God, some recent scholars have sought to show that this was never the whole story. God is not always described as a male. There is a small number of cases where God is described as a female. These texts occur in the Scriptures, particularly in the context of describing God's faithfulness to Israel and suffering on behalf of Israel. Here the labours of a woman in travail, giving birth to a child, and the fidelity of a mother who loves the child unconditionally, seemed to be more striking human analogies for these attributes of God than anything to be found in male activity. Thus in Isaiah we find:

> Yahweh goes forth, now I will cry out like a woman in travail, I will gasp and pant. (Isa. 42:13, 14).

> For Zion said, "Yahweh has forsaken me; my Lord has forgotten me. Can a woman forget her suckling child, that she should have no compassion on the son of her womb? Even these may forget, yet I will not forget you." (Isa. 49:14, 15).

These analogies of God as female in Scripture have been collected in Leonard Swidler's *Biblical Affirmation of Woman* (Philadelphia: Westminster 1979).

There is a second use of the female image for God in Scripture. The female image also appears as a secondary *persona* of God in the work of mediation to creation. In biblical thought this is found primarily in the Wisdom tradition. Here Holy Wisdom is described as a daughter of God through whom God mediates the work of creation, providential guidance, revelation, and reconciliation to God. In relation to the Solomon, the paradigmatic royal person, Wisdom is described as a "bride of his soul." Of her Solomon says:

> I loved her and sought after her from my youth, and I desired to take her for my bride, and I became enamoured of her beauty. . . . Therefore I determined to take her to live with me, knowing that she would give me good counsel (Wisd. of Sol. 8:2, 9).

The same view of Wisdom as mediating creatrix is found in Proverbs (8:23–31). Here she is imaged as the mother who mediates wisdom to her sons.

Behind this powerful image of Divine Wisdom undoubtedly lies remnants of the ancient Near Eastern Goddess, Isis or Astarte. These Goddesses were imaged as creators and redeemers. They are linked particularly with Wisdom, defined as both social justice and harmony in nature, over against the threatening powers of Chaos. Raphael Patai, in his book, *The Hebrew Goddess* (Ktav 1967), has delineated the heritage of this ancient Near Eastern Goddess as she appeared in suppressed form in Hebrew theology.

Although the Sophia image disappears in rabbinic thought after the advent of the Christian era, possibly because of its use in gnosticism, a new image of God's mediating presence as female appears in the form of the *Shekinah*. The *Shekinah* is both the mediating presence of God in the midst of Israel, but also the reconciler of Israel with God. In rabbinic mystical speculation on the *galut* (exile), the *Shekinah* is seen as going into exile with Israel when God-as-father has turned away his face in anger. Each Shabbat celebration is seen as a mystical connubial embrace of God with his *Shekinah*, anticipating the final reuniting of God with creation in the messianic age. The exile of Israel from the land is seen ultimately as an exile within God, divorcing the masculine from the feminine "side" of God.

In Christianity this possibility of the immanence of God as feminine was eliminated. Christianity translated the Sophia concept into the Logos concept of Philo, defined as "son of God." It related this masculine mediating *persona* of God to the human person, Jesus. Thus the maleness of Jesus as a human person is correlated (or even fused into) the maleness of the Logos as "son of God." All possible speculation on a "female side" of God within trinitarian imagery was thus cut off from the beginning.

Some Sophia speculation does get revived in the Greek Orthodox tradition in relation to creation, the Church and Mariology. One somewhat maverick modern Orthodox thinker (Sergius Bulgakov *The Wisdom of God*, London 1937) even relates this sophiological aspect of God to the *ousia* or Being of God. Sophia is the matrix or ground of Being of the three (male) persons of God! But it is doubtful if most Orthodox thinkers would be comfortable with that idea.

In western thought speculation on feminine aspects of God were probably rejected early because of links with gnosticism. Some recent Catholic thinkers (i.e., Leonard Swidler) have tried to revive the Sophia/*Shekinah* idea and link it with the Holy Spirit. But this does not have roots in western trinitarian thought. Basically the Spirit is imaged as a "male" but non-anthropomorphic principle. As the power of God that "fecundates" the waters at creation and the womb of Mary, its human referent would seem to be closer to the male semen as medium of male power.

This means that in western Christian theology, the female image is expelled from any place within the doctrine of God. It appears instead on the creaturely side of the God/creation relation. The female is used as the image of that which is created by God, that which is the recipient of God's creation; namely, Nature, Church, the soul, and, finally, Mary as the paradigmatic image of the redeemed humanity.

One partial exception to this rule is found in the Jesus mysticism of the middle ages that finds its culmination in Juliana of Norwich. Here Jesus, as the one who feeds us with his body, is portrayed as both mother and father. Eucharistic spirituality particularly seems to foster this mothering, nurturing image of Jesus. However since both the divine and the human person of Jesus is firmly established in the orthodox theological tradition as male, this feminine reference to Jesus remains an attribute of a male person. Female-identified qualities, such as mothering and nurturing, are taken over by the male. But the female is not allowed "male" or "headship" capacities.

What I wish to argue then is that all of these suppressed feminine aspects of God in patriarchal theology still remain fundamentally within the context of the male-dominant structure of patriarchal relationships. The female can never appear as the icon of God in all divine fullness, parallel to the male image of God. It is allowed in certain limited references to God's faithfulness and suffering for Israel. Or it appears as a clearly subordinate principle that mediates the work and power of the Father, much as the mother in the family mediates to the children (sons) the dictates of the father. She can be daughter of the divine king; bride of the human king; mother of his sons; but never an autonomous person in her own right.

The "feminine" in patriarchal theology is basically allowed to act only within the same limited, subordinate or mediating roles that women are allowed to act in the patriarchal social order. The feminine is the recipient and mediator of male power to subordinate persons; i.e., sons, servants. In Christianity even these covert and marginal roles of the feminine as aspects of God disappear. Here the feminine is only allowed as image of the human recipient or mediator of divine grace, not as an aspect of the divine. In every relationship in which this "feminine" aspect appears in patriarchal theology, the dominant sovereign principle is always male; the female operating only as delegate of the male.

3. "PAGAN FEMINISM": THE REVOLT AGAINST THE BIBLICAL PATRIARCHAL GOD

In the 1970s the feminist movement, particularly in the United States, began to develop an increasingly militant wing that identified partriarchal religion as the root of the problem of women's subordination. These women saw that efforts to create a more "androgynous" God within the biblical tradition would be insufficient. The female aspect of God would always be placed within this fundamentally male-centred perspective. They concluded that biblical religion must be rejected altogether.

In its place they would substitute a Goddess and nature religion that they believe to be the original human cult of matriarchal society before the rise of patriarchy. They believe that the witches of the European middle ages preserved this Goddess-centred nature religion. They were persecuted for this faith by the Christian Church who falsely accused them of malevolence and "devil worship." Feminist Wicca (or witchcraft) believes itself to be reviving this ancient Goddess religion. The book by Starhawk (Miriam Simos), *The Spiral Dance* (New York 1979), is a good expression of this feminist Goddess movement.

It is possible that we are witnessing in this movement the first strings of what may become a new stage of human religious consciousness. This possibility cannot be ruled out by the critical Christian. It may be that we have allowed divine revelation through the prophets and through Jesus to be so corrupted by an idolatrous androcentrism, that a fuller understanding of God that truly includes the female as person must come as superseding and judging patriarchal religion. However, Goddess religion in its present form manifests a number of immaturities that are open to criticism, even from the point of view of feminism.

Following outdated matriarchal anthropology from the nineteenth century, much of the pedigree claimed by this movement is of doubtful historicity. In fact, the patterns of Goddess religion reveal very clearly their roots in nineteenth-century European romanticism. The dualistic world view that sets the feminine, nature and immanence on one side, and the masculine, history and transcendence on the other, is fundamentally preserved in this movement. It simply exalts the feminine pole of the dualism and repudiates the masculine side. One must ask whether this does not entrap women in precisely the traditional stereotypes. The dualisms are not overcome, but merely given a reverse valuation. But, in practice, this still means that women, even in "rebellion," are confined to a powerless Utopianism in which males own and run "the world."

Moreover, within their own community, instead of transforming the male monotheist model, they have reversed it. Now the great Goddess is the predominant image of the Divine. Woman then becomes the one who fully images the Goddess and communicates directly with her. Males are either excluded or given a subordinate position that is analogous to the position traditionally accorded women in the patriarchal cult. This *coup d'etat* may feel satisfying in the short run, but in the long run would seem to reproduce the same fundamental pathology.

4. DOES THE ANCIENT GODDESS REPRESENT THE FEMININE?

Both biblical feminists, who search for the suppressed feminine in the Judaeo-Christian tradition, and Goddess worshipers, who wish to exalt the feminine at the expense of the masculine, share a common assumption. Both assume that the recovery of the female as icon of the divine means the vindication of the "feminine." Neither ask the more fundamental question of whether the concept of the feminine itself is not a patriarchal creation. Thus the vindication of the "feminine," as we have inherited that concept from patriarchy, will always be set within a dualistic scheme of complementary principles that segregate women on one side and men on the other. Even if this scheme is given a reversed valuation, the same dualism remains.

A recent study by Judith Ochshorn, *The Female Experience and the Nature of the Divine* (Indiana University Press 1980) raises some important questions about the appropriateness of identifying this patriarchally-defined feminine with the ancient goddesses of polytheistic cultures. What Ochshorn has discovered is that, in polytheistic cultures of the Ancient Near East, gods and goddesses do not fall into these stereotyped patterns of masculinity and femininity. A God or Goddess, when addressed in the context of their own cult, represents a fullness of divine attributes. The Goddess represents sovereignty, wisdom, justice, as well as aspects of sexual and natural fecundity. Likewise the God operates as a sexual and natural principle, as well as a principle for social relations. The Goddess displays all the fullness of divine power in a female image. She is not the expression of the "feminine." Ochshorn also believes that this more pluralistic schema allows women to play more equalitarian and even leading roles in the cultus.

The subordinate status of women, in which relation to God is mediated only through the patriarchal class, is absent from religions which have a plurality of divine foci in male and female forms. Although such a lost religious world is probably not revivable as an option today, such studies may help to point us to the relativity of our patriarchally-defined patterns of masculine or feminine. They alert us to the dangers of simply surfacing the suppressed "feminine side" of that dualism as part of the image of God, without further criticism.

5. TOWARDS AN IMAGE OF GOD BEYOND PATRIARCHY

If we are to seek an image of God(ess) beyond patriarchy, certain basic principles must be acknowledged. First we must acknowledge that the male has no special priority in imaging God(ess). If male roles and functions; i.e., fathering, are only analogies for God, then those analogies are in no way superior to the parallel analogies drawn from female experience; i.e., mothering. God(ess) as Parent is as much Mother as Father.

But even the Parent image must be recognised as a limited analogy for God(ess), often reinforcing patterns of permanent spiritual infantilism and cutting off moral maturity and responsibility. God(ess) as creator must be seen as the Ground of the full personhood of men and women equally. A God(ess) who is a good parent, and not a neurotic parent, is one that promotes our growth towards responsible personhood, not one who sanctions dependency. The whole concept of our relation to God(ess) must be reimaged.

If God(ess) is not only creator, but also redeemer of the world from sin, then God(ess) cannot be seen as the sanctioner of the priority of male over female. To do so is to make God the creator and sanctioner of patriarchy. God becomes the architect of injustice. The image of God as predominantly male is fundamentally idolatrous. The same can be said of an image of God(ess) as predominantly female.

The God(ess) who can be imaged through the experience of men and women alike does not simply embrace these experiences and validate them in their traditional historical form. We cannot simply add the "mothering" to the "fathering" God, while preserving the same hierarchical patterns of male activity and female passivity. To vindicate the "feminine" in this form is merely to make God the sanctioner of patriarchy in new form.

God(ess) must be seen as beyond maleness and femaleness. Encompassing the full humanity of both men and women, God(ess) also speaks as judge and redeemer from the stereotyped roles in which men as "masculine" and women as "feminine" have been cast in patriarchal society. God(ess) restores both men and women to full humanity. This means not only a new humanity, but a new society, new personal and social patterns of human relationships. The God(ess) who is both male and female, and neither male or female, points us to an unrealised new humanity. In this expanding image of God(ess) we glimpse our own expanding human potential, as selves and as social beings, that have remained truncated and confined in patriarchal, hierarchical relationships. We begin to give new content to the vision of the messianic humanity that is neither "Jew nor Greek, that is neither slave nor free, that is neither male nor female" (Gal. 3:28) in which God(ess) has "broken down the dividing wall of hostility" (Eph. 2:14).

66. Why Women Need the Goddess

CAROL P. CHRIST

. . . What are the political and psychological effects of this fierce new love of the divine in themselves for women whose spiritual experience has been focused by the male God of Judaism and Christianity? Is the spiritual dimension of feminism a passing diversion, an escape from difficult but necessary political work? Or does the emergence of the symbol of Goddess among women have significant political and psychological ramifications for the feminist movement?

To answer this question, we must first understand the importance of religious symbols and rituals in human life and consider the effect of male symbolism of God on women. According to anthropologist Clifford Geertz, religious symbols shape a cultural ethos, defining the deepest values of a society and the persons in it. "Religion," Geertz writes "is a system of symbols which act to produce powerful, pervasive, and long-lasting moods and motivations" in the people of a given culture. A "mood" for Geertz is a psychological attitude such as awe, trust, and respect, while a "motivation" is the *social* and *political* trajectory created by a mood that transforms mythos into ethos, symbol system into social and political reality. Symbols have both psychological and political effects, because they create the inner conditions (deep-seated attitudes and feelings) that lead people to feel comfortable with or to accept social and political arrangements that correspond to the symbol system.

Because religion has such a compelling hold on the deep psyches of so many people, feminists cannot afford to leave it in the hands of the fathers. Even people who no longer "believe in God" or participate in the institutional structure of patriarchal religion still may not be free of the power of the symbolism of God the Father. A symbol's effect does not depend on rational assent, for a symbol also functions on levels of the psyche other than the rational. Religion fulfills deep psychic needs by providing symbols and rituals that enable people to cope with limit situations in human life (death, evil, suffering) and to pass through life's important transitions (birth, sexuality, death). Even people who consider themselves completely secularized will often find themselves sitting in a church or synagogue when a friend or relative gets married, or when a parent or friend has died. The symbols associated with these important rituals cannot fail to affect the deep or unconscious structures of the mind of even a person who has rejected these symbolisms on a conscious level—especially if the person is under stress. The reason for the continuing effect of religious symbols is that the mind abhors a vacuum. Symbol systems cannot simply be rejected, they must be replaced. Where there is not any replacement, the mind will revert to familiar structures at times of crisis, bafflement, or defeat.

Religions centered on the worship of a male God create "moods" and "motivations" that keep women in a state of psychological dependence on men and male authority, while at the same time legitimating the *political* and *social* authority of fathers and sons in the institutions of society.

Religious symbol systems focused around exclusively male images of divinity create the impression that female power can never be fully legitimate or wholly beneficent. This message need never be explicitly stated (as, for example, it is in the story of Eve) for its effect to be felt. A woman completely ignorant of the myths of female evil in biblical religion nonetheless acknowledges the anomaly of female power when she prays exclusively to a male God. She may see herself as like God (created in the image of God) only by denying her own sexual identity and affirming God's transcendence of sexual identity. But she can never have the experience that is freely available to every man and boy in her culture, of having her full sexual identity affirmed as being in the image and likeness of God. In Geertz' terms, her "mood" is one of trust in male power as salvific and distrust of female power in herself and other women as inferior or dangerous. Such a powerful, pervasive, and longlasting "mood" cannot fail to become a "motivation" that translates into social and political reality.

In *Beyond God the Father*, feminist theologian Mary Daly detailed the psychological and political ramifications of father religion for women. "If God in 'his' heaven is a father ruling his people," she wrote, "then it is the 'nature' of things and according to divine plan and the order of the universe that society be male dominated. Within this context, a *mystification of roles* takes place: The husband dominating his wife represents God 'himself.' The images and values of a given society have been projected into the realm of dogmas and 'Articles of Faith,' and these in turn justify the social structures which have given rise to them and which sustain their plausibility."

Philosopher Simone de Beauvoir was well aware of the function of patriarchal religion as legitimater of male power. As she wrote, "Man enjoys the great advantage of having a god endorse the code he writes; and since man exercises a sovereign authority over women it is especially fortunate that this authority has been vested in him by the Supreme Being. For the Jew, Mohammedans, and Christians, among others, man is Master by divine right; the fear of God will therefore repress any impulse to revolt in the downtrodden female."

This brief discussion of the psychological and political effects of God religion puts us in an excellent position to begin to understand the significance of the symbol of Goddess for women. In discussing the meaning of the Goddess, my method will first be phenomenological. I will isolate a meaning of the symbol of the Goddess as it has emerged in the lives of contemporary women. I will then discuss its psychological and political significance by contrasting the "moods" and "motivations" engendered by Goddess symbols with those engendered by Christian symbolism. I will also correlate Goddess symbolism with themes that have emerged in the women's movement, in order to show how Goddess symbolism undergirds and legitimates the concerns of the women's movement, much as God symbolism in Christianity undergirded the interests of men in patriarchy. I will discuss four aspects of Goddess symbolism here: the Goddess as affirmation of female power, the female body, the female will, and women's bonds and heritage. There are, of course, many other meanings of the Goddess that I will not discuss here.

The sources for the symbol of the Goddess in contemporary spirituality are traditions of Goddess worship and modern women's experience. The ancient Mediterranean, pre-Christian European, native American, Mesoamerican, Hindu, African, and other traditions are rich sources for Goddess symbolism. But these traditions are filtered through modern women's experiences. Traditions of Goddesses, subordination to Gods, for example, are ignored. Ancient traditions are tapped selectively and eclecticly, but they are not considered authoritative for modern consciousness. The Goddess symbol has emerged spontaneously in the dreams, fantasies, and thoughts of many women around the country in the past several years. Kirsten Grimstad and Susan Rennie reported that they were surprised to discover widespread interest in spirituality, including the Goddess, among feminists around the country in the summer of 1974. *WomanSpirit* magazine, whch published its first issue in 1974 and has contributors from across the United States, has expressed the grass roots nature of the women's spirituality movement. In 1976, a journal, *Lady Unique*, devoted to the Goddess emerged. In 1975, the first women's spirituality conference was held in Boston and attended by 1,800 women. In 1978, a University of Santa Cruz course on the Goddess drew over 500 people. Sources for this essay are these manifestations of the Goddess in modern women's experiences as reported in *WomanSpirit*, *Lady Unique*, and elsewhere, and as expressed in conversations I have had with women who have been thinking about the Goddess and women's spirituality.

The simplest and most basic meaning of the symbol of Goddess is the acknowledgement of the legitimacy of female power as a beneficent and independent power. A woman who echoes Ntosake Shange's dramatic statement, "I found God in myself and I loved her fiercely," is saying "Female power is strong and creative." She is saying that the divine principle, the saving and sustaining power, is in herself, that she will no longer look to men or male figures as saviors. The strength and independence of female power can be intuited by contemplating ancient and modern images of the Goddess. This meaning of the symbol of Goddess is simple and obvious, and yet it is difficult for many to comprehend. It stands in sharp contrast to the paradigms of female dependence on males that have been predominant in Western religion and culture. The internationally acclaimed novelist Monique Wittig captured the novelty and flavor of the affirmation of female power when she wrote, in her mythic work *Les Guerilleres*,

> There was a time when you were not a slave, remember that. You walked alone, full of laughter, you bathed bare-bellied. You say you have lost all recollection of it, remember . . . you say there are no words to describe it, you say it does not exist. But remember. Make an effort to remember. Or, failing that, invent.

While Wittig does not speak directly of the Goddess here, she captures the "mood" of joyous celebration of female freedom and independence that is created in women who define their identities through the symbol of Goddess. Artist Mary Beth Edelson expressed the political "motivations" inspired by the Goddess when she wrote,

> The ascending archetypal symbols of the feminine unfold today in the psyche of modern Every woman. They encompass the multiple forms of the Great Goddess. Reaching across the centuries we take the hands of our Ancient Sisters. The Great Goddess alive and well is rising to announce to the patriarchs that their 5,000 years are up—Hallelujah! Here we come.

The affirmation of female power contained in the Goddess symbol has both psychological and political consequences. Psychologically, it means the defeat of the view engendered by patriarchy that women's power is inferior and dangerous. This new "mood" of affirmation of female power also leads to new "motivations"; it supports and undergirds women's trust in their own power and the power of other women in family and society.

If the simplest meaning of the Goddess symbol is an affirmation of the legitimacy and beneficence of female power, then a question immediately arises, "Is the Goddess simply female power writ large, and if so, why bother with the symbol of Goddess at all? Or does the symbol refer to a Goddess 'out there' who is not reducible to a human potential?" The many women who have rediscovered the power of Goddess would give three answers to this question: (1) The Goddess is divine female, a personification who can be invoked in prayer and ritual; (2) the Goddess is symbol of the life, death, and rebirth energy in nature and culture, in personal and communal life and (3) the Goddess is symbol of the affirmation of the legitimacy and beauty of female power (made possible by the new becoming of women in the women's liberation movement). If one were to ask these women which answer is the "correct" one, different responses would be given. Some would assert that the Goddess definitely is *not* "out there," that the symbol of a divinity "out there" is part of the legacy of patriarchal oppression, which brings with it the authoritarianism, hierarchicalism, and dogmatic rigidity associated with biblical monotheistic religions. They might assert that the Goddess symbol reflects the sacred power within women and nature, suggesting the connectedness between women's cycles of menstruation, birth, and menopause, and the life and death cycles of the universe. Others seem quite comfortable with the notion of Goddess as a divine female protector and creator and would find their experience of Goddess limited by the assertion that she is not *also* out there as well as within themselves and in all natural processes. When asked what the symbol of Goddess means, feminist priestess Starhawk replied, "It all depends on how I feel. When I feel weak, she is someone who can help and protect me. When I feel strong, she is the symbol of my own power. At other times I feel her as the natural energy in my body and the world." How are we to evaluate such a statement? Theologians might call these the words of a sloppy thinker. But my deepest intuition tells me they contain a wisdom that Western theological thought has lost.

To theologians, these differing views of the "meaning" of the symbol of Goddess might seem to threaten a replay of the trinitarian controversies. Is there, perhaps, a way of doing theology, which would not lead immediately into dogmatic controversy, which would not require theologians to say definitively that one understanding is true and the others are false? Could people's relation to a common symbol be made primary and varying interpretations be acknowledged? The diversity of explications of the meaning of the Goddess symbol suggests that symbols have a richer significance than any explications of their meaning can express, a point literary critics have long insisted on. This phenomenological fact suggests that theologians may need to give more than lip service to a theory of symbol in which the symbol is viewed as the primary fact and the meanings are viewed as secondary. It also suggests that a *thea*logy of the Goddess would be very different from the *theo*logy we have known in the West. But to spell out this notion of the primacy of *symbol* in thealogy in contrast to the primacy of the *explanation* in theology would be the topic of another paper. Let me simply state that women, who have been deprived of a female religious symbol system for centuries, are therefore in an excellent position to recognize the power and primacy of symbols. I believe women must develop a theory of symbol and thealogy congruent with their experience at the same time as they "remember and invent" new symbol systems.

A second important implication of the Goddess symbol for women is the affirmation of the female body and the life cycle expressed in it. Because of women's unique position as menstruants, birthgivers, and those who have traditionally cared for the young and the dying, women's connection to the body, nature, and this world has been obvious. Women were denigrated because they seemed more carnal, fleshy, and earthy than the culture-creating males. The misogynist anti*body* tradition in Western thought is symbolized in the myth of Eve who is traditionally viewed as a sexual temptress, the epitome of women's carnal nature. This tradition reaches its nadir in the *Malleus Maleficarum* (*The Hammer of Evil-Doing Women*), which states, "All witchcraft stems from carnal lust, which in women is insatiable." The Virgin Mary, the positive female image in Christianity does not contradict Christian denigration of the female body and its powers. The Virgin Mary is revered because she, in her perpetual virginity, transcends the carnal sexuality attributed to most women. . . .

Western culture also gives little dignity to the postmenopausal or aging woman. It is no secret that our culture is based on a denial of aging and death, and that women suffer more severely from this denial than men. Women are placed on a pedestal and considered powerful when they are young and beautiful, but they are said to lose this power as they age. As feminists have pointed out, the "power" of the young woman is illusory, since beauty standards are defined by men, and since few women are considered (or consider themselves) beautiful for more than a few years of their lives. Some men are viewed as wise and authoritative in age, but old women are pitied and shunned. Religious iconography supports this cultural attitude towards aging women. The purity and virginity of Mary and the female saints is often expressed in the iconographic convention of perpetual youth. Moreover, religious mythology associates aging women with evil in the symbol of the wicked old witch. Feminists have challenged cultural myths of aging women and have urged women to reject patriarchal beauty standards and to celebrate the distinctive beauty of women of all ages.

The symbol of Goddess aids the process of naming and reclaiming the female body and its cycles and processes. In the ancient world and among modern women, the Goddess symbol represents the birth, death, and rebirth processes of the natural and human worlds. The female body is viewed as the direct incarnation of waxing and waning, life and death, cycles in the universe. This is sometimes expressed through the symbolic connection between the twenty-eight-day cycles of menstruation and the twenty-eight-day cycles of the moon. Moreover, the Goddess is celebrated in the triple aspect of youth, maturity, and age, or maiden, mother, and crone. The potentiality of the young girl is celebrated in the nymph or maiden aspect of the Goddess. The Goddess as mother is sometimes depicted giving birth, and giving birth is viewed as a symbol for all the creative, life-giving powers of the universe. The life-giving powers of the Goddess in her creative aspect are not limited to physical birth, for the Goddess is also seen as the creator of all the arts of civilization, including healing, writing, and the giving of just law. Women in the middle of life who are not physical mothers may give birth to poems, songs, and books, or nurture other women, men, and children. They too are incarnations of the Goddess in her creative, life-giving aspect. At the end of life, women incarnate the crone aspect of the Goddess. The wise old woman, the woman who knows from experience what life is about, the woman whose closeness to her own death gives her a distance and perspective on the problems of life, is celebrated as the third aspect of the Goddess. Thus, the women learn to value youth, creativity, and wisdom in themselves and other women. . . .

A third important implication of the Goddess symbol for women is the positive valuation of will in a Goddess-centered ritual, especially in Goddess-centered ritual magic and spellcasting in womanspirit and feminist witchcraft circles. The basic notion behind ritual magic and spellcasting is energy as power. Here the Goddess is a center or focus of power and energy; she is the personification of the energy that flows between beings in the natural and human worlds. In Goddess circles, energy is raised by chanting or dancing. According to Starhawk, "Witches conceive of psychic energy as having form and substance that can be perceived and directed by those with a trained awareness. The power generated within the circle is built into a cone form, and at its peak is released—to the Goddess, to reenergize the members of the coven, or to do a specific work such as healing." In ritual magic, the energy raised is directed by willpower. Women who celebrate in Goddess circles believe they can achieve their wills in the world.

The emphasis on the will is important for women, because women traditionally have been taught to devalue their wills, to believe that they cannot achieve their will through their own power, and even to suspect that the assertion of will is evil. . . .

In a Goddess-centered context, in contrast, the will is valued. *A woman is encouraged to know her will, to believe that her will is valid, and to believe that her will can be achieved in the world,* three powers traditionally denied to her in patriarchy. In a Goddess-centered framework, a woman's will is not subordinated to the Lord God as king and ruler, nor to men as his representatives. Thus a woman is not reduced to waiting and acquiescing in the wills of others as she is in patriarchy. But neither does she adopt the egocentric form of will that pursues self-interest without regard for the interests of others.

The Goddess-centered context provides a different understanding of the will than that available in the traditional patriarchal religious framework. In the Goddess framework, will can be achieved only when it is exercised in harmony with the energies and wills of other beings. Wise women, for example, raise a cone of healing energy at the full moon or solstice when the lunar or solar energies are at their high points with respect to the earth. This discipline encourages them to recognize that not all times are propitious for the achieving of every will. Similarly, they know that spring is a time for new beginnings in work and love, summer a time for producing external manifestations of inner potentialities, and fall or winter times for stripping down to the inner core and extending roots. Such awareness of waxing and waning processes in the universe discourages arbitrary ego-centered assertion of will, while at the same time encouraging the assertion of individual will in cooperation with natural energies and the energies created by the wills of others. Wise women also have a tradition that whatever is sent out will be returned and this reminds them to assert their wills in cooperative and healing rather than egocentric and destructive ways. This view of will allows women to begin to recognize, claim, and assert their wills without adopting the worst characteristics of the patriarchal understanding and use of will. In the Goddess-centered framework, the "mood" is one of positive affirmation of personal will in the context of the energies of other wills or beings. The "motivation" is for women to know and assert their wills in cooperation with other wills and energies. This of course does not mean that women always assert their wills in positive and life-affirming ways. Women's capacity for evil is, of course, as great as men's. My purpose is simply to contrast the differing attitudes toward the exercise of will *per se,* and the female will in particular, in Goddess-centered religion and in the Christian God-centered religion.

The fourth and final aspect of Goddess symbolism that I will discuss here is the significance of the Goddess for a revaluation of woman's bonds and heritage. As Virginia Woolf has said, "Chloe liked Olivia," a statement about a woman's relation to another woman, is a sentence that rarely occurs in fiction. Men have written the stories, and they have written about women almost exclusively in their relations to men. The celebrations of women's bonds to each other, as mothers and daughters, as colleagues and coworkers, as sisters, friends, and lovers, is beginning to occur in the new literature and culture created by women in the women's movement. While I believe that the revaluing of each of these bonds is important, I will focus on the mother-daughter bond, in part because I believe it may be the key to the others.

Adrienne Rich has pointed out that the mother-daughter bond, perhaps the most important of woman's bonds, "resonant with charges . . . the flow of energy between two biologically alike bodies, one of which has lain in amniotic bliss inside the other, one of which has labored to give birth to the other," is rarely celebrated in patriarchal religion and culture. Christianity celebrates the father's relation to the son and the mother's relation to the son, but the story of mother and daughter is missing. So, too, in patriarchal literature and psychology the mothers and the daughters rarely exist. Volumes have been written about the Oedipal complex, but little has been written about the girl's relation to her mother. Moreover, as de Beauvoir has noted, the mother-daughter relation is distorted in patriarchy because the mother must give her daughter over to men in a male-defined culture in which women are viewed as inferior. The mother must socialize her daughter to become subordinate to men, and if her daughter challenges patriarchal norms, the mother is likely to defend the patriarchal structures against her own daughter. . . .

The symbol of Goddess has much to offer women who are struggling to be rid of the "powerful, pervasive, and long-lasting moods and motivations" of devaluation of female power, denigration of the female body, distrust of female will, and denial of the women's bonds and heritage that have been engendered by patriarchal religion. As women struggle to create a new culture in which women's power, bodies, will, and bonds are celebrated, it seems natural that the Goddess would reemerge as symbol of the newfound beauty, strength, and power of women.

67. The True Church and the Poor

JON SOBRINO

. . . If justice is a form of love then the practice of justice is automatically an essential requirement of the gospel message. I believe that this is in fact the case. But we need to clarify the meaning of justice and its relation to love.

By love I understand the proper relationship that exists among human beings when certain relations are established between them. Concretely, love makes the "other" or "others" the addressees of our activity in order that they may exist more fully, may have life and have it in increasing abundance, and that thus we may all be united. Since the relationships among human beings vary according to the different states in which they live, the type of love will differ according as the relationships are those of the family, or marriage, or friendship.

By justice I mean the kind of love that seeks effectively to humanize, to give life in abundance to the poor and oppressed majorities of the human race. Justice is thus a concrete form of love in which account is taken of the quantitative fact that its recipients form majorities and of the qualitative fact that they are poor and oppressed.

For the purposes of this study these general descriptions of love and justice will be enough. I must however dispel two possible misunderstandings, lest it be thought that the basis for the requirement of justice is purely verbal, obtained by including justice in the definition of love.

The first misunderstanding would be to assume that we already know what the generic concept of love is independently of its specific applications. It would be to assume that an understanding of the essence of love is best gotten from matrimonial love, familial love, or the love of friendship. It would then be up to justice to prove that it is a historical form of love, whereas the other forms of love are quite clearly exactly that: forms of love.

The second misunderstanding would be to think that justice is a secondary form of love, either because its existence is required only when charity is absent or because its practice is usually accompanied by conflict, whereas the unitive character of love leaves the element of conflict in the shadow.

I think that justice is a primordial and irreducible form of love because it is called for both by the historical reality of the human race and by the social dimension of the human person. To ignore these basic realities and to reduce love to its other forms would be to indulge in idealism and to disregard the gospel. It would be a similar betrayal of reality to reduce love to justice.

My concern here is to show that the form of love we call justice was practiced by Jesus and that when put into practice this form of love is the best way of embodying important Christian values.

If we do not assume that we already know how Jesus practiced love and if, instead, we attend closely to the gospel narrative, two characteristics of the practice of Jesus emerge clearly (I am speaking of passages other than those occasional ones describing his friendships): his tender mercy toward sinners and his identification with the poor for the purpose of giving them life. These two characteristics are not really separate, but I shall focus on the second and analyze it briefly.

The fact that the kingdom of God provides the purview for Jesus' ministry points to a historical situation in which justice is done to the poor majority. Jesus directs his ministry to the multitudes; the emphasis on sheer numbers alerts us to something fundamental about the service he renders. He loves "the many." Soteriology has been very much aware of this point, but it needs to be reevaluated if we are to understand the historical form that Jesus' love took. Jesus also has compassion on the multitudes. The statement "I have compassion on the crowd" (Mt. 15:32; cf. Mk 6:34) expresses a basic fact that the gospel narratives use to organize the story of the life and ministry of Jesus according to a logical pattern.

To this quantitative fact must be added the qualitative one: "He has anointed me to preach the good news to the poor" (Lk. 4:18). The "other" to which Jesus directs his practice of love is a collectivity that is well defined in sociological terms: the world of the poor. It is to these impoverished multitudes that Jesus directs his ministry; he serves them and seeks to restore their life precisely because their life has been diminished, and this at the most elementary level. The crippled, the blind, and the paralyzed are symbols of those who have no life or who have it in a lesser degree.

To this collective "other," made up for the most part of the poor, Jesus comes as savior and re-creator. We see this expressed in a positive way in those symbolic scenes in which Jesus makes his own the interests of these others: the poor, the sick, the lepers, the sinners, the tax collectors, the Samaritans. This solidarity of Jesus with the poor finds implicit but no less clear expression in his dealings with the social groups that cause the poverty of the multitudes. An analysis of the disputes in which Jesus is involved and the curses he utters shows that he is defending the poor and not simply solving problems of religious casuistry or denouncing forms of hypocrisy. We can see from his denunciations what it is he is defending.

In the final analysis Jesus is defending life and the right of the poor to life, a right denied them by other groups. Here are but a few examples: The anathemas that Jesus utters are directed not only at the hypocrisy of the leaders but at the oppression in which they engage. The Pharisees are blind guides with no concern for justice; the scribes impose intolerable burdens; they have taken away the key of knowledge and left the people in ignorance (Lk. 11:37–54). Jesus shows up false traditions not only in order to defend God's will in its authentic and orthodox form but also to prevent widows from having their houses devoured (Mk. 12:38–40) and elderly parents from being deprived of support (Mk. 7:11–12). He engages in controversies about the sabbath not simply in order to defend general anthropological truths about human beings and their dominion over the world, but also in order to defend the right of the hungry to eat (Mk. 2:23–28).

The fate of Jesus can be explained historically only in light of his solidarity with the poor masses and his energetic defense of them and attacks on their oppressors. He certainly does meet death because of his fidelity to the Father's will, but historically his death is the result of a specific love that leads to a specific practice. From the historical standpoint Jesus was put to death by unjust authorities who saw him as a threat.

This brief description of the practice of Jesus does not mean that his entire life is reducible to practice, nor that his mission of evangelizing the poor is reducible to their salvation and liberation. It does not mean that Jesus thought of justice as the only form of love. It does not mean that he idealized the poor and the oppressed with whom his practice was concerned. Neither does it imply that he developed a body of social thought regarding models for a new society and the means of bringing this society into existence.

Nonetheless, the fact remains that Jesus practiced the form of love we call justice; that the gospel narratives give a good picture of this practice; and that such narratives make up a substantial part of the gospels. Whatever Jesus' explicit idea of the kingdom of God was and whatever its apocalyptic or prophetic nuances may have been, one thing remains certain: the service to the kingdom of God that he proclaims is to an important degree one of efficacious love for the poor and oppressed majorities.

This type of love has some historical characteristics that distinguish it from love in general. The possession of these characteristics generates—or can generate—a series of values that I believe to be essential to the gospel and to revelation generally. Justice as a form of love is therefore validated not only by the fact that Jesus practiced it but also by its internal features, which make it consonant with the message as a whole.

I shall list some of these characteristics. They are to be discovered not simply by a conceptual analysis of justice but by observation of the actual practice of justice.

1. Justice takes seriously the primordial fact of the *created world* in its given form; that is to say, it takes seriously the existence of the oppressed majorities. The existence of these majorities is not a fact that can be lightly passed over in speaking of the essence of the Christian message. Otherwise we would have to look for God's will in the signs of the times or by means of subtle efforts to discern it. Justice begins with a judgment, a small but decisive judgment, on the present state of the created world.

2. This initial honesty in dealing with reality leads to the discovery of *sin*. Injustice and the oppression of the majorities reveal to us that which is the most radical denial of God's will and of his very person: the destruction of the created

order and the death of human beings. Offense against God and its correlative, subjective guilt, find objective expression in the death inflicted on human beings, either slowly through oppressive structures or quickly through the techniques used by oppressors. The tradition is fully justified, therefore, in speaking of "mortal" sin, provided the "death" in question be understood as the death not only of the sinner but of the victim as well.

3. When faced with the negation of the life of the majorities, or with the threat to this life, justice tries to re-create human beings and give them *life*. Justice extends to all levels of their existence and seeks to give life in abundance. But justice does not plan too hastily on the fullness of life; it tries first to see to it that life at the most elementary levels is ensured. It endeavors to make God's creation begin to be precisely that. Christianity provides the real possibility of affirming the sublimity of God and, correlatively, the sublimity of the human person. Justice tries to keep these affirmations from being only ideals and to see to it that they start off with the unpretentious reminder of the God of creation and his will that human beings should have life.

4. Justice, operating within history, urges the adoption of a *partisan and subjective perspective* in the practice of love and in the development of Christian existence. This perspective is from below, from the standpoint of wretchedness and oppression, from the underside of history. By taking this approach, one effectively adopts the evangelical perspective, which avoids succumbing to an idealist and alienating universalist attitude by taking as its point of reference the weak, the poor, and the oppressed.

5. Justice fosters objective solidarity with the oppressed and thus an *objective kenosis* or self-emptying. The self-deflation and self-humbling that faith requires takes the concrete form of solidarity with the poor and the adoption of their situation, cause, and fate.

6. The practice of the justice that tries to renew the poor majorities often leads to a personal *conversion*, and a radical conversion at that. Solidarity with the poor may be for the sake of serving them, but it often turns into a service rendered by the poor to those who are trying to secure justice for them. Because of the complex reality of their poverty, and by reason of the fact that their existence acts as a call to break with life as hitherto lived or, to put it in Christian terms, by reason of the fact that they are the sacraments of the Lord and the suffering face he turns to the world, the poor evangelize those whose initial intention was to serve them. The otherness of the poor gives rise to effective and even affective impulses and conceptual categories that will enable those who serve them to become different, to act differently, and to look on themselves differently; in other words, to be converted, and converted once and for all.

7. By its structure as a historical reality justice highlights one characteristic of love, namely, *service*. In other forms of love, service may be accompanied by personal gratification. In the practice of justice, too, gratification may be present, at least in the form of a profound sense of one's own possession of life. But by reason of those to whom the love and justice are directed and of the kind of relationship that is established with them, personal gratification does not emerge

as an immediate affective component. This makes the service aspect of love stand out more clearly; it highlights the fact that love gives rather than receives.

8. Justice recovers the biblical idea of the *neighbor* as being not just someone in close proximity to me but someone I *make* my neighbor. Justice is the movement by which we go out, unconditionally and with a sense of urgency, to the poor and oppressed in order to make of them our neighbors. The situation of the majorities, which is like that of the wounded man by the wayside in the gospel parable, shows clearly what it means to a neighbor. It also shows the fundamental wickedness of passing by, of not actively being a neighbor.

9. Usually, and more clearly than in other forms of love, justice brings *persecution* on those who practice it. Genuine love, of course, implies a readiness to suffer, and this suffering may be very great. Justice, however, brings with it the kind of suffering to which we give the name *persecution*. Sin in its historical reality shows its might and power against those who practice justice. "Taking up one's cross" becomes an unavoidable necessity and turns the life of one who promotes justice into a journey very like that of Jesus: a journey that ends in some kind of historical cross and death.

When I assert that the practice of justice is a basic demand of the gospel, I mean that Jesus practiced this kind of love and that it is therefore essential to the following of Jesus. But I also mean that as a specific kind of love, it generates a series of basic evangelical values. The acknowledgement of God's creation as precisely that, the unmasking of sin as basically the practice of murder, union with the poor in order to give them life, the adoption of a partisan subjective outlook, the achievement of an objective conversion and kenosis, the practice of being a neighbor, the setting aside of self in order to serve, the readiness to suffer persecution—all these to a greater or lesser degree accompany the practice of justice and demonstrate its authenticity from the standpoint of the gospel.

The practice of justice is therefore a basic material demand of the gospel. Without it the gospel would be substantially mutilated.

68. A Theology of Liberation

GUSTAVO GUTIERREZ

THE CHURCH IN THE PROCESS OF LIBERATION

The Latin American Church has lived and to a large extent continues to live as a ghetto church. The Latin American Christian community came into being during the Counter-Reformation and has always been characterized by its defensive attitude as regards the faith. This posture was reinforced in some cases by the hostility of the liberal and anticlerical movements of the nineteenth century and, more recently, by strong criticism from those struggling to transform the society to which the Church is so tightly linked.

This hostility led the Church to seek the support of the established order and economically powerful groups in order to face its adversaries and assure for itself what it believed to be an opportunity to preach the Gospel peacefully.

But for some time now, we have been witnessing a great effort by the Church to rise out of this ghetto power and mentality and to shake off the ambiguous protection provided by the beneficiaries of the unjust order which prevails on the continent. Individual Christians, small communities, and the Church as a whole are becoming more politically aware and are acquiring a greater knowledge of the current Latin American reality, especially in its root causes. The Christian community is beginning, in fact, to read *politically* the signs of the times in Latin America. Moreover, we have witnessed the taking of positions which could even be characterized as daring, especially compared with previous behavior. We have seen a commitment to liberation which has provoked resistance and mistrust.

All this has required a task of reflection on the questions posed by this new attitude; hence the new theological thinking now occurring in Latin America comes more from the Christian groups committed to the liberation of their people than from the traditional centers for the teaching of theology. The fruitfulness of reflection will depend on the quality of these commitments.

The process is complex and things are changing before our very eyes. Here we focus our attention on participation in the process of liberation and thus do not concern ourselves with other aspects of the life of the Church. It will be helpful to point out some of the highlights which characterize the new situation now being created.

The Commitment of Christians

The different sectors of the People of God are gradually committing themselves in different ways to the process of liberation. They are becoming aware that this liberation implies a break with the status quo, that it calls for a social revolution. In relation to the entire Latin American Christian community it must be acknowledged that the number of persons involved is small. But the numbers are growing and active and every day they are acquiring a larger hearing both inside and outside the Church.

Lay Persons   What we have referred to as the pastoral approach of "New Christendom" brought about, among large groups of Christians, a political commitment to the creation of a more just society. In the past, the lay apostolate movements, especially among youth, have given a considerable number of their better leaders to the political parties of socio-Christian inspiration. The "distinction of planes" stage allowed for purification of the motivation of these commitments as well as for the discovery of new perspectives for the action of Christians in the world, in collaboration with persons of different points of view. Today, apostolic youth movements have radicalized their political options. It has been true for some time now that in most Latin American countries young militants do not share the orientation of moderate renewal groups.

The ever more revolutionary political options of Christian groups—especially students, workers, and peasants—have frequently been responsible for conflicts between lay apostolic movements and the hierarchy. These options have likewise caused the movement members to question their place in the Church and have been responsible for the severe crises experienced by some of them.

Moreover, many have discovered in these movements evangelical demands for an ever more resolute commitment to the oppressed peoples of this exploited continent. But the inadequacy of the theologico-pastoral plans which until recently were considered viable by these movements, the perception of the close ties which unite the Church to the very social order which the movements wish to change, the urgent albeit ambiguous demands of political action, the impression of dealing with the "concrete" in the revolutionary struggle—all these factors have caused many gradually to substitute working for the Kingdom with working for the social revolutions—or, more precisely perhaps, the lines between the two have become blurred.

In the concrete, all this has often meant a commitment to revolutionary political groups. The political situation in Latin America, together with the subversion of the status quo advocated by these groups, force them to become at least partially clandestine. Moreover, as awareness of existing legalized violence grows, the problem of counterviolence is no longer an abstract ethical concern. It now becomes very important on the level of political efficacy. Perhaps more accurately, it is on this latter level that the question of human nature is concretely considered. Under these conditions, the political activity of Christians takes on new dimensions which have caught by surprise not only the ecclesial structures but also the most advanced pedagogical methods of the lay apostolic movements. It is clear, for example, that the kind of apostolic movement represented by the Catholic Action groups among the French workers—that is, communities of Christians with different political options who meet for a *révision de vie* in the light of the faith—is, as such, not viable. Among other reasons, this is so because political radicalization tends to lead to united—and impassioned—positions and because the kind of activity which develops does not allow for entirely free expression of ideas. The model of the Workers' Catholic Action is valid in a more or less stable society where political commitments can be lived out publicly. This model presupposes and facilitates, moreover, a theoretical dialogue with Marxism in a way which holds little interest for Latin America. On this continent, the oppressed and those who seek to identify with them face ever more resolutely a common adversary, and therefore, the relationship between Marxists and Christians takes on characteristics different from those in other places.

On the other hand, meetings between Christians of different confessions but of the same political option are becoming more frequent. This gives rise to ecumenical groups, often marginal to their respective ecclesiastical authorities, in which Christians share their faith and struggle to create a more just society. The common struggle makes the *traditional* ecumenical programs seem obsolete (a "marriage between senior citizens" as someone has said) and impels them to look for new paths toward unity.

A profound renewal or renaissance of various lay apostolic movements is nevertheless apparent. After the initial impact of a radical *politicization* for which they were inadequately prepared theologically, pedagogically, and spiritually, everything seems to indicate that they are beginning to find new approaches. There are also arising new kinds of groups as well as close collaboration among existing movements. These go beyond any particular specialization, yet recognize the need for specialized pedagogies and are oriented toward a specific social milieu; the "cement" holding them together is their particular posture within the Church and within the Latin American political process. A clear option in favor of the oppressed and their liberation leads to basic changes in outlook; there emerges a new vision of the fruitfulness and originality of Christianity and the Christian community's role in this liberation. This is not a matter merely of a reaffirmation of a choice but also of concrete experiences of how to witness to the Gospel in Latin America today. But many questions remain unanswered. The new vitality that can be foreseen does not have before it a completely clear path.

Priests and Religious   A clearer perception of the tragic realities of the continent, the clear options which political polarization demand, the climate of more active participation in the life of the Church created by Vatican II, and the impulse provided by the Latin American Bishops' Conference at Medellín—all these factors have made priests and [the] religious today one of the most dynamic and restless groups in the Latin American Church. Priests and religious in ever increasing proportions seek to participate more actively in the pastoral decisions of the Church. But, above all, they want the Church to break its ties with an unjust order, and they want it—with renewed fidelity to the Lord who calls it and to the Gospel which it preaches—to cast its lot with those who suffer from misery and deprivation.

In a considerable number of countries, we observe the creation of groups of priests—with characteristics not foreseen by canon law!—who have organized to channel and reinforce their growing concern. These groups are characterized by their determination to commit themselves to the process of liberation and by their desire for radical change both in the present internal structures of the Latin American Church as well as in the manner in which the Church is present and active on this continent of revolution.

These concerns, as well as other factors, have led in many cases to friction with local bishops and apostolic nuncios. We can say that unless deep changes take place this conflictual situation will spread and become more serious in the immediate future.

Moreover, there are many priests who consider it a duty to adopt clear and committed personal positions in the political arena. Some participate actively in politics, often in connection wth revolutionary groups. As a matter of fact, this participation is not essentially something new. In many ways the clergy has played and still plays a direct participation in political life (barely veiled in some cases under pretexts of a religious nature). The new dimension is that many priests clearly admit the need and obligation to make such a commitment and above all that their options in one way or another place them in a relationship of subversion regarding the existing social order.

There are other factors: for example, the effects of a certain weariness caused by the intensity of the resistance that must be overcome within the Church; and then there is the disenchantment caused by the apparent futility of work regarded as "purely religious," which has little contact with the reality and social demands of the continent. We are facing an "identity crisis." For some this means a reassessment of the current lifestyle of the clergy; and for others it means even a reevaluation of the meaning of the priesthood itself. On the other hand, the numbers are growing of those who have found a renewed meaning for their priesthood or religious life in the commitment to the oppressed and their struggle for liberation. For them, the Gospel, the Word of the Lord, the message of love, is a liberating force which attacks the roots of all injustice. This leads them to put in second place the questions now being debated—with different priorities in other parts of the world—regarding the priestly or religious life.

Frequently in Latin America today certain priests are considered "subversive." Many are under surveillance or are being sought by the police. Others are in prison, have been expelled from their country (Brazil, Bolivia, Colombia, and the Dominican Republic are significant examples), or have been murdered by terrorist anti-communist groups. For the defenders of the status quo, "priestly subversion" is surprising. They are not used to it. The political activity of some leftist groups, we might say, is—within certain limits—assimilated and tolerated by the system and is even useful to it to justify some of its repressive measures; the dissidence of priests and religious, however, appears as particularly dangerous, especially if we consider the role which they have traditionally played.

Bishops   The new and serious problems which face the Latin American Church and which shape the conflictual and changing reality find many bishops ill-prepared for their function. There is among them, nevertheless, an awakening to the social dimension of the presence of the Church and a corresponding rediscovery of its prophetic mission.

The bishops of the most poverty-stricken and exploited areas are the ones who have denounced most energetically the injustices they witness. But in exposing the deep causes of these injustices, they have had to confront the great economic and political forces of their countries. They naturally leave themselves open to being accused of meddling in affairs outside their competence and even of being friendly to Marxist ideas. Often this accusation is made, and vigorously, in conservative sectors, both Catholic and non-Catholic. Some of these bishops have become almost political personalities in their respective countries. The consequence has been tightened police vigilance and in some cases death threats on the part of groups of the extreme right.

But it is not just a question of isolated personalities. It is often entire conferences of bishops who openly take a position in this arena. We should also mention the efforts of many bishops to make changes—of varying degrees of radicalness—in Church structures. The results are still much below what is desired and necessary. The first steps do appear to have been taken, but the danger of retreat has not been eliminated, and, above all, there is much yet to be done.

In the majority of cases, options at the episcopal level regarding social transformation have been expressed in written statements, but there have also been cases in which these declarations have been accompanied by very concrete actions: direct intervention in workers' strikes, participation in public demonstrations, and so forth.

Statements and Attempts at Reflection

From these commitments on which we have commented briefly, there have emerged statements explaining them and outlining a theologico-pastoral reflection upon them.

    During the past three years there have appeared a great number of public statements by lay movements, groups of priests and bishops, or national conferences of bishops. As regards doctrinal authority and impact, the most important text we will mention is, of course, that of the Episcopal Conference at Medellín (1968). To a certain extent, the others can be ordered around it. But without these others, it would not be possible to grasp accurately the process which led to Medellín or the repercussions flowing from it. These other statements go beyond Medellín. Their options are clearer and less easily neutralized by the system. They are also closer to concrete commitments. Moreover, these statements express the sentiments of large sectors of the People of God. It is a somewhat muffled voice which still does not actually arise from the oppressed—condemned as they have been to a long silence except through many filters. It is, however, a first attempt at speaking out.

    From the point of view of the issues being discussed here, we can classify these texts into two necessarily related themes: the transformation of the Latin American reality and the search for new forms of the Church's presence on the contemporary scene.

Towards a Transformation of the Latin American Reality   One unifying theme which is present throughout these documents and which reflects a general attitude of the Church is the acknowledgment of the *solidarity of the Church* with the Latin American reality. The Church avoids placing itself above this reality, but rather attempts to assume its responsibility for the injustice which it has supported both by its links with the established order as well as by its silence regarding the evils this order implies. "We recognize that we Christians for want of fidelity to the Gospel have contributed to the present unjust situation through our words and attitudes, our silence and inaction," claim the Peruvian bishops. More than two hundred lay persons, priests, and bishops of El Salvador assert that "our Church has not been effective in liberating and bettering the Salvadoran. This failure is due in part to the above-mentioned incomplete concept of human salvation and the mission of the Church and in part to the fear of losing privileges or suffering persecution."

    As for the bishops' vision of reality, they describe the misery and the exploitation in Latin America as "a situation of injustice that can be called institutionalized violence"; it is responsible for the death of thousands of innocent victims. This view allows for a study of the complex problems of counterviolence without falling into the pitfalls of a double standard which assumes that violence is acceptable when the oppressor uses it to maintain "order" and is bad when the oppressed invoke it to change this "order." Institutionalized violence violates fundamental rights so patently that the Latin American bishops warn that "one should not abuse the patience of a people that for years has borne a situation that would not be acceptable to anyone with any degree of awareness of human rights." An important part of the Latin American clergy request, moreover, that "in considering the problem of violence in Latin America, let us by all means avoid equating the *unjust violence* of the oppressors (who maintain this despicable system) with the *just violence* of the oppressed (who feel obliged to use it to achieve their liberation)." Theologically, this situation of injustice and oppression is characterized as a "sinful situation" because "where this social peace does not exist, there we will find social, political, economic, and cultural inequalities, there we will find the rejection of the peace of the Lord, and a rejection of the Lord Himself." With this in mind, an important group of priests declared, "We feel we have a right and a duty to condemn unfair wages, exploitation, and starvation tactics as clear indications of sin and evil."

The reality so described is perceived ever more clearly as resulting from a situation of dependence, in which the centers of decision-making are to be found outside the continent; it follows that the Latin American countries are being kept in a condition of neocolonialism. It has been asserted that underdevelopment "can be understood only in terms of the *dependency relationship* with the developed world that it results from. In large measure the underdevelopment of Latin America is a *byproduct* of capitalist development in the West." The interpretation of Latin American reality in terms of dependency is adopted and considered valid "insofar as it allows us to seek a causal explanation, to denounce domination, and to struggle to overcome it with a commitment to liberation which will produce a new society." This perspective is also clearly adopted by a seminar on the problems of youth sponsored by the Education Department of the Latin American Episcopal Council. It stresses that "Latin American dependency is not only economic and political but also cultural."

Indeed, in texts of the Latin American Church of varying origins and degrees of authority, in the last few years there has been a significant although perhaps not completely coherent replacement of the theme of *development* by the theme of *liberation*. Both the term and the idea express the aspirations to be free from a situation of dependence; the "Message of the Bishops of the Third World" states that "an irresistible impulse drives these people on to better themselves and to free themselves from the forces of oppression." In the words of 120 Bolivian priests: "We observe in our people a desire for liberation and a movement of struggle for justice, not only to obtain a better standard of living, but also to be able to participate in the socio-economic resources and the decision-making process of the country." . . .

A New Presence of the Church in Latin America

A call to struggle against oppressive structures and to construct a more just society would have very little impact, however, if the whole Church did not rise to the level of these demands by means of a profound revision of its presence in Latin America.

A) The first evidence of this revision which can be culled from the texts mentioned is that, having acknowledged the Church's responsibility in the current situation, they strongly insist that the Church and in particular the bishops fulfill a role of *prophetic denunciation* of these grave injustices rampant in Latin America, which have already been characterized as "sinful situations." The bishops at Medellín asserted, "To us, the Pastors of the Church, belongs the duty . . . to denounce everything which, opposing justice, destroys peace." They are moved to make this denunciation by the "duty of solidarity with the poor, to which charity leads us. This solidarity means that we make ours their problems and their struggles, that we know how to speak with them. This has to be concretized in criticism of injustice and oppression, in the struggle against the intolerable situation which a poor person has to tolerate." Even further, the bishops are asked to go "beyond statements about situations . . . to concentrate on concrete events, and . . . to take positions regarding them." The Peruvian bishops commit themselves to denounce injustice, supporting these denunciations, if necessary, "by concrete gestures of solidarity with the poor and the oppressed." Aware of the difficulties which this solidarity with the poor may bring to those who practice it, the bishops assembled in Medellín declared: "We express our desire to be very close always to those who work in the self-denying apostolate with the poor in order that they will always feel our encouragement and know that we will not listen to parties interested in distorting their work." There is likewise an awareness of the political implications of these actions and of the criticisms which arise from certain sectors: "No one should be intimidated," say the Mexican bishops, "by those who—apparently zealous to preserve the 'purity' and 'dignity' of priestly and religious activity—characterize this intervention of the Church as 'political.' Frequently this false zeal veils the desire to impose a law of silence when the real need is to lend a voice to those who suffer injustice and to develop the social and political responsibility of the People of God."

The denunciation of social injustices is certainly the prevailing theme in the texts of the Latin American Church. This denunciation is a manner of expressing the intention of becoming disassociated from the existing unjust order. "When a system ceases to promote the common good and favors special interests, the Church must not only denounce injustice but also break with the evil system." The denunciation of injustice implies the rejection of the use of Christianity to legitimize the established order. It likewise implies, in fact, that the Church has entered into conflict with those who wield power. And finally it leads to acknowledging the need for the separation of Church and state because "this is of primary importance in liberating the Church from temporal ties and from the image projected by its bonds with the powerful. This separation will free the Church from compromising commitments and make it more able to speak out. It will show that in order to fulfill its mission, the Church relies more on the strength of the Lord than on the strength of Power. And the Church will be able to establish . . . the only earthly ties which it should have: communion with the disinherited of our country, with their concerns and struggles."

The prophetic task of the Church is both constructive and critical and is exercised in the midst of a process of change: "The prophetic task of justice demands, on the one hand, that the Church point out those elements within a revolutionary process which are truly humanizing and encourage the determined, dynamic, and creative participation of its members in this process. On the other hand, the Church must point out the dehumanizing elements also to be found in a process of change. But this function is not appropriate if the creative participation of the Christian community within the society has not already occurred. The Cuban Church is called to this twofold task within our revolution."

B) A second thematic line in the texts we have examined is the urgent need for a *conscienticizing evangelization*. "To us, the Pastors of the Church, belongs the duty to educate the Christian conscience, to inspire, stimulate, and help orient all of the initiatives that contribute to the formation of man," asserted the bishops at Medellín. This awareness of being oppressed but nevertheless of being masters of their own destiny is nothing other than a consequence of a well-understood evangelization: "As we see it, a perhaps faulty presentation of the Christian message may have given the impression that religion is indeed the opiate of the people. And we would be guilty of betraying the cause of Peru's development, if we did not stress the fact that the doctrinal riches of the gospel contain a revolutionary thrust." Indeed, "the God whom we know in the Bible is a liberating God, a God who destroys myths and alienations, a God who intervenes in history in order to break down the structures of injustice and who raises up prophets in order to point out the way of justice and mercy. He is the God who liberates slaves (Exodus), who causes empires to fall and raises up the oppressed." The whole climate of the gospel is a continual demand for the right of the poor to make themselves heard, to be considered preferentially by society, a demand to subordinate economic needs to those of the deprived. Was not Christ's first preaching to "proclaim the liberation of the oppressed?" The content of the message itself, the process of liberation in Latin America, and the demands for participation on the part of the people, all determine "the priority of a conscienticizing evangelization. This evangelization will free, humanize, and better man . . . and will be nourished by the recovery of a living faith committed to human society." The same idea appears in another important text: "In Latin America today evangelization in the context of the youth movements is closely linked to conscientization—insofar as this is understood as an analysis of reality which has Christ as its center and which seeks the liberation of the person." At Medellín the bishops have resolved "to be certain that our preaching, liturgy, and catechesis take into account the social and community dimension of Christianity, forming men committed to world peace." Others point out that this conscienticizing evangelization is a form of "service and commitment to the poorest; evangelizing action ought to be directed preferentially to this group, not only because of the need to understand their life, but also to help them become aware of their own mission, by cooperating in their liberation and development." It is then to the oppressed that the Church should address itself and not so much to the oppressors; furthermore, this action will give true meaning to the Church's witness to poverty. "Poverty in the Church will only be truly achieved when the Church focuses on the evangelization of the oppressed as its primary duty."

C) *Poverty* is, indeed, one of the most frequent and pressing demands placed on the Latin American Church. Vatican II asserts that the Church ought to carry out its mission as Christ did "in poverty and under oppression" (*Lumen gentium*, no. 8). This is not the image given by the Latin American Christian community as a whole. Rather, poverty is an area in which countersigns are rampant: "Instead of talking about the Church of the poor, we must be a poor Church. And we flaunt this commitment with our real estate, our rectories and other buildings, and our whole style of life." At Medellín it was made clear that poverty expresses solidarity with the oppressed and a protest against oppression. Suggested ways of implementing this poverty in the Church are the evangelization of the poor, the denunciation of injustice, a simple lifestyle, a spirit of service, and freedom from temporal ties, intrigue, or ambiguous prestige.

D) The demands placed on the Church by prophetic denunciation, by the conscienticizing evangelization of the oppressed, and by poverty sharply reveal the *inadequacy of the structures of the Church* for the world in which it lives. These structures appear obsolete and lacking in dynamism before the new and serious challenges. "The very structures in which we operate," says a group of Bolivian priests, "often prevent us from acting in a manner that accords with the gospel. This, too, deeply concerns us; for we see that it greatly complicates the chances of bringing the gospel to the people. The Church cannot be a prophet in our day if she herself is not turned to Christ. She does not have the right to talk against others when she herself is a cause of scandal in her interpersonal relations and her internal structures." There arises, therefore, the urgent need for a profound renewal of the present ecclesial structures. It is the opinion of lay movement representatives that "pastoral structures are insufficient and inadequate. The overall pastoral structure must be reworked if it is to be adequate to the sociological situation in which it is to be carried out." This has been the sense of the seminal effort at Medellín; its implementation is urgent.

E) "The profound changes in Latin America today necessarily affect the priest in his ministry and in his lifestyle," assert the Latin American bishops. The need to change the current *lifestyle of the clergy* is to be considered in this light, especially regarding its commitment to the creation of a new society. Although the denunciation of injustice has political overtones, it is first of all a fundamental demand of the gospel, since it concerns, according to a group of Argentinian priests, "the great option of human beings for their rights, their freedom, and their personal dignity as offspring of God. Moreover, we feel that if we did not denounce injustice we would be responsible for and accessory to the injustices being committed. The exercise of our ministry inevitably leads us to commitment and solidarity." There is need for change also with regard to ways of earning a living: "New ways must be found to support the clergy. Those who do not wish to live on stipends or from teaching religion should be allowed to experiment. . . . A secular job could be very healthy: they would find themselves in the real human world (*Presbyterorum ordinis*, no. 8); it would lessen the temptation to servility on the part of those who depend totally on the clerical institution; it would likewise diminish the financial problems of the institutional Church. It would give a great deal more independence from the government and the armed forces; and finally it would contribute in many of us to the development of a strong apostolic vocation disengaged from all unhealthy ties." Changes are also urged regarding greater participation of lay persons, religious, and priests in the pastoral decisions of the Church.

The documents produced by various sectors of the Latin American Church over the last several years are especially abundant and worthy of a more complete and detailed technical analysis. . . . The issues discussed are markedly different from those being dealt with up to a short time ago. Moreover, in the approach to the problems there is apparent a *growing radicalization*. Although there is still a long road ahead, positions are being taken which are no longer so ambiguous or naive. There is a new attitude—ever more lucid and demanding— suggestive of a qualitatively different society and of basically new forms of the Church's presence in it.

Bibliography

Atkinson, Clarissa W., Constance H. Buchanan, and Margaret R. Miles, eds. *Immaculate and Powerful: The Female in Sacred Image and Social Reality*. Boston: Beacon Press, 1985.

———. *Shaping New Vision: Gender and Values in American Culture*. Ann Arbor, Mich.: University of Michigan Research Press, 1987.

Augustine, Saint. *The City of God*. New York: Random House, 1950.

Aykara, Thomas, ed. "Feminine Aspect of God." *Journal of Dharma* 5 (April–June 1980): 127–211.

Bachofen, J. J. *Myth, Religion and Mother Right*. Princeton, N.J.: Princeton University Press, 1967.

Barrett, Leonard E. *Soul-Force: African Heritage in Afro-American Religion*. Garden City, N.Y.: Anchor Press, 1974.

Barth, Karl. *The Church and the Political Problem of Our Day*. New York: Scribner's, 1939.

Bennett, Anne McGrew. *From Woman-Pain to Woman-Vision: Writings in Feminist Theology*. Edited by Mary E. Hunt. Minneapolis, Minn.: Fortress Press, 1989.

Berryman, Phillip. *Liberation Theology: Essential Facts about the Revolutionary Movement in Latin America—and Beyond*. Philadelphia: Temple University Press, 1987.

Blau, Joseph. *Cornerstones of Religious Freedom in America*. Boston: Beacon Press, 1949.

Bohannan, Paul. *A Source Notebook on Tiv Religion*. New Haven, Conn.: Human Relations Area Files, 1969.

Broughton, John M. "Women's Rationality and Men's Virtues: A Critique of Gender Dualism in Gilligan's Theory of Moral Development." *Social Research* 50 (August 1983): 597–642.

Brown, Harold O. J. *What Is Liberation Theology?* Edited by R. Nash. Maryknoll, N.Y.: Orbis Books, 1981.

Budapest, Z. *The Holy Book of Women's Mysteries*, parts 1 and 2. Los Angeles: Susan B. Anthony Coven, 1979, 1980.

Buxton, Jean Carlisle. *Religion and Healing in Mandari*. Oxford: Clarendon Press, 1973.

Cady, Susan, Marian Ronan, and Hal Toussig. *Sophia: The Future of Feminist Spirituality*. San Francisco: Harper and Row, 1986.

Calvin, John. *God and Political Duty*. New York: Liberal Arts Press, 1950.

Childs, John Brown. *The Political Black Minister: A Study in Afro-American Politics and Religion*. Boston: Hall, 1980.

Christ, Carol. "Why Women Need the Goddess: Phenomenological, Psychological and Political Reflections." In *Womanspirit Rising: A Feminist Reader in Religion*, edited by Carol Christ and Judith Plaskow, 273–87. San Francisco: Harper and Row, 1979.

Cone, James H. *A Black Theology of Liberation*. Philadelphia: Lippincott, 1970.

———. *For My People: Black Theology and the Black Church*. Maryknoll, N.Y.: Orbis Books, 1984.

———. *Speaking the Truth: Ecumenism, Liberation, and Black Theology*. Grand Rapids, Mich.: Eerdmans, 1986.

Cox, Harvey. *The Secular City*. New York: Macmillan, 1969.

Daly, Mary. *Beyond God the Father: Toward a Philosophy of Women's Liberation*. Boston: Beacon Press, 1973.

———. *The Church and the Second Sex*. Boston: Beacon Press, 1985.

Dart, John. "Balancing out the Trinity: The Genders of the Godhead." *Christian Century* 100 (February 16–23, 1983): 147–50.

Fiorenza, Elizabeth. *In Memory of Her: A Feminist Theological Reconstruction of Christian Origins*. New York: Crossroads, 1983.

———. "Commitment and Critical Inquiry." *Harvard Theological Review* 82 (1989): 1–11.

Garcia, Ismael. *Justice in Latin American Theology of Liberation*. Atlanta: Knox Press, 1987.

Gardiner, James J., and J. Deotis Roberts, eds. *Quest for a Black Theology*. Philadelphia: Pilgrim Press, 1971.

Gleason, Judith Illsley. *Oya: In Praise of the Goddess*. Boston: Shambhala; New York: Random House, 1987.

Goldenberg, Naomi. "Women and the Image of God: A Psychological Perspective on the Feminist Movement in Religion." *International Journal of Women's Studies* 1 (1978): 468–74.

———. *Changing of the Gods*. Boston: Beacon Press, 1979.

Grant, Jacquelyn. *White Women's Christ and Black Women's Jesus: Feminist Christology and Womanist Response*. Atlanta, Ga.: Scholars Press, 1989.

Graves, Robert. *The White Goddess: A Historical Grammar of Poetic Myth*. New York: Octagon, 1972.

Hacker, Helen. *Toward a Feminist Reformation of Biblical Religion*. Garden City, N.Y.: Adelphi University, 1984.

Hampson, Daphne. "The Challenge of Feminism to Christianity." *Theology* 88 (September 1985): 341–50.

Harenberg, Werner. *Der Spiegel on the New Testament*. New York: Macmillan, 1970.

Healy, Margaret I. "Mary, Seat of Wisdom: Reflection on the Femininity of God." In *Mary According to Women*, edited by C. Jegen, 1985, 33–50.

Heine, Suzanne. *Christianity and the Goddesses: Systematic Criticism of a Feminist Theology*. London: Student Christian Movement, 1988.

Hennelly, Alfred T. "The Theology of Liberation: Origins, Content, and Impact." *Thought* 63 (1988): 147–61.

Hobbes, Thomas. *Leviathan.* Oxford: Clarendon Press, 1909.

Holden, Pat. *Women's Religious Experience.* London: Croom Helm; Totowa, N.J.: Barnes and Noble, 1983.

Holloway, Joseph E., ed. *Africanisms in American Culture.* Bloomington: Indiana University Press, 1990.

Hopkins, Dwight N. *Black Theology USA and South Africa: Politics, Culture, and Liberation.* Maryknoll, N.Y.: Orbis Books, 1989.

Hurtado, Larry W., ed. *Goddesses in Religions and Modern Debate.* Atlanta, Ga.: Scholars Press, 1990.

Idowu, E. Bolaji. *African Traditional Religion: A Definition.* Maryknoll, N.Y.: Orbis Books, 1973.

James, E. O. *The Cult of the Mother Goddess: An Anthropological and Documentary Study.* New York: Barnes and Noble, 1959.

Jones, Major J. *Black Awareness, a Theology of Hope.* Nashville, Tenn.: Abingdon Press, 1971.

———. *The Color of God: The Concept of God in Afro-American Thought.* Macon, Ga.: Mercer, 1987.

Jones, William Ronald. *Is God a White Racist? A Preamble to Black Theology.* Garden City, N.Y.: Anchor Press, 1973.

King, Noel Quinton. *African Cosmos: An Introduction to Religion in Africa.* Belmont, Calif.: Wadsworth, 1986.

Kinsley, David R. *The Goddesses' Mirror: Visions of the Divine from East and West.* Albany: State University of New York Press, 1989.

Lavaud, B. "Toward a Theology of Woman." *Thomist* 2 (October 1940): 459–518.

LeFevre, Perry D. "Liberation Theology: Feminist." *CTS Register* 72 (Spring 1982): 33–39.

Leo XIII, Pope. "Encyclical on the Constitution of States." In *The Great Encyclical Letters of Pope Leo XIII.* New York: Benzinger, 1903.

Little, Joyce A. "Mary and Feminist Theology." *Thought* 62 (1987): 343–57.

Livingston, James C. *Modern Christian Thought: From the Enlightenment to Vatican II.* New York: Macmillan, 1971.

Loades, Ann. *Feminist Theology: A Reader.* Louisville, Ky.: Westminster/Knox Press, 1990.

Macquarrie, John. *Twentieth-Century Religious Thought.* New York: Harper and Row, 1963.

Maguire, Daniel. *The Mermaid and the Minotaur: Sexual Arrangements and Human Malaise.* New York: Harper and Row, 1976.

Mahan, Brian, and L. Dale Richesin, ed. *The Challenge of Liberation Theology.* Maryknoll, N.Y.: Orbis Books, 1981.

Maloney, Thomas J. "The Catholic Social Justice Tradition and Liberation Theology." *Thought* 63 (1988): 125–46.

Maritain, Jacques. *Christianity and Democracy.* London: Bles, 1945.

Marty, Martin E., and Dean G. Peerman, eds. *New Theology.* New York: Macmillan, 1964.

Mbiti, John S. *An Introduction to African Religion.* New York: Praeger, 1974.

McFague, Sallie. *Metaphorical Theology: Models of God in Religious Language.* Philadelphia: Fortress, 1982.

Meyer, Fortes. *Religion, Morality, and the Person: Essays on Tallensi Religion.* Edited by Jack Goody. Cambridge: Cambridge University Press, 1987.

Middleton, John. *Lugbara Religion.* Washington, D.C.: Smithsonian Institution Press, 1987.

Miller, John W. "In Defense of Monotheistic Father Religion." *Journal of Religion and Health* 21 (Spring 1982): 62–67.

Milton, John. *Areopagitica.* New York: Macmillan, 1927.

Murray, Margaret. *The Witch Cult in Western Europe.* London: Oxford University Press, 1921.

———. *God of the Witches.* 2d ed. London: Oxford University Press, 1952.

Muzorewa, Gwinyai H. *The Origins and Development of African Theology.* Maryknoll, N.Y.: Orbis Books, 1985.

Newman, Richard. *Black Power and Black Religion: Essays and Reviews.* West Cornwall, Conn.: Locust Hill Press, 1987.

Novak, Michael. "Liberation Theology in Practice." *Thought* 59 (1984): 136–48.

———. *Will It Liberate?: Questions about Liberation Theology.* Wisconsin: Madison Books, 1991.

Obiego, Cosmas Okechukwu. *African Image of the Ultimate Reality: An Analysis of Igbo Ideas of Life and Death in Relation to Chukwu-God.* New York: Lang, 1984.

Ochshorn, Judith. *The Female Experience and the Nature of the Divine.* Bloomington: Indiana University Press, 1980.

Paris, Arthur E. *Black Pentecostalism: Southern Religion in an Urban World.* Amherst: University of Massachusetts Press, 1982.

Parrinder, Edward Geoffrey. *West African Religion, a Study of the Beliefs and Practices of Akan, Ewe, Yoruba, Ibo, and Kindred Peoples.* New York: Barnes and Noble, 1970.

———. *African Traditional Religion.* 3d ed. London: Sheldon Press, 1974.

Pero, Albert, and Ambrose Moyo, ed. *Theology and the Black Experience: The Lutheran Heritage Interpreted by African and African-American Theologians.* Minneapolis, Minn.: Augsburg, 1988.

Petersen, Kirsten Holst, ed. *Religion, Development, and African Identity.* Uppsala: Almquist and Wiksell, 1987.

Pfeffer, Leo. *Church, State, and Freedom.* Boston: Beacon Press, 1953.

Plaskow, Judith. *Sex, Sin and Grace: Women's Experience and the Theologies of Reinhold Niebuhr and Paul Tillich.* Washington, D.C.: University Press of America, 1980.

Plaskow, Judith, and Carol P. Christ. *Weaving the Visions: New Patterns in Feminist Spirituality.* New York: Harper and Row, 1989.

———. *Women and Judaism.* New York: Harper Collins, 1991.

Pobee, J. S. *Toward an African Theology.* Nashville, Tenn.: Abingdon, 1979.

Raphael, Patai. *The Hebrew Goddess.* Philadelphia: Ktav, 1967.

Richardson, Marilyn. *Black Women and Religion: A Bibliography.* Boston: Hall, 1980.

Roberts, J. Deotis. *Black Theology in Dialogue.* Philadelphia: Westminster Press, 1987.

Robinson, John A. T. *Honest to God.* Philadelphia: Westminster Press, 1963.

Ross, Isabel. *Margaret Fell: Mother of Quakerism.* London: Longmans, Green, 1949.

Rowbotham, Sheila. *Women, Resistance and Revolution: A History of Women and Revolution in the Modern World.* New York: Random House, 1974.

Ruether, Rosemary Radford. *Sexism and God-Talk: Toward a Feminist Theology.* Boston: Beacon Press, 1983.

———. *Womanguides: Texts for Doing Feminist Theology.* Boston: Beacon Press, 1985.

———. *Women-Church: Theology and Practice of Feminist Liturgical Communities.* San Francisco: Harper and Row, 1985.

———, ed. *Religion and Sexism: Images of Women in the Jewish and Christian Traditions.* New York: Simon and Schuster, 1974.

Schall, James V. *Liberation Theology in Latin America.* San Francisco: Ignatius Press, 1982.

Schillebeeckx, Edward, and Johannes B. Metz. "God as Father." *Concilium* 143 (1981).

Starhawk. *The Spiral Dance: The Rebirth of the Ancient Religion of the Goddess.* New York: Harper and Row, 1979.

Stokes, Anson Phelps. *Church and State in the United States.* 3 vols. New York: Harper, 1950.

Suchocki, Marie. "A Servant Office: The Ordination of Women." *Religion and Life* 47 (1978): 197–210.

Tamez, Elsa, ed. *Through Her Eyes: Women's Theology from Latin America.* Maryknoll, N.Y.: Orbis Books, 1989.

Trible, Phyllis. *God and the Rhetoric of Sexuality.* Philadelphia: Fortress, 1978.

van Binsbergen, Wim, and Matthew Schoffeleers, eds. *Theoretical Explorations in African Religion.* London: Kegan Paul, 1985.

Washington, Joseph R. *Black Sects and Cults.* Garden City, N.Y.: Doubleday, 1972.

———. *Black Religion: The Negro and Christianity in the United States.* Lanham, Md.: University Press of America, 1984.

Weaver, Mary Jo. "Who Is the Goddess and Where Does She Get Us?" *Journal of Feminist Studies in Religion* 5 (1989): 49–64.

Weidman, Judith L. *Women Ministers.* New York: Harper and Row, 1981.

Wilmore, Gayraud S. *Black Religion and Black Radicalism.* Garden City, N.Y.: Doubleday, 1972.

Witvliet, Theo. *A Place in the Sun: Liberation Theology in the Third World.* Maryknoll, N.Y.: Orbis Books, 1985.

———. *Religion and Change in African Societies.* Edinburgh: Centre of African Studies, University of Edinburgh, 1979.

Bibliography

Abernethy, George L., and Thomas A. Langford, eds. *Philosophy of Religion: A Book of Readings.* 2d ed. New York: Macmillan, 1968.

Alston, W. P. *Religious Belief and Philosophical Thought.* New York: Harcourt, Brace and World, 1963.

Ayer, A. J. *Language, Truth and Logic.* London: Gollancz, 1946.

Bambrough, Renford. *Reason, Truth and God.* London: Methuen, 1969.

Britton, Karl. *Philosophy and Meaning of Life.* Cambridge: Cambridge University Press, 1969.

Brody, Baruch A., ed. *Readings in the Philosophy of Religion.* Englewood Cliffs, N.J.: Prentice-Hall, 1974.

Bronstein, D. J., and H. M. Schulweis. *Approaches to the Philosophy of Religion.* Englewood Cliffs, N.J.: Prentice-Hall, 1954.

Cahn, Steven M. *Philosophy of Religion.* New York: Harper and Row, 1970.

Cahn, Steven M., and David Shatz, eds. *Contemporary Philosophy of Religion.* New York: Oxford University Press, 1982.

Campbell, C. A. *On Selfhood and Godhood.* London: Allen and Unwin, 1957.

Christian, W. *Meaning and Truth in Religion.* Princeton, N.J.: Princeton University Press, 1964.

Davies, Brian. *An Introduction to the Philosophy of Religion.* Oxford: Oxford University Press, 1982.

Diamond, Malcolm L., and Thomas V. Litzenburg, Jr. *The Logic of God.* Indianapolis, Ind.: Bobbs-Merrill, 1975.

Donnelly, J. *Logical Analysis and Contemporary Theism.* New York: Fordham University Press, 1972.

Ducasse, C. J. *A Philosophical Scrutiny of Religion.* New York: Ronald Press, 1953.

Edwards, Rem B. *Reason and Religion.* New York: Harcourt Brace Jovanovich, 1979.

Ferré, Frederick. *Language, Logic and God.* New York: Harper and Row, 1961.

———. *Basic Modern Philosophy of Religion.* New York: Scribner's, 1967.

Ferré, Frederick, Joseph J. Kockelmans, and John E. Smith. *The Challenge of Religion: Contemporary Readings in Philosophy of Religion.* New York: Seabury Press, 1982.

Flew, Antony. *God and Philosophy.* New York: Harcourt Brace Jovanovich, 1966.

Flew, Antony, and Alasdair MacIntyre, eds. *New Essays in Philosophical Theology*. London: Student Christian Movement; New York: Macmillan, 1955.

Geach, P. T. *God and the Soul*. London: Routledge and Kegan Paul, 1969.

Geisler, Norman L. *Philosophy of Religion*. Grand Rapids, Mich.: Zondervan, 1974.

Hartshorne, Charles, and William I. Reese, eds. *Philosophers Speak of God*. Chicago: University of Chicago Press, 1953.

Hegel, Georg W. *Lectures on the Philosophy of Religion*. London: Paul, Trench, Trübner, 1895.

Hepburn, R. W. *Christianity and Paradox*. London: Watts, 1958.

Hick, John. *Philosophy of Religion*. London: Prentice-Hall, 1963.

———. *An Interpretation of Religion: Human Responses to the Transcendent*. New Haven, Conn.: Yale University Press, 1989.

———, ed. *The Existence of God*. New York: Macmillan, 1964.

———. *Faith and the Philosopher*. London: Macmillan, 1964.

Hocking, William Ernest. *The Meaning of God in Human Experience: A Philosophic Study of Religion*. New Haven, Conn.: Yale University Press, 1928.

Hook, S., ed. *Religious Experience and Truth*. New York: New York University Press, 1961.

Kant, Immanuel. *Religion within the Limits of Reason Alone*. Chicago: Open Court, 1934.

Kaufmann, Walter. *Critique of Religion and Philosophy*. New York: Harper and Row, 1958.

Kenny, Anthony. *The God of the Philosophers*. Oxford: Clarendon Press, 1979.

King-Farlow, John, ed. *The Challenge of Religion Today: Essays on the Philosophy of Religion*. New York: Science History Publications, 1976.

Lessa, W., and E. Vogt, eds. *Reader in Comparative Religion*. New York: Harper and Row, 1958.

Lewis, H. D. *Our Experience of God*. London: Allen and Unwin, 1959.

MacIntyre, Alasdair. *Difficulties in Christian Belief*. London: Student Christian Movement, 1959.

Mackie, J. L. *The Miracle of Theism: Arguments for and against the Existence of God*. Oxford: Clarendon Press, 1982.

Martin, C. B. *Religious Belief*. New York: Cornell, 1959.

Matson, Wallace I. *The Existence of God*. Ithaca, N.Y.: Cornell University Press, 1965.

Mavrodes, George I. *The Rationality of Belief in God*. Englewood Cliffs, N.J.: Prentice-Hall, 1970.

Mavrodes, George I., and Stuart C. Hacket, eds. *Problems and Perspectives in the Philosophy of Religion*. Boston: Allyn and Bacon, 1967.

Maynell, H. "Truth and Witchcraft." *Bulletin of Philosophy* 36 (1910): 392–98.

McPherson, T. *Philosophy of Religion*. London: Van Nostrand, 1965.

Miller, Ed. L. *God and Reason*. New York: Macmillan, 1972.

———, ed. *Classical Statements on Faith and Reason*. New York: Random House, 1970.

Mitchell, Basil. *The Philosophy of Religion*. London: Oxford University Press, 1971.

———, ed. *Faith and Logic: Oxford Essays in Philosophical Theology*. London: Allen and Unwin, 1957.

Mitchell, Basil, ed. *The Philosophy of Religion* (Oxford Readings in Philosophy). London: Oxford University Press, 1971.

Munson, Thomas N. *Reflective Theology: Philosophical Orientations in Religion*. New Haven, Conn.: Yale University Press, 1968.

Nielsen, Kai. *An Introduction to the Philosophy of Religion.* London: Macmillan, 1982.

Owen, Huw Parri. *Christian Theism: A Study in Basic Principles.* Edinburgh: Clark, 1984.

Penelhum, Terence. *Religion and Rationality: An Introduction to the Philosophy of Religion.* New York: Random House, 1971.

Plantinga, Alvin, ed. *Faith and Philosophy.* Grand Rapids, Mich.: Eerdmans, 1964.

Purtill, Richard L. *Reason to Believe.* Grand Rapids, Mich.: Eerdmans, 1974.

Radhakrishnan, S. *East and West in Religion.* London: Allen and Unwin, 1958.

Ross, James. *Philosophical Theology.* Indianapolis, Ind.: Hackett, 1969.

Rowe, William L. *Philosophy of Religion; An Introduction.* Belmont, Calif.: Wadsworth, 1978.

Rowe, William L., and William J. Wainwright, eds. *Philosophy of Religion: Selected Readings.* New York: Harcourt Brace Jovanovich, 1973.

Stewart, David. *Exploring the Philosophy of Religion.* Englewood Cliffs, N.J.: Prentice-Hall, 1980.

Swinburne, Richard. *The Existence of God.* Oxford: Clarendon Press, 1979.

Thomas, George F. *Philosophy and Religious Belief.* New York: Scribner's, 1970.

Wainwright, William J. *Philosophy of Religion.* Belmont, Calif.: Wadsworth, 1988.

Wells, Donald A. *God, Man and the Thinker: Philosophies of Religion.* New York: Random House, 1962.

Yandell, Keith E. *Basic Issues in the Philosophy of Religion.* Boston: Allyn and Bacon, 1971.

———. *Christianity and Philosophy.* Grand Rapids, Mich.: Eerdmans, 1984.

———, ed. *God, Man and Religion.* New York: McGraw-Hill, 1973.

Note on the Editor

Dr. Burton F. Porter received his undergraduate education in philosophy at the University of Maryland and did his graduate studies in philosophy at St. Andrews University, Scotland, and Oxford University, England. During his academic career, he has taught at several universities, including the University of Maryland, European Division in London, and Drexel University in Philadelphia. At present he holds the position of dean of arts and sciences at Western New England College.

Dr. Porter's previous publications include *Reasons for Living, a Basic Ethics* (Macmillan, 1988); *The Good Life, Alternatives in Ethics* (Macmillan, 1980, and Ardsley House, 1991); *Philosophy, a Literary and Conceptual Approach* (Harcourt Brace Jovanovich, 1976, rev. ed. 1980); *Personal Philosophy, Perspectives on Living* (Harcourt Brace Jovanovich, 1974); and *Deity and Morality* (Allen and Unwin, and Humanities Press, 1968).

Acknowledgments (continued from copyright page)

1. William Howells: From *The Heathens* by William Howells. Copyright 1948 by William Howells. Used by permission of Doubleday, a division of Bantam Doubleday Dell Publishing Group, Inc.

2. E. E. Evans-Pritchard: Reprinted from *Witchcraft, Oracles, and Magic among the Azande* by E. E. Evans-Pritchard (1937) by permission of Oxford University Press.

3. Bronislaw Malinowski: "Magic" from "Culture" by Bronislaw Malinowski. Reprinted with permission of Macmillan Publishing Company from *Encyclopaedia of the Social Sciences*, Edwin R. A. Seligman, editor in chief., Vol. IV, pp. 634–639. Copyright 1931, and renewed 1959, by Macmillan Publishing Company.

4. Clifford Geertz: "Religion as a Cultural System" from *Anthropological Approaches to the Study of Religion*, ed. Michael Banton, London: Tavistock Publications. Reprinted by permission.

5. Ninian Smart: Reprinted with the permission of Macmillan Publishing Company from *World Views: Cross Cultural Explorations of Human Beliefs*, by Ninian Smart. Copyright © 1983 Charles Scribner's Sons.

6. Rudolph Bultmann: From *New Testament and Mythology* by Rudolph Bultmann, London: The Society for Promoting Christian Knowledge. Reprinted by permission.

7. H. J. McCloskey: "The Nature and Attributes of God" in *God and Evil*, Chapter 4, four pages. Reprinted by permission of Kluwer Academic Publishers.

8. Charles Hartshorne: Reprinted from *Omnipotence and Other Mistakes* by Charles Hartshorne by permission of the State University of New York Press.

9. Mordecai Kaplan: "The Changing Conception of God" by Mordecai Kaplan in *The Meaning of God in Modern Jewish Religion*, 1947. Reprinted by permission.

10. Mircea Eliade: *A History of Religious Ideas* by Mircea Eliade. Copyright © 1982, pp. 91–106. Reprinted by permission of the University of Chicago Press.

11. T. M. P. Mahadevan: With the permission of Chetana Pvt. Ltd., 34 Rampart Row, Bombay 400 023, India, publishers of "Outlines of Hinduism" by T. M. P. Mahadevan.

12. Huston Smith: "Islam" from *The Religions of Man* by Huston Smith. Copyright © 1958 by Huston Smith. Reprinted by permission of HarperCollins Publishers.

13. Paul Tillich: *Christianity and the Encounter of the World Religions* by Paul Tillich, Columbia University Press, New York. Used by permission.

14. John Hick: Reprinted from *God Has Many Names*, by John Hick. Copyright © John Hick 1980, 1982. Reprinted by permission of Westminster/John Knox Press.

15. Saint Anselm: "Proslogion" by St. Anselm from *A Scholastic Miscellany: Anselm to Ockham*, edited and translated by Eugene R. Fairweather (Volume X: The Library of Christian Classics). First published in MCMLV by SCM Press Ltd., London and the Westminster Press, Philadelphia. Used by permission of Westminster/John Knox Press.

16. René Descartes: "Meditations on First Philosophy" by René Descartes in *The Philosophical Works of Descartes*, Vol. I, translated by Haldane and Ross. Reprinted by permission of Cambridge University Press.

17. Immanuel Kant: Public domain.

18. Saint Thomas Aquinas: From *Summa Theologica* by Thomas Aquinas, (Mission Hills: Benziger Publishing Company). Reprinted by permission.

19. Richard Taylor: *Metaphysics*, 4e, by Richard Taylor. Copyright © 1992, pp. 99–108. Reprinted by permission of Prentice Hall, Englewood Cliffs, N.J.

20. William Paley: Public domain.

21. David Hume: Public domain.

22. Richard Swinburne: *The Existence of God* by Richard Swinburne. Reprinted by permission of Oxford University Press.

23. Blaise Pascal: *Pensées* by Blaise Pascal, translated by W. F. Trotter. Reproduced from the Everyman's Library Edition, 1932, with permission of David Campbell Publishers, Ltd.

24. William James: Public domain.

25. W. K. Clifford: Public domain.

26. William James: Public domain.

27. Rudolf Otto: *The Idea of the Holy* by Rudolf Otto. Translated by John W. Harvey. Reprinted by permission of Oxford University Press.

28. Bertrand Russell: *Religion and Science* by Bertrand Russell. Reprinted by permission of Oxford University Press.

29. Immanuel Kant: Reprinted with the permission of Macmillan Publishing Company from *Immanuel Kant: Critique of Practical Reason* by Lewis White Beck (translator). Copyright © 1956 by Macmillan Publishing Company.

30. A. E. Taylor: A. E. Taylor's "Does God Exist?" in *Does God Exist?* Copyright © 1947. Reprinted by permission of The Macmillan Press, Ltd.

31. John Stuart Mill: Reprinted with the permission of Bobbs-Merrill Company, an imprint of Macmillan Publishing Company, Inc., from *John Stuart Mill: Nature and the Utility of Religion* by George Nakhnikian (editor). Copyright © 1958 by Bobbs-Merrill Company.

32. John Hick: John Hick, *Philosophy of Religion*, 4e, © 1990, pp. 39–55. Reprinted by permission of Prentice Hall, Englewood Cliffs, New Jersey.

33. Moses Maimonides: Moses Maimonides, *Guide for the Perplexed*, New York: P. Shalom Publishers, 1969; translated by M. Friedlander. Reprinted by permission.

34. G. W. Leibniz: From the *Theodicy* by G. W. Leibniz, translated by E. M. Huggard. Reprinted by permission of Routledge Publishers.

35. David Hume: Public domain.

36. John Stuart Mill: Public domain.

37. Emil Brunner: *The Divine Imperative* by Emil Brunner; translated by Olive Wyon. Copyright © MCMXLVII W. L. Jenkins. Used by permission of Westminster/John Knox Press.

38. Kai Nielsen: "God and the Basis of Mortality" by Kai Nielsen. *The Journal of Religious Ethics*, Vol. 10, No. 2 (fall 1982): 335–350. Reprinted with permission of Religious Ethics, Incorporated.

39. David Hume: Public domain.

40. C. S. Lewis: *Miracles* by C. S. Lewis. Reprinted by permission of HarperCollins Publishers, London.

41. John Locke: Public domain.

42. Paul Tillich: Excerpt from *Dynamics of Faith* by Paul Tillich. Copyright © 1957 by Paul Tillich. Renewed 1985 by Hanna Tillich. Reprinted by permission of HarperCollins Publishers.

43. Jacques Maritain: Reprinted with the permission of Charles Scribner's Sons, an imprint of Macmillan Publishing Company from *The Range of Reason* by Jacques Maritain. Copyright 1952 by Jacques Maritain; copyright renewed © 1980 Evelin Garnier.

44. Miguel de Unamuno: Miguel de Unamuno's "The Tragic Sense of Life" in *The Tragic Sense of Life*. Copyright © 1921. Reprinted by permission of The Macmillan Press, Ltd.

45. Plato: Reprinted from *The Dialogues of Plato* translated by Benjamin Jowett (4th edition, 1953), Vol. I, by permission of Oxford University Press.

46. Joseph Campbell: From *The Masks of God: Oriental Mythology* by Joseph Campbell. Copyright © 1962 by Joseph Campbell, renewed copyright © 1990 by Jean Erdman Campbell. Used by permission of Viking Penguin, a division of Penguin Books U.S.A., Inc.

47. A. Seth Pringle-Pattison: Public domain.

48. George Santayana: George Santayana, *Ideal Mortality*. Reprinted by permission of the MIT Press.

49. Ludwig Feuerbach: Public domain.

50. Karl Marx: Public domain.

51. Freud: Reprinted from *The Future of an Illusion* by Sigmund Freud. Translated and edited by James Strachey. Reprinted by permission of W. W. Norton & Company, Inc. Copyright © 1961 by James Strachey. Copyright renewed 1989.

52. Albert Einstein: Public domain.

53. H. J. Paton: From *The Modern Predicament* by H. J. Paton. Reprinted by permission of Routledge Publishers and International Thomson Publishing Services Ltd.

54. A. J. Ayer: *Language, Truth and Logic* by A. J. Ayer. Reprinted by permission of Dover Publications, Inc.

55. Antony Flew, R. M. Hare, and Basil Mitchell: Reprinted with the permission of Macmillan Publishing Company from *New Essays in Philosophical Theology* by Antony Flew and Alastair MacIntyre. Copyright © 1955 and renewed 1983 by Antony Flew and Alastair MacIntyre.
56. Friedrich Nietzsche: From *The Portable Nietzsche* by Walter Kaufman. Copyright 1954 by The Viking Press, renewed © 1982 by Viking Penguin Inc. Used by permission of Viking Penguin, a division of Penguin Books U.S.A., Inc.
57. Søren Kierkegaard: Kierkegaard, Søren; *Fear and Trembling.* Translated by Walter Leuirie. Copyright © 1941 by Princeton University Press. Renewed 1969. Reprinted by permission of Princeton University Press.
58. Martin Buber: Reprinted with the permission of Charles Scribner's Sons, an imprint of Macmillan Publishing Company from *I and Thou* by Martin Buber, translated by Ronald Gregor Smith. Translation copyright © 1958 Charles Scribner's Sons; copyright renewed.
59. William Hamilton: *The New Essence of Christianity* by William Hamilton. Copyright © 1966 by Darton Longman & Todd Ltd. Reprinted by permission.
60. Joseph Fletcher: *Situation Ethics: The New Morality* by Joseph Fletcher. Copyright © MCMLXVI, W. L. Jenkins. Used by permission of Westminster/John Knox Press.
61. Corliss Lamont: *The Philosophy of Humanism* by Corliss Lamont. Copyright © 1965 by Corliss Lamont. Reprinted by permission of The Crossroad Publishing Company.
62. Erich Fromm: Erich Fromm, *Psychoanalysis and Religion.* Copyright © 1950. Reprinted by permission of Yale University Press.
63. Martin Luther King, Jr.: Excerpt from *The Trumpet of Consciousness* by Martin Luther King, Jr. Copyright © 1967 by Martin Luther King, Jr. Reprinted by permission of HarperCollins Publishers.
64. Desmond Mpilo Tutu: Taken from *Hope and Suffering: Sermons and Speeches* by Desmond Mpilo Tutu, copyright © 1983 by Desmond Mpilo Tutu. First published by Skotaville Publishers, Johannesburg, S.A., in 1983, and published in the United States in 1984 by William B. Eerdmans Publishing Company. Used by permission.
65. Rosemary Radford Reuther: Rosemary Radford Reuther, "The Female Nature of God," *Concilium* 163: 1981. Reprinted by permission.
66. Carol P. Christ: "Why Women Need the Goddess" from *Womanspirit Rising* by Carol P. Christ and Judith Plaskow. Copyright © 1979 by Carol P. Christ and Judith Plaskow. Reprinted by permission of HarperCollins Publishers.
67. Jon Sobrino: Jon Sobrino, "The True Church and the Poor," *A Theology of Liberation.* Copyright © 1988. Reprinted by permission of Orbis Books.
68. Gustavo Gutierrez: Gustavo Gutierrez, "A Theology of Liberation," *A Theology of Liberation.* Copyright © 1988. Reprinted by permission of Orbis Books.